The Acquisition of French

Language Acquisition and Language Disorders (LALD)

Volumes in this series provide a forum for research contributing to theories of language acquisition (first and second, child and adult), language learnability, language attrition and language disorders.

Volume 51 (Monographs on the Acquisition of Specific Languages 2)

The Acquisition of French. The development of inflectional morphology and syntax in L1 acquisition, bilingualism, and L2 acquisition
by Philippe Prévost

The Acquisition of French

The development of inflectional morphology and syntax in L1 acquisition, bilingualism, and L2 acquisition

Philippe Prévost
François-Rabelais University, Tours

John Benjamins Publishing Company
Amsterdam / Philadelphia

The paper used in this publication meets the minimum requirements of American National Standard for Information Sciences – Permanence of Paper for Printed Library Materials, ANSI Z39.48-1984.

Library of Congress Cataloging-in-Publication Data

Prévost, Philippe, 1966-

The acquisition of French : the development of inflectional morphology and syntax in L1 acquisition, bilingualism, and L2 acquisition / Philippe Prévost.

p. cm. (Language Acquisition and Language Disorders, ISSN 0925-0123 ; v. 51)

Includes bibliographical references and index.

1. Language acquisition. 2. French language--Acquisition. 3. Second language acquisition. 4. Bilingualism in children. I. Title.

P118.P663 2009

445--dc22 2009033054

ISBN 978 90 272 5312 5 (Hb ; alk. paper)

ISBN 978 90 272 8885 1 (Eb)

John Benjamins Publishing Co. · P.O. Box 36224 · 1020 ME Amsterdam · The Netherlands

John Benjamins North America · P.O. Box 27519 · Philadelphia PA 19118-0519 · USA

Table of contents

PART III. **Determiner phrases**

Preface

The main objective of this book is to describe linguistic knowledge developed by learners of French in different learning situations: first language (L1) acquisition, second language acquisition (SLA), bilingualism, and L1 acquisition by children suffering from Specific Language Impairment (SLI). This knowledge will be discussed using the theoretical tools of generative grammar, drawing on its various developments since the 1980s, including Principles and Parameters (P&P) (Chomsky 1986) and the Minimalist Program (Chomsky 1995, 2000, 2001, 2002). In turn, I hope to demonstrate how data on the acquisition of French can advance our understanding of the nature of linguistic knowledge. For instance, we will see how such data can be used to confirm or disconfirm particular hypotheses about language acquisition that have been proposed in the various learning situations explored in this volume. In addition, numerous comparisons with acquisition data from other languages will be drawn throughout this book, so as to better evaluate the scope of the findings that have been reported on the acquisition of French.

Another objective of this book is to compare the acquisition process across the various learning situations. Acquisition researchers (of necessity) work mainly within their own field of investigation, only occasionally drawing comparisons with other acquisition domains. The advantage of this book is the possibility for systematic review and comparison of studies across different fields. For instance, researchers in L2 French and in the acquisition of L1 French by monolinguals, bilinguals, and children with SLI have been investigating the status and role in developing systems of the functional categories that underlie grammatical notions such as tense, agreement, Case, and definiteness. They also have recently been investigating the issue of variability, particularly with respect to inflectional morphology. The time is now ripe to take a step back and look at the whole spectrum of reported results, in the hope of better understanding general as well as specific properties of language acquisition. As research in different domains has expanded in the last few years, new types of comparisons have become possible, such as between the experience of adult L2 learners and L1 acquisition by children with SLI. With this book, I hope to strengthen such comparisons.

While French has received considerable attention in acquisition studies, it has not been thoroughly investigated in all learning contexts. For instance, while verb placement has been investigated in detail, noun placement (with respect to adjectives, for example) has received much less attention. Similarly, the development of embedded clauses and question formation has been studied in L1 acquisition, but has largely been ignored in L2 acquisition. Another objective of this book is therefore to identify areas underrepresented in existing research on the acquisition of French and to propose new avenues of investigation.

The volume is divided into four parts, each focusing on one domain of acquisition: (1) the verbal domain (with focus on inflectional morphology and verb placement in main declaratives); (2) the pronominal domain (with focus on both overt and null subject and object pronouns); (3) the nominal domain (with focus on determiners, gender, number and noun placement with respect to adjectives); (4) the CP domain (with focus on question formation, embedded clauses and relative clauses). This division is simply an organizational device and is not meant to imply that the different domains should be kept separate, an impossibility in any case since the acquisition of particular properties ranges over several domains. For example, it is impossible to talk about verbal morphology in French (see Part I) without discussing subject pronouns, which are viewed by some linguists as inflectional markers (see Part II). Therefore, numerous cross-referencing remarks are made throughout the book. Acquisition facts in different domains are also compared. For example, the various acquisition chapters of Part III compare results on the verbal and nominal domains, since proposals have been made that relate the development of the functional categories Infl and Det.

Each part contains four chapters. The first chapter presents the facts of French that are relevant to the domain under discussion, and the various theoretical accounts provided to explain them, as background information for the subsequent acquisition chapters. These chapters should be viewed as an overview of the basic facts and theoretical analyses of particular properties of French, not as a thorough investigation; properties that are not covered in the subsequent acquisition chapters will not be discussed. The subsequent chapters in each part address child L1 French, the acquisition of French by children in a bilingual setting and by children with SLI, and the acquisition of L2 French. Bilingualism and acquisition by children with SLI are grouped into one chapter for both theoretical and practical reasons: they are both subcases of L1 acquisition, and they have attracted the attention of fewer researchers, in comparison to L1 and L2 French, so there are fewer data on which to report than in the two other learning contexts.

Linguistic properties of French that have been investigated in each of the four learning contexts were given priority, so as to facilitate comparisons. This is particularly the case in the verbal and pronominal domains. In some cases, however, some properties were included that have significant implications for theory but have only been investigated in a subset of learning contexts, such as the binding properties of pronouns (which have not been examined in L2 French), or the constraints on wh-movement (which have mainly been explored in TD monolinguals). Within each chapters, the facts are presented first and their theoretical implications second, under the assumption that it is easier to understand the theoretical implication of learners' behaviour once the details of that behaviour are known. Incidentally, this organization makes the volume easily usable for those who are only interested in the results of the studies presented.

Some linguistic properties are not discussed at all, simply because of lack of acquisition data. This particularly applies to French phonology, as the investigation of the phonology of French within the generative program is relatively new in some of the learning situations considered in this book. A substantial comparison of phonological development in the different acquisition contexts considered will hopefully be possible in the near future.

Writing this book has been a rather long process mainly due to too many other commitments. I should thank several people for their patience, including Harald Clahsen, Lydia White, and Kees Vaes. Many thanks also to Harald, Lydia, and an anonymous reviewer for their fruitful comments on previous versions of this book. This volume is dedicated to all the people with whom I discussed its content across the four acquisition contexts over the years and who never ceased to encourage me. I know that many of them have been waiting for the final product; there it is! Special thanks to Silvina Montrul, who wrote a similar volume on the acquisition of Spanish, for her support. This book could not have been the same without the wonderful editing skills of Jennifer Ormston. Her advice far extended beyond style, grammar, and typos, and she deserves my warmest gratitude. Finally, many thanks to Bill, Nicola, Phil, and Verena, who despite their many ironic inquiries as to whether the book would ever come out, never really stopped believing that one day it would (I hope!).

Abbreviations

ACC	accusative
Adj	adjective
AdjP	Adjective Phrase
Adv	Adverb
Agr	Agreement (as a functional category)
AgrO	Object Agreement (as a functional category)
AgrP	Agreement Phrase
AgrS	Subject Agreement (as a functional category)
ATOM	Agreement or Tense Omission Model
AUX	auxiliary
AUXP	Auxiliary Phrase
C(omp)	Complementizer
CCH	Computational Complexity Hypothesis
cl	clitic
CM	code mixing
COND	conditional
CP	Complementizer Phrase
CS	code switching
D	Determiner (as a functional category)
DAT	dative
DM	Distributed Morphology
DP	Determiner Phrase
ec	empty category
F	Finite (as a functional category)
FC	functional category
FEM	feminine
FIN	Finite
FP	Finite Phrase
FQ	floating quantifier
FUT	future
I(nfl)	Inflection (as a functional category)
I(nfl)P	Inflection Phrase
IL	interlanguage
INF	infinitival
L1	first language
L2	second language
L3	third language
MA	Moroccan Arabic
MASC	masculine
MDG	Minimal Default Grammar
MLU	Mean Length of Utterance
Mod	modal verb
N	Noun
nc	null constant
NEG	Negative particle
Neg	Negation (as a functional category)
NegP	Negation phrase
NMP	Nominal Mapping Parameter
NOM	nominative
NP	Noun Phrase
Num	Number
NumP	Number phrase
OI	optional infinitive
P(rep)	Preposition
Ph	placeholder
PL	plural
POSS	possessor
POSSP	Possessive Phrase
PP	Prepositional Phrase
PtP	present participle

PtP	past participle
PLU	Predominant Length of Utterance
Q	Question marker
QP	Quantifier Phrase
RC	relative clause
rec	recording
refl	reflexive
RI	root infinitive
S	subject
SG	singular
SLA	second language acquisition
SLI	Specific Linguistic Impairment
SM	sentence matching
Spec	specifier
STR	strong pronoun
T	Tense (as a functional category)
t	trace
TD	typically developing
TNS	tense (as a feature)
TP	Tense Phrase
UCC	Unique Checking Constraint
UG	Universal Grammar
V	Verb
V2	verb second
V3	verb third
VP	Verb phrase
WM	working memory

Introduction

What is linguistic knowledge?

According to the theoretical model adopted in this book, all human beings have a mental representation of language. This particular linguistic knowledge, our linguistic competence as it is called, consists of a grammar that contains rules and constraints pertaining to (at least) phonology, morphology, syntax, and semantics, on the one hand, and a lexicon made up of words and morphemes, on the other. The rules and constraints allow us to manipulate the limited number of words and morphemes in our lexicon to produce (and understand) an infinite number of sentences; this is known as our linguistic performance. The task of any language learner (whether in first or second language acquisition) is to acquire and develop this knowledge. In the case of L1 acquisition at least, this learning is assumed to be achieved via the combined action of an innate language faculty and exposure to linguistic input.

The innate language faculty

According to Chomsky, all children are equipped with a language faculty that guides their learning of their mother tongue (Chomsky 1981, 1986, 1995, 2001). This language faculty includes a linguistic module called Universal Grammar (UG). It is the role played by UG in the acquisition of French in the various learning contexts identified above which is explored in this book. Some of the main arguments for the existence of innate linguistic knowledge in L1 acquisition include rapidity of acquisition (in the span of about four years, children manage to acquire most of the grammar of their mother tongue), uniformity of acquisition (all normally developing children reach a similar level of competence), and the underdetermination of the input (children accumulate complex knowledge about their language that is not explicitly evident in the input). Although input plays a crucial role in acquisition (after all, a child being exposed to French will acquire French, not Chinese), a large part of the knowledge children develop does not seem to be externally driven. For instance, knowledge of the ungrammaticality of certain sentences would be difficult to explain if learning relied solely on general learning mechanisms; the grammaticality of the utterances children produce is rarely corrected, so the input children receive does not include information about what is grammatical, yet children acquire such knowledge very quickly.[1] The question of how complex linguistic knowledge can be attained based on limited input is also called the logical problem of language acquisition. UG is viewed as an solution to this problem; it guides children in their acquisition process and limits the range of possible grammars that can be constructed. In other words, there are a number of grammars that would be possible in principle if acquisition were guided by general learning mechanisms such as observation and deduction that will simply never be hypothesized by children because they are not allowed by the properties of UG. This is not to say that such general learning mechanisms have no role to play in acquisition; they certainly do. But they cannot explain everything, and in particular they cannot explain the (unconscious) knowledge of the ungrammaticality of particular constructions.

The content of Universal Grammar

The shape of UG has evolved along with the different developments of linguistic theory in the last thirty years or so. No particular version of linguistic theory will be favoured in this book, since acquisition studies focusing on French followed the development of the theory itself over the years. However, given that a large proportion of the existing research on the acquisition of French has been published in the last decade and has assumed the principles of the Minimalist Program, that instantiation of the general principles of generative grammar, especially in its early or traditional version (Chomsky 1995), will receive particular attention.

UG can be roughly characterized as containing a set of grammatical categories and features and a set of rules and constraints that are together assumed to underlie the grammars of all natural languages. Grammatical categories are divided into two main types, namely lexical categories (such as N(oun), V(erb), and A(djective)) and functional categories (such as Infl(ection), D(eterminer), and C(omplementizer)). Lexical categories project from elements that carry conceptual information, such as verbs, nouns, adjectives, and adverbs, whereas functional categories underlie grammatical distinctions and relationships, such as tense, agreement, definiteness, number, and Case. Functional categories are also involved in syntactic operations, such as movement. As such, they are crucial participants in the derivation of word order. With respect to the rules and constraints

1. In fact, caregivers have a tendency to correct the truth value of a child's utterance rather than its grammatical correctness (Bowerman 1988; Brown & Hanlon 1970; Marcus 1993; Morgan & Travis 1989). Besides, even when children are exposed to corrections (either explicit or implicit), it is not clear that they recognize such corrections for what they are, or whether they can make use of the information that a correction provides.

of UG, an early distinction was made between *principles* and *parameters* (Chomsky 1981). Principles are assumed to be present in the grammar of all natural languages, while parameters allow (limited) crosslinguistic variation, via so-called parametric values. Within principles and parameters theory, principles include Subjacency, which determines the contexts from which wh-extraction can take place, and binding, which governs the possible relationships between nominal and pronominal elements with potential antecedents. A well-known example of a parameter is the null subject parameter, which accounts for the fact that some languages, such as Spanish and Italian, allow subject omission (they have the [+null subject] value of the parameter), whereas others, such as French and English, do not (they have the [–null subject] value).

Under the Minimalist Program, the concept of parameters has been largely restricted to the lexicon and, more specifically, to functional categories (FCs). FCs are seen as a collection of features, such as [±finite] and [±nominative Case] for Infl. In traditional Minimalism, such features are assumed to vary in strength, which creates different possibilities for head-movement and XP-movement (which is assumed to occur for feature checking purposes), and ultimately results in different word orders. Languages may thus vary in the specific functional categories and features that they instantiate, as well as in feature strength; some features may be strong in some languages and weak in others. Features also come in two types: interpretable features, typically categorial features and the so-called phi-features of nouns (person, number, and gender), and uninterpretable features, which are all other features, and are typically involved in the syntactic derivation. In traditional Minimalism, uninterpretable features need to be checked by elements bearing similar features. When an uninterpretable feature is checked, it is removed from the derivation. Each feature is assumed to be strong or weak, and feature strength is key to determining the nature of the checking operation. Checking of a strong feature triggers overt movement, which can affect word order, while checking of a weak feature triggers covert movement, which is assumed to take place at the level of logical form (LF) where sentences are interpreted semantically. Covert movement does not change word order. For example, as will be shown in Section 1.2, the feature [+finite] is strong in French, which triggers (finite) verb movement to Infl. This is reflected by the fact that finite verbs in French must precede negative adverbs, such as *pas* 'not', as in *Je n'aime pas les films d'horreur* lit. 'I like not movies of horror', or more naturally in English, 'I don't like horror movies'.

Along with the inventory of grammatical categories and features, a number of computational operations are involved in building phrase structure. Among the most prominent ones are Numeration, Merge, and Move. Numeration selects a subset of items from the lexicon associated with certain features, Merge takes these elements and brings them together into phrases, and Move takes an element of the phrase structure, raises it and merges it with another element whose features it needs to check. Such computations are constrained by the general principle of Economy, which says that the least complex computation must always be selected. For example, Merge is considered more economical than Move, covert movement is more economical than overt movement, and overt movement is so costly that it is assumed to apply only as a last resort.

In more recent developments of Minimalism, uninterpretable features are assumed to lack value; consequently, they need to be valued (and not checked). Valuation takes place in a defined relation with a corresponding interpretable feature via the operation Agree (which does not involve overt movement). Movement will occur when necessary, as a result of strong morphology (as in French), for example, or because of the requirement that a head associated with the so-called Extended Projection Principle (EPP) feature must have a specifier. In terms of computational complexity, Merge is viewed as the most economical operation, followed by Agree, and then Move.

Once the syntactic structure is complete, it is fed into each of two other components of the grammar, the phonetic form (PF) component, which maps the structure onto a phonetic representation, and a logical form (LF) component, which is in charge of mapping the syntactic derivation onto a semantic representation. The model is summarized in (1). Ultimately, a derivation must only contain interpretable features, so that it can receive phonetic and semantic representations. This means that all uninterpretable features must be removed from the derivation, either via checking or valuation.

(1)

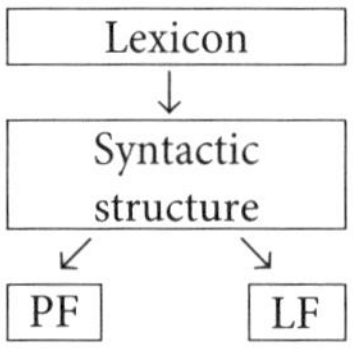

The acquisition task

According to the theory, UG is a kind of blueprint for language. The invariant components of UG, such as principles of computational operation, are deemed by theorists to be available to the child right from the start. Among acquisition researchers, however, whether or not all these elements are active right from day one or require some 'learning' time, is in fact the focus of intense debate in the literature, as will become apparent throughout this book. The properties of UG that allow crosslinguistic variation, it is generally agreed, have to be fixed based on the input. Under Minimalism, the task of the child is to infer from the input what subset of the categories and features (and their strengths) in the UG inventory is instantiated in the language being learned (and construct their mental grammar accordingly). In L2 acquisition, the task remains the same. Learners must acquire the parametric values, the categories and the features of the L2, possibly influenced by their L1 grammar (see below). The question of whether or not native-like acquisition of L2 properties is possible and whether L2 learners build native-like grammars turns on the question of whether UG is available as a guiding tool in (adult) L2 acquisition. As will become clear below, opinions differ on this issue.

Naturally, reaching adult-like or target-like grammars takes some time, for both L1 and L2 learners. Learners are assumed to construct intermediate grammars during linguistic development, as can be seen in (2). In L2 acquisition, these are called interlanguage (IL) grammars. This books aims to investigate the content of grammars developed by learners of French, at both the initial and intermediate stages, as well as at the endstate stage in the case of L2 acquisition.

(2) [G1] → [G2] → [G3] → [Gn] → [G Final]

In L1 acquisition, such intermediate systems are commonly assumed to be constrained by UG. That is, even though the intermediate grammars may differ from the final state of the grammar (the grammar imputed to adult speakers of the mother tongue), they still respect the properties of UG. Again, whether the IL grammars constructed by L2 learners are also UG-constrained is subject to debate.

It is important to point out that UG is not meant to explain the totality of language acquisition. Certain properties of language are not relevant to UG yet still need to be learned. Vocabulary and morphological markers are chief among the characteristics that are specific to the language being learned and that are unrelated to the kinds of generalizations made by UG about language. For example, a child learning French will have to learn the word designating the piece of furniture on which one can sit (*chaise*) and that *-ons* express 1st person plural. While we will not be concerned about lexical acquisition in this book, we will see that the acquisition of certain forms, especially inflectional markers, can play an important role in deciding whether underlying categories or features are present in developing grammars.

General assumptions about French

As in other Romance languages, basic word order in French is Subject-Verb-Object (SVO). The basic clausal representation for French assumed throughout this book is given in (3).

(3)

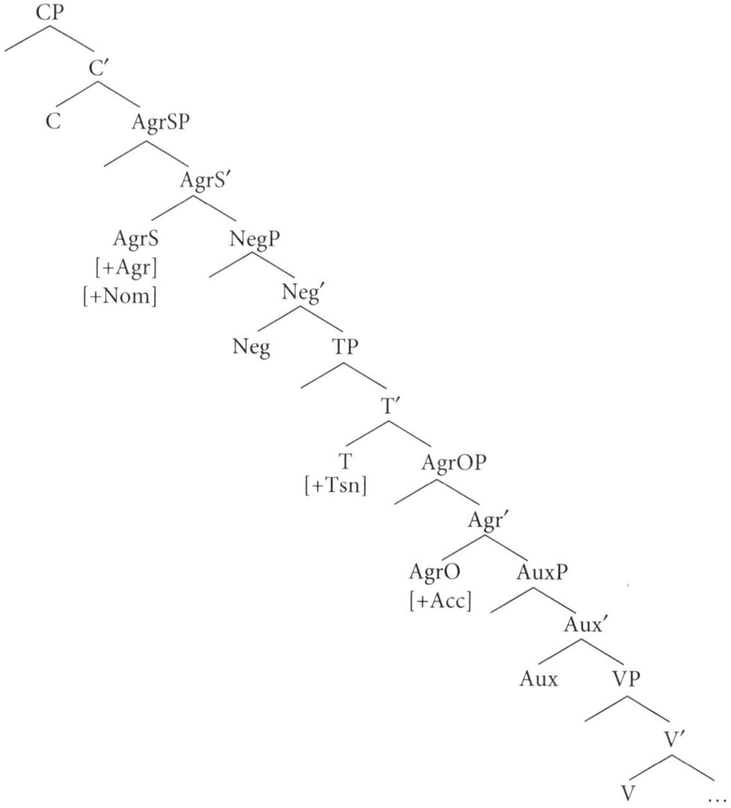

Two important assumptions are made here. First, following Pollock (1989), I assume a split version of Infl, with tense and agreement projecting their own categories, T and AgrS. These categories are associated with tense and (subject) agreement features. The AgrS position is also associated with nominative Case checking.[2] There is also an AgrO projection for object agreement and accusative Case checking. I follow Belletti (1990, 2001) and Brousseau & Roberge (2000) in assuming that AgrsP dominates TP in French, in contrast to Pollock's original proposal. Throughout the book, the Infl notation is used for ease of exposition when the difference between AgS and T is not crucial to the discussion. Second, following Pollock (1989) again, I assume that negation projects its own category, Neg, which is located between AgrS and T. I also assume that *ne* is the head of NegP and that negative adverbs, such as *pas*, occupy the specifier position of NegP. The representation in (3) also includes a specific position for auxiliaries (AuxP) below AgrO, although

2. The projection of Agr is maintained although its existence has been questioned for some time (Chomsky 1995). A discussion of whether or not Agr should be dispensed with goes beyond the scope of this book.

for some researchers, auxiliaries are directly generated in T (e.g. Guasti 1993/1994). This divergence is not crucial to our discussion of the acquisition of French.[3,4]

Most discussions will focus on the acquisition of standard French in L1 and L2 learning contexts, although occasional references will be made to acquisition of other varieties, such as nonstandard French, Belgian French, and Quebec French.

The different learning situations

In this book, the acquisition of French is discussed from the perspective of four different learning situations: L1 acquisition, L2 acquisition, bilingualism, and acquisition by children with SLI. This section offers a review of some of the general assumptions and hypotheses that form the background of the discussions throughout the book. In all cases, acquisition means building a grammar, that is, a linguistic system containing categories and features, rules, and constraints. Naturally, constructing a grammar is a gradual process. Over time, new properties are added to the existing system, while others are deleted, as illustrated in (2) above.

First language acquisition

Assuming UG, one of the main research questions in L1 acquisition is the issue of continuity, that is, to what extent do child grammars compare to adult ones?. According to the Weak Continuity Hypothesis, initial grammars are different from adult ones in that some of the principles or categories of the mature grammar may not be readily available to children. These properties initially lacking will develop later on, either via maturation, much like a biological clock (Borer & Wexler 1987; Lebeaux 1988; Radford 1990), or via the acquisition of specific lexical or morphological items related to them (Clahsen, Eisenbeiss & Penke 1996). Under the Strong Continuity Hypothesis, the other account of early child grammars, child systems are assumed to contain all the principles and categories present in adult grammars (Guasti 1993/1994; Hyams 1996; Poeppel & Wexler 1993). What children must do is acquire the target properties of these categories and the

3. Arguably, there is also an AgrPstPartP node located between AuxP and VP, which underlies participle agreement. Participle agreement can be overt in French when the direct object of the verb precedes the auxiliary, as in the following exchange *A: Et la voiture? B: Jean l'a prise* 'A: And the+FEM car+FEM? B: John it+FEM has taken.FEM'. Participle agreement has rarely been addressed in the literature on the acquisition of French within the generative framework (see Pirvulescu & Belzil 2008), so the AgrPstPrt position will not be included in the syntactic representations appearing in this book.

4. Other categories have been proposed over the years, such as Asp, Mod, and Voice (see Belletti 1990; Cinque 1999). See Belletti (2001) for discussion.

parametric values of their language. Under the hypothesis that early grammars contain all the categories and constraints of adult grammars, the question is how to account for the errors children make during the acquisition process. Recently, a number of hypotheses have been proposed to answer this question, which assume the underspecification of particular functional categories, such as Tense (Wexler 1994) or Number (Hoekstra & Hyams 1998), or of principles, such as the Root Principle (Rizzi 1993/1994). Other Proposals appeal to the notion derivational complexitity and reduced computational capacities in young children to explain, among other things, initial difficulties with tense and object clitics (Jakubowicz 2004, 2005; Jakubowicz & Nash 2001; Jakubowicz, Nash, Rigaut, & Gérard 1998) (see below).These hypotheses, and some of their latest developments, will be further discussed in Section 2.2. The same questions about the continuity between child and adult (or target) grammars are raised in all cases of acquisition by children, such as bilingual acquisition and acquisition by children with SLI.

Bilingualism

Definitions of bilingualism in the literature range from 'demonstrates native-like proficiency in two languages' to 'has minimal contact with more than one language' (see Romaine 1996). Here, I take bilingualism to be a situation where a child is learning two languages at the same time from birth. In this context, it is interesting to ask how exposure to two languages at once affects language development. In other words, is bilingual development like L1 acquisition, or like L2 acquisition, or radically different from these two processes? Researchers have been particularly interested in investigating whether the child starts with one or with two grammatical systems. Those who assume only one grammar to start with also assume that the initial unified grammatical system later splits into two grammars (between the ages of two and three) (see Redlinger & Park 1980; Volterra & Taeschner 1978, among others). Evidence for this view is the fact that *code mixing* (CM) and *code switching* (CS) are abundant in early bilingual acquisition. Both refer to the mixing of elements of the two languages (such as lexical items and morphemes) in production, which can take place either within a sentence, as in code mixing, or across sentence boundaries, as in code switching (see Bhatia & Ritchie 1996). Those who argue that the child has two grammars, one for each language, right from the outset of acquisition (see De Houwer 1995; Genesee 1989, among others) point to the fact that bilingual children do not code mix or code switch all the time; they also produce long stretches of speech in either one of the two languages with no intervention from the other. This suggests that bilingual children have command of both grammars (see also de Houwer 2005; Genesee 2001; Genesee & Nicoladis 2006; Meisel 2001, 2004). Under this view, CS and CM are assumed to be performance phenomena (greatly influenced by pragmatic and sociolinguistic factors) that do not reflect an underlying unitary grammatical competence.

If two separate grammars are indeed constructed from the outset, the question of whether, and to what degree, they influence each other then arises. There may be interactions between the two grammars, in the sense that some properties may transfer from one grammar to the other (see Paradis & Genesee 1996) and may accelerate or impede the development of particular linguistic properties. Such interactions could stem from language dominance (Schlyter 1993) and be facilitated by particular structural properties (Müller & Hulk 2001). Under the dual grammar view, then, the degree and the nature of the interaction between the two grammars determine the extent to which bilingual acquisition differs from monolingual L1 acquisition.

Acquisition by children with SLI

Children with Specific Language Impairment have difficulty with certain aspects of language but no impairment to their cognitive abilities. These children typically obtain low scores on language tests and may particularly struggle with phonology and morphosyntax (Leonard 1998). The diagnosis of SLI is often reached by a process of elimination, i.e. if no abnormality is detected in non-verbal IQ, hearing, and physical and social interactions, and if no brain damage is found. Heredity is also a factor in the SLI condition (see Gopnik 1990).

Research in language acquisition by children with SLI has focused on how acquisition in this population should be understood with respect to L1 acquisition by typically developing (TD) children. Acquisition by children with SLI is considered to be either deviant (radically different from that of TD children) or delayed (particular properties emerge more slowly than in TD children, but they emerge in the same order). Researchers who consider SLI acquisition to be deviant argue that grammars developed by children with SLI are defective with respect to certain properties, and often consider functional categories and their features to be the source of the impairment (e.g. Gopnik 1990). Other researchers believe that acquisition is delayed rather than deviant. For them, the impairment in SLI is not specifically linguistic, in fact. Rather, they argue that SLI is related to a limitation in general processing capacities, perhaps due to a restriction in the size of the computational region of memory, which may prevent children from learning parts of the grammar. According to Leonard's (1998) Surface Hypothesis, the difficulty that SLI learners experience with certain linguistic elements is due to the combination of their limited processing capacities and the fact that some linguistic forms, such as inflectional morphemes, are inherently difficult to perceive.[5] As a result, grammar may be slow to develop and acquisition may be incomplete, with non-target-like utterances persisting into adulthood. According to

5. Another processing account assumes a deficit in phonological memory, whereby children with SLI have difficulties storing new linguistic material in working memory (Gathercole & Braddeley 1990).

the Computational Complexity Hypothesis (CCH), children with SLI have particular difficulties with the computation of syntactic complexity, which may depend on several factors, such as whether the presence of specific categories in the underlying representation of utterances is obligatory or optional (children with SLI have little trouble with categories that are systematically part of the representation but struggle with categories whose projection is not always required) and whether there is overt movement or not (children have less computational difficulties with Merge than with Move and they 'prefer' constructions with fewer overt movement operations which are deemed to be computationally costly) (see Jakubowicz 2004, 2005; Jakubowicz & Nash 2001, to appear; Jakubowicz et al. 1998).

Second language acquisition

A fundamental question that has received much attention in second language acquisition research for over 20 years is, if there really is a language faculty that guides children in the acquisition of their mother tongue, what happens to this faculty when a second or third language is being learned? Is it still operational? Does it still guide language acquisition? Also, given that child L2 learners seem to be 'better' at learning a foreign language than adults, could it be that UG is only available to child learners? Finally, what is the role of the L1 in the L2 acquisition process?

UG is not available in L2 acquisition

Many researchers argue that UG is not available in (adult) L2 acquisition because L2 acquisition is considered to be very different from L1 acquisition. In particular, learning an L2 can be very slow and take quite a long time, it is not uniform (great differences in proficiency can exist between L2 learners of the same language, even after the same number of years of exposure or instruction under similar learning conditions), and the final level reached by learners often falls short of being native-like. For researchers who have adopted this view (e.g. Bley-Vroman 1990; Clahsen 1988; Clahsen & Muysken 1986; Meisel 1991, 1997; Schachter 1990), L2 acquisition is not guided by UG but by general learning mechanisms such as problem solving and trial and error. This means that the nature of IL grammars is fundamentally different from that of the grammars of native speakers.[6] According to the UG-is-unavailable hypothesis, UG would become inaccessible at around puberty, a view related to the proposed existence of a critical period for language acquisition.

---

6. According to some researchers, there is transfer of the parametric values and principles of the L1 into the IL grammars (Hawkins 2001; Hawkins & Chan 1997). In other words, UG is available through the L1, so to speak, but it is not an active force in the acquisition of the L2. This means that although UG-constrained, IL grammars cannot be native-like, since L2 parametric values and principles that differ from those of the L1, will never be acquired.

In recent years, some researchers have used the term impairment to characterize non-UG-constrained IL grammars. Impairment is deemed global when UG is considered to be fully unavailable to L2 learners (Meisel 1997) and local if it only affects some aspects of linguistic knowledge. In particular, some researchers have proposed that specific features, such as finite features, may be valueless in IL grammars, that is, neither strong nor weak (Beck 1998; Eubank, Bischof, Huffstutler, Leek & West 1997; Eubank & Grace 1996). Such impairments, whether global or local, are assumed to be permanent.[7]

UG is available in L2 acquisition

For other researchers, the fact that adults may struggle with L2 learning does not mean that they cannot develop IL grammars whose content goes beyond the input they receive (often by means of instruction) or the grammar of their L1. In other words, the logical problem of language acquisition – the fact that the input learners receive does not entirely determine the content of the grammars they build – remains in L2 acquisition (see White 1989 for discussion). That L2 competence may differ from native speakers' does not mean that UG is unavailable to L2 learners: the content of the grammars may differ, but the nature of linguistic competence may be the same (for a review, see White 2003). This viewpoint has led researchers to look more closely at the content of IL grammars and attempt to determine if they are UG-constrained.

The role of the L1

Opinions differ widely as to the extent of transfer that occurs from the L1 at the beginning of L2 acquisition. For some researchers, there is no transfer at all; the L2 is learned in the same way as the L1 (Epstein, Flynn & Martohardjono 1996). Learners are assumed to be equipped with UG and not to use their prior knowledge of language (in the form of the L1); parametric values and operating principles of the L2 are activated solely on the basis of the input. At the other extreme are researchers who assume that the entire grammar of the mother tongue is transferred into the initial IL grammar (Schwartz & Sprouse's (1994, 1996) Full Transfer/Full Access Hypthesis). That is, L2 learners start with all the parametric values and the operating principles of the L1 and maintain these properties until counterevidence is found in the input, at which point a restructuring of the IL grammar is triggered. Crucially, such changes are constrained by UG, which is deemed available to L2 learners. Thus, parameters may be reset to the target value and

7. Note that the proponents of the Local Impairment approach otherwise assume that UG is available to L2 learners. However, there seems to be a contradiction between their proposal and the fact that feature strength must be specified as either strong or weak in natural languages. The IL grammars thus proposed are therefore incompatible with UG constraints.

principles only operative in the L2 may be acquired. Still other researchers take an intermediate view, according to which only part of the L1 grammar transfers; exactly what part varies according to the researchers. For some, lexical categories transfer, but functional ones do not (Vainikka & Young-Scholten 1994, 1996, 2005); for others, both lexical and functional categories transfer, but the strength of L1 features does not (Eubank 1993/1994), leaving the strength specification of features in the L2 to be acquired based on the input (and the availability of UG).

Methodological issues

Determining what language learners know about their language is by no means an easy task, since this knowledge, their linguistic competence, is unconscious and cannot be accessed directly. As will be reported throughout this book, researchers use a variety of psycholinguistic techniques, such as spontaneous production and grammaticality judgment tasks, to attempt to understand learners' linguistic competence. Such techniques are not without their limitations, so it is important to raise some of the issues that have been discussed in the literature with respect to the interpretation of test results.

Production data

One way of investigating linguistic knowledge is to examine spontaneous production data. This may be particularly suitable to young language learners to whom complicated psycholinguistic tasks cannot be administered. However, the interpretation of production data can sometimes be difficult, as discussion in the literature makes abundantly clear. What can a researcher conclude about underlying knowledge of a particular property when its related tokens are produced only seldom or not at all, or when they are used in a non-target fashion? Opinions differ on the answers to these questions. For some, at least some tokens must be produced by the learners (or a certain percentage of target-like use must be present) if the underlying property is to be assumed to be part of the grammar (Clahsen et al. 1996 for L1 acquisition and Vainikka & Young-Scholten 1996 for L2 acquisition), while for others, this is not necessarily the case (Borer & Rohrbacher 2002 for L1 acquisition and Lardiere 1998 for L2 acquisition). One way to address these shortcomings is use elicited production tasks, where the learner is forced to use the linguistic properties under investigation. But here again, should a low incidence or non-target like use of particular items be synonymous with absence of underlying knowledge? Ideally, production tasks should be coupled with other tests, such as comprehension tests and grammaticality judgments. This will offer different insights into the content of developing grammars. Alternatively, a wide variety of interrelated properties, not just a few, should be investigated in spontaneous production before any conclusions are drawn about the nature of underlying knowledge.

Judgment tasks

The advantage of experimental tasks, such as grammaticality judgment (GJ) tasks, is that they allow researchers to manipulate language and focus exactly on what they are looking for. One aspect of knowledge that can be tested with such tasks is knowledge of ungrammaticality, which cannot be achieved via experiments relying on production. However, the validity of GJ tasks has been under scrutiny for a number of years (see, Schütze 1996, for example). In the case of adult L2 learners, for example, it is sometimes difficult to tell whether the results truly reflect linguistic intuitions, which is what is sought, or whether other factors, such as metalinguistic knowledge, have intervened in the judgments. Recently, on-line tests have been developed in order to obtain indirect grammaticality judgments from learners, notably based on measuring reaction time to particular tasks. Where applicable, different kinds of tasks should be developed and administered to the same set of learners to test knowledge of a particular property, given that the results may be affected by the nature of the task itself (Murphy 1997).

PART I

The verbal domain

CHAPTER 1

The verbal domain

Syntactic assumptions

The first part of this book is concerned with the acquisition of different aspects of morphosyntactic properties related to the verbal domain, such as verbal morphology and verb placement with respect to adverbs and negation. Investigating the verbal domain can give us insight into the development of functional categories, (such as Inflection (Infl), which underlies tense and agreement properties) and their features, which are involved in word order (e.g. in French, finite verbs must occur in front of the negative adverb *pas*, as in *Je ne travaille pas* 'I work not'). One of the questions that will be addressed is how knowledge of finiteness (tense and agreement) develops in the first stages of acquisition. We will also look at the development of knowledge of verb placement in L1 and L2 French. On the theoretical level, we will look at the development of Infl and its features. Is Infl part of initial developmental grammars? If not, how does it develop? In particular, when are its features acquired in child L1 French? Can these features ever be acquired by L2 learners? Do learners' L1 Infl features that differ from those of the target language impact their acquisition of L2 Infl features?

This first chapter lays out the main linguistic facts of French that have been investigated in acquisition research. In particular, properties pertaining to verbal morphology and verb placement are reviewed, along with the theoretical analyses that have been proposed to account for these facts. Acquisition questions will then be raised, which will be addressed in the upcoming chapters.

1.1 Verbal morphology

The verbal inflection paradigm of spoken French is relatively poor. Although inflectional markers are in general graphically distinct from each other, the distinctions are not audible in most cases. Moreover, one of the audible agreement markers, namely *-ons* (1PL), is rare in spoken French since first person plural forms tend to be replaced by third person singular ones with *on* 'one' as subject, rather than *nous* 'we'. Whether verbal inflections can be heard depends on the class the verb belongs to, and on the subject. French verbs are traditionally divided into three groups: the first group includes verbs ending in *-er* in the infinitival form (these make up the majority of verbs in

French); verbs of the second group end in *-ir* and display the finite regular plural markers *-issons* (1PL), *-issez* (2PL), and *-issent* (3PL); the third group comprises all other verbs, including irregular verbs ending in *-ir* and *-re*. As can be seen in Table 1, first, second, and third person singular forms within each group are audibly indistinguishable from each other in the present and the imperfect. For example, although the orthography differs, in the present only the final consonant of the stem of first group verbs is produced in first, second, and third person singular and in third person plural, e.g. *je/tu/il/elle/on/ils/elles chan[t]* 'I/you/he/she/one/they sing(s)'. For second group verbs, again in the present, first, second, and third person singular forms all end in [i]. In all these cases, it is the subject (and usually the subject pronoun) which disambiguates the verb form.[8]

Table 1. French inflectional paradigm

		1st group ***chanter*** **('sing')**	**2nd group** ***finir*** **('finish')**	**3rd group** ***vendre*** **('sell')**
Infinitival form		chant-er [e]	fin-ir	vend-re
Past participle		chant-é [e]	fin-i [i]	vend-u
Present	1/2/3SG	chant-e/-es/-e [t]	fin-is/-is/-it [i]	vend-s/-s/-ø [vɑ̃]
	1PL	chant-ons [ɔ̃]	fin-iss-ons [isɔ̃]	vend-ons [ɔ̃]
	2PL	chant-ez [e]	fin-iss-ez [ise]	vend-ez [e]
	3PL	chant-ent [t]	fin-iss-ent [is]	vend-ent [d]
Imperfect	1/2/3SG	chant-ais/-ais/-ait [ɛ]	fin-iss-ais/-ais/-ait [isɛ]	vend-ais/-ais/-ait [ɛ]
	1PL	chant-i-ons [jɔ̃]	fin-iss-i-ons [isjɔ̃]	vend-i-ons [jɔ̃]
	2PL	chant-i-ez [je]	fin-iss-i-ez [isje]	vend-i-ez [je]
	3PL	chant-aient [ɛ]	fin-iss-aient [isɛ]	vend-aient [ɛ]
Future	1SG	chant-er-ai [re]	fin-ir-ai [ire]	vend-r-ai [re]
	2/3SG	chant-er-as/-a [ra]	fin-ir-as/-a [ira]	vend-r-as/-a [ra]
	1PL	chant-er-ons [rɔ̃]	fin-ir-ons [irɔ̃]	vend-r-ons [rɔ̃]
	2PL	chant-er-ez [re]	fin-ir-ez [ire]	vend-r-ez [re]
	3PL	chant-er-ont [rɔ̃]	fin-ir-ont [irɔ̃]	vend-r-ont [rɔ̃]

In fact, some researchers hold that subject pronouns (or subject clitics) are agreement prefixes in some varieties of spoken French, such as nonstandard French

8. Except for singular and plural third person pronouns which are phonetically indistinct (*il/ils* ([il]) and *elle/elles* ([ɛl])). They can be distinguished only when the following verb starts with a vowel, in which case there is obligatory fusion between the final sound of the pronoun and the vowel in oral speech, a phenomenon called liaison, e.g. *il/elle arrive*' he/she arrives' ([il/ɛlariv]) vs. *ils/elles arrivent* ([il/ɛlzariv]).

(Lambrecht 1981; Zribi-Hertz 1994) and Quebec French (Auger 1994; Roberge 1990). Evidence for this claim comes from the frequent use of clitic doubling in oral speech. Subject clitics are very often used in combination with a subject DP without a pause between them (1a), which suggests that the DP is in subject position and not in a (non-argumental) topic position. Moreover, clitics must be repeated in cases of coordination in these varieties, as in (1b), suggesting that they are attached to the verb (for more on French clitics, see Section 5.1)

(1) a. Le prof il donne beaucoup de travail.
The prof he gives much work
'The prof assigns a lot of work'

b. Je travaille et *(je) dors, c'est tout.
I work and I sleep that is all
'I work and sleep, that's all'

Suppletive forms of verbs such as *aller* 'go', *avoir* 'have', and the copula *être* 'be' display a greater range of audible distinctions, although homophonous forms can also be found in the finite paradigm of these verbs, especially second and third person singular in the present and all singular forms in the imperfect (Table 2).

Table 2. Inflectional paradigm of *être* 'be', *avoir* 'have', and *aller* 'go'

		être **('be')**	***avoir*** **('have')**	***aller*** **('go')**
Infinitival form		être	avoir	aller [e]
Past participle		été	eu	allé [e]
Present	1SG	suis [sɥi]	ai [e]	vais [vɛ]
	2/3SG	es/est [ɛ]	as/a [a]	vas/va [va]
	1PL	sommes [sɔ̃m]	av-ons [ɔ̃]	all-ons [ɔ̃]
	2PL	êtes [ɛt]	av-ez [e]	all-ez [e]
	3PL	sont [sɔ̃]	ont [ɔ̃]	vont [vɔ̃]
Imperfect	1/2/3SG	ét-ais/-ais/-ait [ɛ]	av-ais/-ais/-ait [ɛ]	all-ais/-ais/-ait [ɛ]
	1PL	ét-i-ons [jɔ̃]	av-i-ons [jɔ̃]	all-i-ons [jɔ̃]
	2PL	ét-i-ez [je]	av-i-ez [je]	all-i-ez [e]
	3PL	ét-aient [ɛ]	av-aient [ɛ]	all-aient [ɛ]
Future	1SG	ser-ai [re]	aur-ai [re]	ir-ai [re]
	2/3SG	ser-as/-a [ra]	aur-as/-a [ra]	ir-as-a [ra]
	1PL	ser-ons [rɔ̃]	aur-ons [rɔ̃]	ir-ons [rɔ̃]
	2PL	ser-ez [re]	aur-ez [re]	ir-ez [re]
	3PL	ser-ont [rɔ̃]	aur-ont [rɔ̃]	ir-ont [rɔ̃]

Past tense is either perfective (*passé composé* or *plus-que-parfait*) or imperfective (*imparfait*). The perfective past tense involves an auxiliary (*être* or *avoir*) conjugated either in the present (in the case of *passé composé*) or in the imperfect (in the case of *plus-que-parfait* (or plu-perfect)) followed by the past participle of the verb (e.g. *j'ai chanté* 'I sang', *je suis parti* 'I left'). The *imparfait* is marked by homophonous [ɛ] markers in the singular, and by the imperfective marker *-i* in the plural (e.g. *nous chantions* 'we were singing').

Future tense is either synthetic or analytic. Regular synthetic future is based on the infinitival form of the verb, to which distinctive suffixes are added (see Table 1). The analytic form, also called *futur proche*, involves the verb *aller* 'go' used as an inchoative auxiliary followed by the infinitival form of the verb (e.g. *Il va partir* 'he is going to leave').

Homophony of forms extends across tense, since some of the nonfinite endings in French are homophonous with certain finite markers, although they differ in their spelling. As illustrated in Table 1, an ending in [e] in the first verb group could correspond to one of three markers: the infinitival marker itself, the past participle *-é*, or the second person plural suffix *-ez*. Potential ambiguity also arises with verbs of the second and third groups and the ending [i]. This ending could either be a singular present marker (for first, second, and third person), or the past participle marker. In contrast, the infinitival markers of the 2nd and 3rd groups are unambiguous, e.g. *-ir* as in *finir* 'finish', and *-re* as in *boire* 'drink' and *prendre* 'take'.

The paucity of audible distinctions in the verbal paradigm is a challenge to acquisition researchers because it is difficult to determine whether a given form produced by a learner includes information about agreement and tense. As we will see in upcoming chapters, in the early stages especially, children tend to produce verb forms that lack distinctive, audible morphology (called default or elsewhere forms (Ferdinand 1996)) and not to produce the accompanying clitic pronouns that, in adult speech, identify the person/number intended. Additionally, learners of French produce a significant number of utterances that include nonfinite verbs (called root infinitives) where a finite form would be expected in the target language. Since the majority of lexical verbs in these utterances are first group verbs, it is not easy to tell whether or not these forms are in fact infinitive (entirely unmarked for tense).

1.2 Verb placement

In French, finite verbs appear before, and not after, frequency, manner and negative adverbs, as shown in (2), (3) and (4). They also precede so-called floating quantifiers (FQs) such as *tous* 'all', as illustrated in (5). Negation is marked by the preverbal particle *ne*, which is rare in informal speech, and a negative adverb, such as *pas* 'not', which follows the finite verb.

(2) a. Mes amis regardent souvent la télévision.
my friends watch often the television
'My friends often watch television'

b. *Mes amis souvent regardent la télévision.

(3) a. Mes amis regardent passivement la television.
my friends watch passively the television
'My friends watch television passively'

b. *Mes amis passivement regardent la télévision.

(4) a. Mes amis (ne) regardent pas la télévision.
my friends NEG watch not the television
'My friends don't watch television'

b. *Mes amis (ne) pas regardent la télévision.

(5) a. Mes amis regardent tous la télévision.
my friends watch all the television
'My friends all watch television'

b. *Mes amis tous regardent tous la télévision.

Note that adverbs may also appear clause initially, as with speaker-oriented adverbs such as *évidemment* 'obviously' (e.g. *Évidemment, la France gagnera la Coupe du monde* 'Obviously France will win the World Cup'), or clause finally, as with manner adverbs (e.g. *Mes amis regardent la télévision passivement* 'My friends watch TV passively'). We will not be concerned with such possibilities here because they provide no information relevant to word order within the clause. What is crucial to our discussion is that when an adverb appears clause internally in French, it follows – rather than precedes – the finite verb.[9]

In Minimalist theory (Chomsky 1995), it is the strength of Infl features (tense and agreement features) that determines verb placement in the sentence. In French, these features are assumed to be strong, in contrast to their English counterparts, which are weak. In Minimalist terms, strong features have to be checked overtly within their respective categories (Chomsky 1995). Consequently, the finite verb must leave its base position in V and raises to T and Agr in French to check tense and agreement features.[10] This is illustrated in (6), where this movement results in the verb appearing

9. For an account on the various positions held by adverbs, see Cinque (1999).

10. Several modifications have been made to the Minimalist Program since 1995, in particular concerning the nature of movement and feature checking mechanisms (Chomsky 2001, 2002). However, the fundamental idea presented here has remained the same: every uninterpretable feature must be checked and every strong feature triggers 'visible' movement.

in front of the negative *pas*, adverbs, and floating quantifiers.[11] The representation in (6) also shows that the subject originates within VP and moves to SpecAgrSP to check (strong) nominative Case features.

(6)

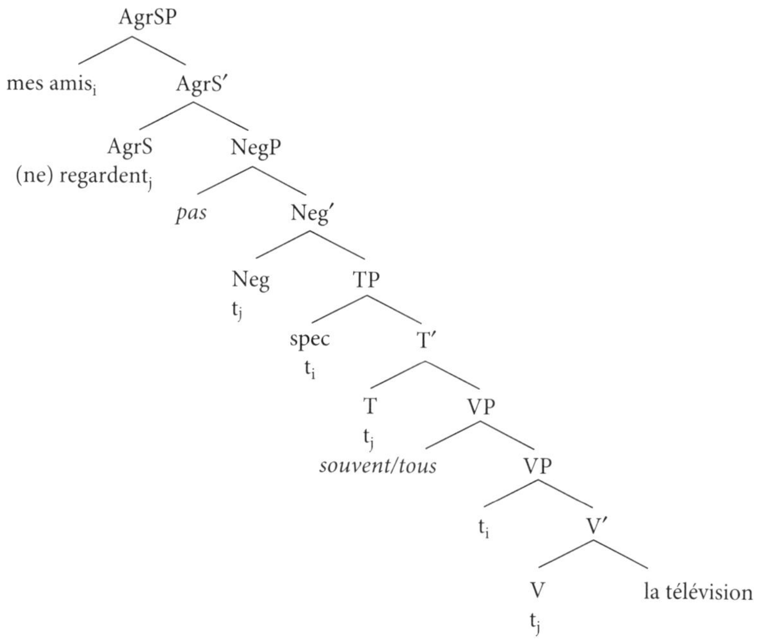

In English, Infl features are assumed to be weak, which means that the finite verb stays in V; it does not move overtly to T and AgS. Consequently, it appears after the negator *not*, frequency and manner adverbs, and floating quantifiers, such as *all*, as can be seen in the English translations of (2) through (5). The crosslinguistic differences in Infl feature strength can be accounted for in terms of the verb movement parameter. Languages such as French where Infl features are strong are said to have the [strong] value of the parameter, while languages with weak Infl features are assumed to instantiate the [weak] setting.

When the verb is nonfinite, it may precede or follow frequency/manner adverbs in French, as in (7) and (8), and floating quantifiers, as in (9) and (10).

(7) a. Mes amis ont souvent /passivement regardé la télévision.
my friends have+3P often passively watched the television
'My friends often watched television'

b. Mes amis ont regardé souvent/passivement la télévision.

---

11. Divergent accounts of floating quantifiers abound (Baltin 1995; De Cat 2000; Dowty & Brodie 1984; Sportiche 1988). I will not commit to one particular view, as they all hold that floating quantifiers are generated between TP and VP, which is all that matters for my discussion.

(8) a. Souvent/passivement regarder la télévision est abrutissant.
Often/passively watch.INF the television is stupefying
'To often watch television is stupefying'

b. Regarder souvent/passively la télévision est abrutissant.

(9) a. Mes amis ont tous regardé la télévision.
my friends have+3P all watched the television
'My friends all watched television'

b. Mes amis ont regardé tous la télévision.

(10) a. Tous regarder la télévision, tel est le voeux de mes amis.
All watch.INF the television such is the wish of my friends
'My friends all wish to watch television'

b. Regarder tous la télévision, tel est le voeux de mes amis.

However, nonfinite lexical verbs can only follow negative adverbs, as shown in (11) and (12).

(11) a. Mes amis (n') ont pas regardé la télévision.
my friends NEG have+3P not watched the television
'My friends didn't watch television'

b. *Mes amis (n') ont regardé pas la télévision.

(12) a. Ne pas regarder la télévision est une bonne chose.
NEG not watch.INF the television is a good thing
'Not watching television is a good thing'

b. *Ne regarder pas la télévision est une bonne chose.

To account for this difference, nonfinite features are assumed to be weak in French. Nonfinite verbs can only raise to T (short movement), not to Agr (long movement), which explains why they may precede adverbs and quantifiers, but not negators. However, movement to T seems to be optional; hence, nonfinite verbs may also follow adverbs and quantifiers. This is illustrated in (13).[12]

12. According to Iatridou (1990), the V_{inf}-Adv order is not derived from verb raising, but results from the adjunction of the adverb to the verb (in the sense of Di Sciullo & Williams 1987). In other words, V_{inf}-Adv sequences should be considered complex verbs. Some authors also question the judgments reported in the syntax literature. Ayoun (1999) reports that in a grammaticality judgment task, French native speakers overwhelmingly favour V_{inf}-Adv over Adv-V_{inf}, suggesting that optionality may not obtain to start with (see also Ayoun 2003). Such patterns should be confirmed by other studies manipulating different types of verbs and adverbs in order to establish, among other things, whether there is any kind of lexical and/or phonological effect in the judgments.

(13)

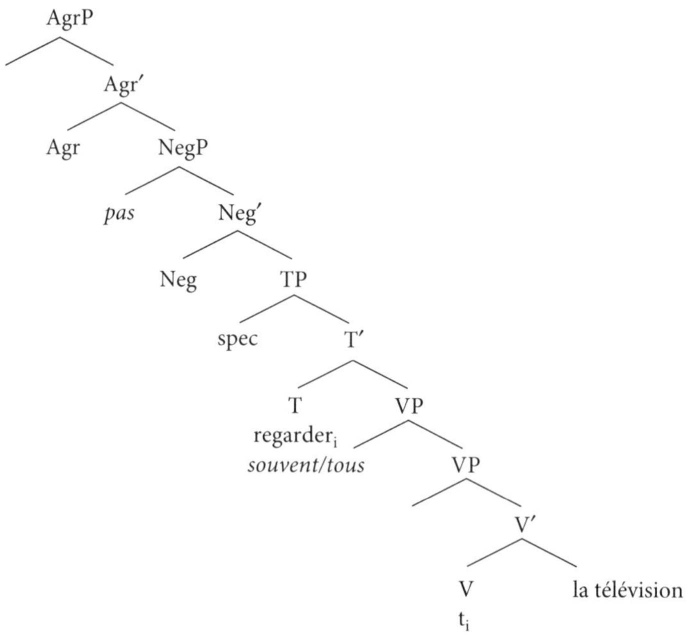

1.3 Questions for acquisition

At first sight, the acquisition of morphology may seem to have little to tell us about whether the fundamental principles of Universal Grammar are operative in learners' early grammars. Inflectional morphemes are language-specific and must be learned. For instance, there is nothing universal in the fact that the first person plural marker is *-ons* in French. Of interest to the acquisition researcher, however, is that these morphological elements are lexical realizations of underlying functional projections such as Tense and Agreement. As such, their production or their omission may reflect the presence or the absence of the functional categories themselves in learners' grammars. A related question researchers have investigated concerns the development of these categories. Are they all present in initial French child and interlanguage grammars or do they develop gradually? In particular, does T emerge before Agr or vice-versa? In bilingual acquisition, do Agr and T develop at the same time in French as in the other language? For children with specific language impairment, is the acquisition of these categories or their features affected by the children's condition? For instance, is the development of functional categories slower compared to typically developing children?

The investigation of acquisition of appropriate word order (verb placement) can also shed light on whether or not functional categories are part of early systems. In child L1 French, is there evidence of verb movement early on, or do verbs tend to stay in V? In L2 acquisition of French, do learners adopt the parametric setting of their L1 first, only to reset it (if necessary) to the target value later on, based on properties of the input? Can they in fact ever acquire the French value? All these questions will be addressed in the next chapters.

CHAPTER 2

The verbal domain in child L1 French

This chapter focuses on the acquisition of inflectional morphology and verb placement in child L1 French. Most of the data on which theoretical claims are based come from spontaneous (longitudinal) production data. At the beginning of the recording sessions, the children have typically started producing sentences containing a verb (between 20 and 24 months), and are generally followed for several months to over a year. Recording sessions usually take place every three to four weeks. (Note that throughout this book ages are given either in year;month;week or year;month.day.) The chapter starts with a discussion of the development of finite morphology, focusing on the first finite verbs, the production of root infinitives, and the development of tense. Several theoretical analyses of the findings are then presented. Not all of these approaches are systematically evaluated at this point, since crucial data supporting or disconfirming them will be introduced in upcoming chapters. Where appropriate, the reader will be referred to the relevant sections for discussion. The chapter ends with the findings on knowledge of verb movement in child L1 French and its theoretical implications.

2.1 Inflectional morphology in child L1 French

Verbal inflection is used relatively early by children learning L1 French (at around 20 months). However, these children go through a period during which they also produce nonfinite verbs (such as infinitives and past participle forms), in utterances where a finite verb is expected in the target language. This phenomenon, which has also been reported in the acquisition of a wide variety of languages, such as Dutch, Faroese, German, Icelandic, and Russian (see Guasti 2002), is referred to as the root infinitive (RI) or optional infinitive (OI) phenomenon.

2.1.1 The first finite verbs in child L1 French

The first utterances produced by children learning French are largely made of one or two words, from which the verb is often absent, such as *là nounours* 'there teddy', *voilà papillon* 'here butterfly' (Marie, aged 15–17 months), *bébé beau* 'baby pretty' (Charles, 1;5.11) (examples from Boysson-Bardies 1999). This said, there is tremendous variation across children, and longer utterances are not infrequent in some cases, e.g. *canard dans l'eau* 'duck in the water' (Léo, aged 15–17.5 months) (Boysson-Bardies 1999). In general, the canonical word order of French is respected, although word order may vary according to the situation.

Verbs appear quite early in the speech of young children, although it is not clear whether their first verbal utterances are truly analysed as different units or whether they should be considered formulaic expressions or routines, namely constructions that are rote-learned, such as *c'est Grégoire* 'it's Grégoire', and *y a poupée* 'there is doll' (Marie, 15–17 months). There is also a high incidence of imperatives in early speech (e.g. *regarde!* 'look!'). Although the Mean Length of Utterance (MLU) is not always reported by researchers, it seems that the first finite forms appear at around an MLU value of 1.50. However, the data on which these findings are based do not always involve children of the same age, which in turn can affect the MLU values reported. For instance, Rasetti (2003) reports that the three children of her Geneva corpus (Augustin, Marie, & Louis) have an MLU of 2.37, 1.64, and 1.33 respectively at the time of their first recording (at 2;0.2 for Augustin, 1;8.26 for Marie, and 1;9.26 for Louis). The three children all produced finite forms at that time. What is not clear, however, is whether they produced finite utterances earlier on, especially Augustin, whose MLU at the first recording is much higher than that of the two other children.

Once verbs start being used productively, agreement is expressed. However, it is important to note that not all markers are used early on. First, verb forms may appear in the infinitive where a finite verb is required in adult speech, the so-called root infinitive or optional infinitive phenomenon (e.g. *moi pousser* 'me push.INF' Daniel, 1;9;3) (see Section 2.1.2 below). Second, the first finite verbs used by children are in the present form; past and future constructions emerge later on. Third, plural forms are not produced initially (e.g. *finissent* 'finish.3PL' and *partent* 'leave.3PL'). The 1st person plural marker *-ons* is only rarely used in spoken French, which means that it is very seldom present in the input to which children learning French are exposed. Not surprisingly, *-ons* emerges quite late in child French. In fact, children have a tendency to use – and overuse – 3rd person singular forms initially, such as *est* 'is', *a* 'has' and *va* 'goes'. Researchers often consider these forms to be default finite forms or elsewhere forms (Ferdinand 1996, based on terminology from Halle & Marantz 1993), in contrast to what they call specified forms, which bear specific agreement morphology. For example, in the paradigm of the first group verb *chanter* 'sing', the form *chan[t]* does not bear any specific (audible) person marker since it can be used with 1st, 2nd, 3rd singular and 3rd plural subjects (see Table 1 in Section 1.1). It is therefore considered an elsewhere form. In contrast, *chant-ons* 'sing.1PL' is clearly specified for 1st person plural. In the paradigm of *être* 'be', [ɛ] is the elsewhere form because it can appear with second and third person singular subjects, as in *tu es* 'you are', *il est* 'he is', *elle est* 'she is', and *on est* 'one is'. Specified forms are *je suis* 'I am', *nous sommes* 'we are', and *ils sont* 'they are'.[13] Initially, children tend to use elsewhere forms in contexts where a specified form is required.

Another characteristic of children's first verbal productions is that they mostly include lexical verbs or the copula *être* 'be'; significant use of modal verbs and auxiliaries emerges later. Table 1 summarizes the incidence of the different verb types across the three children of the Geneva corpus (Rasetti 2003). This table further distinguishes between finite and nonfinite main verb forms. Note that all verbs appearing in RIs are lexical.

Table 1. Incidence of different verb types in the Geneva corpus (from Rasetti 2003)

Child	Age	+ Finite Lexical	Copula	Modal	Aux	– Finite (Lexical)	Total
Augustin	2;0.02 – 2;9.30	326 (41.8%)	200 (25.6%)	44 (5.6%)	111 (14.2%)	99 (12.7%)	780
Marie	1;8.26 – 2;6.10	687 (41.2%)	520 (31.2%)	200 (12%)	64 (3.8 %)	195 (11.7%)	1666
Louis	1;9.26 – 2;3.29	607 (49.8%)	312 (25.6%)	90 (7.4%)	43 (3.5%)	167 (13.7%)	1219

In short, the first tensed verbs found in child speech are present 3rd person singular forms (of lexical verbs or the copula), as in (1) (examples from Pierce 1992).

(1) a. Elle la voit l' auto. (Nathalie, 2;0;2)[14]
she it see.FIN[15] the car

b. Il mange. (Grégoire, 1;10;0)
he eat.FIN

c. (ils) est tout tombé. (Daniel, 1;8;3)
(they) is all fallen

13. In languages with rich inflectional paradigms, such as Italian and Spanish, all verb forms differ from each other overtly. In other words, their paradigms contain no elsewhere forms, and all verbal markers are specified for person and number. In turn, no default (3rd person) singular forms or elsewhere forms are reported in the speech of children acquiring those languages. Instead, children use specified forms from the outset.

14. Data from Nathalie and Daniel were collected by Lightbown (1977). Grégoire's data are from the Champaud corpus. All these data are available in CHILDES (MacWhinney 2000).

15. Throughout this book the abbreviation FIN will be used to refer to a finite verb form whose ending is not distinctive in terms of person and number.

Acquisition of the inflectional paradigm is gradual. In other words, the production of elsewhere forms does not end abruptly. Instead, there is a period of variability between the use of specified forms, which enter the lexicon of the children little by little, and the use of elsewhere forms, as illustrated in (2) and (3).

(2) a. (Ils) a bobo. (Daniel, 1;11;1)
(they) has pain

b. Je l' ai mis là.
I it have+1SG put there

(3) a. (Je) va assis. (Grégoire, 2;1;25)
(I) go+3SG sit

b. (Je) vais chercher hélicoptère moi.
(I) go+1SG look+for.INF helicopter me

In general, verbal agreement is largely correct in the early stages of L1 French. Rasetti (2003) reports that over 90% of irregular verbs (e.g. *aller* 'go', *avoir* 'have' and *être* 'be') used with an overt subject in the Geneva corpus bear target-like morphology. In Augustin's data, the rate of correct inflection is 92% (155/169); for Marie, it is 97% (337/349); for Louis, 100%. Interestingly, inflectional errors are almost always of the same kind: 3rd person singular forms (which are elsewhere forms) are used for other forms but not vice-versa. In other words, specified forms do not substitute for elsewhere forms. That is, utterances such as *papa vont* 'daddy go+3PL' or *des motos vais* 'some motorcycles go+1SG' are not observed in child speech. Similar results are reported by Franck et al. (2004) on elicited production (see Section 3.2.1.1 for a description of the task). The authors show that although substitution of plural forms by singular verbs can be found until the age of seven, children are nonetheless sensitive to the presence of a plural subject as of a relatively young age (the youngest children in their study were five years old). One possible explanation for the end of the elsewhere stage, suggested by Ferdinand (1996), relates it to indirect negative evidence received by children. Given that elsewhere forms do not substitute for specified forms in adult language, once children acquire specified forms, they start ranking all verb forms in their lexicon, gradually placing specified forms higher than elsewhere ones.

2.1.2 Root infinitives in child L1 French

In addition to finite forms, children often use infinitival verbs or past participles instead of tensed verbs in the early stages of acquisition, as in (4), which is erroneous with respect to the target language.[16]

16. Researchers do not always distinguish between infinitives and past participles when discussing RIs. One of the potential reason for this is that the infinitival form and the past participle of first group verbs are homophonous (ending in [e]), as *jouer* 'play.INF' and *joué*

(4) a. Michel dormir là. (Philippe, 2;2;3)[17]
Michel sleep.INF there

b. Monsieur conduire. (Daniel, 1;8;7)
mister drive.INF

c. Moi pousser. (Daniel, 1;9;3)
me push.INF

d. Toi venir. (Grégoire, 2;3;0)
you come.INF

e. Lancer la balle. (Philippe, 2;1;3)
throw.INF the ball

f. Dormir tout nu. (Daniel, 1;10;2)
sleep.INF all naked

Although the observed variation across children is large, the incidence of root infinitives can be quite high early on (as high as 70% in some cases). Table 2 summarizes the global incidence of nonfinite verbs for children whose spontaneous production has been studied longitudinally. The incidence of infinitival forms gradually decreases with age and is reported to be quite low by age 2;6. Note that the ratio of RIs is comparable to what is reported in L1 acquisition of Danish, Dutch, German, and Swedish, and is much higher than what is reported in child Italian, Spanish and Catalan (see Guasti (2002), Hoekstra & Hyams (1998), and Rasetti (2003) for overviews).

Interestingly, not all kinds of verbs occur in RIs. As observed by Ferdinand (1996), noneventive verbs (such as stative verbs (like *rester* 'stay'), the copula *être,* auxiliaries, and modals) do not appear in such utterances; instead, they are systematically found as tensed forms, as in (5a). In contrast, the vast majority of RI utterances include verbs denoting an event (such as *jouer* 'play' or *marcher* 'walk'), as in (5b).

(5) a. Est froid le camion. (Philippe: 2;2;0)
is cold the truck

b. Moi aller dehors. (Daniel: 1;10;2)
me go.INF outside

'play. PtP (see Section 1.1). Moreover, most lexical verbs initially used by children are first group verbs. Despite these drawbacks, Rasetti (2003) calculated that unambiguous past participles, such as *vu* 'seen', make up between 8% and 20% of RIs used by children learning French.

17. Philippe's data are from Suppes, Smith and Leveillé (1973). All these data are available in CHILDES (MacWhinney 2000).

Table 2. Incidence of RIs in early child L1 French

Study	Child	Age	RI stage(s)	Post RI stage(s)
Hamann et al. (1996)[18]	Augustin	2;0.2 – 2;9.30	2;0.2 – 2;4.22 *46/263 (17%)*	2;4.22 – 2;9.30 *23/374 (6.1%)*
vd Velde (1999)	Hugo	1;8.14 – 2;5.19	1;8.14 – 2;1.29 *53/132 (40%)*[a]	2;2.27 – 2;5.19 *6/463 (1.3%)*
Rasetti (2000)	Nathalie	1;9;3 – 2;3;2	1;9;3 – 2;3;2 *69/372 (18.5%)*	–
	Daniel	1;8;1 – 1;11;1	1;8;1 – 1;11;1 *227/635 (35.7%)*	–
Labelle (2000)	Mélanie[b]	1;7.1 – 2;3.23	1;7.1 – 2;3.23 *35/385 (9%)*	–
Legendre et al. (2002)	Grégoire[c]	1;9;2 – 2;3;0	– 1;9 – 1;10 *82/297 (28%)* – 2;0 – 2;3 *46/287 (16%)*	2;5 *6/711 (1%)*
	Stéphane[c, d]	2;2 – 3;3	– 2;2 – 2;3 *51/106 (48%)* – 2;6–2;8 *25/205 (12%)*	3;3 *3/152 (2%)*
	Philippe	2;1;3 – 2;3;0	2;1 – 2;2 *102/476 (21%)*	2;6 *11/260 (4%)*
De Cat (2002)	Anne	1;10.12 – 3;1.4	1;10.12 – 2;8.3 *131/1323 (9.9%)*	2;8.20 – 3;1.4 *10/1273 (0.8%)*
	Max[b]	1;9.19 – 2;10.24	1;9.19 – 2;4.18 *111/509 (21.8%)*	2;5.1 – 2;10.24 *55/1148 (4.7%)*
	Tom[e]	2;1.11 – 2;10.7	2;1.11 – 2;4.9 *76/505 (15%)*	2;5.24 – 2;10.7 *13/645 (2%)*
Rasetti (2003)	Marie	1;8.26 – 2;6.10	1;8.26 – 2;3.03 *172/1115 (15.4%)*	2;3.13 – 2;6.10 *23/551 (4.2%)*
	Louis	1;9.26 – 2;3.29	1;9.26 – 2;2.04 *153/775 (19.8%)*	2;2.17 – 2;3.29 *14/444 (3.1%)*

a. Based on vd Velde Table IV, excluding imperatives and expressions such as *c'est* and *il y a*, as well as legitimate RIs.

b. These children were learning Quebec French.

c. The data are reported in different phases of acquisition by the researchers.

d. Data from Rondal (1985).

e. This child was learning Belgian French.

18. Calculations by Rasetti (2003) yielded similar results (Table 20, p. 59).

Another difference between RIs and tensed declaratives is that most RIs have a modal reading. For instance, they may express necessity, will or capacity, as in (6). This reading is apparent when the discursive and situational contexts in which the child's utterance is produced are considered. Tensed declaratives, on the other hand, almost always receive a strictly temporal interpretation, referring to either past or present events.

(6) Cabinets ouvrir. (Grégoire, 1;9.28)
restroom open.INF
'(I will) open the restroom (door)'

In the Geneva corpus, Rasetti (2003) reports that at least 80% of the three children's RIs have a modal reading, versus at most 12.3% a descriptive interpretation. Similar correlations are reported in the acquisition of other languages that have overt infinitival markers and that do not allow subject omission, such as German and Dutch (Hoekstra & Hyams 1998; Hyams 2001; Wijnen 1998).[19]

2.1.3 Development of tense in child L1 French

As said earlier, past and future tenses emerge later than present tense forms. Moreover, *passé composé* emerges before *imparfait*, and analytic future (e.g. *je vais manger* 'I'm going to eat') is found before syntactic future (e.g. *je mangerai* 'I will eat'). In Hugo's data (1;8.14–2;5.19) analysed by van der Velde (1999), the first finite verbs are found in the second recording (at age 1;9.21), and they are in the present. The first instance of *passé composé* appears in the sixth sample (at age 2;1.7), namely over four months later. This is consistent with the finding that auxiliaries emerge after lexical verbs and the copula (recall Table 1). Verbs in the *passé composé* are then found throughout the rest of the data. As for future tense, it is usually expressed analytically and appears slightly after the emergence of the first verbs in the *passé composé*, at age 2;1.29. There is only one instance of synthetic future in Hugo's data (at age 2;1.29). Very few instances of other tenses (*imparfait*, *plus-que-parfait* and the conditional) are recorded, and all of them appear at or after age 2;4.8. In Pauline's data (Bassano 1998), *passé composé* emerges between months 18 and 21 and its incidence increases as of month 22 (see also Bassano et al. 2001). Prior to month 18, utterances include forms in the present or in the infinitive. The imperfect appears between months 26 and 29. Unfortunately, few studies have focused on the development of tenses other than the present and *passé*

19. In contrast, the modal interpretation of RIs is less often observed in child L1 English. For Hoekstra and Hyams (1998), this is due to the fact that English does not have overt infinitival markers.

composé in child L1 French. More research is therefore needed, including research on the development of mood and aspect.

2.1.4 Development of regular vs. irregular morphology in child L1 French

As seen above, children produce correctly inflected verbs early on, but it is not always clear whether these first forms result from rote learning, which may be related to frequency in the input, or from the application of a productive rule that has been acquired. In this respect, overgeneralization can be used as a diagnosis for the acquisition of a particular rule, and for the nature of acquisition. We already saw that children learning French produce overgeneralized forms, as elsewhere forms and RIs, but what is actually produced, albeit non-target-like, corresponds to forms that are attested in the language. What is interesting here is overgeneralization of regular paradigm to irregular forms. Anecdotal evidence point to overuse of regular inflection in spontaneous speech in child L1 French, such as past participle forms ending in *-é*, e.g. *batté* instead of *battu* 'beaten' and *voulé* instead of *voulu* 'wanted'. While *-é* is the most frequent overregularized marker in past participles, other endings may also be overgeneralized, such as *-u*, as in *prendu* instead of *pris* 'taken' and *éteindu* instead of *éteint* 'switched off'.

Similar results are reported by Royle (2007) in an elicited production task focusing on *passé composé*. Thirty-two verbs were targeted, 16 regular and 16 irregular, equally divided between frequent verbs (e.g. *laver* 'wash' for regular and *ouvrir* 'open' for irregular) and infrequent verbs (e.g. *brider* 'bridle' for regular and *fendre* 'split' for irregular). Results show that children aged 2;11 to 4;6 (n=15) are sensitive to frequency and regularity effects, regardless of age. With frequent verbs, they produced significantly more target-like regular forms (78.1%) than irregular ones (40.6%). Moreover, close to 11% of irregular forms were overregularized, as illustrated above. With infrequent verbs, the accuracy rate also favoured regular verbs (29.7%) vs. irregular ones (3.1%).[20] In the latter case, the vast majority of the verbs produced were regular forms. In brief, we can see that with both frequent and infrequent verbs, target-like production was mostly observed with regular forms. Interestingly, while most cases of overregularization were in *-é*, some were in *-i* (e.g. *ouvri* instead of *ouvert* 'opened'). None was in *-u* [y]. This corresponds to the productivity of the inflectional rules, past participles in *-é* being the most productive type and past participles in *-u* the least productive. Crucially, the fact that children use overregularized forms in *-i*, even with verbs that do not end in *-ir* in the infinitive, such as *répondi* instead of *répondu* 'answered' for the verb *répondre* 'answer', shows that children are sensitive to regularity, even when it is not frequent in the input (see also Say & Clahsen 2002 for child L1 Italian).

20. This was calculated on eight children only, who had obtained a 50% accuracy rate with frequent verbs.

This supports the view that children are able to induce generative rules from the input they receive, presumably via the language faculty (Bartke, Marcus & Clahsen 1995; Marcus 1996; Pinker 1999). Children apply this capacity to lexical items they hear in the input, regardless of the frequency of these items. They end up with a lexicon, a set of lexical entries, and a set of rules that they apply in order to form larger lexical expressions. In other words, children are able to build (and inversely decompose) lexical items into larger/smaller units. This account clashes with the view according to which lexical words are stored and learned as unanalysed chunks, with frequency being one of the main factors behind the learning process (Bybee 1995; Marchman & Bates 1994). In this view, inflected forms are learned via the establishment of patterns. Here, frequency is crucial since the more frequent the forms with a similar shape, the more likely they are to form a pattern, and then for the pattern to be integrated and used. We will see in Section 3.2.1.1 that children with SLI, in contrast to typically developing children, tend to treat inflected forms as wholes rather than as decomposable units.

2.2 Functional categories in child L1 French

The fact that finite verbs are produced in early stages, although sometimes to a very limited extent, suggests that children have some knowledge of finiteness. This means that at least one functional layer is present in initial underlying grammars, which is usually labeled either IP or F(unctional)P:

(7)

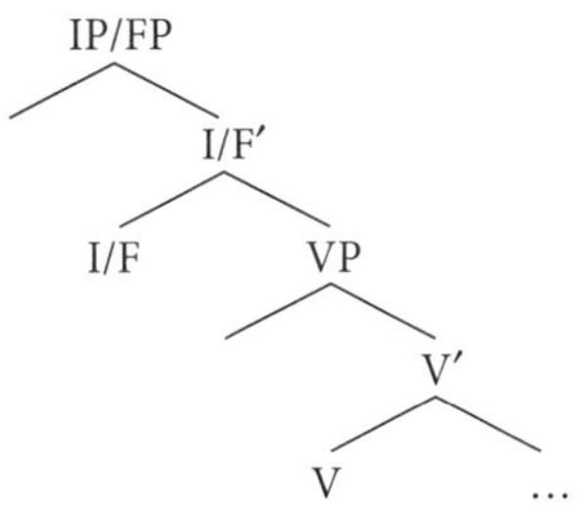

Another argument in favour of the availability of at least one functional category in early child grammars is that subject clitics, such as *je/tu/il/ils* 'I/you/he/they+MASC', which need to attach to a finite verb in Infl, are used very early by children and become quickly productive. Indeed, the first instances of subject clitics (mostly 3rd person clitics) are reported to occur at around the age of two (see Section 6.1.1 for more detailed discussion). Moreover, subject clitics rarely appear with nonfinite forms; rather, they seem to be restricted to finite clauses. This is reported in both longitudinal data (Table 3) and cross-sectional studies (Jakubowicz & Rigaut 2000). The few overt subjects reported to occur in RIs are NPs and strong pronouns, namely elements that do not bear or need nominative Case (see Section 6.1.1).

Table 3. Incidence of subject clitics with finite and nonfinite verbs in child L1 French[21]

Children	+Finite	%	–Finite	%
Marie (1;8.26 – 2;6.10)	872/1219	84.1%	0/179	0%
Jean (1;7.16 – 2;0.28)	261/303	86.1%	0/8	0%
Nathalie (1;9;3 – 2;3;2)	156/301	51.8%	0/71	0%
Louis (1;9.26 – 2;3.29)	588/871	67.5%	0/141	0%
Philippe (2;1.19 – 2;6.20)	988/1471	67.2%	2/247	0.8%
Daniel (1;8;1 – 1;11;1)	154/436	35.3%	3/221	1.4%
Augustin (2;0;2 – 2;9;30)	378/646	58.4%	8/82	9.8%
Hugo (1;8.14 – 2;5.19)[a]	428/567	75.5%	1/71	1.4%
Anne, Max, and Tom[b]	4114/5007	82.1%	11/386	2.8%

a. Data from vd Velde (1999: 96), Table V. Note that in contrast to vd Velde, relative clauses were not compiled in the present table. In addition, 38 RIs out of the 71 reported are deemed indeterminate (e.g. *souffler* 'blow.INF'). An additional 11 instances do not appear to be nonfinite declaratives (e.g. *pour jouer* 'to play.INF'). Thus, 22 cases of true (illegitimate) RIs remain. Nonetheless, the ratio of subject clitics remain low in these cases (1/22 = 4.5%).

b. For these children, the data are collapsed over the following periods: Anne (1;10.12–3;1.4), Max (1;9.19–2; 10.24), and Tom (2 ;1.11–2;10.7) (De Cat 2002). Note that De Cat makes a distinction between 'real' RIs and RIs with an embryonic modal or auxiliary, as in *e cacher les fleurs* '(I want to/I'm going to) hide.INF the flowers', Anne 2;1.19). No subject clitic is reported in the 77 utterances of the latter type found in the data.

Early knowledge of finiteness is further evidenced by the fact that the distribution of finite and nonfinite forms is target-like from the outset. Recall that, in adult French, finite forms precede negative adverbs as in *Je n'aime pas les carottes* 'I don't like carrots', while nonfinite forms follow them, as in *Je n'ai pas aimé les carottes* 'I didn't like the carrots'. Children's early forms respect this distinction. For example, nonfinite verbs rarely appear before negative adverbs (see Table 5 below); rather, they are mainly found to follow *pas*, as in (8a). Finite verbs, on the other hand, precede rather than follow negation (8b).

(8) a. Pas attraper papillon. (Daniel 1;8;3)
not catch.INF butterfly

b. Marche pas. (Daniel 1;8;3)
function.FIN not

21. Data on the first seven children in Table 3 (i.e. from Marie to Augustin) are adapted from Rasetti (2003, Tables 39 and 40, pp. 194–195). Slight discrepancies may occur across different studies of the same children. For example, Pierce (1992) reports 14 subject clitics in Daniel's RIs compared to three reported by Rasetti (2003). Despite these differences, the general observation holds: subject clitics largely tend to occur in finite declaratives.

Nonfinite verb forms are also absent from CP clauses (such as embedded clauses and wh-questions). This is target-like behaviour, since CPs imply the projection of functional categories such as Infl. Reviewing data from Philippe (age 2;1.19–2;7.18), Augustin (age 2;0.2–2;0.30) and Marie (1;8.26–2;3.3), Hamann (2000a) looked at verb forms in wh-questions. During the periods considered, the total number of wh-questions produced by each child was 313, 94, and 30 respectively. In all of them, the verb was finite (see also Crisma 1992).[22]

The array of facts presented above strongly argue against the maturational approach to the emergence of functional categories (Lebeaux 1988; Radford 1990). According to this view, initial grammars contain only lexical categories, as in (9), and functional categories develop along a pre-programmed biological clock following this early lexical stage of acquisition.

(9)

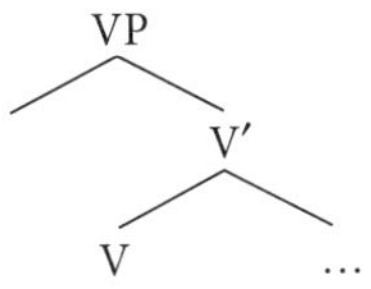

This view is mainly based on the acquisition of English, in which evidence for finite verbs (*-ed* and *-s* forms) is relatively late to emerge. However, if maturation truly guided language acquisition and the development of functional categories, it should apply to all learning situations. In other words, evidence for finite forms should be scarce in the early stages of acquisition of any language, contrary to what we have just seen for L1 French, in which children produce both finite verbs and subject clitics quite early and are quick to distinguish between finite and nonfinite forms.

The fact that the distinction between finite and nonfinite forms seems to be in place very rapidly does not necessarily mean that all categories and all of their features are available or fully specified right away. For instance, the fact that children produce so many root infinitives in the early stages may signal that they lack knowledge of tense or agreement initially. In other words, they may possess Infl, but that category may be underspecified for tense, or agreement, or both. Alternatively, they may have the category Agr but not T, or T but not Agr. They could also have both categories, but fail to

22. Phillips (1995) points out that most of Philippe's wh-questions involve an auxiliary, which we have seen only appear in the finite form throughout the data, including in root declaratives. However, Hamann (2000a) reports that some of the wh-questions produced by Augustin and Marie do include lexical verbs, such as *faire* 'do' and *aller* 'go'. Although the figures are low (23 verbs in Augustin's data and 6 in Marie's), not one of these verbs appears as a nonfinite form. This is especially revealing in Marie's case, given that her RI rate was relatively high (17.9%) during the period where wh-questions were found.

project them systematically. Researchers have explored these various hypotheses, and the following sections will consider each in turn.

2.2.1 Underspecification of Tense values

One possibility, assumed in Ferdinand (1996), is that Agr is present in underlying grammars right from the outset. Although most finite forms are elsewhere forms in the early stages, they nonetheless appear with a range of subjects (such as 1st person singular, 3rd person singular, etc.), which Ferdinand takes to suggest that they are marked for agreement, although they may not be specified for person and number (they are simply [+agreement]). As for Tense (and its [+tense] specification), Ferdinand also assumes it to be available initially, but claims that [±present] values are underspecified. This assumption has important consequences for the distribution of eventive and noneventive verbs. Ferdinand assumes that eventive verbs denote a change in time: 'they consist of beginning, middle, and terminal stages' (Ferdinand 1996: 86). In other words, they have an internal time structure. Therefore, when they are associated to [+tense], they must be related to a specific moment of time: past, present or future. Ferdinand claims that since the [±present] values of Tense are not available in early acquisition, these verbs cannot be associated to [+tense]. Therefore, they appear as nonfinite forms. In contrast to eventive verbs, noneventive verbs, such as statives, do not denote any change in time, so they can be [+tense] without being related to a specific point on the temporal axis. They can therefore be inflected. This would explain the observed correlation between finiteness and verb types in the initial stages of acquisition, illustrated in (6) above.

An important question for this analysis is: if noneventive verbs may be finite, why do they *never* appear in RIs? In other words, not only *can* they be inflected, it seems that they *must* be inflected. Ferdinand argues that RIs contain a null auxiliary with modal or aspectual properties, as illustrated in (10) (see Boser, Lust, Santelmann, & Whitmann (1992) for a similar proposal for early child German).

(10) [$_{IP}$'tascha [$_{INFL}$ Ø] [$_{VP}$ ouvrir]]
Natascha open.INF

This assumption is based on the observation that in some cases nonfinite verbs are preceded by a dummy element, which Ferdinand takes to be a partial phonological realization of an auxiliary, as in *e couper* 'cut.INF' (Daniel, 1;8;3). In the Geneva corpus, these dummy forms are found in a substantial number of RIs: 92 of Augustin's 166 and 64 of Marie's 243 (Rasetti 2003; see also De Cat 2002).[23] Ferdinand further argues

23. Rasetti (2003) argues that these placeholders should not be considered subjects. While they appear in alternation with overt (preverbal) subjects in finite declaratives, such an alternation does not obtain in RIs, given that overt subjects rarely appear in such utterances.

that children are unable, at around age two, to combine the aspectual properties of the null auxiliary with noneventive verbs. This would explain why noneventive verbs cannot appear in RIs. Positing the existence of a null auxiliary/modal also provides an immediate account for the correlation between finiteness and modal interpretation introduced above (recall (6)): null auxiliaries are only present in RIs (not in finite declaratives) and grant these utterances a modal reading, which does not obtain in finite declaratives.

Positing the existence of a null element, however, requires some insight as to its licensing and identification, which Ferdinand does not do. In a related proposal, Boser et al. (1992) argue that the null auxiliary must be licensed in specifier/head agreement relation. In other words, an overt (agreeing) subject must occupy the specifier position. As pointed out by Hoekstra and Hyams (1998), however, this hypothesis runs into trouble when wh-questions and subject types appearing in RIs are taken into consideration. Starting with the latter, we will see in Chapter 6 (Section 6.2.1.1) that null subjects are very frequent in RIs. Yet, if RIs are meant to contain a null auxiliary that should be licensed by an overt subject, the high incidence of subjectless RIs cannot be explained. Similarly, Boser et al.'s (1992) approach predicts that subject wh-questions should be found with nonfinite verbs, since the overt wh-pronoun, *qui* 'who' in French, could act as a licensor of the null auxiliary. Yet, as will be seen in Chapter 14, wh-questions rarely appear with a nonfinite verbs in child language, including child L1 French.[24] Ferdinand's account, coupled with Boser et al.'s (1992) account of null auxiliaries in RIs, is therefore difficult to maintain.

2.2.2 Underspecification of Agreement

Another possible assumption to account for the variation in children's early inflectional forms is that Agr develops after Tense (Legendre, Hagstrom, Vainikka & Todorova 2002). Legendre et al. investigated knowledge of tense and agreement in the corpus of Grégoire, Philippe, and Stéphane (see Table 3). During the acquisition period considered, the children were reported to go through three different stages (named 3b, 4b and 4c). These stages were identified in terms of the Predominant Length of Utterance (PLU), which takes into account both the number of words in the majority of a child's utterances and the proportion of utterances containing a verb (Vainikka, Legendre & Todorova 1999). The authors focused their attention on the occurrence of nonpresent forms, in particular verbs in the *passé composé* and the *futur proche* (analytic future), and of verbal forms other than 3rd person singular (e.g. *je suis* 'I am'). Table 4 summarizes the occurrence of such verbs at the three PLU stages,

24. Nonfinite wh-questions are reported in child L1 English, however (see Bromberg & Wexler 1995).

collapsing across the children.[25] The incidence of nonpresent and non-3rd person singular (non-3SG) forms is also reported in adult speech, as identified in the conversation between the interviewers and the children. Finally, the incidence of RIs was calculated for each child.[26]

Table 4. Incidence of nonpresent, non-3SG, and nonfinite forms in three children (from Legendre et al. 2002)

	Stage 3b	Stage 4b	Stage 4c	Adults
Verbs with nonpresent tense inflection (out of verbs marked for tense)	85/246 (35%)	105/725 (15%)	313/1027 (31%)	418/1365 (31%)
Verbs with non-3SG agreement inflection (out of verbs marked for agreement)	7/199 (4%)	90/584 (15%)	370/1,028 (36%)	500/1,362 (37%)
Nonfinite root forms (out of all verbs)	133/403 (33%)	173/968 (18%)	20/1,123 (2%)	–

The development of nonpresent forms seems to follow a U-shaped pattern, with starting and ending points at mature-like levels (around 30%). In contrast, non-3SG forms develop in a more linear fashion, starting at a very low level (4%) and reaching an adult-like ratio at the final stage. This, the authors argue, suggests that Tense develops prior to Agr in child French. As for RIs, their development is inversely correlated with non-3SG forms: incidence of RIs is high at first and then sharply declines. For Legendre et al. this suggests that there is a connection between RIs and the development of Agr, but not between RIs and Tense.

It should be remembered, however, that this conclusion is based on a calculation of linguistic development, PLU, which is not often used by child L1 researchers who rely rather on MLU or MLU-w statistics. Moreover, it is not clear whether Legendre et al.'s hypothesis can explain the array of facts about RIs that has been identified in the literature, such as the contingencies between verb types and finiteness (with RIs containing almost only noneventful verbs) and between interpretation and finiteness (with RIs largely receiving a modal reading), as well as other phenomena which will be discussed later in the book, such as the simultaneous decline of RIs subjectless finite declaratives in child speech (see Chapter 6) and the lack of RIs in embedded and wh-questions (Chapter 14).

25. The incidence of the reported forms is very similar for the three children at each stage.

26. Here again, the collapsed results reflect individual performance, except perhaps at stage 4b (see Table 2 for the difference between Grégoire and Stéphane).

2.2.3 Underspecification of Number

Yet another possibility, argued for in Hyams and Hoekstra (1998) (H&H), is that it is Number which is initially underspecified. Their proposal relies on the assumption that person and number are specified in separate projections Pers and Num. In French, there is no morphosyntactic person distinction in the singular (recall Section 1.1), so, they argue, the category Pers is not specified. In contrast, Num is operative in French since there are distinctive markers in the plural, like *-ons* (1PL) and *-ez* (2PL). H&H assume that since Number is underspecified initially, children learning French produce verbs with no finite markers, that is, root infinitives. For H&H, RIs are truly nonfinite, which means that the infinitival marker does not act as a substitute for finite inflection. Crucially, infinitival markers possess irrealis properties (they can refer to events that are not yet realized), in contrast to past participles, which denote completeness (Hyams 2001; Wijnen 1998). For H&H, this [−realized] property of infinitival markers is the reason for the future or modal interpretation of RIs. Finally, to explain the correlation between finiteness and verb type, H&H claim that children under three years old do not have yet knowledge of epistemic modality. According to H&H, epistemic modality obtains when a modal is combined with a noneventive predicate (11a), whereas the other types of modality obtain with predicates denoting an event (11b). The utterance in (11b) is not about the 'necessary' truth of the event, in contrast to (11a); rather, it is about the necessity that the event take place.

(11) a. Il doit être 17h.
it must be 5:00pm
'It must be 5:00pm'

b. Je dois lire ce livre pour demain.
I must read this book for tomorrow
'I have to read this book for tomorrow'

Given that RIs most often have a modal interpretation, the lack of knowledge of epistemic modality in children would explain why noneventive verbs do not appear in such utterances.[27]

In Section 6.2.1.2, we will see that H&H's analysis runs into trouble when data from subjects of finite clauses are taken into account. In particular, we will see that null subjects can be found with finite verbs in child language, which, H&H assume, are instances of PRO. Since PRO can only appear in ungoverned positions (see Chomsky 1995), it should not appear with verb forms that occupy the Infl position, such as the copula. However, as we will see in Section 6.2.1.2, the incidence of subjectless utterances with a copula can be quite high in child L1 French.

27. See Hyams (2007) for a detailed analysis of the role played by event structure, aspect, and modality in the temporal and modal interpretation of RIs.

2.2.4 The Unique Checking Constraint (UCC)

Wexler's Unique Checking Constraint (Wexler 1998; Wexler, Gavarró & Torrens 2004) is another hypothesis to explain the observed distribution of finite and nonfinite forms in child L1 French. Wexler elaborates on Schütze and Wexler's (1996) Agreement or Tense Omission Model (ATOM), in which either Tense or Agreement may be absent from early representations. In accordance with standard linguistic theory, Wexler assumes that the Tense category is equipped with a D(eterminer)-feature that needs to be checked by a corresponding feature, typically the D-feature of the subject DP. In French, as in English, the D-feature in T is assumed to be strong, which forces the subject DP to raise overtly to the specifier position of TP. Wexler further assumes that Agr also possesses a D-feature that requires checking, and that, like the D-feature of T, the D-feature of Agr is strong in French. Therefore, the subject DP will need to raise to SpecTP and then move on to SpecAgrP for checking. This is illustrated in (12).

(12)

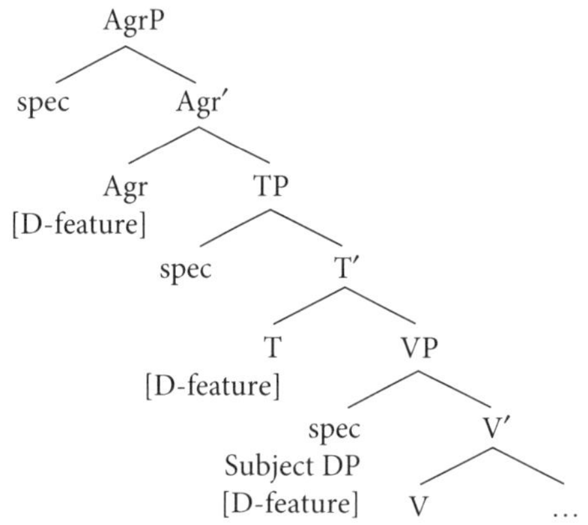

Under the UCC hypothesis, the D-feature of DP can only check one functional category. In other words, the UCC holds that in initial grammars, only one of the two D-features can be checked, either the D-feature of T or that of Agr. This means that only one of the two categories will be projected, as in (13). According to Wexler, once T or Agr is projected, its D-feature will be checked, which prevents any further checking.

(13) a. [$_{AgrP}$ AGR [D] [$_{VP}$ Subject [D] V...]]
b. [$_{TP}$ T [D] [$_{VP}$ Subject [D] V...]]

The nature of the category that is projected has important consequences for the form that the verb will take. In child French, if Tense is projected (and not Agr), the verb will surface as a tensed, nonagreeing form, namely a default finite form or an elsewhere form in the sense of Ferdinand, which generally corresponds to the 3rd person singular. If Agr is projected (and not T), the verb will appear as a nonfinite form, that is, as a root infinitive. Under Wexler's account, children are assumed to have early knowledge of functional categories, D-features, and feature-checking mechanisms. Once the UCC stops operating (via maturation), systematic projection of both T and Agr will obtain, and the RI period will end.

This account has difficulty explaining why most CP clauses produced by children learning French include a finite verb. A priori, the Unique Checking Constraint should apply across the board, including in CPs. Thus, nonfinite verbs should be found in CP-clauses, as in main clauses, when only the D-feature of Agr is checked. Crucially, there exists a period during which child learners produce both CP-clauses with finite verbs and main clauses with root infinitives, which is a problem for the UCC. However, nonfinite verbs are not found in CP-clauses, as seen in Section 2.2, contrary to the predictions of the UCC. Data on object pronouns, which further challenge the UCC, will be presented in Section 6.2.2.2.

2.2.5 Truncation

Another possible explanation for the patterning of finite and nonfinite forms in child language is that all functional categories are available from the outset and are fully specified (along with their features) in early grammars, but they fail to be systematically projected (Rizzi 1993/1994, 1998, 2000; see also Haegeman 1995). Under this hypothesis, the root of declaratives may vary: it may be CP, IP, or VP. In other words, children project truncated structures in the initial stages of acquisition, as in (14).

(14)

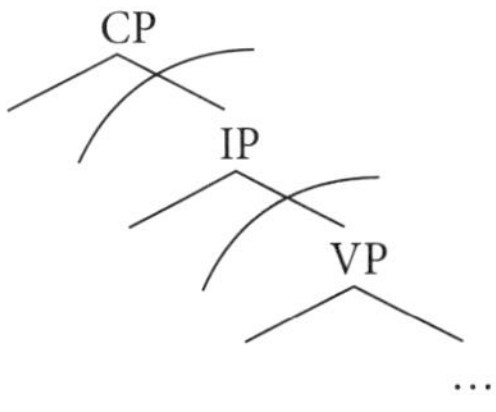

When VP is the root, no functional category is projected, which yields the production of an RI; when at least IP is projected, a finite declarative is produced.

Originally, truncation was couched in terms of the underspecification of the Root Principle, according to which root declaratives are CPs. Basically, children were claimed to be able to project any kind of root prior to their development of the Root Principle, presumably via maturation. More recently, Rizzi (1998, 2000) has proposed that two principles are in competition in early grammars, the Structural Economy Principle (15a) and the Categorial Uniformity Principle (15b):

(15) a. Structural Economy: Use the minimum of structure consistent with well-formedness constraints.

b. Categorial Uniformity: Assume a unique canonical structural realization for a given semantic type

Adult grammars, Rizzi assumes, are constrained by Categorial Uniformity, which yields a uniform projection for the semantic type 'proposition', i.e. CP. Children's grammars, on the other hand, follow Structural Economy, which makes children project representations smaller than CPs, and hence produce RIs. They will do so until they acquire the Categorial Uniformity Principle (presumably via maturation).[28]

In contrast to the UCC hypothesis, the Truncation approach has no problem accounting for the fact that RIs are not found in CP clauses. The Truncation approach holds that all the projections normally appearing below a particular root are projected. It follows that when CP is the root, all functional projections, including IP, will be part of the representation. Hence, a finite verb will be produced. Note that the Truncation hypothesis does not say that CP cannot be the root of the clause; it simply holds that the nature of the root may vary in early L1 child grammars due to economy considerations. We will see in Section 2.3.1 that data on negation may pose a challenge to this hypothesis. For a Truncation account of subject pronouns, see Section 6.1.5.

2.2.6 Computational limitations

For some linguists, children have knowledge of all functional categories, but have computational limitations, presumably due to limited working memory capacities, that prevent them from projecting all categories systematically. This general view has taken the forms of several proposals, such as Computational Complexity Hypothesis (CCH) (Jakubowicz 2004, 2005; Jakubowicz et al. 1998; Jakubowicz & Nash 2001) and Labelle's (2000) Computational Limitation Hypothesis. Other proposals, such as the UCC and Truncation can also be viewed as resulting from the limited computational capacities of young children (see below). In what follows, I will develop Labelle's Computational Limitation Hypothesis in detail and show how it can account for some of facts presented so far. The CCH, which has also been proposed to address the development of tense in child L1 acquisition, will be presented in the section on SLI in the next chapter (3.2.2). Other views of initial limited computational capacities in children will also be dealt with in various parts of this book.

Following Cowper (1994), among others, Labelle assumes that complex tenses, such as *passé composé* and analytic future, involve the projection of two tense nodes: Ttense and Taspect for the *passé composé*, and Ttense and Tinfinitive for analytic future. Taspect hosts the past participle, and Tinfinitive, the infinitival verb. In the structure in (16), TP1 is Ttense and TP2 can be either Taspect or Tinfinitive.

28. A slightly different approach is proposed in Rizzi (2006) where truncation is presented as a parametric option, available in some adult systems.

(16)

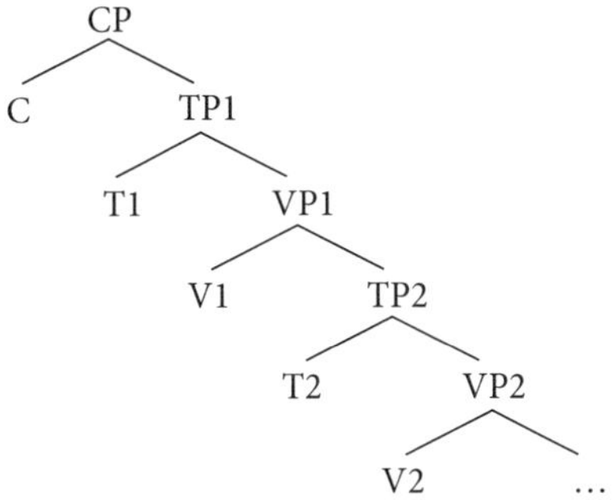

Assuming that the projection of two T nodes implies a composition of temporal information that is too complex for the child, Labelle proposes that children are only able to project one T node in the initial stages of acquisition. If they only project Ttense, a finite declarative will be produced. Labelle further assumes that Ttense only dominates [+present] initially, which is why the first finite verbs produced by children are in the present tense. If Tinfinitive is projected, the resulting declarative is an RI with an infinitival form. Finally, if Taspect is projected, an RI with a past participle will be produced. In the absence of Ttense, the temporal interpretation of RIs is assumed to be done via discourse. Specifically, the time of an RI with an infinitival verb will be interpreted as being prospective with respect to the speech time (hence the frequent modal and future interpretations of RIs observed by researchers); RIs with a past participle, on the other hand, will be interpreted as having taken place prior to the speech time. This hypothesis predicts that children will produce very few utterances with complex tenses initially, which seems to be confirmed by the data. Labelle's analysis also suggests that the projection of C along with Tinfinitive or Taspect (but without Ttense) is possible. This means that children should produce nonfinite questions, counter to the evidence of child L1 French, as seen above. Note that Labelle's account is similar in some respects to the Truncation approach. It could be the case that truncation is in fact related to computational limitations on the part of young children (see also Hamann 2008). However, in contrast to Labelle's account, Truncation correctly predicts that nonfinite verbs should not occur in CPs, since the projection of CP is held to entail that of IP.

Summary

In this section, a range of hypothesis to account for the distribution of finite and nonfinite forms in child L1 French has been considered, from underspecification of various features to computational limitations. The Truncation approach, perhaps re-conceived as a variation of the computational limitation approach, seems the most viable candidate, as it correctly predicts the observed behaviour. In Section 6, further challenging data will be considered that will shed light on the question of children's early functional projections.

2.3 Knowledge of verb movement in child L1 French

As with adult speech, word order in children's speech has been used to argue for the existence of functional categories and their relative order, as well as for the emergence of verb movement. It should be mentioned that evidence for verb movement mostly involves negation as spontaneous production of adverbs and floating quantifiers are quite rare, especially in the early stages of acquisition. This section examines both negation and subject placement, and raises some questions about the existence of an initial lexical stage in language acquisition.

2.3.1 Development of verb placement with respect to negation in child L1 French

Several studies report that verb placement is largely correct in early production data from children (e.g. Ferdinand 1996; Pierce 1992; Rasetti 2003; Verrips & Weissenborn 1992). As Table 5 illustrates, there is a significant contingency between finiteness and verb placement with respect to negation: when the verb precedes the negative adverb, it is finite; when it follows the adverb, it is nonfinite.[29] This is illustrated in (17) and (18). Note that the negative particle *ne* is not attested in the earliest stages.

Table 5. Incidence of finite and nonfinite verbs with respect to negation in child French

Children	Age	V-Neg		Neg-V	
		+finite	– finite	+finite	– finite
Daniel[a]	1;8;1 – 1;11;1	53	1	3	36
Grégoire[a]	1;9;2 – 2;1;3	43	0	0	0
Nathalie[a]	1;9;3 – 2;2;2	68	0	3	82
Philippe[a]	2;1;3 – 2;2;2	52	1	3	4
Benjamin[b]	1;9.19 – 2;03.8	149	1	5	19
Fabienne[b]	1;5.11 – 2;0.23	55	0	2	2
Augustin, Louis, and Marie[c]	1;8.26 – 2;9.30	272	1	2	42

a. Data examined by Pierce (1992)[30]
b. Data examined by Verrips and Weissenborn (1992)
c. Data from Rasetti (2003)

29. The correlation is not evident in the case of Grégoire and Philippe, but this is probably due to the low number of Neg-V sequences produced by these children, in contrast to Daniel and Nathalie. Note also that the ratio of negative utterances is quite similar in finite declaratives and RIs, between 10% and 15%.

30. Ferdinand (1996) examined the same data as Pierce (1992). She reports different numbers for Nathalie and Daniel than those appearing in Table 5 (although they confirm the tendencies identified by Pierce) and does not address the issue of V-Neg sequences in RIs.

(17) a. Elle a pas la bouche. (Nathalie 1;10;2)
she have.FIN not the mouth

b. Marche pas. (Daniel 1;8;3)
function.FIN not

c. Ça tourne pas. (Philippe 2;1;3)
this turn.FIN not

d. Elle roule pas. (Grégoire 1;11;3)
she roll.FIN not

(18) a. Pas la poupée dormir. (Nathalie 1;9;3)
not the doll sleep.INF

b. Pas attraper papillon. (Daniel 1;8;3)
not catch.INF butterfly

c. Pas chercher les voitures. (Philippe 2;1;3)
not look+for.INF the cars

d. Pas rouler en vélo. (Philippe 2;2;1)
not roll.INF on bike

There is no early stage in L1 French during which negation systematically precedes verbs. Moreover, negation is used nonanaphorically even in the earliest recording sessions, that is, it truly negates the utterance in which it appears, not what has been previously said in the discourse. The anaphoric element *non* is also almost never used nonanaphorically, i.e. as a substitute for *pas*, which suggests that children make an early distinction between the two elements. Moreover, there is no initial period where verbs (finite or nonfinite) optionally occur before or after negation. This suggests that the verb movement parameter is set very early by young learners, which is consistent with Wexler's (1998) Very Early Parameter Setting Hypothesis. It also suggests that children have at least one (functional) position available to host finite verbs, as proposed for independent reasons in the various hypotheses considered in the preceding section.

An interesting fact with respect to negation is that children learning French produce negative RIs in the early stages of acquisition. These negative RIs typically display a Neg-$V_{nonfinite}$ order, as is the case in (18) above. This has important consequences for both the UCC and the Truncation approaches. We saw in Section 1 that negation projects a functional category Neg assumed to be located between AgrS and T in French: AgrS > Neg > T. Therefore, Neg-V order with root infinitives is not expected by either of those approaches. Under the UCC analysis, nonfinite forms obtain when the verb raises to AgrS, and no T is projected. Since Neg is lower than AgrS, V-Neg order with root infinitives is predicted, contrary to fact. Wexler's analysis could be saved if the opposite hierarchy between AgrS and T were adopted, whereby T dominates AgrS, which in fact corresponds to Pollock's (1989) original proposal. In that case, Neg, which would still appear between the two functional categories, would dominate AgrS: T > Neg > AgrS. The Neg-V order would then obtain in negative RIs. Under the Truncation analysis,

RIs are produced when VP is the root, and a finite declarative is obtained when at least T is projected. Since Neg is located above T (or AgrS depending on the hierarchy one adopts), negative RIs are not predicted. In fact, all negative roots should at least involve the projection of T (or AgrS), which means that they should all be finite, again contrary to fact. How could the Truncation approach be saved? One possibility is suggested by Zanuttini (1991), who argues that Neg is located below T/AgrS in French, namely right above V: T/AgrS > Neg > V. If truncation occurs right below T/AgrS, then NegP is the root of the declarative. Crucially, no functional category would be involved in the underlying structure and the Neg-$V_{nonfinite}$ order would be derived. Another possibility is to follow Hamann (2000b), who argues that a distinction should be made between past participles and infinitival verbs when investigating verb placement with respect to negation. Maintaining the AgrSP > NegP > TP > VP hierarchy for French, Hamann argues that past participles carry some tense properties, so they may be found after *pas*. However, infinitival forms are truly tenseless and should therefore be banned from negative RIs. This seems to be indeed the case in data from Grégoire, Philippe, and Augustin. For Philippe (2;1 – 2;3) and Grégoire (1;11 – 2 ;3), Hamann reports a total of 6 negative RIs out of 127 negative verbal utterances (4.7%). In Augustin's data (2;0 – 2;4 and 2;6 – 2;10), the proportion is 2 out of 128 (1.6%). In contrast, the incidence of infinitival verbs is much higher in negative utterances produced by children learning L1 German and L1 Dutch (between 14% and 25% in some cases), which could be explained by assuming that NegP is located directly above VP in Germanic languages (see Haegeman 1996).

The other anomalous pattern in child L1 French, with respect to the adult target, is the presence of Neg-V_{finite} word order. Although the incidence of Neg-V_{finite} order is very low, some researchers have tried to formulate an analysis of such sequences, since they apparently violate the theory underlying verb movement. Some studies report that the verbs involved in most of these sequences are so-called main verbs, as in (19) (examples from Verrips & Weissenborn 1992). They further report that initially the vast majority of finite forms occurring before negative adverbs are suppletive forms, i.e. the copula, modals and auxiliaries, as well as forms of *aller* 'go' (de Boysson-Bardies 1976; Verrips & Weissenborn 1992).

(19) a. Pas joue le chat. (Fabienne 2;0.13)
not play.FIN the cat

b. Pas compte. (Fabienne 2;0.23)
not count.FIN

c. Pas chante moi. (Benjamin 2;2.18)
not sing.FIN me

d. Pas saute. (Benjamin 2;2.18)
not jump.FIN

Based on these facts, Verrips and Weissenborn suggest that young children do not yet know that all verbs must be associated with agreement markers, which means that verb movement in the early stages of child French is restricted to T (the Partial Raising Hypothesis). Assuming that NegP is located above TP, verb movement to T would explain the few cases of Neg-V_{finite} errors. In contrast, suppletive forms, i.e. forms that are morphologically marked for agreement, are in Agr and thus precede negation.

A problem for this view, however, is that the number of finite verbs following *pas* is extremely low in some of the corpora investigated (3/39 in Daniel and 3/85 in Nathalie). Verrips and Weissenborn's hypothesis implies that the incidence of such sequences should be much higher. Moreover, nonsuppletive forms do also occur before *pas*, as acknowledged by Verrips and Weissenborn themselves ; see (17b–d), for example. It is not clear how such forms would land in Agr if they do not carry agreement features. Ferdinand (1996) also observes that in the recordings where V_{finite}-Neg sequences are found, there is no variation in the paradigm of the finite verbs being used. She shows that Nathalie only produces one form of *être* 'be' (*est* 'is'), one form of *avoir* 'have' (*a* 'has') and one form of *aller* 'go' (*va* 'goes'). Ferdinand concludes that these forms should have the same status as any other finite forms. In other words, one should not distinguish between *tensed* forms and *agreeing* forms, suggesting that whatever process is allowing children to correctly place suppletive forms before *pas*, it is not agreement per se. As an alternative to the Partial Raising Hypothesis, Ferdinand (1996) proposes that the verb in Neg-V_{finite} sequences occupies the same finite position as in V-Neg sequences (in other words, verb movement has occurred) and that the negative adverb has been fronted to a focus position, as in (20). She claims that in all instances of Neg-V_{finite}, contrastive focus is involved.

(20) $[_{FocusP}$ pas$_i$ $[_{AgrP}$ tombe$_j$ $[_{NegP}$ t_i $[_{TP}$ t_j $[_{VP}$ $t_j]]]]$ (Daniel 1;9;3)
not fall.FIN

Ferdinand fails to provide clear criteria to establish contrastive focus. It is obvious that negation introduces some kind of contrast with what has just been said in the discourse, but this does not mean that focus is systematically placed on the negative. One of the most reliable ways to establish that focus is involved is to analyse them prosodically. It would be interesting to analyses utterances such as (20) as well as other negative finite declaratives produced by children, i.e. those displaying V_{finite}-Neg, to determine whether or not contrastive focus is present.

To summarize, we have seen that verb placement with respect to negation is largely correct from the early stages of acquisition: finite forms largely tend to precede *pas*, whereas nonfinite ones are found to follow it. Some finite forms also occur after the negator, but their incidence is extremely low and cannot question the fact that verb movement in French is acquired very early and that functional categories are present in underlying systems. They could be performance errors or involve some kind of contrastive focus. We have also seen that the occurrence of negative RIs present a challenge to hypotheses such as the UCC and Truncation. However, they can be handled depending on the assumption we make about the exact location of NegP and that of AgrP and TP with respect to each other.

2.3.2 Postverbal subjects in child L1 French

The other area of potential evidence for early implementation of verb movement is subject/verb inversion, as in (21). Postverbal subjects can be quite frequent in child L1 French (Déprez & Pierce 1993; Friedemann 1993/1994; Labelle & Valois 1996; Pierce 1992; Rasetti 2003). Based on Rasetti's (2003) detailed examination of production data from seven children, this type of subjects represents between 10.7% and 70% of overt nonclitic subjects appearing in finite clauses, with an average of 38.8% (see her Table 11, p. 151).[31] Postverbal subjects appear early in production and with different types of verbs, including transitives and intransitives.

(21) a. A bobo fesse Nathalie. (Nathalie, 2;0;1)
has booboo buttocks Nathalie

b. Monte la main. (Grégoire, 1;10;3)
climb.FIN the hand

c. Fait pas du bruit la fifille. (Philippe, 2;1)
make.FIN/PtP not some noise the little girl

d. Veut encore Adrien du pain. (Grégoire, 2;1;3)
want.FIN more Adrien some bread

One way to interpret these data is to assume that the verb has moved to I and that the subject stays within VP. This is most obvious in VS and VSO orders. For Pierce (1992), the subject is in (left-branching) SpecVP and receives Case from I via government, as in (22), leaving aside the details of the projections of I. Note that when the VSO order is found in an RI, Pierce (1992) proposes that the verb moves to AgrO (below I in (22)), and not to I.

31. According to Déprez and Pierce (1993), they make up 85% of nominal subjects in Nathalie's data and around 75% in Grégoire's and Philippe's data. In Rasetti's (2003) count, the ratio is 48.7% for Philippe and 10.7% for Nathalie. Some of the discrepancies between the two studies come from the fact that Rasetti followed Philippe and Nathalie over a much longer period than did Déprez and Pierce.

(22)

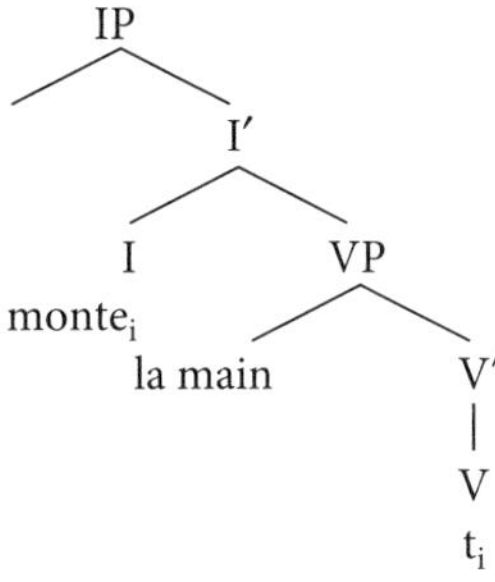

However, this explanation fails to account for the numerous utterances where the subject follows other VP-material in child language, including the object, as shown in (21a,c). According to Friedemann (1993/1994), such VOS orders account for 63% of postverbal subjects. VOS sequences cannot be derived if the subject is in the left-branching specifier of VP; rather, such a configuration should only yield VSO orders. There are two possible solutions to this problem: either the subject moves to a right-dislocated position (adjoined to IP), or SpecVP is right branching in French (and possibly in other Romance languages as well, such as Italian). Friedemann argues in favour of the latter option and proposes that a null constant (nc) occupies SpecIP in child V(O)S declaratives (as in (23)), which satisfies the Extended Projection Principle. In addition, the VP-internal subject is assumed not to need Case, since in most cases, it lacks the DP layer and only appears as an NP, as in (21a) above.[32]

(23)

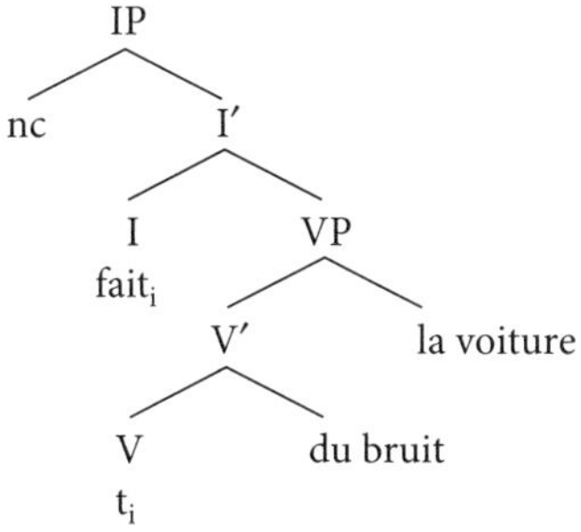

This approach could also account for the frequent RIs displaying a postverbal lexical subject, such as *Manger salade Adrien* 'eat.INF salad Adrien' and *Faire boum sur le*

32. However, there are instances of full DP subjects in postverbal positions in child speech (see (21c) above). Under Friedemann's system, these cannot receive Case, which is problematic.

camion maman 'make.INF boom on the truck mommy' (Philippe, 2;1;3).[33] In such cases, the RIs are VPs with a right branching specifier hosting the subject.

According to the other analysis, adjunction to IP, the specifier of IP is occupied by a null subject and the postverbal subject is adjoined to it (De Cat 2002; Ferdinand 1996; Labelle & Valois 1996). This is illustrated in (24) (from Ferdinand 1996).

(24) a. Veux un autre joujou moi. (Daniel, 1;11;1)
want.FIN a other toy me

b.

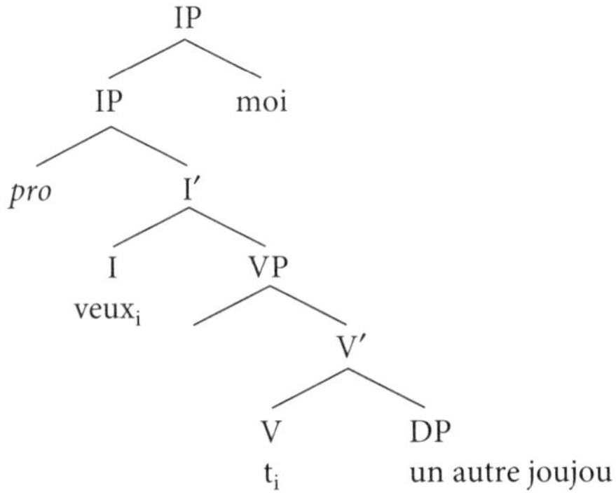

There are four arguments in support of this analysis. First, children use subjectless sentences at the time they produce sentences such as (24a) (see Section 6.2.1). Second, they also produce target-like right-dislocated subjects, such as *Il pousse une pierre, le monsieur* 'He's pushing a rock, the man' (Grégoire, 2;0.5). Third, in utterances involving a postverbal subject and the modifying adverbial *tout seul* 'by oneself', the adverbial systematically precedes the NP, as in (25).

(25) a. Range tout seul Grégoire. (Grégoire, 2;2.25)
cleans+up by himself Grégoire

b. Marche tout seul la voiture. (Philippe, 2;2.3)
works by itself the car

In adult French, the adverbial forms a constituent with the NP, and it follows the NP, as in *Moi/Grégoire tout seul* 'Me/Grégoire by my/himself'. The order *tout seul* – NP in (25) thus suggests that the NP has moved out of that constituent, presumably to a position adjoined to IP (Labelle & Valois 1996). Fourth, acoustic analyses of child utterances containing a postverbal subject are similar to those of right-dislocated subjects in adult French. In particular, the child utterances involve two distinct intonation contours,

33. According to Pierce (1992), postverbal subjects account for 75% of lexical subjects in RIs.

with the postverbal subject being 'marked as an appendix' (see Labelle & Valois 1996: 71, referring to Mertens 1990, 1993). This contrasts sharply with the acoustic analysis of sentences exhibiting a preverbal subject and a direct object, such as *Elle boit le jus* 'She's drinking the juice', which involve only one intonation contour. The difference between the two sentences suggests that the postverbal subject is not part of the VP. Similar arguments are presented in 6.1.1.3 in favour of left-dislocation of NPs in child L1 French.

To sum up, original arguments in favour of verb movement to I based on the occurrence of postverbal subjects brought forward by Pierce (1992) have been challenged by several authors. However, the counter-proposals do not focus on verb movement per se, but on the exact location of the postverbal subject (in the specifier of a right-branching VP or in a topicalized position). This only tells us that we should not consider the existence of postverbal subjects as direct evidence of verb movement in child language any longer.

2.4 Conclusion

In this chapter, we have seen that although children often produce nonfinite verb forms in the initial stages of acquisition, appropriate use of agreement and tense morphology develops rapidly in L1 French. Children also tend to overregulate verb forms with both productive and less productive inflectional markers. This argues in favour of the rapid development of functional categories, although there is debate about whether all functional categories are available right from the onset of speech, and for a treatment of inflectional forms as decomposable units. The root infinitives that children produce are challenging precisely because of their nonfinite properties. Several hypotheses have been proposed to account for them, such as the Unique Checking Constraint, the underspecification of Number, and Truncation, and these will be considered again in upcoming chapters whenever additional aspects of RIs are discussed. Another account of the development of tense draws on the limited computational capacities of young children, which would prevent them from systematically projecting full-fledged derivations (which is reminiscent of the proposals of the Truncation hypothesis). This hypothesis will be expanded on in upcoming chapters, in particular when dealing with children with SLI who can be argued to possess more limited computational capacities than typically developing children. It will also be further discussed with respect to the development of other linguistic phenomena, such as object clitics and wh-questions.

The vast majority of studies on the development of inflectional morphology in French are based on spontaneous production. While these data are interesting, complementing them with elicited production (e.g. Franck et al. (2004) for knowledge of plural agreement and Jakubowicz & Nash (2001) for knowledge of tense (see Section 3.2.1.1); see also Schütze & Wexler (2000) for knowledge of tense in child L1 English) and comprehension tasks (see Jakubowicz & Nash 2001) would offer a more complete understanding of L1 French acquisition. Further research should also be carried out examining the development of other properties of clauses, such as aspect (e.g. *imparfait*) and mood (e.g. the subjunctive).

We have seen that verb placement is largely correct from the outset: finite verbs appear to the left of the negative adverb *pas*, and nonfinite verbs to its right. This is compatible with (indeed, reinforces) the idea that at least one functional category is available to children initially, and suggests that the target value of the verb movement parameter is set quite early by children learning French. However, most of what we know about verb placement has to do with the verb's position with respect to negation; verb placement with respect to adverbs has not been studied in detail. As we will see, verb position with respect to adverbs poses tremendous problems for L2 learners of French, who often accept and produce both Adv-V and V-Adv, whereas only V-Adv is appropriate. It would be interesting to know whether a similar stage of variability also exists in child L1 French.

CHAPTER 3

The verbal domain in French bilingual acquisition and in children with SLI learning French

This chapter looks at the development of inflectional morphology and verb placement in children learning French in a bilingual context and in children with Specific Language Impairment (SLI). Frequent comparisons are made with (typically developing) monolingual children, so as to isolate the specific aspects of learning French in these particular circumstances. In bilingualism, issues pertaining to language dominance and the potential influence of the other language being learned will be discussed. In the case of acquisition by children with SLI, which will be taken up in the second part of this chapter, potential reasons for the delay in their learning process will be explored.

3.1 The verbal domain in French bilingual acquisition

As in acquisition by monolinguals, finite morphology and target-like verb placement is observed early on in spontaneous production data from French bilinguals. Root infinitives are also reported. In most cases, the properties of the other language being learned do not affect development: finite morphology may develop first in French or first in the other language, or may emerge simultaneously in the two languages. Finally, some studies report that language dominance may affect the rate at which finite morphology is acquired in French, while others report no language dominance effect. Clearly, the role of language dominance in bilingual acquisition is far from being perfectly understood.

3.1.1 Inflectional morphology in French bilingual acquisition

3.1.1.1 *Development of finite morphology in French bilingual acquisition*

The first verbs emerge between the ages of 1;3 and 1;5 after an initial period during which utterances generally contain only nouns, but these first verbal clauses may be considered formulaic expressions. There is also a high incidence of root infinitives in early speech. The first evidence of finite forms is the production of finite verbs at around 2;0, as in (1). This roughly corresponds to an MLU close to 1.50, which is similar to what is reported for monolinguals. In addition, as is true for monolinguals, the first finite forms produced by French bilinguals are in the present; perfect tenses, such as *passé composé* and the future, develop later. No auxiliary or modal constructions are reported in the early stages of acquisition. Furthermore, the first finite forms are almost all 3rd person singular; 1st and 2nd person singular morphology emerges two to four months later (see Meisel 1994). In general, person agreement precedes number agreement, which emerges at around age 2;7–2;8, as in (2).

(1) a. va, est, met, monte, ferme, pique, saute
go.FIN is put.FIN climb.FIN close.FIN itch.FIN jump.FIN
(Caroline, German/French, age 2;0) (Meisel 1994)

b. Nounours dort. (Ivar, German/French, age 2;0;2) (Meisel 1994)
teddy sleep.FIN

c. Ça va là-bas. (Mathieu, English/French, age 1;1)
That go.FIN over there (Paradis & Genesee 1997)

d. Je mets là? (Anne, Swedish/French, age 2;6) (Schlyter 1997)
I put.FIN there

e. Il chante. (Yann, English/French, age 2;3) (Paradis & Genesee 1997)
he sing.FIN

(2) ils sont, ils ont, ils dorment (Ivar, German/French, age 2;7–2;8)
they be+3PL they have+3PL they sleep.3PL (Meisel 1990)

Note that the development of *imparfait* in bilingual French has not been studied in detail. As in studies of acquisition by monolinguals, most studies of finite inflection in bilinguals merely comment that *imparfait* is acquired late.

One of the questions often asked by researchers working with bilingual children is whether finiteness develops faster in one language than in the other, and, if there is a difference, whether it is to be explained by variation in the quantity or quality of input received or by language dominance. In French bilinguals, finite forms may develop in French first, as for the English/French bilingual children studied by Paradis and Genesee (1996, 1997). In their two studies of five children (ages from 1;9 to 3;3), Paradis and Genesee report that the incidence of finite forms is much higher in French than in English in all recordings. In their 1996 study, the authors show that for three children interviewed roughly at ages 2;0, 2;6, and 3;0, the global ratio of finite verbs in French is 51%, 74% and 85%, respectively, compared to 10%, 24% and 44% for English. The difference is even more impressive in their 1997 paper: 65% vs. 0% for one child and 43% vs. 3% for the other. They observe a very long delay between the emergence of finite forms in French and finite forms in English for these two children. While finite verbs are found in the earliest recordings in French (at age 1;11 for each child), they do not develop in English until at least age 2;11.[34] Crucially, the incidence of finite

34. Note that the interviews were quite scattered in time, which may misrepresent the actual emergence of finite forms in English: one child (Mathieu) was reported to use no finite form

forms in French and English is not related to the amount of input received in each language by the children or to any kind of measurement of language dominance.[35] Regardless of whether they had access to more input in French or English, or whether they were deemed French dominant, English dominant or balanced, the children produced more finite forms in French than in English. What is interesting here is that the English/French bilingual acquisition process follows what has been reported in the acquisition of each of these languages by monolinguals. In particular, finiteness has been reported to emerge earlier in French-speaking monolinguals than in English-speaking ones (Pierce 1992). In the English/French bilinguals reported on, then, exposure to French, and, specifically, acquisition of finite forms in French does not seem to have any accelerating effect on the acquisition of finiteness in English.

Simultaneous development of finiteness is also reported in the two languages being learned by bilinguals, as for the German/French children analysed in Meisel (1994). In German, evidence for finiteness includes the development of verb second (V2) constructions (with a finite verb), placement of the verb before negation, and the emergence of modals. Based on this evidence, knowledge of finiteness in German is estimated to occur at age 2;3–2;4 for Caroline, 2;4–2;5 for Ivar, and 2;11–3;0 for Pascal. In French, the development of subject clitics, auxiliaries, and modals, and placement of the verb before negation, all evidence of knowledge of finiteness, is observed to take place at the same time as above for each child. In terms of language dominance, the children seem to follow three different paths: Caroline is somewhat dominant in German at first, receiving more input in that language than in French, while Pascal is French dominant, and Ivar is rather balanced. Therefore, as in the case of the English/French bilingual children investigated by Paradis and Genesee, language dominance does not seem to be playing a role in the development of finiteness in German/French bilinguals.

Dominance is reported to have a strong impact over the development of inflectional morphology in other learning situations, however, as in Swedish/French bilinguals. In her investigation of six children, three Swedish dominant and three French dominant, Schlyter (1993) reports that finiteness develops rapidly in the dominant language and more slowly in the weaker one. For Anne, for example, who is French dominant, the incidence of finite forms in her French is 40% at age 2;7 (MLU = 2.7), compared to 6%

at age 2;3 and some at the next recording, at age 2;11. For the other child (Yann), however, no finite form was observed during the entire data collection period, including the last recording at age 3;0.

35. Both subjective and objective criteria can be used to establish language dominance. Subjective criteria include informal parental reports of daily exposure to French and English and the impressions of the researchers visiting and interviewing the children. Objective measures of language dominance rely on statistical analyses of the children's production, such as MLU and code-mixing (see Müller & Pillunat 2008; Nicoladis 1995).

in Swedish at age 2;11 (MLU = 2.5). In contrast, for Jean, who is Swedish dominant, the ratio is 58% in Swedish at age 2;6 (MLU = 2.7) and 9% in French at age 3;1 (MLU = 3.0). The incidence of agreement errors may also be affected by language dominance. Schlyter reports that it can be higher and longer-lasting in the case of the weaker language (see also Schlyter 1997). She quotes examples of number mismatches between the subject and the verb in Jean, at an age when such errors are no longer observed in children for whom French is the dominant language.

(3) Où il est, les glaces? (Jean, Swedish/French 3;1)
where it is the+PL ice-creams

Schlyter argues that bilingualism is not a case of simultaneous L1 acquisition in a dominant/weaker language combination situation. Rather, the dominant language develops as in monolinguals, while the weaker language is acquired as a second language. In particular, the weaker language is likely to be influenced by the dominant language, much as the L1 may influence the development of a second language (but see Meisel (2007) who argues that the development of the weaker language may be simply delayed).

Clearly, the issue of language dominance in the development of verbal morphology in bilingual learning situations involving French is not settled yet, as different studies have reached opposite conclusions. More data need to be analysed from a wider combination of languages to resolve the issue.

3.1.1.2 *Root infinitives in French bilingual acquisition*

Only a few studies mention root infinitives in bilingual acquisition, but those that do report that RIs are produced from the moment the first verbal forms are observed until roughly the age of 3;0, which is slightly later than what is reported in monolinguals. RIs may also appear sporadically later on. For instance, Schlyter reports that out of the 24 RIs produced by the Swedish/French child Jean between the ages of 2;0 and 2;11, 18 are found during the first recordings (2;0 and 2;2), and four in the last file (2;11). For the Dutch/French child Anouk, RIs are found until age 3;03.17 (Hulk 2000). The incidence of RIs is also reported to be quantitatively similar to what occurs in child L1 French, namely 20% at MLU 3.0 (Hulk & Müller 2000). Examples of RIs produced by some of these children are presented in (4).

(4) a. Parti vache. (Mathieu, English/French 2;1)
gone cow

b. Papa chercher Anouk. (Anouk, Dutch/French 2;6.11)
daddy look+for.INF Anouk

c. Lapin baigner dans lolo. (Yann, English/French 3;0)
Rabbit bathe.INF in water

d. Ouvrir chaussures. (Pascal, German/French, 1;10.28)
open.INF shoes

The RIs produced by bilingual children seem to have properties similar to those reported for RIs in monolinguals. In particular, they almost never include clitic subjects. For instance, Paradis and Genesee (1996) report that more than half of the finite forms produced by the three English/French children under investigation contained a subject clitic, compared to only 0.35% of their RIs (see Section 7.1.1.1 for more detail). Subject clitics are not always reported to occur early in bilingual French (in contrast to monolingual acquisition). For example, of the four Swedish/French children that Schlyter (2003) looked at (ages between 2;0 and 3;3), three did not produce subject clitics until the age of 2;6 (see Chapter 7). Similar findings are reported for the Dutch/French child Anouk (Hulk 2000). Yet, interestingly, when subject clitics do appear, they are almost always used with a finite verb form.[36] With respect to negation, the verb systematically occurs after the negative element in negative RIs, as in *Non manger!* 'No eat.INF' (William, English/French, 2;3) (Paradis & Genesee 1996). Finally, it has been reported that RIs generally contain change of state verbs and action verbs, whereas tense seems to be restricted to stative verbs during the RI period Hulk & Müller 2000; Meisel 1994;). No auxiliaries, no modals, and no noneventive verbs are found in RIs, and nonfinite eventive verbs seem to have a modal interpretation, which is similar to what is reported for acquisition by monolinguals.

Although detailed statistics are not always available, these preliminary results suggest that, despite the production of RIs, bilinguals have knowledge of finiteness and that RIs are truly nonfinite, which is similar to what has been found for monolinguals. However, further research into the RI phenomenon in bilinguals is needed to generate a clearer picture of their properties. One area of investigation could focus on the types of verbs occurring in finite and nonfinite declaratives, and on the modality of RIs. Different language combinations should also be examined.

3.1.1.3 *Knowledge of tense and agreement in French bilingual acquisition*

Although most studies on French bilingual acquisition report that finite forms appear at around the same age, namely 2;0, they do not always agree on how to interpret this finding. As in research on acquisition by monolinguals, studies differ in their analysis of finiteness and in the criteria they use to draw conclusions about knowledge of

---

36. Some subject clitics are observed in Anouk's RIs, as in (i). For Hulk, this suggests RIs may include an empty modal verb.

(i)	Tu	couper	un	grand	bout	(Anouk, 3;4.28)
	you	cut.INF	a	big	piece	

Note, however, that these occur late in the data. Moreover, no exact figures are provided, so the incidence of such constructions is difficult to evaluate.

finiteness and the early availability of functional categories. In their studies of five English/French bilinguals, for example, Paradis and Genesee (1996, 1997) simply use the term *finite*, without explicitly distinguishing between agreement and tense. However, the relatively high incidence of finite forms in initial production of French and the early appearance of subject clitics suggest that Infl (in some instantiation) is available to these learners in French, although arguably not in English as their use of finite forms is more limited. As mentioned above, this variable access to Infl seems not to be correlated to the amount of input received in the target language or to their language dominance patterns.

The fact that finiteness does not seem to develop in the two languages simultaneously suggests that the two languages are acquired separately, which goes against approaches claiming that bilingual children start out with only one grammar (e.g. Volterra & Taeschner 1978). It also argues against a maturational account of linguistic development according to which functional categories should mature at the same time in both languages. If the development of finiteness is taken to reflect the emergence of functional categories in child grammars, this prediction is clearly not confirmed by the bilingual data. As seen in the previous chapter, more recent approaches to morphological variability in the early stages of acquisition, such as Truncation and the Unique Checking Constraint, tend to assume that children have (perhaps incomplete) access to functional categories. Nevertheless, the fact that the development of finite forms may differ so widely in the two languages – within each child – means that whatever property is deemed to explain the RI phenomenon, such as the UCC itself or Rizzi's (2000) Structural Economy Principle, cannot be argued to disappear via maturation.

Other authors, such as Meisel (1994) and Schlyter (2003), conclude that Infl is not initially available to bilingual children based on criteria that appear to be more severe than those adopted by Paradis and Genesee. To decide whether finiteness and agreement have emerged, Meisel and Schlyter look for at least two forms of the same verb (e.g. *vais* 'go.1S' and *aller* 'go.INF') in the same recording sample. Meisel also looks for different verb forms appearing in spontaneous oral production, such as infinitives, imperatives, participles, and present tense forms. The ages at which Infl is assumed to emerge according to these two criteria are reported in Table 1.

Table 1. Emergence of Infl in French bilingual children based on two different criteria

Child	Languages	Formal variation of the same verb	Range of verb forms
Caroline	German/French	2;1	2:0
Ivar	German/French	2;5	2;2–2;3
Pascal	German/French	2;9–2:10	2;7
Mimi	Swedish/French	2;0	–
Jean	Swedish/French	2;4	–
Anne	Swedish/French	2;6	–

First and second person singular forms appear more or less together, at 2;3 for Caroline, 2;5 for Ivar, 2;11–3;0 for Pascal, and 2;6 for Anne. At these points, Infl is assumed to have become part of the children's grammars, along with its Agreement property. Meisel also notes a dramatic increase in MLU afterwards, from below 2.0 to above 3.0. Tense, however, is assumed to develop later, although Meisel acknowledges that the emergence of Tense is difficult to evaluate in French (see below).

For researchers who reject the initial availability of Infl, utterances produced earlier than those they consider evidence for the projection of Infl must be accounted for. For Schlyter, these utterances lack functional projections; they are VPs. She notes a high incidence of RIs in the earliest stages, a low incidence of subject clitics in the children's data (except for Mimi), and the lack of auxiliaries and modals initially. According to Meisel, the first utterances are not organized structurally or grammatically; instead they follow semantic-pragmatic principles, e.g. agent-rheme. In other words, the grammar is not yet accessible to the children. Meisel assumes that UG modules mature at around the age of two, as evidenced by the first production of finite forms (see also Meisel 1990, 2001; Meisel & Müller 1992). These first finite forms are not assumed to be evidence for the emergence of Infl (which, for Meisel, can only be assumed to have emerged when multiple forms of the same verbs are observed). Instead, Meisel considers these first finite forms to be default forms, given that they are almost all 3rd person singular. In other words, they are not *agreeing* forms. In short, the first finite utterances are claimed to be instances of VPs, and there is no agreement between the subject and the verb. A significant problem for this analysis is that, if 3rd person forms are truly default verbs, they should be found along with 1st and 2nd person subjects, which is not the case in the data examined. Instead, finite verbs are reported to be solely used with 3rd person subjects, namely they are used *correctly* with respect to agreement, which suggests that there is agreement and that at least one functional category is projected in the early stages.

To summarize, we have seen that French bilinguals use finite forms early on, sometimes much earlier in French than in the other language being learned. In addition, a large proportion of these first verb forms are 3rd person singular, which could be interpreted as default forms. However, since they appear almost only with 3rd person singular subjects in some learners, they can also be considered agreement forms. The data suggest that at least one functional category is available early on, as argued by Paradis and Genesee (1996, 1997) and that functional categories may emerge at different moments in the two languages, which argues against maturation accounts of linguistic development.

Moving now to knowledge of tense, Meisel reports that it is acquired after verbal inflection, around the age of 2;8 (note that the findings are similar to what Paradis, Le Corre & Genesee (1998) report for L2 acquisition of French by children; see Section 4.1.1.1). Meisel observes that initially tense is used only with stative verbs, while change of state verbs and action verbs are only used as nonfinite forms (as participles, infinitives, or imperatives). For Meisel, tense is used initially as a perfectivity marker. Later on, all verb types are used in the present (starting with action verbs), but still not yet in a target-like manner. Moreover, no tense other than the present is used. Meisel argues that only when perfect tense starts being used can we be certain that Tense has been acquired. While it is correct to hold that use of perfect tense suggests the availability of T, the reverse assumption (absence of perfect tense in production means absence of T) seems to be too strong. Children may have difficulties with the exact forms to be selected, or they may not have learned them yet. What would be useful here is comprehension data, for instance via a picture selection task with images displaying on-going and completed events. If T is unavailable to young children, they should randomly select the pictures upon hearing a sentence in the past.

3.1.2 The acquisition of verb movement by French bilinguals

Word order is target-like from the very first word combinations onward in French bilingual children (see, for examples, the utterances in (5) through (7) below). This is particularly striking in learning situations where the other language displays a word order different from French, such as German. In French, the canonical word order is SVO. Some elements may directly precede the subject, such as adverbs (as in *Hier Jean a acheté une voiture* lit. 'Yesterday John has bought a car'). Moreover, in a sentence with an auxiliary and a past participle, the object of the verb appears after the participle, as in the example above. In German, the canonical word order is SOV, an order typically found in embedded clauses. German is also a V2 language since the verb must occupy the second position of main clauses. This is clear in cases where an adverbial appears in the front of the sentence, for example, as in *Gestern hat Hans einen Wagen gekauft* lit. 'Yesterday has Hans a car bought'. This example also shows that with complex tenses the object must precede the past participle, in contrast to French. Work on German/French bilingual children shows that they are able to distinguish target-like word orders in each language from the moment they start producing multiword utterances (at around age 1;10). For instance, they produce verbs at the end of clauses in German, but not in French. There are also cases of VOS orders in the French of German/French children, but not in their German (Köppe 1994; Meisel 1994). In Section 2.3.2, we saw that VOS is quite frequent in the utterances of French monolinguals (although VOS cases seem to be less common in bilingual French than in monolingual French, which should be investigated in more detail).

According to Meisel (1994) and Schlyter (2003), the first instances of verb movement across negation roughly correspond to the emergence of Agreement, which hosts

1st and 2nd person singular verbs, as well as auxiliaries. For instance, Swedish/French child Anne produces her first negative verbal utterances at age 2;6 (see (5)), which is also the age at which she produces different forms of the same verb as well as subject clitics and her first auxiliary. Under the assumption that Tense develops later than Agreement, this suggests that Agr is sufficient for verb movement.

(5) N' aime pas celle-là (Anne, Swedish/French 2;6)
NEG like.FIN not this one

Data also show that verb forms are correctly placed with respect to negative adverbs, as in acquisition by monolinguals: finite forms are located before negation, as in (6), while nonfinite forms follow it, as in (7). With respect to the verb movement parameter, this suggests that the acquisition of the French value does not seem to pose any problem to the learners.[37]

(6) a. Maman veut pas. (Ivar, German/French 2;04.23) (Meisel 1994)
mummy want.FIN not
b. On bouge pas. (Yann, English/French 3;0) (Genesee & Paradis 1997)
we move.FIN not
'We're not moving'

(7) A pas trouvé. (Ivar, German/French 2;05.07) (Meisel 1994)
has not found

As in child L1 French, examples of finite forms following negative adverbs are quite rare, as *Il pas joue dehors* 'He not play.FIN outside' (Gene, English/French 1;11). Such an example may be considered a performance error and not a case of English influence. However, it should be mentioned that negative utterances are often scarce in the data examined: the utterance in (6b) is the only negative utterance found in the English/French data examined by Paradis and Genesee (1997), for example. It would be interesting at this point to further investigate the development of negation in French-speaking bilingual children in order to be able to draw more firm conclusions about their accuracy in placing the verb relative to negation.

3.1.3 Conclusion

In general, the development of inflectional morphology and verb placement in bilingual French is similar to what is found in the acquisition of French by monolinguals. Verbal inflection is used early on and the first verbs often display the 3rd person singular

37. Interestingly, the French parametric value does not seem to transfer to the other language. For example, Paradis and Genesee (1996) did not observe any instance of V-Neg order in their English data (e.g. *I play not*).

present form, which may be interpreted as default forms. Root infinitives are also used, albeit for a slightly longer time than by monolinguals, and they share the properties of the root infinitives produced by monolinguals in that they express finiteness and their nonfinite form may result from Structural Economy (see Section 2.2.5).

There is debate in the literature about whether language dominance influences the development of inflectional morphology in bilingual children. Some consider the influence of the dominant language to be low to minimal, while for others, it plays a significant role and can account for errors produced by children learning the weaker language. Studies of French bilingual acquisition are simply not extensive or varied enough to be able to answer the question. It would be useful to vary language combinations so as to obtain a greater insight into the influence of the other language and of language dominance over the development of the verbal domain in French. Researchers also disagree about the content of underlying IL grammars. While researchers working on bilingual French seem to assume that each language has its own system from the outset, the exact composition of the two grammars is subject to debate. For some, functional categories are available initially, as witnessed by the early production of finite forms and subject clitics, while others argue for an initial strictly lexical stage. The debate largely rests on the criteria used to determine the development of functional categories. On the one hand, the fact that finite forms are being produced may be enough to argue that underlying functional categories are initially available; on the other, the argument that the production of several forms of the same verb shows that functional material is present in the grammar, while correct, may underestimate the moment functional categories become available.

Verb placement is largely correct from the very beginning, as in acquisition by monolinguals. This suggests the early availability of at least one functional category. As with monolinguals, however, data for verb placement comes almost exclusively from the verb's position relative to negation, but data involving negative utterances are scarce. Moreover, as with monolingual development, little is known about the development of verb placement with respect to adverbs, so it is difficult to draw firm conclusions. Accuracy of verb placement also seems to be independent of the properties of the other language being learned. In German/French children, for example, the verb does not appear in a clause-final position in their French, while it can in their German. This confirms the existence of two different grammars from the outset, one for each language.

Many avenues for future research remain, including verb placement with respect to adverbs and negation, as well as how aspect develops in bilingual children. Bilingual studies that elicit data, rather than just recording production, would be helpful in developing a complete picture, as would psycholinguistic tests focusing on comprehension.

3.2 The verbal domain in acquisition of French by children with SLI

The pattern of development of inflectional morphology in children with SLI is generally similar to what is found in typically developing (TD) children (e.g. present tense before *passé composé*), although non-present tenses may take a significantly longer time to emerge. The development of finite morphology has been an important topic of investigation in children with SLI, but much less is known in the development of verb placement in this population.

3.2.1 Development of inflectional morphology in children with SLI learning French

3.2.1.1 *Development of finite inflection in children with SLI learning French*

Children with SLI have been reported to experience tremendous difficulties with tense morphology, especially with past and future tenses. Instead, they use present forms and root infinitives. Such errors are observed in TD children, as we have seen, but they persist for much longer in children with SLI.

Paradis and Crago (2001) elicited production of various tense forms via questions about past, present, and future events from 10 children with SLI and 20 TD children, 10 of whom were MLU matched (mean age 3;3) and 10 age-matched (mean age 7;6). The accuracy rate on the present form was high for all participants, including the SLI children; no significant difference was reported between the participants (see Table 2). On tensed forms, however, the SLI children's performance was significantly poorer than the TD children, including the younger TD group: 74% accuracy on past tense and 64% on future. These results are similar to what has been reported in SLI development of other languages, such as English, where the past tense marker *-ed* is often omitted (Rice, Wexler & Cleave 1995). In the data reported by Paradis and Crago, most errors in past and future contexts were due to children's use of present tense verbs and nonfinite forms. In utterances displaying a nonfinite verb, Paradis and Crago noticed that use of (unambiguous) past participles was restricted to past contexts (as in *Maman bu* 'Mommy drunk'), which suggests the omission of the auxiliary. Forms that are (unambiguously) infinitival, on the other hand, were almost always used in a future context, which could also be interpreted as auxiliary omission, in this case, the inchoative auxiliary *aller* 'go' which forms part of the analytic future. The authors also observed that the copula *être* was sometimes missing in the speech of SLI children (the omission rate was 19%).[38] Higher copula omission rate for SLI children as compared to

38. For comparison's sake, it would be interesting to examine the development of copula omission in TD children learning French.

TD children is also reported in English (e.g. Rice, Wexler & Cleave 1995) and Italian (Leonard, Sabbadini, Leonard & Volterra 1987).

Table 2. Accuracy on tense by children with SLI (from Paradis & Crago 2001)

Subjects	Mean age	Present	Past	Future
7SLI (n=10)	7;6	88.8%	74.3%	64.5%
3TD (n=10)	3;3	95.3%	86.5%*	90.7%*
7TD (n=10)	7;3	99%	98.6%*	99.6%*

* significant difference with the children with SLI

Results on younger children with SLI show poorer performance on *passé composé* as well. In an elicited production task administered to 11 children with SLI (age range: 3;1–4.4; mean age: 3;9) Royle and Thordardottir (2007) report a production rate of only 7.7%. This was obtained on regular verbs; with irregular verbs, performance dropped to 4.4%. In contrast, results of a comparative group of 11 age-matched TD children display production rates of 59.2% for regular verbs and 26.7% for irregular verbs.[39]

Although problems with past tense are persistent in children with SLI, it has been argued that they can eventually be resolved (roughly by age 10). Jakubowicz and Nash (2001) administered a sentence completion task (with pictures) and a sentence-to-picture matching task to 28 children with SLI (age 5;7 to 13 years) and to 36 children without SLI subdivided into three smaller groups based on age (see Table 3). The children with SLI were also placed into three groups based on their responses, SLI3, SLI2 and SLI1, with SLI3 (which included the youngest children) displaying the least accurate performance. In the production task, performance on present tense sentences was high for all groups (higher than performance on past tense), except for SLI3. Interestingly, although SLI3 and SLI2 children performed much worse than the TD groups on past tense (and also significantly worse than on the present), there was no difference between the SLI1 and the 6TD children, and no difference between the use of past and present by the SLI1 group.[40] Errors similar to those reported by Paradis and Crago were observed

39. In another study with children of the same age, but based on spontaneous production, no differences were found between the children with SLI and an age-matched TD group (mean age of 3;11 in both cases) (Thordardottir & Namazi 2007). According to Royle and Thordardottir (2007), the past tense forms used spontaneously by the young children with SLI may not result from productive rules.

40. A recent study on 10-year-old children with SLI (range: 8;1–13; mean age: 9;11, n=10) done in Belgium reports a much higher rate of auxiliary omission than Jakubowicz in an elicited production task (between 20% and 30%) (Pizzioli & Schelstraete 2008). See Section 3.2.2 for more detail.

in the children with SLI. The authors further report that these children often used the form *[fini]* 'finish.FIN/finish.PtP' instead of *passé composé*. This form is ambiguous between a finite form and a past participle, as in *il [fini] son dessin* 'he finishes/finished his drawing' (Elodie, 13, SLI3). The children with SLI often used it to convey the resultative meaning encoded in past tense instead of producing the past form itself.

The results of the comprehension task were comparable to the production task, with increased accuracy in the past tense on the part of the SLI3 group. Similar results are reported by Jakubowicz (2003) for 12 typically developing children and 11 children with SLI followed over a period of three to four years. Overall, the results show that SLI children are not a homogenous group: some children seem to be more affected than others.

Table 3. Developing knowledge of past tense by children with SLI (from Jakubowicz & Nash 2001)

Subjects	**Mean age**	**Production (n=36)**		**Comprehension (n=24)**	
		Present (n=18)	**Past** (n=18)	**Present** (n=12)	**Past** (n=12)
3TD (n=12)	3;3	85.2%	76.8%	86.1%	87.5%
4TD (n=12)	4;2	90.7%**	78.7%	97.2%*	82.6%
6TD (n=12)	6;7	99.1%	97.7%	100%	100%
SLI3 (n=12)	6;10	75%**	12%	77.1%	57.6%
SLI2 (n=10)	8;2	82.2%**	65%	92.5%*	64.2%
SLI1 (n=6)	9;8	97.2%	96.3%	100%	100%

Significant difference between present and past tense: * $p < .05$, ** $p < .01$

In contrast to tense, agreement has often been argued not to pose any major problems for children with SLI. Looking at the production of first person singular forms *suis* 'am' and *ai* 'have.1S', Paradis and Crago (2001) found that all SLI groups (see Table 2) employed them correctly at least 96% of the time. A similarly high level of accuracy was obtained on agreement between a clitic and a lexical subject in subject doubling constructions (e.g. *le garçon il mange* 'The boy he's eating'). This is similar to findings on children with SLI learning other languages, such as English (Rice, Wexler & Cleave 1995) and Italian (Bortolini & Leonard 1996; Leonard, Bortolini, Caselli, McGregor & Sabbadini 1992).[41] However, recent research suggests that plural inflection can be problematic

41. Note that not all research reports high accuracy on verbal agreement in SLI children. Investigating the speech of 6 children learning German (age 5;8–7;11), Clahsen, Bartke and Göllner (1997) report accuracy rates of 60% or less on first person singular markers *-e* and *-ø* (see their Table A4, p. 170). However, for other endings, such as 2nd person singular *-st* and 3rd person singular *-t* (which also marks 2nd person plural in German), accuracy is much higher, at 85% and over.

for children with SLI. Franck et al. (2004) administered an elicited production task to eight children with SLI (aged 5;4–9;4) and four control groups of TD children varying in mean ages (from 4;5 to 8;5). The children were asked to complete sentences using the verb *faire* 'do', a suppletive verb (*font* 'do.3PL'). Interestingly, the subject of the sentence was separated by the verb by either a modifier or an adjunct, as in (8) and (9). In both cases, the postsubject material included a noun matching or mismatching number marking of the subject.

(8) Modifier condition

a. SG-SG:

La	gagnante	du	dernier	championnat
the+SG	winner	of+the+SG	last	championship

(faire du patin)
(do ice-skating)

b. SG-PL:

La	gagnante	des	derniers	championnats
the+SG	winner	of+the+PL	last	championships

(faire du patin)
(do ice-skating)

c. PL-SG:

Les	habitants	du	petit	village
the+PL	inhabitants	of+the+SG	small	village

(faire le sapin)
(do the Christmas tree)

d. PL-PL:

Les	habitants	des	petits	villages
the+PL	inhabitant	of+the+PL	small	villages

(faire le sapin)
(do the Christmas tree)

(9) Adjunct condition

a. SG-SG:

La	grand-mère,	en	parlant	à	la	fille,
the+SG	grandmother	while	talking	to	the+SG	daughter

(faire	la	pâte)
make	the	dough

b. SG-PL:

La	grand-mère,	en	parlant	aux	filles,
the+SG	grandmother	while	talking	to+the+PL	girls

(faire	la	pâte)
make	the	dough

c. PL-SG:

Les	garcons,	en	suivant	le	moniteur,
the+PL	boys	while	following	the+SG	instructor

(faire	du ski)
do	skiing

d. PL-PL: Les garcons, en suivant les moniteurs,
the+PL boys while following the+PL instructors
(faire du ski)
do skiing

Overall, the error rate was significantly higher in the children with SLI (36.3%) than in any TD group (at most 23.3%). Crucially, however, the vast majority of errors were unidirectional, namely singular forms used in plural contexts. With plural subjects, the ratio of agreement errors was 30.5% in the SLI group, compared to less than 6% with singular subjects. In other words, while plural marking is problematic for children with SLI, when plural forms are produced, they are largely used correctly. This strongly shows knowledge of agreement. In addition to these findings, it is reported that the position of the subject (preceding a modifier or an adjunct) did not affect performance in the children with SLI. Their error rates were very similar in both conditions, at about 18%. In contrast, the TD children aged 8;5 tended to commit more errors in the adjunct condition (5%) than in the modifier condition (2.9%), although the figures are low.

Roulet-Amiot (2008) also looked at (elicited) production of number agreement in children with SLI (mean age 9;3) compared to younger TD children (mean age 6;7), but she investigated perception of number agreement mismatching between the verb and the subject as well. The production task involved verbs with overt plural marking, four suppletive verbs (e.g. *faire* 'do') and six lexical verbs with distinctive plural endings (e.g. *lire* 'read'). As can be seen in Table 4, the error rate was higher in the children with SLI than in the TD children. Moreover, errors tended to be more frequent with lexical verbs than with suppletive verbs, in both groups. In particular, it should be noted that the TD children, although they performed better than the children with SLI, displayed a high percentage of errors (over 40%) on these verbs.[42]

Table 4. Mean percentage of errors in number agreement in production (from Roulet-Amiot 2008)

	Mean age	Suppletive verbs	Lexical verbs	Total
SLI group (n=13)	9;3	51.3%	74.4%	62.8%
TD group (n=15)	6;7	10.6%	42.8%	26.7%

42. With irregular lexical verbs, overt plural marking results in the pronunciation of a word-final coda, as in *lisent* [liz] 'read.3PL'). The high ratio of errors reported on these verbs could thus be due to general difficulties with word-final codas. Roulet-Amiot (2008) ruled out this possibility by administering a word repetition task to the children which included nonwords with final codas similar to the ones that should have been used in elicited production (e.g. *kiz*). All children performed perfectly on this task.

Importantly, all the errors occurred with a plural subject (so, singular marking was used instead of plural), which corroborates the findings reported by Franck et al. (2004). Roulet-Amiot (2008) also found a significant correlation between error rate and age in the SLI group, namely the number of errors tended to decrease with age.

In the perception task, the children heard a sentence and were presented with a picture on a computer screen. They had to decide whether the picture corresponded to the sentence or not. The main verb of the sentence was either in the singular or in the plural (e.g. *le garcon va/*vont à l'école* 'the boy goes/*go to school), while the picture represented the action expressed by the sentence, including its subject (e.g. a boy going to school). Therefore, there was either number matching or mismatching between the verb and the subject as represented in the picture. The reaction time taken by the children to give his/her answer was recorded. As indicated in Table 5, reaction time was higher in the number mismatching condition than in the number matching condition, which suggests that children are sensitive to number agreement. Roulet-Amiot further shows that the children with SLI are particularly sensitive to number mismatching with suppletive verbs whereas in the TD group the effect of number mismatching was observed on both suppletive and lexical verbs.

Table 5. Mean reaction time (in ms) according to number or no number agreement in reception (from Roulet-Amiot 2008)

	Meanage	Number agreement	No number agreement
SLI group (n=13)	2;3	2108 ms	2270 ms
TD group (n=15)	6;7	2021 ms	2152 ms

Results from other research suggests that individuals with SLI have trouble with inflectional morphology in general. In particular, they have extreme difficulty decomposing inflected words into root+affix; instead, they treat such words as a whole, in contrast to TD children (see Section 2.1.4). Kehayia (1997) administered a word recognition task to 19 SLI subjects (age 14 to 40), among whom 7 were French speakers, and 24 TD controls. The stimulus included real and nonce words, either inflected or not (e.g. real: *vendu* 'sold' and *vend* 'sells'; nonce: *nendu* and *nend*). Each word was presented individually on a computer screen and each subject had to decide whether or not the word was real by pressing a key. The response time was computed. The results, presented in Table 6, show that the controls took significantly more time to give their answer when the word was inflected than when it was not, for both real and nonce words. The extra time needed to provide the answer with inflected words was interpreted as evidence in favour of decomposition. In contrast, there was no significant difference between the SLI subjects' response times on inflected and uninflected words, with either real or nonce words.[43] The fact that the SLI subjects did not need extra time to process the inflection was taken to suggest that for them both inflected and uninflected forms are treated – and represented – as whole forms (see also Royle, Jarema, & Kehayia 2002).

Table 6. Response times on inflected and simple non-words and real words (in ms) (from Kehayia 1997)

	Control (n=24)	SLI (French) (n=7)
Non-words (simple)	731*	790
Non-words (inflected)	772	795
Real words (simple)	595*	690
Real words (inflected)	673	715

* significant difference with corresponding inflected forms

If individuals with SLI do not process inflectional morphology but rather store apparently inflected forms in their lexicon as unanalysed chunks, then they should not be able to produce inflected forms when facing novel words: by definition, such forms cannot be present in their lexicon. This is what Gopnik and Goad (1997) investigated in an elicited production task in which TD and SLI subjects were presented with novel words (that is words they could not have heard before) and asked to come up with inflected forms. The results showed a significant difference between the TD and SLI subjects' performance: while the incidence of inflected forms reached 92.6% with the TD participants, it was a low 33.3% in the case of the SLI group.

To summarize, we have seen so far that children with SLI have problems with tense, such that present and infinitival forms are often used instead of past and future tenses. However, these difficulties erode with time and children with SLI can eventually perform as well as TD children on the different tenses. Agreement, on the other hand, does not seem to cause particular difficulties to children with SLI, in particular person agreement, as is the case in the acquisition of other languages such as Italian and English. Number agreement generates some errors, but they are almost systematically unidirectional, with singular marking used instead of plural. This suggests knowledge of number, which is confirmed by perception studies. Some researchers argue that children with SLI have fundamental difficulties with inflectional morphology. However, if this was the case, an equally low performance should be observed on tense and agreement, and errors should be found with both singular and plural markings, contrary to fact.

43. Similar tendencies are reported on the 12 English-speaking participants with SLI in comparison with TD controls.

3.2.1.2 *Root infinitives in acquisition of French by children with SLI*

The incidence of utterances containing root infinitives can be quite high in young children with SLI learning French, although variation is observed, and it gradually diminishes with age; it is quite rare after the age of five. Table 7 summarizes findings in two cross-sectional studies on the production of RIs by children with SLI. Recall that for TD children, RIs disappear at around the age of 2;6.

Table 7. Incidence of RIs in children with SLI learning French

Study	Mean age (range)	Number of children	Design	%RIs (range)
Hamann et al. (2003)	4;8 (3;10–5;0)	6	Spontaneous production	7.8% (1.9%–56.2%)
	7;1 (5;7–7;11)	5		0.9% (0%–2.3%)
Paradis & Crago (2001)	7;6	10	Elicited production	12%

The rate of production of RIs also seems to vary greatly between individuals. For instance, Hamann et al. (2003) report that the incidence of RIs is higher with children younger than five, but there are in fact two profiles in that younger group: of the six children investigated, two display an RI ratio of at least 50%, while the four others show a ratio below 10%. In Jakubowicz & Nash's (2001) study, the three SLI groups (36 children altogether) are reported to use a total of 22 nonfinite utterances instead of past tense, but 21 of them are found in one group, SLI3, which, as said earlier, contained the youngest children. In other studies, however, the extent of individual variation is impossible to establish. In Paradis & Crago (2001), only the mean of RI incidence is provided so it is impossible to know whether a correlation exists between age and the RI ratio.

The RIs produced by children with SLI seem to have similar properties to those observed in TD children. First, RIs often contain a null subject, but rarely a clitic subject. For instance, over 90% of subject clitics are used with finite verbs in the children with SLI investigated by Paradis & Crago (2001). Note, however, that Jakubowicz & Nash (2001) do report the use of subject clitics in such utterances (e.g. *il ouvrir très grand la porte* 'he open.INF very wide the door' (Johan, 5;7, SLI3)). In addition, there is a strong contingency between verb form and verb placement with respect to negative adverbs: nonfinite forms largely appear after the negative adverb. Paradis & Crago (2001) report that out of the 142 V-Neg sequences produced by the children with SLI, 139 (97.9%) contain a finite verb; in contrast only one of the 9 Neg-V sequences displays a finite form (11.1%). Finally, some studies suggest a correlation between verb form and modality, as in the case of unambiguous infinitives appearing mostly in future contexts observed by Paradis & Crago (2001). However, this is not reported everywhere: cases of infinitives used instead of *passé composé* are also observed (e.g. *mettre pantalon* 'put+on.INF pants' (Benoît, 7;3, SLI3)) (Jakubowicz & Nash 2001).

RIs have been reported in the speech of children with SLI learning other languages but the incidence of such utterances varies greatly depending on the language being learned. In Italian, the incidence of RIs in children with SLI is very low. In their study of 46 children with SLI, Bottari, Cipriani and Chilosi (1996) report that only seven produce RIs, and the highest incidence of RIs for a single child is 6%. By comparison, the incidence of RIs in children learning English can be quite high. For instance, Rice and Wexler (1996) report a 75% ratio of uninflected forms in obligatory contexts (requiring either *-s* or *-ed*) in the speech of 37 children with SLI.

Conflicting results are also reported on knowledge of finiteness in learners with SLI. In SLI German, Rice, Noll and Grimm (1997) report that nonfinite forms rarely appear in typically finite positions, which suggests knowledge of finiteness. Of the 241 verbs appearing in the V2 position in spontaneous production data of eight children (4;0–4;8), only two were found to be nonfinite (0.8%). In contrast, almost 90% of the verbs found in clause-final position are nonfinite (72/81=88.9%). However, Clahsen et al. (1997) also report an incidence of clause-final finite forms of between 30% and 40% in some German children with SLI, which seems to contradict the idea that there is knowledge of finiteness. A more systematic study of verbal forms occurring in a wide range of finite and nonfinite positions (i.e. not looking only at negation) in children with SLI, including children learning French, could shed light on the question of whether children's errors are related to problems with inflection in general or whether they point to a greater deficit in knowledge of finiteness.

3.2.2 Grammatical knowledge of French in children with SLI

We have seen that children with SLI produce RIs for a longer period of time than TD children and that they have persistent problems with tense, producing present and non-finite forms instead of past tense, for instance. However, the RIs they produce seem to have the same properties as the RIs produced by TD children. A priori, then, children with SLI go through an RI period, just like TD children, only for a longer period of time. This suggests that, theoretically, most accounts of RIs proposed for TD children could apply to children with SLI, and a number of researchers have proposed exactly that. Rice, Wexler and Cleave (1995), for example, propose the Extended Optional Infinitive hypothesis according to which SLI grammars have an underspecified or impaired T. This account builds on Wexler's (1994) Underspecification of Tense hypothesis whereby Tense is held to mature at a certain point in normal development. Rice, Wexler, and Cleave assume that SLI affects maturation mechanisms, which means that the development of Tense is delayed.[44] This would explain SLI children's tendency to

44. Rice, Wexler and Cleave's (1995) Extended Optional Infinitive Period hypothesis was essentially proposed on the basis of facts from English. Data from children with SLI learning French show a shorter period of RIs than for English-speaking children with SLI.

produce present forms in obligatory past contexts, as well as to omit auxiliaries and the copula. For Rice, Wexler and Cleave, the fact that most present forms used in past contexts do not bear any overt inflectional morphology suggests that they are verb stems unspecified for tense and person. This would explain why they can substitute for (more specified) forms such as past and future verbs. Other researchers, such as Hamann (2003), put forward a Truncation approach to early SLI grammars, building on proposals by Rizzi (1993/1994, 1998, 2000) for TD children.

For Gopnik and Goad (1997), the impairment affects inflectional morphology as a whole, which, they argue, explains SLI individuals' incapacity to process inflected forms as such and to produce inflectional morphology on novel words. Note that this does not necessarily mean that inflectional features, such as [±past], are absent from SLI grammars as previously claimed by Gopnik (1990). One challenge for this hypothesis is the fact that not all inflections seem to be equally affected – agreement seems to be much less problematic than tense for children with SLI – which is unexpected if SLI is a general impairment of morphology. Unfortunately, it is almost impossible to tease apart the two types of inflection in French since most inflectional morphology is conflating in this language. We will also see that plural morphology is largely correct in SLI (Section 11.2.2), which is not predicted by the inflectional impairment hypothesis. This said, it could be the case that severely impaired individuals may have more difficulties to deal with inflectional morphology.

For Jakubowicz and Nash (2001), the fact that children with SLI can eventually master the past tense suggests that Tense is not generally impaired in SLI grammars. If it were, they argue, nonfinite forms would be expected to be produced in place of all tenses; yet, nonfinite forms are largely restricted to past tense; present tense forms are generally correctly used. Moreover, nonfinite forms are generally past participles (*sorti* 'gone', *bu* 'drunk' and *mis* 'put') rather than infinitives (*sortir, boire, mettre*), which suggests to Jakubowicz and Nash that children with SLI have a problem with auxiliaries (*avoir* and *être*) rather than tense itself. To account for these facts, Jakubowicz and Nash propose the Computational Complexity Hypothesis according to which the syntactic computation in a given language is less complex when a merged functional category must be present in every sentence (obligatory Merge). Jakubowicz and Nash assume that sentences in the present have a different representation from sentences in the past tense. While both structures are projections of IP (which they call PersonP, given the pronominal nature of Romance Infl), the representation of past tense sentences includes an additional functional layer between VP and PersP, which projects from the auxiliary. This projection is called PastP:

(10) a. Present sentences: PersP > VP
b. Past sentences: PersP > PastP > VP

Since PastP is not systematically part of the representation of utterances (nonobligatory Merge), in contrast to PersP, children with SLI have difficulty projecting it. They sometimes project only PersP, which explains why they use verbs in the present instead of the past tense. This analysis would also explain why subject clitics (in Pers) may appear along with a past participle or an infinitival form (in V). Another argument in favour of the idea that computational complexity causes tremendous difficulties to children with SLI comes from the observed high accuracy with agreement compared to the much lower accuracy with tense. This finding is reported not only in SLI populations, but also in agrammatic aphasic patients (see, e.g. Friedmann & Grodzinsky 2000). While computation involved in agreement can be conceived as a very local operation (which involves a specifier/head relationship between the subject and Agr), tense computation involves a more complex relation between, at least, utterance time possibly expressed in the C-system (see Guéron & Hoekstra 1989), and event time. This relation may be less local than feature checking or copying, which in turn would increase complexity.

This notwithstanding, it is not entirely true to say that agreement is not problematic in children with SLI, especially when it comes to plural. In Franck et al.' s (2004) study, we saw that when the subject and the verb were separated by some extra material, either a modifier of the subject or an adjunct, children with SLI made a significant number of agreement errors. According to the authors, this extra material presumably increased computational complexity which made it very difficult for the children to establish the necessary syntactic relationships. It is worth pointing out that the oldest TD children in the study (average age of 8;5) made significantly more errors in the adjunct condition than in the modifier condition. This can be explained by the fact that in the adjunct condition, agreement is achieved via a trace, which is more complex than the more local spec/head relationship of the modifier condition. This is illustrated in (11).

(11) [$_{IP}$ [Les garçons]$_i$ … [$_{CP}$ en suivant le moniteur] … [$_{AgrP}$ t$_i$ font du ski]]]]
the.PL boys while following the instructor do skiing

Agreement via a trace would thus require more computational resources, which would yield more errors.

Naturally, appealing to computational complexity, and decreased computational capacities in children with SLI to explain the results, require a precise – and appropriate – definition of what makes a derivation complex. We have already discussed the proposal that nonobligatory Merge leads to greater complexity than obligatory Merge. Another candidate for determining complexity is sentence length. However, findings so far do not seem to confirm this possibility. In Pizzioli and Schelstraete's (2008) study, *passé composé* was elicited with transitive and intransitive verbs. It was anticipated that the presence of an additional element, the object, with a transitive verb may increase complexity which would result in higher auxiliary omission. In addition, short and long sentences were used in the prompts, with longer sentences displaying an adjective next to every noun (the subject and the object in the case of transitives, the longest sentences). None of these factors (transitivity and sentence length) affected the results. The rate of auxiliary omission did not differ significantly in any subcondition in the children with SLI. In Section 14.1.6, we will examine Jakubowicz' (2005) Derivational Complexity Metric whose aim is to quantify derivational complexity by counting the number of Merge operations involved in the derivation (essentially, the more overt movements, the more complex the derivation).

3.2.3 Conclusion

We have seen in this section that children with SLI experience problems with past tense similar to those experienced by TD children, but for a much longer period of time. Interestingly, this obtains in both production and comprehension data, although comprehension results are better. Root infinitives can also be quite frequent in children with SLI, and can be found until the age of 5, while they usually drop out by the age of 2;6 in TD children. In contrast, agreement errors, especially person agreement, are less frequent. Therefore, errors involving tense and the persistent use of nonfinite forms could be considered clinical markers of SLI. At the theoretical level, several hypotheses have been proposed, such as Underspecification of Tense, Truncation, inflectional impairment, and computational complexity. As we will see in upcoming chapters, data from the development of subject and object pronouns, determiners, and questions will argue in favour of the computational complexity approach.

Given that most studies involved only a small number of subjects studied for only a short time, it would be interesting to collect more longitudinal data to confirm the findings reported so far. In particular, the incidence and the properties of RIs should be further investigated. While some researchers argue that RIs produced by children with SLI have the same properties as those found in TD monolinguals, including a modal interpretation, others have tried to relate them to difficulties with tense. Since individual variation in the production of RIs has also been reported, it would also be interesting to see whether there is a correlation between the use of RIs and that of non-present tense. Do the children who use few RIs tend to have fewer problems with past tense, or do they use other verb forms, such as the present, to express past tense? What is the difference, then, between the production of RIs and erroneous use of present tense?

CHAPTER 4

The verbal domain in French L2 acquisition

This chapter addresses the development of inflectional morphology and verb placement in French L2 acquisition by children and adults. The boundary between child and adult L2 learners was placed at the pre-adolescent period, around age 12, while the age of four was taken as the point after which acquisition of another language is considered L2 acquisition (Schwartz 2004).

4.1 The verbal domain in child L2 acquisition of French

Much like children learning L1 French, child L2 French learners take little time to master the inflectional morphology of the target language, although they do use default forms for a while, such as nonfinite verbs. Moreover, verb placement is largely correct from the outset, especially with respect to negative adverbs such as *pas* 'not'.

4.1.1 Inflectional morphology in child L2 French

4.1.1.1 *Development of finite inflection in child L2 French*

Some studies report that finite forms are used in initial stages of acquisition, with present forms developing first, followed by past and future forms. Moreover, agreement is largely correct in early child L2 French, although 3rd person singular forms are often overgeneralized, as in child L1 French.

Grondin and White (1996) investigated spontaneous production data from two anglophone children, Kenny and Greg, who learned French in Montreal. At the time of their first interview, Kenny was 5;4 and Greg, 5;8, and they had had very limited exposure to French. Adopting Meisel's (1994) criterion for acquisition of finiteness (see Section 3.1.1.3), Grondin and White report that the two children have acquired finiteness, as they use a variety of verbal forms early on, including auxiliaries and lexical verbs, such as imperatives, infinitival verbs, past participles and finite forms. This is illustrated in (1). They also use the same verbs in different forms, as in (2).

(1) Infinitives: *sauter* 'jump.INF', *monter* 'climb.INF' (Kenny, L1=English, month 3)[45]
Participles: *fait* 'done'
Imperatives: 2SG = *regarde* 'look.2SG'
2PL = *regardez* 'look.2PL'
Present: 1SG = *sais* 'know.1SG'
2SG = *fais* 'do.2SG'
3SG = *est* 'be+3SG', *aime* 'love.3SG'
Past: 3SG = *était* 'was+3SG'

(2) a. J'ai petite famille. (Greg, L1=English, month 5)
I have+1SG little family

b. Moi avez/er.
Me have.2PL/INF

Moreover, subject clitics are present in the earliest recording samples, and are used only in appropriate clitic positions, that is, together with finite verbs (see Section 8.1.1.1). Assuming that clitics are morphological markers, their presence suggests that verbal morphology is acquired rather quickly. Verbal agreement is also largely correct when used. In particular, irregular verbs *aller* 'go', *avoir* 'have', and *être* 'be' are usually correctly inflected: the accuracy rate is 94.6% in Kenny's data (470/497) and 92% in Greg's (324/352) (Prévost 2001). As in child L1 French, most errors involve an overgeneralization of 3rd person singular forms, such as *a* 'has', *est* 'is' and *va* 'goes', as illustrated in (3).[46]

(3) a. Les cinq animaux i(ls) va là. (Greg, L1=English, month 14)
the five animals they go+3SG there

b. Tous les méchants animaux est noirs. (Kenny, L1=English, month 8)
all the naughty animals is black

Not all researchers agree with this picture, however. For Paradis, Le Corre and Genesee (1998), for example, tense is acquired after agreement. Paradis et al. (1998) investigated the development of tense and agreement in production data from 15 anglophone children learning French (mean age 6;7) and a group of 10 native child speakers (mean age 7;3). The children were interviewed once a year for three years. The L2 learners were attending French-language schools in the Montreal area. At the time of their first recording, they were at the end of grade one and had been exposed to French for two years. The control group were grade-matched monolinguals. The interviews were designed to elicit use of present, past, and future tenses. As shown in Table 1, during the first two years, significant differences were found between the learners and the native speakers with respect to the use of tense-related elements, whereas the two

45. Month x indicates the number of months of exposure to French.

46. Note that in Quebec French, the variety of French being learned by the two children, the sequence *je va* 'I go.3SG' is acceptable in informal speech. Its use was therefore not considered an error.

groups did not differ significantly with respect to agreement, where agreement was primarily established on the basis of subject clitic use. The authors report that at least 95% of clitic subjects produced by the learners were used with finite verbs at each year. Moreover, the two groups did not differ with regard to verb movement (across negation), which was almost systematically correct. It is important to point out that the production of present forms was investigated via the incidence of the 3rd person plural form of certain verbs, i.e. irregular forms such as *ils vont* 'they go' and forms with an audible final consonant, such as *ils prennent* [prɛn] 'they take.3PL'. Such forms were chosen because they are among the few that are audibly distinct in the present tense, although, arguably, they are also associated with agreement.

Table 1. Development of tense and agreement in child L2 French (L1=English) (from Paradis et al. 1998)

	Verb movement	Subject clitics	Present (3PL)	Past	Future
Learners 1	.947	.859	.138	.327	.255
Learners 2	.929	.943	.197	.669	.347
Learners 3	.959	.953	.375	.706	.424
Natives 1	.984	.972	.846	.872	.718
Natives 2	.992	.986	.934	.924	.882
Natives 3	.992	.982	1.00	.948	.898

Very little is known about the development of tenses other than the present in child L2 French. In her studies of acquisition of French by English-speaking children enrolled in early French immersion programs in Canada,[47] Harley (1989, 1992) has shown that children make early distinctions between the present, the past and the future based on auxiliaries such as *avoir* 'have' and *aller* 'go' which are used as temporal cues. However, use of infinitival and past participle forms is not always target-like early on. Harley also observes the frequent production of [ʒe] initially, which may be used as an unanalysed chunk rather than the target *je* + auxiliary form *j'ai* 'I have'. Aspectual distinctions between *passé composé* and *imparfait* also pose tremendous difficulties for the children. For a while, verbs occurring in the *imparfait* are restricted to typically durative verbs such as *avoir* 'have', *être* 'be' and *savoir* 'know'. Action verbs which should appear in the *imparfait* in the target language are either used in the present or the *passé composé*. Finally, the conditional is reported to develop relatively late in the children; instead, the analytic future is frequently used to express hypotheses. In addition to these findings, no study has systematically investigated knowledge of tense and aspect development in child L2 French within the generative paradigm.

47. These programs start in kindergarten with a half-day in French. In elementary schools, schooling is entirely in French as of grade one.

4.1.1.2 *Root infinitives in child L2 French*

According to some studies, children learning L2 French go through an RI period in the early stages of acquisition, as is observed in monolinguals (Paradis & Crago 2000; Prévost 1997; Prévost & White 2000a). Analysing data from Kenny and Greg (see above), Prévost (1997) reports that RIs are used during the first 18 months of acquisition, as shown in Table 2. Examples are given in (4).

Table 2. Finite and nonfinite root declaratives in child L2 French before and after month 18 (L1=English) (from Prévost 1997)

Child	Before month 18	After month 18
Kenny	76/504 (15.1%)	3/527 (0.6%)
Greg	58/659 (8.9%)	4/911 (0.4%)

(4) a. Moi jouer avec le train. (Greg, L1=English, month 5)
me play.INF with the train

b. Toi faire ça. (Kenny, L1=English, month 8)
you do.INF this

Prévost reports that the RIs produced during the 18-month period have the same properties as those produced by monolingual children. First, they rarely occur with clitic subjects or DP subjects, as shown in Table 3 (see also Paradis et al. 1998). Instead, RIs are generally found with strong pronoun subjects (which bear default case in French) or null subjects.

Table 3. Subject types found in child L2 French RIs (L1=English) (from Prévost 1997)

Learner	Finiteness	Clitics	DPs	Strong pron	Null
Kenny	+Finite (n=428)	159 (37.1%)	115 (26.9%)	65 (15.2%)	87 (20.3%)
	–Finite (n=76)	3 (3.9%)	6 (7.9%)	45 (59.2%)	23 (30.3%)
Greg	+Finite (n=591)	411 (69.5%)	99 (16.7%)	32 (5.4%)	59 (10%)
	–Finite (n=58)	13 (22.4%)	0 (0%)	15 (25.9%)	31 (53.4%)

In addition, nonfinite forms are quite rare in the finite context of CPs. Of the 147 questions and embedded clauses Kenny produced, only 9 exhibit a nonfinite verb (6.1%). For Greg, the ratio is 6/160 (3.8%). Third, the vast majority of RIs the children produced have a modal interpretation, in contrast to their finite utterances, which generally receive a purely temporal reading, as shown in Table 4. Table 4 further shows a relationship in the child L2 data between finiteness and verb type: RIs appear almost exclusively with eventive verbs; noneventive predicates occur almost exclusively in finite utterances.

Table 4. Interpretation and verb types in child L2 French root declaratives (L1=English) (from Prévost 2001)

Child	Finiteness	Interpretation		Verb types	
		Past/Present	Future/Modal	Eventive	Noneventive
Kenny	+Finite	86 (89.6%)	10 (10.4%)	69 (66%)	36 (34%)
	–Finite	20 (35.1%)	37 (64.9%)	73 (100%)	0
Greg	+Finite	166 (93.8%)	11 (6.2%)	78 (43.5%)	99 (56.5%)
	–Finite	11 (22.9%)	37 (77.1%)	56 (98.3%)	1 (1.7%)

Finally, nonfinite verbs are placed to the right of negative adverbs in negative RIs. This is observed in the 18 negative RIs produced by Kenny and the 6 found in Greg's data (e.g. *Pas ouvrir ça* 'Not open.INF this', Kenny, month 5).

Other studies of child L2 French report a low production of RIs. In a study on L2 French acquisition on the part of two children, Elisa and Lorenzo, whose L1s were German and Italian respectively, Belletti and Hamann (2004) report that RIs represent at most 2% of all declaratives in spontaneous speech. Elisa and Lorenzo were aged 4;0 and 3;5 when data collection began and they were followed for seven months. Crucially, they had been exposed to French for 13 and 14 months, respectively, at the time of the first interview, which is much more than Kenny and Greg. They may therefore have already gone through an RI period. Clearly more investigation needs to be undertaken on this topic.

4.1.1.3 *Finite forms in nonfinite positions in child L2 French*

Although children use nonfinite forms instead of target-like finite verbs, the opposite is not systematically observed. In other words, in positions requiring a nonfinite form (following a preposition, an auxiliary, or another verb), target-like nonfinite verbs are correctly used, as shown in Table 5. Use of nonfinite forms in nonfinite contexts is illustrated in (5) through (7).[48] Note that although the forms may not be 'native-like', as shown in (5b), where an infinitival form is used instead of a past participle, they at least respect the finite/nonfinite distinctions of the target language.

48. The children were found to produce a number of utterances involving *c'est va* 'it's go.FIN', as in *C'est va là* 'It's go.FIN there (Kenny, month 11). This sequence seems to qualify as a routine in the children's speech. First, the finite form *va* only replaces the infinitive *aller* when used with *être*. With any other verb, the target-like form *aller* is used, as in (i). Second, other occurrences of *va* indicate that this form is considered finite by the children, especially when it is used with a negative adverb. In this case, it always precedes the adverb, as in (ii). *C'est va* utterances are not taken into account in Table 5.

Table 5. Incidence of finite forms in nonfinite positions in child L2 French (L1=English) (from Prévost 2001)

	Greg		Kenny	
	– Finite	+ Finite	– Finite	+ Finite
Prep + V	8	0	7	1
Aux + V	213	6	111	7
V + V	40	0	15	0
Total	261 (*97.8%*)	6 (*2.2%*)	133 (*94.3%*)	8 (*5.7%*)

(5) a. Kenny a crié. (Kenny, L1=English, month 4)
K. has scream.INF

b. Moi j' ai écrire. (Greg, L1=English, month 11)
me I have+1SG write.INF

(6) a. Il va dans ça pour dormir. (Kenny, L1=English, month 18)
he go.FIN in this to sleep.INF

b. C'est pour jouer. (Greg, L1=English, month 14)
it is to play.INF

(7) a. Le crocodile peut manger le tigre. (Kenny, L1=English, month 7)
the crocodile can.FIN eat.INF the tigre

b. Moi vais mettre le hibou brun. (Greg, L1=English, month 10)
me go.FIN put.INF the owl brown

Interestingly, the low rates of finite verbs found in nonfinite positions (2.2% for Greg and 5.7% for Kenny) are extremely close to the low percentages of nonfinite forms in finite contexts: 2.8% for Greg (19/683) and 4.2% for Kenny (18/430). In other words, although both children produce RIs, they seem to have knowledge of finiteness.

4.1.2 Development of verb placement in child L2 French

In the vast majority of cases, verb forms are correctly placed with respect to negation in child L2 French, as in child L1 French. For instance, in 321 of the 331 finite

(i) a. C'est va aller juste là. (Greg, L1=English, month 10)
it is go.FIN go.INF just there

b. Je va aller à la toilette. (Kenny, L1=English, month 4)
I go.FIN go.INF to the toilet

(ii) a. Moi je va pas là. (Greg, L1=English, month 5)
me I go.FIN not there

b. Moi j'y va pas. (Kenny, L1=English, month 10)
me I there go.FIN not

negatives found in Kenny's data, the finite verb is correctly placed to the left of the negative adverb (97%). A similar ratio obtains in Greg's corpus (447/449 = 98%). This is illustrated in (8). Similar findings are reported in Devitt's (1992) study of (finite) verb placement in the corpus of five English-speaking children. Data collection started shortly after the children arrived in France (between ages 8 and 11;6).[49]

(8) a. Ça c'est pas ma maman. (Kenny, L1=English, month 2)
this it is not my mummy

b. Moi je veux pas. (Kenny, L1=English, month 3)
me I want.FIN not

c. Ça c'est pas le ferme. (Greg, L1=English, month 5)
this it is not the farm

d. Non j'ai pas joué avec. (Greg, L1=English, month 9)
no I have+1SG not played with

Moreover, target-like verb placement with respect to negation seems to be acquired relatively early. Devitt (1992) reports that negative sentences with lexical verbs are used productively as early as sample 2 in his data. However, for most examples reported in the literature on early verb placement in child L2 acquisition, including those in (8a–c), it is possible that the children treat them as unanalysed chunks. Few studies address the question of the productivity of verb placement with respect to negation, that is, whether it occurs with different verbs or not.

Verb placement with respect to adverbs and floating quantifiers is reported to be correct in child L2 French, although evidence is scarce, and examples with adverbs and quantifiers are not observed until later in longitudinal data (see (9)).

(9) a. Ils ont toujours un parachute. (Kenny, L1=English, month 27)
they have+3PL always a parachute

b. mais en hiver i' prend tous des pantalons.
but in winter he/they take.FIN all some pants
(Kenny, L1=English, m 29)

In general, there is a very strong contingency between verb form and verb placement in child L2 French: nonfinite forms are restricted to nonfinite positions, such as following a preposition, negation or another verb (including auxiliaries), whereas finite verb generally appear in finite contexts (e.g. above negation).

49. Devitt (1992) also reports 6 cases of *ne*-V (with no *pas*) in which one cannot be sure whether or not verb movement has applied, since *ne*, when it is produced, always precedes the verb in adult French.

4.1.3 The content of child interlanguage grammars of French

There are several views on the content of initial child L2 grammars and their subsequent development. Some researchers consider child L2 learners to have knowledge of finiteness from the outset, which means that initial child interlanguage (IL) grammars possess at least one functional category usually assumed to be Infl. This is sometimes held to be the result of transfer from the L1 (see Section 8.1.1.3 for more discussion). The idea that child L2 learners have knowledge of finiteness is based on several observations: finite verbs are produced initially, subject clitics are correctly used with finite verbs, and verb forms are correctly placed with respect to negation, prepositions, and other verbs (including auxiliaries). Consider Kenny, for example. His very first recordings contained NPs, with only a few verbal utterances, but this was rather short-lived. He started using verbs, finite and nonfinite forms, as well as subject clitics quite rapidly.

Child L2 learners' success in appropriately placing the verb with respect to negation suggests that the target strength of Infl features is acquired relatively quickly by children and thus that parameter (re)setting takes place early in child L2 acquisition. Indeed, these facts appear to call into question approaches claiming that the L1 grammar makes up the very first IL systems (see Schwartz & Sprouse 1996), but more data should be gathered on verb placement with respect to adverbs and floating quantifiers in the early stages of child L2 French before a definitive judgment can be made.

Other researchers, Paradis et al. (1998) for example, argue that knowledge of finiteness is absent from initial grammars. As in L1 acquisition and bilingual acquisition, the formal distinction between knowledge of Tense and knowledge of Agreement is not always made in studies on child L2 French, but Paradis et al. (1998) looked at the development of tense and agreement separately. They argue that, as in bilingual acquisition, Agr is part of initial grammars (where it realizes agreement and acts as a host for verb movement), but T is not. They also argue that acquisition of functional categories is lexically driven, with Agr acquired before T in L2 French because of the rich input about agreement to which learners are exposed (mostly due to the frequency of subject clitics, which Paradis et al. consider to be agreement markers). Interestingly, seven of the 15 child learners Paradis et al. interviewed showed evidence of acquisition of past and future tenses in the first interview. For these children, therefore, it is impossible to know whether or not Agr was acquired prior to T. The authors also report that future morphology is acquired after past tense, but offer no explanation for this fact. It might be due to problems with the lexical forms of tense, rather than to the lack of T in early grammars. Finally, the fact that the learners struggled with 3rd person plural forms may be an indication of a problem with (number) agreement, rather than with tense.

It is important to point out that the hypothesis that child learners have knowledge of functional categories early on does not imply that these categories are systematically projected. For example, the utterances including RIs produced by Kenny and Greg have been argued to support a Truncation analysis of early grammars: for a while, children project either VPs, yielding (truly) nonfinite declaratives, or IPs/CPs yielding finite utterances (Prévost 1997; Prévost & White 2000a). This approach has recently received additional support from a study examining the incidence and nature of verbless utterances in child L2 French (Prévost 2008). Prévost's investigation of Kenny's and Greg's data reveals that verbless sentences, and in particularly sentences with copula omission, are found and that they disappear roughly at the same time as RIs, at around month 18. Verbs are also rarely omitted in CP-related clauses, namely in exactly the same contexts from which main infinitival verbs are largely excluded (see Section 4.1.1.2). Assuming that the copula is a grammatical reflex of finiteness and Tense, these findings suggest that utterances in which the copula has been dropped lack T and are represented as root NPs, APs, or PPs (see Caprin & Guasti (2006) for a similar proposal for copula omission in child L1 Italian).[50]

Finally, child L2 facts have interesting implications for theories of L1 development. In particular, the properties of RIs in L1 French and L2 French argue against the concept of maturation as an explanation for the end of the RI period in L1 French because maturation cannot explain the end of a similar period, with similar properties, in L2 French. Instead, the inflectional variability that RIs represent could be argued to result from similar difficulties in both acquisition contexts, perhaps related to the restricted computational capacities of children. Konhert, Windsor, and Danahy Ebert (2009), for instance, found that children aged 8 to 13 learning L2 English performed worse than control children on working memory tasks in English. Assuming that the computational load becomes heavier as more structural layers are projected, children may sometimes fail to project the full representation until they can better handle the multiple computations that it implies. As seen earlier, reduced computational capacities in children have also been argued to constrain language development in young children, especially in the case of SLI populations (see Jakubowicz's (2004, 2005) Computational Complexity Hypothesis, among others).

4.2 The verbal domain in adult L2 acquisition of French

In contrast to child learners, adolescents and adults learning L2 French seem to struggle with inflectional morphology. They produce RIs for a much longer period and their RIs have different properties from those produced by children. In particular,

50. This analysis differs from Ionin and Wexler's (2002) interpretation of copula omission as missing surface inflection in child L2 English.

adult learners seem to use nonfinite markers as substitutes for finite inflection. In other words, they use RIs as default finite markers. With respect to verb placement, knowledge of verb raising in French is attested in negative utterances, with the verb appearing above the negative adverb, but verb placement with respect to adverbs and floating quantifiers is much less accurate.

4.2.1 Inflectional morphology in adult L2 French

4.2.1.1 *Development of finite inflection in adult L2 French*

Development of inflectional morphology can take quite a long time in adolescent and adult L2 learners. In the initial stages, verbless sentences, as in (10), and formulaic expressions such as *c'est X* 'it is X', *il y a* 'there is' and *je ne sais pas* 'I don't know' are frequent.

(10) Taxi dans la bois. Après, pluie pluie pluie. (Henry 1, beginner, L1=Swedish)
taxi into the wood then rain rain rain [=we took a taxi to go into the wood, but then it started raining all the time] (Schlyter 2003)

Myles (2005) followed the acquisition of French morphosyntax by 14 anglophone adolescents aged 12–13 at the time of their first interview (year 1). By then, they had been exposed to French for one year in a classroom context. A second recording took place a year later (year 2), with the same experimental task, namely an elicited verbal narrative based on a cartoon story. Myles reports that the incidence of verbal utterances is quite low at year 1, averaging 54.6% of all utterances produced by the children. For seven of the learners, the incidence of verbal utterances is below 50%. At year 2, the mean of verbal utterances rises to 75.7%.

In initial stages, many verbs often appear in just one form regardless of tense and person, such as *comprendre* 'understand' in *je comprendre* 'I understand.INF' and *la dame comprendre* 'the lady understand.INF' (Henry 1, beginner, L1=Swedish) (Schlyter 2003). This tendency decreases with time. Similarly, Myles (2004) argues that many of the first utterances containing inflected verbs are unanalysed chunks, many of them involving *j'* 'I', such as *j'adore* 'I adore', *j'habite* 'I live', and *j'aime* 'I like' (see also Myles, Hooper, & Mitchell 1998). Myles (2004) reports that of the 329 occurrences of such chunks in the speech of beginner (English-speaking) learners of French, nearly half were overextended to other persons, as in *Monique j'aime* 'Monique I like = Monique likes'. Moreover, *j'* appeared outside of these chunks only three times. For Myles, learners start to break down chunks as they start mastering the pronominal system, that is, when they try to relate the verb with a subject pronoun other than the one appearing in the chunk (in particular 3rd person pronouns).

A similar overgeneralization happens with respect to tense, with past forms often expressed by an infinitive or a present form (typically a 3rd person singular form), as in *Il y avait quelques-uns qui a oui* 'There were some who has yes' (Yvonne I) (Bartning 1997; Schlyter 2003). Such erroneous uses decrease as acquisition proceeds. In particular, recourse to auxiliaries increases, quite rapidly in some learners. However, Schlyter (2003) reports that for most learners target-like tense morphology, at least for *passé composé,* is not in place before about two years. Other past tenses such as *imparfait* and *plus-que-parfait* are acquired later. Indeed, Coppierters (1987) reports that aspectual properties of *imparfait* may fail to be fully acquired, even by very advanced learners. However, his conclusions are based on a preference task involving only five sentences. Moreover, these sentences are decontextualized, which, according to Birdsong (1992) is an important methodological shortcoming. Therefore, much more thorough investigation of the development of aspect in L2 French is required before firm conclusions can be drawn.

Other studies do show evidence of auxiliaries and subject verb agreement very early on, as illustrated in (11) (data in (11a–b) are from Prévost 2004).

(11) a. J'ai étudié heu secondaire. (Ann, beginner, L1=English)
   I have+1SG studied secondary

b. Elle est boire du thé. (George, beginner, L1=English)
   she is drink.INF some tea

c. Je suis vingt-deux (Lisa, beginner, L1=Swedish)
   I am twenty-two (Schlyter 2003)

There is also correct placement of the verb with respect to the negative adverb *pas*, such as *Je (ne) comprends pas* 'I don't understand' (Lisa 1, beginner, L1=Swedish), although it is not always easy to decide whether learners are producing unanalysed chunks or fully analysed utterances.

Leung (2002) is one of the few studies that looked at knowledge of tense and agreement in elicited and judgment data. Two groups were investigated: a group of 12 Vietnamese speakers who were learning French in Montreal (at the beginner level) (the L2 French group) and a group of 84 Cantonese speakers learning French in Hong Kong (at three different levels). The latter learners also had advanced knowledge of English (the L3 French group). Chinese does not have overt tense and agreement markers, and there is debate over whether or not T is present in Chinese at all (e.g. Huang (1984) vs. Hu, Pan & Xu (2001)). In her work, Leung assumes that it is not and that, likewise, finiteness and tense features are also absent. Chinese sentences, Leung assumes, have AspP instead of TP. In contrast to Chinese, Vietnamese has tense markers, such as *sê* and *dâ*, which (optionally) mark future and past, respectively (N'Guyen 1997). They can therefore be considered to instantiate finiteness and tense features, along with T. However, like Chinese, Vietnamese does not have agreement markers.

Knowledge of tense in French was tested via a written composition task (e.g. asking the learners about their past summer holiday) and a preference task where participants were asked to select appropriate tense forms in sentences set either in the past or the present (e.g. *Sophie a beaucoup parlé/parle beaucoup à la réunion hier* 'Sophie spoke/ speaks a lot at the meeting yesterday'). In the written production test, accuracy in tense selection in obligatory contexts was a high 80% in the two groups, including the beginner learners. The results of the preference task are given in Table 6. The L2 French group's performance was lower than that of the beginner L3 learners, whose overall accuracy was close to 80% (as in the production task). However, all beginners, as well as the intermediate L3 learners, struggled with [+past] marking, in comparison to [−past]. The advanced learners' performance was similar to that of the controls.

Table 6. Accuracy at selecting target-like tense in adult L2/L3 French (L1 = Vietnamese or Chinese) (preference task) (from Leung 2002)

Group	L1	[+past]	[−past]	Total
L2 French Beginn (n=12)	Vietnamese	69.3%	76.2%	72.7%
L3 French Beginn (n=44)	Chinese	74.9%	82.6%	78.7%
L3 French Interm (n=30)	Chinese	78.9%	87%	83%
L3 French Adv (n=10)	Chinese	98.3%	93%	95.7%
Controls (n=30)	French	93.1%	95.6%	94.3%

Agreement was tested via the same preference task as above (e.g. *J'aime/aimons écouter de la musique* 'I like.1S/like.1P to listen to music') and via a sentence completion task in which participants were asked to place (and adapt) missing words into a sentence (e.g. *aller au* 'go.INF to+the' in *Marc et Pete ... cinéma* 'Mark and Pete ... cinema'). As shown in Table 7, accuracy on agreement was very high in the L3 group, above 90% accurate, while the performance of the L2 group was much lower, below 65%.

Table 7. Accuracy at production and selection of agreement in adult L2/L3 French (L1 = Vietnamese or Chinese) (from Leung 2002)

Group	L1	Sentence completion	Preference
L2 French (n=12)	Vietnamese	61.5%	64.2%
L3 French Beginn (n=44)	Chinese	96.9%*	94.1%*
L3 French Interm (n=30)	Chinese	99.1%	97.7%
L3 French Adv (n=10)	Chinese	100%	96.7%
Controls (n=30)	French	100%	98.8%

As mentioned above, Chinese and Vietnamese do not mark agreement overtly. However, English does, at least in the 3rd person singular. Since the Chinese native speakers had an advanced knowledge of English, they had presumably acquired Agr. This category, or at least the agreement features, could have transferred to their L3 French grammar, which would explain their better results (Leung 2002).

4.2.1.2 *Root infinitives in adult L2 French*

The incidence of RIs can be quite high in the speech of adult L2 French learners with different L1s, such as English, Moroccan Arabic (MA), Spanish, and Swedish (Myles 2004; Prévost 2004; Prévost & White 2000a; Schlyter 1997, 2003). In addition, RIs are not restricted to the early stages: they are also found in more advanced learners, although their ratio tends to decrease with proficiency. In Myles' (2004) study, only half of the verbs are finite at year 1 (65/126 = 51.6%) and a little more than half the following year (105/186 = 56.4%), which is a small but significant difference.

It is important to point out that tremendous variation can be observed across learners, including beginner learners. The incidence of RIs, for example, can be quite high for some (higher than what is found in child learners), whereas for others it is very low. For instance, among four beginner anglophone learners in a language-course setting followed over a year, Prévost (2003a) reports that RIs amount to 42% of the declarative clauses produced by one person (Mary: 39/93), and only 2.9% for another (Ian: 4/140). Similarly, in cross-sectional data, the incidence of RIs can be over 25% for some learners, and lower than 5% for others at similar proficiency levels (Prévost 2004).[51]

Regardless of these variations, the nature of adult RIs seems to differ from child nonfinite declaratives. While child RIs are truly nonfinite and are structurally determined (that is, they are VPs underlyingly), adult RIs seem to have finite properties. In particular, as shown in Table 8, nonfinite forms are used in finite contexts, such as with clitics or DP subjects (see the examples in (12)); in contrast, they almost never appear with a strong pronoun subject. Table 8 summarizes findings of a longitudinal study that began when the learners were at the beginner level (Prévost 2003a); compare with the child data reported in Table 3. Such results are confirmed in cross-sectional studies (Prévost 2004). Note that some tokens of the copula used as an infinitive are reported in the adult L2 data (12e), which never occurs in child L2 corpora.

51. Herschensohn (2001) reports few RIs in a longitudinal study of spontaneous production from two English-speaking teenagers (Emma and Chloe). The learners were between 16- and 17-years old when data were collected for the first time and had been studied French for several years. Each learner was interviewed three times over a six-month period. Only nine RIs were found in Emma's data out of a total of 215 root declaratives (4.2%) and in Chloe's, only seven out of a total of 228 (3.1%). However, these learners were considered to be at the intermediate level at the time of their first interview, so it is impossible to know about their early development of inflectional morphology.

Table 8. Subject types in adult L2 French declaratives (from Prévost 2003a)

Learner	L1	Finiteness	Clitics	DPs	Str. pron.	Null
Abdelmal.[a]	MA	+Finite	532 (81.5%)	53 (8.1%)	13 (2%)	52 (8%)
		–Finite	168 (61.8%)	15 (5.5%)	19 (7%)	67 (24.6%)
Zahra[a]	MA	+Finite	392 (65.3%)	71 (11.8%)	26 (4.3%)	111 (18.5%)
		–Finite	120 (50.8%)	32 (13.6%)	23 (9.7%)	60 (25.4%)
Frank	English	+Finite	163/191 (85.3%)	34/303 (11.2%)	0	4/303 (1.3%)
		–Finite	25/30 (83.3%)	3/38 (7.9%)	0	0
Mary	English	+Finite	125/193 (64.8%)	47/237 (19.8%)	0	5/237 (2.1%)
		–Finite	37/63 (58.7%)	14/70 (20%)	1/70 (1.4%)	11/70 (15.7%)
Jane	English	+Finite	421/596 (70.6%)	108/631 (17.1%)	5/631 (0.8%)	42/631 (6.7%)
		–Finite	39/87 (44.8%)	18/94 (19.1%)	0/94 (0%)	27/94 (28.7%)

a. data from the European Science Foundation project on L2 acquisition (Perdue 1984)

(12) a. Tu boire. (Abdelmalek, month 27, L1=MA)
you drink.INF

b. Tu couper tout. (Zahra, month 24.5, L1=MA)
you cut.INF everything

c. Il laver les serviettes. (Frank 1, L1=English)
he wash.INF the towels

d. Le bateau faire beaucoup de bruit. (Jane 7, L1=English)
the boat do.INF much noise

e. Il être marié. (Joe 1, L1=English)
he be.INF married

In addition to being used with finite subjects, nonfinite forms may also appear in CPs (13) and above negation (14), which is rarely observed in child L2 French (see also Meisel 1997; Rule & Marsden 2006). For instance, nonfinite verbs are found in around one third of Abdemalek's and Zahra's CPs (Prévost 1997).

(13) a. Combien tu rester ici? (Abdel., month 24, L1=MA)
how (long) you stay.INF here

b. Et Malika, pourquoi téléphoner à toi à la maison?
and Malika why call.INF to you at the house
(Zahra, month 38.5, L1=MA)

c. parce qu' il trouver le sable rapide (Jane 6, L1=English)
because he find.INF the sand quick

d. Quand on être dans la # la 'eller' dans la pays (Lisa 4, L1=Swedish)
when one be.INF in the the 'or' in the country

(14) a. Consulat du Maroc tu donner pas de feuille.
consulate of Morocco you give.INF not some paper
(Abd., month 24.5, L1=MA)

b. Maintenant payer pas deux mois. (Zahra, month 36.5, L1=MA)
now pay.INF not two months

c. Il ne venir pas. (Joe 1, L1=English)
he NEG come.INF not

d. Je ne connaître pas. (Lisa 2, L1=Swedish)
I NEG know.INF not

Finally, in contrast to child L2 data, there is no apparent relationship between finiteness and modal interpretation in adult production: the vast majority of both finite and nonfinite declaratives have a temporal interpretation, as shown in (15) (see also Herschensohn 2001). It is not the case that RIs have a future or modal reading (at most 20% in Prévost's (2003a) study), which corroborates the idea that RIs do not have nonfinite properties in adult language. In adult L2 French, infinitival markers seem to be employed as a substitute for finite inflection. According to Schlyter (2003), the opposition between finite and nonfinite forms is established at the same time as the present/nonpresent distinction. However, this predicts that finite and nonfinite forms should alternate in nonfinite positions for a while, contrary to fact (see Section 4.2.1.3).

(15) a. Il dormer. (Jane 1, L1=English)
he sleep.INF
[J. is describing a picture]

b. Mon frère visiter aussi. (Mary 1, L1=English)
my brother visit.INF too
[M. is talking about her brother's visit the preceding Christmas]

Crucially, for adults, just as for children, the production of nonfinite verb forms does not stem from a lack of knowledge of finite morphology. Indeed, when finite inflection is used, it is used correctly, as illustrated in Table 9. Of the few agreement errors that are observed, the majority involve overgeneralization of 3rd person singular forms, such as *a* ('has') and *est* ('is') (see also Bartning 1997):

(16) a. J'a fait la bagarre avec lui-même.
I have+3SG made the fight with him
(Abdelmalek, month 52.7, L1=MA)

b. Quand moi est pas là. (Zahra, month 39.5, L1=MA)
when me is not there

Table 9. Accuracy in verbal agreement in adult L2 French (L1=MA) (from Prévost & White 2000b)

Verb form	**Abdelmalek**		**Zahra**	
	Correct	Incorrect	Correct	Incorrect
Regular affixation	447 (94.7%)	25	552 (93.4%)	39
homophonous inflection	445 (94.7%)	25	538 (93.2%)	39
distinctive inflection	2 (100%)	0	14 (100%)	0
être, avoir and *aller* forms	264 (97.8%)	6	156 (98.7%)	2
Total	711 (95.8%)	31	708 (94.5%)	41

In her study, Leung (2002) investigated knowledge of finiteness via the same sentence completion task and preference task (e.g. *Je rencontre/rencontrant beaucoup de monde chaque jour* 'I meet.1SG/meet.PrP a lot of people') as described in Section 4.2.1.1. The preference task represented the first attempt to collect data on finite vs. nonfinite declaratives using a methodology that did not involve production. The results, reported in Table 10, show that the L3 French learners performed significantly better than the L2 French group, even at the beginner level. Accuracy was over 80% at all levels in the L3 group. All participants showed higher accuracy on the sentence completion task than on the preference task.

Table 10. Accuracy at production and selection of finiteness in adult L2/L3 French (L1 = Chinese and Vietnamese) (from Leung 2002)

Group	**L1**	**Sentence completion**	**Preference**
L2 French (n=12)	Vietnamese	79.1%	70.3%
L3 French Beginn (n=44)	Chinese	97.6%*	83.1%*
L3 French Interm (n=30)	Chinese	98.3%	83.3%
L3 French Adv (n=10)	Chinese	100%	94.2%
Controls (n=30)	French	100%	99.2%

4.2.1.3 *Incidence of finite forms in nonfinite positions in adult L2 French*

Another difference between child and adult L2 French is that verbs that superficially look finite may occur in nonfinite positions in adult data, especially in the early stages of acquisition, as shown in Table 11. These are present forms that do not bear any overt person or number marker, as in (17); no instance of overt agreement marker is reported in such positions, as in (18).

Table 11. Finite forms in nonfinite positions in adult L2 French (L1 = English) (from Prévost 2004)

Level	Finiteness	Prep+V	Aux+V	Mod+V	V+V	Neg+V	Total
Begin (n=5)	– finite	5	14	6	2	0	27
	+ finite	3	17	4	0	1	25 (48.1%)
Int 1 (n=5)	– finite	55	146	92	8	18	319
	+ finite	3	16	7	1	2	29 (8.3%)
Int 2 (n=6)	– finite	130	269	192	17	29	637
	+ finite	14	16	11	1	3	45 (6.6%)
Int 3 (n=5)	– finite	181	278	158	19	28	664
	+ finite	3	3	4	2	1	13 (1.9%)

(17) a. J'ai difficile demande des questions. (Ann, beginner, L1=English)
I have+1SG difficult ask.FIN some questions

b. Il est prépare pour dormer. (George, beginner, L1=English)
he is prepare.FIN for sleep.INF

c. Comment tu vas arrive à mon travail?
how you go.FIN arrive.FIN to my work
(Jen, Interm 1, L1=English)

d. .. mais je ne peux pas parle ... (Sophie, Interm 1, L1=English)
but I NEG can.FIN not speak.FIN

e. qui uh j'ai rencontre à Nouvelle-Ecosse (Jill, Interm 2, L1=English)
who I have+1SG meet.FIN in Nova-Scotia

(18) a. *pour mangeons (unattested)
for eat.1PL

b. *pour suis (unattested)
for am

Similarly, Rule & Marsden (2006) report a nonnegligible production rate of *pas*+V_{finite} sequences in an elicitation task administered to 60 English-speaking adolescents (age 13–16) learning French in England. The learners were divided into three groups according to their schooling in French, and about 180 negative clauses were collected in each group. The percentage of *pas*+V_{finite} was highest (10.8%) for those learners whose proficiency was presumably the lowest, with production ratios declining to below 10% afterwards (see also Section 4.2.2.1).

Crucially, the use of finite forms in nonfinite contexts is not observed in all L2 French learning situations. In particular, the errors reported above are mainly attested in L2 French acquisition by English native speakers, that is, learners whose L1 does not exhibit any overt infinitive marker. It is therefore possible that the finite forms used in nonfinite contexts in French are in fact considered nonfinite by the learners, based on the morphological properties of their L1. Almost no such forms are used by learners whose L1 possesses overt infinitival markers. For instance, only rare cases of *pas*+V_{finite} orders are reported in L2 French data from native speakers of Spanish (Meisel 1997; Prévost 2006b; Trévise & Noyau 1984) and similar facts are reported in the acquisition of L2 German by Spanish and Portuguese learners (Prévost & White 2000b). In other words, the production of finite forms in nonfinite contexts seems to be affected by the presence (or absence) of the relevant morphology in the L1.[52] Further research is needed to pinpoint exactly what factors are involved, including, possibly, the influence of L1 phonology, as suggested in Lardiere (2003) and Goad, White & Steele (2003).

4.2.1.4 *Theoretical analyses*

As we have seen, the incidence of verbless utterances and RIs can be high in the initial stages of L2 acquisition by adult learners. Moreover, many verbs are used in only one form and tense is expressed via present forms. At first sight, this looks like evidence that there are no functional categories in initial adult IL grammars (Vainikka & Young-Scholten 1994, 1996, 2005). Under this view, these grammars contain only lexical categories, which are transferred from the L1. Myles (2004) argues that the majority of the 12- to 14-year-old anglophones she interviewed twice over two years failed to project IP, at both recording sessions. In particular, over 40% of the verbal utterances produced at year 2 were still nonfinite. Myles assumes that the lack of functional categories is due to processing problems caused by the projection of verbs and their argument structure. Evidence for IP is found in only three learners, who used finite forms and clitic subjects productively (at year 2). To explain the transition from the VP-stage to a functional stage, Myles suggests that the copula and auxiliaries *être* and *avoir* act as a trigger for the projection of functional layers (see Hawkins 2001).[53] Prior to the VP-stage, Myles argues, L2 learners produce utterances that receive no syntactic analysis. They

52. Some cases are mentioned in Swedish learners of French (Schlyter 2003), but it is difficult to evaluate their overall incidence since statistical counts are not provided.

53. In the same vein, Klein & Perdue (1997) argue that the initial stages of adult L2 acquisition are best characterized as the Basic Variety (BV), 'a well-structured, efficient and simple form of language' used by learners acquiring the language in naturalistic setting (Klein & Perdue 1997: 301). The BV mainly consists of (uninflected and often phonologically distorted) open-class items. Strikingly absent from the BV are (a) free or bound morphemes with purely grammatical function and (b) complex hierarchical structures, in particular, subordination (Klein & Perdue 1997: 333). From this point of view, evidence for functional categories is rare in the BV.

are simple mappings between semantic representations and phonological strings, for example [give name] = [*je m'appelle*] (Myles 2004: 20). This would account for the unanalysed chunks that L2 learners use initially to break into the communicative situation. At that stage, many utterances consist only of juxtapositions of NPs, as in *Nom... le garçon?* 'Name... the boy?'. VPs appear later, according to Myles, because they are more structurally complex than NPs. A similar view is shared by Rule and Marsden (2006) who report a high rate of Neg+NP utterances in a production task meant to elicit verbal negatives (e.g. *Elle non télévision* lit. 'She no television'). Such verbless sentences represent about 30% of the negatives obtained from the least proficient learners. Moreover, these learners were found to produce a large number of Neg+VP sentences (e.g. *Il ne pas jouer au basketball* lit. 'He not play basketball'), and a large proportion of the target V_{finite}-*pas* sequences observed in their production data were analysed as chunks by the authors (e.g. *Je n'aime pas* 'I don't like'). These facts are taken to indicate the absence of functional categories in early interlanguage systems.

In spite of these arguments, there is evidence for early use of auxiliaries and subject/verb agreement in beginner learners of French. Although it is true that the ratio of RIs can be quite high in some cases, when finite morphology is produced, it is largely correct. This includes suppletive forms of verbs such as *être*, *avoir*, and *aller*. In the data investigated by Myles (2005), although the incidence of subject clitics is low (less than 25%), they almost always occur with a finite form across both recordings (31/33 = 93.4%). There is also tremendous variety across learners. As Myles (2005) acknowledges, at least 75% of the verbs produced by three of her learners at year 1 are in the finite form (see also Prévost 2003a). In Leung's data, tense accuracy in production is a high 80% for the beginner learners. Taken together, these facts suggest that functional categories cannot be altogether absent from early IL grammars.[54]

Furthermore, we have seen that knowledge of functional categories cannot be determined based solely on the production of inflectional morphology; syntactic consequences of the projection of such categories must also be investigated. For instance, while the incidence of RIs is high in Myles' data, the relationship between finiteness and verb position is strong (with nonfinite forms occurring in nonfinite positions and finite forms restricted to finite contexts) and verbs are correctly placed with respect to negation, both of which suggest knowledge of finiteness. We have also seen that (apparently) nonfinite forms may appear in finite contexts (such as above negation and with clitic subjects), which suggests that they are not within VP, but rather are hosted by a functional category, presumably Infl. In addition, although it may be true, as argued by Rule and Marsden (2006), that some V_{finite}-*pas* sequences are used as

54. In Myles' (2004) study, some learners produce *être* and *avoir* forms at year 2, but are not considered to be in the IP-stage. It would be interesting to know how the utterances in which such forms occur could be accounted for under Myles' assumptions.

chunks by beginner L2 learners of French, it does not quite follow that such sequences necessarily lack functional structure. The learners may simply experience lexical gaps, which leads them to produce what looks like systematic and inappropriate sequences (with respect to what is expected), but such sequences nonetheless exhibit target word order and target inflectional marking. These facts further argue against the idea of an initial stage at which functional categories are absent from IL grammars.

If, contra Vainikka and Young-Scholten (1994, 1996, 2005), we posit the presence of functional categories in initial IL grammars, how can we explain the incidence of infinitival forms in positions where finite morphology is normally required? A number of possible responses to this question have been proposed. One possibility is that L2 learners have knowledge of underlying syntactic properties (including functional categories), but that they have problems with the overt morphological realization of these properties. This approach, known as the Missing Inflection Hypothesis, was originally proposed by Haznedar and Schwartz (1997) and was renamed the Missing Surface Inflection Hypothesis by Prévost and White (2000a) to highlight the fact that the problem lies at the superficial level. This approach makes a clear distinction between abstract morphosyntactic properties, such as the [+finite] feature, and their morphophonological realization, such as *-ons* '1PL' (see also Beard 1995). Another hypothesis is that adult L2 learners have problems mapping morphology and syntax (Lardiere 1998, 2000). Finally, drawing on Distributed Morphology (DM) (Halle & Marantz 1993), which distinguishes between abstract features, on the one hand, and forms, which are part of the Vocabulary, on the other, Prévost and White (2000b) propose that default nonfinite forms are underspecified with respect to finiteness in IL grammars. In other words, nonfinite forms are not [–finite] or [+finite], but [0finite]. In DM, the forms of the Vocabulary are associated with a bundle of features, such as finiteness, person, number, gender, etc. Once the syntactic derivation is complete, these forms must be inserted into the representation, which requires that there be a correspondence between the features of the forms and those of the terminal nodes targeted. So, a Vocabulary form specified as [+verb, +finite, +1st person, +plural], such as *mangeons* 'eat.1PL', could be inserted in a terminal node associated with these features.[55] If there is a mismatch in features, insertion cannot take place. This would prevent, for example, the insertion of nonfinite forms (that is, forms specified as [–finite]) into finite positions (positions specified as [+finite]). If, in (adult) L2 acquisition, nonfinite forms are underspecified for finiteness ([0finite]), they should be able to appear in

55. Total matching between features is not obligatory. The inserted form may be associated with only a subset of the features of the host node. Prior to insertion, a competition takes place between several forms of the Vocabulary, with the winner having the highest number of matching features.

finite or nonfinite positions without triggering any feature mismatch with the [+finite] or [–finite] specification of the host node (either Infl or V). This would explain why infinitival verbs may be found in finite positions (e.g. above negative adverbs) or nonfinite ones (e.g. following a modal). A similar approach could be adopted to account for (finite) present forms used instead of past tense verbs, under the assumption that such present forms are underspecified for tense ([0tense]), but specified for finiteness. Finally, forms that are obviously finite, i.e. that bear an overt finite marker, are associated with [+finite], which means that they can only appear in finite positions: insertion into a nonfinite node would yield a feature mismatch and the derivation would crash. This explains the ungrammaticality of (18) above. Interestingly, this hypothesis could also explain how, in Leung's (2002) (preference) judgment task, nonfinite forms could be wrongly selected as main verbs. In Leung's study, accuracy at selecting a finite form was at 70% for the beginner L2 French learners, and accuracy was overall higher on the sentence completion task than on the preference task. If nonfinite forms are underspecified for finiteness in the learners' grammars, the fact that RIs are rated grammatical by the beginners is not problematic. It remains unclear why there should be a difference between the two tasks, however. Perhaps it is due to only some individuals, or to particular sentences that were problematic. Unfortunately, not enough detail is provided to assess such possibilities.

We also saw that English speakers learning French may produce finite and nonfinite forms in both finite and nonfinite contexts. At first sight, this seems to go against the claim that there is knowledge of finiteness on the part of adult L2 learners because finite forms should be restricted to finite contexts. These data seem instead to favour impairment views of IL grammars according to which there is no relationship between verb form and position (Beck 1998; Eubank et al. 1997; Meisel 1997). According to Meisel, for instance, given that finite forms almost never occur in nonfinite positions in child L1 production, and assuming that L1 learning is UG-driven, the fact that such errors are found in L2 speech suggests that L2 acquisition differs fundamentally from L1 acquisition. In other words, UG is not the guiding force underlying the acquisition of a second language. However, in contrast to what an impairment hypothesis would predict, it is almost exclusively English-speaking learners who make such errors. Learners whose L1 has overt infinitival marking on verbs rarely use finite forms in nonfinite positions in their L2 French. This difference across learning situations suggests that the errors committed by the English-speaking learners do not stem from a lack of abstract knowledge of finiteness. Rather, it suggests that the bare forms that appear in nonfinite contexts are specified as [–finite] in their IL grammars.[56] Meisel (1997) also argues that

56. Alternatively, these forms could be [0finite], which would mean that they could appear in either finite or nonfinite contexts.

the few cases where finite forms arise in nonfinite positions in adult L2 data indicate that verb placement is unrelated to finiteness in L2 acquisition, but in that case, one would not expect to find such a discrepancy between the incidence of nonfinite forms in finite contexts (which is quite high) and that of finite forms in nonfinite positions (which is very low). Meisel's (1997) Impairment Hypothesis predicts much more variation in error types than is observed.

The data also argue against the so-called Failed Functional Features Hypothesis (FFFH) (Hawkins & Chan 1997; Hawkins & Hattori 2006; Hawkins & Liszka 2003). According to this approach, L2 features that are not activated in the L1 cannot be acquired, since the activation of new functional features is assumed to be subject to a critical period that ends at adolescence. The absence of a feature from the IL grammar is held to render its overt realization approximate and to lead to morphological variability. Let us take the example of the L3 French learners investigated by Leung (2002). As previously discussed, Leung assumes that Chinese lacks T, and hence [± past] features. On the other hand, English and French, the two languages learned by the Chinese-speakers involved in the study, do have T and temporal features. According to the FFFH, these learners should not be able to acquire [±past] features in either the L2 or the L3.[57] However, the results reported by Leung argue otherwise. In particular, past tense morphology was accurately selected over 93% of the time by the advanced learners in the preference task (Table 6). This score, which was not significantly different from the French native speakers, suggests that the [±past] features have been acquired by the learners.

As seen above, evidence for the presence of functional categories in early IL systems disconfirms the existence of an initial lexical stage in L2 acquisition. The question then arises as to the origin of such categories. In principle, they could be transferred from the L1 grammar (see, e.g. Schwartz & Sprouse 1996) or come from direct access to UG, without transfer, combined with exposure to the relevant input (as argued by Epstein et al. 1996). In many learning situations reviewed so far, both the L1 and the L2 share similar FCs, so while the early availability of FCs may be viewed as a simple case of L1 influence, it is not totally incompatible with the direct-access-to-UG account either. However, when comparing different learning situations involving L1s that are either similar to, or different from French with respect to particular functional properties, the transfer approach is clearly supported. In Leung's (2002) results on agreement in L2 French, a better performance was displayed by beginner learners whose previously acquired language has agreement (English) than

57. Hawkins and Liszka (2003) also looked at the acquisition of English by Chinese native speakers. Although they assume that T is active in Chinese (contra Leung), they nonetheless hold that [± past] features are not (on a par with Leung).

by learners whose L1 does not (Vietnamese).[58] Many other instances of L1 influence will be exposed throughout the book (for a more general discussion on transfer in L2 acquisition, see White 2003).

Finally, the question of the impact of instruction on acquisition can be reviewed in the studies discussed above. Schlyter (2003) noted that the impact of instruction was limited, and these studies tend to confirm that. Instruction seems to have a limited impact on the production of target inflectional morphology. In particular, the incidence of RIs can be quite high, regardless of whether acquisition is taking place in formal settings or more natural immersion environments. For example, RIs were frequently used by some of the English-speaking learners investigated by Prévost (2003a, 2004), Myles (2004), and Rule & Marsden (2006) who were all taking French classes, and by the learners investigated by Prévost & White (2000a) who were learning the language in natural settings. However, no study has specifically looked at the impact of the learning conditions over the acquisition of inflectional morphology in the long run. Another issue that might affect the reported results is the *amount* of input to which the learners are exposed. We know that tremendous variation may exist across learners in that respect, even in apparently similar learning conditions. For instance, when learning takes place in a country where the L2 is being spoken by the community, although all learners could, in principle, have extensive access to the target language, some of them may seek exposure to various sources of natural L2 input, while others may remain in groups with other speakers of their L1 and be exposed to the L2 mainly through classes. It seems plausible that the poor performance reported for learners with limited access to French outside of the classroom may stem from a lack of access to the kind of primary linguistic data necessary for language development. Lack of exposure to appropriate linguistic data may also have an impact on the duration of the RI period. This may explain the differences in the results reported by Myles (2004) and Prévost (2003a, 2004) on the performance of beginner English-speaking learners of French. In these studies, the learners had roughly received the same amount of in-class instruction prior to the first recording session, about 150 hours. According to Myles (2004), this corresponds to the very first stages of acquisition. However, the participants to her study were learning French in the United Kingdom, with limited access to French outside of the classroom, while the ones investigated by Prévost were immersed in the French-speaking community

58. Although Epstein et al.'s (1996) hypothesis was originally proposed for L2 acquisition, it should in principle be true of all subsequent language learning, since UG is held to be available to adult learners. In L3 acquisition, this means that there should be no evidence of influence of the L1 or the L2; acquisition remains a combination of direct access to UG and relevant triggering data in the input.

of Quebec City. This natural exposure may have allowed these learners to advance more quickly than Myles'.

4.2.2 Acquisition of verb placement by adult L2 learners of French

Most studies focusing on the acquisition of verb placement in adult L2 French have investigated the positioning of the verb with respect to negation, frequency and manner adverbs, and floating quantifiers such as *tous* 'all' on the part of English-speaking learners. English and French have different settings of the verb movement parameter, which raises the question of whether learners can acquire the target value of the parameter and abandon their L1 setting. Furthermore, given that each parametric value is associated with mutually exclusive clusters of properties, if learners have acquired the French value, not only should they produce or accept orders such as V-Neg, V-Adv, and V-FQ with finite verbs, they should also reject Neg-V, Adv-V, and FQ-V, which are typical of languages without verb raising, such as English. The discussion of the acquisition of the L2 value of the verb movement parameter goes hand in hand with the question of the status of functional categories and their features in early IL grammars. In particular, if there is an initial stage with no functional categories, verb movement should not be observed and the only orders allowed should be Neg-V, Adv-V, and FQ-V. In general, results suggest that English-speaking learners have little difficulty placing the finite verb above negation, in contrast to their L1. However, verb placement with respect to adverbs and FQs is not always target-like: although learners may acquire the fact that finite verbs can appear above adverbs and FQs, they do not always reject their L1 order. In experimental studies looking at the acquisition of other parametric values, such as the location of finiteness features in either Infl or in C (as is the case for German- and Dutch-speaking learners of French), it is reported that resetting can eventually take place (Hulk 1991).

4.2.2.1 *Production data*

Studies of adult spontaneous production mostly report on verb placement in negative constructions. Generally, too few relevant utterances are produced to assess verb placement with respect to adverbs and floating quantifiers. It is widely reported that in negative utterances involving a simple verb and the negative adverb *pas*, the order is V-*pas*. This is the case regardless of the form of the verb, finite or infinitival. Under the assumption that RIs in adult L2 data are truly finite, then the conclusion is that placement of finite forms with respect to negation is largely correct in L2 French.

Negation has also been found to be solely expressed by the negative particle *ne* in adult L2 speech, as in *je ne parle bien* lit. 'I NEG speak well' (M2) (Trévise & Noyau 1984). Such utterances are target-deviant since in French negatives, a negative adverb is obligatory (e.g. *pas* 'not', *rien* 'nothing'), while *ne* is optional, especially in informal speech. However, *ne* negatives are mostly used by learners whose L1 expresses negation via a preverbal element phonologically close to French *ne*, such as Spanish *no* (e.g. *no quiero vino* 'NEG want.1SG wine'). Although variation between individuals is great, *ne*-negatives were found to range from 11% to 58% in negative utterances produced by three of the eight Spanish-speaking learners interviewed by Trévise and Noyau. By comparison, Prévost (2004) found only four instances of *ne*-V pattern out of a total of 293 negatives (1.4%) produced by 21 English speakers learning French at the beginner and intermediate levels. Crucially, when *ne*-negatives were found, they never represented more than 10% of the negatives produced by the learners.

In Rule & Marsden's (2006) study of elicited production obtained from English-speaking learners, group results show that the verb (regardless of whether it is finite or not) may occur either before or after *pas*. Crucially, however, it is reported that both orders are almost never found in the same production sample. In other words, learners either use Neg-V, presumably due to L1 influence, or V-Neg, the target order.

4.2.2.2 *Experimental data*

Experimental investigation of verb placement provides data on the various constructions subsumed under the verb movement parameter. In general, studies report target-like verb placement with respect to negation, as is the case in spontaneous production, but problems with word orders involving an adverb or a floating quantifier.[59]

Hawkins, Towell & Bazergui (1993) administered a 124-sentence grammaticality judgment (GJ) task to 104 English-speaking learners of French. The learners were placed into two groups according to how long they had studied French formally and how much time they had spent in a francophone country. Note that the age of the participants is not mentioned; they were simply labeled adult learners. A group of 37 controls, native speakers of French, was also included in the study. The task tested all three properties of verb placement, with both finite and nonfinite verbs. Results reveal variability across groups, properties and finiteness, as shown in Tables 12 and 13. As far as finite verbs are concerned, both experimental groups correctly accepted grammatical verb placement in French to a large extent, except in cases involving the quantifier *tous*. Moreover, advanced learners were better at rejecting ungrammatical sentences than lower proficiency learners. In other words, they were better at rejecting properties typical of their L1. However, the accuracy rate depended on the property being tested: performance was higher on negation than adverbs, and it was the lowest on *tous*, as can be seen in Table 12.

59. This pattern of results is similar to L2 acquisition of English (e.g. White 1992).

Table 12. Accuracy rate on placement of finite lexical verbs in adult L2 French (L1=English) (from Hawkins et al. 1993)

Group	Neg sentences		Adv sentences		FQ sentences	
	V-Neg	*Neg-V	V-Adv	*Adv-V	V-FQ	*FQ-V
Intermediate (n=75)	95.8	79.4	86.5	52.6	46.3	31.7
Advanced (n=29)	93.1	86.2	94.5	72.4	44.8	55.7
Controls (n=37)	89.2	79.3	93.7	50.5	89.2	85.1

In nonfinite contexts, Neg-V (with a lexical verb) is the only grammatical order in French; with adverbs and FQs, verb placement is more free. Curiously, as shown in Table 13, the controls did not like the V-Adv order, nor sentences with *tous*, regardless of verb placement. The advanced learners performed much like the controls on negative sentences (with high accuracy) and adverbs (preferring Adv-V). Lower accuracy was obtained on *tous*, with a preference for V-FQ. The intermediate learners correctly rejected the V-Neg order, but also failed to completely accept Neg-V. They also accepted both orders with adverbs and scored at around 60% on sentences with *tous*.

Table 13. Accuracy rate on placement of nonfinite lexical verbs in adult L2 French (L1=English) (from Hawkins et al. 1993)

Group	Neg sentences		Adv sentences		FQ sentences	
	*V-Neg	Neg-V	V-Adv	Adv-V	V-FQ	FQ-V
Intermediate (n=75)	85.7	51.1	72.6	85	64	56
Advanced (n=29)	82.8	82.8	43.1	81	51.7	69
Controls (n=37)	93.2	93.2	50	81.1	48.7	43.2

Interestingly, Herschensohn (1997) administered Hawkins et al.'s test to five superior English-speaking learners of French. The learners showed an accuracy rate of above 90% on both grammatical and ungrammatical sentences (i.e. they accurately accepted grammatical sentences and rejected ungrammatical ones), except for nonfinite verbs with respect to *tous* where the accuracy rate was 87%. The results are comparable to those obtained by native speaker controls and to results reported by Birdsong (1992) who looked at verb placement in learners who had reached a steady (superior) state. Both Herschensohn's and Birdsong's results suggest that acquisition of the target parametric values can be achieved. One possible explanation for the difference between the results of Herschensohn's study and Hawkins et al.'s is that the advanced learners in Hawkins et al.'s study were not as advanced as the ones tested by Herschensohn.

In a more recent study, Herschensohn (1999) administered an elicited production task to 45 intermediate learners of French whose L1 was English. They were divided into two groups: 25 low intermediate and 20 advanced intermediate. A third group comprised four French native speakers and six superior English-speaking learners. Participants were asked to construct written sentences with specific lexical verbs and adverbs, such as frequency adverbs (e.g. *rarement* 'rarely', *souvent* 'often' and *jamais* 'never') and so-called quality adverbs (e.g. *bien* 'well', *mal* 'badly' and *pas* 'not'). Each subject produced 40 sentences with an adverb, 10 of which were negative adverbs. Results show that there were very few errors involving Neg-V and Adv-V orders, which may indicate that resetting had taken place. However, there were many errors (16%) displaying the adverb in a sentence final position, even with frequency adverbs, which is target-deviant (e.g. *Jean mange des escargots souvent* lit. 'John eats snails often'). Adverb placement shows greater variability than negation, even in advanced learners.

In yet another study, Ayoun (1999) combined a GJ task and a production task that she administered to 83 English-speaking learners of French. The learners were divided into three groups depending on their level of French study (2nd year, 3rd year, and 4th year). A control group of 85 native speakers of French was also included. The GJ test included 47 sentences (reduced to 25 items for the controls). In the elicited production task, the participants were instructed to add an adverb or a quantifier into 49 sentences (different from the ones on the GJ test).[60] Results on the finite sentences of the GJ task are summarized in Tables 14 and 15. The last column of Table 14 reports on sentences displaying quantification at a distance (QD) where a finite auxiliary precedes the quantifier (V-Q), as in (19a). In such sentences, verb movement has occurred over the quantifier, with lack of movement yielding ungrammaticality, as in (19b).

(19) a. Nous avons beaucoup acheté de cd.
we have.1PL many bought of cds
'We bought a lot of cds.'

b. *Nous beaucoup avons acheté de cd.

Note that the tables do not include the controls' scores since they were not asked to rate finite verb placement. As can be seen, accuracy improved with proficiency, with advanced learners scoring above 80% on negation and frequency adverbs in finite contexts. All learners also performed with high accuracy in rejecting Q-V in sentences with quantification at a distance. As with Hawkins et al. (1993), however, accuracy was much lower with nonfinite verbs and with floating quantifiers. Also as with Hawkins et al., the controls' performance was not perfect either. Ayoun reports low accuracy with nonfinite auxiliaries occurring above negation (which the controls tended to incorrectly reject) and with sentences displaying QD.

60. A preference task involving five pairs of sentences was also developed, but it was only administered to the control group.

Table 14. GJ task: Accuracy rate on finite verb placement in adult L2 French (L1=English) (from Ayoun 1999)

Group	Neg sentences		Adv sentences		FQ sentences		QD sentences	
	V-Neg	*Neg-V	V-Adv	*Adv-V	V-FQ	*FQ-V	V-Q	*Q-V
2nd year (n=27)	72.7	65	59.3	50.6	43.2	49.4	65.4	86.4
3rd year (n=30)	70	61.2	61.1	50	38.9	55.6	63.3	87.8
4th year (n=26)	82.2	67.3	85.9	71.8	55.1	66.7	67.9	96.1

Table 15. GJ task: Accuracy rate on nonfinite verb placement in adult L2 French (L1=English) (from Ayoun 1999)

Group	Neg sentences		Adv sentences	
	V-Neg	*Neg-V	V-Adv	Adv-V
2nd year (n=27)	33.9	45.7	33.3	51.8
3rd year (n=30)	52.9	52.2	46.7	33.3
4th year (n=26)	58.2	44.8	76.9	51.9

Scores were quite high on the production task, as can be seen in Table 16. The controls behaved according to the predictions of the verb movement parameter. In nonfinite contexts, for instance, they produced V-Adv, but not V-Neg. The learners' accuracy rate almost always exceeded 80%, except for the two lower groups who performed slightly above chance level on adverbs in finite and nonfinite clauses. Note however, that the most advanced learners obtained high scores on these clauses.

Table 16. Production task: Accuracy rate on verb placement in adult L2 French (L1=English) (from Ayoun 1999)

Group	Finite				Nonfinite	
	Neg	Adv	FQ	QD	Neg	Adv
2nd year (n=27)	83.7	58	85.2	87.1	80.2	54
3rd year (n=30)	83.7	65.6	90	87.8	80	58
4th year (n=26)	92.5	85.9	92.9	93.6	92.3	83.8

Finally, Leung (2002) investigated verb placement with respect to adverbs in L2 and L3 French by Vietnamese and Cantonese native speakers, respectively. Neither Vietnamese nor Chinese has overt verb movement, which means that adverbs occur between the subject and the verb, in contrast to French. The Chinese L3 speakers spoke English, a language that also lacks overt raising, as their L2. Two tasks were administered to the learners, a preference task and a sentence completion task (see Section 4.2.1.1). As can be seen in Table 17, accuracy was better in the sentence completion task. In the preference task, the beginner learners scored at around chance level, which is similar to what we saw in the other studies. Overall accuracy also increases with level: it is above 80% in the intermediates, and above 90% in the advanced, which suggests that acquisition has taken place.

Table 17. Accuracy in verb placement with respect to adverbs in adult L2/L3 French (L1=Vietnamese and Chinese) (from Leung 2002)

Group	Preference task			Sentence completion
	Frequency	Manner	Total	(frequency Adv)
L2 French Beginn (n=12)	44.5	48.2	46.2	73.5%
L3 French Beginn (n=44)	59.7	64.1	61.6	79.4%
L3 French Interm (n=30)	79.9	83.6	83.3	95.3
L3 French Adv (n=10)	86.7	98	92.3	96.7
Controls (n=30)	99.2	97.3	98.5	100%

Hulk (1991) also looked at the acquisition of verb raising to Infl in French, but not from the point of view of the placement of the verb with respect to elements such as negation and adverbs. Rather, she investigated knowledge of verb movement in French on the part of learners whose L1 exhibits verb raising to a position other than Infl, namely C. She assumes that finiteness can be expressed by a [+Finiteness] operator whose location is subject to parametric variation: it is in Infl in French, and in C in other languages such as Dutch and German. In these languages, so-called verb-second (V2) languages, the finite verb moves to C in root declaratives while the subject or any other XP occupies SpecCP.[61] This is illustrated in the Dutch examples in (20). Note that in this language, VP and IP are traditionally held to be head-final, whereas CP is head-initial.

(20) $[_{CP}$ Gisteren $[_{C}$ heeft$_i]$ $[_{IP}$ Jan $[_{VP}$ aardbeien gegeten$]$ $t_i]]$.
yesterday has John strawberries eaten
'Yesterday John ate strawberries'

In embedded clauses, a complementizer occupies the C position, which prevents the verb from moving there. It will therefore raise to Infl only and appear in clause-final position. This is illustrated in (21).

61. In Minimalist terms, the C head of V2 languages may contain two strong features which need to be checked off: a verbal feature (which forces overt verb movement to C) and a topic feature (which forces overt XP-movement to SpecCP) (see Herschensohn 2000).

(21) … [$_{CP}$ [$_{C}$ dat] [$_{IP}$ Jan [$_{VP}$ aardbeien t_i] eet_i]].
that John strawberries eats
'… that John eats strawberries'

Another difference between V2 languages and French is that in French, topicalization is restricted to adjunction to IP, as in (22), whereas in Dutch, for example, it involves the CP node, as in (20) above, or the IP node, as in (23). Dutch learners must therefore learn to restrain topicalization in French.

(22) [$_{IP}$ Hier [$_{IP}$ Jean a mangé des fraises]].
yesterday John has eaten some strawberries
'Yesterday John ate strawberries'

(23) … [$_{CP}$ dat [$_{IP}$ gisteren [$_{IP}$ Jan aardbeien gegeten heeft]]].
that yesterday John strawberries eaten has
'… that John ate strawberries yesterday'

It is assumed that sentences exhibiting the order XSVO, as in (22), which is disallowed in main clauses of V2 languages, should lead the learners to reset the [+Finiteness] parameter to the French value, and to restrict topicalization possibilities, even if adjunction to IP is also allowed in Dutch.

A grammaticality judgment task of 40 sentences was administered to four groups of Dutch learners of French. Each group was selected according to their schooling in French, from 1st year French (Group 1) to university students (Group 4). Tables 18 and 19 report results on the topicalization of arguments and non-arguments to SpecCP (ungrammatical in French) and on adjunction to IP (grammatical in French with non-arguments). The tense of the clause was also considered, present (simple tense) and *passé composé* (complex tense).

Table 18. Acceptance rates of topicalization to SpecCP in adult L2 French (L1=Dutch) (from Hulk 1991)

	Non arguments			Arguments	
	*s.t.	*c.t. (OV)	*c.t. (VO)	*s.t.	*c.t.
Group 1 (n=26)	92	92	38	58	19
Group 2 (n=21)	50	38	64	26	7
Group 3 (n=25)	32	0	8	16	12
Group 4 (n=16)	10	0	6	19	0

s.t.=simple tense; c.t.=complex tense

Table 19. Acceptance rates of IP adjunction in adult L2 French (L1=Dutch) (from Hulk 1991)

	Non arguments			Arguments	
	s.t.	*c.t. (OV)	c.t. (VO)	*s.t.	*c.t.
Group 1 (n=26)	38	30	19	11	15
Group 2 (n=21)	80	38	85	10	4
Group 3 (n=25)	100	0	100	0	0
Group 4 (n=16)	100	6	100	0	0

s.t.=simple tense; c.t.=complex tense

The learners wrongly accepted topicalization to SpecCP until Group 4, especially with simple tense and a fronted argument (e.g. *Les fraises mangeait Jean* 'The strawberries ate John'). Adjunction of non-arguments to IP was accepted rather early, as of Group 2, with either simple or complex tense. Note that adjunction of an argument was never really considered a possibility in simple or complex tense, and even the beginner learners accurately rejected adjunction of arguments to IP. For a while, then, the learners accepted fronting either via topicalization to SpecCP or adjunction to IP. Because V3 order was accepted as of Group 2, this suggests that the learners had also acquired the fact that Infl may be a destination for the finite verb, and that they had reset the verb movement parameter to the target value. However, topicalization to SpecCP seems to be quite difficult to abandon.

4.2.2.3 *Theoretical accounts*

The interpretation of the findings on verb placement in adult L2 French has lead to a debate in the literature about the possibility of parameter resetting. For Hawkins et al. (1993), the results obtained in their study suggest that parameter resetting did not occur, since property clustering was not observed. In particular, the results on negative sentences were target-like, but the results on sentences involving an adverb or a floating quantifier were not. The results on adverb placement also seem to be compatible with the proposal that finite features are (permanently) inert in L2 acquisition, namely they are neither strong nor weak in IL grammars (Beck 1998; Eubank et al. 1997). This would account for the fact that the finite verb is allowed to precede or follow the adverb in L2 French. Note, however, that the Adv-V order is not fully rejected by native speakers of French either. For Hawkins et al., the high performance displayed by several learners is not due to the development of native-like grammars. The authors contend that these learners' grammars differ significantly from that of native speakers in that they do not include the target parametric settings (see also Bley-Vroman 1990;

Smith & Tsimpli 1995; Tsimpli & Roussou 1991). Instead, the IL grammar, despite appearances, is argued to be similar to the L1 grammar. In those constructions for which native-like judgments are given, the learners are claimed to use linguistic means made available by UG to resemble native speakers. Crucially, however, they retain fundamental properties of their L1 grammar. For example, in order to explain the good scores obtained on negative sentences, Hawkins et al. suggest that the learners consider *pas* an affix generated under Agr in French, and adverb placement as 'rightward adjunction of the verb complement to VP over a VP-final adverb (Hawkins et al. 1993: 215). In other words, the learners are deemed not to have acquired verb movement in French.

In more recent work, Hawkins (2001) proposes the Modulated Structure Hypothesis. According to this approach, functional categories are *in principle* absent from initial IL grammars, which are claimed to only contain lexical projections. *In principle*, these projections have L1 properties (due to transfer). Here, *in principle* means that depending on the learning situation, the input, and the learner, restructuring may take place very quickly, so quickly that the lexical stage or L1 transfer may not be apparent. Following the lexical stage, functional categories are assumed to be established based on the nature of the input available to the learner. It is only once functional layers start being posited that influence of L1 functional categories can take place. In other words, structure building is influenced by the properties of the L1 at the relevant points in the construction of the grammar, not prior to them. To come back to the L2 acquisition of verb movement in French, the fact that lexical verbs are systematically placed before negation in the target language is generally assumed to force learners to posit Infl and to implement movement. But, according to Hawkins, the positing of Infl and movement that arises from observing V-*pas* does not imply acquisition of strong inflectional features. Rather, it arises because of the 'complement requirement of Neg': the fact that the V-Neg order conflicts with an initial Neg > VP assumption forces L2 learners to perform verb movement above Neg. This is why learners do not generalize movement to other contexts, i.e. adverbs. It could also explain why learners may place nonfinite verbs before *pas* in the initial stages of L2 French acquisition, although nonfinite verbs have weak features in French (recall that Hawkins et al. (1993)'s GJ task included four sentences with $V_{nonfinite}$-*pas*, which were wrongly accepted almost 40% of the time). The main problem here, however, is that the nature of verb movement assumed by Hawkins is not made explicit, and it seems to enter in conflict with some basic principles of UG, which Hawkins assumes is at work in IL grammars. According to Minimalism, movement occurs because strong features need to be checked. Since Hawkins argues that there is verb movement over Neg in French IL grammars, it then follows that there is checking of strong features in I, which in turn means that parameter resetting has taken place. If movement occurs for any other reason in IL grammars, then these systems are not UG-compatible, in contrast to Hawkins' assumptions. The analysis proposed by Hawkins is also contradicted by the results of the superior learners reported by Herschensohn (1997) which show that parameter resetting can take place in adult L2 acquisition.

Rather than positing fundamental differences between target and IL grammars, Herschensohn (1999, 2000) proposes a constructivist approach to L2 acquisition, whereby L2 learners use cognitive strategies in addition to having access to the properties of UG. According to this view, parameter resetting is possible in second language acquisition, but it does not occur in an across-the-board way; rather, it takes place item by item. Thus, learners may initially show only partial control of the target parametric value. For the acquisition of verb placement in L2 French, this translates into the following sequence:

(24)
1. The L1 value is adopted
2. The L1 value is abandoned but [±interpretable] features are underspecified
3. Some target constructions are acquired which involve specific lexical items, such as *pas*
4. [±interpretable] morphology is acquired
5. The target construction is generalized to a morpholexical class, e.g. negation
6. The target parametric value is acquired; morphology is complete

At the intermediate stages, Herschensohn assumes, feature strength is neither weak nor strong in IL grammars, as if learners are looking for the right specification. This could explain the mixed results reported by Hawkins et al. (1993) and those reported by Leung (2002) for her beginner learners.[62] Herschensohn proposes that phi-features may be unspecified in the grammars developed by Hawkins et al.'s learners. This would be caused by the incomplete acquisition of verbal morphology, which prevents verb movement from stabilizing (see also Eubank 1993/1994). It is only once morphology is acquired that resetting takes place. Note that such a scenario strongly relies on a close relationship between the richness of the inflectional paradigm and properties of verb movement (see Clahsen et al. 1996 for similar proposals in L1 acquisition). However, such a relationship is far from being clearly established in theoretical linguistics: whereas languages exhibiting verb movement tend to possess distinct inflectional markers, there are languages that have verb raising and no overt verbal morphology (such as Kronoby Swedish) (see Sprouse 1998). Herschensohn also tries to account for the difference between intuitions about negation and intuitions about adverb placement in Hawkins et al.'s results. She suggests that verb placement with respect to negation belongs to the core grammar, whereas verb placement with respect to adverbs and quantifiers relates to the periphery, since these elements do not occupy a fixed position in the sentence. Therefore, the learners' choice with negation is binary, whereas with adverbs and quantifiers it is not, which would explain why verb placement with respect to negation is acquired first. Moreover, quantifiers and frequency and manner adverbs may be less frequent than negative sentences in the input. Positive evidence pertaining to the properties subsumed under the target parametric value, based on which parameter resetting could take place, may therefore be unequal. Crucially,

62. Alternatively, learners may entertain the two parametric settings at the same time until one of them stabilizes. This has also been proposed by Déprez (1994) for L1 acquisition.

though, parameter resetting is deemed possible in Herschensohn's model, due to access to UG, as witnessed by the high accuracy reached by advanced and very advanced learners with respect to adverb placement (Herschensohn 1997, 1999; Leung 2002).

Ayoun (1999) takes the same position, and further proposes that so-called short adverbs such as *bien* 'good' and *souvent* 'often' are relevant to the resetting process and that the position of adverbs of place and time, as well as the placement of long adverbs (adverbs typically ending in *-ement*, such as *lentement* 'slowly'), may have to be acquired one by one (see also Herschensohn 1999; Müller 1998).

In the study reported by Hulk (1991), we saw that one of the target properties under investigation, namely the L2 value of the localization of the [+Finiteness] operator, was acquired, but that the other one, topicalization, still caused problems for the learners. French represents a subset of Dutch with respect to topicalization: topicalization in Dutch can be achieved either via movement to SpecCP or adjunction to IP. When acquiring French, Dutch learners will therefore have to restrict their grammar. In particular, they will have to come to know that topicalization to SpecCP is not an option in French. Although the input is compatible with IP adjunction, it does not contain evidence suggesting that topicalization to SpecCP is impossible, which would lead the learners to keep applying it for a while. Negative evidence may be necessary for these learners to lose their L1 property.

4.2.2.4 *Methodological considerations*

So far, research on verb placement in L2 French reports different results in production and judgment tasks. Based on the results of her production test, Ayoun (1999) concludes that parameter resetting can take place in L2 acquisition (see also Ayoun 2003). She further argues that the lower accuracy rates obtained on GJ tests may be problems inherent to such tasks. Ayoun's study clearly raises the issue of what constitutes evidence for acquisition. It is well known that results – and their theoretical implications – largely depend on the mode through which the data were obtained (see Murphy 1997). The validity of traditional (pencil and paper) GJ tasks has been fiercely debated over the years. The discussion essentially focuses on whether or not such tests are able to effectively tap (unconscious) intuitions about the well-formedness of sentences. Many researchers argue that it is impossible to know on what basis learners render their judgments. In particular, it is difficult to evaluate the amount of consciousness brought into their decisions. New methodologies have been designed to avoid directly asking learners about their intuitions on sentences, such as sentence matching (see Section 8.1.2.2.2). These methods rely on variables such as reaction times, as a reflex of grammaticality knowledge.

Results are also largely dependent on test design, which calls for extreme rigor on the part of researchers. Details such as sentence length, number of items per sentence type, and lexical variety should be seriously taken into account. In Hawkins et al.'s (1993) GJ task, although exact figures are not given, there seem to be few tokens instantiating each sentence type and the number of tokens are not evenly distributed across types. For example, there is only one sentence instantiating nonfinite verb placement with an adverb, which is not enough. In addition, many sentences are quite long, which may have caused processing difficulties for some learners.

Finally, it is essential that learners' proficiency be established via an independent test. It is simply not enough to rely on notions such as 'number of years of schooling or exposure' or 'amount of time spent in a country where the target language is spoken'. The way the learners are grouped in most studies investigating verb movement in L2 French, including Hawkins et al.' s (1993) and Ayoun's (1999) studies, thus appear not to be rigorous enough. The results may have been affected by some learners having been assigned to a group which does not correspond to their proficiency.

4.3 Conclusion

This chapter has looked at child and adult L2 development of verbal inflection and verb placement. Several differences and similarities between the two groups of learners have been uncovered.

With respect to inflection, it was shown that children make systematic use of finite markers faster than adults do. Although both types of learners may produce RIs initially, the RI period may last much longer in the case of adults. In particular, the adults tend to use nonfinite forms as substitutes for finite verbs, whereas the distribution of RIs in child L2 French data is largely structure-dependant (they are truly nonfinite). Despite the recourse to RIs and verbless sentences, when finite inflection is used by child and adult learners, it is largely correct. Moreover, there is knowledge of finiteness given that finite forms rarely appear in nonfinite positions. When they do, they seem to be restricted to one particular profile of learners, namely English speakers. This observation needs to be confirmed by further research combining different languages. Both child and adult learners also seem to struggle with aspect, e.g. *imparfait*, but not enough research has been done to understand the development of this property in L2 French. Knowledge of finiteness argues in favour of the presence of at least one functional category in initial interlanguage grammars developed by child and adult learners. Aside from the fact that inflectional morphology must be learned, the problems that adult learners tend to have with producing it appropriately likely stem from problems in mapping syntax and morphology or from underspecification of nonfinite forms, not from the lack of relevant functional categories or from impaired grammars. In the case of children, production of nonfinite forms may stem from truncation due to computational difficulties.

With respect to verb placement, both child and adult learners seem to have little difficulty in positioning the verb accurately with respect to negative adverbs. However, adult learners have much greater difficulty in accurately placing the verb relative to adverbs and floating quantifiers. However, studies of very advanced learners suggest that acquisition of the target value of the verb movement parameter is possible. Future studies examining this issue will have to use extreme caution with methodology, such as control of sentence length and complexity, so as to minimize test effects. For child learners, there is little relevant data available, since children tend not to produce utterances that include adverbs and floating quantifiers. Future research should look at acquisition of verb placement with respect to adverbs and floating quantifiers in child L2 learners of French, preferably with various language combinations (Chinese – French, for example).

PART II

Subject and object pronouns

CHAPTER 5

Subject and object pronouns

Morphosyntactic background

The second part of this book is concerned with the acquisition of the morphosyntactic properties of subject and object pronouns. Particular attention will be paid to pronominal clitics, namely pronouns, such as *je* 'I', *tu* 'you+SG', *il* 'he' and *le* 'it/him', *la* 'it/her', and *les* 'them', which need to attach to a verbal form. As this chapter will show, there is considerable controversy about their nature. Some researchers consider them to be verbal agreement markers while others claim that they are element whose position is derived via movement. However, it is generally agreed that investigating the acquisition of subject and object pronouns can provide insight into knowledge of finiteness and the status of functional categories in developmental grammars. The binding properties of pronouns, that is, the syntactic relationship between a pronoun and its antecedent, will also be discussed in this chapter. Since these properties are argued to stem from principles of Universal Grammar, investigating their acquisition is crucial in determining the role of UG in the learning process.

5.1 French pronouns: Types and formal representations

In this section, we present the different types of pronouns in French, along with their distributional properties, and discuss different theoretical analyses that have been proposed to account for these properties.

5.1.1 French pronouns and their distributional properties

French pronouns are traditionally divided into two types: weak pronouns (also called clitics) and strong (or tonic) pronouns. Pronouns are the only elements displaying overt Case in French. For instance, *je* 'I', *tu* 'you' and *il(s)* 'he/they+MASC' are nominative, *le* 'it/him', *la* 'it/her' and *les* 'them' are accusative, and *leur* 'to them' is dative. A list of clitics and strong pronouns is given in Table 1. Note that some pronouns have the same form whether they are weak or strong, such as *elle* 'she/her', *nous* 'we/us', and *vous* 'you', while others have the same form whether accusative and dative, such as *me* 'me/to me' and *te* 'you/to you'. Finally, while most 3rd person clitics distinguish between genders (e.g. *il* 'he' and *elle* 'she'), some do not (e.g. *les* 'them' and *leur* 'to them'). Note that in spoken French, *on* has almost completely supplanted subject *nous* 'we'.

Table 1. Clitics and strong pronouns in French

		Clitics			Strong pronouns
		Subject	**Direct object**	**Indirect object**	
Singular	1 pers	je	me	me	moi
	2 pers	tu	te	te	toi
	3 pers	il (masc) elle (fem) on (neuter)	le (masc) la (fem) se (refl)	lui se (refl)	lui (masc) elle (fem)
Plural	1 pers	nous	nous	nous	nous
	2 pers	vous	vous	vous	vous
	3 pers	ils (masc) elles (fem)	les	leur	eux (masc) elles (fem)

The other clitics are *en* and *y*, which typically stand for prepositional phrases. For *en*, the corresponding PP is usually introduced by *de* 'of', as in (1a), while *y* stands for PPs introduced by other prepositions, such as *à* 'to', as in (1b).

(1) a. Je suis certain de son amour. / J' en suis certain.
I am certain of his love I of+it am certain
'I'm certain of his love / I'm certain of it'

b. Je vais à Paris demain / J'y vais.
I go to Paris tomorrow I there go
'I'm going to Paris tomorrow / I'm going there tomorrow'

Clitics and strong pronouns differ in their distribution. Basically, the distribution of strong pronouns patterns with lexical nominals, whereas the distribution of subject and object clitics does not. Clitics are pronominal elements that need to be adjoined (or attached) to a verb (see (2a–b)). Because of this, object clitics do not appear in the canonical (postverbal) object position (2c). (For cliticization in restructuring and causative contexts, see Section 8.1.2.2.2.)

(2) a. Il rencontrera Marie.
he meet.FUT.3SG Mary
'He will meet Mary.'

b. Il la rencontrera.
he her meet.FUT.3SG
'He will meet her'

c. *Il rencontrera la.

Clitics form a morphological unit with the verb that cannot be broken by any element other than another clitic. For example, adverbs cannot come between a clitic and the verb (3a–b). This is not true for strong pronouns and lexical nominals (4) (see Kayne 1975).

(3) a. *Il, bientôt, rencontrera Marie.
he soon meet.FUT.3SG Mary

b. *Il la, bientôt, rencontrera.

(4) Jean / Lui, bientôt, rencontrera Marie.[63]
John him soon meet.FUT.3SG Mary
'John/he will soon meet Mary.'

Furthermore, clitics cannot be conjoined, whether with a nominal or with another clitic (5a–b), and they cannot appear after a preposition (6a). Again, strong pronouns and lexical nominals pattern differently (5c and 6b).

(5) a. *Mon père et il rencontreront Marie.
my father and he meet.FUT.3PL Mary

b. *Mon père la et le rencontrera.
my father her and him meet.FUT.3SG

c. Mon père et mon frère / lui rencontreront Marie.
my father and my brother him meet.FUT.3PL Mary
'My father and my brother /him will meet Mary.'

(6) a. *Marie a parlé avec le.
Mary has spoken with him

b. Marie a parlé avec mon père / lui.
Mary has spoken with my father him
'Mary spoke to my father / him.'

Clitics cannot appear alone, in contrast to strong pronouns and nominals, for example as an answer to a question (7).

63. Strong third person pronouns, such as *lui* and *eux*, pattern like nominative clitics, insofar as they may appear as the (superficial) subject of a finite verb (with a contrastive meaning). Despite this similarity, strong pronouns may not occur as inverted subjects in interrogatives, in contrast to nominative clitics (for more on subject/verb inversion, see Chapter 13).

(i) a. Est-il parti?
is he gone
'Has he gone?'

b. *Est lui parti?

Note that the similarity between strong third person pronouns and clitics does not apply to other strong pronouns (e.g. **Moi rencontrerai Marie* lit. 'Me will meet Mary').

(7) a. Qui a rencontré Mary? *Il/Lui/Mon père.
who has met Mary he/him/my father
'Who met Mary? He/Him/My father.'

b. Qui as- tu rencontré? *Le/ Lui/ Alexandre.
whom have you met him+CL/ him+STR Alexandre
'Whom did you meet? Him / Alexandre.'

Finally, clitics cannot receive contrastive stress (8a–b), in contrast to strong pronouns and nominals (8c) (but see Cardinaletti & Starke 1999).

(8) a. *IL rencontrera Marie.
he meet.FUT.3SG Mary

b. *Mon père LA rencontrera.
my father her meet.FUT.3SG

c. MON PÈRE / LUI rencontrera Marie.
my father him+STR meet.FUT.3SG Mary
'My father /he will meet Mary.'

Note that there is a difference between subject and object clitics in that object clitics, but not subject clitics, may appear to the left of a nonfinite verb, such as an infinitival form (9). Instead of a clitic subject, a strong pronoun 'subject' is required in such contexts (9b).

(9) a. *Il les aimer? Pas possible!
him them love.INF not possible

b. Lui les aimer? Pas possible!
him them love.INF not possible
'Him love them? Impossible!'

Apart from the distributional differences discussed above, clitics and strong pronouns further contrast in that clitics can refer to either [+animate] or [–animate] items, as shown in (10) and (11), whereas strong pronouns typically refer to [+animate] entities, as in (12).

(10) a. Cet homme$_i$, il$_i$ apprend le japonais.
this man he learns the Japanese
'This man, he's learning Japanese.'

b. Ce voyage$_i$, il$_i$ me fait rêver.
this trip it me makes dream
'This trip, it makes me dream.'

(11) a. Cet homme$_i$, je le$_i$ connais depuis des années.
this man I him know since some years
'This man, I've known him for years.'

b. Ce voyage$_i$, je le$_i$ ferai l' année prochaine.
this trip I it do.FUT the year next
'This trip, I'll do it next year.'

(12) a. Cet homme$_i$, j'entends parler de lui$_i$ depuis des années.
this man I hear talk of him since some years
'This man, I've heard about him for years.'

b. *Ce voyage$_i$ j'entends parler de lui$_i$ depuis des années.
this trip I hear talk of him since some years

Instead of a strong pronoun, (12b) requires a clitic:

(13) Ce voyage$_i$, j'en$_i$ entends parler depuis des années.
this trip I of+it hear talk since some years
'This trip, I've heard about it for years.'

Finally, clitics ending in a vowel (*je, tu, me, te, le, la, se*) appear as reduced forms in certain contexts, typically in front of a form phonetically starting with a vowel, as in (14).[64]

(14) a. J' aime Mozart.
I love Mozart
'I love Mozart'

b. Je l' aime.
Je him love
'I love him'

5.1.2 Formal accounts of pronouns

The exact nature of clitics is subject to debate in the literature, and I will not commit to any particular position in this volume (for a review, see Heap & Roberge 2001). There are two main points of view: either clitics are generated directly on the verb, as affixes, or they cliticize onto the verb. I will outline the main arguments of each position below.

---

64. Moreover, the liaison between a clitic and the following vowel is obligatory, as in (i), whereas in a similar context the liaison is disallowed with a DP, as in (ii).

(i) Ils [z] ont beaucoup mangé.
they have much eaten
'They ate a lot.'

(ii) Les gens *[z] ont beaucoup mangé.
the people have much eaten
'The people ate a lot.'

Finally, in clitic/verb inversion, an epenthetical consonant [t] appears between the verb and the clitic; this does not obtain with subject DPs:

(iii) a. Où jouera-t- il?
where play.FUT he
'Where will he play?'

b. *Où jouera-t- Étienne?
where play.FUT Étienne

5.1.2.1 *The cliticization approach*

According to Kayne (1975), object pronouns are base-generated in the canonical object position within VP, and then undergo movement to their preverbal position, as in (15).

(15) Pierre la_i rencontre t_i
Peter her meet
'Peter is meeting her'

One of the arguments Kayne puts forward in favour of this analysis is that object clitics cannot co-occur with a postverbal object DP (e.g. **Jean* le_i *lit le* $livre_i$ 'John it reads the book'), leaving aside the possibility of clitic doubling right dislocation for the moment. For Kayne, this suggests that the pronoun occupies the object position prior to superficially becoming a preverbal clitic (or a proclitic). If the clitic were generated directly on the verb, he argues, the sentence above should be grammatical, contrary to fact.

Under more recent theory, the clitic is assumed to be generated as the head of the AgrO(bject) layer, while the canonical object position is occupied by a coindexed null element *pro*. The verb then 'picks the pronoun up' on its way to Infl, as illustrated in (16).

(16) $[_{IP}$ Peter $[_{I}$ la_i+$rencontre_j]$ $[_{AgrOP}$ $[_{AgrO}$ $t_j]$ $[_{VP} t_j$ $pro_i]]]$

Under this view, the impossibility of an object clitic co-occurring with a postverbal object DP suggests that the clitic absorbs Case. The object DP then cannot be assigned Case or check Case, which renders the construction ungrammatical.[65]

For Uriagereka (1995) and Belletti (1999), object clitics are determiners, that is, instances of D^0. This idea is based on the fact that object clitics have the same forms as definite determiners in many Romance languages, including French (*le, la , les*). The DP whose head is the clitic is generated in the canonical object position, and the clitic is then assumed to move to AgrO, from which it can cliticize onto the verb.[66]

---

65. In Spanish, an object DP may appear in postverbal position along with a preverbal object clitic, but it must be preceded by the preposition *a*, which is assumed to be a Case assigner (Aoun 1979) (e.g. *Juan la vio a Maria* lit. 'John her saw to Mary').

66. The two approaches differ with respect to the nature of the object clitic and its movement. For Uriagereka, object clitics are transitive determiners that take *pro* as an object: $[_{DP}$ Specifier $[_{D'}$ $[_{D}$ clitic$]$ *pro* $]]$. AgrO is assumed to be associated with properties such as referentiality and specificity, so the clitic moves there to check the AgrO head; it also licenses *pro* (which is assumed to move to SpecAgrOP) via spec/head agreement. For Belletti, object clitics may not take a (null) object. Rather, they are assumed to carry a strong Case feature which needs to be checked within AgrO prior to LF.

Subject pronouns are assumed to occupy the typical subject position, SpecIP, before undergoing cliticization at the phonological level (see Kayne 1975). Arguments for the occurrence of subject clitics in SpecIP come from the fact that, in standard French, a subject clitic cannot be doubled by a DP without a pause occurring between them, which suggests that both elements are fighting for the same position. This is illustrated in (17).

(17) *Le prof$_i$ il$_i$ donne beaucoup de travail.
The prof he gives much work

Subject pronouns have often been argued to differ from object clitics. For instance, Kayne considers that cliticization takes place phonologically in the case of subjects and syntactically in the case of objects. Under his analysis, subject pronouns are weak pronouns and object pronouns are clitics. One distributional difference between the two types of pronouns is their behaviour in coordinated structures. In standard French, the subject clitic does not need to be repeated in such constructions, as in (18a), while repetition of the object clitic is obligatory, as showed in (18b).[67]

(18) a. Il ira à Paris et Ø visitera la Tour Eiffel.
He go.FUT to Paris and visit.FUT the Tower Eiffel
'He'll go to Paris and will visit the Eiffel Tower.'

b. Pierre le prend et *(le) jette à la poubelle.
Peter it takes and it throws to the trash
'Peter takes it and throws it into the trash.'

One final point that needs to be made here is that according to the cliticization view sequences involving a DP followed by a coindexed subject clitic, such as (17), are interpreted as cases of subject dislocation. That is, the subject clitic is in SpecIP and the DP occupies a dislocated position, which for the time being I assume is adjoined to IP: $[_{IP}$ Le prof $[_{IP}$ il $[_{I}$ donne$]$ du travail $]]$.

5.1.2.2 *The affix approach*

Without disputing the claim that pronouns may undergo a cliticization process in some varieties of French, such as standard French, some linguists propose that clitics are base-generated as affixes in their preverbal position in other varieties (Auger 1994;

67. Repetition of the subject clitic is obligatory in clitic/verb inversion in standard French, namely when the subject pronoun is an enclitic (see Kayne 1975):

(i) Viendra-t- il et apportera-t- *(il) quelque chose?
come.FUT he and bring.FUT he something
'Will he come and will he bring something?'

Borer 1984; Jaeggli 1982; Zribi-Hertz 1994). These varieties include Quebec French and spoken/informal French (or advanced French, see Zribi-Hertz 1994). I refer to these varieties as nonstandard French.[68] Under this view, subject clitics are inserted directly under Infl; alternatively, they may be considered (agreement) prefixes, as seen in Chapter 1, and in that case, are inserted into the representation attached to the verb.

(19) $[_{IP}$ Le prof $[_{I}$ il+donne] beaucoup de travail]]

Interestingly, this view leaves the possibility open for a DP subject to occupy the SpecIP position, as in (19). According to some researchers, subject clitic doubling (without an intermediate pause) occurs frequently in Quebec French and spoken/informal French (Auger 1994; Lambrecht 1981; Roberge 1990). In addition, repetition of the subject clitic in conjoined contexts is frequent in these varieties. It is worth mentioning that if clitics are indeed agreement markers, then French is arguably a null subject language, namely a language in which overt subjects may be omitted, on a par with Italian and Spanish. The idea is that the inflectional marker, i.e. the subject clitic, is strong enough to identify the null subject *pro* in SpecIP, as in (20a). If there is no overt subject and no clitic, the result is ungrammatical, as in (20b), except in specific registers such as diaries (Haegeman 1990).[69]

(20) a. $[_{IP}$ *pro*$_i$ $[_{I}$ il$_i$+donne] beaucoup de travail]]
he gives much work
'He assigns a lot of work.'

b. *$[_{IP}$ *pro* $[_{I}$ donne] beaucoup de travail]]

---

68. According to Zribi-Hertz (1994: 460–461), standard French is 'the productive formal style, i.e. formal French rid of various archaisms'. In contrast, advanced French is 'a group of dialects which, at various degrees, disregard the norms taken as characterizing 'good usage' and which thus reveal ongoing grammatical mutations'. It includes at least two layers, namely colloquial French ('the unmarked informal style used by those speakers who also master standard French'), as in (ib), and very advanced French (which includes 'all forms regarded as substandard or dialectally marked by standard and colloquial French speakers'), as in (ii). The latter is also referred to as popular French and child French.

(i) a. Cela inquiète beaucoup Marie. (standard)
b. Ça inquiète beaucoup Marie. (colloquial)
'That worries Marie much.'

(ii) a [=elle] part. (very advanced)
'She's leaving'

69. For Jakubowicz (2003), subject clitics are obligatory in spoken French because the verbal paradigm is too weak to check the [+nominal] feature of T. This is in contrast to languages such as Spanish and Italian, which exhibit rich inflectional marking. In those languages, the inflectional suffixes are strong enough to check the [+nominal] feature in T.

Another argument in favour of the affix status of subject clitics is that subject doubling can be found with quantified DPs in nonstandard French, as in (21). Given that dislocation cannot take place with such elements (see Rizzi 1986), it follows that the quantified expression must occupy SpecIP.[70]

(21) Personne i(l) m' aime. (from Zribi-Hertz 1994)
Nobody he me likes
'Nobody likes me.'

Finally, clitic/verb inversion, which is possible in questions in standard French, as shown in (22) (see Section 13.1.2.1), is reported to have become quite rare in nonstandard French, with the exception of *tu* 'you+SG' in yes/no questions of Quebec colloquial French (Auger 1994).

(22) À quelle heure part- il?
At what time leaves he
'At what time is he leaving?'

If subject clitics are held to be verbal prefixes, the impossibility of inversion as in (22) is to be expected.

Most of the arguments offered in favour of the affix analysis come from the distribution of nominative pronouns. Much less is said about object clitics. However, the fact that object pronouns must be repeated in coordinated structures (recall (18b) above) could be used to show that a similar analysis applies to them. In that case, the canonical object position would be occupied by a coindexed *pro*: Pierre la_i+rencontre pro_i (see Borer 1984; Jaeggli 1982). As seen above, the clitic is taken to absorb Case, which prevents a realized object DP from occurring directly after the verb.

Before moving to alternative accounts of clitics in French, it is important to note that some of the arguments put forward by the proponents of the affix analysis of clitics are not unanimously accepted. For instance, in a sample of adult data from Belgium, France, and Canada, De Cat (2002) shows that of all the nominal subjects, only 40% occur preverbally and involve a doubling clitic (so, DP-cl). Another 40%, also doubled with a clitic, are found in postverbal position, typically at the end of the sentence (so, cl…DP). Moreover, clitic/verb inversion is still frequent in Belgian French and Canadian French (going beyond inversion with *tu* in the latter case). Finally, she argues, careful prosody analyses should be undertaken to determine whether or not subject DPs doubled with a clitic have the same intonation pattern as subject DPs occurring without the clitic. If the results show differences, then DP-cl sequences should be considered instances of left dislocation.[71]

70. But see Côté (2001) for a counter-argument to this view.

71. Based on her preliminary prosodic analyses of DP-cl-V and DP-V sequences, De Cat (2002) offers a number of acoustic diagnoses that can be used to distinguish between a subject

5.1.2.3 *Alternative accounts*

In an attempt to integrate the two views presented above, Sportiche (1996) suggests that clitics project their own categories called Clitic Voice: Nom(inative)V for nominative clitics and Acc(usative)V for accusative clitics. The clitic is generated as the head of the projection and must appear in a spec/head configuration with an element in the specifier position (which may be *pro*). This element is base-generated within the VP and then moves to the specifier of either NomV" or AccV", as in (23). In the case of object *pro*, it is assumed to raise through AgrO on its way up.

(23) a. [$_{\text{NomV''}}$ *pro*$_i$/Jean$_i$ il [$_{\text{AccV''}}$ *pro*$_j$ la [$_{\text{VP}}$ t$_i$ rencontre t$_j$]]]
John he her meet.FIN
'(John), he is meeting her.'

b.

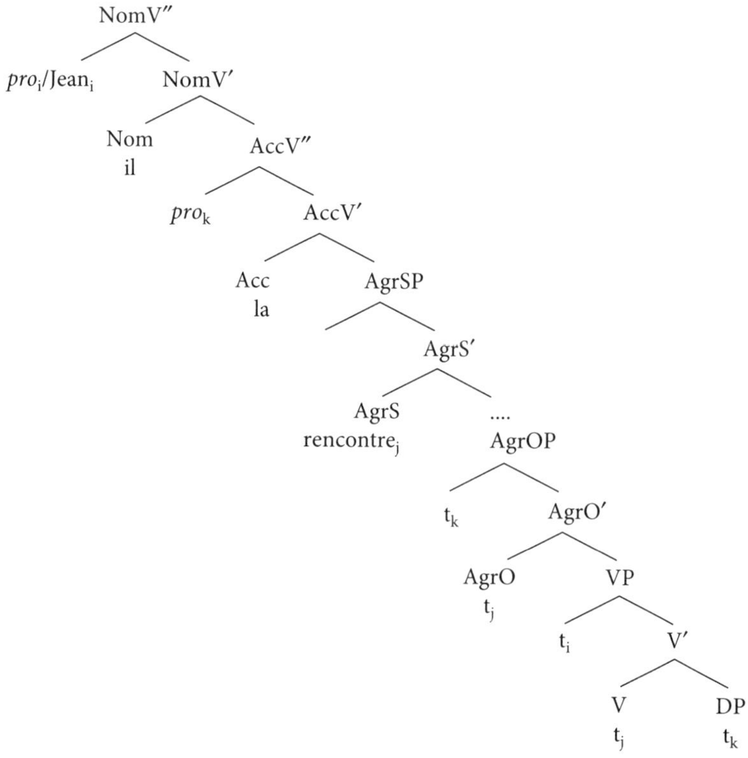

---

interpretation and a dislocation interpretation of subject nominals. Interestingly, the pause between the DP and the clitic, which is often used in the literature to distinguish the two, does not appear in De Cat's list. De Cat also points out that when the DP is used emphatically or contrastively, it is extremely difficult to tell the two interpretations apart.

Another account of pronominal elements, proposed by Cardinaletti and Starke (1999, 2000), distinguishes between three classes of pronouns on the basis of the amount of 'deficient structure' they project: (1) strong pronouns, such as *moi*, (2) subject pronouns, which Cardinaletti and Starke consider weak pronouns, and (3) object pronouns, which they analyse as clitics. The structure underlying each type of pronoun is given in (24). Both strong and weak pronouns are analysed as XPs, but weak pronouns are somehow structurally deficient relative to strong pronouns. In particular, strong pronouns include the C_LP layer, whose head contains referential and human features; weak pronouns are instances of Σ_LP, whose head is the locus of prosody-related features. In contrast, object pronouns are I_LPs, whose head is where phi-features are located, and are considered to be the most deficient pronouns.

(24) a. strong pronouns

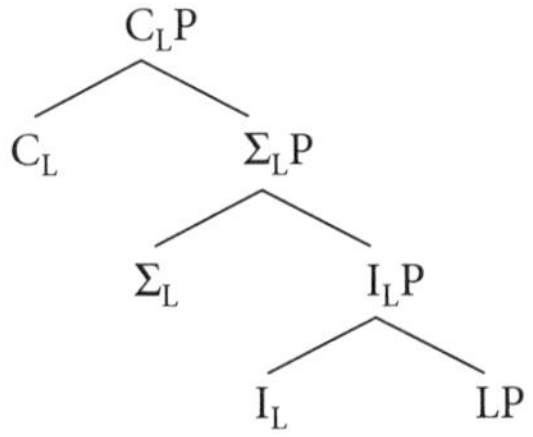

b. weak pronouns

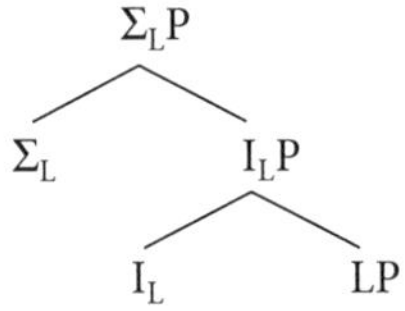

c. clitics

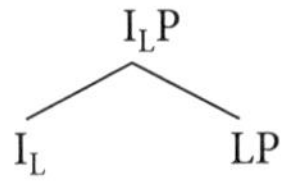

Cardinaletti and Starke assume that weak and clitic pronouns need to compensate for their structural deficiency by finding an element that will host them (the verb), which explains their distributional similarities. In contrast, strong pronouns are not structurally deficient, which allows them to appear in typical XP positions. Note that if examples of subject clitic doubling such as (19) are frequent in informal French, then the representation of nominative pronouns as weak pronouns, as in (24b), should be revised in favour of a structure typical of clitics, as in (24c).

5.2 Binding properties of French pronouns

Pronouns do not have any intrinsic reference; rather, their reference is established by the (discursive) context. For example, it is clear that in (25a), the pronoun *il* 'he' refers to the noun *Jean* 'John'. This is also the case in (25b) where *Jean* precedes the pronoun in the lower clause. Note that the pronoun may also refer to another person.

(25) a. Jean$_i$ a 20 ans. il$_i$ vit à Paris.
John has 20 years he lives in Paris
'John is 20 years old. He lives in Paris.'

b. Jean$_i$ pense qu' il$_{i/j}$ est intelligent.
John thinks that he is intelligent
'John thinks that he is intelligent.'

However, when the pronoun precedes the noun in sentences like (26a,b), coreference leads to ungrammaticality, regardless of the distance separating the two elements.

(26) a. Il$_i$ pense que Jean$_{*i/j}$ est intelligent.
he thinks that John is intelligent
'He thinks that John is intelligent.'

b. Il$_i$ pense que la femme qui travaille à l' agence croit que
he thinks that the woman who works at the agency believes that
Jean$_{*i/j}$ est sympa.
John is nice
'He thinks that the woman who works at the agency believes that John is nice.'

That said, co-reference is possible when a pronoun precedes the noun in sentences like (27).

(27) La femme qu' il$_{i/j}$ aime pense que Jean$_i$ est intelligent
the woman who he loves thinks that John is intelligent
'The woman he loves thinks John is intelligent.'

Finally, co-reference is impossible when the noun precedes the object pronoun in a configuration such as (28a). Coreference can only obtain via the use of an anaphor, such as *se* 'himself/herself/itself/themselves' (28b). In contrast, anaphors are not possible in contexts where pronouns are possible, as in (28c).

(28) a. Jean$_i$ le$_{*i/j}$ considère intelligent.
John him considers intelligent
'John considers him intelligent.'

b. Jean$_i$ se$_i$ considère intelligent.
John himself considers intelligent
'John considers himself intelligent.'

c. Jean$_i$ pense que Marie se$_{*i}$ /le$_i$ trouve intelligent.
John thinks that Mary self him finds intelligent
'John thinks that Mary finds him intelligent.'

It appears that the difference between (28a) and (25b) is that in (25b) the noun and the pronoun are in two different clauses whereas in (28a) they belong to the same clause. But what about the grammatical sentence (29a), where *Jean* and *le* are in the same proposition? Note that the anaphor *se* cannot refer to *Jean* in such a sentence; it can only refer to the possessor *père* 'father'.

(29) a. Le père de Jean_i $\text{le}_{i/j}$ considère intelligent.
the father of John him considers intelligent
'John's father considers him intelligent.'

b. Le père_i de Jean_j $\text{se}_{i/*j}$ considère intelligent.
the father of John self considers intelligent
'John's father considers himself intelligent.'

c. Jean_i pense $\text{se}_{i/*j}$ raser demain
John thinks self shave.INF tomorrow
'John thinks he'll shave tomorrow.'

Let us see how Binding Theory (Chomsky 1981, 1982), which establishes the referential interpretation of anaphors, pronouns and R-expressions, can account for these facts:

(30) Binding: A binds B if A and B are co-indexed and A c-commands B

(31) C-command: a node A c-commands a node B if and only if:
i. A does not dominate B
ii. B does not dominate A
iii. the first branching node dominating A also dominates B.

(32) a. Principle A: an anaphor must be bound within its governing category
b. Principle B: a pronoun must be free within its governing category
c. Principle C: a referential expression must be free everywhere

(33) Governing Category: The governing category for A is the minimal domain containing it, its governor and an accessible subject/SUBJECT.

The c-command principle is illustrated in (34). In this example, A c-commands C: it does not dominate C and the first branching node dominating A, namely Y, also dominates C. C does not c-command A (or B) since the first branching node dominating B, i.e. Z, does not dominate A (or B). Similarly, A does not c-command B: Y, the first branching node dominating A, does not dominate B.

(34)
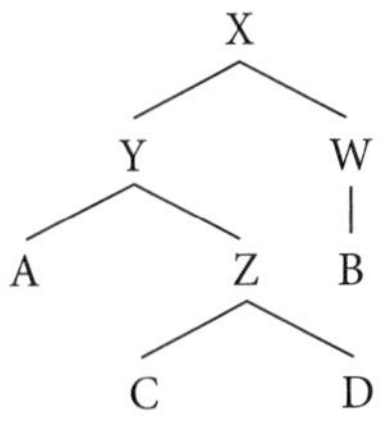

According to Principle C, referential expressions such as *Jean* cannot be bound by anything. This is the case in (25a). In (25b), *Jean* binds *il*, but *il* does not bind *Jean* since it does not dominate (or c-command) *Jean*. The reverse obtains in (26a): since *Jean* is not free in this sentence, the result is ungrammatical. In (27b), although *il* precedes *Jean*, there is no binding relation between the two. Their configuration is similar to that of B and C in (34), so there is no c-command relation between the two of them. *Jean* is thus free, and the sentence is grammatical.

According to Principle B, pronouns must be free (not bound) within a particular domain, which is defined as their governing category. In the examples given above, the governing category is the IP in which the pronoun occurs. In (25b) and (28c), *il* occurs in the lower IP, its governing category, and it is bound by *Jean*. Since *Jean* is in the specifier position of the higher IP, *il* is not bound within its governing category. The sentences are therefore grammatical. In (28a), *il* is bound by the subject *Jean* and both belong to the same IP. Hence, coreference is ungrammatical. In (29a), *Jean* does not bind *il*, since there is no c-command relation between the two (as between B and C in (34)). The pronoun is therefore free within its governing category.

Principle A states that anaphors must be bound within their governing category. Again, in the examples above, this category is the IP in which the anaphor occurs. In (28b), the anaphor *se* is bound by *Jean* and both belong to the same IP. Coreference is therefore grammatical. This contrasts with (28c) where *se* and *Jean* belong to two different IPs. Consequently, *se* cannot co-refer with *Jean*. Finally, although *Jean* and *se* are within the same IP in (29b), *se* cannot refer to *Jean* because there is no c-command relation between them. Again, their relationship is akin to that between B and C above. The anaphor is therefore left unbound. The example in (29c) shows that in French the governing category for an anaphor is the first *finite* IP, since an anaphor in a nonfinite verbal complement must refer to the subject of the main clause.

5.3 Questions for acquisition

Pronominal elements raise a number of questions for acquisition researchers: Do learners have an early knowledge of clitics? Is there a particular order in the acquisition of clitics: do all clitics emerge at the same time, or do some of them emerge later than others? Do learners make an early distinction between the different types of pronouns (in particular, between strong and clitic pronouns)? Researchers hope that answers to these questions will shed light on the issue of learners' knowledge of the distributional properties of pronouns and the status of functional categories in initial grammars. Given that there is a strong association between clitics and functional categories (most obvious under the assumption that clitics head their own category), if language learners show early knowledge of clitics, this suggests that functional categories are available early on in acquisition. The binding properties of pronouns and reflexives are also interesting to acquisition researchers because they are constrained by principles of Universal Grammar. If language acquisition is guided by an innate language faculty, the argument goes, then children learning French as their L1 should display knowledge of such properties as soon as they have acquired the target pronominal forms.

CHAPTER 6

Subject and object pronouns in child L1 French

Research on child L1 French has shown that children use both overt and null pronouns (clitics) in the early stages of acquisition and that object pronouns develop after nominative pronouns. The binding properties of pronominal and nominal elements are also in place quite rapidly, which suggests early availability of the three binding principles discussed in Section 5.2. This chapter is divided into three main parts. The first two address the development of overt and null pronouns, while the third deals with the acquisition of the binding properties of pronominal elements.

6.1 Overt pronouns in child L1 French

Overt pronouns appear in the early stages of child L1 French, with subject clitics developing before object clitics. Moreover, nominative and accusative pronouns appear in appropriate clitic positions from the moment they start being produced.

6.1.1 Development of subject clitics in child L1 French

Nominative pronouns are reported to start developing slightly after the emergence of two-word combinations, namely at around age 1;8–1;10. In fact, clitics are among the first overt subjects children use, appearing at roughly the same time as finite verb forms (see Chapter 2). Moreover, subject clitics are almost always found attached to a finite verb; very few utterances display any non-clitic elements in between. For those researchers who assume that subject clitics are agreement markers in French, this suggests that agreement is acquired fairly rapidly by young children.

6.1.1.1 *General development of subject clitics in child L1 French*

Table 1 summarizes the general development of subject clitics in several children. It focuses on finite environments since, as will be seen below, clitics almost never appear in nonfinite declaratives in child L1 French. Table 1 can therefore be taken as a solid summary of the emergence and development of subject clitics. The first two columns identify the moments at which verbal utterances and subject clitics were produced for the first time by the children. Note that there is almost always a correspondence between the two, which supports the conclusion that subject clitics appear very early in spontaneous production and that they appear as soon as verbal utterances are used. The third column of the table identifies the moment at which subject clitics have clearly become productive, with an incidence ratio of at least 50%. The figures clearly show that such productivity is reached extremely rapidly by almost all children. For five of the eight children listed in Table 1, the 50% ratio landmark is reached within at most one month following the first appearance of subject clitics (Marie, Louis, Jean, Nathalie, and Philippe). For Marie, Louis and Nathalie, it is even reached before the age of two, while Louis reaches it shortly thereafter (2;0.8). For the other children, the ratio of subject clitics is not low in the early stages. For Daniel, it is at around 40% as of 1;8.3. In Augustin's case, it is over 45% between 2;0.23 and 2;2.13 (with a peak at 60% at 2;1.15), while it decreases slightly to between 30% and 40% in the next three files. As for Hugo (1;8.14 – 2;5.19), while subject clitics account for 10% of the subjects of finite verbs before the age of two, their ratio rapidly climbs to around 35% at age 2;1.7 and over 50% thereafter. Examples attesting the early use of pronoun clitics in other children are given in (1) (see also Ferdinand 1996; Pierce 1992).

Table 1. General development of subject clitics in child L1 French

Child	Age	First verbal utterance	First subject clitics	50% incidence ratio
Marie[a]	1;8.26 – 2;6.10	1;8.26	1;8.26	1;8.26
Jean[a]	1;7.16 – 2;0.28	1;7.16	1;7.16	1;7.16
Nathalie[a]	1;9;3 – 2;3;2	1;9;3	1;9;3	1;10.2
Louis[a]	1;9.26 – 2;3.29	1;9.26	1;9.26	2;0.8
Philippe[a]	2;1.19 – 2;6.20	2;1.19	2;1.19	2;1.19
Daniel[a]	1;8;1 – 1;11;1	1;8;1	1;8;1	–
Augustin[a]	2;0;2 – 2;9;30	2;0.2	2;0.2	2;6.16
Hugo[b]	1;8.14 – 2;5.19	1;9.21	1;10.6	2;1.7
Victor[c]	1;11.10 – 2;5.29	1;11.10	1;11.10	2;0.14
Chloé[c]	1;11.19 – 2;5.14	1;11.19	1;11.19	1;11.19

a. data adapted from Rasetti (2003)[72]
b. data adapted from van der Velde (1999)
c. data adapted from van der Velde, Jakubowicz and Rigaut (2002)

72. These figures include instances of presentative *c'est* 'it is' and locative *il y a* 'there is', as well as subject placeholders, as in *e veux pas nounours* '(I) don't want the teddy bear' (see Section 6.1.1.2). According to Rasetti (2003), placeholders account for 7.3% of all subject clitic pronouns in the data she looked at.

(1) a. I ku(r) apE. (Augustin, 2;0;2)
he run.FIN after

b. 'l est gros. (Augustin, 2;0;2)
he is fat

c. I(l) vole (Hugo, 1;10.6)
he fly.FIN

d. On met. (Hugo, 1;10.24)
we put.FIN

e. Elle dort. (Daniel, 1;8;1)[73]
she sleep.FIN

f. Il mange. (Grégoire, 1;10;0)
he eat.FIN

Early production of subject clitics is reported in cross-sectional studies as well. Jakubowicz and Rigaut (2000) looked at the acquisition of subject and object pronouns in 12 children. The children were divided into two groups based on several criteria, including MLU levels (Group 1 (n = 5): MLU < 3.2, age: 2;0;13–2;7;3; Group 2 (n = 7): MLU > 3.2, age: 2;3;22–2;7). The study involved a spontaneous production task and an elicited production task based on pictures. In the elicited production task, children were shown pictures representing an action involving one or two characters and were asked questions such as *Que fait X?* 'What is X doing?' and *Que fait X à/avec Y?* 'What is X doing to/with Y?'. These were meant to elicit an answer displaying a subject clitic, a transitive verb and an object clitic, as in (2). (Object pronouns are discussed in Section 6.1.2).

(2) [Picture of a little boy throwing a ball]

a. Question: Que fait le garçon avec la balle?
what does the boy with the ball
'What is the boy doing with the ball?'

b. (Expected) answer: Il la lance.
He it throws
'He's throwing it.'

For Group 1 children (MLU < 3.2), subject clitics represented 60% of the subjects in spontaneous speech (135/224), and over 85% in the elicited production task (58/67) (see Table 4 below). The youngest child, Claire (age 2;0,13), produced a total of 54 subject clitics out of 73 utterances with a finite verb (74%) in the spontaneous task. Even for

73. Note that although the pronoun *elle* is taken into account in studies on the development of subject clitics, its status is ambiguous between a clitic and a strong pronoun (see Chapter 5). In other words, it is impossible to tell whether *elle* in *elle dort* is a clitic or a strong pronoun unless the context is taken into account and an acoustic analysis is carried out.

those children who used few subject clitics in spontaneous speech, the incidence of such elements in elicited production was sometimes quite high. Such is the case of Gaëtan (age 2;3.20) for whom the incidence of subject clitics was the lowest in the spontaneous production (11/32 = 34.4%) but a high 94.1% (16/17) in the elicited production task. Note that for almost all children, the vast majority of subject pronouns in spontaneous production were 3rd person clitics (see Section 6.1.1.2).

Clitics quickly become the most common type of subjects in child L1 French. Incidence ratios ranging between 65% and 90% are reported for all the children listed in Table 1 by the end of the recording sessions.[74] The incidence of other types of overt subjects, such as lexical subjects and *ça* 'this', remains below that of subject clitics throughout the various observation periods.[75] In some cases, other overt subjects emerge slightly later than subject clitics, and their incidence remains low throughout the early developmental phases. In Hugo's corpus, the incidence of lexical subjects and *ça* generally stays below 10% (van der Velde 1999). Lexical subjects emerge at age 2;1.29 (compared to 1;10.6 for clitics) and their incidence hovers at around 3%, with a peak at 7.2% (2;2.27). *Ça* makes up 12% of finite subjects when it emerges at age 2;1.7, but then quickly falls to 7.5% and eventually to around 5%. In other children, the incidence of lexical subjects can be relatively high, but it still remains below that of subject clitics. Such is the case of Augustin (2;0.2 – 2;9.30) for whom the ratio of lexical subjects is at around 20% until age 2;6.16 (compared to an incidence ratio of subject clitics ranging between 29% and 60% during the same period). The incidence of lexical subjects then falls abruptly to 7.3%, right when the ratio of subject clitics climbs to 70%. Interestingly, only eight instances of *ça* are reported for Augustin (Hamann et al. 1996). In fact, the only subjects with which clitics seem to compete during the early stages of development are null subjects (see Section 6.2.1).

In an interesting comparison between bilinguals and monolinguals, Schmitz and Müller (2008) report the incidence of subject types in French in both adult data and in developmental data of one monolingual child, Grégoire (1;9.18–2;5.27). The adult data come from spontaneous interactions with children. In this corpus, clitics represent the vast majority of the subjects, at about 85%. Other subjects include strong pronouns (about 5%) and null subjects (about 10%). There is almost no subject lexical DP in the data that were analysed. In Grégoire's data, subject clitics are observed as of the

---

74. In her investigation of data from Anne (1;10.12–3;1), Max (1;9.19–2;10), and Tom (2;1.11–2;10), De Cat (2002) found that out of a total of 5007 finite utterances, 4114 (82.2%) contained a subject clitic.

75. Among non-clitic overt subjects, *ça* is the most frequent, followed by proper nouns (including *maman* 'mommy' and *papa* 'daddy'), DPs, bare NPs, and non-nominative pronominals (such as *moi* 'me') (Rasetti 2003: 153).

first sample (1;9.18), just like the other children mentioned so far, and they represent between 20 % and 40% of the subjects until 2;1.15. Their incidence reaches adult-like figures as of 2;5.1. Lexical DPs are frequent at first (between 40% and 60% of subjects), they stabilize at around 20% until 2;3, and decline to less than 10% as of 2;5.1. As can be seen, his development profile closely resembles that of Augustin.

6.1.1.2 *Detailed development of subject clitics in child L1 French*

Table 2 summarizes the order in which subject clitics develop in child speech. The first clitics to emerge are third person singular pronouns, such as *il*, *elle* and *on*, as seen in the examples above. First person form *je* usually develops later (see (3a–b)). Although children often talk about themselves in the first stages of acquisition, they have a tendency to refer to themselves in the third person. For instance, the child P. is reported to say *P. est malade* 'P. is ill' (P. 1;8) instead of *je suis malade* 'I am ill' (Heinen & Kadow 1990). Among the singular pronouns, second person singular *tu* (3c) is usually acquired late, and plural pronouns appear even later. The early emergence of third person singular pronouns, and the delayed development of plural pronouns, is reported in other languages as well, such as German (Clahsen 1986).

Table 2. Emergence of specific subject clitics in child L1 French

Clitic	**Augustin**[a] (2;0;2 – 2;9;30)	**Grégoire**[b] (1;9;2 – 2;1;3)	**Nathalie**[b] (1;9;3 – 2;2;2)	**Daniel**[b] (1;8;1 – 1;11;1)	**Hugo**[c] (1;8.14 – 2;5.19)
il	2;0.2	1;9;2	1;10;2	1;8;3	1;10.6
elle	2;2.13	1;10;0	2;2;2	1;8;1	1;10.24
on	2;0.2	1;10;0	2;2;2	1;8;1	1;10.24
je	2;9.2	1;10;0	2;2;2	1;8;1	2;1.7
tu	2:4.1	2;1;3	–	–	2;1.29

a. data from Hamann et al. (1996)
b. data from Pierce (1992)
c. data from van der Velde (1999)

(3) a. Et je veux. (Natalie, 2;2;2)
and I want.FIN

b. Je suis là. (Grégoire, 2;3;0)
I am here

c. Tu peux me la donner. (Hugo, 2;5.19)
you can me it give.INF

Although subject clitics are used early, Ferdinand (1996) argues that the acquisition of paradigms starts with the use of elsewhere forms, namely forms that are generalized to all other environments (see Section 2.1.1). In the acquisition of subject clitics, she reports the use of elsewhere forms that do not belong to the target paradigm (see also Heinen & Kadow 1990). The elsewhere form in this case is simply a vowel (some kind of 'tone' that children use instead of the actual form) either [e], [ə], or [a], which can act as any subject, as illustrated in (4). These forms are also sometimes referred to as fillers. Given that they can stand for any subject, as they are presumably unspecified for person, gender, and number.

(4) a. [e] ouvre. (Grégoire, 1;11.22)
e open.FIN
'I am opening.'

b. [e] fait. (Grégoire, 1;11.22)
e do.FIN
'She is doing.'

c. [ə] marche pas. (Grégoire, 2;3.0)
ə work.FIN not
'It doesn't work.'

d. [a] va dodo. (Nathalie, 2;2;2)
a go.FIN sleep
'She is going to sleep.'

Specified forms, such as *il* 'he' and *je* 'I', develop sometime after the first presence of these elsewhere forms. Note that when specified forms start being used, they always appear in the appropriate contexts. That is, *je* always occurs with first person singular verb forms, and *il* with third person singular ones.[76]

6.1.1.3 *Distribution of clitic subjects in child L1 French*

Not only do children use subject pronouns relatively early, they also display early knowledge of pronouns' distributional properties. Subject clitics almost never occur in postverbal position, in contrast to lexical subjects (5) and strong pronouns (6). In addition, clitics do not appear in right- or left-dislocated positions; instead, when a pronoun is used in such positions, it takes the form of a strong pronoun (7). In short, sequences such as *Pleure pas il* 'Cries not he', *Bois peu je* 'Drink little I', or *je moi* 'I me' are not observed.

(5) a. Pleure pas garçon. (Daniel, 1;8;3)
cry.FIN not boy

b. Fait pas du bruit la fille. (Philippe, 2;2;0)
make.FIN not some noise the girl

c. A plus papa. (Grégoire, 2;1;3)
have.FIN no+more daddy

76. This does not prevent gender errors, however, as observed by Jakubowicz and Rigaut (2000) (for knowledge of gender in French in children with SL1, see Section 11.2.2).

(6) a. Bois peu moi. (Daniel, 1;8;1)
drink.FIN little me

b. Est tombé moi. (Philippe, 2;1;3)
is fallen me

c. A peur moi. (Grégoire, 2;3;0)
have.FIN fear me

(7) a. Moi je vais faire café moi. (Daniel, 1;11;1)
me I go+1SG make.INF coffee me

b. Moi je tousse encore. (Philippe, 2;2;2)
me I cough.FIN still

c. Moi je veux regarder. (Grégoire, 2;3;0)
me I want.FIN watch.INF

Furthermore, clitics are always repeated in coordination contexts (8) and they are never conjoined with any another element.

(8) a. Moi je saute et je descends. (Philippe, 2;2;1)
me I jump.FIN and I go+down.FIN

b. Il se ouvre et il se ferme. (Philippe, 2;3;0)
it itself open.FIN and it itself close.FIN

Another fact suggesting early knowledge of clitics is the observed contingency between finiteness and pronominal forms. As seen in Section 2.1.4.1, subject clitics are very rarely found in root infinitives in child L1 French, in contrast to subject DPs and strong pronoun subjects; rather, subject clitics are restricted to finite clauses (see Table 4 in Section 2.1.4.1, repeated below as Table 3). Similar facts are reported in child L1 Dutch, where subject clitics such as *'k* 'I' and *ze* 'she' do not appear in RIs (Haegeman 1995).

Table 3. Incidence of subject clitics with finite and nonfinite verbs in child L1 French

Child	Age	+Finite	%	–Finite	%
Marie	1;8.26 – 2;6.10	872/1219	84.1%	0/179	0%
Jean	1;7.16 – 2;0.28	261/303	86.1%	0/8	0%
Nathalie	1;9;3 – 2;3;2	156/301	51.8%	0/71	0%
Louis	1;9.26 – 2;3.29	588/871	67.5%	0/141	0%
Philippe	2;1.19 – 2;6.20	988/1471	67.2%	2/247	0.8%
Daniel	1;8;1 – 1;11;1	154/436	35.3%	3/221	1.4%
Augustin	2;0;2 – 2;9;30	378/646	58.4%	8/82	9.8%
Hugo	1;8.14 – 2;5.19	428/567	64.3%	1/22	4.5%
Anne, Max, and Tom[a]		4114/5007	82.1%	11/386	2.8%

a. Anne (1;10.12–3;1.4), Max (1;9.19–2;10.24), and Tom (2;1.11–2;10.7)

Of particular interest is the fact that the difference between clitics and strong pronouns is established quite early by children. As seen above, strong pronouns are restricted to non-clitic positions in spontaneous production. Only a few cases of strong pronoun subjects occurring with finite forms are reported in the literature (De Cat 2002; Ferdinand 1996; Heinen & Kadow 1990; Rasetti 2003). In her study of three children learning French, De Cat found 124 strong pronoun subjects (what she calls non-nominative apparent heavy subjects), of which 81 appeared with a finite verb. These make up only 1.6% of all subjects in finite declaratives (81/5007). Similarly, Rasetti (2003) found only 38 strong pronouns as subjects of 3425 finite utterances (1%) in the data of eight children (Table 1). Some examples are given in (9); note that (9c) is possible in adult French.

(9) a. Moi a tout bu. (Philippe, 2;01.19)
me have.FIN all drunk

b. Moi est dedans. (Grégoire, 2;03)
me is inside

c. Lui mange. (Philippe, 2;01.19)
him eat.FIN

d. et moi a gagné. (Tom, 2;4.8)
and me have.FIN won

Since strong pronouns do not bear nominative Case, it is not clear whether or not the strong pronoun occupies the subject position in (9a–d). It could be proposed that children have no knowledge of Case in the early stages of acquisition. If this were true, however, one would expect many more instances of utterances such as those above. One might also expect to observe instances of prepositions followed by nominative clitics (e.g. *pour il* 'for he'), which children do not produce. Alternatively, the strong pronouns in (9) could be assumed to occupy a left-dislocated position, with a null clitic in subject position (De Cat 2002; Legendre et al. 2002). This is illustrated in (10). Under this analysis, the strong pronoun is adjoined to IP (or CP) and does not occupy the subject position.[77] A similar dislocation analysis was proposed for postverbal subjects in Section 2.3.2, assuming right-branching adjunction to IP.

(10)

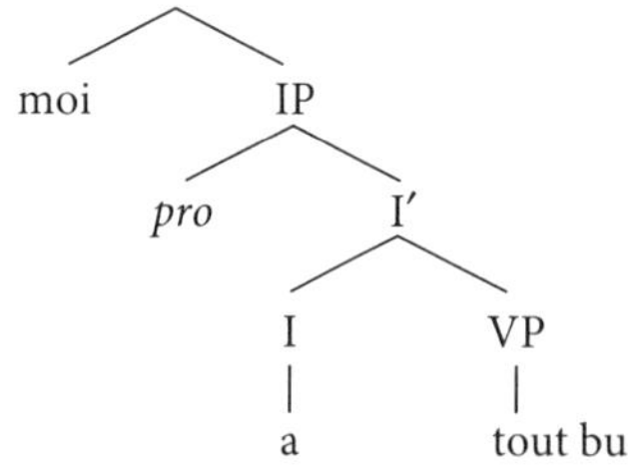

77. Ferdinand (1996) proposes a similar analysis, with the strong pronoun in SpecFocusP. For arguments against this analysis, see De Cat (2002).

Interestingly, acoustic analyses of such utterances reveal that the acoustic profile of the strong pronoun is similar to what is found in adult language with an overt clitic occupying the subject position (see De Cat 2002), as in (11).

(11) $[_{IP}$ Moi $[_{IP}$ j'ai tout bu]].
me I have all drunk

Crucially, unambiguous evidence of left-dislocation related to the subject was found in the data examined by De Cat, as illustrated in (12). These also have an acoustic contour typical of dislocation.

(12) a. Et ça, c' est là. (Anne, 2;2.30)
and that it is there

b. Et toi aussi t' as tapé # comme ça. (Tom, 2;3.22)
and you too you have hit like that

The dislocation analysis outlined in (10) differs from Schütze and Wexler's (1996) ATOM hypothesis in which Tense and Agreement may be underspecified independently from each other. Below, we will be concerned with the possibility of Tense being specified and Agreement being either specified or underspecified, i.e. [+tns, +agr] and [+tns, −agr]. The first possibility corresponds to the production of specified finite forms, such as *ai* 'have+1SG' and *suis* 'am'; the second possibility yields the production of finite elsewhere forms, e.g. *a* 'has' and *est* 'is'. Each possibility makes predictions about the kinds of subjects that should be observed. When Agreement is fully specified, a nominative subject is expected to occur, e.g. *j'ai* and *je suis*; when Agr is underspecified, a non-nominative subject is predicted, e.g. *moi a* and *moi est*. In the latter case, the strong pronoun is assumed to be in the specifier position of AgrP, in contrast to the dislocation analysis illustrated in (10). A problem for this analysis is that reverse combinations of pronouns and verb forms can be observed in child L1 French. De Cat noticed cases of strong pronoun (apparent) subjects with fully specified verb forms, such as *Moi ai cassé ça là* 'Me have+1SG broken that there' (Anne, 2;2.0). In fact, De Cat reports that strong pronoun (apparent) subjects appear with fully specified forms (2%) and with elsewhere forms (3%) in similar proportions. She also counted 60 unambiguous cases of underspecified agreement in the data. These involve a finite (elsewhere) form and non-matching subject, as *moi j'est pas méchant* lit. 'Me I is not nasty' (Tom, 2;4.8). In 15 cases (60%), the subject was a subject clitic, as above, whereas in only three cases was it a strong pronoun, as in (9d), in contrast to the ATOM predictions.[78]

To summarize, we have seen that children display early command of distributive properties of subject clitics. In particular, they do not appear in topicalized positions,

78. For De Cat (2002), preverbal lexical DP subjects in child L1 French are also left-dislocated (with a null subject clitic). See also Ferdinand (1996).

they are repeated in coordination contexts, and they almost always appear with a finite verb form. Children also seem to distinguish between strong pronouns and clitics relatively early, restricting strong pronouns to non-clitic positions. However, in some cases strong pronouns seem to play the role of the subject of finite verbs in early production. Following De Cat (2002), these are amenable to instances of left or right dislocations, with an empty subject occupying SpecIP, contra Schütze and Wexler (1996).

6.1.2 Development of accusative clitics in child L1 French

Most of the studies which have looked at the development of object clitics in French monolinguals report that these elements appear later than subject clitics, several months later in some cases. Before object clitics, children use *ça* 'this', object DPs or strong pronominal objects, such as *à moi* 'to me' or *à toi* 'to you' where the target language requires object clitics *me* or *te* (Heinen & Kadow 1990), or they omit the object altogether (see Section 6.2.2). Once object clitics do appear, however, they are correctly positioned.

Table 4 shows that object clitics can emerge up to four months after nominative pronouns (as with Augustin). Moreover, their incidence remains low for a while. In many cases, it remains close to 10% at the end of the respective production periods. The incidence of object clitics can also be sporadic even in the case of children who seem to acquire them more rapidly, such as Marie, for example. Although the ratio is above 15% in her first two recording samples, it is below 10% in seven of the remaining 15 samples, including two toward the end of the data collection period (at ages 2;3.3 and 2;3.13) (Rasetti 2003, Table 7: p. 258).[79] Moreover, the incidence of object clitics in her transitive contexts does not exceed 25%. In contrast, the incidence of subject clitics is over 50% throughout the data collection period. In Grégoire's data (Schmitz & Müller 2008), although the incidence of object clitics reaches 10% at age 1;11.22, no object clitic is found until age 2.3.0.[80] Examples of object clitics are given in (13).

---

79. Similarly, as shown in Table 4, Chloé's ratio of object clitics is high in her first recording, at 1;11.19. However, it plunges to below 10% in the second sample, at 2;0.10, and does not go above 20% before 2;2.4. Moreover, of the 18 object clitics produced at 1;11.19, 16 involve the verb *voir* 'see', as in *Le vois pas* lit. 'It see not'. It is possible that these sequences are not analysed by the child (van der Velde et al. 2002).

80. In contrast, Hulk (2000) reports no delay in the emergence of object clitics in Philippe's data (2;1–2;6), showing that both nominative and accusative clitics are used from early on, as in (ia) and (ib).

(i) a. Tu appuies là. (Philippe, 2;01.19)
you press here

b. Les mettre dans le garage (Philippe, 2;01.26)
them put.INF in the garage

(13) a. Ateinds- le! (=éteinds-le) (Augustin, 2;2.13)
switch+off it

b. T' as vu, en a par terre aussi. (Augustin, 2;9.2)
you have seen some has on+floor too

c. parce qu'il le coupe puis le plie. (Augustin, 2;9.2)
because he it cuts then it folds

d. Je le démolis. (Hugo, 2;2.27)
I it destroy

Table 4. General development of object clitics in child L1 French

Child	Age	First subject clitic	First object clitic	10% incidence in transitive contexts
Marie	1;8.26 – 2;6.10	1;8.26	1;8.26	1;8.26
Louis	1;9.26 – 2;3.29	1;9.26	1;10.19	2;2.17
Augustin	2;0;2 – 2;9;30	2;0.2	2;4.1	2;9.30
Hugo	1;8.14 – 2;5.19	1;10.6	2;1.7	2;2.27
Victor	1;11.10 – 2;5.29	1;11.10	2;1.0	2;3.0
Chloé	1;11.19 – 2;5.14	1;11.19	1;11.19	1;11.19
Grégoire	1;9.18 – 2;7.15	1;9.18	1;11.22	1;11.22

The development of object clitics is confirmed in cross-sectional studies. Jakubowicz and Rigaut (2000) report that all children in the two groups they investigated tend to use subject clitics more frequently than object clitics (Table 5).[81] In particular, results in the elicited production task show that subject clitics are used in almost 90% of the utterances, whereas the ratio of object clitic use is below 20%. Recall that in this task, both clitics were deemed obligatory in the children's anticipated answers (see Section 6.1.1.1).[82] Similar results are reported by van der Velde (1999) who administered the same elicited production task to Hugo at age 2;5.19.

However, the incidence of object clitics is much lower than that of subject clitics in Philippe's early recordings (6% vs. 48% at age 2;01.19), which is similar to the pattern observed in other children.

81. Jakubowicz and Rigaut also interviewed adult speakers of French. No subject/object asymmetry was observed in their use of clitics.

82. Results for subject clitics take into account the number of nominal pronouns produced with all finite verbs, while results for object clitics consider the number of object pronouns produced with transitive verbs.

Table 5. Incidence of subject and object clitics in early child L1 French (from Jakubowicz & Rigaut 2000)

Group	Age	Subject clitics		Object clitics	
		Spontaneous	Elicited	Spontaneous	Elicited
Group 1	2;0.13 – 2;7.3	135/224 (60.3%)	58/67 (86.6%)	9/109 (8.3%)	13/67 (19.4%)
Group 2	2;3.22 – 2;7.0	566/604 (93.7%)	105/113 (92.9%)	75/285 (26.3%)	62/113 (54.9%)

It generally takes children learning French quite a while to master object clitics. Chillier et al. (2001), in one of the few studies that has looked at the development of object clitics after the age of 4, administered an elicited production task to 99 children aged between 3;5 and 6;5 and divided into five age groups. In the youngest group (mean age 4;0), the ratio of object clitics in obligatory contexts is 68.5%, which is higher than the results reported by Jakubowicz and Rigaut (2000) for their Group 2 (2;3.22 – 2;7.0) on the elicitation task (54.9%). The incidence of object clitic use gradually climbs to 88.1% in the fourth group (mean age 4;9) and to 90% in the oldest children (mean age 6;3). Similar results are reported by Van der Velde (2003) on children with comparable ages (see Section 6.1.4, Table 6). It would be interesting to look at longitudinal data to further explore the later development of object clitics.

Contrary to subject clitics, it is not clear whether object clitics emerge according to any particular order in spontaneous speech. For example, before age 2;9.2, there are only four instances of object clitics in Augustin's data: two instances of *me*, one of *le*, and one of *y* 'there'. At 2;9.2, and later at 2;9.30, almost all object clitics are produced, except for *la*. A more visible trend can be observed in Philippe's speech, however, in which 3rd person singular forms are found early on (between 2;01.26 and 2;02), while *te* and *vous* appear much later (2;06) (see Hulk 2000). As illustrated in (14), *me* is attested very early (2;01.19), but it may be unanalysed at that point.

(14) e me gratter (Augustin, 2;9.2)
me scratch.INF

Another early asymmetry between subject and object clitics concerns their appearance in RIs: the proportion of object clitics in such utterances is much higher than that of subject clitics. Hamann et al. (1996) report that of the 36 object clitics used by Augustin, four occur in RIs (11.1%), as in (14), compared to 1.8% of his subject clitics (5/278).

Despite these asymmetries, object clitics, like their nominative counterparts, are almost always placed in target-like positions once they start being used, as illustrated in the examples given so far.[83] The distribution of clitics differs from that of other

83. Heinen and Kadow (1990) mention erroneous postverbal placement (e.g. *je veux le* 'I want it' (Ch)), which may be induced from the V-cl order heard in positive imperatives in the target language (e.g. *dis-le!* 'say it'). Difficulty with the placement of object clitics is also

(non-clitic) elements frequently used by children in the early stages, including *ça* 'this'. In Augustin's data, for example, 121 of the 129 instances of *ça* appear in non-clitic positions, namely after a verb or a preposition, as in (15) (Rasetti 2003).

(15) a. Manger ça? (Augustin, 2;0;2)
eat.INF this

b. C' est pour ça. (Augustin, 2;9;2)
it is for this

One construction where erroneous positioning of object clitics has been found is the positive imperative (Haverkort & Weissenborn 1991). In such constructions, the clitic usually follows the imperative verb in French, as in *fais-le* 'do it', which can be accounted for by adopting a V-to-C movement analysis: $[_{CP}\text{Fais}_i\ [_V\ t_i\ \text{le}]]$. Instead of the target V-cl, monolingual children initially produce imperatives with cl-V, as in (16). At that initial stage, children also produce imperatives with NP objects, which systematically occupy their canonical postverbal position, as in (17).

(16) a. Le mets là-dedans! (2;00.13)
it put therein

b. Les prête! (2;03.16)
them lend

(17) a. Papa, donne les lunettes (2;03;06)
daddy give the glasses

b. Mets ça! (2;04;12)
put that

This stage is followed by a stage of optionality, where objects clitics either precede or follow the imperative verb. Finally, systematic correct clitic placement is observed. Haverkort and Weissenborn argue that this development is due to the early unavailability of V-to-C movement, presumably because the emergence of the C position is delayed (see Chapter 14).

6.1.3 Development of reflexive clitics in child L1 French

Reflexive pronouns are reported to emerge prior to their non-reflexive (accusative) counterparts. According to Ferdinand (1996), the acquisition of reflexives starts with the use of an elsewhere form, namely third person *se* 'himself/herself/itself/oneself/themselves' (henceforth 'self'), as illustrated in (18). In support of the claim that this *se* is an elsewhere form, she notes that specified forms, such as *me* 'myself', are never

reported with respect to auxiliaries (e.g. *il a me pas dit oui* 'he has me said not yes' (FC 2;7)). However, the authors do not discuss the incidence of these errors. We will see that they can be quite frequent in adult L2 French (Section 8.1.1.2) and, to a lesser extent, in bilingual acquisition (Section 7.1.2.2).

used in contexts requiring a third person reflexive, as shown by the fact that utterances such as (19) never occur in the data.

(18) a. Moi je s' accroche. (Philippe, 2;2.10)
me I self attach.FIN

b. Je s' ennuie pas. (Philippe, 2;11.0)
I self bore.FIN not

c. Ne s' amuse avec elle, moi. (Augustin, 2;9.2)
NEG self enjoy.FIN with her me

(19) Il me souvient pas. (unattested)
he myself remembers not

However, not all studies report such a pattern in the early development of reflexive clitics. The incidence of reflexive clitics has been reported to be quite low in spontaneous speech (Jakubowicz & Rigaut 2000; Schmitz & Müller 2008; van der Velde et al. 2002), but quite high in elicited production. Some of the pictures Jakubowicz and Rigaut (2000) used in their elicited production task (see Section 6.1.1.1) were meant to make the children produce reflexive pronouns, as in (20).

(20) [Picture of a teddy bear washing itself]

a. Question: Que fait le nounours?
'What is the teddy bear doing?'

b. (expected) answer: Il se lave.
he himself is+washing
'He's washing (himself)'

The incidence of answers including the targeted pronoun was higher in the case of reflexive pronouns than for non-reflexive object clitics, in both learner groups. Questions such as *What is X doing to Y?*, for which only answers including a non-reflexive pronoun could be used, did not trigger the production of any reflexives. In contrast, the question *What is X doing?*, which could result in the use of either reflexive or non-reflexive pronouns depending on the picture, yielded the production of nine reflexive clitics. For Jakubowicz and Rigaut, this suggests that reflexive clitics are acquired before accusative clitics.[84] Note that Jakubowicz and Rigaut's study was meant to elicit 3rd person singular anaphors. It is therefore inconclusive as to the acquisition of other reflexive pronouns, such as *me* 'myself' and *te* 'yourself'. Similar results are reported for Chloé, Victor, and Hugo: their ratio of reflexive pronouns was higher than their ratio

84. Maybe the spontaneous production task did not trigger the use of reflexive pronouns. Note that the incidence of reflexive pronouns is significantly higher in elicited production than in spontaneous speech. In contrast, there is no significant difference in the case of non-reflexive pronouns: the incidence of such clitics is low in both tasks, especially in Group 1 children.

of non-reflexive object pronouns in the elicited production task, although the children used few reflexive clitics in spontaneous production (van der Velde et al. 2002).

6.1.4 Production vs. comprehension

Interestingly, children do better at comprehension of object clitics than at production. In a series of two studies, van der Velde (2003) looked at both the production and comprehension of clitics in groups of children aged between 3 and 7. The studies each involved an elicited task similar to the one used in Jakubowicz and Rigaut (with pictures representing either reflexive or non-reflexive actions), but they differed in the animacy of the referents of the clitics: referents were animate in the first study and inanimate in the second one. In addition, the first study involved a comprehension task. In this task, the child was presented with a series of three pictures and was instructed to choose one based on a question from the experimenter. The question included either an accusative pronoun, as in (21) or a reflexive pronoun, as in (22).

(21) Experimenter: Montre- moi l' image sur laquelle tu vois:
'Show me the picture in which you see'
Donald Duck dit que le Petit Chaperon Rouge
Donald Duck says that the Little Red Riding Hood
l' arrose avec un tuyau
him is+spraying with a hose
'Donald Duck says that Little Red Riding Hood is spraying him with a hose'

(22) Experimenter: Montre- moi l'image sur laquelle tu vois:
'Show me the picture in which you see
Schtroumpfette voit que Barbie se coiffe.
'Schtroumpfette sees that Barbie herself is+combing
'Schtroumpfette sees that Barbie is combing herself.'

The three pictures were distributed as follows: (a) the target picture, (b) a picture representing the reflexive or non-reflexive counterpart of the test sentence (namely a reflexive action if the test sentence displayed a non-reflexive accusative clitic, or a non-reflexive action if the test sentence involved a reflexive clitic), and (c) a distractor picture.[85] In the production task (see Table 6), the incidence of object clitics did not reach the adult level until the last group (roughly age 6). In contrast, the ratio

85. The distractor displayed the same action as in the target picture, but either the relationship between the main subject and the embedded subject was inversed (so, with respect to (21), Donald Duck would be spraying Little Red Riding Hood), or there was a character different from the embedded subject (e.g. Donald Duck sprays Barbie).

of subject clitics and reflexive pronouns was high from the age of three onward. In addition, animacy did not appear to play a role in the children's performance: the pattern of results was similar regardless of whether accusative clitics referred to animate or inanimate antecedents. Instead of the accusative clitic, children tended to use a full DP or to omit the pronoun.

Table 6. Accuracy rate in the production of subject and object clitics in early child L1 French (from van der Velde 2003)

Participants	Study	Subject clitics		Accusative clitics		Reflexive clitics
		[+animate]	[−animate]	[+animate]	[−animate]	[+animate]
Group 1 (Younger children)	Study 1 (n=12) (mean 3;3)	95.8%	–	44.1%	–	85.4%
	Study 2 (n=12) (mean 3;5)	–	95.6%	–	53.2%	–
Group 2 (Interm. children)	Study 1 (n=12) (mean 4;2)	98.2%	–	78.6%	–	96.3%
	Study 2 (n=12) (mean 4;2)	–	98.0%	–	74%	–
Group 3 (Older children)	Study 1 (n=12) (mean 6;7)	99.7%	–	91.7%	–	99.5%
	Study 2 (n=12) (mean 6;4)	–	99.8%	–	97.6%	–
Adults	Study 1 (n=12)	100%	–	–	–	100%
	Study 2 (n=12)	–	–	100%	–	–

Comparing Table 7 (results on the comprehension task) with Table 6 shows that comprehension of accusative clitics is better than production in Group 1, while comprehension and production are at similar levels thereafter.[86] For reflexive pronouns, there is very little difference between comprehension and production for any group. Comprehension of reflexive clitics is higher than the comprehension of accusative clitics in Groups 1 and 2, as was the case with production. In most cases, errors involved the selection of the distractor picture, especially when the main subject and the embedded subject were interchanged. No differences in the production or comprehension of the two types of clitics was observed in the adults.

86. Weissenborn, Kail and Friederici (1990) also found that object clitics did not pose any particular comprehension problems for young French children. Interestingly, they found that the comprehension of object pronouns posed greater challenges to children learning languages in which such elements are not clitics, for instance Dutch and German.

Table 7. Accuracy rate in the comprehension of accusative and reflexive clitics in early child L1 French (from van der Velde 2003)

Group	Mean age	Accusative clitics	Reflexive clitics
Group 1 (n=12)	3;3	69.8%	80.2%
Group 2 (n=12)	4;2	73%	92.7%
Group 3 (n=12)	6;7	94.8%	100%
Adults (n=12)		100%	100%

6.1.5 Theoretical implications

Studies on the development of pronouns in L1 French suggest that children are able to distinguish clitics from other types of elements, in particular DPs and strong pronouns, relatively early. The incidence of subject clitics also increases very rapidly from the earliest stages onward and is much higher than that of subject DPs.[87] These findings suggest that children have early knowledge of finiteness, which tends to confirm similar arguments based on children's use of inflectional morphology and verb placement discussed in Chapter 2. In other words, functional categories, at least Infl, are present very early in underlying child grammars.

Some findings can be seen as confirming the Truncation hypothesis, according to which functional categories are not systematically projected. In particular, the fact that subject clitics do not appear in RIs, but object clitics do, tends to support the Truncation analysis for RIs. A structure truncated below TP would include AgrOP (AgrOP > VP) but not AgrSP (AgrSP > TP). Under the assumption that object clitics are in AgrO and subject clitics in AgrS in French, then the Truncation analysis explains why object clitics, but not subject clitics may be found in child French RIs.[88] As appealing as this interpretation may be, it cannot be the whole story of the acquisition of subject and object clitics, however, since it says nothing about why the number of object clitics in RIs is so low (only four in Augustin's data, among which two instances of the same sequence, *se gratter* 'scratch. INF oneself' during the same interview at 2:9.30), or why subject clitics are acquired so quickly while object clitics appear later and with much lower frequency.

---

87. According to Hulk (1987, 1995), the lower incidence of subject NPs may be due to pragmatic reasons related to the realization of the discourse topic. Instead of using NPs, children mark the topic using gestures, eye-movements, and similar cues. In other words, topics are realized non-verbally.

88. Nonfinite object clitics are not observed in all child languages; for example, they are not observed in child Dutch. Cross-linguistic differences of this type may be due to differences in the site of cliticization of the pronoun: AgrO in French, as suggested here, and AgrS in Dutch (Haegeman 1995). If RIs are truncated structures, then they do not include AgrS, which would explain the lack of object clitics in child Dutch RIs.

A number of explanations have been put forward to account for the differences in the acquisition of subject and object clitics, based on a wide range of notions including deficiencies in the input, markedness, pragmatic considerations, and computational complexity. I will outline them below. One obvious possibility that is easily discounted is that object pronouns are not very frequent in the input. Analyses of the speech of the adults recorded along with children' spontaneous production data reveal that the incidence of object clitics can be quite high. In Augustin's data, they represent 25% of all clitics used by the adults (Hamann et al. 1996), while Schmitz and Müller (2008) report a 40% production rate based on all the objects used. Another potential explanation for the delayed development of object clitics is that transitive verbs are slow to develop in young children. For example, van der Velde (1999) points out that in Hugo's data only five transitive verbs appear prior to the first production of an object clitic. It is only after transitive verbs have become productive, at age 2;1.7, that object clitics are used. This, however, is not systematically reported in all studies on the development of clitics.

Cardinaletti and Starke (1999) appeal to the notion of markedness, whereby non-marked elements or properties are acquired earlier than marked ones. According to their analysis of pronominal elements, subject clitics are less deficient structurally than object clitics (see Section 5.1.2.3). Under this approach, subject clitics are considered to be less marked than their object counterparts (see Hamann et al. 1996), which, it is argued, explains why subject clitics are acquired first. The problem with this account, as argued by Jakubowicz and Rigaut (2000), is that reflexive object clitics seem to be acquired before non-reflexive ones, despite reflexive object clitics having a more deficient structure according to Cardinaletti and Starke's model. Moreover, Schmitz and Müller (2008) observe that object clitics and strong pronouns (in object position) appear at the same time in Grégoire's data (at around age two), as well as in child Italian data. This is not predicted by the analysis proposed by Cardinaletti and Starke since strong pronouns are assumed not to be structurally deficient, and thus they are expected to appear earlier than clitics in language development. Instead, Schmitz and Müller (2008) propose that the internal structure of strong pronouns and subject clitics includes a lexical N-layer which allows them to check off the EPP feature of T. In contrast, the structure of reflexive and accusative clitics lacks this layer; instead, these clitics are assumed to spell out the phi-features of the arguments with which they are coindexed, and are thus argued to project up until a Φ category (see Déchaine & Wiltschko 2002). Under this model, which awaits further research, elements with an internal N-layer are acquired first.

According to the pragmatic factors argument, since VPs introduce new information, the information encoded by the object is more likely to be introduced as a full DP rather than as a clitic (Jakubowicz & Rigaut 2000). Subjects, in contrast, are more likely to express information already known to the listener, so they are prone to appear as clitic pronouns. A problem for this view, however, is that the incidence of object clitics is lower than that of subject clitics in the elicited production based on pictures. In this task, no new information needs to be introduced by the participants with respect to the subject and the object. Recall that children are typically presented with pairs of characters, who are identified, and to whom they need to refer as arguments of a transitive verb (e.g. *Que fait nounours à bébé? Il le peigne* 'What is Teddy Bear doing to Baby? He is combing him'). In other words, use of subject and object clitics is equally required in the responses. Note that no subject/object asymmetry was obtained in the data from the adult controls.

The last account that will be considered here, the Computational Complexity Hypothesis, suggests that the development of object clitics is delayed because of computational difficulties. According to Jakubowicz et al. (1998), clitics are semantically deficient and do not occupy canonical argument positions in French. Concerning semantic deficiency, the authors assume that clitics are unspecified for animacy, given that they do not intrinsically refer to animate or inanimate items (see Section 5.1.1; see also Cardinaletti & Starke 1995). As such, they contrast with nouns, with French strong pronouns like *lui* 'him', and with English pronouns like *he* and *him*. The authors further propose that lexically deficient elements cannot act as canonical arguments and cannot occupy canonical argument positions. They argue that the placement of such deficient elements in a non-canonical argument position creates computational problems for children initially. In the case of subject clitics, the cost of this complexity is balanced by the fact that subjects must be present in all utterances. Moreover, under the assumption that subject clitics are agreement markers, they must be part of the functional skeleton of the sentence. Thus, the acquisition of subject clitics should pose little problem to children, which is indeed what is observed. In contrast to subjects, objects are not obligatory. Therefore, the cost of deriving object clitics, leaving the canonical object position empty, is such that they will be omitted. In short, children omit the object rather than fill the object position with a semantically deficient element. One piece of evidence in favour of this approach is that object clitics almost never occur postverbally in child L1 French; once they emerge, they almost always appear in a target-like preverbal position. Moreover, during the null object period, children produce object DPs, namely, elements that are fully specified for animacy. This suggests that the difficulty generated by object clitics is not related to a general problem with objects; rather, it has to do with the fact that object clitics lack descriptive content. To account for the fact that reflexive pronouns are acquired before accusative clitics, Jakubowicz et al. argue that reflexive pronouns are intrinsically specified as [person] and point out that reflexive pronouns always refer to the subject of the clause, which means that their content can easily be recovered. Thus, they come to be used rather rapidly. By comparison, the antecedent of an object clitic cannot be part of the same clause, and it may not even be part of the same sentence. This means that the object clitic may be avoided and a full NP may be used instead, which is exactly what is observed (e.g. *Il peigne Nounours* 'He's combing Teddy' instead of *Il le peigne* 'He's combing him'). Naturally, subject clitics must also be related to a clause-external antecedent, but the computational complexity involved in this operation is compensated for by the fact that they also express finiteness in French. Not only can the computational complexity approach explain the delayed development of object clitics with respect to subject clitics, it also has widespread implications, as it can account for why children produce finite and nonfinite verb forms in early stages, which would stem from the children's incapacity to systematically project full-fledged structures initially (see Chapter 2).

One final account of the delayed development of object clitics in child French, which is also based on computational complexity, rests on the fact that the presence of an object clitic in the sentence implies chain crossing between the chain of the object clitic (assuming a movement account of object clitics (see Belletti 1999)) and that of the subject raised from the specifier of VP to the I-domain (Chillier-Zesiger et al. 2006). This is illustrated in (23):

(23) a. Pierre$_i$ le$_j$ prend [$_{VP}$ t$_i$ V t$_j$]

b. Pierre$_i$ se$_j$ lave [$_{VP}$ t$_j$ V t$_i$]

For Chillier-Zesiger et al. chain crossing is a complex operation which young children cannot perform systematically at first due to reduced computational capacities. In contrast there is no chain crossing with reflexive clitics, assuming that *se* is generated as the external argument of the verb as argued by Chillier et al. (see 23b), which would explain why reflexive clitics seem to be less problematic than non-reflexive object clitics for children. As pointed out by Grüter (2006), however, this account cannot really explain, why it is the object clitic, and not the subject, which is affected by the complexity of chain crossing. In particular, why should there be more object drop than subject drop in this case?

In Section 6.2.2.1, which deals with object drop, we will explore other accounts of the late development of object clitics, which are related to Wexler's (1998) UCC and Müller and Hulk's (2001) Minimal Grammar accounts. It will be shown that these approaches have difficulties meeting some of the predictions that they make.

6.2 Null arguments in child L1 French

Children learning L1 French go through a period during which they produce main declaratives without a subject and transitive verbs without an overt object. Although the phenomenon of argument drop does not occur across the board (for example, null subjects are rarely found in wh-questions), it is nevertheless reported by researchers despite the fact that French is not considered a null subject or a null object language.

6.2.1 Null subjects in child L1 French

French generally requires the presence of an overt subject, contrary to null subject languages such as Italian and Spanish. According to linguistic theory, null elements must be properly licensed and identified. It is generally accepted that null (lexical) subjects, called *pro*, appear in the specifier of IP in such languages and are licensed and identified by a strong Infl head. In French, however, Infl is not assumed to be strong enough for the licensing and identification of *pro*.[89] Indeed, the inflectional paradigm in French is rather poor, compared to the richness of verbal inflection in Spanish and Italian. Hence, an overt subject must be produced. However, early utterances produced by monolingual children sometimes contain no lexical subject and no clitic subject, which is ungrammatical in mature French.

6.2.1.1 *The findings*

Subject drop in child L1 French happens in both finite and nonfinite clauses, as in (24) and (25) (examples from Pierce 1992).

(24) a. Va chercher l' auto. (Nathalie, 2;2;2)
go.FIN look+for.INF the car

b. Veut lait. (Daniel, 1;11;1)
want.FIN milk

c. Est cassé. (Philippe, 2;1;3)
is broken

d. Est tombé. (Grégoire, 1;10;3)
is fallen

(25) a. Pas manger. (Nathalie, 1;10;2)
not eat.INF

b. Lancer la balle. (Philippe, 2;1;3)
throw.INF the ball

c. Enlever papier. (Daniel, 1;9;3)
remove.INF paper

d. Regarder Adrien (Grégoire, 1;11;3)
watch.INF Adrien

Subjectless utterances are found early in child French and persist for quite a while. In general, null subjects represent between 30% and 50% of the total number of subjects appearing with a finite or nonfinite verb, with peaks at 60% and 70% (see Table 8). This is comparable to the incidence of null subjects in child Dutch, English, and German, but it is much lower than what is reported for child Italian, where the mean of subject drop can be as high as 70% (Valian 1990). Nonetheless, the ratio of

89. As seen in Section 5.1.2.2, under the view that clitic subjects are agreement markers, French is considered a *pro*-drop (null subject) language. However, this does not bear on the issues discussed in the present section.

null subjects, including in finite declaratives, can be very high in the earliest stages of L1 French. Van der Velde (1999) reports ratios of 90% for null subjects in Hugo's finite roots before the age of two (this was observed in the first two recordings in which 33 and 18 verbal utterances were produced, respectively). This phase is short-lived, however. Subjectless utterances can also persist for a long time, as for Augustin, for example, whose ratio of null subjects was 30% to 40% between ages 2;6.16 and 2;9.2 (it was still 16% in his last sample at age 2;9.30). In fact, Pierce (1992) observes that the period during which null subjects are encountered is longer in child French than in child English.

Cross-sectional data confirm the findings of longitudinal studies, although subject omission can be significantly higher in spontaneous speech than in elicited production (37.9% vs. 17.9% in Jakubowicz et al.' s (1997) study).

Table 8. Null subjects in child L1 French

Child	Age	High rate	Decrease	Lowest rate
Augustin[a]	2;0.2 – 2;9.30	49.5% (2;0.2 – 2;2;4.22)	32.4% (2;6.16 – 2;9.2)	16.2% (2;9.30)
Philippe[a]	2;1.19 – 2;6.20	39.5% (2;1.19 – 2;3.21)	11% (2;6.13 – 2;6.20)	9.9% (2;6.20)
Marie[a]	1;8;2 – 2;3;3	38.7% (1;8.2 – 2;3;3)	–	27.8% (1;10.1)
Nathalie[a]	1;9;3 – 2;3;2	55.8% (1;9;3 – 2;0;1)	34.2% (2;2;2 – 2;3;2)	25.8% (2;3;2)
Jean[a]	1;7.16 – 2;0.28	26% (1;7.16)	11.2% (1;8.24 – 1;10.16)	4.5% (2;0.28)
Daniel[a]	1;8;1 – 1;11;1	71.6% (1;8;1 – 1;9;3)	53.8% (1;10;2)	41.6% (1;11;1)
Hugo[b]	1;8.14 – 2;5.19	62.6% (1;8.14 – 2;1.29)	7.2% (2;2.27 – 2;5.19)	2.7% 2;5.5
Anne[c]	1;10.12 – 3;1.4	38% (1;10.12 – 2;8.3)	–	4.7% (2;8.20 – 3;1.4)
Max[c]	1;9.19 – 2;10.24	51% (1;9.19 – 2;4.18)	–	9.8% (2;5.1 – 2;10.24)
Tom[c]	2;1.11 – 2;10.7	39.4% (2;1.11 – 2;4.9)	–	6.7% (2;5.24 – 2;10.7)

a. from Rasetti (2000)
b. from van der Velde (1999)
c. from De Cat (2002)

Finally, although null subjects appear in both finite and nonfinite declaratives, the incidence of null subjects is higher in RIs (at least 75%), as shown in Table 9. These various results hold for both longitudinal and cross-sectional studies. Note that the data are collapsed over the data collection periods in Table 9. However, the discrepancy between subjectless finite and nonfinite declaratives also obtains when only the null subject stage is considered (see Table 10).

Table 9. Incidence of null subjects in finite and nonfinite declaratives in child L1 French

Children	Age	Subject	+Finite	–Finite	Total
Longitudinal data					
Augustin[a]	2;0.2 – 2;9.30	Overt	428	5	433
		Null	155 (26.8%)	66 (93%)	222 (33.9%)
Philippe[a]	2;1.19 – 2;6.20	Overt	1075	21	1096
		Null	322 (23%)	225 (91.5%)	547 (33.3%)
Marie[a]	1;8;2 – 2;3;3	Overt	406	4	410
		Null	154 (27.5%)	130 (97%)	284 (40.9%)
Nathalie[a]	1;9;3 – 2;3;2	Overt	211	17	228
		Null	92 (30.4%)	52 (75.4%)	144 (38.7%)
Jean[a]	1;7.16 – 2;0.28	Overt	281	0	281
		Null	22 (7.3%)	8 (100%)	30 (9.6%)
Daniel[a]	1;8;1 – 1;11;1	Overt	217	38	255
		Null	191 (46.8%)	189 (83.3%)	380 (59.8%)
Louis[a]	1;9 – 2;4	Overt	658	4	662
		Null	213 (24.5%)	130 (97%)	343 (34.1%)
Hugo[b]	1;8.14 – 2;5.19	Overt	490	1	491
		Null	105 (17.6%)	70 (98.6%)	175 (26.3%)
Anne[c]	1;10.12 – 3;1.4	Overt	2025	8	2033
		Null	430 (17.5%)	133 (94.3%)	563 (21.7%)
Max[c]	1;9.19 – 2;10.24	Overt	1283	1	1284
		Null	208 (13.9%)	165 (99.4%)	373 (22.5%)
Tom[c]	2;1.11 – 2;10.7	Overt	906	0	906
		Null	155 (14.6%)	89 (100%)	244 (21.2%)
Cross-sectional data (Jakubowicz et al. 1998)					
Group 1 (n=5)	2;0.13 - 2;7;3	Overt	122	0	122
		Null	89 (42.2%)	21 (100%)	110 (47.4%)
Group 2 (n=7)	2;3.22 - 2;7	Overt	527	0	527
		Null	38 (6.7%)	14 (100%)	52 (9%)

a. from Rasetti (2000)
b. from van der Velde (1999)
c. From De Cat (2002)

6.2.1.2 *Theoretical accounts*

Several explanations have been proposed to account for the subject-drop phenomenon in early L1 French. First, it might be the case that children consider French a *true* null subject language, on a par with Spanish and Italian. That is, they may assume that subject clitics are not necessary for the identification of *pro*. This idea was proposed by Hyams (1986), who suggested that the null subject parameter has a default [+null subject] setting, which means that all children, regardless of the language they are acquiring, allow subject *pro*. However, there is no evidence for the properties subsumed under the [+pro-drop] parametric value (namely null referential subjects, null expletive subjects, and subject/verb inversion) in child L1 French. Hulk (1987, 1995) examined production data from five children between the ages of two and four. Overall, she found that only about 10% of the subjects were omitted (with a higher incidence for the younger learners). She also reports that expletive subjects are not systematically omitted, as in (26), and that nominal subjects are almost never postposed (in contrast to what we saw in Section 2.3.2).

(26) a. Faut pas arracher les feuilles. (Lucien)
must not tear the pages

b. Il manque ça. (Lucien)
it miss.FIN this

Another argument against the null subject parameter analysis is that null subjects are restricted to root clauses; very few are found in wh-questions (but see below). Reviewing data from Philippe, Grégoire, Daniel, Nathalie, and Augustin, Hamann (2002) reports that in a total of 166 constituent questions, 161 (97%) have an overt subject, as illustrated in (27). Similar tendencies are reported by Roeper and Weissenborn (1990). If null subjects were *pro*, they would be expected to appear in a variety of contexts, including root declaratives, wh-questions, and embedded clauses, as is the case in genuine *pro*-drop languages.[90,91]

(27) a. Où est la main de maman? (Philippe, 2;02.10)
where is the hand o mommy

b. Pourquoi il met du sucre dedans? (Philippe, 2;07.11)
why he put.FIN some sugar inside

90. Incidentally, this disconfirms an explanation for early null subjects in terms of limited processing capacities in the initial stages of acquisition. According to this view, since the subject often carries old information (shared by the listener), the child will delete it in order to focus his/her attention on the rest of the sentence (Bloom 1990). But if indeed subjects are omitted because of limited processing capacities then it remains to be explained why they are only missing in certain contexts (e.g. declaratives) and not in others (e.g. wh-questions).

91. Rasetti (2003) reports that embedded clauses appear in the last recordings of Augustin, Marie, and Louis. The children each produced three null embedded subjects. However, because the number of their embedded clauses is low, the ratio of null subjects appear to be high, especially in Augustin (3/16 =18.8%) and Marie (3/19 = 16.5%). In Louis's data, the ratio is 9.4% (3/32). Conclusions are difficult to draw based on these low figures. It would therefore be useful to obtain more data on the types of subjects in the embedded clauses produced by children learning L1 French.

Phillips (1995) minimizes the significance of the findings regarding the lack of null subjects in wh-questions, given that a large proportion of these interrogatives contain an auxiliary (as in Philippe's data) and that in general auxiliaries do not occur with null subjects in child language (but see below). The same could be said of the copula which occurs frequently in the first wh-questions produced by children (see Section 14.1.1). However, as will be made clear below, the incidence of null subjects in matrix declaratives involving the copula can be quite high in child L1 French (as much as 40%). If null subjects can be found with the copula in matrix clauses, the question of why they do not occur with the copula in wh-questions remains.

Instead of *pro*, Rizzi (1994) proposes that early null subjects in French are null constants (nc), namely non-variable R-expressions with the characteristics ⟨–anaphora⟩, ⟨–pronominal⟩, and ⟨–variable⟩. According to Rizzi, these elements must appear in the specifier of the root (VP in the case of RIs and IP for finite declaratives) where they can be identified by discourse. This would explain why subjectless wh-questions are so rare in child data: null constants are not permitted in such contexts because they do not occupy the specifier of the root (CP), which prevents them from being identified:

(28)

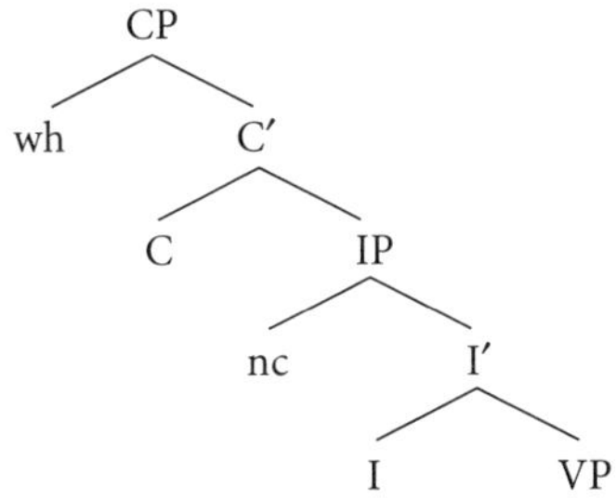

Likewise, once children acquire the fact that declaratives are CPs underlyingly, under Rizzi's analysis, and not IPs, identification of the null constant will be prevented in such utterances. Subjectless finite declaratives will therefore stop being produced at that point.[92] (In the same vein, Roeper and Weissenborn (1990) propose a close connection between the development of CP, and its generalization to declaratives, and the sharp decrease of null subjects.) Indeed, there seems to be a close relationship between the decrease of RIs and that of null subjects in finite declaratives in child L1 French.

92. Rizzi further assumes that null constants are posited in subjectless declaratives found in diary registers and colloquial speech (Haegeman 1990), as in (i). In such utterances, the underlying root is claimed to be IP, and not CP.

(i) __ suis allé à l' église
am gone to the church

This is shown in Table 10. Analysing Marie's data (1;8.26–2;3.3), Rasetti (2000) reports that RIs and finite null subjects drop simultaneously right before age 2;4. A similar trend can be found in the data analysed by De Cat (2002). For instance, in Anne's case, the RI stage is held to end at age 2;8.3, while the incidence of subjectless finite declaratives decreases sharply at age 2;8.20. In Max, the RI stage and the null subject stage end at 2;4.9 and 2;5.24 respectively. Similar findings are reported in L1 Dutch (Hamann & Plunkett 1998).

Table 10. RIs and null subjects in finite declaratives in child L1 French

Child	Age	Phenomenon	High rate	Decrease
Augustin[a]	2;0.2 – 2;9.30	NS in finite roots	38.8% (2;0.2–2;4.22)	18.9% (2;6.16–2;9.30)
		RIs	15.6% (2;0.2–2;4.22)	6.6% (2;6.16–2;9.30)
Philippe[a]	2;1.19 – 2;6.20	NS in finite roots	29.1% (2;1.19–2;3.21)	8.8% (2;6.13–2;6.20)
		RIs	17.4% (2;1.19–2;3.14)	3.5% (2;3.21–2;6;20)
Marie[a]	1;8.26 – 2;3.3	NS in finite roots	11–41% (1;8.26–2;3;3)	
		RIs	6–29% (1;8.26–2;3;3)	
Nathalie[a]	1;9;3 – 2;3;2	NS in finite roots	38.2% (1;9;3–2;2;2)	21.9% (2;3;2)
		RIs	24.3% (1;9;3–2;2;2)	4.5% (2;3;2)
Jean[a]	1;7.16 – 2;0.28	NS in finite roots	12.5% (1;7.16–1;8.24)	3.4% (1;10.16–2;0.28)
		RIs	10.3% (1;7.16)	0% (1;8.24–2;0.28
Hugo[b]	1;8.14 – 2;5.19	NS in finite roots	41.1% (1;8.14–2;3.17)	3.5% (2;4.8–2;5.19)
		RIs	26.7% (1;8.14–2;2.27)	3.1% (2;3.17–2;5.19)

a. from Rasetti (2000)
b. from van der Velde (1999)

In some cases (e.g. Augustin and Nathalie), the rate of null subjects in finite root declaratives remains relatively high (close to 20%). For Rasetti, this is to be expected under the tension created between the Categorial Uniformity Principle and the Structural Economy Principle proposed by Rizzi (2000) for developing child grammars. We saw in Section 2.2.5 that according to Rizzi, early child grammars are constrained by

Structural Economy ('Use the minimum of structure consistent with well-formedness constraints'), whereas mature systems follow Categorial Uniformity ('Assume a unique canonical structural realization for a given semantic type'). Rasetti argues that once Categorial Uniformity arises (roughly by the time children acquire embedded clauses), it is enforced in gradual steps. That is, children do not renounce Structural Economy altogether right away. Rather, they first drop the most economical representations, VP roots, which leaves some tension between the projection of IP roots, the heirs of Structural Economy, and that of CP roots. The projection of IP roots explains the production of subjectless finite declaratives for a while, despite the disappearance of RIs. Null subjects in finite roots cease once Categorial Uniformity becomes fully enforced.

Before moving to the next account of the subject-drop phenomenon (in terms of PRO) in early child French, let us briefly come back to the issue of null subjects in interrogative constructions. It was said earlier that null subjects are quite rare in wh-questions. This is not exactly true. For instance, although they are almost never found in wh-questions where the wh-word has been fronted, they occur in interrogatives introduced by *pourquoi* 'why', as illustrated in (29).

(29) Pourquoi coupe le bois? (Philippe, 2;02.17)
why cut.FIN the wood

Null subjects are also found in wh-questions where the wh-word is in situ, as in *est où?* lit. 'is where?' (Augustin, 2;6.16). This is found in Augustin (23/86) and Marie (2/25) (Hamann 2002), as well as in the finite wh-questions initially produced by Max (2;0.14 – 2;0.28: 13/15) and Anne (1;11.13 – 2;2.20: 18/23) from the York corpus (Plunkett 2004b).[93] Finally, null subjects are reported in yes/no questions (see Crisma 1992; Levow 1995). In Grégoire's data, for example, the incidence of subjectless yes/no questions is 53.3% (16/30). Putting together the results given by Crisma, Levow, and her own research, Hamann reports that null subjects can be found in 32% of such questions. This is illustrated in (30).

(30) a. Veut de la fumée? (Philippe, 2;02.10)
want.FIN some the smoke
b. A des gâteaux au chocolat? (Philippe, 2;01.26)
have.FIN some cakes at+the chocolate

93. At the next stage, Anne is reported to produce null subjects in wh-questions with a preposed wh-phrase. Between the age of 2;2.30 and 2;10.18, Anne uses 159 wh-questions, of which 33 (21%) have a null subject. Unfortunately, no figures are given for the number of subjectless wh-questions displaying a preposed wh-word at that stage. It is only reported that 'Anne had begun to used some moved questions in this second stage' (Plunkett 2004b: 396). This remarks seems to suggest that there were few interrogatives displaying a null subject and a preposed wh-word.

How could we account for these facts? One possibility is that early wh-questions are not instances of CP; rather, they are IPs (Hulk 1995; Pierce 1992). According to this view, wh-words are in SpecIP, and the subject clitic occupies Infl with the verb:[94]

(31)

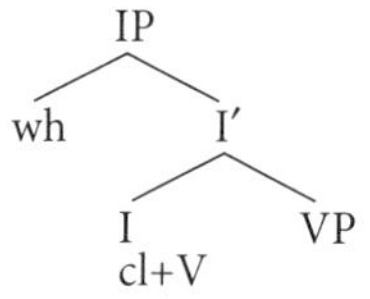

This approach crucially assumes that C and verb movement to C are not available in initial grammars (see Chapter 14). Subjectless interrogatives, as in (30), involve a null clitic under I (see also Ferdinand 1996). According to Hulk (1995), there are few null subjects in child wh-questions because phonological reduction is easier when the word is at the beginning of the utterance. This could explain the higher incidence of subjectless yes/no questions and subjectless wh-questions with the wh-word in situ, but not the fact that null subjects are found with *pourquoi* (see Section 14.1.5 for more discussion).

Another hypothesis put forward in the literature to explain subject drop in child language is that child null subjects are instances of PRO (Sano & Hyams 1994). For these authors, there is no verb movement to Infl in child language because number features are initially underspecified (see Section 2.2.3). According to linguistic theory, PRO must appear in ungoverned positions. Since it is assumed that there is no verb movement initially, the Infl position is empty, which means that SpecIP is ungoverned. This allows PRO to appear there. The problem with this account is that numerous instances of subjectless matrix clauses are found with the copula *être* 'be' and with auxiliaries, namely with elements that occur in Infl and that govern the SpecIP position. For instance, the incidence of null subjects with the copula is around 34% for Augustin (age 2;0–2;10), 19.2% for Nathalie (age 1;9–2;3) and 14% for Daniel (age 1;8–1;11) (see Hamann 2004), and around 15% for Marie (see Rasetti 2003).[95] This is illustrated in (32a). With auxiliaries *avoir* and *être*, the omission rate is between 20% and 40% in the Geneva corpus (Rasetti 2003). There are also examples of null subjects despite the

94. Hulk (1995) observes that the vast majority of Philippe's wh-questions are of the form Wh-word – clitic subject – finite verb (– dislocated NP).

95. Augustin's and Marie's figures are obtained once all the instances of *c'est* 'it is', which could be rote-learned, are removed from the statistics.

occurrence of verb movement, as in (32) (from Hamann 2003), with both lexical and nonlexical verbs.

(32) a. Est pas mort. (Philippe, 2;1.6)
is not dead

b. Trouve pas. (Philippe, 2,2;3)
find.FIN not

Finally, some authors have proposed topic drop to account for null subjects produced by children learning a non–*pro*-drop language (see Bromberg & Wexler 1995; Hyams & Wexler 1993; Wexler 1994). Topic drop is usually found in languages such as German and Chinese. In such languages, subject drop involves a discourse-bound null operator in SpecCP that binds a variable in subject position (Huang 1984). This is illustrated in (33).

(33) a. Question: Was hat dein Vater$_i$ gekauft?
what has your father bought
'What did your father buy?'

b. Answer: [$_{CP}$ OP$_i$ hat [$_{IP}$ t$_i$ ein neues Auto gekauft]].
has a new car bought
'He bought a new car.'

According to Bromberg and Wexler (1995), topic drop applies in finite declaratives, while null subjects of RIs are instances of PRO. Although not originally proposed for French, at first glance, it appears that the topic drop analysis could be a plausible explanation for null subjects in child French. For example, it seems to be supported by the data on wh-questions. Given that an operator must occupy the SpecCP position, the subject cannot be omitted in contexts where that position is not available, namely in wh-questions. We have seen that, indeed, subjects are rarely omitted in such contexts in child L1 French. What the topic drop analysis for finite declaratives fails to explain, however, is why RIs and subjectless finite declaratives are found to decline at the same time in early child French, as seen in Table 10 above. The topic drop account bears no direct relation to Tense. Therefore, there is no obvious reason to expect that the systematic projection of Tense should yield a significant decline of subjectless finite declaratives. Another problem for the topic drop analysis is that children are claimed to detect its presence in the input and to extend it to a wider range of contexts than what is allowed in the adult language. In adult English, topic drop is possible, as in the following exchange (from Bromberg & Wexler 1995: 243):

(34) A : What happened to Mary?
B : __ went away for a while.

This may explain the relatively high ratio of subjectless finite declaratives in child L1 English. However, Rasetti (2003) found only four null subjects in 2150 finite utterances produced by adult French speakers in six of the recording samples that she analysed. This clearly suggests that topic drop is not an option in spoken French, and, therefore, that children do not perform topic drop based on the input when they produce subjectless finite declaratives in French.

6.2.2 Null objects in child L1 French

In French, the object of a transitive verb cannot be easily omitted, but French does license some null objects, specifically, (generic) null objects, as in (35), and discourse-controlled null objects, as in (36). In the latter case, the null object refers to a salient discourse topic, which is either specifically mentioned (and emphasized) in a preceding question or declarative clause, as in (36a), or present physically in the environment, as in (36b). See Cummins and Roberge (2005) for an overview.

(35) Cette musique rend __ heureux. (Rizzi 1986)
this music renders happy
'This music makes one happy'

(36) a. Les couleurs? Oui, j'aime __ beaucoup. (Fónagy 1985)
the colors yes I love much

b. J' abaisse __ ? (referring to curtains) (Fónagy 1985)
I pull+down

Note that the possibility of discourse-controlled null objects is restricted to a limited class of verbs, such as *aimer* 'love', *adorer* 'adore', *connaître* 'know', and *voir* 'see', as in (37b) and (38b). They are much more difficult to obtain with *rencontrer* 'meet' and *porter* 'carry', for example, as in (37b') and (38b'). In those cases, the definite null object must be identified by an object clitic.

(37) a. Jean-Marc, il est vraiment sympa.
Jean-Marc he is really nice

b. Oui, j' aime beaucoup __. b′. Oui, je *(le) rencontre souvent __.
yes I like much yes I (him) meet often

(38) a. Le sac à dos de Luc pèse un tonne le vendredi soir.
the backpack of Luke weighs a ton the Friday evening
(from Tuller 2000)

b. T' as déjà vu __ ? b′. T' *(l') as déjà porté __?
you have ever seen you it have ever carried?

Object omission is reported in the early stages of child French, although the distinction between licit and illicit omission is not always clearly made (and sometimes hard to establish).

6.2.2.1 *The findings*

Studies focusing on illicit omission in longitudinal spontaneous production report mean rates below 30% (see Table 11).[96] Note that the ratios displayed in Table 11 are calculated on the basis of finite and nonfinite clauses.

Table 11. Incidence of illicit object drop in L1 child French

Child	Age	Mean	Higher rate of omission	Lower rate of omission
Augustin[a]	2;0.2 – 2;9.30	16.7%	27% (2;0,2 – 2;4.1)	9.5% (2;4.22 – 2;9.30)
Marie[a]	1;8.26 – 2;3.3	20.1%	24% (1;8.26 – 2;3.13)	8.4% (2;5.26 – 2;6.10)
Louis[a]	1;9.26 – 2;3.29	27.3%	61.6% (1;9.26 – 2;0.8)	15.3% (2;1.4 – 2;3.29)
Hugo[b]	1;8.14 – 2;5.19	14.3%	30.9% (1;8.14 – 2;1.29)	6.7% (2;2.27 – 2;5.19)
Victor[c]	1;11.10 – 2;5.9	11.8%		
Chloé[c]	1;11.19 – 2;5.14	7.7%		

a. data from Rasetti (2003).

b. data from van der Velde (1999)

c. data from van der Velde (1998)

Although some variation is found across children, the incidence of object omission is globally lower than the incidence of null subjects (compare the third column of Table 11 to the last column of Table 9). In some cases the rate of null objects is twice as low as that of null subjects. This is true of Augustin (16.7% vs. 33.9%), Marie (20.1% vs. 40.9%), and Hugo (14.3% vs. 26.3%). These figures are confirmed in cross-sectional studies. For instance, in Jakubowicz et al.' s (1997) cross-sectional data presented above, 11% of objects were dropped by children with an MLU below 3, compared to 35% for subjects. Examples of illicit object drop are given in (39). Sometimes, multiple argument drop can occur, as in (39e).

96. Interestingly, the phenomenon of object drop seems to be strongly restricted to accusative clitics. In sequences involving two object clitics, namely one accusative clitic and one dative clitic, and a finite verb, the tendency is for children to omit the accusative pronoun (as in adult French). It is clear that such sequences represent a double source of difficulty for the learners: not only do they have to place two clitics in non-canonical object positions, they must also acquire the orders in which they can appear. However, the fact that two object clitic sequences are not systematic in production data does not mean that they are not comprehended by the children (Connors & Nuckle 1986).

(39) a. On met__. (Hugo, 1;10.24) (van der Velde 1999)
we put.FIN

b. Maman aide__. (Augustin, 2;0.23) (Rasetti 2003)
mommy help.FIN

c. Je veux__ là-haut. (Marie, 1;9.10) (Rasetti 2003)
I want.FIN over there

d. I(l) brosse__. (Louis, 2;0.8) (Rasetti 2003)
he brush.FIN

e. __ Habille__. (Raphaël, 2;5,17) (Jakubowicz et al. 1997)
dresses

As showed in Table 11, two periods can generally be found in the production of illicit null objects: one during which null objects are quite productive followed by a second period with a much lower incidence rate. Sometimes, the decrease can be quite spectacular, as with Hugo. In his data, the incidence of null objects ranges from 18.2% to 100% between 1;8.14 and 2;1.29 (mean 30.9%), and from 2.9% to 9.9% between 2;2.27 and 2;5.19 (mean 6.7%) (from van der Velde 1999, Table X, p. 112). The moment at which null objects start declining does not always coincide with a drop in null subjects. If we compare Tables 9 and 10, we can see that for Augustin and Hugo, null objects start declining before null subjects do (Augustin: 2;4.22 vs. 2;16.16; Hugo: 2;1.4 vs. 2;4.8), while the reverse order obtains for Marie (2;5.26 vs. 2;3.3).

In general, the incidence of object drop in child French is much lower than in child speech of topic-drop languages such as German. In child German, the rate of object omission is similar to the ratio of null subjects (around 40%). Nonetheless, the rate of object omission in child L1 French can be quite high in elicited production, as high as 50% (Jakubowicz et al. 1997). In Müller, Schmitz, Cantone, and Kupisch (2006) object drop is between 25% and 30% in elicited production data collected from 21 French children (age 2;3–3;1.15) divided into two groups (mean ages 2;8 and 2;11). It is possible that the extent of object omission is underestimated in spontaneous production, given that some verbs can be ambiguous between transitive and nontransitive use. As argued by Pirvulescu (2006), what should be used as a denominator for the calculation of clitic omission in spontaneous production is not the total number of transitive verbs used by the child, but the number of contexts in which a clitic should be obligatorily produced, that is when the referent is the topic of the discussion (see also Pirvulescu & Roberge 2005). This is exactly what happens in (controlled) elicited production, where obligatory clitic contexts are provided. Hence, failure to produce the object clitic is presumably incorrect from the point of view of the adult language. When obligatory clitic contexts are taken into account in spontaneous production, the rate of object omission climbs to between 40% and 100% (Pirvulescu 2006), which is comparable to the findings in elicited production. It is important to note that the children produce lexical objects at the same time as object drop is observed in the data. In other words, children are able to realize objects. This is particularly true in elicited production, where approximately 50% of objects are realized as either object clitics or full NPs.

Pérez-Leroux, Pirvulescu and Roberge (2008) looked at object omission in two different contexts, when the object has a salient (specific) referent in the discourse (*What is X doing to Y?* – the individuated condition) and when the object has no specific referent in the discourse (*What is X doing?* – the generic or nonindividuated condition). In the individuated context, targeted answers should include an object clitic while in the nonindividuated condition, answers may include a lexical DP or appear with a null object. An elicitation task manipulating these two contexts was administered to three groups of French-speaking learners aged three to five and to three groups of age-matched children learning English, a language less permissive than French with respect to object drop. The results are given in Table 12.

Table 12. Incidence of object lexical DPs, object clitics and null objects in Individuated and Nonindividuated conditions (L1 French) (from Pérez-Leroux et al. 2008)

Participants	**Age**	**Individuated**			**Nonindividuated**		
		Lexical	**Clitic**	**Null**	**Lexical**	**Clitic**	**Null**
Group 1 (n=10)	3;0 – 3;10 (M= 3;5.3)	50.7%	13.2%	34.5%	55.8%	0%	33.2%
Group 2 (n=10)	4;1 – 4;8 (M = 4;3.9)	31%	41.7%	25.7%	65%	0%	33.3%
Group 3 (n=9)	5;0 – 5;5 (M = 5;2.8)	29.6%	52.6%	11.5%	66.7%	1.9%	25.9%
Adults (n=12)		18.1%	81.9%	1.4%	72.2%	0%	27.8%

In the individuated condition, the proportion of illicit null objects was high in the three-year olds and four-year olds, and it was higher in the five-year olds than in the adults. Clitic objects appeared in the youngest group and their incidence climbed rapidly to over 40% in the four-year olds. In the oldest children the incidence of clitics did not reach adult level. In the nonindividuated condition, null objects represented one third of the responses given in all groups. Interestingly, clitic objects were almost never produced, which means that children as young as three know that clitic objects are restricted to individuated contexts. The performance of the English-speaking children was globally similar to the French children in the nonindividuated condition: few pronouns and between 25% and 40% object omission (26.4% in the adults). The individuated condition, however, yielded different results in the English learners. In particular, although the ratio of null objects was similar to that of the French children at three years of age (35%), it quickly dropped to less than 10% in the four-year olds. Therefore, it takes the French children longer than the English-speaking children to abandon null objects in such contexts. Note that a 35% object omission rate is much higher than what has been reported in studies investigating the acquisition of object pronouns in English. Hyams and Wexler (1993), for example, found a 9% object omission rate in Adam (2;5–3;0) and 8% in Eve (1;6–2;1) (data from CHILDES). Another difference is observed in the ratio of pronouns in the three-year-old children: it is much higher in English (35%) than in French (13.2%), although later on the two ratios become more similar. In other words, the development of object pronouns is delayed in French with respect to English.

The discussion so far has focused on production data. What about comprehension? In particular, if children omit object complements in production, do they also accept object omission in comprehension? This question is addressed in Grüter (2006) which reports, among other things, on a truth-value task administered to 10 French children aged 3;6 to 4;10 (mean age 4;4). The children were presented with pictures and were asked one question about each picture, to which they were expected to answer yes or no. Four verbs that can be used transitively or intransitively in French were involved in the experiment: *plonger* (trans. 'to plunge', intrans. 'to dive'), *sortir* (trans. 'to move (something) out', intrans. 'to come out'), *monter* (trans. 'to move (something) up', intrans. 'to climb up'), and *descendre* (trans. 'to move (something) down', intrans. 'to climb down'). The pictures contained actions depicting the transitive or intransitive interpretation of each verb (for example, intransitive *monter* was illustrated with a character climbing up a tree and transitive *monter* with a character moving a bag up into a tree house). The corresponding questions were *Est-ce que le garçon monte dans l'arbre?* 'Is the boy climbing up the tree?' (Target: true) and *Est-ce que le garçon le monte dans la maison?* 'Is the boy moving it up into the house?' (Target: true). The transitive interpretation was also associated to a stimulus question with object omission, which is not possible in this context: *Est-ce que le garçon monte __ dans la maison?* 'Is the boy moving __ up into the house?' (Target: false). Grüter also added sentences in which the targeted verbs were included into an embedded clause, as in *Crois-tu que le garçon (le) monte dans la maison?* 'Do you think that the boy is moving (it) up into the house?'. This was to compare acceptance of object omission in simple and complex clauses. The results are reported in Table 13.[97]

Table 13. Acceptance rate of True answers in simple and complex clauses (from Grüter 2006)

Clause types	Intransitive (True)	Transitive with overt object (True)	Transitive with null object (False)
Simple clauses	97.1%	88.9%	14.3%
Complex clauses	100%	87.5%	13.9%

97. Two experiments using the same technique were designed by Grüter (2006). The data reported here come from her Experiment 1. Experiment 2, which slightly differed from Experiment 1 and was administered to other children, yielded similar results.

These results clearly show that children accept null objects to a very low extent in French, although, as seen above, they tend to omit the object in production. However, one of the limitations of Grüter's (2006) results is that the verbs that she used are very infrequent with their transitive interpretation in French. Thus, it is possible that the children have the null object option but that their replies only reflect a strong preference in favour of the intransitive reading. While this may indeed be the case, note that the children accepted the transitive use of these verbs, as attested by the high performance on the transitive in the overt object condition. This acceptance was confirmed by the results of an elicitation task targeting the four verbs in question administered to a subset of six children.

6.2.2.2 *Theoretical accounts*

One explanation for the phenomenon of object drop in child French draws on the difficulty that children seem to have with object clitics. We saw that the emergence of clitic objects is delayed compared to the production of clitic subjects in child French. So, it could be the case that the problems posed by object clitics, in particular the fact that they occur in non-canonical object positions, could explain the recourse to missing objects. That is, object drop is actually 'clitic drop'. As it turns out, there seems to be a correlation between the end of the null object period and the emergence of object clitics. This is particularly visible in Augustin, Louis and Hugo, as shown in Table 14, which collapses data from Tables 4 and 11 above; see also Pirvulescu (2006).

Table 14. The development of object clitics versus the decline of illicit null objects in child L1 French

Child	Age	First object clitic	10% incidence in transitive contexts	Declining incidence of null objects
Marie	1;8.26 – 2;6.10	1;8.26	1;8.26	2;5.26
Louis	1;9.26 – 2;3.29	1;10.19	2;2.17	2;1.4
Augustin	2;0;2 – 2;9;30	2;4.1	2;9.30	2;4.22
Hugo	1;8.14 – 2;5.19	2;1.7	2;2.27	2;2.27

In addition, the incidence of lexical objects remains stable throughout the various data collection periods. In other words, the sudden increase of object clitics does not seem to affect the ratio of lexical objects in any of the children listed in Table 14. In the case of Augustin, for example, we saw that object clitics emerge at 2;4.1 which almost corresponds to the beginning of a strong decline in the incidence of object drop (at 2;4.22). In comparison, the ratio of lexical objects is constantly above 60% throughout the recording period (except at 2;4.22 where it is at 44%), and even during the last recording, at age 2;9.2, it is still at 73.9% (Rasetti 2003). Similar patterns obtain in the other children's data, which suggests that object omission is largely due to the lack of object clitics.

Another possibility is that object omission is related to the early unavailability of the CP layer. We saw above that the end of the null subject period may be related to the emergence of CP. A similar proposal was made by Müller, Crysmann, and Kaiser (1996). Before the CP layer starts developing, null objects are assumed to be an instance of discourse-identified PRO adjoined to IP, as shown in (40a). Once Comp emerges in the representation, it governs the IP-adjoined position, which prevents PRO from being licensed, as in (40b) (see also Jakubowicz et al. 1997; Müller, Hulk & Jakubowicz 1999). Müller and Hulk (2001) suggested that the licensing strategy in (40) corresponds to a property of a Minimal Default Grammar, as originally proposed by Roeper (1999), i.e. a set of default representations determined by UG (see Section 15.2.2 for more detail on such grammars).

(40) a. $[_{IP}$ PRO$_i$ $[_{IP}$ Ivar répare t$_i$]]
Ivar repairs

b. *$[_{CP}$ … $[_{IP}$ PRO$_i$ $[_{IP}$ Ivar répare t$_i$]]

In more recent development, Müller et al. (2006) suggest that early null objects in French are similar to null objects found in Japanese, namely *pro* in object position bound by a based-generated zero topic, as in (41).

(41) $[_{IP}$ $[_{TOP}$ e$_i$] $[_{IP}$ Jean a vu *pro*$_i$]]

In all cases, the prediction is that there should be a simultaneous increase of CP-related structures, such as questions and embedded clauses, and a dramatic decrease of object drop in spontaneous production data. Under the more recent account of object drop in early L1 French, children will need to find out that their language is not a discourse-language like Japanese, and that it involves feature checking in the C-domain (such as the *que/qui* alternation; see Section 13.3).[98] In Jakubowicz et al.' s (1997) cross-sectional study on the acquisition of pronouns, we saw that two groups of children were distinguished, based, among other things, on MLU counts. Crucially, the groups also differed in their usage of CP-related constructions: children in Group 1 (with the higher ratio of object drop in spontaneous and elicited production – 50% in the latter case) did not produce finite subordinate clauses with an overt complementizer. In contrast, each child in Group 2 (for whom object omission was much lower – 14% in the elicited data) did produce at least one. At first sight, then, there seems to be a strong relationship between the production of CP structures and the incidence of object drop. However, it is not clear whether or not CP constructions were productive in Group 2 children. For example, we do not know whether complementizers and wh-words were used.

98. This is not necessarily the case, however. It could be that two different grammars are activated simultaneously for a while by the children (Roeper 1999). Under this approach the so-called Universal Minimal Grammar, which generates constructions such as (40), can co-exist with a language-specific grammar (which includes CP) for a while.

Individual profiles would be particularly informative in this regard, but they were not provided by the researchers. Particularly problematic for the null object account under discussion is that in the Champaud corpus there is a 5-month gap between the emergence of the CP-domain, based on production of wh-questions at age 2;0.5, and the emergence of object clitics at age 2;5.1 (Pirvulescu 2006).

Other researchers have proposed a parallel between the production of root infinitives and clitic omission. One proposal draws on Wexler's (1998) Unique Checking Constraint according to which only one D-feature can be checked in early grammars. In Chapter 1, we saw how the UCC could account for the RI phenomenon. Wexler, Gavarró and Torrens (2004) further claim that the UCC predicts that null objects should occur in the acquisition of languages that display object agreement on the past participle. In French, such agreement obtains when the object precedes the past participle, as in (42).

(42) a. Pierre a pris la tasse.
Peter has taken the+FEM cup
'Peter took the cup.'

b. Pierre l' a prise.
Peter it+FEM has taken.FEM
'Peter took it.'

Following Sportiche (1996), Wexler et al. assume that clitics project their own category, AccV in the case of object clitics, and that the canonical object position is occupied by *pro*. The object *pro* is further assumed to raise to the specifier of AccV to check the definiteness feature of AccV. But before reaching that position, it will stop in the specifier of AgrOP to check another D-feature, this time a Case feature (which triggers agreement with the past participle in AgrO). In other words, *pro* needs to check off two D-features, one in AgrO and one in AccV.

(43)
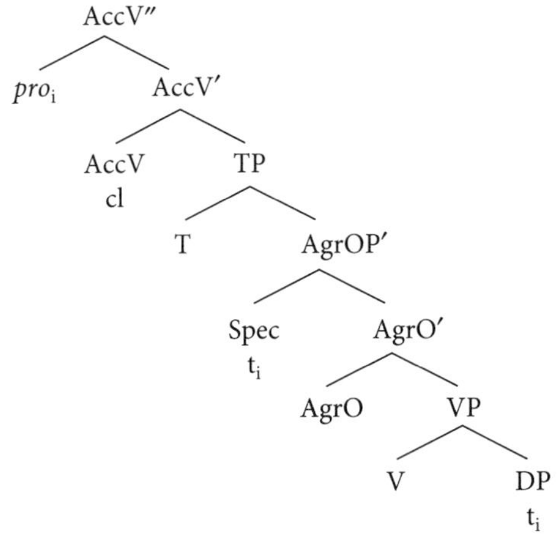

Since initial grammars are held to be subject to the UCC, this double checking cannot take place. In particular, when the D-feature of AgrO is checked, an object clitic cannot be produced. Therefore, object clitic omission will occur until the UCC disappears (via maturation). This predicts that null objects and RIs should stop being produced at the same time. Another prediction is that children should display knowledge of past participle agreement, which results from one checking operation only, during the null object phase.

Preliminary results suggest that there is no parallel development between RIs and object clitics in child French. As shown in Table 15 (which collapses data presented in Tables 4 and 10 above), object clitics may either develop after RIs start declining (as with Augustin), before the decline of RIs (as with Marie), or at the same time (as with Hugo).[99] Note that researchers have just started to look into the developmental relationship between RIs and object drop. More research is needed before firm conclusions can be drawn.

Table 15. The decline of RIs and the development of overt object clitics in child L1 French

Child	**Age**	**RIs**		**Overt object clitics**	
		High rate	**Decrease**	**First object clitic**	**10% incidence in transitive contexts**
Augustin[a]	2;0.2 – 2;9.30	15.6% (2;0.2 – 2;4.22)	6.6% (2;6.16 – 2;9.30)	2;4.1	2;9.30
Marie[a]	1;8.26 – 2;3.3	6–29% (1;8.26 – 2;3;3)		1;8.26	1;8.26
Hugo[b]	1;8.14 – 2;5.19	26.7% (1;8.14 – 2;2.27)	3.1% (2;3.17 – 2;5.19)	2;1.7	2;2.27

a. from Rasetti (2000)
b. from van der Velde (1999)

Finally, Pirvulescu and Belzil (2008) looked at knowledge of past participle agreement in children learning Quebec French, where agreement is optionally realized, especially in informal speech. Results from a preference task reveal that object agreement is selected 30% of the time by three-year olds and four-year olds, versus 43.3% by five-year olds and 60% by adults. Crucially, all groups performed perfectly well on adjective agreement and subject-verb agreement. However, three-year-old children also selected overt past participle agreement with postverbal DPs (e.g. **Le père a ouverte la fenêtre* 'The father has opened.FEM the+FEM window'), which is ungrammatical in French. For Pirvulescu and Belzil, these results are too weak to support the UCC,

99. In Augustin's case, although object clitics emerge roughly at the moment his RIs start to disappear (at age 2;4.1), the incidence of accusative pronouns remains extremely low (one per recording) until age 2;9.2, namely four months later. See also Hamann et al. (2003).

although they clearly show an early sensitivity to past participle agreement at a time when object omission is high in children.

For Pérez-Leroux et al. (2008), all children should go through an initial null object period. According to this account, children start off with a default transitive strategy according to which any V, regardless of whether it is considered to be transitive or unergative, merges with a nominal complement which may be null. Following Hale and Keyser (2002), Pérez-Leroux et al. propose that children assume that this noun enters a 'semantic hyponymic relation with the V root' (Pérez-Leroux et al. 2008: 384), as in (44).

(44)

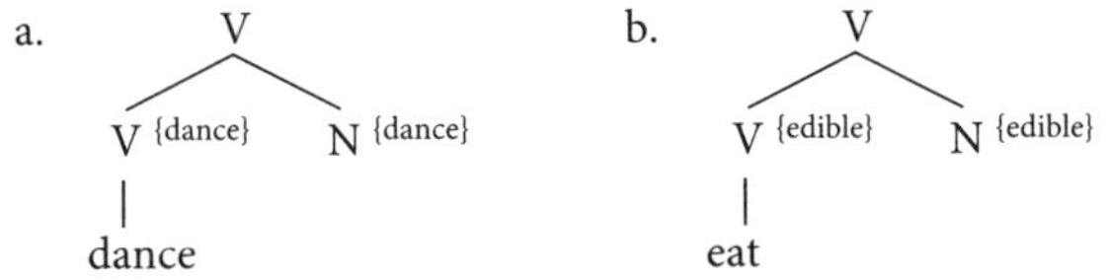

This initially leads to an overextension of generic bare nouns to individuated contexts, which explains the high ratio of object omission reported by Pérez-Leroux et al. in the youngest English children they tested. Such initial null nouns will be gradually replaced by overt elements. In child French, this process will take longer than in child English because there is ample evidence for null objects in the input, so children learning French will retain this possibility longer than child learners of English. This explains why in individuated contexts the ratio of null objects, while similar in the youngest groups of French and English learners investigated by Pérez-Leroux et al. (around 33% at age 3), drops faster in English children (below 10% at age 4) than in the French children (around 25% at age 4) (recall Table 12 and subsequent comments).

If null objects are represented in the grammar, it is predicted that they should not only appear in production, but also that they should be accepted as grammatical options in contexts where an overt object should appear in French. Although few experiments have been conducted on the acceptance of null objects so far, the available data suggest that this prediction is not borne out. In particular, as shown by Grüter (2006), children who accept overt objects with verbs that may be used transitively or intransitively do not accept null objects with the transitive interpretation.

Based on the observation that null objects are largely confined to production, Grüter proposes the Decayed Feature Hypothesis (DFH) which relies on the interaction between the derivation of syntactic representations with the limited Working Memory (WM) capacities of young children (see also Jakubowicz 2005). According to the DFH, children are unable to fully process long distance relations between two elements due to their reduced WM abilities (see also Gibson 1998, 2000 on the notion of distance and processing). The idea is that the features, or some of the features, of an element h1 that should be related to another element h2 may have 'decayed below the required threshold level by the time h2 is merged' into the representation. This will in turn affect the choice of the relevant Vocabulary item to be inserted into the structure. Under the DFH, object omission is explained in the following way. Assuming Sportiche's (1996) account of object clitics according to which an object *pro* must check the uninterpretable specificity feature of the object clitic (in AccV), the interpretable specificity of *pro* is activated when it is merged with the verb. It must then 'wait' until the uninterpretable specificity feature of the head of AccV is part of the representation. Crucially, several Merge operations may take place in between, which may increase the distance between *pro* and AccV to a point where the limited WM capacities of the children do not allow them to maintain the specificity feature of *pro* available. In other words, the feature has decayed. This hypothesis, like Jakubowicz's CCH, is an attempt at characterizing syntactic derivations in young children while taking into account their computational capacity limitations. However, in contrast to the CCH which relies on a precise metric of derivation, the Derivational Complexity Metric (a. Merging α_i n times is less complex than merging α_i (n+1) times; b. Internal Merge of α gives rise to a less complex derivation than Internal Merge of $\alpha + \beta$ (Jakubowicz 2005; see Sections 11.2.2 and 14.1.6 for more detail), the DFH does not offer any clear definition of distance. Under the current version of this hypothesis, it is thus impossible to make predictions as to the exact point at which feature decay will occur. Moreover, we may wonder whether features will all decay at the same time once the threshold limit has been reached, whatever that limit may be, or whether some can sustain different thresholds. Clearly more research is needed in order to make some of the claims of the DFH more precise.

6.3 L1 acquisition of the binding properties of French pronouns

We saw in Chapter 5 that the binding properties of anaphors, pronouns, and full DPs are captured by three principles, namely Principles A, B, and C of the Binding Theory. Studies investigating knowledge of binding principles in child English suggest that anaphors are correctly interpreted before pronouns are (Chien & Wexler 1990). Children as young as four years old correctly treat *herself* as an anaphor in *Mama Bear touches herself*, but fail to interpret *her* as a pronoun in *Mama Bear touches her*; instead, they tend to treat the pronoun as an anaphor, accepting coreference with the subject DP *Mama Bear*. Some scholars have proposed that Principle B emerges later than Principle A, via maturation (Felix 1988). Others argue that all binding principles are available from the outset and that children initially experience difficulties with pragmatics (Chien & Wexler 1990) or with the processing of pronouns (Grodzinsky & Reinhart 1993). Research on the acquisition of French suggests that children have early knowledge of the binding properties of pronominal and nominal elements. Although children may experience difficulties with pronouns at first, this is not necessarily due to the initial unavailability of Principle B.

Jakubowicz (1991) looked at the acquisition of the binding properties of anaphors and pronouns in L1 French by 104 children (aged 3 to 7.5). The children were divided into four groups according to age: Group 1 (3.0–3.5; mean 3.4), Group 2 (3.6–4.0; mean 3.9), Group 3 (5.0–6.0; mean 5.8), and Group 4 (6.1–7.5; mean 6.11). The children were administered a picture matching task with four sentences with the anaphor *se* and four sentences with the pronouns *le* and *la*, and an elicited production task where the experimenter asked 16 questions about particular pictures depicting reflexive or nonreflexive scenes (see Jakubowicz & Rigaut 2000). Overall, the children performed better with anaphors than with pronouns. In the picture matching task, almost all sentences including an anaphor were correctly interpreted by all groups (90% and higher). In contrast, some interpretation errors occurred with sentences including a pronoun. Accuracy in the interpretation of pronouns was around 60% in Group 1, which was significantly lower than for anaphors ($p < .0005$). The frequency and the nature of the errors were also found to change with age. In Group 1, errors were binding errors, but they concerned only nine children out of 26. In all other groups, errors did not involve binding. Rather, children in those groups often switched the subject and the object, which led them to point to the wrong picture. Crucially, the picture selected was not the one depicting a reflexive scene, which suggests that the children rightfully considered pronouns to be free. Jakubowicz also reports a significant difference between Group 1 and Group 2 in the accuracy of interpretation of pronouns, but not between Group 2, Group 3, and Group 4. She suggests that a change in linguistic behavior in the interpretation of pronouns occurs between ages 3;4 and 3;9.

In the elicited production task, there were few errors in the reflexive condition. That is, there were very few answers where a non-reflexive pronoun was used instead of the reflexive *se* (e.g. *elle lave elle* lit. 'she washes her'). In contrast, many errors occurred with pronouns in the non-reflexive condition. Most errors (close to 50% of errors in Groups 2 and 3) concerned erroneous gender (as in (45)) or the use of incorrect Case (as in (46)).[100] This was observed in the first three groups.

(45) a. Elle la [target: le] coiffe. (Barbie brushes Little bear's hair) (age 3;0)
she her brushes

b. Elle le [target: la] brosse. (Kiki brushes Little bear's hair) (age 3;0)
she him brushes

(46) a. Elle le brosse ses cheveux (Little bear brushes Kiki's hair) (age 3;4)
she him brushes her hair

b. Il lui brosse Kiki (Little bear brushes Kiki's hair) (age 3;3)
he to+him brushes K.

100. It should be pointed out that in Group 3 (n = 18), the vast majority of errors (11/16) were due to two children, and gender errors were only observed when the pictures showed two characters of different genders, for 12 children. This suggests that these children had knowledge of gender.

Other errors, observed in Groups 1 and 2 only, involved the use of an anaphor for a pronoun, as in (47), and accounted for 34.4% of the errors in Group 1 and 21.3% in Group 2.

(47) a. Il se coiffe Schtroumpfette. (Kiki brushes Schtroumpfette's hair)
he himself brushes S. (age 3;2)

b. Elle se coiffe lui. (Barbie brushes Little bear's hair) (age 3;2)
she herself brush him

This study suggests that the trouble that monolinguals experience with pronouns is not always related to binding. Rather, the errors they commit often pertain to Case and gender. In other words, problems may arise due to inadequate lexical acquisition rather than to the unavailability of grammatical principles. Even cases of overgeneralization of *se* instead of a pronoun do not necessarily indicate that Principle B is initially inoperational. First, not all children who made such errors in the elicited production task made errors in the picture matching task. Second, most of the overgeneralization errors involved the production of the lexical object, as in (47) above. Jakubowicz argues that in such cases, the production of *se* stems from an incomplete acquisition of the paradigm of pronominal forms. In other words, children know that they can use a pronoun in their answer, but they do not yet know which one (decisions about gender, number, and Case must be made). Since they already have command of reflexives, they use an anaphor. But, Jakubowicz pursues, they know that this answer is somehow insufficient, which is why they produce the object afterwards.

Another argument against the unavailability of Principle B is that if the errors reported in the first two groups were due to late maturation of this principle, we would expect maturation to take place at around the same age cross-linguistically. However, in child English and child Dutch, errors with pronouns occur until age 6 (Jakubowicz 1994). In contrast, the study described here reports errors only until age 3;9. In addition, the unavailability of Principle B would predict that children should make binding errors with both subject and object pronouns, which is not the case. In a study on 80 children aged 3;1 to 5;0, Jakubowicz (1991) reports a significant difference between errors with subject and object pronouns in an act-out task ($p < .01$). The interpretation of subject pronouns was almost always correct at all ages, whereas accuracy on object pronouns was around 60% at age 3;1–3;6, and around 80% for the rest of the children.

Hamann, Kowalski and Philip (1997) administered a truth-value judgment task based on pictures to 33 children aged 4 to 7 years. The task involved two experimenters and a series of pictures depicting characters in a variety of actions. One experimenter was sitting with the child, and both could see the pictures. The other experimenter, who could not see the pictures, had to guess what was going on in the pictures. The child's job was to decide whether the second experimenter's guess was correct or not. Take the example of a picture showing an old woman sitting on a chair and a little girl scratching her own head. The first experimenter would first tell the 'guesser' about the characters depicted in the picture (*une grand-mère et une petite fille* 'a grandmother and a little girl'), the guesser would then repeat the clues out loud, pretending to be involved in deep thinking (*euh.. une grand-mère et une petite fille*) and would then come up with the guess, in the form of a question (e.g. *Est-ce que la petite fille la touche?* 'Is the girl touching her?'). The child's answer was then recorded. Input questions to the child included the anaphor *se* or the pronoun *la*. Three types of sentences where used: sentences including a non-quantified subject antecedent as in the example above (LA and SE sentences), sentences including a quantified subject antecedent, as in *Est-ce que chaque maman la sèche*? 'Is every mom drying her off?' (QLA and QSE sentences), and sentences with a finite verb followed by an infinitive complement, where clitic climbing can occur, as in *Est-ce que la fille la voit faire des bulles?* 'Does the girl see her blow bubbles?' (VLA and VSE sentences). The answers provided by the children on *la*- and *se*-sentences are summarized in Tables 16 and 17, respectively.

Table 16. Percentage of accurate 'yes' and 'no' responses on *la*-sentences (from Hamann et al. 1997)

Group	LA		QLA		VLA	
	Yes	No	Yes	No	Yes	No
4 yrs (3;5–4;8) (n=9)	82%	78%	89%	70%	70%	48%
5 yrs (5;3–5;11) (n=8)	100%	100%	100%	88%	63%	54%
6–7 yrs (6;0–7;3) (n=16)	100%	100%	98%	94%	94%	62%

As showed in Table 16, accuracy was generally high in all groups, including the youngest children, on LA and QLA sentences. The fact that accuracy on questions requiring a 'no' answer in the LA and QLA conditions was lower than their 'yes' counterparts may be explained by a general tendency to reply 'yes' on the part of the children. Results for LA and QLA guesses suggest that children had early knowledge of the binding properties of pronouns. Accuracy was lowest on VLA guesses, especially on questions requiring a negative answer. For these VLA-'no' sentences, accuracy was significantly lower than for all other conditions requiring 'no', in each group.

Table 17. Percentage of accurate 'yes' and 'no' responses on *se*-sentences (from Hamann et al. 1997)

Group	SE		QSE		VSE	
	Yes	No	Yes	No	Yes	No
4 yrs (3;5–4;8) (n=9)	96%	74%	85%	74%	93%	70%
5 yrs (5;3–5;11) (n=8)	100%	96%	96%	92%	96%	92%
6–7 yrs (6;0–7;3) (n=16)	96%	100%	96%	85%	100%	96%

With respect to *se*-sentences (Table 17), accuracy was high overall, although performance on wrong guesses was lower, which may reflect a tendency to reply 'yes' to the questions asked by the experimenter, as seen above. Interestingly, accuracy was very high on VSE sentences, including the ones where 'no' was the targeted answer. In contrast to what was observed with the pronoun *la*, there was no statistically significant difference between VSE sentences and SE and QSE guesses requiring 'no', in any group.

The three experiments reported so far suggest that children learning French have early knowledge of the binding properties of anaphor and pronouns. This is in contrast to children learning English and Dutch, for whom the binding properties of pronouns are slow to emerge. For instance, accuracy in dissociating reference between a pronoun and a non-quantified subject is at chance level for children learning English (Chien & Wexler 1990) and below chance for children learning Dutch (Philip & Coopmans 1996), compared to around 80% for French-speaking children reported by Hamann et al. (1997) (Table 16). The difference may ultimately boil down to the nature of object pronouns in the different languages involved: they are clitics in French and strong pronouns in English and Dutch.[101] Hamann (2002), for example, has suggested that it is much easier to obtain 'accidental coreference', namely pragmatically determined coreference between a pronoun and a clausemate antecedent, when the pronoun is strong, as in (48a), than when it is a clitic, as illustrated in (48b).

(48) a. If everyone hates Oscar, then Oscar$_i$ hates him$_i$.
b. Si tout le monde déteste Oscar, alors Oscar$_i$ *le$_i$ déteste.

Following Cardinaletti and Starke (1999), Hamann assumes that clitics (and weak pronouns) are deficient with respect to reference. Recall from Section 5.1.2.3 that according to Cardinaletti and Starke, only strong pronouns include a C_LP layer, whose head contains referential features. Weak pronouns and clitics therefore crucially rely on the context to be identified. As a result, the antecedent will often be provided in the discourse preceding the clause in which the pronoun occurs. This means that a (potential) referent is very likely to have been assigned to the clitic before the subject of the clause in which the clitic occurs is produced. As a result, accidental coreference is very rare with clitics in French. In English, object pronouns are ambiguous between being weak and being strong. This leads children to accept (accidental) coreference between the subject DP and the object pronoun more frequently, as in *Mama Bear$_i$ touches her$_i$*.[102]

101. Acquisition of the binding properties of object pronouns in child Spanish appears similar to what has been reported in child French (Baauw 2000). Spanish, just like French, has object clitics.

102. Performance of English-speaking and Dutch-speaking children is reported to be adult-like on object pronouns when the subject is quantified. This is presumably due to the fact that quantification does not allow accidental coreference.

In contrast, French object pronouns are clear cases of clitics, which children come to know very quickly, namely from the moment they start using them (see Section 6.1.2). This automatically prevents an accidental coreference scenario and in turn explains children's adult-like performance on the binding properties of pronouns. Now, if this is on the right track, something needs to be said about the poor performance on sentences involving clitic climbing (*La petite fille la voit danser*) reported by Hamann et al. (1997). In these sentences, Hamann (2002) proposes that accidental coreference may occur because an extra potential referent is introduced, in the form of the entity performing the action of the lower verb. The child may therefore associate the pronoun to that referent, which turns out to be the same referent as the main subject.

Research on Principle C, according to which free expressions cannot be bound, also confirms early knowledge of binding principles in French. In a study reported in Goodluck and Solan (2000), an act-out task and a grammaticality judgment task (with dolls) were administered to 40 children, 20 aged 3 to 5 and 20 aged 6 to 7, and to 20 adults. In the act-out task, there were four biclausal sentences involving a pronoun in the matrix clause and a subject DP in the lower clause. Knowledge of coreference between the pronoun (subject or object) and the subject of the embedded clause (adjoined or argument) was investigated. Examples are given in (49). Only in (49d) can there be coindexation between the pronoun and the embedded subject. In such constructions, the object pronoun of the main clause does not c-command the embedded subject, so co-reference can obtain. In the other examples in (49), there is a c-command relationship between the higher pronoun and the embedded subject, which means that co-reference between the two would result in the embedded subject being bound (by the pronoun), in violation of Principle C. Two tokens of each sentence type were presented to the children, four in the case of the adults.

(49) a. Il$_{*i}$ dit au cheval que le zèbre$_i$ mange.
he says to+the horse that the zebra eats
'He says to the horse that the zebra eats'
(subject pronoun and complement)

b. Le cheval lui$_{*i}$ dit que le zèbre$_i$ mange.
the horse to+him says that the zebra eats
'The horse tells him that the zebra eats'
(object pronoun and complement)

c. Il$_{*i}$ touche le cheval avant que le zèbre$_i$ mange.
he touches the horse before that the zebra eats
'He touches the horse before the zebra eats'
(subject pronoun and adjunct)

d. Le cheval le$_i$ touche avant que le zèbre$_i$ mange.
the horse him touches before that the zebra eats
'The horse touches him before the zebra eats'

(object pronoun and adjunct)

Children were provided with several props, including a zebra and a horse, and were asked to act out the sentence. For each sentence, the experimenter recorded which prop was used as a reference for the pronoun. If children had early knowledge of Principle C, it was predicted that they should not use the zebra prop for *il* and *lui* in 49(a–c), and that they could use it in (49d), which would indicate a coreference reading with the embedded subject. Results show that for all participants, coreference was most accepted for (49d). Reference to an antecedent outside of the sentence, namely neither the zebra nor the horse, which is possible in all four types, was preferred for (49a), (49b), and (49c), but not for (49d). In (49d), coreference within the sentence was chosen more often by all groups. It is also worth mentioning that young children provided more incorrect act outs (or no act out at all) for sentences (49a), (49b) and(49c) than for sentence (49d), which suggests that they acknowledged the ungrammatical status of the first three utterances. The younger children also tended to chose an inside antecedent more often than any other group, even for (49a), (49b) and (49c) sentences, so it might be the case that the faculty for looking for an antecedent outside of the sentence is delayed.

The grammaticality judgment task was administered to eight adults and the older children (three of them were later excluded after an initial training phase). In this task, an experimenter first performed a scene with dolls, which was set up to establish coreference or disjoint reference between the matrix pronoun and the embedded subject. The experimenter then pretended that another doll produced a sentence which was supposed to describe the scene. The sentence was either correct, as in (49d), or incorrect, as in (49c). While the adults performed perfectly, the children accepted coreference in sentences such as (49c). They also accepted it in (49d). Goodluck and Solan suggest that the results on the (49c) sentences may be due to the fact that the context in which the sentences were presented was not rich enough. For this kind of task, the authors recommend against the use of isolated sentences (see also McDaniel, McKee & Smith Cairns 1996).

To summarize, French-speaking children's performance on a variety of tasks targeting binding theory, such as picture identification, elicited production, grammaticality judgments and act-outs, suggests early knowledge of binding principles. Errors that are recorded on pronouns in the youngest children are not due to problems with binding per se, but with other properties, such as gender and Case, and with difficulties mastering the pronominal paradigm. The nature of pronominal elements could also explain the good performance displayed by French-speaking children on object pronouns. Since they are clitics, children would be less prone to a binding relationship with the subject than if they were strong or weak, as observed in the delayed development of binding properties of object pronouns in children learning languages such as Dutch and English.

6.4 Conclusion

This chapter has addressed the development of pronominal elements in L1 French. We saw that subject clitics emerge early and become productive very quickly in child speech, and that they are generally accurately placed. In other words, the distinction between clitics and strong pronouns is made very early. This suggests that the Infl category is available from the outset, whether or not subject clitics are considered agreement markers in French. The fact that subject clitics almost never appear with nonfinite verbs suggests that nonfinite verbs are truly considered nonfinite, which in turn is compatible with a Truncation analysis of root infinitives (see Section 2.2.5). Object clitics are delayed with respect to nominative clitics. Moreover, object clitics take time to develop, although little is known about what happens beyond the age of four, an unfortunate lack. Reflexive pronouns develop before their non-reflexive counterparts, as shown by elicited production and comprehension data. The difference between the emergence of nominative and accusative clitics has been explained by a number of analyses, including those relying on the internal structure of pronominal elements (Hamann et al. 1996; Schmitz & Müller 2008) and computational complexity, either via chain crossing (Chillier-Zesiger et al. 2006) or the merging of deficient elements in nonargument positions (Jakubowicz et al. 1998). Accounts based on computational limitations of children, especially Jakubowicz's Computational Complexity Hypothesis, seem the most promising, as they can account for more data, including the development of reflexive pronouns.

Children are also found to produce null subjects and null objects for a while, with both finite and nonfinite verbs, although the incidence of null subjects is higher in RIs than in finite declaratives. Null subjects are also quite rare in wh-questions, although more research is required to understand the development of interrogatives; in particular, research involving elicited production tasks and focusing on the types of verbs that they contain (lexical vs. non-lexical) would be helpful. Finally, null subjects decline at about the same time as RIs. All these facts have been argued to support a Truncation approach to early child grammars, under which Structural Economy is an operating principle from the outset. The issue of object drop is more challenging to investigate because null objects are not impossible in adult French, especially when the referent is obvious in the discourse or the immediate environment. It is therefore difficult to establish whether null objects reported in children's speech are licit or illicit. While early research reported a lower incidence of object drop compared to subject drop, more recent studies taking into account the (il)licit status of null objects found a higher incidence of object omission. Object omission has been accounted for in terms of clitic drop, the initial unavailability of CP, the Unique Checking Constraint, decayed features, or the use of a default transitivity strategy. The findings so far seem to privilege the idea the object omission in production is related to problems with clitics in general, presumably due to computational complexity.

Finally, children demonstrate early knowledge of the binding properties of pronominal and nominal elements, which are captured in terms of Binding Principles A, B, and C. Although more errors are reported with pronouns than with reflexives in experimental settings, these errors rarely involve binding. Instead, they are related to gender or Case, which ultimately point to lexical difficulties. The rapidity with which the binding properties of pronouns are acquired in child French may be due to their status as clitics, in contrast to other languages, such as English and Dutch, in which the full array of binding properties of pronouns take longer to develop.

CHAPTER 7

Subject and object pronouns in French bilingual acquisition and in children with SLI learning French

This chapter deals with the development of French subject and object pronouns in two learning situations: bilingualism and SLI. We will see that the general findings reported for (typically developing) monolinguals obtain in these two contexts as well, although development may be delayed in bilinguals and children with SLI. In particular, the delay in the development of object clitics can be quite significant in children with SLI. We start with acquisition in a bilingual context (Section 7.1) and then discuss acquisition of pronouns in children with SLI (Section 7.2). For each learning setting, the presentation of the findings is divided between overt pronouns and null arguments. Knowledge of binding will only be discussed in the case of children with SLI since it has not been systematically investigated in French bilinguals.

7.1 Subject and object pronouns in French bilingual acquisition

Bilinguals learning French, just like monolinguals, produce both overt and null arguments in the early stages of acquisition, and they do so even when the other language being learned does not allow null subjects and null objects.

7.1.1 Overt pronouns in French bilingual acquisition

In a bilingual setting, the acquisition of French pronouns proceeds in a way similar to acquisition by monolinguals. In particular, subject clitics appear early (with third person singular pronouns occurring first) and object clitics develop later. The only difference is that emergence of clitics, including subject clitics, may be delayed in bilingual children as compared to monolinguals. Note, however, that there can be tremendous variation across children.

7.1.1.1 *Development of subject clitics in French bilingual acquisition*

The first subject clitics are reported in the earliest recordings of bilingual children, but they may be either rote-learned (e.g. *c'* 'this' in *c'est* 'this is') or part of imitations from adult speech. For some children, the first instance of a non-imitated and non-formulaic subject clitic occurs at around age two, which is comparable to observations in acquisition by monolinguals. This is the case, for instance, of the German/French children Caroline, Ivar and Pascal (Kaiser 1994; Köppe 1994), as in (1a–b), and of the Swedish/French child Mimi (1c) (Schlyter 1993). Early use of subject clitics is also reported in English/French children (Paradis & Genesee 1997).

(1) a. Maman elle est là. (Pascal, German/French, 2;1)
mommy she is there

b. (il) dort. (Ivar, German/French, 2;2)
he sleep.FIN

c. Ils sont là. (Mimi, Swedish/French, 2;2)
they are there

Productive use of subject clitics, that is, in combination with different verbs, is attested right from the outset for Caroline and Mimi, and as of 2;3 for Ivar and Pascal, as in (2) (see Table 1).

(2) a. Il promème (=promène). (Pascal, German/French, 2;3)
he walk.FIN

b. (i)l écoute. (Ivar, German/French, 2;3)
he hear.FIN

c. Il a écrit comme ça. (Mimi, Swedish/French, 2;2)
he has written like that

In other children, productive usage of subject clitics is slightly delayed. This is the case of the Swedish/French children Anne and Dany (at 2;6) (Schlyter 2003) and Dutch/French child Anouk (at age 2;7) (Hulk 2000). Prior to using subject clitics, bilingual children mainly resort to full NPs, null subjects and, to a lesser extent, strong pronouns.

Table 1. Emergence of productive use of overt clitic subjects in child bilingual French

Child	Languages	Age	Age of productive use of subject clitics
Caroline[a]	German/French	1;6.26–4;1.06	1;11
Mini[b]	Swedish/French	2;0–3;2	2;0
Ivar[a]	German/French	1;10.12–3;4.23	2;3
Pascal[a]	German/French	1;8.22–3;4.14	2;3
Jean[b]	Swedish/French	2;0–2;11	2;4
Anne[b]	Swedish/French	2;3–3;3	2;6
Dany[b]	Swedish/French	2;2–3;6	2;6
Anouk[c]	Dutch/French	2;3.13–3;10.07	2;7

a. Data from Meisel (1994)
b. Data from Schlyter (2003)
c. Data from (Hulk 2000)

As in acquisition by monolinguals, third person singular clitics are acquired first, as illustrated in Table 2. However, the other clitics appear shortly thereafter, which suggests that the clitic paradigm is mastered rather quickly. Plural pronominal subjects are acquired later.

Table 2. Emergence of subject clitics in child bilingual French

Clitic	Caroline (German/French) 1;6.26–4;1.06	Ivar (German/French) 1;10.12–3;4.23	Pascal (German/French) 1;8.22–3;4.14	Anouk (Dutch/French) 2;3.13–3;10.07
il	1;11	2;3	2;3	2;8.03
elle	1;11	2;3	2;3	–
on	2;0	2;5	2;5	2;6.11
je	2;0	2;5	2;5	2;7.05
tu	2;3	2;5	2;5	–

Subject clitics are reported to appear in clitic-like positions from the moment they start being used. For instance, they almost all appear with finite forms as they are emerging. We saw in Section 3.1 that fewer than 1% of the French RIs produced by three English/French speaking children investigated by Paradis and Genesee (1996) contained a subject, compared to over 50% of their finite declaratives. This is true from the very first recordings, in which the incidence of subject clitics in finite declaratives was 71% for one child (Olivier, age 1;11) and 96% for another (Gene, age 1;11).[103] The incidence of pronominal subjects with finite and nonfinite forms in these children's English, in contrast, was very similar (around 20% in each case). Furthermore, while they mixed English pronouns with finite and nonfinite verbs in French, as shown in (3), they only mixed French (strong) pronouns with uninflected forms in English (4a). No mixing involved a French clitic and an English uninflected form (4b).[104] This strongly suggests that bilingual children acquire the clitic status of French nominative pronouns very quickly, and that they do not treat them as strong pronouns.[105]

---

103. The third child (William) produced no subject clitic together with a finite verb during his first recording (2;2), but 67% of his finite forms had a subject clitic at the second recording (2;10).

104. For more on code-mixing in English/French bilinguals, see Paradis, Nicoladis and Genesee (2000).

105. Note that of the few attested cases of RIs with a clitic subject in bilingual French, some involve *elle* 'she', which is ambiguous between a clitic and a strong subject, as in *Elle sucer la glace* 'She suck.INF the ice-cream' (Anouk 3;13.17) (Hulk 2000).

(3) a. I pousse là. (Gene, English/French, 2;7)
push.FIN there

b. They manger bonbon. (William, English/French, 2;10)
eat.INF candy

(4) a. Moi play this. (William, English/French, 3;3)

b. Je find this (unattested)

Moreover, elision of the clitic in front of a vowel occurs very early, which suggests that these subject pronouns are considered clitics, not XPs, in the early stages of acquisition. Granfeldt and Schlyter (2004) report that Mimi produces 13 cases of elided subject clitics as of age 2;2, as in (5), versus only one non-elided clitic.

(5) J' ai trouvé! (Mimi, Swedish/French, 2;2;2)
I have found

Finally, no clitic subjects are reported in a dislocated or postverbal position, or following a preposition (e.g. *pour il* 'for he'). In such cases, strong pronouns are used instead. In the numerous cases of clitic doubling constructions that are reported, the clitic systematically appears in a position adjacent to the finite verb, as in (6).

(6) a. La grand-mère elle est là. (Pascal, German/French, 2;3)
the+FEM grandmother she is here

b. Ivar, i(l) répare. (Ivar, German/French, 2;5)
Ivar he repair.FIN

c. Il est pas à toi ce camion. (Jean, Swedish/French, 2;6)
it+MASC is not to you this+MASC truck

d. Oui, la place elle est comme ça. (Mimi, Swedish/French, 2;2;2)
yes the+FEM place it+FEM is like that

Interestingly, dislocated NPs start appearing in the German/French data as subject clitics are emerging. In Ivar's data, for example, NPs occupy the subject position, that is, they are found adjacent to the verb. Once clitics start appearing, at 2;3, NP subjects are no longer found in subject position; instead, they appear in a left-dislocated position, as in (6b), and in right-dislocated ones, as in *C'est kaputt nounours* 'It is broken teddy' (Ivar, 2;4). Similar tendencies are found in Pascal's data. The fact that clitics and NPs do not appear in the same positions strongly suggests that the two elements are different in nature in initial grammars and that clitics are interpreted as such as soon as they start being used. Note that this developmental trend does not obtain in these children's German, which suggests that the two languages are distinguished from the outset.

Occasionally children resort to a strong pronoun as the (apparent) subject of a finite verb (see (7)). Strong pronoun subjects otherwise appear with infinitives, as in *Mais toi manger l'autre* 'But you eat.INF the other one' (Anouk, 3;03.17) (Hulk 2000).

(7) a. Moi comprends. (Anouk, Dutch/French, 3;03.17)
me understand.FIN

b. Toi peux avoir un N. (Anouk, Dutch/French, 3;06.25)
you can have a N

It is tempting to analyse utterances such as (7) as cases of left-dislocation, with the strong pronoun occupying a position adjoined to IP or CP and a null subject clitic, as was the case with monolinguals (recall Section 6.1.1.3). However, in the Dutch/French data that she investigated, Hulk observes that dislocations with an overt clitic subjects are quite rare (e.g. *Moi je la croque* 'Me I bite+into it' Anouk 3;03.17). Thus, she claims that the examples in (7) most likely are what they appear to be: strong pronouns in subject position. Yet, no acoustic analysis was carried out to further support this conclusion (see De Cat 2002) (see Section 6.1.1.3).

The emergence of clitic subjects is often compared to the emergence of finite verb forms in an attempt to characterize the development of Infl. In some cases, there is correspondence between the two, as with Ivar (at around age 2;3). In other cases, there is a mismatch, as with Pascal. In his case, the examination of verb forms reveals that Infl seems to be slightly delayed (at age 2;7) compared to the first use of subject clitics (2;3) (Meisel 1994). Recall, however, that determining the age at which Infl develops largely depends on the criteria being adopted by the researcher. In the research involving Ivar and Pascal, the criteria placed on the development of Infl were quite constraining: a range of verb forms or the formal variation of the same verb had to be observed in order to conclude that Infl was present in underlying grammars (see section 3.1.1.3). Under less restrictive criteria, or if subject clitics were also taken into account, Infl might be seen to emerge earlier than originally claimed in the grammars of these bilingual children.

Other researchers are interested in the emergence of clitics because of their relationship to the null subject parameter. Kaiser (1994) for example, assumes that clitics are agreement markers and French is a *pro*-drop language. Under this view, as seen in Section 5.2.2.2, the clitic is held to be a licensor and identifier of subject *pro*. Moreover, subsumed under the positive value of the null subject parameter is subject/verb inversion. The relationship between the development of subject clitics and right-dislocated subjects found in German/French data (as seen above) is interpreted as evidence for the setting of the null subject parameter to the [+null subject] value in French. Indeed, right-dislocated subjects in the bilingual data are interpreted as inversion cases. For Kaiser, then, the emergence of subject clitics shows that the children have set the null subject parameter to the target-value, which is corroborated by the fact that postverbal subjects appear shortly afterwards (see the next section for more discussion).

7.1.1.2 *Development of object clitics in French bilingual acquisition*

Object clitics are delayed with respect to the emergence of subject pronouns in some French bilinguals, as is the case in monolinguals, but for others, subject and object clitics appear at around the same time (Table 3). For instance, Ivar masters subject clitics at age 2;3, but his first object clitics do not emerge before age 3;1, eight months later (*elle se lève* 'she is getting up'). A delay is also mentioned in the case of another German/French bilingual child, Céline, although the exact emergence of her subject clitics remains vague (Müller 2004). A similar situation obtains with Swedish/French children: object clitics are said to emerge 'somewhat later than subject ones', at age 2;6 (Granfeldt & Schlyter 2004: 352). However, we saw that some of these children started using subject clitics a little late as well (recall Table 1).

Table 3. Emergence of subject and object clitics in child bilingual French

Child	Age	Languages	Subject clitics	Object clitics
Ivar	1;10.12–3;4.23	German/French	2;3	3;0
Pascal	1;8.22–3;4.14	German/French	2;3	2;4
Céline	2;0.9–5.0	German/French	2;0 – 3;1	3;4.9
Anouk	2;3.13–3;10.07	Dutch/French	2;7	2;7

In other cases, Pascal and Anouk, for example, there is no delay between the production of subject and object clitics (8).

(8) a. Veux le remè (=remettre). (Pascal, German/French, 2;4)
want it put+back

b. M' aider maman. (Anouk, Dutch/French, 2;7.05)
me help.INF mommy

Regardless of whether there is a delay between the first subject clitics and the first object clitics, the incidence of subject clitics is much higher than that of object clitics. For example, between the ages of 2;07.05 and 3;03.17, Anouk produced only six object clitics (all with a nonfinite verb). In comparison, subject clitics represented close to 30% of her subjects at age 3;01.04. Moreover, the development of the object clitic paradigm tends to take much longer than the nominative pronoun paradigm. For instance, while Pascal has acquired the subject clitics *je* and *tu* by 2;5, he does not master accusative *me* and *te* before the age of 3;2–3;3.

As with subject clitic pronouns, the first object clitics are third person singular (Table 4), a developmental trend that seems to be more firmly established than for monolinguals. The reflexive *se* (see (9)) is also reported to be produced relatively early, as in child monolingual French.[106]

106. Hulk argues that the somewhat delayed emergence of object clitics may be explained by the fact that children initially use few transitive verbs. Moreover, with the few transitive verbs

(9) a. On s' déguise. (Pascal, German/French, 2;4)
one oneself disguise

Finally, plural clitics are acquired last: there are just two instances of *nous* in Pascal's and Ivar's data, and no instances of *vous*.

Table 4. Emergence of object clitics in child bilingual French

Clitics	Ivar[a] (1;10.12–3;4.23)	Pascal[a] (1;8.22–3;4.14)	Céline[b] (2;0.9–5.0)
le(s)/la	3;1	2;4	3;3.12
se	2;11	2;5	3;3.12
me	3;2	3;2	–
te	3;0	3;3	–
lui/leur	–	3;3	–
nous/vous	3.1 (?)	3;3 (?)	–

a. data from Kaiser (1994)
b. data from Müller (2004)

Interestingly, Kaiser (1994) notes that the delay between the acquisition of subject clitics and the acquisition of object clitics in some children parallels what is observed in the acquisition of languages in which subject and object agreement are overtly marked on the verb, such as Basque. In such languages, research has shown that object agreement initially fails to be overtly realized by children, while subject agreement appears early on (Ezeizabarrena 1996). If clitics are agreement markers (see Section 5.1.2.2), their late appearance can be seen as part of a general tendency for object markers to be acquired late. Note that the fact that subject and object clitics frequently appear in addition to a DP from the moment they start being produced may constitute evidence that they are inflectional affixes in early child grammars. Examples of object clitic doubling are given in (10).

(10) a. Je vais les prendre les jaunes. (Pascal, German/French, 2;8)
I go+1SG them take.INF the+PL yellow

b. Moi je le prend(re) le bus. (Ivar, German/French, 3;1)
me I it+MASC take the+MASC bus

Different explanations for the delay in the development of object clitics have been proposed. As mentioned in Section 6.2.2.2, for Müller et al. (1996) the acquisition of object clitics is related to the emergence of the CP layer, which they consider to be unavailable in the early stages of acquisition. In a more recent analysis, Müller and

they do produce, the object may be realized as an NP or *ça* 'this'. Hulk notes that the incidence of object clitics increases as the number of transitive verbs goes up.

Hulk (2001) argue that crosslinguistic influence in bilingual acquisition is likely to occur at the interface between pragmatics and syntax, which involves the C-domain. The authors propose that before the C-domain is in place, children use a universal discourse licensing strategy for dropped constituents, which involves PRO-movement to SpecIP (recall Example (40) in Section 6.2.2.2). According to Müller and Hulk (2001: 2), 'if (the adult) language A [French, in this case] allows more than one grammatical analysis from the child's perspective and language B [Dutch or German, in this case] contains a lot of positive evidence for one of those possible analyses, crosslinguistic influence is probable.' In other words, confronted with the fact that the canonical object position may remain empty in French, German/French and Dutch/French bilingual children adopt the strategy of leaving it empty because they also receive input from the other language they are learning, in which objects are dropped in topic position. Recourse to this strategy becomes impossible once CP develops. This account hence predicts that the sudden emergence of the CP layer should correspond to a dramatic drop in object omission and a dramatic increase in the use of object pronouns. This is indeed observed in Ivar's data. There is no evidence for the CP layer before the age of 3;0 (see Section 15.1). Crucially, object clitics are found to emerge at the same moment, and the incidence of null objects (which is relatively high until age 3;0) drops dramatically after that point. However, this does not obtain for other children, as recent research on English/French bilinguals has shown (Paradis et al. 2003) (see below for discussion).

Paradis et al. (2003) suggest instead that the delay in the use of object clitics may have to do with the specific characteristics of clitics rather than with difficulties with object pronouns in general, or with the absence of the CP layer. Looking at spontaneous production data in French and English, Paradis et al. found that, in both languages, the most frequent object type was object pronouns (clitics in French), at around 80%, but that the incidence of object omission was statistically higher in French than in English. Null objects were in fact the second most frequent object type in French, which was not the case in English. Moreover, when object pronouns were used, they were more frequently correct in English than in French (with respect to number, person, and gender). If CP had emerged in these children, it is difficult to explain why null objects persisted in one language and not in the other. Conversely, if CP had not yet developed, then why were so few null objects observed in English? Interestingly, the bilinguals were not found to differ from age-matched French monolinguals with respect to object clitic use. The fact that English/French bilinguals are reported to experience specific difficulties with object clitics and not with object pronouns in general (as evidenced by their high performance on object pronouns in English) points to computational problems related to object clitics – which do not occur in canonical object position in French, in contrast to English object pronouns (see Jakubowicz et al. 1998) (see also Section 6.1.5).

With respect to clitic placement, some differences arise across children. Whereas no errors are reported in Ivar's and Pascal's data, 10% of Anouk's object clitics are incorrectly placed, even in later recordings (Hulk 2000). In particular, object clitics may appear after the verb, as in (11a–b), before the auxiliary in a complex verbal construction, as in (11c), or between the auxiliary and the past participle, as in (11d). Incorrect placement similar to (11d) is also reported in Swedish/French children, but it is very rare and it occurs in the later recordings examined (Granfeldt & Schlyter 2004).

(11) a. Je prends la. (Anouk, Dutch/French, 3;03.23)
I take.FIN it+FEM

b. Je couper le pas. (Anouk, Dutch/French, 3;04.28)
I cut.INF it+MASC not

c. Tu le vas fermer. (Anouk, Dutch/French, 3;07.29)
you it+MASC go.FIN close.INF

d. Il a le mis à l'envers. (Anouk, Dutch/French, 3;09.01)
he have.FIN it+MASC put inside out

Such errors almost never occur in acquisition by monolinguals, as seen in Section 6.1.2, but they are found in L2 acquisition (see Chapter 8). One potential explanation for these errors is the fact that children may receive contradictory evidence in the input with respect to the position of object clitics. In complex constructions, for instance, object clitics can occur between verb forms, as in *Je vais le manger* lit. 'I will it eat', or in front of the first (auxiliary) verb, as in *Je l'ai mangé* lit. 'I it have eaten'. This explanation is unlikely to be correct, however, since such constructions are also part of the input received by monolinguals and by other bilingual children, but almost no placement errors are found with those children. Alternatively, erroneous object clitic placement may be due to some crosslinguistic influence from Dutch, the other language being learned by Anouk. In this language, object pronouns follow the finite verbs and are considered weak pronouns (e.g. *Ik wil't* 'I want it'). Hulk speculates that Anouk might hesitate in her analysis of object clitics, sometimes treating them as weak pronouns (as in Dutch), and other times considering them clitics (as in French). This pattern is compatible with the idea of bilingual bootstrapping proposed by Gawlitzek-Maiwald and Tracy (1996), according to which a possible pattern is activated in one of the two languages by the input of a superficially similar and frequent pattern in the other language, at a stage where the other language is more developed. However, it should be pointed out that none of the German/French bilingual children is reported to commit placement errors with object clitics, despite the fact that German shares some of the Dutch properties with respect to object pronoun placement. At this point, it is not clear why some children exhibit some initial difficulties with clitic placement. Such errors hover at around 10% and disappear by about age 5.

7.1.2 Null arguments in French bilingual acquisition

7.1.2.1 *Null subjects in French bilingual acquisition*

Like monolinguals, bilingual children drop subjects in the early stages of acquisition, a phenomenon that decreases over time. This obtains in children whose other language is not a null subject language, such as German and Dutch. Incidence of null subjects is relatively similar to what is observed with L1 French children (Table 5).[107]

Table 5. Null subjects in child bilingual French

Child	Languages	High rate	Decrease	Lowest rate
Ivar (2;4–3;5)	German/French	37.9% (2;4–2;8)	11% (2;9)	Below 10% (after 2;9)
Céline (2;0–3;6.12)	German/French	24.4% (2;0–3;1)	Below 10% (3;3.12–3;6.12)	0% (3;4.9–3;4.23)
Anouk[a] (2;3.13–3;10.07)	Dutch/French	38.9% (2;03.13–2;07.05) 57.6% (2;07.28–3;01–04)	13.6% (3;03.17–3;04.28)	2.8% (3;06.25–3;10.07)

a. This was calculated from finite declaratives only

As illustrated in (12) and (13), null subjects are found in both finite and nonfinite declaratives. However, little is known about the relationship between subject drop and finiteness in bilingual acquisition. In acquisition by monolinguals, we saw that the incidence of subject drop was higher in RIs than in finite declaratives. It would be interesting to see whether or not the same trend obtains in bilingual children.

(12) a. Pousse la table. (Anouk, Dutch/French, 2;07.05)
push.FIN the table

b. A pas touvé. (Ivar, German/French, 2;05.07)
have.FIN not found

(13) a. Couper ça. (Anouk, Dutch/French, 2;04.17)
cut.INF that

b. Maintenant faire autre chose. (Anouk, Dutch/French, 2;11.27)
now do.INF something else

There also seems to be a coincidence between the end of RIs and the end of null subjects in finite declaratives in bilingual French, although the findings await further confirmation. In Section 3.1.1.2, we saw that RIs were mainly found until the age of 3;03.17 in Anouk's data. Interestingly, this is also the age at which subjectless finite declaratives are reported to decrease dramatically in her data (Table 5). The same relationship between the end of the RI period and the decrease in the use of null subjects in finite root

107. Note that subjectless utterances are also reported in Swedish/French children (Schlyter 2003).

clauses is also reported in acquisition by monolinguals (recall Section 6.2.1.2). This further confirms that RIs may be of the same nature in both acquisition contexts; presumably, they are instances of truncated structures.

Recent research suggests that convergence to the target system obtains at about the same moment regardless of the dominance status of French with respect to the other language being learned. Müller and Pillunat (2008) looked at subject omission in French in three German/French children, Alexander (2;2.6–3;8.11), Céline (2;0.9–3;7.17), and Caroline (2;8.5–3;7.28). The three children stand in different situations with respect to language dominance: Alexander is relatively balanced, although his MLU is higher in French than in German, Céline is German-dominant, and Caroline is balanced, but with two weak languages (her development is delayed compared to the two other children).[108] Müller and Pillunat (2008) show that the three children omit subjects to different degrees at first, with the highest ratio found in Caroline. Interestingly, while Alexander stops omitting subjects at an earlier age (at around age 3) than Céline and Caroline (at around age 3;8), all three children converge to the target system at the same moment when MLU is taken into account, namely at MLU 3–3.49. The authors argue that MLU, in addition to age, should be taken into account when tracking the development of any linguistic phenomenon.

Although bilingual children produce subjectless declaratives in French, the data examined so far suggest that they do not considered French a null subject language. For instance, the German/French children are found to produce (overt) expletive pronouns, which is incompatible with the [+null subject] setting. As in acquisition by monolinguals, null subjects are likely not instances of *pro* but are some other null element, such as null constants. However, more data must be investigated, such as the incidence of null subjects in CP-clauses, before this statement can be made conclusively. In monolinguals, it was found that null subjects were largely restricted to main declaratives; in comparison, their incidence was very low in wh-questions. It would be interesting to know whether the same obtains in bilingual acquisition. It would also be interesting to collect data from bilingual children learning French and a null-subject language, to see whether this has an impact on the incidence of null subjects in their French.

7.1.2.2 *Null objects in French bilingual acquisition*

In bilingual acquisition, the incidence of null objects in French can be quite high, especially if the other language being acquired is a topic-drop language, such as German

108. Caroline showed characteristics of SLI development, although she had not been diagnosed for language impairment.

or Dutch (see Table 6). It averages around 40% for some children in spontaneous production data. For Ivar, the rate of object omission is 50% between ages 2;5 and 2;8 and as high as 25% at age 2;11 (mean: 39.5%). In Céline's data, the average rate of object drop is 34.4% during her first developmental phase (2;0–3;1), and it remains relatively high until the age of 3;4.23. It is below 20% until 3;5.29 and falls to 0% at 3;6.12. In another German/French bilingual child investigated by Schmitz and Müller (2008), Alexander, object omission is at about 60% at 2;2.6 and it quickly drops to a maximum of 40% afterwards, stabilizing below 10% as of 2;6. In Anouk's data, the incidence of object omission is high until 2;8.22 (on average, 40%), and stays relatively high (around 20%) for most of the rest of the data, namely until the age of 3;10.7 (Müller, Hulk & Jakubowicz 1999).

Table 6. Null objects in child bilingual French

Child	Age	Languages	High rate	Decrease	Lowest rate
Ivar	2;4–3;5	German/French	39.5% (2;4–2;11)	below 10% (3;0–3;5)	0% (3;3–3;5)
Céline	2;0–3;6.12	German/French	34.4% (2;0–3;1)	24.2% (3;3.12–3;5.29)	0% (3;6.12)
Alex.	2;2.6–2;11.20	German/French	About 60% (2;2.6)	15%-35% (2;2.15–2;5.25)	Below 10% (2;6–2;11.20)
Anouk	2;3.13–3;10.07	Dutch/French	40.3% (2;3.13–2;8.22)	17.5% (2;09.17–3;10.07)	7.5% (3;7.9)

In English/French bilinguals, it seems that object omission in French occurs to a lesser extent than in German/French children. Paradis, Crago and Genesee (2005/2006) report that in spontaneous production collected from nine TD English/French bilinguals aged three on average, the rate of object pronouns is higher in the children's English (96.2%) than in their French (77.1%). In French, object omission was identified as the most productive non-clitic option, although no detailed figures are provided. Nevertheless, it would place null object at a maximum of 23.9%, which is lower than the ratios observed in bilingual children who are learning French alongside a topic-drop language.

It is often held that the figures for object omission are higher in bilinguals than in monolinguals (Hulk & Müller 2000: 230). This appears to be true in some cases, as in Jakubowicz et al.'s (1997) cross-sectional study of seven French monolinguals aged 2;0.13–2;7;3 for whom a 12% object omission rate is reported. However, in other cases, object drop can be quite high in monolinguals, especially in the early recordings. As seen in Section 6.2.2.1, the incidence of object omission is between 25% and 40% for Augustin between 2;0,2 and 2;4.1 and still as high as 20% in the last recording at age

2;9.30 (Rasetti 2003). In Hugo, the mean is 31.1% between 1;8.14 and 2;1.29 (range: 17–100%) (van der Velde 1999).

Object omission occurs with a number of verbs, such as *changer* 'change, *faire* 'make', *mettre* 'put', and *prendre* 'take'. These verbs may appear with an object, or without one, during the course of the same interview (14).

(14)	a.	Met __	dedans.			(Ivar, German/French, 2;5;7)
		put.FIN	inside			
	b.	Ça	on	met.		(Ivar, German/French, 2;5;7)
		this	one	put.FIN		

Children may also drop more than one argument, as in (15).

(15)	a.	__	répare __.	(Ivar, German/French, 2;4.9)
			repair.FIN	
	b.	__	allume __	(Anouk, Dutch/French, 2;7.5)
			switch+on.FIN	

Crucially, the children are also able to use multi-argument structures, as illustrated in (16).

(16)	a.	Je	cherche	petit	nounours,	(Anouk, Dutch/French 2;7.28)
		I	look+for.FIN	little	teddy bear	
	b.	Elle	fait	le	bruit.	(Céline, German/French, 2;9.20)
		she	make.FIN/PTP	the	noise	

The decrease in null objects is usually taken to occur later than the decrease in null subjects in bilingual children. Ivar's object omission reaches 10% three months later than subject omission, i.e. 3;2 vs. 2;9. In Anouk's data, the incidence of null subjects is well below 10% as of 3;06.25, while the ratio of null objects remains at around 20% until 3;10,7. However, when MLU is taken into account, there seems to be convergence between subject drop and object drop. In their investigation of three German/French children (see Section 7.1.2.1), Müller and Pillunat (2008) found that object omission stabilizes between 10% and 20% in all three children at MLU 3–3.49. Crucially, this is the same MLU value at which subject drop was found to reach target-like level in French in these children.

In elicitated production, which has not been used widely in research on null objects in bilingual children, the ratio of object omission can be quite high. Pérez-Leroux, Pirvulescu, and Roberge (2009) administered a task similar to the one used by Pérez-Leroux et al. (2008) on monolinguals (for the results, see Table 11 in Section 6.2.2.1) to 21 bilingual children (mean age 3;7.2) and 13 age-matched monolinguals (mean age 3;6.9). The task included two conditions: an individuated condition (*What did X did to Y?*)

which requires production of an object clitic and a nonindividuated condition (*What is X doing?*) in which a lexical object or a null object can be used. The results are summarized in Table 7.

Table 7. Incidence of object lexical DPs, object clitics and null objects in individuated and nonindividuated conditions in French in bilinguals and monolinguals (from Pérez-Leroux et al. 2009)

Children	Age	Individuated			Nonindividuated		
		Lexical	Clitic	Null	Lexical	Clitic	Null
Bilinguals	3;1–4;2 (M=3;7.2)	33.1%	11.1%	50.4%	34.6%	0.2%	53.6%
Monolinguals	3;0–4;1 (M=3;6.9)	47.5%	14%	36.8%	63.5%	0%	28.1%

In the individuated condition, clitic use was the least frequent option (with no difference between the two groups). The ratio of clitic production (10–15%) is similar to that of the three-year-old monolingual children reported by Pérez-Leroux et al. (2008) (recall Table 11, Section 6.2.2.1). With respect to null objects, a difference was observed between the bilingual and monolingual groups: the ratio of object omission was much higher in the bilinguals than in the monolinguals. The same was observed in the nonindividuated condition, where null objects appeared almost twice as much in the bilingual group (53.6%, which is comparable to what obtains in individuated contexts) as in the monolinguals (28.1%). The extent of object drop is similar to what is reported in language combinations where one of the two languages is a topic-drop language. This is surprising, given the fact that null objects are found to decline quickly in English monolinguals (see Pérez-Leroux et al. 2008). As such, it could have been expected that the influence of English may have shortened the period during which French children drop objects in a bilingual setting. Such is not the case however. For Pérez-Leroux et al. (2009), bilinguals can be characterized by a general tendency to drop objects in French in the early phases of acquisition, as shown in Table 7. Children would start off by assuming the default transitive strategy (see Section 6.2.2.2) according to which any V merges with a nominal complement which may be null. This possibility would be entertained longer in a bilingual learning situation than in a monolingual setting due in part to the fact that lexical acquisition takes a long time in bilingual children because less input is available in each language in comparison with a situation where only one language is being acquired. What would be interesting to obtain now is results on null objects in English in English/French bilinguals and compare them with the results on French to see whether or not these children tend to drop object, presumably under the influence of French, for a longer period than their English monolingual peers.

We saw above that the end of the object omission period in Ivar's data happens at around the same time as the emergence of CP-constructions. However, in other children (Anouk and Céline), there is a long period of overlap between CP-clauses and object drop. In these children, there seems to be a transition period characterised by an increase in CP-constructions and a decrease in object omission. For Anouk, this transition period starts at around the time she first begins to use wh-words (2;8.22). At that age, object omission drops from around 40% to 20%. It is impossible to say with certainly that this is truly a temporary period, given that object omission remains at the same level throughout the rest of the data collection period (until 3;3.17). In Céline's data, there is evidence for CP-constructions during her first development phase (between 2;0 and 3;1): she uses *parce que* 'because', *où* 'where', and other wh-words in matrix questions. The incidence of subordinate questions then increases, but the figures remain low throughout. Note that in the last file (3;6.12), there is no object drop but only one CP-construction.

How can the facts from Anouk and Céline be accounted for under Müller et al.' s (1996) model? Perhaps these children assume, based on ample evidence in the input from Dutch and German, that empty categories may be licensed via discourse, and they generalize this possibility to French (see Müller & Hulk 2001). This assumption would cause the children to use the (universal) discourse licensing strategy for dropped constituents, such as the one illustrated in (40) in Section 6.2.2.2, for a longer period of time than the monolinguals. Crucially, the influence from Dutch and German does not seem to be direct, i.e. children do not seem to treat French as a topic drop language. As seen above, there is evidence for multiple argument drop in French, whereas only one topic may be dropped in Dutch or German. Moreover, object drop in the children's data is not restricted to V1 constructions, in contrast to adult German (e.g. *Ivar répare* __ *lit.* 'Ivar repairs __' (Ivar, 2.4.9)), Finally, the possibility of object drop does not seem to be related to the issue of language dominance. Indeed, object omission can be quite high in bilingual children even when German is not the dominant language. Ivar is reported to be a balanced child with respect to French and German, yet his object drop ratio in French is a high 39%. It is even higher than Céline's, for whom German is dominant. Celine's object omission rate is 26.3% between 2;0 and 3;5.29 (40/152). In brief, cross-linguistic influence may obtain regardless of language dominance, in contrast to proposals by Schlyter (1993) and by Hulk (1997) who notes that Anouk's Dutch was more advanced than her French in the period considered.

There seems to be a connection between the end of the null object period and the emergence of object clitics, much like what was reported for French monolinguals (see Table 8, based on data from Tables 3 and 6 above). More data are needed to verify this possibility, though. For example, it would be useful to know the incidence of object NPs, because if null objects are truly instances of null clitics, the rate of object NPs should remain stable throughout the various data collection periods.

Table 8. Object omission vs. emergence of object clitics in child bilingual French

Child	Languages	Object omission			Emergence of object clitics
		High rate	Decrease	Lowest rate	
Ivar (2;4–3;5)	German/French	39.5% (2;4–2;11)	below 10% (3;0–3;5)	0% (3;3–3;5)	3;0
Céline (2;0–3;6.12)	German/French	34.4% (2;0–3;1)	24.2% (3;3.12–3;5.29)	0% (3;6.12)	3;4.9
Anouk (2;3.13–3;10.07)	Dutch/French	40.3% (2;3.13–2;8.22)	17.5% (2;09.17–3;10.07)	7.5% (3;7.9)	2;7

7.1.3 Conclusion

We have seen that subject clitics were generally produced early by bilingual children, although a delayed emergence can sometimes be observed (as with Dutch/French child Anouk). The first subjects clitics are third person singular, as in monolinguals. Moreover, object clitics appear later, and sometimes much later, than nominative pronouns. In general, then, the pattern of development of overt clitics is similar to what is reported in young French monolinguals, modulo occasional delays. Several accounts have been proposed to explain the late development of object clitics, such as the unavailability of C and difficulties posed by object clitics, which can be related to the Computational Complexity Hypothesis proposed by Jakubowicz et al. (1998). Another possibility, yet to be explored, is Wexler's (1998) Unique Checking Constraint: if only one D-feature can be checked in early child grammars, there should be a relationship between the decline of RIs and the development of object clitics in bilingual children.

It has also been reported that clitics frequently appear with a coindexed DP in the speech of bilingual French children, which some researchers take as evidence in favour of an agreement analysis of clitics in the children's grammars. However, figures on clitic doubling are not systematically provided in studies on French bilinguals, so it is difficult to truly evaluate this account. Further investigation of the phenomenon should be undertaken, perhaps incorporating acoustic analyses of the kind performed by De Cat (2002) (see Section 6.1.1.3) to better determine the structure of the clauses in which clitic doubling appears.

We also saw that subject and object pronouns have a clitic status from the moment they are produced. In particular, a difference is clearly made between clitics and strong pronouns in French, and between French clitics and non-clitic pronouns in the other language being learned. The latter finding further suggests that the two languages have two distinct underlying grammars. In some cases, placement of clitics, especially object clitics, is non target-like. However, this seems to be the exception rather than the norm. Moreover, it is not clear that placement errors should be imputed to cross-linguistic influence. Further research should tell us whether or not such placement errors are found in other bilingual children.

As with monolinguals, bilingual children produce null arguments in French even when the other language being learned does not allow them. Not much is known about the nature of null subjects. For instance, we do not yet know whether they should be treated as instances of *pro* or as null constants. The first possibility seems less likely, since overt expletives are reported in bilingual French. Investigation of null subjects in CP-clauses such as wh-questions should be undertaken to settle the issue and draw comparisons with the findings and proposals for monolingual child French. Moreover, the relationship between the RI phenomenon and the incidence of null subjects in finite main declaratives should be investigated in French bilinguals. In monolinguals, we saw strong evidence that these two phenomena are related, and the few observations on this issue in bilinguals point to a similar relationship, but more explicit investigation is required.

The issue of object drop has received considerable attention in the literature on bilingual acquisition. The main finding here is that the incidence of object omission can be higher than in French monolinguals, especially when the other language being learned is a topic-drop language, such as German. Interestingly, high object omission rates are observed regardless of whether the topic-drop language is dominant or not. Cross-linguistic influence seems to be quite restricted as well, that is, although they do drop objects, the children do not consider French a topic-drop language. Null objects have been related to the early unavailability of C and the recourse to a universal strategy (Hulk & Müller 2001; Müller et al. 1996), but this possibility has not been tested in many children. In particular, there is no comparative data from bilingual children learning French along with a non-topic-drop language, such as Italian or Spanish. In monolingual French, we saw that there was a strong relationship between the end of object drop and the emergence of overt object clitics, suggesting that object omission is a case of clitic omission. As mentioned above, this could be due to (computational) problems posed by object clitics. Such an explanation seems plausible in the context of bilingual acquisition as well, but it should be addressed in more detail. It could be the case that cross-linguistic influence reinforces the kind of difficulty that child learners seem to have with these elements. Again, studies of children learning both French and a non-topic-drop language would be useful. According to yet another account of object omission, children's initial grammars include a default transitive strategy, which leads them to use null objects (Pérez-Leroux et al. 2009). This account needs to be further investigated by looking at object omission in the other language being learned, preferably a language where object drop is strongly constrained, such as English.

The final piece of research that seems to be missing in French bilingualism is any systematic investigation of binding. Virtually nothing is known about French bilinguals' knowledge of the binding properties of nominals and pronominals. It would be particularly interesting to consider learning contexts in which the other language being acquired displays binding possibilities different from French, such as Japanese or Chinese. In these languages, an anaphor may be bound by an antecedent located in a higher clause, in contrast to French, so if children learning one of these languages as well as French allow binding of an anaphor across finite clauses in French, it would argue for cross-linguistic influence. Another learning situation worth investigating is English/French bilingualism. We saw that in language acquisition by monolinguals, children learning English have longer-lasting problems with the binding properties of pronouns than children learning French, which may boil down to the nature of pronouns in the two languages, strong pronouns in English and clitics in French. In a bilingual English/French acquisition context the question therefore arises as to whether the acquisition of the binding properties of English pronouns would be sped up due to the acquisition of French or whether the acquisition of the binding properties of French clitics would be slowed down due to the acquisition of English.

7.2 Acquisition of French pronouns by children with SLI

In Section 3.2, we saw that children with SLI experience tremendous difficulty with tense. Here, we will see that they also have problems with overt pronouns, especially object clitics, whose emergence is more delayed than in typically developing children. These problems lead them to produce a high ratio of null objects.

7.2.1 Development of overt pronouns in children with SLI learning French

The development of subject and object pronouns in children with SLI shows similarities and differences with typically developing (TD) children. It is similar in that the incidence of subject clitics is higher than that of object pronouns in spontaneous and elicited production data, with the incidence of reflexive clitics falling somewhere in between. It is different because in general the incidence of clitics is much lower in children with SLI than in age-matched TD children. Another difference between the two groups has to do with the ultimate level of acquisition. While children with SLI eventually manage to master subject clitics and reflexive pronouns, they rarely fully master object clitics. In contrast, TD children eventually acquire all types of pronouns. The difference is sufficiently great that some researchers have proposed that the low incidence of object clitics be used as a clinical marker for SLI in French (Paradis, Crago & Genesee 2003).

Jakubowicz et al. (1998) administered the same elicited production task discussed in Section 2.1.1 to 13 children with SLI (age 5;7–13;0, mean 8;11) and 20 TD children learning L1 French (age 5;6–5;11, mean 5;7). A picture-matching comprehension task, similar to the one described in Section 6.1.3, was also administered, to test the children's knowledge of the binding properties of reflexive and accusative pronouns. Results are summarized in Table 9. The TD children scored very high in both tasks, although their performance was lower for accusative clitics than other pronouns (below 80%) in elicited production. Crucially, there was no difference between comprehension and production. In contrast, the children with SLI showed significant differences between comprehension and production. While their performance on comprehension was comparable to that of TD children, their scores on elicited production were systematically lower. The difference is most spectacular in the case of accusative clitics, for which the children with SLI showed a low 25% production rate. Moreover, the children with SLI performed less well on reflexive clitics than on nominative clitics in the elicited production task, in contrast to the typically developing children. Instead of accusative object clitics, the children with SLI tended to use lexical NPs or null objects (see Section 7.2.2).

Table 9. Production and comprehension of clitics by TD and SLI children learning French (from Jakubowicz et al. 1998)

Clitics	**TD children (n=20) (age 5;6–5;11, mean 5;7)**		**SLI children (n=13) (age 5;7–13;0, mean 8;11)**	
	Elicitation	**Comprehension**	**Elicitation**	**Comprehension**
Nominative clitics	97.8%	–	75.4%	–
Reflexive clitics	95.6%	98.1%	56.7%	86.5%
Accusative clitics	78.7%	85%	25.2%	80.8%

Similar results are reported in spontaneous production obtained from children by Paradis & Crago (2003) and Hamann et al. (2003). Paradis & Crago (2003) looked at the production of object clitics in a group of 10 children with SLI (mean age 7;6) and two groups of TD children, one MLU-matched (mean age 3;3) and the other age matched (mean age 7;3). They found that the incidence of object clitics in direct object pronominalization contexts was slightly above 40% for the children with SLI, compared to over 80% for the MLU-matched TD children and close to 100% for the age-matched TD children. As to Hamann et al.' s (2003) study, one of its interests is that some of the children with SLI who were tested were younger than in the other studies. These young children were grouped together (n=6; age 3;10–5;0), and their performance was compared to a group of older children with SLI (n=5; age 5;7–7;11). As shown in Table 10, the incidence of object clitics did not change much with age, remaining at around 20% in obligatory contexts. The ratio of object clitics with respect to the total number of clitics produced was then computed and compared with the ratio found in adults and in Augustin, a TD developing child (see Hamann et al. 1996) (see Section 6.1.2). The ratio of object clitics is below 10% in the group of young children with SLI, which is comparable to Augustin's object clitic ratio before the age of 2;9. However, while for Augustin the ratio increased with age to an almost adult-like level (at around 20%), it remained below 10% in the older group of children with SLI (see Table 10).

Table 10. Ratio of subject and object clitics in one TD child, in children with SLI learning French, and in French-speaking adults (from Hamann et al. 2003)

	Subject clitics	%	Object clitics	%	Total clitics
Augustin (2;0–2;9)	179	92.7%	14	7.3%	193
Augustin (2;10)	99	81.8%	22	18.2%	121
Adults	2332	76.4%	719	23.6%	3051
SLI (3;10–5;0)	333	91.7%	30	8.3%	363
SLI (5;7–7;11)	681	92.5%	55	7.5%	736

Results of a longitudinal study reported in Jakubowicz (2003) revealed similar trends and also showed that SLI children's production of nominative and reflexive clitics can reach target-like level. However, performance on object clitics lags behind systematically. The same elicited production and comprehension tasks were administered three times, over three to four years, to 12 TD children and 11 children with SLI. At time 1, the mean age of the TD group was 3;3, compared to 6;4 for the SLI group. In the elicited production task, the incidence of subject and reflexive clitics was at ceiling at time 1 for TD children, while the incidence of object clitics hovered around 40% at time 1 and reached ceiling at time 2, at roughly age 4. In contrast, the incidence of clitics including subject pronouns (between 50% and 60%) was much lower for children with SLI at time 1. Reflexive pronouns were at around 20% and accusative clitics were below 10%. At time 2 (mean age 7;8), the incidence of subject clitics was similar to that of TD children, but the ratio of the other pronouns was still low, with accusative clitics at the lowest (slightly above 10%). At time 3 (at roughly age 9), reflexive pronouns were used in a target-like manner, but accusative pronouns, although more productive than at previous stages, were still used as low as 50% of the time.[109] In the comprehension task, TD children performed at high levels on both accusative and reflexive clitics at times 1 and 2, although comprehension of reflexives was higher. At time 3, both types of clitics were understood at ceiling. The children with SLI once again lagged behind the TD children.[110] While comprehension of both categories of clitics was much better

109. Note that one child reached 100% at time 3, and three reached 80%.

110. Similar tendencies were obtained on English/French bilingual children with SLI (mean age of 7;3) when compared to TD bilinguals (mean age 3;3), although the difference was not as dramatic as what is reported in other studies (Paradis et al. 2003). In spontaneous production

than production, it remained lower than for the TD children at times 1 and 2. At time 3, comprehension of the reflexive was similar to the TD children, but comprehension of accusative clitics remained below 80%. Note that there was no difference between comprehension and production for reflexive clitics at times 2 and 3. For accusative clitics, a difference between the two modalities persisted throughout.

These results have interesting theoretical implications. If children with SLI suffer from perceptual difficulties, as argued by Leonard (1989), they should have equal difficulty in perceiving and producing. However, this is clearly not the case: comprehension is much better than production, especially with respect to accusative clitics. The results also go against the idea that children have problems with movement operations (van der Lely 1998). Under a movement approach to accusative and reflexive pronouns, whereby these elements are base-generated within VP and end up in their surface preverbal position via movement, if children with SLI have problems with movement operations, then they should show similar problems with both types of clitics. Moreover, if they are not able to apply movement, one should expect to find errors such as *il lave le* or *il lave se*. However, none of these predictions is borne out in the data. Instead, Jakubowicz (2003) argues that the data support the Computational Complexity Hypothesis (see Section 6.1.5), according to which the placement of semantically deficient elements (such as object clitics) in non-canonical positions creates computational difficulties for children. These problems, which are also claimed to affect TD children, are argued to be more severe in the case of children with SLI. As a result, the development of object clitics is even more delayed than in acquisition under normal conditions.

7.2.2 Null arguments in acquisition of French by children with SLI

Just like TD children, children with SLI produce null subjects and null objects in an early stage of acquisition (with tremendous individual differences). Also as for TD children, the incidence of null arguments decreases with age. In Hamann et al.'s (2003) study of 11 children with SLI (see Section 3.2), the mean of subject omission is 22.5% in the younger children (reaching 70% for two of them), compared to 5.9% for the older ones (see Table 11). The incidence of object drop is slightly below that of overt object pronouns (16.4% vs. 18.2%) in the younger group (close to 50% for one child) and it decreases dramatically in the older group (to around 8%), with only one child displaying an omission rate above 10%. Given that the incidence of object clitics does not otherwise increase much with respect to the younger children with SLI, we are forced to conclude that most objects in Group 2 were lexical NPs.

---

data, the incidence of object clitics was 70% for the SLI group versus over 75% for the TD children, although object omission was more frequent with the children with SLI.

Table 11. Null arguments in TD and SLI children learning French (from Hamann et al. (2003))

Arguments	Overt vs. null	Group 1 (n=6; age 3;10–5;0)	Group 2 (n=5; age 5;7–7;11)
Subjects	subject clitics	333/533 (62.5%)	681/747 (91.2%)
	null subjects	140/533 (22.5%)	44/747 (5.9%)
Objects	object clitics	30/165 (18.2%)	55/242 (22.7%)
	null objects	27/165 (16.4%)	19/242 (7.8%)

These results are similar to what is reported in longitudinal data. In Jakubowicz's (2003) study, object omission in elicited production was observed at times 1 and 2, but not at time 3, where errors consisted solely in the use of NPs instead of object clitics. These are grammatically correct in isolation, but inappropriate in the context of the question-answer design of the task.

Paradis & Crago (2003) report a much higher incidence of null objects in the speech of children with SLI than the two studies reviewed above. We have already seen that the 10 children with SLI recorded by Paradis and Crago produced object clitics in only 40% of direct object pronominalization contexts (see Section 7.2.1). The authors also found that in the vast majority of cases (over 80%), a null object was used instead of an accusative clitic.[111] It could be the case that the children involved in that study were more severely affected than the children examined by Hamann et al. (2003).

There does not seem to be a strong correlation between the end of the RI period and the decline of object drop. The correlation is observable for some children, but not for others. In particular, one child examined in Hamann et al. (2003) produced few RIs (0.3%) but displayed a high ratio of null objects (22.5%). This goes against the UCC account of RIs of Wexler (1998) whereby RIs and null object have a common source, the possibility of checking only one D-feature in early grammars. Moreover, there does not seem to be any developmental link between the decline of RIs and the emergence of object clitics, which should also be related under the UCC approach. Hamann et al. (2003) report that the incidence of object clitics remains low in some children although RIs have phased out of their production data. For the authors, these types of disconnections in SLI suggests that the disappearance of RIs, the decline of null objects, and the emergence of objects clitics may not be related in normal development either.

What remains to be seen is whether there is a connection between the decline of null subjects in finite declaratives and that of RIs, as was discovered in the case of

111. Interestingly, null objects were also the option most often selected by the MLU-matched children, although to a lesser extent (60%). In other words, although the TD children provided object clitics in the target language, when they did not, they strongly tended to opt for a null object instead.

TD children. Another connection should be investigated in SLI children as well, that between the development of CP clauses and the end of the null object period. As previously seen, such a correlation was observed in some TD monolinguals and bilinguals.

7.2.3 Acquisition of the binding properties of French pronominal elements by children with SLI

Binding principles do not seem to be too deeply affected in children with SLI. In elicited production, Jakubowicz et al. (1998) and Jakubowicz (2003) report almost no case of substitution of a non-reflexive accusative clitic for a reflexive clitic, and only infrequent observation of the reverse (a reflexive clitic substituted for a non-reflexive one). These observations match those for TD children (recall Section 6.3). Moreover, although NPs may be used instead of reflexives, they are mostly possessive NPs, as in (17a). Crucially, the children never use an NP which is coreferential with the subject, as (17b), which suggests that they also have knowledge of Principle C.

(17) a. i lave ses dents. (Johan)
he wash.FIN his teeth

b. i lave Kiki. (unattested)
he wash.FIN Kiki

In comprehension, we saw that TD children may experience more (short-time) binding difficulties with pronouns than with anaphors. For SLI children, the difference between the two pronominal elements, with respect to interpretation errors, is minimal. In Jakubowicz et al. (1998), binding errors represent 9.8% of the sentences with a pronoun and 7.1% of sentences with an anaphor. Although these findings should be complemented with more research, they nonetheless suggest that SLI is not a condition affecting the language capacity as a whole. In fact, binding problems have been reported in children with SLI learning other languages, such as English (van der Lely & Stollwerck 1997). It could be the case, as argued in Section 6.3, that the clitic properties of object pronouns in French facilitates the development of binding operations.

7.2.4 Conclusion

We have seen that although there are some similarities between TD and SLI children with respect to the order of acquisition of subject and object clitics, children with SLI seem to have substantial and persistent difficulties with the latter. Instead of object clitics, SLI children tend to use null elements or overt lexical NPs. Their problems do not seem to extend to comprehension, although their comprehension levels lag behind those of TD children, since they display less difficulty comprehending than producing object clitics. Some researchers consider the difficulties with object clitics to be computational in nature since they appear in non-canonical object positions

(Jakubowicz et al. 1998). The fact that comprehension of object clitics is better than their production argues against a perception analysis of the problems suffered by SLI children. Furthermore, the appearance of object clitics in the speech of children with SLI does not seem to be related to the end of the RI period, contrary to the predictions of the UCC hypothesis (Wexler 1998).

Children with SLI produce null arguments, just as TD children do. However, contradictory results are reported with respect to the incidence of null elements, especially null objects. Some studies report a high level of object omission (e.g. Paradis & Crago 2003), while others do not (e.g. Hamann et al. 2003). This difference may have to do with the severity of the children's condition. It may also be related to the way obligatory contexts for overt objects were computed in the various studies. More research is therefore necessary to settle the issue. Note that the low level of null objects reported by Hamann et al. (2003) does not go hand in hand with a low level of RIs, contrary to the predictions of the UCC. In order to better characterize null subjects in the speech of children with SLI learning French, more research is needed into their appearance in CP-clauses, such as wh-questions, and into whether their incidence in finite declaratives drops at the same time as the production of RIs. Investigating these two issues would further help building comparisons with TD children learning French.

Finally, we saw that binding properties do not seem to create problems for children with SLI. However, knowledge of binding has not been extensively addressed in research on children with SLI learning French, at least not in the same way it has been addressed in research on TD French children (recall Section 6.3). A more thorough investigation of the development of knowledge of binding in French children with SLI is therefore warranted.

CHAPTER 8

Subject and object pronouns in L2 French acquisition

As with monolingual and bilingual children, the development of the pronominal system in L2 French involves the production of both overt and null pronouns. However, as we will see below, the properties of these elements in IL grammars, particularly in adult systems, may differ greatly from what we saw was characteristic of acquisition by monolinguals and bilinguals. For example, null subjects in IL adult grammars seem to be greatly influenced by the properties of null subjects in the L1, and overt clitics may appear in contexts from which they are absent in child L1 French. Specifically, subject clitics may be found alongside nonfinite verbs in adult L2 speech, and object clitics may follow the finite verb. There are also important differences between child and adult L2 learners of French, with child L2 development resembling L1 acquisition. However, research involving experimental setups different from simple production tasks reveal that adult IL grammars may attain native-like properties.

8.1 Development of overt pronouns in L2 French

Studies focusing on the L2 acquisition of clitics in French report important differences between child and adult learners that involve the contexts in which clitics are used: while acquisition of clitics by children is quite similar to what is observed in L1 acquisition, for adult learners there is ample evidence of non-target uses. In particular, clitics are often found to occur with infinitival forms, and they can appear in non-clitic positions, such as following the finite verb.

8.1.1 Overt pronouns in child L2 French

In child L2 acquisition, knowledge of clitics has mainly been investigated in spontaneous production data. In general, subject clitics are found quite early in child L2 speech, whereas the emergence of object clitics is delayed. Moreover, the distribution of clitics is largely target-like from the moment they start being used. These general tendencies are comparable to what is reported in acquisition by monolinguals. However, some differences do arise as well (with respect to the order of acquisition of clitics, for example), and there is evidence of L1 influence.

8.1.1.1 *Development of subject clitics in child L2 French*

In her investigation of clitic pronouns in two English-speaking children learning French in Montreal, Greg and Kenny, White (1996) reports that clitic subjects are used as of the earliest interviews. By then, Kenny and Greg were 5;10 and 5;9, and they had been exposed to French for only two months and five months, respectively (see Section 4.1.1.1). Examples are given in (1). Subject clitics are also reported to occur with a variety of verbs early on, as in (2).

(1) a. Je sais pas. (Kenny, L1=English, month 2)[112]
I know.FIN not

b. Moi j' ai deux lapins. (Greg, L1=English, month 5)
me I have+1SG two rabbits

(2) I(l) crie. … I(l) tombe. I(l) pas vient. (Kenny, L1=English, month 4)
he shout.FIN he fall.FIN he not come.FIN

Early use of subject clitics is corroborated by a cross-sectional study of 15 English-speaking children learning French, although the participating children had received at least two years of daily exposure to French before being interviewed (Paradis et al. 1998).

The order of development of pronominal subjects also differs from what is observed in child L1 French. In particular, third person pronoun clitics are not reported to be dominant at first (White 1996). First person singular *je* 'I' is attested from the outset. *Tu* 'you+SG' may also be found early on, but it becomes productive only later, which is also true of *on* 'one'. As in acquisition by monolinguals, plural pronouns such as *vous* 'you+PL' and *nous* 'we' are acquired last.

Distributional evidence of pronominal subjects suggests that they are considered clitics by the learners from the moment they are used. For example, the contiguity between a clitic and the verb is largely respected: almost no element is found to intervene between the clitic and the verb, except another clitic (3a). Such is not the case with strong pronouns, which are often involved in clitic doubling constructions. In that construction, a subject clitic may appear between the pronoun and the verb (3b–c), but not the opposite (3d). Moreover, adverbs may be found between the strong pronoun and the subject clitic (4a), but not between the clitic and the verb (4b).

112. For White, (1a) is unlikely to be an unanalysed form, given that the verb *sais* also appears with a strong pronoun during the same interview (*Moi sais* 'Me know').

(3) a. Je le sais (Kenny, L1=English, month 11)
I it know.FIN

b. Moi j' ai deux lapins (Greg, L1=English, month 5)
me I have+1SG two rabbits

c. Moi je veux pas (Kenny, L1=English, month 3)
me I want.FIN not

d. *Je moi veux pas (unattested)

(4) a. Moi aussi j' ai besoin (Kenny, L1=English, month 27)
me too I have+1SG need

b. *Moi je aussi ai besoin (unattested)

Paradis et al. (1998) also report that their child L2 French learners tended to repeat the subject pronoun in co-ordinated structures as monolingual French children. In particular, no statistically significant difference was found between the learners and a group of five native speakers with respect to subject clitic use in these utterances.

Finally, there is a strong contingency between pronominal forms and finiteness in early child L2 French, similar to what is reported in acquisition by monolinguals. As shown in Table 1 (partly reproducing Table 3 in Section 4.1.1.2), the incidence of strong pronoun subjects is higher in root infinitives and verbless sentences than in finite clauses, as illustrated in (5).

(5) a. Toi animaux. (Kenny, L1=English, month 3)
you animals

b. Moi chercher. (Greg, L1=English, month 5)
me search.INF

In contrast, subject clitics are strongly restricted to finite environments. In all, 98.8% of Kenny's subject clitics appear with a finite verb (840/850); for Greg, the ratio is 99% (1365/1378). Similar ratios are reported by Paradis et al. (1998) and by Belletti and Hamann (2004) on two children (Elisa and Lorenzo) whose L1s are German and Italian, respectively (see Section 4.1.1.2).

Table 1. Incidence of clitic and strong pronoun subjects in finite and nonfinite clauses in child L2 French L1=English) (from White 1996)

Child	Finiteness	Total utterances	Clitic subjects	Strong pronouns
Kenny	+ finite	1132	840 (74.2%)	83 (7.3%)
	– finite	89	10 (11.2%)	53 (59.5%)
Greg	+ finite	1765	1365 (77.3%)	32 (2.3%)
	– finite	67	13 (19.4%)	21 (31.3%)

Note that Belletti and Hamann (2004) also found some cases of subject clitics occurring with nonfinite forms in the data they investigated, as in (6). Similar utterances are found in Kenny's and Greg's speech, mostly in the last recordings.

(6) a. … on faire comme ça. (Elisa, L1=German, month 16)
we do.INF like this

b. Comme je boire. (Elisa, L1=German, month 16)
how I drink.INF

An instance of subject clitic used in a verbless utterance and with stress is also observed in Elisa's data:

(7) mais JE maman (Elisa, L1=German, month 16)
but I mommy

However, the figures are extremely low: there are only seven nonfinite verbs used instead of finite forms in Elisa's corpus (of which two occur in a root declarative), and four in Lorenzo's. Of these eleven cases, four involve a subject clitic. In Kenny's data, seven of the ten nonfinite clitics occur at months 27 and 29, long after the period during which root infinitives are reported to be productively used (Prévost 1997; Prévost & White 2000a). As for the utterance in (7), it is the only such utterance found in Elisa's speech. These findings are therefore best analysed as production errors, or, alternatively, as cases of missing inflection.

8.1.1.2 *Development of object clitics in child L2 French*

As in child L1 French, object clitics emerge later than subject clitics in child L2 acquisition. In Kenny's and Greg's data, they appear at month 11, compared to months 2 and 5 for subject clitics. Productive use of these elements is not observed until much later (month 20 for Greg and month 25 for Kenny). Examples are given in (8).

(8) a. Je le sais. (Kenny, L1=English, month 11)
I it know.FIN

b. On le laisse comme ça. (Greg, L1=English, month 11)
we it leave.FIN like that

In earlier stages, both children use non-clitic elements such as *ça*. As in L1 acquisition, object *ça* is restricted to non-clitic positions, as illustrated in (9).

(9) a. Pas ouvrir ça. (Kenny, L1=English, month 5)
not open.INF this

b. Le papa-vache fait ça. (Kenny, L1=English, month 7)
the father+cow do.FIN this

Comparative examination of Elisa's and Lorenzo's data reveals interesting results. In Elisa, whose L1 is German, a language that lacks preverbal clitic (like English), the development pattern follows what is observed in Kenny and Greg. Object clitics, although they are reported in the second recording (at month 16), do not become productive until the fourth sample (at month 24). In contrast, the ratio of subject clitics is high from the first session onward (23 out of 24 subjects). The tendency is different in Lorenzo, whose mother tongue, Italian, has preverbal object clitics. In his case object clitics become productive earlier than in Elisa's, as of the second recording (at month 15). These findings are consistent with L1 influence. Nevertheless, Belletti and Hamann (2004) report no instance of enclisis with nonfinite forms in Lorenzo's French, in contrast to what is found in Italian. In all cases, the clitic appears in the target position in French, to the left of the nonfinite verb, as illustrated in (10). Such examples were found in the first recording session (at month 13), which plays down the role of the L1.

(10) a. No, c' est pas moi qui devrais l' amener (Lorenzo, L1=Italian, month 13)
no it is not me who should it take

b. Faut le mettre là. (Lorenzo, L1=Italian, month 13)
must it put there

When object clitics emerge, they tend to be correctly placed in a preverbal position. White (1996) reports that all of Kenny's 67 object clitics appear in a preverbal position; for Greg, placement is target-like in 89.6% of the cases (86/93). Moreover, clitics almost never appear in other non-clitic positions, such as following a preposition. In such cases, a strong pronoun is used (e.g. *de moi* 'of me'). Finally, object clitics do not receive contrastive stress, in contrast to strong pronouns (11). This further reinforces the conclusion that an early distinction is made between the two types of pronouns.

(11) a. C' est de MOI! (Kenny, L1=English, month 3)
it is of me

b. C' est à TOI celui- là. (Greg, L1=English, month 20)
It is of you this one

Clitic-placement errors are occasionally observed, as in (12), but it should be stressed that such errors are rare. Sometimes, a strong pronoun is used instead of an object clitic (12d). Note, however, that although the latter case is ungrammatical in French, the strong pronoun is correctly placed in a non-clitic position.

(12) a. Moi j' ai trouvé le. (Greg, L1=English, month 14)
me I have+1SG found it

b. Alors, tu joues avec le. (Elisa, L1=German, month 16)
so you play.FIN with him

c. On laisse le. (Elisa, L1=German, month 16)
one leave.FIN it

d. Moi j' ai fait toi aussi. (Greg, L1=English, month 15)
me I have+1SG made you too

These errors are presumably due to L1 influence: in English and German, object pronouns follow the verb (at least with simple verb clauses in the case of German). Moreover, German has demonstrative (strong) pronouns which are undistinguishable from determiners (e.g. *der* 'this/the+MASC', *die* 'this/the+FEM') and which are often used instead of personal pronouns in colloquial speech. Since third person object clitics have the same form as determiners in French (*le/la/les*), German-speaking children may interpret French clitics as strong pronouns (see Belletti & Hamann 2004). This would explain why they may occur, albeit infrequently, after prepositions (12b). No such instances are reported in the data obtained from the native speakers of English, a language where object pronouns differ from demonstratives and determiners. Finally, it is worth pointing out that the erroneous placement of object clitics reported in Elisa's data involves only four tokens (at month 16), and that these errors are found before object pronouns start being used productively, eight months later.

In an experimental setting, Grüter (2005) administered an elicited production task and a sentence-picture matching task to three groups of children, ages 6 to 9: one group of TD French native speakers, one group of French children with SLI, and one group of English-speaking children learning French (with a year and a half of exposure to the language). The production task roughly followed Jakubowicz et al.'s (1998) technique, except that it was integrated within little stories. The picture identification task involved a series of eight verbs that may either be used transitively or intransitively in French (e.g. *plonger* 'plunge', *descendre* 'go+down/take+down', and *bouger* 'move'). The interviewer told the child a little story, illustrated with pictures, but with the last picture missing. Upon reaching the last sentence of the story, the child was presented with a choice of three pictures, from which he/she was invited to select the one that would best match the sentence. The verb in the sentence was in either an intransitive context (e.g. *Il bouge* 'he's moving'), or a transitive one. In the transitive sentences, the object was either an object clitic (e.g. *Il la bouge* 'he's moving it') or an object DP (e.g. *Il bouge la table* 'he's moving the table'). Two of the pictures illustrated the intransitive and transitive use of the verb (e.g. a little boy moving or a little boy moving a table), while the third was a picture previously used in telling the story. If children do not have a syntactic representation for accusative clitics, a similar performance on sentences with an intransitive verb and sentences with its transitive counterpart and an accusative clitic was predicted. The results show that neither the L2 learners nor the children with SLI used object clitics much in the production task (7.5% for the SLI group and 25.4% for the L2 learners, compared to 72.6% for the TD children).[113] However, as shown in Table 2, both the SLI children and the L2 learners selected the target pictures with high accuracy in the picture identification task (Table 2 does not include the results on the picture previously shown, as it was almost never selected). In particular, matching of an object clitic with a transitive action was 64.3% accurate for the L2 learners and 75% accurate for the children with SLI. Similarly high accuracy rates were obtained in the intransitive conditions (75% for each group).

---

113. The percentage of use of an overt object DP was similar in each group: 16.4% for the children with SLI and 19.5% for the L2 learners. The omission rates were 67.2% and 53.7%, respectively.

Table 2. Frequency of response-type (transitive or intransitive action) by condition in the picture–sentence matching task (from Grüter 2005)

Group	Age (mean)	Condition	Transitive action	Intransitive action
L1 (n=12)	6;7	Lexical	89.6%	8.3%
		Clitic	87.5%	8.3%
		Intransitive	18.8%	80.2%
SLI (n=6)	8;2	Lexical	100%	0%
		Clitic	75%	22.9%
		Intransitive	22.9%	75%
L2 (n=7)	6;8	Lexical	96.4%	3.6%
		Clitic	64.3%	32.1%
		Intransitive	23.2%	75%

Interestingly, at the individual level, a correlation was observed between production and comprehension in the L2 learners: those who produced the fewest object clitics also obtained the lowest results on the comprehension task, while those who produced the highest number of object clitics also understood them the best. No such correlation was observed in children with SLI. Note that in another study comparing the acquisition of French by English-speaking children (n=10, mean age 6;10), and aged-matched French children with SLI (see Section 7.2.1), Paradis & Crago (2003) report a similar incidence of obligatory object clitics in both groups, namely 40%. This ratio is significantly lower than the 80% rate displayed by MLU-matched TD monolinguals (mean age 3;3).

8.1.1.3 *Theoretical implications*

The data reviewed so far suggest that clitics are considered clitics from the earliest stages of French L2 acquisition: children display early use of clitics and early knowledge of their distributional properties in French. This suggests that they have acquired the relevant functional categories underlying clitics, and that such categories are present in child L2 grammars from the earliest stages of acquisition. This contradicts the Minimal Trees approach to the initial state, according to which functional categories are absent from the first IL systems (Vainikka & Young-Scholten 1994, 1996, 2005). The results also have a bearing on the issue of UG access in L2 acquisition. In English, subject and object pronouns are generally not considered clitics: adverbs may appear between the subject pronoun and the verb (13a), subject pronouns can be modified (13b), they can be conjoined (13c), and they may receive contrastive stress (13d).

(13) a. He usually meets Mary at 3:00pm
b. We two will meet Mary
c. My father and I will meet Mary
d. HE will meet Mary

Assuming Sportiche's (1996) hypothesis that clitics project their own (functional) Clitic voice categories (see Section 5.1.2.3), it follows that these categories are not active in English. The English/French data then suggest that child L2 learners can acquire functional categories which are not active in their L1, presumably via access to the categorial inventory assumed to be part of UG.[114]

For White (1996), target functional categories may even be part of the children's initial IL grammars, as evidenced by the early and error-free production of subject clitics in child L2 French. Likewise, the Italian/French data reported by Belletti & Hamann (2004) on the lack of enclisis on nonfinite verbs in French, which differs from properties of the L1, as early as the first language samples collected also suggest that target properties can be acquired very early. These findings seem to provide evidence that initial grammars are not solely constrained by L1 properties, contrary to approaches arguing for a total transfer of the L1 grammar in the initial stages of L2 acquisition (Schwartz & Sprouse, 1994, 1996).

However, the extent of L1 influence, or lack of thereof, is difficult to establish in what has been examined so far. First, the data may not fully represent the initial state of acquisition, especially in the case of Greg, since he had already been exposed to French for five months at the time of his first interview.[115] Moreover, as pointed out by Schwartz (1999), English does have clitics, such as *y´* (vs. *you*), *'m* (vs. *him* and *them*), and *'r* (vs. *her*) (see van Riemsdijk 1999). Just like French clitics, these elements cannot be conjoined, they cannot receive contrastive stress and they cannot appear stranded, as shown in (14) and (15).

(14) a. You / * Y´, it appears, can't do that
b. John and you / * y´ can't do that
c. YOU / * Y´ can't do that

(15) a. *John sees him and her / * 'm and 'r
b. *John prefers HIM / * 'M
c. Question: Who did you see? Answer: Him / * 'm

114. Naturally, on another account of clitics, i.e. one where they do not project their own categories, the task of L2 learners would not be to acquire new categories, but to figure out that these elements are heads (e.g. of AgrS and AgrO), namely elements that are weaker than their English counterparts.

115. White argues that the changes that are observed in the data are quantitative rather than qualitative. In other words, changes pertain to the number of clitics being used, not to the way they are used. Somewhat problematic with this view is that the appearance of object clitics is delayed, which suggests the abrupt emergence of the functional category which underlies them (AccV, in Sportiche's system). In response, White points out that in the initial stages there are few appropriate contexts where object clitics could be used. Moreover, the data examined were spontaneous production data, so if particular elements or constructions are not uttered, it does not necessarily mean that they are unknown to the learners.

The only difference between French and English clitics is that, in English, object clitics appear after the verb in non-imperative clauses. The fact that there are clitics in English, Schwartz argues, suggests that the functional categories underlying these elements are part of the grammar of English. Therefore, if anglophone children learning French show target-like knowledge of the properties of clitics, this cannot be taken as evidence against full transfer of the L1 grammar. In addition, Schwartz reviews some of the facts reported by White, arguing that they can be explained by L1 syntax. She claims that the data are compatible with an account of early subject pronouns as strong pronouns rather than clitics. In particular, she points out that in the early stages, there are instances of elements intervening between the clitic and the verb, as in *i pas vient* lit. 'he not come.FIN' (Kenny, month 4). She also argues that some of the facts reported by White may simply be cases of translation from English. For instance, instead of considering clitic doubling constructions to involve a strong pronoun and a clitic, such as *moi je*, she suggests that they be viewed as a translation of *me I*. Finally, she notes that the only object pronouns occurring in the early data are precisely those that can be found in the L1, i.e. postverbal pronouns in imperative constructions (e.g. *Excuse-moi* 'Excuse me'). In fact, she argues, it is exactly where there exists a difference between the L1 and the L2, namely preverbal versus postverbal object pronouns, that a delay in the acquisition of the target properties is observed. This scenario could also explain some of the individual results reported by Grüter (2005) on her L2 child learners. For those learners who produced and comprehended the lowest number of object clitics, the target property of French AccV may not yet have been in place. A final element compatible with early L1 influence stems from the fact that object clitics seem to develop earlier and more rapidly in children whose L1 also instantiates these elements, as seen in the comparative study of Elisa and Lorenzo. However, such comparative data are scarce at the moment, and efforts should be made to pursue this line of investigation in order to better assess the role of the L1 in the acquisition of object clitics in French.

8.1.2 Overt pronouns in adult L2 French

As with child learners, adult L2 learners of French use subject clitics early, and their development of object clitics is delayed. However, the status of nominative and accusative pronouns in adult IL grammars is ambiguous: it is not clear whether L2 learners treat them as clitics or not.

8.1.2.1 *Development of subject clitics in adult L2 French*

Subject clitics appear in the earliest utterances produced by adult learners, and their incidence increases very rapidly throughout the early stages of acquisition. They quickly become the most productive type of subjects. In the speech of two speakers of

Moroccan Arabic (MA) learning French, Prévost (1997) reports that subject clitics are used in 75% of verbal utterances for one learner (Abdelmalek) and in over 60% for the other (Zahra), as shown in Table 2 below. Although these learners had been exposed to French for over a year when recording began, they produced very few verbal utterances during the first interview, which suggests that their proficiency level was extremely low. Yet, subject clitics were used right away, and their incidence was high from the outset. In longitudinal L2 French data from English-speaking adults, the incidence of subject clitics is over 50% in the first recordings (Prévost 2003a, 2004). Again, these learners were at the beginner level at the time of the first interview. Similar trends are reported for Swedish learners of French (Schlyter 2003). This is especially the case of one learner, Henry, who produced subject clitics early on despite having been exposed to the language for only about 3 months. Importantly, he had never used French for communication prior to his first interview. As seen in Section 6.1.1.1 for L1 acquisition, early uses of subject clitics could be unanalysed. We saw that many instances of *j'* 'I' were used with non-first person referents by English-speaking learners of French, as in *Monique j'aime* 'Monique I like = Monique likes' (Myles 2004; Myles et al. 1998). Moreover, the incidence of subject clitics can be low at the beginning, as reported by Myles (2005) on beginner English-speaking learners of French. As seen in Section 4.2.1.4, subject clitics represent less than 25% of the learners' subjects initially.

Although researchers seem to agree on the early use of pronominal subjects by adult L2 learners, there is less agreement as to their distribution, and as to whether they have a clitic status in IL grammars. In some cases, the distribution of pronominal subjects is argued to be target-like, in that they are never found separated from the verb, they never occur in conjoined NPs, and they never appear in verbless clauses, i.e. in clauses lacking Tense (Prévost 2006a; Prévost & White 2000a). Moreover, no subject clitic is reported in dislocated positions. There is also evidence of elision, as in the target-like form *j'entends* 'I hear' (Herschensohn 2001). In contrast, other studies report just the opposite. They show that subject pronouns may be used contrastively (16a), they may be separated from the verb (16b), and they are not systematically elided (16c) (Granfeldt & Schlyter 2004).

(16) a. JE comprendre. (Henry 1, L1=Swedish)
I understand.INF

b. Je seulement habite. (Lisa 1, L1=Swedish)
I only live.FIN

c. Je je aime. (Henry 1, L1=Swedish)
I I love.FIN

One clear difference between child and adult L2 learners, which may not be directly related to the issue of the status of nominative pronouns as clitics in adult IL grammars, is that subject pronouns often appear with (apparently) nonfinite verb forms in L2 adult French, as seen in Section 4.2.1.2. Table 3 (which reproduces part of Table 8, Section 4.2.1.2) and the examples below (repeated from Section 4.2.1.2) illustrate the phenomenon.[116] In some cases, more than half of RIs contain a nominative pronoun. This is much higher than what has been found in child L2 French (below 5%).

Table 3. Incidence of subject clitics in finite and nonfinite clauses in adult L2 French (from Prévost 2003a)

Learner	L1	Finiteness	Total utterances	Subject clitics	% clitics
Abdelmalek[a]	MA	+Finite	653	532	81.5%
		–Finite	272	168	61.8%
Zahra[a]	MA	+Finite	600	392	65.3%
		–Finite	236	120	50.8%
Frank	English	+Finite	191	163	85.3%
		–Finite	30	25	83.3%
Mary	English	+Finite	193	125	64.8%
		–Finite	63	37	58.7%
Jane	English	+Finite	596	421	70.6%
		–Finite	87	39	44.8%

a. data from the European Science Foundation project on L2 acquisition (Perdue 1984)

(17) a. Tu boire. (Abdelmalek, L1=MA, month 27)
you drink.INF

b. Tu couper tout. (Zahra, L1=MA, month 24.5)
you cut.INF everything

c. Il laver les serviettes (Frank 1, L1=English,)
he wash.INF the towels

d. Le bateau faire beaucoup de bruit (Jane 7, L1=English,)
the boat do.INF much noise

e. Il être marié (Joe 1, L1=English,)
he be.INF married

116. Note that for the English-speaking learners, root clauses displaying subjects such as *elle* 'she', *nous* 'we', and *vous* 'you+PL' have been discarded because these elements are ambiguous between clitics and strong pronouns. Nonetheless, such utterances reveal tendencies similar to those observed with clitics.

Another difference between adult and child L2 learners is that adults very rarely use strong pronouns as subjects of RIs (Table 4). In contrast, strong pronouns may account for at least 30% of RI subjects in child L2 French data. Note that adult learners almost never use strong pronouns as subjects in finite clauses either.

Table 4. Incidence of strong pronoun subjects in finite and nonfinite clauses in adult L2 French (from Prévost 1997)

Learner	L1	Finiteness	Total utterances	Strong pronouns	% Strong pronouns
Abdelmalek	MA	+Finite	653	13	2%
		–Finite	272	19	7%
Zahra	MA	+Finite	600	26	4.3%
		–Finite	236	23	9.7%
Frank	English	+Finite	303	0	0%
		–Finite	38	0	0%
Mary	English	+Finite	237	0	0%
		–Finite	70	1	1.4%
Jane	English	+Finite	631	5	0.8%
		–Finite	94	0	0%

The status of pronominal subjects in adult IL grammars remains unsettled in the literature. Researchers who report placement errors with pronominal subjects tend to argue that adult L2 learners treat pronominal subjects as XPs. On the other hand, researchers who report no placement errors on the part of their learners tend to assume that L2ers consider pronominal subjects to be clitics. Additionally, it is often difficult to interpret the claims of published reports because the findings are not always quantified. For instance, although the contrastive use of clitics has been reported, data that would help determine the extent of its productivity are not available. Similarly, cl-Adv-V sequences are produced by adult learners, but these sequences are not always quantitatively contrasted with target-like cl-V-Adv orders, so it is difficult to determine the extent of this error. In other cases, such as elision, there is a relatively high level of variability. For example, not *all* instances of first person singular pronoun *je* appear as a non-elided subject in front of a vowel; some cases of elision are also reported in the early stages of acquisition. Additionally, adult learners of L2 French produce errors of a type not reported for child learners, which calls for an explanation. More research is clearly needed in this area.

The fact that adult L2 learners use clitics, but not strong pronouns, as subjects of finite roots suggests that they distinguish between the two types of pronominal elements quite early and that they have knowledge of Case. This in turn suggests that functional categories are available to adult learners in the early stages of acquisition, contra Vainikka and Young-Scholten (1996, 2005) who argue for an initial lexical stage. Moreover, the fact that adult L2 learners do not use strong pronoun subjects in RIs, coupled with the finding that a high ratio of RIs have clitic subjects, suggest that adult RIs have finite properties. In other words, adult learners use infinitival markers as substitutes for finite morphology, which in turn means that finite declaratives and RIs are equally finite in adult systems. This contrasts with child L2 RIs, which were argued earlier to be truly nonfinite and to result from truncation (see Section 4.1.3).

8.1.2.2 *Development of object clitics in adult L2 French*

In this section a distinction is made between studies on object clitics in spontaneous production and in experimental settings.

8.1.2.2.1 Spontaneous production data

As with child (L1 and L2) learners, object clitics tend to be delayed in adult L2 acquisition, when compared to the development of subject clitics. For instance, Schlyter (2003) reports that production data from two Swedish speakers at the beginner level, Henry and Lisa, include almost no object clitics, whereas the incidence of subject clitics is quite high: Henry produced a total of 93 subject clitics and not one object clitic; for Lisa the figures are 566 subject clitics and only four object clitics (Schlyter 2003: 35). Similar discrepancies also obtain for more advanced Swedish learners of French, which suggests that the properties of object clitics take quite some time to develop.

In addition, adults learning L2 French have difficulty with the distributional properties of object clitics, in contrast to child L2 learners who tend to place object clitics correctly once they start using them. In adult speech, object clitics may appear in canonical object position rather than preceding the verb, as in (18), or they may be omitted, as in (19). They may also be placed in between the auxiliary and the past participle in sentences in the *passé composé*, as in (20). This is observed in acquisition of L2 French by English-speaking learners (Adiv 1984; Herschensohn 2000, 2004) and by adolescents and adults whose L1 is Arabic, Berber, or Swedish (Schlyter 1997; Véronique 1986). See Hawkins (2001) for an overview.

(18) Il prend nous. (from Schlyter 1997)
he take.FIN us

(19) J' ai mangé __. [In the context of a mother asking who ate the cake.]
I have+1SG eaten (from Adiv 1984)

(20) Vous avez la pris. (from Herschensohn 2004)
you have+2PL it taken

Interestingly, the distributional errors produced by adult learners with respect to object clitics do not seem to affect reflexive pronouns. Such elements are reported to appear early in production data, and they are correctly placed in a preverbal position:

(21) a. Je m' appelle Petra. (Petra 1, L1=Swedish)
I myself call.FIN Petra

b. Il s' en va. (Karl 1, L1=Swedish)
he himself go.FIN

However, it is not clear whether these first reflexive clitics are truly analysed as such. Schlyter (1997) notes that such sequences are found with a very restricted number of verbs (e.g. *je m'appelle, tu t'appelles, il s'appelle*).

In the case of English-speaking learners of French, Towell & Hawkins (1994) and Hawkins (2001) propose that errors with object clitics correspond to different stages prior to target-like placement:

(22) 1. Postverbal positioning
2. Omission
3. Intermediate position
4. Target-like position

The first stage is characterized by the appearance of object pronouns in postverbal position (as in (18)), presumably due to transfer from the L1 (English, in Towell & Hawkins' study). Similar findings are reported for Swedish learners (Schlyter 1997). Reviewing data from six learners with different patterns of exposure to French, Schlyter found that of the first 39 object pronouns, 31 were placed after the verb and the remaining eight occurred in an intermediate position. Such results are compatible with L1 influence, given that object pronouns in Swedish share the same properties as their English counterparts: they are postverbal and they may optionally cliticize onto the verb as enclitics, as shown in (23) (from Granfeldt & Schlyter 2004). Therefore, at stage 1, French accusative pronouns may be considered either strong pronouns or enclitics by the learners.

(23) Jag sag henne / 'na.
I saw her

At the second stage, object clitics are very often omitted. Given that object drop is not a marginal phenomenon in French and that (preverbal) object clitics are often used (Cummins & Roberge 2005; Fónagy 1985; Tuller 2000), L2 learners of French may be exposed to a relatively high amount of input pointing to the possibility that the canonical object position can be left empty in that language (see Section 6.2.2). It follows that the production of sentences such as (19) may not result from difficulties with object pronouns per se. At the third stage, the clitic may intervene between the auxiliary and the past participle. One explanation is that learners may overgeneralize the fact that clitics can attach to the left of other nonfinite verbs in French, such as infinitives (e.g. *Je veux le faire* lit. 'I want it do.INF'). Herschensohn proposes that the object clitic is in AgrO but that movement of the clitic to TP is not forced due to the underspecification of functional categories in the IL grammar at that stage. At the final stage, target-like placement of object clitics has been reached. In particular, all functional categories are fully specified by then.

The existence of these proposed four stages is very difficult to assess. To start with, it is not always easy to evaluate the extent of the errors involving object clitics, as researchers often provide examples without any statistics. Moreover, a large amount of overlap between the proposed stages can be observed. For example, intermediate positioning of clitics in L2 French is found in early stages of acquisition, although it is proposed to occur at stage 3. The Swedish learners of French studied by Schlyter (2003), for example, show intermediate positioning of clitics in early stages. In this case, L1 influence is not at play since object pronouns follow the last verb in Swedish verbal sequences, as shown in (24). Instead, the production of Aux-cl-V, albeit incorrect, shows that the learners are starting to learn the fact that object clitics do not occupy the canonical postverbal object position in French.

(24) a. Jag har sett den
I have seen it

b. *Jag har den sett

Also problematic is the fact that the proposed stages are claimed to affect both child and adult L2 learners. However, as seen above, the incidence of errors in object clitic placement is minimal in child L2 acquisition. Finally, some of the errors used as evidence for the existence of particular stages do not necessarily involve clitics per se. In particular, learners are reported to frequently use strong pronouns in postverbal position at the postverbal stage, as in (25). Similarly, in (18) above, the object pronoun *nous* 'us' is ambiguous between a clitic and a strong pronoun.

(25) a. Je veux regarde toi. (Petra 1, L1 Swedish)
I want.FIN watch.FIN you

b. Il dit moi. (Petra 1, L1 Swedish)
he say.FIN/PTP me

Although these utterances are clearly deviant from the perspective of the target language, where a preverbal object clitic should be used instead, the strong pronouns are still used in a correct non-clitic position. In other words, in addition to acquiring the positioning of clitics, learners must acquire the fact that strong pronouns cannot appear in object position in French.

In brief, a more thorough examination of object clitics in L2 French is necessary to investigate the existence of the four stages. It would be particularly interesting to obtain spontaneous production data from native speakers whose L1 includes preverbal object clitics, such as Italian and Spanish, which would provide insight into the issue of L1 influence in the acquisition of object clitics and the role the L1 plays in the proposed stages.

8.1.2.2.2 Experimental data

Since accusative clitics may be infrequent in spontaneous production from L2 learners, experimental data are important in shedding light on knowledge of these elements in L2 French. In particular, some studies have looked at knowledge of the placement of object clitics in complex constructions involving infinitival complement. Most of this research focuses on Spanish-speaking learners of French. Just like French, Spanish has object clitics that are systematically placed before the highest finite verb in simple clauses, as illustrated in (26) and (27).

(26) a. Juan lo ve.
John him see.3SG
'John sees him.'

b. *Juan ve lo.

(27) a. Juan lo ha visto.
John him has seen
'John saw him.'

b. *Juan ha lo visto.

However, the two languages differ with respect to biclausal sentences involving a modal or aspectual verb followed by an infinitival complement. In Spanish, the accusative clitic associated with the lower verb can 'climb' into the main clause and attach to the modal or aspectual verb, as shown in (28a). Clitic climbing is extremely restricted in French, as shown in (28b) (it is possible with perception verbs, however). French accusative clitics almost always attach to the left of the lower (infinitival) verb (28c), an order ungrammatical in Spanish (28d).

(28) a. Lo quiero ver.
him want.1SG see
'I want to see him.'

b. *Je le veux voir.
I him want see.INF

c. Je veux le voir.

d. *Quiero lo ver.

Additionally, clitic climbing is optional in Spanish, which means that the accusative clitic can also appear to the right of the lower verb (29a). This is impossible in French, as shown in (29b).

(29) a. Quiero ver lo.
want.1SG see.INF him

b. *Je veux voir le.
I want see.INF him

The differences between the two languages are imputable to feature strength (Kayne 1989; Roberts 1997). Infinitival verbs are equipped with nonfinite features that need to be checked in the nonfinite AgrS position of the lower clause. In Spanish, nonfinite features are assumed to be strong, which forces the infinitival verb to raise overtly to (the lower) AgrS, as shown in (30). From there, it can left-adjoin to the object clitic in AccV. It then has the option of incorporating into the higher aspectual or modal verb (i.e. restructuring), thus forming one verbal entity. In this case, it is as if the whole sentence contained one single verb, with one VP and its clitic projection. In French, nonfinite features are assumed to be weak, so there is no overt verb movement to AgrS, and the clitic precedes the infinitival verb. Since the infinitival verb cannot raise in the first place, restructuring is impossible in French.

(30)
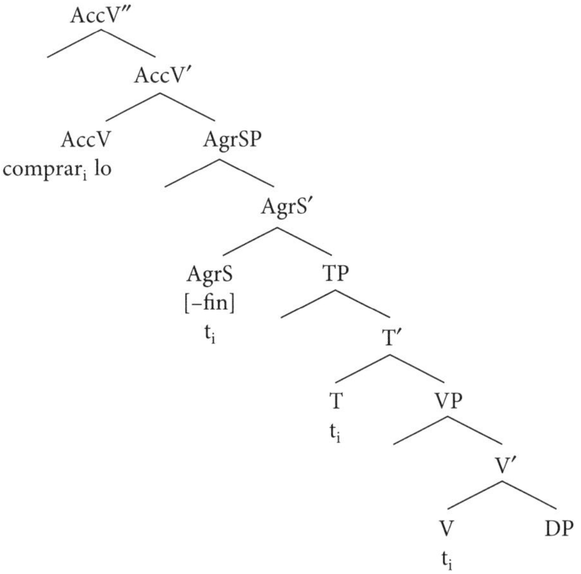

In causative constructions, clitic climbing is obligatory in Romance languages, including French and Spanish (Guasti 1996; Kayne 1975).

(31) a. Marie le fait marcher
Marie him makes walk
'Mary makes him walk.'

a'. María lo hace caminar
Mary him makes walk

b. * Marie fait le marcher

b'. * María hace lo caminar

c. * Marie fait marcher le

c'. * María hace caminar lo

In contrast to restructuring contexts involving an aspectual or a modal verb, causative constructions remain biclausal. Because causatives have an additional (external) theta-role, the higher verb and the lower predicate do not fall within the same extended projection, which prevents restructuring. Since the structure is biclausal, both the higher and the lower clauses project their own clitic voice projections. It is assumed that the accusative clitic base-generated in the lower AccV can raise to the high AgrS and attach to the finite verb.

Bruhn-Garavito & Montrul (1996) looked at knowledge of accusative clitic placement in French and Spanish in two groups of French-Spanish bilingual adults: native speakers of Spanish whose French was at the intermediate level, and native speakers of French with intermediate-level Spanish. The learners were administered a grammaticality judgment task investigating knowledge of clitic placement in simple and restructuring contexts. Results show that accusative clitics were accurately placed with respect to finite forms and past participles. In L2 French participants accepted target placement (cl-V, e.g. *Je le vois* 'I see him' and *Je l'ai vu* 'I saw him') and rejected non-target sequences (V-cl, e.g. **Je vois le*, **J'ai vu le*). However, accuracy was much lower in contexts involving restructuring for both groups of learners. The Spanish speakers learning French were quite accurate at accepting target clitic placement between the two verbs ($V_{+finite}$-cl-$V_{-finite}$), as in *Je veux le voir* 'I want to see him', which is impossible in their L1, and they also accurately rejected $V_{-finite}$-cl, as in **Je veux voir le*, which is possible in Spanish but not in French. However, they failed to reject clitic climbing, as in **Je le veux voir*. They incorrectly accepted it about 50% of the time. Similar results were obtained for the French learners of Spanish: they appropriately accepted $V_{-finite}$-cl sequences and rejected $V_{+finite}$-cl-$V_{-finite}$, but performed at around chance level on clitic climbing. The results suggest that these learners had acquired the strength of the [–finite] feature of nonfinite AgrS in the target language (since clitics were accurately placed between the two verbs), but failed to accept or reject clitic climbing. Note that long-lasting problems with clitic climbing are also reported in L2 Italian (Sorace 1993).

Duffield et al. (2002) investigated knowledge of clitic placement in complex contexts involving either a causative verb or a modal/aspectual verb. Participants were native speakers of Spanish and native speakers of English (for which the researchers assumed clitics are absent) learning French. The learners' proficiency ranged from high intermediate to advanced. Duffield et al. used a Sentence Matching (SM) task (see Freedman & Forster 1985) to obtain grammaticality judgments on clitic placement. Participants were shown pairs of sentences on a computer screen and were instructed to decide (using the keyboard) whether the sentences were the same or different within each pair. In this methodology, the pairs of interest are the ones with similar sentences, as they involve grammatical or ungrammatical sentences, as in (32) and (33).

(32)

Paul	veut	le	manger.
Paul	wants	it	to eat

Paul	veut	le	manger.
'Paul	wants	to	eat it.'

(33)

Paul veut manger le.
Paul veut manger le.

The rationale behind the SM procedure is that the reaction time needed by participants to respond that the two sentences are the same will be indicative of grammaticality judgments: if target properties have been acquired, it should take the learners less time to respond that the two sentences are the same when they are grammatical, as in (32), than when they are ungrammatical, as in (33).[117]

Results on simple clauses were as expected (e.g. learners took longer to respond when the two sentences were ungrammatical, in comparison to grammatical pairs), although statistically significant differences were not always found.[118] With biclausal sentences displaying an aspectual or modal verb followed by an infinitive, learners responded faster on sentences with the target order cl-$V_{\text{-finite}}$ (32), where there is no movement of the infinitival verb, than on sentences exhibiting the reverse order (33), in which the infinitival verb has raised. This suggests that they have acquired the (weak) feature strength of nonfinite AgrS in L2 French. This is confirmed by the data on clitic climbing, which was disallowed by the learners: they responded faster on sentences not displaying it (e.g. *Paul veut le manger* 'Paul wants to eat it') than on sentences where the clitic appeared attached to the higher verb (e.g. **Paul le veut manger*).

With causatives, the English-speaking learners did not really distinguish the grammatical from the ungrammatical sentences, since their response time was similar in both cases. The Spanish speakers, however, did make the target distinction. They particularly rejected ungrammatical causatives where the object clitic appeared between the causative verb and the infinitival verb (e.g. **Antoine fait le courir* 'Antoine makes him run').

---

117. Despite criticisms of the SM procedure (Crain & Fodor 1987; Stowe 1992), this methodology resolves many of the problems associated with more traditional pencil and paper GJ tasks, in particular the fact that traditional GJ tasks do not control for the effect of metalinguistic knowledge (Birdsong 1989; Ellis 1991; Schütze 1996). This is especially problematic when the properties being investigated are explicitly taught in the classroom.

118. Importantly, the French native speakers responded significantly faster on grammatical sentences than on ungrammatical ones in all test conditions but one, that of causatives with cl-Causative-$V_{\text{-finite}}$ (e.g. *Antoine le fait courir* 'Antony makes him run') versus * Causative-cl-$V_{\text{-finite}}$ (e.g. **Antoine fait le courir*).

In their 1998 study, Hoover & Dwivedi looked at knowledge of clitic placement in complex constructions similar to those later examined in Duffield et al.' s study. Hoover and Dwivedi's learners were native speakers of English highly proficient in French. The authors compared parsing strategies used by learners and native speakers of French in reading tasks. Results reveal no differences between the two groups. In causative constructions, it took the participants longer to read the lower verb when the object was a clitic than when it was a full DP (e.g. *Je le fais courir* 'I make him run' and *Je fais courir Jean* 'I make John run'). In the latter case, the object clearly follows the infinitival verb, whereas in the former, Hoover & Dwivedi argue, the readers must reanalyse the clitic (which appears on the higher verb) as the object of the lower verb, which takes them some time. In constructions with a modal/aspectual verb, opposite results were obtained. It took the readers longer to read the infinitival verbs when associated with a full DP object (e.g. *Paul veut manger le pain* 'Paul wants to eat the bread') than with an accusative clitic (e.g. *Paul veut le manger* 'Paul wants to eat it'). In such contexts, the clitic is readily associated with the lower verb, since there is no clitic-climbing. The results suggest that the learners have acquired the properties of clitics in French, including knowledge of the underlying position in which they are base-generated.

8.1.2.2.3 Theoretical analyses

The experimental data clearly show that target-like properties of object clitics can be acquired by L2 learners of French, regardless of whether or not their L1 has clitics. First of all, L2 learners come to know that accusative clitics do not occupy the canonical object position in French, since they allow them in preverbal position and reject them post-verbally. L2 French learners also manage to acquire the weak value of infinitive AgrS since they strongly favour an intermediate placement of the clitic between the modal and the infinitival verb to orders typical of (infinitival) verb movement (i.e. Mod-V-cl). The errors in object clitic placement reported in spontaneous production data may come from learners at lower proficiency levels than those of the participants in the experimental studies. They may also reflect problems that are more closely related to processing issues or communicative pressure. In any case, the fact that more target-like results were obtained in the experimental studies suggests that the investigation of underlying knowledge cannot solely be based on spontaneous oral production data.

In addition, the experimental results from learners whole L1 exhibits strong infinitival AgrS values show that parameter resetting is possible in L2 acquisition, in contrast to claims by Hawkins (2001) and Tsimpli & Roussou (1991). Furthermore, it is not the case that accusative clitics are allowed to appear in all kinds of positions; rather, their placement seems to be strongly restricted. This argues against the Impairment Hypothesis according to which a high level of variability is to be expected, owing to the proposed absence of features, feature strength, and feature checking mechanisms from IL grammars. In the same vein, the fact that the target strength of infinitival AgrS can be acquired is evidence against a more local view of impairment according to which feature strength is (permanently) inert in IL grammars (Beck 1998). The data show that French infinitival AgrS is specified as weak in grammars developed by learners of at least intermediate proficiency level. Finally, although L2 learners may have problems with clitic climbing, in the sense that they allow it for a while in French, they can eventually acquire its properties to a target-like extent, sometimes as early as the intermediate level of proficiency.

8.2 Null arguments in L2 acquisition of French

Most of the research on null arguments so far has been on null subjects. The results show that null subjects may be produced by child and adult learners, but that the nature of the null elements may differ in the two acquisition contexts. As to object drop, research on child L2 learners shows that it can be as frequent as with monolinguals.

8.2.1 Null arguments in child L2 French

8.2.1.1 *Null subjects in child L2 French*

As in acquisition by monolinguals, null subjects are reported in child L2 French, even when the L1 does not allow them (such as English). Moreover, they are found in both finite and nonfinite clauses, with a higher incidence in RIs. Finally, null subjects seem to be restricted to root declaratives: few are reported to occur in questions and embedded clauses. Analysing spontaneous data from the two English-speaking children Greg and Kenny, Prévost (1997) found that null subjects account for between 10% and 20% of finite subjects and between 30% and 50% of nonfinite subjects during the first 18 months of acquisition, which corresponds to the period during which they produce RIs. Examples are given below.

Table 5. Null subjects in root declaratives vs. finite CPs in child L2 French (L1=English)

Learner	Clause types	# of utterances	Null subjects	% Null subjects
Kenny	Finite roots	428	87	20.3%
	RIs	76	23	30.3%
	CP	104	6	5.5%
Greg	Finite roots	591	59	10%
	RIs	58	31	53.4%
	CP	128	5	4%

(34) a. Va là. (Kenny, L1=English, month 4)
go.FIN there

b. Veux jouer avec ça. (Kenny, L1=English, month 11)
want.FIN play.INF with this

c. Et là sont jaunes. (Greg, L1=English, month 9.5)
and there are yellow

d. Est l' auto. (Greg, L1=English, month 11)
is the car

(35) a. Jouer de hockey. (Kenny, L1=English, month 9.5)
play.INF of hockey

b. Séparer les deux singes (Kenny, L1=English, month 15)
separate.INF the two monkeys

c. Manger les oreilles (Greg, L1=English, month 10)
eat.INF the ears

d. Enlever les dents (Greg, L1=English, month 14)
remove.INF the teeth

Table 5 further shows that there is a contingency between (finite) clause type and the omission of subjects: null subjects tend to occur in root contexts rather than in CPs.

The last interesting finding is that, just like in L1 French, null subjects in finite clauses and RIs decrease dramatically at the same time. In Kenny's and Greg's data, this simultaneous decrease occurs around month 18, as shown in Table 6.

Table 6. Nonfinite root declaratives and null subjects before and after month 18 in child L2 French (L1=English) (from Prévost 1997)

Child	Period	RIs	%	Null subjects	%
Kenny	Before month 18	76/504	15.1%	87/428	20.3%
	After month 18	3/527	0.6%	15/524	2.9%
Greg	Before month 18	58/659	8.9%	59/591	10%
	After month 18	4/911	0.4%	15/907	1.7%

The data from these English-speaking children are consistent with the Truncation approach: before the children systematically project CP roots, they produce null subjects in root declaratives and significantly fewer in CPs. This suggests that the null pronoun is not *pro*, in contrast to what is observed in typical *pro*-drop languages where null subjects can be found across clause types. Once declaratives are systematically represented by CP, null subjects decrease dramatically. This suggests that during the first 18 months of acquisition, null subjects in finite root declaratives are null constants, that is, null elements occurring in the specifier of the root, IP. Once CP becomes the root of main declaratives, null constants in SpecIP can no longer be licensed, which triggers a dramatic decrease in finite subjectless utterances.

Belletti & Hamann (2004) is one of the few studies focusing on the L2 acquisition of French by a child (named Lorenzo) whose L1 is a null-subject language, namely Italian. Interestingly, the incidence of null subjects in his spontaneous production data is extremely low, even in the first recording (age 3;5). In all, only four cases of unambiguous null subjects are reported out of a total of 601 finite clauses (0.7%). In comparison, 77% of his finite clauses had a null subject in Italian (the child was interviewed in each language). The data from Lorenzo suggest that he had acquired the French [-*pro*-drop] value of the null subject parameter very rapidly. Note that he also produced overt expletive clitics in French (e.g. *il faut que* 'it is necessary that'), which are typical of non-*pro*-drop languages.

8.2.1.2 *Null objects in child L2 French*

As noted above, null objects have not yet been thoroughly investigated in child L2. Some researchers report that their incidence can be quite high. In the acquisition of French by English-speaking children, for example, we saw that object clitics were not used very frequently, at least in the early stages of acquisition. Instead, they tend to be omitted and not replaced by NP objects. In Paradis & Crago's (2003) study, omission represented over 60% of the errors produced by 10 English-speaking children (mean age 6;10).[119] In all, object omission was observed in over 25% of the contexts in which an accusative clitic should have been used.

One problem in the investigation of null objects in spontaneous production data is that object omission is not impossible in French, as seen previously. Prévost (2006a), drawing on Cummins & Roberge's (2005) account of null objects, distinguished between licit and illicit object omissions in Greg & Kenny's data, the two English-speaking children previously examined by Grondin & White (1996) and White (1996). A similar three-phase developmental trend was found in the two children: (a) a first period during which all cases of object omission were illicit (until month 14), (b) a second period when both licit and illicit null objects were produced (until month 20), and (c) a third period with a vast majority of licit omissions. The sharp decrease in use of illicit omission is illustrated in Table 7.

Most cases of illicit omission are due to clitic drop, as illustrated in (36). Interestingly, as seen in Section 8.1.1.2, object clitics did not start being used productively before month 20 by the two children. There is therefore a correlation between the end of illicit use of object omission and the development of object clitics in the data.

119. These children also used *ça* in object position.

Table 7. Production and omission of objects in child L2 French before and after month 20 (adapted from Prévost 2006a)

Child	Period (in months)	Overt objects	Null objects		Total	% Illicit
			Licit	Illicit		
Kenny	1–20	176	29	31	234	13.2%*
	20–29	353	46	13	412	3.1%
Greg	5–20	221	47	53	321	16.5%*
	20–29	534	154	56	744	7.5%

* Significant difference between the two periods

(36) a. Interviewer: Tu l' mets pas.
you it put not
Kenny: Mets pas __. (Kenny, month 1)
put not

b. Interviewer: Attends un peu ton train là j' vais l' attacher.
Wait a little your train there I will it attach
Greg: Moi j' ai attaché __. (Greg, month 9)
Me I have attached

These correlations can be explained by appealing to computational complexity, as proposed by Jakubowicz et al. (1998) and Jakubowicz and Nash (2001) for L1 acquisition. According to this hypothesis, French object clitics are semantically deficient elements that cannot occupy the canonical object position. Rather, they must be placed in a preverbal position, which requires computational operations initially too costly for the learners (see section 6.1.5). Hence, object clitics are almost not produced initially. This also explains why most cases of object omission correspond to clitic drops before month 20 in Greg and Kenny's data. Once the processing load decreases, around that time, the children are able to place object clitics correctly and produce them. We already saw that an increase in computational capacity could also account for the end of the period during which RIs and null subjects are produced by these two children, which was observed at month 18 (see Section 4.1.1.2), which is very close to the point when illicit object omission is observed to fall. However, more data are needed to strongly conclude that the end of the RI period and the development of object clitics are related in (L2) language acquisition.[120]

Finally, there does not seem to be any clear relationship between object omission and the development of CP in Greg and Kenny's data, since there is at least an

120. In L1 acquisition, the simultaneous decline of RIs and null objects is predicted by Wexler's (1998) UCC account, according to which only one D-feature can be checked off in initial grammars. However, this account contains a strong maturational component (the UCC is assumed to disappear via maturation). This means that it cannot apply to the learning situation considered

eight-month period of overlap between the use of interrogatives and object omission in the data (for a detailed account of the emergence of C in the two children, see Section 16.1). This argues against Müller et al.'s (1996) hypothesis adapted to (child) L2 acquisition.

8.2.2 Null arguments in adult L2 French

Like child learners, adults learning L2 French produce null arguments. Unlike for child learners, however, the incidence and nature of null elements (especially null subjects) in adult L2 learners is strongly influenced by the L1. The nature of null objects is difficult to establish, as the difference between licit and illicit use is not clearly reported.

8.2.2.1 *Null subjects in adult L2 French*

In L2 acquisition by adults, the production of null subjects seems to depend on whether the L1 allows null subjects or not. For example, the incidence of subjectless root declaratives is low in English-speaking and Swedish-speaking learners, but it can be high in learners whose L1 is Moroccan Arabic, a null-subject language, including in embedded clauses. This suggests that the null subject for adult learners is *pro*, rather than a null constant, in contrast to the findings for child learners.

In his longitudinal study of four English-speaking learners who were at the beginner level at the first recording, Prévost (2003a) reports that null subjects are found in at most 9% of their finite clauses (it is lower than 6% for one and less than 3% for another). RIs show more cross-individual differences: while the incidence of null subjects was zero in one case (0/30), it was much higher for two other learners (11/60 and 27/91, respectively). However, even in the cases where the rate of subjectless RIs seems high, the incidence of null subjects in finite roots is quite low. These findings were confirmed in cross-sectional data, in which five English-speaking adults at the beginner level produced few subjectless root declaratives (Prévost 2004). Similar results are reported for native speakers of Swedish, another non-*pro*-drop language (Schlyter 2003).

In contrast, the Moroccan learner Zahra produced a relatively consistent ratio of finite null subjects throughout the data, varying between 12% and 33% across the recordings (total incidence for all recordings: 111/600 = 18.5%). She exhibited similar consistency in the development of root infinitives (60/236 = 25.4%). Examples of subjectless declaratives produced by Zahra appear in (37) and (38).

(37) a. Gonfle beaucoup. (Zahra, L1=MA, month 28.2)
swell.FIN much

b. Part à la mer. (Zahra, L1=MA, month 40)
go.FIN to the sea

---

here given that Kenny and Greg were about five years old when they started learning French, which means that they were over the UCC stage (assuming that such a stage exists).

(38) a. Parler le maroccain. (Zahra, L1=MA, month 14)
speak.INF the Moroccan

b. Marcher à la maison. (Zahra, L1=MA, month 36)
walk.INF to the house

Moreover, Zahra consistently produced embedded null subjects throughout the recordings. This was rarely observed in the child L2 French corpora. Embedded null subjects account for 39 of her 109 CPs (26.4%). In fact, Zahra's null subjects tend to occur proportionally more in finite CPs than in finite main declaratives ($\chi^2 = 4.565$, $p < .05$). Some examples of subjectless finite CPs are given in (39).[121]

(39) a. … quand toujours dort (Zahra, L1=MA, month 21.7)
when always sleep.FIN

b. … quand cherche l' autre maison (Zahra, L1=MA, month 29.2)
when look+for.FIN the other house

c. … quand entre dans le bus (Zahra, L1=MA, month 41)
when enter.FIN in the bus

These results clearly differ from what was found with child L2 French learners. There is no connection between the production of null subjects in finite declaratives and the production of RIs in the adult data. In fact, for speakers of non-*pro*-drop languages, the incidence of null subjects is low during the RI period. Moreover, even when null subjects are observed in parallel with the production of RIs (which is what obtains in L2 child data as well), there is no simultaneous drop in the incidence of null subjects and RIs. All this tends to confirm the hypothesis that adult learners do not project truncated structures, in contrast to child learners. At this point, much more data should be analysed from learners whose L1 is a *pro*-drop language in order to verify the findings on Zahra. Data about the incidence of null subjects in CPs would be particularly helpful in determining the nature of null subjects.

8.2.2.2 *Null objects in adult L2 French*

The issue of null objects in adult L2 French was introduced within the discussion on the acquisition of object clitics in Section 8.1.2.2. There, we saw that adult learners seem to go through a phase during which they omit these elements. We also saw, however, that most of the discussion in the literature on the use of null objects instead of an accusative clitic lacks statistical grounding, and that when null objects are reported, it is not always clear whether omission is licit or not. Further studies, ideally including experimental data as was done with child learners, are needed to provide answers to this question.

121. Data from the other Moroccan learner, Abdelmalek, are slightly different from Zahra's. His ratio of null subjects is higher in RIs (24.6%) than in root finite declaratives (8%), and the incidence of null subjects is low in CPs (8.1%).

According to Herschensohn (2000), the empty object in adult L2 French is *pro*, and the clitic is not expressed due to defective morphology. We already saw that L2 learners experience difficulties with inflectional morphology (e.g. verbal inflection), presumably due to access or mapping problems in the case of the adults (see Section 4.2.1.4), which results in the production of infinitival verb endings instead of finite forms. Under this view, infinitival markers are underspecified with respect to finiteness. Consequently, default infinitival verbs may be inserted under functional projections without creating featural mismatching. Herschensohn extends this idea to the domain of clitics, which she considers to be inflectional markers. This approach suggests that default object agreement markers are null, and that such null markers are underspecified for person. Again, insertion of the verb with the null agreement marker would not yield any feature mismatch with the host. Note that with default infinitival verbs, there is optionality in inflectional marking: some verbs show agreement, while others bear the infinitival ending. In other words, verbs do not appear only in the infinitive in L2 learners' speech. It is not clear whether this kind of optionality obtains with clitic omission as well. It would be interesting to find out if adult learners go through a period where they do not produce object clitics at all, as predicted by the four stage development discussed in Section 8.1.2.2.1.

8.3 Conclusion

This chapter has explored the development of subject and object pronouns in child and adult L2 French. Important differences between the two types of learners were identified, as was the case with the development of the verbal domain (see Chapter 4). With respect to overt pronouns, we saw that in child L2ers subject and object clitics develop in a fashion largely similar to what is reported in L1 acquisition: subject clitics develop before object clitics, and clitic placement is by and large correct from the moment they emerge, suggesting that they are considered clitics from the very beginning. Evidence of L1 influence was also uncovered, especially with respect to object clitics. Occasional cases of enclisis were discussed, but it seems that their incidence remains relatively low. The fact that subject clitics emerge early in beginner learners and that they are restricted to finite contexts was argued to show that functional categories are available from the outset, contra the Minimal Trees approach. Whether or not transfer of clitic categories has occurred from the L1 depends on the analysis of the L1 pronominal system, as seen in the conflicting positions adopted by White (1996) and Schwartz (1999) for English.

Although there are some similarities in the acquisition of clitics in child L2 learners and in adult L2 learners (subject clitics appear early in both groups, and the development of object pronouns is delayed relative to subject clitics), clitics do not seem to have the same status in adult IL grammars as they do in child IL systems. In adult (but not child) L2 learners, subject clitics may appear with nonfinite forms, may receive contrastive stress, and sometimes fail to be elided in obligatory elision contexts, and object clitics often appear in postverbal position. This suggests that clitics are first considered XPs by adult L2 learners. While this interpretation may be true, the data are not always reported in a manner that makes interpretation and accurate comparison with other studies possible, which means that more research on the nature of clitics in adult IL systems is needed. In any case, the reported fact that nominative clitics appear as subjects rather than strong pronouns suggests that there is knowledge of Case in early adult grammars, which in turn suggests that at least T is present in their underlying grammars. As suggested in Section 4.2.1.4, the fact that subject clitics are found with (apparently) nonfinite forms is compatible with the Missing Surface Inflection Hypothesis, specifically, these nonfinite forms have finite properties. With respect to object clitics, a four-stage process of development has been proposed, involving postverbal placement, omission, intermediary positioning, and target-like placement. This possibility needs further examination, using more refined linguistic analysis, one which distinguishes, for example, between obligatory and optional contexts for clitic use. Learners whose L1 allows preverbal clitics should also be tested. In experimental tasks, it has been shown that target-like placement of object clitics is possible, especially in potential restructuring contexts (so, $V_{+finite}$-cl-$V_{-finite}$ in French), which are generally considered to create tremendous difficulties to L2 learners whose L1 allows clitic climbing. A more detailed comparison between these results and results from spontaneous production should be undertaken.

L2 learners were also shown to produce subjectless utterances. Here again, a difference between child and adult learners was found. In child L2 acquisition, null subjects are restricted to main declaratives, and their incidence in finite main clauses has been found to decline sharply at the same time as RIs. This, coupled with the fact that subjects clitics are largely restricted to finite contexts, was shown to support a Truncation approach to child L2 acquisition. In contrast, null subjects in adult L2 acquisition seem to follow the properties of the L1, as subjectless utterances are found more in the speech of learners whose L1 allows them than in the speech of those with non-*pro*-drop L1s. This includes the possibility of null subjects in CP-clauses, which are rarely found in child L2 French.

Two important areas remain largely understudied in L2 French: null objects and binding. So far, null objects have mainly been discussed within investigations of object clitics, but they have not been examined in their own right. Prévost (2006a) is an exception, as he explored licit and illicit object omission in child L2 French. He suggested that most illicit omissions are cases of clitic object omission, which can be explained in terms of computational complexity, thus echoing proposals accounting for the production of RIs and null subjects in child L2 French. These first results need confirmation in other learning situations. Given the recent attention that L1 researchers have been placing on the phenomenon of object omission, it would be interesting to start looking at object omission more thoroughly in the context of foreign language learning, including acquisition by adults. Finally, while knowledge of binding properties has been extensively explored in L2 English, it has received virtually no attention in French L2 acquisition. Not much is known about the development of binding properties in child and adult L2 French, a lack that should be corrected.

PART III

Determiner phrases

CHAPTER 9

Determiner phrases

Morphosyntactic assumptions

The third part of this book deals with the acquisition of various aspects of the noun phrase, such as the determiner, number, gender, and noun placement with respect to the adjective. Some of the questions addressed in the subsequent chapters relate to when these elements and properties are acquired, namely whether they appear in production from the outset or whether their development is delayed. In L2 French acquisition, the question is whether they can ever be fully acquired and to what degree the L1 influences the course of acquisition.

At the theoretical level, determiners have been considered to play a crucial role in the underlying representation of noun phrases since the late eighties (e.g. Abney 1987). One of the main arguments in favour of this representation is that determiners are instrumental in anchoring noun phrases in the discourse. As a result, noun phrases are considered to be incorporated into a projection headed by the corresponding functional category D(eterminer) and are therefore part of a DP projection. Questions about the acquisition of the properties of noun phrases are thus directly relevant to the general issue of the knowledge and development of functional categories in learners' grammars.

This chapter is divided into three main sections. The first section discusses the properties of French DPs, mainly focusing on the determiner system and noun placement, the second presents a formal account of French DPs, and the third explores particular acquisition questions with respect to the four learning situations investigated in this book.

9.1 French DPs

This section addresses the properties of the determiner system in French, including definiteness, specificity, gender, and number, as well as agreement concord and noun placement with respect to adjectives.

9.1.1 The determiner system in French

In French, nouns are usually accompanied by a determiner, be it definite, indefinite, possessive or demonstrative, as shown in (1). Very few nouns are determinerless, with the notable exception of proper names (for a review of the incidence of such 'bare' NPs, see Section 9.1.3 below).

(1) a. le / un / ce / mon chien
the+MASC a+MASC this+MASC my+MASC dog+MASC

b. la / une / cette / MA chienne
the+FEM a.FEM this.FEM my+FEM dog.FEM

c. les / des / ces / mes chiens / chiennes
the+PL some these my+PL dog+MASC.PL dog.FEM.PL

d. le / un / ce / mon véhicule
the+MASC a+MASC this+MASC my+MASC vehicle+MASC

e. la / une / cette / MA voiture
the+FEM a.FEM this.FEM my+FEM car+FEM

Determiner-like elements also include numerals (*un* 'one', *deux* 'two', etc.) and quantifiers (*plusieurs* 'several', *quelques* 'some', and *chaque* 'each', for example).[122] While the term 'determiner' applies to all these elements, the term 'article' is reserved for definite (*le, la, les*) and indefinite (*un, une*) determiners.[123] We will see in Section 9.2 that all these elements may be represented by different categories.

9.1.1.1 *Gender and number*

Nouns are associated with masculine or feminine gender in French, as illustrated above, with the majority of nouns being masculine. In the singular, gender is usually signaled by the form of the determiner, as shown in Table 1. In the plural, the determiner does not carry any gender specification; it is simply *les*. Possessive markers are phonetically distinct for both genders when there is a single possessor, but determiners referring to several possessors are identical in the masculine and the feminine (*notre* 'ours', *votre* 'yours', and *leur* 'their').[124] Note that definite determiners are elided when the following noun starts with a vowel (e.g. *l'arbre* 'the+MASC tree', *l'école* 'the+FEM

---

122. As pointed out by Granfeldt (2003), certain indefinite adjectives can also qualify as determiners, such as *divers/ses* 'several.PL/.FEM.PL', *different(e)s* 'different.PL/.FEM.PL', and *certain(e)s* 'certain.PL/.FEM.PL' (see also Jones 1996).

123. It is noteworthy that definite determiners in French (*le, la, les*) have the same form as accusative clitics.

124. The gender of possessive markers corresponds to the gender of the noun they modify, and not to the gender of the possessor, in contrast to English. This is illustrated in (ia) and (ib):

(i) a. Cette femme a perdu son sac.
This woman has lost POSS+MASC bag+MASC
'This woman lost her bag'

school'). Moreover, the masculine definite determiner can combine with prepositions *de* 'of' (yielding *du* 'of+the+MASC') and *à* 'at' (yielding *au* 'at+the+MASC), as in *du vin* 'some wine' and *au lit* 'in bed'.[125]

Table 1. Gender and number specification on determiners in French

Determiners	Person	Masculine	Feminine	Plural
Definite determiners		le	la	les
Indefinite determiners		un	une	des
Demonstrative determiners (definite)		ce	cette	ces
Possessive determiners (definite)	1/2/3 SG 1/2/3 PL	mon/ton/son notre/votre/leur	ma/ta/sa/ notre/votre/leur	mes/tes/ses nos/vos/leurs

The assignment of grammatical gender is purely arbitrary and even with natural gender, the correspondence between gender and sex is not systematic, especially in the animal kingdom. For example, one can distinguish between *un lion* 'a+MASC lion' and *une lionne* 'a.FEM lion', but *girafe* 'giraffe', which is feminine, refers to both male and female giraffes. Similarly, *tamanoir* 'ant-eater', is only used in the masculine regardless of whether the animal referred to is male or female. When referring to human beings, the correlation between gender and sex is more consistent, although sometimes no gender distinction is made between men and women. This is particularly true with words designating professions, e.g. *un mannequin* 'a+MASC mannequin', and *un médecin* 'a+MASC doctor'.

It is possible to find strong correlations between the ending of a noun and its gender in French. For example, all nouns ending in *-tion* (e.g. *nation* 'nation') are feminine, and nouns ending in *-isme* (e.g. *capitalisme* 'capitalism') are systematically masculine. The phonological form of the last sound (or sounds) of a noun can also be a strong indicator of its gender. Corbett (1991: 57–61) indicates that at least 99% of words ending in /ã/ and /ɛ̃/ are masculine (e.g. *un appartement* 'an apartment' and *un larcin* 'a theft'); 90% of nouns ending in /z/ are feminine (e.g. *une église* 'a church'). Gender regularities may also be found beyond the last sound of the word. For instance,

---

b. | L'homme | ne | retrouve | plus | sa | voiture.
|---|---|---|---|---|---|
| The man | NEG | finds | anymore | POSS+FEM | car+FEM |

'The man cannot find his car anymore'

125. Note that only mass nouns, such as *sable* 'sand', may be introduced by the partitive *de* combined with a definite article. Compare the grammaticality of *Je veux du vin* 'I want some wine' vs. the ungrammaticality of *Je veux du livre* 'I want some book'.

while only 70% of nouns ending in /ɔ̃/ are feminine, the ratio increases to 99.8% when considering the ending /jɔ̃/ (e.g. *la nation* 'the nation'). In many cases, though, there is no clear association between phonology and gender. For instance, nouns in /e/ and /t/ are evenly distributed between masculine and feminine (e.g. *le papier* 'the paper' and *la poupée* 'the doll'; *le parachute* 'the parachute' and *la date* 'the date').[126]

Number marking is overtly signaled by the determiner and by certain endings such as *-aux* (e.g. *animal* 'animal+SG' → *animaux* 'animal.PL'). However, overt plural affixes are rather rare in spoken French. In the written system, plural is generally marked by the morpheme *-s*, but it is left unpronounced in the spoken variant (2b). Note that when the noun starts with a vowel, there is obligatory liaison between the /s/ of the determiner and the vowel in oral speech. Liaison also obtains between the /n/ of the masculine indefinite determiner *un* (normally pronounced [ɛ̃]) and the following vowel:

(2) a. un animal [ɛ̃nanimal] → des animaux [dezanimo]
a animal some animals

b. un homme [ɛ̃nɔm] → des hommes [dezɔm]
a man some men

9.1.1.2 *Definiteness and specificity*

Definite and indefinite determiners in French have different roles. Definite determiners refer to entities known to the listener or previously mentioned in the discourse; indefinite determiners refer to entities that are unknown to the listener or that are mentioned for the first time in the discourse. There is no overt specificity marker in French. Although definite determiners often refer to entities that are specific (3a), they can also receive a non-specific interpretation, as is the case of generics (3b). Likewise, indefinite determiners tend to refer to entities that are non-specific, as in (4a) where the speaker has no specific cat in mind, they can also refer to specific entities as well, as in (4b) where the speaker – but not the listener – knows which cat is involved in the event.

(3) a. [+definite] and [+specific]

Le chat a encore miaulé toute la nuit.
The cat has again meowed all the night
'The cat meowed all night again'

b. [+definite] and [–specific]

Le chat est un animal qui miaule souvent.
The cat is a animal that meows often
'The cat is an animal that often meows'

126. Note that here again, when the penultimate sound is also considered, the systematicity of gender correspondence may increase dramatically. This is the case of words ending in /te/ which are almost all feminine (e.g. *la vérité* 'the truth').

(4) a. [–definite] and [–specific]

Un chat a miaulé toute la nuit.
A cat has meowed all the night
'A cat meowed all night long'

b. [–definite] and [+specific]

Un chat s' est assis sur mes genoux.
A cat self is sit on my lap
'A cat sat on my lap'

9.1.2 Agreement concord

Adjectives agree in number and gender with the head noun they modify. As a result, the adjective may signal the gender and number of the noun. In (5a), for example, the adjective *petites* 'small.FEM.PL' is the one element in the NP which overtly signals that the head noun *chemises* 'shirts' is feminine, the same goes for *petits* 'small+MASC.PL' in (5b) which carries masculine gender. However, the adjective often provides no gender clue at all, as in (5c).

(5) a. des petites chemises
some small.FEM.PL shirt+FEM.PL
'some small shirts'

b. des petits pantalons
some small+MASC.PL pants+MASC.PL
'some small pants'

c. des chemises/ pantalons rouges
some shirt+FEM.PL pant+MASC.PL red.PL
'some red shirts'

As to number agreement, it is rarely heard in spoken language because the *-s* plural marker is mostly left unpronounced, as in (5c) above. When the adjective is located before the noun and when the following word starts with a vowel sound, liaison is obligatory, which signals number agreement, as in *des petits animaux* [pətizanimo] 'some little.PL animal.PL'. Only a few adjectives possess an overt distinctive ending in the plural, such as *tropical* 'tropical+MASC+SG' versus *tropicaux* 'tropical+MASC.PL'. Number agreement with these adjectives is therefore overtly marked. Note, however, that such marking only applies to the masculine form. In the feminine, the singular and the plural sound the same. For instance, *tropicale* 'topical.FEM+SG' and *tropicales* 'topical.FEM.PL' are both pronounced [trɔpikal].

9.1.3 Determinerless NPs

Languages vary widely in the extent to which they allow overt determiners to be omitted (cf. Longobardi 2001 for an overview). French is one of the most restrictive languages in this respect. In French, NPs without determiners can only be found in non-argumental positions: predicates, especially when the noun identifies the subject as a member of a class (6a–c),[127] idioms (6d),[128] vocatives (6e), and complements of certain prepositions (6f).[129]

(6) a. Pierre est avocat.
Peter is lawyer
'Peter is a lawyer.'

b. Pierre, avocat à Paris, est impliqué dans un trafic de drogue.
Peter lawyer in Paris is involved in a trafficking of drug
'Peter, a lawyer in Paris, is involved in drug trafficking.'

c. Pierre a été nommé gérant.
Peter has been appointed manager
'Peter was made a manager.'

d. porter chance / avoir faim / faire attention
bring luck have hunger do care
'to bring luck' / 'to be hungry' / 'to be careful'

e. Salaud!
bastard

127. In such contexts, it is possible to use the determiner as well, with a slight nuance in meaning: while the bare NP denotes some kind of property of the NP it refers to, the presence of the determiner serves to identify that NP, e.g. to someone who is not familiar with the person being referred to, as in (i):

(i) Pierre, l' avocat de ma femme, est passé à la maison.
Peter the lawyer of my wife is come to the house
'Peter, my wife's lawyer, came by to the house'

128. Not all nouns can be found in such constructions, but the semantic/syntactic constraints are difficult to establish. Moreover, as pointed out by Jones (1996), bare nouns may not easily be replaced by synonyms or close terms. So, one can say *porter secours* 'to bring help' but not *porter aide* 'to bring aid', *sur mer* 'on sea' but not *sur lac* 'on lake'. Furthermore, bare NPs may not be modified by an adjective: *rendre hommage à quelqu'un* 'to render hommage to someone' is fine, but not *rendre hommage sincère à quelqu'un* 'to render sincere hommage to someone'. This strongly suggests that we are dealing with idiosyncractic expressions which have to be memorized.

129. Other contexts where determinerless NPs may be found involve the presence of the preposition *de*:

(i) a. Le trafic de drogue.
the trafficking of drug
'Drug trafficking'

b. Un chien de berger.
a dog of sheperd
'A sheep dog'

f. par hasard / sur demande / en avance
by chance on demand in advance
'by chance' / 'on demand' / 'in advance'

Determinerless subjects and objects (of a verb) are not possible in French, as in (7).

(7) a. *(Les) lions vivent en Afrique.
the lions live in Africa
'Lions live in Africa'

b. J' ai acheté *(du) café.
I have bought of+the coffee
'I bought (some) coffee'

In contrast, English and Dutch allow a much wider range of bare nouns, especially in argument positions. For example, generics and mass nouns may be determinerless in English, as illustrated by the glosses in (7a) and (7b). French also differs from other Romance languages in which restrictions on bare arguments are less rigid. Such is the case of Italian and Spanish, which both allow mass nouns and plural bare nouns in object position. The examples in (8a) and (8b) are from Spanish.

(8) a. Preparé arroz para esta noche.
prepared.1SG rice for this night
'I prepared some rice for tonight.'

b. Aveces compro manzanas.
sometimes buy.1SG apples
'I sometimes buy apples.'

9.1.4 Noun placement

In French, nouns usually appear before adjectives as shown in (9). This is particularly true of adjectives of color (e.g. *blanc* 'white'), shape (e.g. *rond* 'round'), identity (i.e. derived from proper nouns, such as *anglais* 'English', *freudien* 'Freudian'), size (e.g. *grand* 'tall'), and quality (e.g. *intelligent* 'intelligent'). Note that past participles used as adjectives are postnominal (e.g. *détesté* 'detested'). This differs from Germanic languages such as English and German in which adjectives typically appear before the noun.

(9) a. une voiture blanche / *une blanche voiture
a car white

b. Un portefeuille volé / *un volé portefeuille
a wallet stolen

c. Les fromages français / *les français fromages
the cheeses French

d. Une bouteille ronde / *une ronde bouteille
a bottle round

However, a small number of high-frequency adjectives are found almost exclusively in prenominal position: *beau* 'beautiful', *bon* 'good', *grand* 'big', *gros* 'fat', *haut* 'high', *jeune* 'young', *joli* 'pretty', *mauvais* 'bad', *meilleur* 'better', *petit* 'small', *vaste* 'vast', and *vieux* 'old'.[130] In addition, some adjectives may be found either before or after the noun, and the meaning of the adjective may change according to its placement. By and large, postnominal adjectives are said to be predicative, that is, they refer to some property of the noun they modify. As such, they can appear in a copular construction such as NP *est Adj* or *qui est Adj* 'which/who is *Adj*', as in (10a), (11a) and (12a). This is typical of adjectives of size, shape, identity, color, and quality. A predictive interpretation is generally banned from prenominal position. Instead, an adjective placed in front of the noun often reflects the attitude of the speaker vis-à-vis the noun. Hence, an intensional or attitudinal meaning can obtain, as in (10b) and (11b). In (12b), the phrase *un sale type* does not refer to a man who has not washed (this would be expressed by *le type sale*); rather, it refers to a man whose behavior is questionable. Prenominal adjectives may also denote the specificity of the following noun, as illustrated in (12b). Finally, adjectives of time are largely prenominal, as they cannot appear in a predicative relationship with the noun, as shown in (13).[131]

(10) a. une question simple (= qui est simple)
a question simple which is simple
'a simple question'

b. une simple question (intensional)
a simple question
'a mere question'

(11) a. des draps sales (= qui sont sales)
some sheet dirty which are dirty

---

130. These adjectives are often referred to as 'short' adjectives. This does not seem to reflect reality, however, since some adjectives on the list are not monosyllabic, and some short (monosyllabic) adjectives can occur postnominally, as *seul* 'lonely' in *un homme seul* 'a lonely man'.

131. A number of exceptions can be found to this general tendency. For instance, the prenominal adjective *dernier* 'last' in (ia) is clearly predicative, and the intensional adjective *éventuel* 'likely' in (ib) occurs after the noun. For a detailed discussion, see Grévisse 1980, Jones 1996.

(i) a. la dernière réunion
the last meeting

b. un problème éventuel
a problem likely
'a likely problem'

b. un sale type (attitudinal)
a dirty guy
'a bad guy'

(12) a. une preuve certaine (= qui est certaine)
a proof certain which is certain
'sure proof'

b. un certain individu (specific)
a certain individual
'a particular individual'

(13) a. Mes futurs beaux-parents (≠ qui sont futurs)
my future parents-in-law who are future
'My future parents-in-law)

b. *Mes beaux-parents futurs

A further division of predicative adjectives into intersective and non-intersective adjectives will be presented in Section 12.2.2.

9.2 The formal representation of DPs

In this section we discuss the underlying structure of DPs, with particular reference to French. A formal account of agreement concord is also presented. The nature of the various determiners (articles, possessives, demonstratives, and quantifiers), the positions they hold in the representation of DPs, and the clitic status of definite determiners are discussed.

9.2.1 The DP hypothesis

It is now widely accepted, since at least Abney (1987), that noun phrases should be represented as D(eterminer) phrases (DPs), whose head is a functional category taking NP as its complement, as in (14):

(14) $[_{DP}$ $[_{D}$ la $[_{NP}$ $[_{N}$ chemise]]]]
the shirt

One of the ideas behind such a treatment of noun phrases is that their structure should parallel that of main clauses where the VP is dominated by functional projections, such as Infl and C. The idea is that D, just like C, serves to anchor the phrase that follows in the discourse. The D can play this role, it is argued, because it encodes such grammatical notions as definiteness and specificity, much like C, which encodes temporal specificity. Moreover, there seem to be strong similarities in the internal structure of verbal clauses and nominal phrases with respect to the distribution of verbs and nouns (see also Szabolcsi 1983, 1987). In French, for example, both the verb and the noun may appear in front of their modifiers (adverbs and adjectives, respectively). In Section 1.2, we saw that the order V-Adv was obtained by verb raising to I. Similarly, N-Adj is assumed to be derived by movement of the noun. Several researchers have proposed that N moves to Num(ber), an intermediary category located between D and N (Berstein 1993; Valois 1991, 1997). This is illustrated in (15b) where the noun *chemise* 'shirt' moves from N to Num above the adjective *rouge* 'red' generated in the specifier of NP.[132,133]

(15) a. La chemise rouge.
the shirt red
'The red shirt'

b.

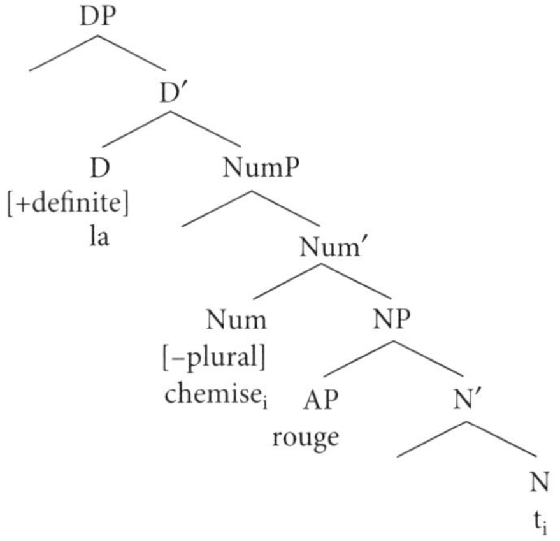

As seen in the previous sections, nouns are either singular or plural, masculine or feminine. They are held to be associated with (intrinsic) interpretable [±plural] and [±masculine] features. The Num head is also assumed to be equipped with such features. However, the features of Num are uninterpretable and need to be checked before LF (Chomsky 1995).[134] In French, these features are held to be strong, which means that N-movement must take place overtly (before Spell Out). Assuming that

132. Just as for the clausal domain, a variety of studies have looked at the internal structure of DPs, proposing functional layers to account for a varity of properties such as gender and agreement within the DP (see Longobardi 2001 for a review).

133. Alternative accounts involve head incorporation, adjunction, and complementation (Bouchard 1998; Lamarche 1991).

134. Under current theory, gender features are checked under Num, although proposals have been made for a Gender phrase (Picallo 1991) or a Word marker phrase (Ritter 1991).

adjectives are generated within an adjective phrase in the specifier of NP, as in (15) above, N-movement to Num yields the order N-Adj.[135,136] In languages where adjectives systematically appear prenominally, such as Germanic languages (e.g. *the red shirt*), number features are assumed to be weak, which means that N-movement does not take place overtly.

If this analysis is correct, then we must account for the fact that prenominal adjectives can also be found in French. Since movement is by definition obligatory (for feature-checking purposes), we are forced to assume that N-raising also applies in such contexts. Recall however, that prenominal adjectives generally have a non-predicative reading, in contrast to adjectives appearing after the noun. To capture this difference, it is assumed that prenominal adjectives are generated higher than Num. This is illustrated in (16).[137]

(16) a. Un sale type
a dirty man
'A dirty man'

b.

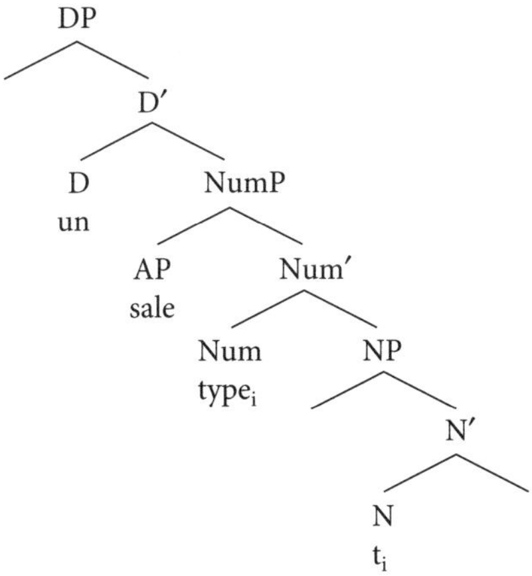

135. Alternatively, adjectives may be assumed to project their own categories above NP (see, e.g. Cinque 1994 ; Laenzlinger 2005; Scott 2002). See also footnote 137

136. For some researchers, it is NP-raising rather than N-raising. However, a discussion of the nature of the movement goes beyond the scope of this book. For details, see Laenzlinger (2005) and the references therein.

137. A hierarchical projection of adjectives in the DP has also been proposed (see, among others, Cinque 1994; Scott 2002). I will not review this proposal as almost no research has been carried out on the acquisition of the ordering of adjectives with respect to each other in French, and of the restrictions underlying such ordering.

The other operation occurring in DPs, which is systematic in every language, is N-to-D movement, as shown in (17) (Longobardi 1994, 1996). According to Longobardi, such movement, which takes place at the level of Logical Form, allows the noun to receive its referential value. This operation is akin to verb movement to C in the clausal domain (see Chapter 13).

(17) $[_{DP}\ [_{D}$ la chemise$_i$] $[_{NumP}\ [_{Num}\ t_i][\ _{NP}\ [_{N}\ t_i]]]]$
the shirt

9.2.2 The different types of determiners and their status

The different types of determiners are argued to be distinguished by the different positions in which they are generated. While definite and indefinite articles are assumed to be instances of D, demonstratives and quantifiers are held to be generated in the specifier position of NumP, while possessives are argued to be in the specifier of NP (Valois 1991). Demonstratives, quantifiers and possessives then move out of their positions: demonstratives raise to the specifier of DP, possessives end up in D after having first gone through both the specifier of NumP and the specifier of a Possession Phrase (PossP) located between DP and NumP, and quantifiers (and numerals) move to the specifier of a quantifier phrase (QP) projected above DP. According to these assumptions, the internal structure of French DPs is as follows: QP > DP > PossP > NumP > NP. In the literature on acquisition, however, the distinction between the different positions is not always made, and determiners are generally considered instances of D, except for quantifiers which are assumed to be QPs. In other words, while searching for evidence of the presence of D in developing grammars, researchers not only look at the occurrence of definite and indefinite articles, they also consider possessive determiners and demonstratives.

The status of definite determiners, in particular in French, has received a lot of attention in the theoretical literature. They are assumed to be heads, as we have just seen. This assumption is further supported by the contraction between *à/de* and *le/les* (into *au/aux* and *du/des*), given that contractions of this kind can only involve elements of the same syntactic level. If *à* and *de* are heads, the argument goes, then *le* and *les* must also be heads.[138] Definite determiners are also often considered clitics (Abney 1987; Zribi-Hertz 1999). For example, they must be repeated in a sequence of nouns, as in (18).

138. Interestingly, contraction is impossible with demonstratives (e.g. *à/de ce/cette/ces*), which suggests that demonstratives are maximal projections.

(18) *(le) chien, *(le) chat et *(la) souris
the dog the cat and the mouse

In addition, their form is dependent on the phonological form of the noun they attach to, as evidenced by the elision cases mentioned above (e.g. *le arbre* 'the+MASC tree' → *l'arbre*).

Finally, determiners are obligatory in French, in contrast to Germanic languages (where bare nouns are quite frequent) and Chinese (where there are no determiners). For Chierchia, Guasti, & Gualmini (2001), the difference between the various languages can be accounted for by the Nominal Mapping Parameter (NMP). According to the NMP, nouns are universally marked for either [+argument] or [+predicate]. Nouns that are [+argument] do not need a determiner to behave as arguments. They can therefore appear as bare NPs in argument positions, as in Chinese. In contrast, [+predicate] nouns cannot appear as arguments; they need to be attached to a determiner to do so. Such is the case of French, where, as we have seen, bare NPs are strongly restricted to non-argument positions. In Germanic languages, nouns can be either [+argument] or [+predicate]; this is why determinerless nouns are found so frequently in these languages. The task for child learners is to set the NMP to the target value. We will see in the next chapter that they are assumed to start off with a default [+predicate] value.

9.2.3 The representation of agreement concord

With respect to agreement concord, Carstens (2000) proposes that determiners and adjectives have no intrinsic gender specification, in contrast to nouns. Instead, determiners and adjectives are associated with an uninterpretable [*u*gender] feature which needs to be checked or valued (Chomsky 2000). This operation takes place through a specifier/head or head/head agreement relationship with the interpretable gender feature of the noun. The relevant configuration obtains thanks to noun movement, either overt or covert, as illustrated in (19). Note that in (19), an NP-shell is assumed, in which an *n*P phrase dominates NP. According to Marantz (1997), the root N must move to the functional category *n* in order to become a noun. Following Kihm (2005) and van der Velde (2003), we assume that *n* is associated with gender and that N-movement to *n* takes place so that gender feature checking can take place. After raising to *n*, the noun overtly raises to Num. This will result in checking the [*u*gender] features of adjectives *vert* 'green' and *grand* 'large' in (19), via a spec/head configuration. Covert noun raising then applies to D, with the resulting head/head relationship allowing checking of the [*u*gender] of D.

(19) a. la grande chemise verte
the+FEM large.FEM shirt+FEM green.FEM
'The large green shirt'

b.

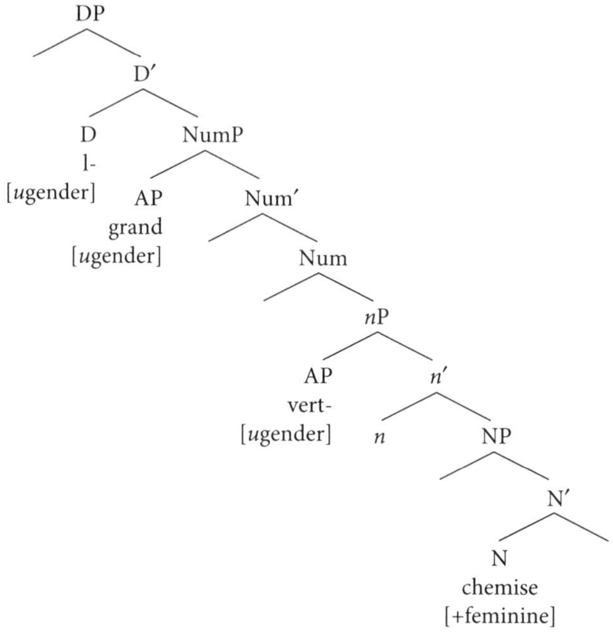

Once the [*u*gender] features of the adjective and of the determiner have been checked, the terminal nodes A and D will be specified for a specific gender, [+feminine] in the example given above. Following Distributed Morphology (Halle & Marantz 1993), whereby lexical items of the Vocabulary are inserted into terminal nodes of syntactic derivations via feature matching (see Section 4.2.1.4), the appropriate forms, i.e. those bearing a matching gender feature, will then be inserted into A and D. In (19), the relevant [+feminine] forms are *la*, *grande* and *verte*.

9.3 Questions for acquisition

The research question that has received the most attention is whether or not overt determiners are produced from the outset, or whether their development is somewhat delayed. In children with SLI, there is the additional question of whether or not the determiner system is affected by their condition, as is the case with past tense morphology and object clitics. Other research questions pertain to knowledge of number and gender (e.g. do learners produce the correct gender/number right from the beginning or do they use default determiners? Does gender appear before number or vice versa?). As mentioned in Chapter 1, the status of functional categories and their features in developing grammars is currently the subject of a vivid debate. Are they part of initial grammars? In L2 acquisition, do they transfer from the L1 grammar into the IL system?

Can L2 categories and features be acquired? These questions have been investigated from the perspective of the D category and its features. Moreover, comparisons have been made between the development of D and I: do these projections develop at the same time or are they acquired independently of each other? Research into these questions will be reviewed in the upcoming chapters.

CHAPTER 10

Determiner phrases in child L1 French

Fewer studies have focused on the acquisition of D-elements in L1 French than on properties related to the verbal domain. Investigations so far suggest that children are quite fast at acquiring determiners in French, although they seem to go through an initial phase where they produce determinerless nouns (Heinen & Kadow 1990). In this initial phase, children name objects and people using bare NPs. Target-like forms make their first appearance at around the age of two, although there is some variation across children. The determiner system then takes quite some time to develop, as children seem to struggle with gender and definiteness.

10.1 L1 acquisition of determiners in French

As shown in Table 1, investigation of spontaneous production by children learning French shows that determiners appear slightly before the age of two, but they are not

Table 1. Incidence of overt determiners in child L1 French

Child	Age	First appearance	50% incidence rate	90% incidence rate
Louis[a]	1;9.26–2;3.29	around 1;10	around 2;0.15	around 2;3
Marie[b]	1;8.26–2;6.10	1;9	around 2;2	around 2;6
Grégoire[c]	1;9.18–2;5.27	1;9,28	btw 2;0.5 and 2;1.25	2;5.1
Augustin[b]	2;0.2–2;9.30	2;0.2	btw 2;5 and 2;6	btw 2;8 and 2;9
Hugo[d]	1;8.14–2;5.19	1;10.6	2;1.7	2;1.29
Pauline[e]	1;2–2;6	1;6	2;2	2;6
Chloé[f]	1;11.19–2;5.14	1;11.19	1;11.19	2;0.10
Victor[f]	1;11.10–2;5.29	1;11.10	1;11.10	2;3.0
Tim[g]	1;5–2;3	1;5	1;11	–
Marie[g]	1;6–2;5	1;6	2;1	2;5 (89%)

a. Data from Hamann et al. (2002)

b. Data from Hamann (2003)

c. Data from Kupisch (2003)

d. Data from van der Velde (1999)

e. Data from Bassano (1998)

f. Data from van der Velde, Jakubowicz and Rigaut (2002)

g. Data from Demuth and Tremblay (2008)

used systematically until the age of two and a half. Between age two and two and a half, children appear to treat them as optional. For example, in Louis' data (1;9.26–2;3.29), of the Geneva corpus, determiners emerge at around 1;10. A stage of optionality then follows until the age of 2;3, at which point a 90% production rate is reached in obligatory contexts (Hamann et al. 2002). Example of bare NPs are given in (1).

(1) a. tiens couteau (Louis, 1;10.5) (Hamann et al. 2002)
hold knife

b. Ai caché lumière. (Grégoire, 1;11)
have hidden light

c. Je veux voiture comme ça. (Grégoire, 2;3)
I want car like that

d. Est chat.... Veux biberon. (Pauline, 1;6) (Bassano 1998)
is cat want baby bottle

The existence of an initial bare NP stage is difficult to establish across children. While Louis and Hugo are reported to only use bare nouns for a period prior to the emergence of their first determiners, other children have been found to produce determiners as soon as their first recording samples. For instance, Louis's determiner omission rate is 85% at age 2;0.2, whereas it is as low as 30% in Marie's first sample at age 1;8,26. It is at 20% in Victor and Chloé in their first recordings at ages 1;11.19 and 1;11.10, respectively. It could be the case that the latter three children had already passed the bare NP stage at the time of their first interview. In all cases, however, there is a period of optionality before determiners start to be systematically used. Examples of target-like use of determiners are given in (2) (from Bassano 1998).

(2) a. C'est la culotte. (Pauline, 1;11)
it is the+FEM underwear

b. Cherche une serviette. (Pauline, 2;3)
look+for a.FEM towel

One of the general difficulties in investigating the acquisition of the determiner system is to decide whether the production of a determiner (e.g. *l'école* 'the school') corresponds to the occurrence of a genuine article, i.e. analysed as such, for example as a realization of the definite feature, or whether it is considered part of the word, i.e. as a result of erroneous segmentation. There is no across-the-board solution to this problem; the decision should be based on the behavior of each individual. For example, in each learner, one should look at whether nouns appearing in Det+N sequences also occur without determiners or accompanied by an indefinite marker. It is likely that the decomposition into a determiner followed by a noun is achieved once the child realizes that the sequence can be broken down, separated by an adjective, for example, or that the noun can appear on its own, i.e. without its determiner component.

The development of determiners in three phases (omission, optionality, and target-like usage) is reported in the acquisition of other languages, such as English, Swedish, and Italian (Chierchia, Guasti & Gualmini 2001). Interestingly, it seems that children learning French and Italian go through the different stages faster than children learning languages such as English and Swedish. In particular, their optionality stage is reported to be much shorter.

Children are also reported to use a number of placeholders in the early stages of acquisition of French, such as [ə], [a], [e], and [am], which seem to be reduced forms of determiners (Bassano 1998; Clark 1998; Demuth & Tremblay 2008). Some examples are given in (3).

(3) a. [a] lapin, [e] bébé, [am] lit. (Bassano 1998)
rabbit baby bed

b. [e] seau, [a] pe(lle) (Francis, 1;10.17) (Clark 1998)
bucket shovel

c. [ə] tito (=bouton) (Francis, 1;11) (Clark 1998)
button

In her investigation of Pauline's data (1;2–2;6), Bassano (1998) reports that the incidence of these placeholders – which are also called fillers – can be quite high at the beginning (see also Demuth & Tremblay 2008). During the first phase of acquisition identified by Bassano (1;2–1;5), NPs that should be accompanied by a determiner are either bare (84%) or preceded by a filler (16%). The incidence of fillers then increases, with fillers produced in approximately 30% of obligatory contexts for determiners between the ages of 1;6 and 2;1. A sharp decline to around 10% is then observed. In a study specifically looking at filler syllables in prenominal and preverbal positions in a child's spontaneous production (1;3.2–2;2.6), Veneziano & Sinclair (2000) report a very high percentage of fillers where grammatical morphemes are required in French. They also observe a correlation between the reduction in the percentage of filler syllables and the increase of target-like morphemes. Target-like morphemes are rare until 1;10.12 (7.7%), but much more frequent thereafter (60.5% at age 2;2.6). In contrast, fillers are found in front of 40% of lexical items between 1;7.18 and 1;9.3, 20.9% at 1;10.12, and 12.6% at 2;2.6. This strongly suggests that fillers are precursors of determiners in child L1 acquisition.

The other area of interest in the acquisition of determiners is whether there is any difference in the acquisition of the different types. Although insufficient research has been done on this topic, initial studies suggest that demonstratives and possessives develop later than definites and indefinites. In Hugo's data, for example, van der Velde (1999) reports that articles emerge at 1;10.6 while demonstratives and possessives are first found three months later, at age 2;1.09.

10.2 Development of definiteness in child L1 French

Definite articles are produced before indefinites, and for a while, definite determiners are used in all contexts, whether they are appropriate or not. According to Clark (1998), appropriate use of definite and indefinite articles may not be fully mastered before the age of three or four. However, as Granfeldt (2003) points out, whether children have mastered the pragmatic relations of definiteness is a different question from whether the forms themselves have emerged or whether the [± definite] feature is present in underlying grammars.

In elicited production tasks, the results suggest that knowledge of definite and indefinite determiners is in place by the age of three. Van der Velde (2003) reports on two tasks based on pictures. In the first task, the pictures represent a little girl and a little boy, and occasionally a pet, involved in some kind of action. For each picture, the child is asked a question about the patient or the agent, in either a passive (4a–b) or active (4c) setting. For each of the 22 questions asked, a definite determiner is expected in the answer (11 feminine and 11 masculine).

(4) a. Question: Qui est coiffé par le petit garçon?
who is brushed by the little boy

Expected answer: La petite fille.
the little girl

b. Question: Qui est lavé? Expected answer: Le petit garçon.
who is washed the little boy

c. Question: Qui boit le lait? Expected answer: Le chat.
who drinks the milk the cat

The results summarized in Table 2 clearly show that determiners were almost always provided, even in the youngest group, and that the determiners used were always definite.

Table 2. Percentage of production of definite DPs and bare nouns in elicited task 1 (from van der Velde 2003)

Group	Age	% Definite	% Bare
Group 1 (n=12)	3;3	95.1%	4.9%
Group 2 (n=12)	4;2	96.9%	3.1%
Group 3 (n=12)	6;7	100%	0%
Adults	–	100%	0%

In the second task, a definite DP was elicited within a verbal clause. In all, 24 articles were targeted, 8 masculine, 8 feminine, and 8 plural. Two sets of drawings were used in this task. In the first set, the children were presented with pictures of different objects and asked to describe what they saw. One of the objects, the target item, was a different color from the others. In each case, an indefinite noun was elicited, as in (5).

(5) Question: Qu'est-ce que tu vois ici? Expected answer: Un livre bleu.
what you see here a+MASC book blue
'What do you see here?' 'A blue book.'

Once the child had become familiar with the target object, a second drawing, in which a character was doing something with the object, was presented to him or her. The child was asked to described the action and was expected to answer using the target object along with a definite determiner, as in (6).

(6) Question: Et ici, que fait le petit garçon?
and here what does the little boy
'And here, what is the little boy doing?'

Expected answer: Il lit le livre bleu.
he reads the book blue
'He's reading the blue book.'

The different types of answers used by the participants are given in Table 3. Discarding answers labeled *Others*, such as *il les prend* 'he's taking them' (instead of *Il prend les voitures rouges* 'He's taking the red cars'), it is clear that when a noun was provided, it was almost always accompanied by a determiner. In addition, when a determiner was used, it was almost always a target definite article. Very few demonstratives or possessives were used. Crucially, very few indefinite articles were produced, even by the youngest children.

Table 3. Percentage of production of the different answers in elicited task 2 (from van der Velde 2003)

Group	Age	% Definite DP	% Indefinite DP	% Bare[139]	Other (e.g. accusative clitic)
Group 1 (n=12)	3;5	80.4%	4.5%	5.9%	9.1%
Group 2 (n=12)	4;2	77.8%	7.7%	7.7%	6.8%
Group 3 (n=12)	6;4	97.3%	1.7%	0%	1%
Adults	–	100%	0%	0%	0%

The results of the two experiments are therefore similar and show that determiners are well mastered by the age of three. Details about the naming of objects in the first

139. It is not clear what the answer Bare means. The few examples provided by van der Velde illustrate cases of object omission rather than bare nouns, such as *Il répare* 'He's repairing' (instead of *Il répare les chaussettes vertes* 'He's repairing the green socks'). Therefore, the percentage of true bare nouns produced by the children is even lower than what is reported in Table 3.

part of the second experiment, where an indefinite determiner was expected, should have been reported, for the sake of completeness. If it is true that children go through an early period during which definite determiners are used across the board, erroneous production of such elements is to be expected in that task.

Naturally, research on knowledge of definiteness should be very careful about the discursive and situational context when analysing the way children introduce new information. For instance, introducing new information with a definite article may not be erroneous if the reference can be found in the context. Therefore, asking a child to tell a story based on pictures that both the child and the experimenter can see may not be the best way to elicit definite and indefinite determiners, given that all participants can be assumed to have knowledge of the characters and actions represented by the pictures. In particular, when the referent associated with the new information is salient enough (from the physical context, for example), it can be directly introduced as the topic of the sentence, namely via dislocation (e.g. *Le cochon, il est là* 'The pig it is here'). In such cases, use of an indefinite determiner is not possible. Conversely, as argued by De Cat (2004), resorting to dislocation (with a definite DP) would be erroneous if the referent is new and not salient enough. Reviewing spontaneous production data from five children learning L1 French (from age 1;10 to 3;16), De Cat found no errors involving the non-target-like use of a definite determiner introducing new and non-unique information. Moreover, when new information was introduced via existential constructions (e.g. *Il y a* DP *qui...* 'There is DP that...'), the DP was systematically indefinite, as required in French (see (7)).

(7) a. (il) (y) a un poisson derrière. (Tom, 2;5.24)
there is a fish behind

b. Mais il y a un petit bouton qui va le faire rouler.
but there is a little button that will it make roll
(Max, 3;1.25)

Finally, no errors involving definiteness were observed in dislocated constructions. Indefinites were never used in reference to a specific antecedent, and dislocation was not used to introduce new information that was not salient in the context.

Hickmann, Hendriks, Roland & Liang (1996), however, report a relatively high incidence of errors of the latter type in a study relying on an elicitation experiment in which children (aged on average 4;10, 7;6 and 10;6) were asked to tell a story based on pictures to a blindfolded person. The children in this study used definite DPs in dislocation constructions to introduce new information which was clearly non-salient given that the receiver of that information could not see. As De Cat (2004) argues, these errors might be due to immature cognitive development, rather than to a shortcoming in linguistic knowledge. In particular, the children may not fully grasp the fact that saliency needs to be based not only on their own perspective, but also on the perspective of the listener. For De Cat, the elicitation task used in the study may have exacerbated such cognitive immaturity.

10.3 Development of number and gender in child L1 French

With determiners, number seems to be mastered earlier than gender. The few number errors reported in the literature tend to occur in the early phases of acquisition (Heinen & Kadow 1990). The acquisition of gender seems to vary widely across children; it can take quite some time in some cases and be much faster in others. In terms of errors, children tend to overgeneralize masculine forms *le* and *un*, which they use as default forms (e.g. *un maison* 'a+MASC house' for *une maison* 'a.FEM house'), but this is not systematically found in all children (e.g. *la couvercle* 'the+FEM lid' instead of *le couvercle* 'the+MASC lid') (see Clark 1985).[140] In the two elicited production experiments reported by van der Velde (2003), which targeted feminine and masculine nouns equally, almost no gender errors were reported, even for the youngest group (age 3;3 and 4;2, respectively).

At first, children seem to rely on word ending in order to assign gender. Karmiloff-Smith (1979) administered an elicited production task based on made-up words to children aged three to nine. In it, the experimenter used word endings that are typically feminine (e.g. *goltine*, *plichette*), typically masculine (e.g. *bicron*, *golicheau*), or typical of neither gender (e.g. *coumile*, *chalique*). The children were introduced to the words by way of pictures. The words were accompanied either with an indefinite article likely to match its ending (e.g. *une goltine*), a nonmatching determiner (e.g. *un goltine*), or a numeral (i.e. carrying no gender information at all). The children then had to use the given word with a definite determiner. Children younger than six chose the gender of the determiner based on the ending of the word. When given an unmatched construction, they ignored the gender of the determiner with which the word was introduced and used the word with the other gender, the one more likely to match the ending of the word. So, when given *un goltine*, children under six years of age had a strong tendency to say *la goltine* afterwards. In contrast, by the age of nine, children had stopped using the ending of the noun as a cue for its gender. So, when hearing *deux goltines*, they produced either *la goltine* or *le goltine* despite the fact that *-ine* is a prototypical feminine ending.

140. These examples are from Lightbown (1977).

10.4 Theoretical implications

The results reported above have bearing on the theoretical questions of the initial availability of D, the development of NumP and the [*u*gender] feature, and the relationship between the development of determiners and object clitics.

10.4.1 The initial availability of D

The fact that children tend to omit determiners and produce bare nouns in the early stages of acquisition raises the question of whether or not the corresponding functional projections are present in children's early grammars. This question is at the heart of the debate between adherents of the Strong Continuity and Weak Continuity approaches. According to the Weak Continuity approach, functional categories are not part of initial underlying systems, and their development is assumed to be constrained by either maturation (Radford 1990) or lexical learning (Clahsen, Eisenbeiss & Vainikka 1994). If the development of functional categories is related to maturation, then all functional categories should emerge at around the same age. At first sight, this prediction seems to be borne out in child L1 French, since inflectional morphology and determiners start being produced at about the same time, around the age of two. However, a closer look at the development of finiteness and determiners shows large discrepancies between the two, which are not predicted by the maturation approach (see Section 10.4.3 below). Similar disconfirmation of the maturation view is found in bilingual children, in whom D and I show different developmental trends (see Section 11.1.3.2).

According to the lexical learning approach, functional categories are not present in children's grammars until the morphological forms that they are supposed to underlie are mastered. Under this approach, D is assumed not to be activated until target-like determiners have been learned. This does not appear to be the case in the French data examined so far. In particular, children were found to use placeholders or fillers before they truly master the production of corresponding determiners. These fillers can be argued to instantiate the D category, since, as we saw, they are almost always found in positions where grammatical morphemes are expected, including determiners (but see below). D therefore appears to be part of initial grammars *before* the acquisition of target-like determiners.

Instead of postulating the existence in initial child grammars of a purely lexical phase, meaning a phase without D, one could appeal to Rizzi's (2000) Structural Economy Principle, according to which children use 'the minimum of structure consistent with well-formedness constraints'. According to this analysis, NP can be the root of nominal phrases, as well as DP (see also Friedemann 1993/1994). This can explain why not all NPs lack a determiner in the early stage of acquisition. Children project truncated (NP) structures until the emergence of the so-called Categorial Uniformity Principle, which underlies adult grammars, according to which a unique canonical structural realization for a given semantic type, nominals in the case at hand, should be assumed. As previously stated (see Section 2.2.6), the development of Categorial Uniformity can be related to computation complexity issues, in that the projection of the whole structure, full-fledged DPs in this case, entails computational operations, such as the projection of multi-layered structures and computations involving definiteness and specificity, which children may not be able to perform systematically at first.

However, this analysis needs to be nuanced in the light of recent findings in prosodic analysis of fillers. In their study of fillers in child L1 French, Veneziano & Sinclair (2000) found that these elements appeared significantly more often with monosyllabic words (between 60% and 80%) than with polysyllabic ones (between 7% and 20%). This asymmetry is unexpected if fillers have a grammatical function. It could be the case that these elements act as 'bootstrappers' for the acquisition of target-like morphemes. In particular, their first appearance may not be a grammatical phenomenon but a phonoprosodic one; they may be part of the child's construction of the metrical structure of the target language. French is usually considered an iambic language, meaning that stress tends to fall on the right-edge of the foot, as in [ʃapó] (*chapeau* 'hat') and [ləʃá] (*le chat* 'the cat'). Before the sudden occurrence of fillers observed by Veneziano & Sinclair in their data (see Section 10.1), most monosyllabic words are produced as CV or display reduplication (CVCV). As soon as fillers appear, these words are produced as VCV, which corresponds to a iambic structure. This analysis would explain why fillers occur quite frequently with monosyllabic words but quite rarely with polysyllabic ones. Once the iambic structure of the language has been established, the child is ready to acquire determiners. Fillers, which still precede 30% of nouns at this stage, may acquire a grammatical function while target-like determiners start being productive. Demuth & Tremblay (2008) found similar tendencies with the occurrence of determiners in early production data of two children, Marie (1;6–2;5) and Tim (1;5–2;3). After excluding elided articles as well as cases of determiners occurring before an adjective (for prosodic reasons), they found that determiners first tend to occur with monosyllabic words, and only later with disyllabic and trisyllabic words. This is particularly striking in Tim's data. While the proportion of determiners with monosyllabic words is over 30% from the first recording at age 1;5, it only reaches the same ratio with disyllabic words six months later (at age 1;11) and five months thereafter with trisyllabic words (at age 2;1). Crucially, disyllabic and trisyllabic words occur early in the data at ages 1;5 and 1;7 respectively. In Marie's case, determiners appear with disyllabic words as of the first recording (1;6), but the ratio of disyllabic words used with a determiner lags far behind that of determiners used with monosyllabic words throughout the data until age 2;5. As to trisyllabic words, they are frequently used as of age 1;10, but only so with a determiner (i.e. above 30%) as of 2;2. For Demuth & Tremblay (2008), these asymmetries suggest that early determiners in child French first appear in positions that are prosodically licensed (as part of a binary foot). They become to be gradually used with multisyllabic words once more complex prosodic representations have been acquired. Although this account remains to be further investigated, it points to the need of integrating prosodification issues into the investigation of the development of grammatical morphemes in language acquisition. Concerns such as the way grammatical morphemes are prosodified in the target language and the acquisition of prosodic constraints should therefore be considered more systematically (see also Demuth 2001; Lleó & Dumuth 1999).

When investigating the question of the presence of D in child L1 grammars, it is also important to look at the distributional properties of omitted and overt determiners. Are bare NPs found in contexts where DPs are to be expected? For example, is the incidence of bare NPs similar in argument and predicative positions? Interestingly, Bassano (1998) reports target-like use of bare NPs in the longitudinal and cross-sectional data she examined. The proportion of such bare NPs with respect to the total number of NPs produced is 30% in the longitudinal data (44% between 1;2 and 1;5) and 25% in the cross-sectional data (at each time). Although this could result from a tendency to omit determiners on the part of children in the early stages of acquisition, more thorough investigation of the contexts in which bare NPs are found should be looked at. In Chapter 11, it will be shown that making this adjustment for bilinguals gives a more accurate picture of their rate of production of determiners.

In RIs, it has been reported that lexical subjects are by and large bare, which can be explained by Case theory. If RIs are VPs, then overt nominal subjects cannot bear nominal Case because there is no place within VP for Case to be checked. Since bare NPs do not need Case, their appearance as subjects of RIs follows. What is needed here is a comparison of the incidence of bare NP subjects in RIs and main finite declaratives. If children have knowledge of D, the production of determiners should be restricted to subjects of main finite clauses. Similarly, if postverbal subjects following the object are within VP (see Friedemann 1993/1994), they should not be accompanied by a determiner, again for Case reasons.

One analysis of the development of determiners, Chierchia et al.'s (2001) Nominal Mapping Parameter (NMP) Hypothesis, has attempted to take into account the positions that nominals can occupy. As seen in Section 9.2.2, the values of the NMP are [+argument] (where a determiner is needed for a noun to appear in argument position, as in French), [+predicate] (where determiners are not needed in argument positions, as in Chinese), or [+argument]/[+predicate] (where determinerless argument NPs are possible, as in Germanic languages). According to the NMP Hypothesis, all children start off by assuming that nouns are [+predicate], which is the default value of the NMP. This explains why children learning languages where determiners are obligatory, such as French, omit these elements initially. Being exposed to input containing determiners then forces children learning French to change the initial setting of the parameter. But instead of switching directly to the target [+predicate] setting, they first adopt the Germanic value, i.e. they assume that nouns may be either [+argument] or [+predicate]. Chierchia et al. argue that this explains the period of optional use of determiners in child L1 French. The target value is eventually adopted, and target-like production of determiners is observed.[141] Note that this account does not postulate the initial unavailability of D in child L1 acquisition.

10.4.2 Knowledge of definiteness, gender, and number

Results of research on definiteness, gender, and number in child L1 French suggest that number is acquired first. This points to the early availability of NumP. With respect to definiteness, results from experimental elicitation tasks suggest that definiteness is mastered by age three. Unfortunately, we do not really know how children treat indefinite determiners prior to that age, since there are very few elicitation tasks focusing on them. If an adult-like understanding of definiteness takes time to emerge, and the definite determiner is initially a kind of default, then a high incidence of definite determiners is expected in tasks seeking to elicit indefinite determiners.

Regarding gender, results of elicited production tasks also show that children have perfect command of gender by the age of three or four. However, these results were obtained on tasks involving only a narrow range of nouns and based on the production of definite articles only. In would be interesting to know whether the same level of accuracy is reached as rapidly with other determiners, including indefinites, demonstratives, and possessives. In any case, research suggests that children initially rely on the phonological shape of the word ending in order to establish the gender of the noun. Hawkins & Franceschina (2004) interpret this to mean that the uninterpretable [*u*gender] feature of D is not available initially. Once it has emerged, children start relying on the shape of the determiner to decide on the gender of the noun. In other words, 'there is a shift from a phonologically-based concord system to a syntactically-based one' (Hawkins & Franceschina 2004: 189).

10.4.3 Relationship between the development of determiners and finiteness

Some researchers have tried to relate the production of bare NPs to the RI phenomenon in child language development. Hoekstra & Hyams (1998), for example, suggest that both bare NPs and RIs are due to the underspecification of Number in early systems, as seen in Section 2.2.3. Given that Number is also involved in the derivation of DPs, its underspecification will yield the production of bare NPs in the early stages of acquisition. In both the clausal and nominal domains, the underspecification of

141. For children learning English, Chierchia et al. argue that although they zoom in to the target value of the NMP (i.e. [+argument] and [+predicate]) sooner than children learning French, they still have to learn which nouns appear with a determiner and which ones do not. This takes quite a while, which is why optionality is observed for a longer time in child English than in child French.

Number prevents main declaratives and nominals from being temporally and referentially anchored in the discourse. This suggests that the development of root clauses and nominal expressions should be parallel. In particular, the incidence of bare nouns and RIs should start decreasing at around the same time, once Number start being fully specified.

Under hypotheses based on computational complexity, there may not be any developmental relation between the two phenomena. According to the Structural Economy Principle (Rizzi 2000), for example, children's RIs are VPs and bare nominal phrases are NPs, as seen above. Children project such structures until the development of the Categorial Uniformity Principle. If this development has to do with children gradually being able to handle structures increasing in complexity, there is in principle no reason why full-fledged structures should start being projected simultaneously in the clausal and nominal domains, since the computational costs involved may be different in the two contexts.

Studies that have looked at the relationship between the incidence of bare nouns and RIs in the early stages of L1 child French suggest that the two do not develop in parallel. In Hugo's data, while the incidence of determinerless DPs drops below 10% quite early, at 2;1.7, his ratio of RIs declines sharply much later, as of 2;2.27 (van der Velde 1999). The findings are slightly different in Louis' and Marie's data. There, Hamann (2003) found that the incidence of determiner omission and RIs dropped at around the same moment, as of age 2;0 for Louis and 2;3 for Marie. However, prior to that point, there is a difference between the development of bare NPs and RIs in that the incidence of bare NPs is much higher than that of RIs in each child. In Louis' first recording (1;9.26), for example, the ratio of bare NPs is 100% compared to about 30% for RIs (Hamann et al. 2002).

While these results are compatible with Rizzi's Structural Economy Principle, they argue against Hoekstra and Hyams' proposal that RIs and bare NPs stem from the same deficit (lack of development of Number) in child learners, since the predicted parallel development is not observed. These results are also incompatible with a maturational view of linguistic development, since that view also suggests that these phenomena should disappear together when the appropriate system matures within the child.[142]

142. As pointed out by an anonymous reviewer, there is also accumulating evidence for the fact that nominal and verbal categories (and presumably the functional structures associated with them) are processed in different regions of the brain, as shown by neuroatomical evidence from brain imaging studies on adult brain-damaged patients (see, among others, Shapiro & Caramazza 2003; Shapiro, Moo & Caramazza 2006). Disjoint development of the nominal and verbal domains may therefore be expected.

10.4.4 Relationship between the development of determiners and object clitics

As discussed in Chapter 9, one analysis of object clitics is that they are instances of D. Object clitics, it was also noted, have the same forms as definite determiners (*le, la, les*). If object clitics are in fact instances of D, then we might expect their development to parallel the development of other determiners. Such parallels do seem to exist. For example, we saw that there is a period in early child L1 French where determiners are not produced. In parallel to this, the development of object clitics is delayed (see Section 6.1.2). According to Schaeffer (1997, 2000), the delay in both cases is because the specificity feature is underspecified in early child grammars, which means that elements that usually mark specificity, such as determiners and object clitics, are optionally produced in the early stages of acquisition. Schaeffer's approach predicts another parallel in the development of determiners and object clitics. In particular, the incidence of bare NPs and clitic drop should be found to decline at the same time. These prediction are not borne out by the data on child L1 French, however. In fact, determiners seem to develop well in advance of object clitics. Moreover, the increase of object clitics is not quite as sharp as that of overt determiners. Table 4 brings together some of the findings on determiners and object clitics on the same children (from Table 1 and Table 4 in Section 6.1.2).

Table 4. Development of determiners versus object clitics in child L1 French

Child	**Determiners**			**Object clitics**	
	First appearance	**50% incidence rate**	**90% incidence rate**	**First appearance**	**10% incidence in transitive contexts**
Marie (1;8.26–2;6.10)	1;9	around 2;2	around 2;6	1;8.26	1;8.26
Louis (1;9.26–2;3.29)	around 1;10	around 2;0.15	around 2;3	1;10.19	2;2.17
Augustin (2;0;2–2;9;30)	2;0.2	btw 2;5 and 2;6	btw 2;8 and 2;9	2;4.1	2;9.30
Hugo (1;8.14–2;5.19)	1;10.6	2;1.7	2;1.29	2;1.7	2;2.27
Victor (1;11.10–2;5.29)	1;11.10	1;11.10	2;3.0	1;11.10	2;3.0
Chloé (1;11.19–2;5.14)	1;11.19	1;11.19	2;0.10	1;11.19	1;11.19

These data show that determiners may emerge earlier than object clitics (for Augustin and Hugo). Moreover, for most of the children, the production of clitics is still at a low rate (10%) when the incidence of overt determiners is already quite high (90%). This is true even for those children who start producing determiners and object clitics at roughly the same time (Louis and Victor). For these children, the ratio of determiners is already over 50% at the time when object clitics start being produced in 10% of obligatory contexts. In Augustin's data, clitic production is a low 3.9% at age 2;6.16, whereas he produces overt determiners 89.2% of the time (see Hamann 2003). His production of object clitics rises only later, at age 2;9.2. In addition, while the mean rate of determiner and clitic omission is similar in his early recordings (20.9% and 26%, respectively, between ages 2;0.2 and 2;6.16), a gap opens between the two in later samples: the rate of determiner drop decreases to below 10% (1% in the last sample), whereas the rate of clitic drop remains between 15% and 20%. Finally, we saw in Section 6.1.2 that in both Marie and Chloé, a strong initial performance on object clitics was followed by a declining production of these elements. In contrast, their use of determiners remains quite high throughout, especially in Chloé's case. In short, there does not seem to be any strong relationship between the development of determiners and that of complement clitics in child L1 French, in contrast to Schaeffer's predictions. The findings can also be interpreted to argue against a prosodic account of the development of determiners. If determiners are initially slow to emerge because children must first figure out the prosodic constraints of French and the prosodic representation of these elements, it is not clear why object clitics should not be learned at the same time, once these constraints are mastered, given their prosodic similarities to determiners.

10.5 Conclusion

In this chapter, we saw that the development of determiners tends to proceed in three stages: omission, optionality, and target-like use. It is important to note, however, that not all children drop determiners altogether in the initial stage. Moreover, some children produce a prenominal vocalic element very early on that has been argued to be a placeholder for the determiner, suggesting that D is available from the outset. The optionality of determiners can be accounted for by Rizzi's (2000) Structural Economy Principle, according to which the minimum structure is projected for a semantic kind, nominals in this case, which we have seen could be related to computational complexity issues. An alternative explanation is the Nominal Mapping Parameter, under which children are assumed to adopt non-target like settings initially (Chierchia et al. 2001). We saw that there appears to be no evidence of any strong link between the development of determiners and the development of either finiteness or some property – Number for Hoekstra & Hyams (1998) or specificity for Schaeffer (1997, 2000) – in child grammars. In contrast, the observed lack of any developmental relationship between determiners, finiteness, and object clitics is compatible with Rizzi's (2000) account of early child grammars in terms of structural minimality, suggesting that this account may be on the right track.

Other findings suggest that number develops relatively early, before gender and definiteness, both of which generate errors until the age of about three or four. Some researchers assume children's difficulty with gender arises because uninterpretable gender features are not initially available. It does appear that children initially assign gender based on the phonological shape of the word ending, rather than on any strictly grammatical evidence available in the context, which seems to support this hypothesis. However, more research on the development of gender is needed to determine, for instance, the extent to which children make recourse to a default gender. It would also be interesting to know if gender errors affect definite and indefinite determiners similarly. Another aspect of knowledge of gender that has been overlooked so far is gender concord between the noun and the adjective. Such errors are reported to be quite frequent in early child French (e.g. *gros porte* 'big+MASC door+FEM' instead of *grosse porte* 'big.FEM door+FEM' [Clark 1985]), but studies on this topic are rare. Definiteness errors are also frequently reported in early child French, with definite markers apparently overgeneralized to indefinite contexts, but further investigation of this phenomenon, via elicited production tasks, for example, is required.

One property of DP that has largely been ignored in research on child L1 French is the development of the strength of number features. Virtually no study has looked at knowledge of noun placement with respect to adjectives. Studies occasionally mention that only one element, which may be either an adjective or a determiner, can appear before the noun in the earliest stages of child L1 French, but no systematic statistics are provided. It would be useful to further investigate this phenomenon and report on the kinds of adjectives that are found in the prenominal position. Such studies would give us a fuller understanding of the acquisition of the DP in child L1 French.

CHAPTER 11

The development of DPs in French bilingual acquisition and in children with SLI learning French

This chapter addresses the development of DPs in bilingual acquisition and in children with SLI learning French. In general, the findings are comparable to what has been observed in (TD) monolinguals, although with bilinguals instances of delayed development of determiners and cross-linguistic influence are reported. In the case of children with SLI, the findings suggest that the acquisition of determiners, in contrast to the acquisition of tense and object clitics, is not strongly affected by their pathology.

11.1 DPs in French bilingual acquisition

The development of determiners and of the internal structure of the nominal phrase is well documented in bilingual French children. By and large, it resembles what is found in monolingual French children, although target-like production of determiners can be delayed in some cases (up to a year).

11.1.1 Production of determiners in obligatory contexts by French bilinguals

As shown in Table 1, determiners emerge at around the age of two or slightly after in French bilingual children. Their production in obligatory contexts then increases gradually, usually taking significantly longer to reach the 90% ratio than in monolinguals, often around a year following the production of the first determiner.

As in monolinguals, the incidence of null determiners can be quite high in the first stages of French bilingual acquisition, as illustrated in (1) and (2). It is impossible to say exactly how high because while researchers often note the phenomenon of null determiners, they do not always provide exact figures.

(1)	Mother:	Qu'est-ce que	tu	vas	manger?	
		what	you	will	eat	
	Anouk:	Ø pain				(Anouk, Dutch/French, 2;3.13)
		bread				

(2) Mother: Qu'est-ce qu'il fait le petit minou?
what he does the little kitty
Jean: Il mange Ø carottes (Jean, Swedish/French, 2;2)
he eats carrots

Table 1. Frequency of lexical determiners in early child bilingual French

Child	Other language	Age	First appearance	50% incidence rate	90% incidence rate
Anouk[a]	Dutch	2;3.13–3;10.7	2;4.17	2;7.28 (2 < MLU < 3)	3;3.17 (MLU > 3.5)
Mathieu[b]	English	1;9 – 2;11	1;11	2;11 (MLU ≈ 1.50)	–
Yann[b]	English	1;11 – 3;0	1;11	–	–
Alexander[c]	German	2;2.6 – 2;11.20	before 2;2.6	2;4.6	2;4.20 (MLU = 2.74)
Celine[d]	German	1;6 – 3;0	slightly after 2;0.9	around 2;7	3;0.27
Anne[e]	Swedish	2;3 – 4;0	before 2;3	2;6 (MLU: 1.9)	3;7 (MLU = 3.6)
Jean[e]	Swedish	1;10 – 3;9	around 1;10	2;6 (MLU: 2.0)	3;9 (MLU = 4.4)
Mimi[e]	Swedish	2;0 – 4;2	before 2;0	before 2;0 (MLU = 2.1)	2;2 (MLU= 3.2)

a. Data from Hulk (2004)

b. Data from Paradis and Genesee (1997). Note that in the case of Mathieu, there is no recording between 2;3 and 2;11.

c. Data from Kupisch (2003)

d. Data from Müller (1994a)

e. Data from Granfeldt (2000)

As noted by Granfeldt (2000), many contexts in which learners produce bare nouns are elliptical, as in (3).

(3) a. Qu'est-ce que c'est? [with deictic reference to an object X]
b. (DET) X

These contexts are predicative by nature, and predicative contexts are the ones in which bare nouns can be grammatical (although not every such context). Therefore, learners may be *overgeneralizing* the idea that bare nouns can be used in any predicative contexts. Thus, to tease out the presence of 'truly inaccurate' bare nouns, examples such as (3) should be ignored, or at least treated separately. When only noun phrases selected by verbs are considered, the ratio of determiner omission decreases dramatically. For example, with this new calculation method, Swedish/French child Jean reaches the 90% production ratio much earlier than what is reported in Table 1, namely 2;9

(instead of 3;7) (Granfeldt 2003). It would be interesting to take this into account in other learning situations (e.g. acquisition by monolinguals) when investigating determiner omission.

Placeholder determiners are also observed during the initial phases of bilingual French, but not in all children. For example, the German/French child Alexander (Kupisch 2003) does not produce any.[143] In the early stages of acquisition, adjectives and numerals may occasionally appear as prenominal elements, but determiners as such are relatively rare in these early stages. As in acquisition by monolinguals, the first instances of Det+N constructions may not be analysed by the child, that is, the determiner may be considered an integral part of the noun. This often seems to be the case of elided articles, as in *l'eau* 'the water'. There are also examples of Det+N constructions appearing with another determiner, as *des l'écharpes* 'some the scarves' (Granfeldt 2003).

As pointed out above, the emergence of target-like use of determiners can be delayed in bilingual French, when compared to acquisition by monolinguals.[144] In some cases, it takes at least a year from the moment determiners start being used (Table 1), compared to just about 6 months for monolinguals. In the German/French child Céline, omission rates above 10%, usually involving mass nouns (e.g. *et sucre* 'and sugar' 3;11.5), are occasionally reported even after use has become target-like (Kupisch 2003). The delay in target-like production of determiners may be due to cross-linguistic influence of the other language being acquired. Indeed, the studies mentioned above all involve a Germanic language where the incidence of bare nouns is higher than in French, given that these languages allow, for instance, bare mass and bare plural nouns to occur as arguments. To get a clearer picture of the potential influence from the other language being learned, we would need data from bilingual children whose other language imposes strong restrictions on the occurrence of bare nouns. Nevertheless, it is important to point out that whatever the influence of the other language may be, it is not total. In Céline's case, Kupisch (2003) reports that she does not use bare nouns in French in all the contexts where they are allowed in German. Kupisch observes that Céline correctly produced 30 determiners in 37 contexts in French where they could be omitted in German. Moreover, Céline reached target-like use of German determiners

143. Alexander was already aged 2;2.6 at his first interview, so it is possible he passed through a stage of using placeholder determiners prior to the first recording session.

144. One exception is Alexander, who achieves a 90% ratio of determiners quite quickly, but note that determiners had already appeared in his speech before the first recording, so it is impossible to determine exactly how quickly. His transition between 50% use and 90% use is significantly shorter than that of the other children so his overall learning time is also likely to have been shorter.

six months earlier than for French determiners, namely at around age 2;4.13. If there were a strong cross-linguistic influence from German, the incidence of determiners should be higher in her French.[145] For instance, she is reported to omit determiners with singular count nouns in French after 2;4.13, which is impossible – and which she does not do – in German.

Even after children begin to use determiners, they produce nominal expressions made of only two elements, either an adjective or a determiner and the noun. In other words, Det+Adj+N sequences are quite rare for a while. Table 2 summarizes omission rates of determines with adjectives and nouns in Swedish/French children. It identifies an initial period of high omission of determiners, followed by a second period with a lower omission ratio.[146]

Table 2. Determiner omission in Adj-Noun sequences in Swedish/French bilinguals (from Granfeldt 2000)

Child	Age	Higher omission rate	Lower omission rate
Jean	1;10 – 3;9	1;10 – 2;6 16/17 (94.1%)	2;9 – 3;9 11/65 (16.9%)
Anne	2;3 – 4;0	2;3 – 3;5 3/13 (23%)	3;7 – 4;0 0/12 (0%)
Mimi	2;0 – 4;2	2;0 3/4 (75%)	2;2 – 4;2 1/25 (4%)

In the Dutch/French child Anouk's data, 80% of the nouns preceded by an adjective are determinerless (Hulk 2004), as illustrated in (4), which also shows the same phenomenon as in the Swedish/French child Jean (see Table 2). Müller (1994a) reports that the German/French child Ivar does not produce Det+Adj+N sequences until age 2;5.7, whereas he does produce A+N without a preceding determiner.

(4) a. Petit bonnet. (Jean, Swedish/French, 2;2)
little hat

b. Petit poisson. (Anouk, Dutch/French, 2;4.17)
little fish

145. In monolingual acquisition, it is usually reported that determiners develop earlier in French than in German and that determiner omission is larger in child German (see Kupisch 2008). The six-month difference between German and French, in favour of German, observed in Céline's target-like use of determiners could therefore result from crosslinguistic influence of French, as argued by Kupisch. This is all the more interesting since French is Céline's weaker language, thus granting evidence that crosslinguistic influence may be observed not only from the dominant language to the weaker language, but also in the opposite direction (see also Müller & Hulk 2001).

146. Anne's omission rate is lower than that of the other children, presumably because her first recording took place at a later age.

Although determiners may not be systematically used right from the outset, once they start being produced, they seem to be correctly treated as clitics. Granfeldt (2003) reports that out of a total of 132 contexts requiring an elided determiner in the Swedish/French data he examined, 123 determiners (93%) correctly appear in their reduced forms, as in (5). The few errors that are found, which include use of non-elided determiners and of elided articles doubled with other determiners, occur in later samples, as illustrated in (6). It is possible that children consider such elided determiners to be part of the noun, but in any case, the fact that elided determiners are produced where they are supposed to appear suggests that children acquire determiners' target clitic status very quickly.

(5) Il passe aussi, l' auto. (Mimie 2, Swedish/French, 2;2)
it passes too the car

(6) a. le élastique. (Jean 6, Swedish/French, 2;9)
the+MASC elastic

b. est un l' éléphant. (Anne 9, Swedish/French, 3;7)
is a+MASC the elephant

Another piece of evidence suggesting that the target-like status of determiners is acquired very quickly by French bilingual children comes from the use of contracted forms *du* (*de+le*) and *au* (*à+le*). Such forms appear relatively early in the Swedish/French data, as illustrated in (7).[147] Crucially, no instances of *de le* sequences are reported in the data.

(7) Jean: Fini. (Jean 2, Swedish/French, 2;0)
finished
Mother: Qu- est-ce que tu as fini?
what you have finished
Jean: Du lait.
of+the milk

11.1.2 Development of definiteness, gender, and number in French bilingual acquisition

11.1.2.1 *Development of definiteness in French bilingual acquisition*

Systematic research on the development of definiteness in bilingual French is lacking. Anecdotal evidence suggests that as in acquisition by monolinguals definite determiners seem to be overgeneralized to contexts requiring the indefinite, as illustrated in (8)

147. Granfeldt acknowledges that some early occurrences of partitive *du* may not be analysed. Indeed, there is no production of *de* itself (as in *de la*) and the emergence of prepositional *du* is delayed.

(from Granfeldt 2003). In this example, the child should have used the indefinite article *un* when mentioning the egg for the first time.

(8)	Mother:	C'	est	pas	du	pain	ça?
		this	is	not	some+MASC	bread	this
	Jean:	Non.					
		no					
	Mother:	C'	est	quoi?			
		this	is	what			
	Jean:	L'œuf.					(Jean 4, Swedish/French, 2;4)
		the egg					

However, erroneous production of definite articles may not be due to a problem with definiteness *per se*. Rather, it could result from the failure to correctly analyse Det+N sequences. In the example above, two facts point to such a conclusion: (a) the fact that Jean's determiner omission rate is 70% at 2;4 and (b) the fact that the determiner is elided in *l'œuf* (Granfeldt 2003).

11.1.2.2 *Development of number in French bilingual acquisition*

Addressing the acquisition of number requires a distinction between number as a semantic concept and number as a grammatical feature. In particular, studies report that children may acquire concepts such as unicity/multiplicity before the grammatical entities *singular* and *plural*. Children use numerals and quantifiers quite early (e.g. *un* 'one' and *deux* 'two', Ivar (German/French; age 1;10 (Koehn 1994)). Moreover, they use plural expressions to correctly refer to more than one object, which suggests that they have the concept of multiplicity. However, determiners, including plural determiners, are quite rare at first. For Swedish/French children, for example, Granfeldt (2000) reports that *les* emerges at 2;9 for Jean and at 2;6 for Anne. In Mimi's case, quantifiers emerge at age 2;0, but plural determiners are not used productively until age 2;2. In addition, Paradis & Genesee (1997) found no plural determiners at all in the data from Yann (1;11–3;0), one of the two English/French bilinguals they investigated. In contrast, all of these children are reported to have command of *un/une* from their first recordings.

Interestingly, in the German/French data examined by Müller (1994a), first use of the plural form *les* seems to refer to one or more than one object (until the age of 2;11 for Ivar and 2;6 for Caroline). This is also observed in the children's German. The German equivalent of *les* is *die*, which has the same form as the feminine singular definite article. Some confusion may therefore arise with respect to this determiner, which may influence the way these children use *les* in French.[148]

148. In the German data, Müller notes that *die*+$N_{singular}$ sequences always refer (correctly) to unique items. In contrast, *die*+N_{plural} combinations may refer to plural or singular items. For

11.1.2.3 *Development of gender in French bilingual acquisition*

The incidence of gender errors reported in studies on bilingual French is low: around 10%, although productive use of both genders is initially quite rare. While the errors mostly involve overgeneralization of the masculine form of the indefinite determiner, masculine and feminine definite forms seem to be largely used accurately from the moment they arise. Table 3 reports the number of gender errors in Swedish/French children (from Granfeldt 2003). It displays the number of determiners found in the data, and for each type, how many were used in the wrong context. Although the number of errors is low, the majority involve the masculine (except perhaps for Jean).[149] Similar results are found in German/French bilingual children Ivar and Caroline (Müller 1994a). For example, Caroline makes more gender errors with indefinite determiners (36%) than with definite ones (17%) at MLU 2.6.

Table 3. Gender errors in Swedish/French bilinguals (from Granfeldt 2003)

Child	Age	Definite		Indefinite		Total
		Masculine	Feminine	Masculine	Feminine	
Jean	1;10 – 3;9	2/61	1/33	4/56	5/23	12/173 (6.9%)
Anne	2;3 – 4;3	3/73	3/38	4/81	1/33	11/225 (4.9%)
Mimi	2;0 – 4;2	3/46	2/28	8/53	2/37	15/163 (9.2%)

That gender distinctions first develop with definite determiners may be related to the fact that indefinite articles are first considered numerals by children (Koehn 1994; Müller 1994a). In the initial stages of acquisition they are assumed to use *un* as a mean to express the semantic notion of unicity and not the grammatical concept of number. The non-grammatical use of *un* is also devoid of gender specification. Of course, some variation is observed across learners. The Dutch/French child Anouk, for example, shows errors in both definite and indefinite forms (Hulk 2004), and for the Swedish/French child Anne, gender errors tend to occur toward the end of the recording period (as of age 3;3).

With respect to gender agreement within DP, it is reported that agreement between a determiner and an adjective is first achieved with definite articles. Agreement is also largely performed with masculine nouns at first. For the Swedish/French child Jean, the first agreement with a feminine adjective is found at age 3;1 (*la petite lusionne (=luciole)* 'the+FEM small.FEM firefly') (Granfeldt 2003)); by then, Jean had already

Müller, this suggests that the unmarked feature associated with *die* – and *les* – is [+singular] and that this initial setting is changed later based on evidence from the input.

149. Jean produced the same error involving the feminine indefinite determiner *une* three times in the same interview (3;1), i.e. *une fil* 'a.FEM thread'.

performed 32 agreement concords in the masculine beginning at the age of 2;2. In Mimi's data, only three instances of feminine agreement are found (two of them correct), versus 21 masculine ones. Finally, agreement is by and large correct: one error is reported in Jean's data (out of 60 occurrences) and three in Mimi's (out of 24).[150] Note that most agreement concord patterns involve only three adjectives in the early stages, namely *petit(e)* 'small', *gros(se)* 'fat', and *grand(e)* 'big'.

11.1.2.4 *Development of noun placement in French bilingual acquisition*

Although no study has been devoted solely to knowledge of noun placement with respect to adjectives in a bilingual context, results from Swedish/French and Dutch/French longitudinal studies suggest that nouns are initially placed after adjectives. We saw above that in an early developmental phase there seems to be only one prenominal position available and it can be filled by either a determiner or an adjective. Most of the adjectives reported in this position are from the group of adjectives that regularly occur prenominally in French, such as *petit* 'small'. Development of correct placement of postnominal adjectives varies across children: it is reported to emerge at around age 2;6–2.7 for Anouk (Dutch/French) and Mimi (Swedish/French) and much later for Swedish/French bilingual children Jean and Anne, at around age 4. Note that errors in noun placement are recorded for some time after correct placement begins to occur. These involve adjectives that should normally occur after the noun, as the adjective *rose* 'pink' in (9). Such errors may be due to cross-linguistic influence from the other language (Swedish), where adjectives are prenominal.

(9)	une	rose	papillon	(Mimi, Swedish/French, 3;7)
	a	rose	butterfly	

11.1.3 Theoretical implications

11.1.3.1 *The development of D*

Given the high incidence of bare nouns in the earliest stages of bilingual acquisition, some authors argue in favour of an initial lexical stage where no functional categories are projected. At the next stage, where noun phrases are made of two elements, namely, the head noun preceded by either a determiner or an adjective, there is assumed to be only one prenominal position available, which can host only one item, as in (10). However, the nature of the prenominal position is not clear: should the lexical elements be assumed to head the same category? Do adjectives have the status of determiners at this stage? Can numerals be considered adjectives?

150. Granfeldt (2003) reports 25 cases of adjective agreement in Mimi's data, but one of them is given without gender indication.

(10)

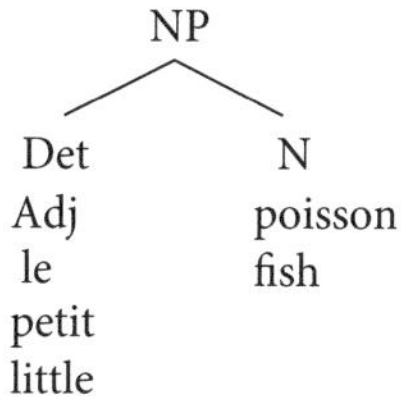

Note that at this stage, no functional category is projected above NP, which suggests that noun movement does not apply in early grammars. Further layers are then assumed to be gradually projected. At the next stage, Det-Adj-N constructions emerge, which suggests that two positions are projected above the head noun, as in (11):

(11)

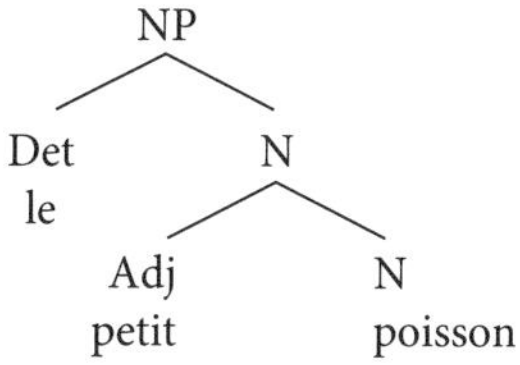

The status of these projections is not certain. According to Hulk (2004), they could be created either through adjunction or Merge.

In the last developmental stage, postnominal adjectives make their appearance, which suggests, under this analysis, that a functional projection is projected as the host of noun movement, as in (12).

(12)

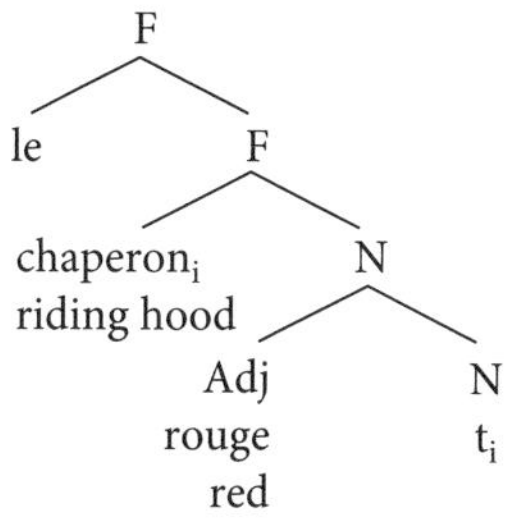

In contrast to this view of the developmental process, it can be argued that D is present in the earliest underlying grammars. First, when noun phrases occurring in argument positions are considered, the ratio of determiner omission is quite low, in contrast to predicate NPs (see (3) above). This suggests that the functional category D may be present quite soon in underlying grammars. Moreover, whenever determiners are produced, they are correctly used as clitics, which means that their head status is established extremely early. Similarly, contracted forms, which are used early by bilingual children, are only possible when the preposition and the determiner occur in head positions. Finally, cross-linguistic influence from the other language being acquired may also imply the early development of D. As previously mentioned, the studies discussed above all involve a Germanic language where bare nouns are allowed in argument positions. It is generally assumed that such bare nouns are DPs with a null D. Such an analysis could very well be adopted to account for the initial stages of the acquisition of bilingual French, meaning that once the children correctly assume DPs in German, they generalize DPs to their bare nouns in French.[151] Cross-linguistic influence could also account for the late emergence of the target N-Adj order among the children discussed above, given that N-movement only occurs at LF in the other language being acquired. It would be interesting to look at a learning situation where both languages allow noun raising to see whether the N-Adj order appears earlier in these children than in the Germanic/French children investigated so far.

Language dominance in bilingual children may also play a role in linguistic development. However, although it can account for the development of determiners in some children, it fails to explain development in others. For example, delayed appearance of determiners in French for the German/French child Céline may be related to French being her weaker language. In contrast, French is the strong language of the Swedish/French child Mimi, who was found to use determiners in French in her very first recording. However, delayed productivity is also observed in children for whom French is deemed to be dominant. Such is the case of the Swedish/French child Anne in whose data determiners only start being used in 90% of obligatory contexts at age 3;7. In contrast, high productivity rates are reported in children for whom French is weaker. For instance, although the 90% incidence rate is only found at age 3;9 in Jean, few determiner omissions are observed in his Det+Adj+Noun sequences between 2;6 and 2;9.

11.1.3.2 *The development of number and gender*

What triggers the acquisition of number and gender is not clear. For number, the fact that children can distinguish between unicity and multiplicity suggests that they associate nouns with an interpretable number feature. The same would be true for indefinite articles interpreted as numerals initially by the children. According to current theory, grammatical [±singular] features on determiners are uninterpretable (Carstens 2000). It might be the case that uninterpretable features take some time to develop (see Radford 2000). Alternatively, Granfeldt (2003) proposes that the late emergence of *les* can be explained by the delayed development of definiteness. This, however, does not seem to be strongly supported by the data he investigated. For example, Anne and

151. Cross-linguistic influence may account for some of the data, but not all. In Celine's data, for example, it does not explain why so few bare nouns are found in her French utterances; rather, she seems to know that nouns should be preceded by a determiner in French.

Mini produced almost as many definite determiners *le/la* as indefinite *un/une* in the samples investigated. As for Jean, although he produced more indefinite articles, he also used at least some definite determiners in all samples. Finally, Hulk (2004) reports that in Anouk, definite and indefinite determiners emerge at the same time. For Müller (1990, 1994a), it is the recategorization of indefinites from numerals to determiners which triggers the development of number (and gender) features. In particular, once indefinite determiners are correctly understood to be instances of D, agreement concord with the adjective starts taking place, which occurs for the German/French child Caroline, for example, at age 2;7 (Müller 1990).

The details of the development of gender are also poorly understood. Recall from chapter 10 that several studies in L1 acquisition argue for the role of morphophonological properties of nouns in the early attribution of gender (Carroll 1989; Karmiloff-Smith 1979). In bilingual acquisition, Koehn (1994) suggests that gender attribution is based on the use of schemas, at least initially. For instance, she shows that nouns ending in /o/ or in a nasal are systematically assigned masculine gender, which reflects patterns in the adult language, as in (13a) and (14a), which yields the production of target-deviant forms, as in (13b) and (14b).

(13) a. le cacao, le manteau
the cocoa the coat

b. *le photo, *le moto
the photo the motorcycle

(14) a. le train, le capuchon, le lapin
the train the hood the rabbit

b. *le main, *le dent
the hand the tooth

Another hypothesis is that children look for syntactic cues for gender assignation, namely the form of the determiner and the adjective (if there is one) accompanying the noun (Carroll 1989). One possibility is that gender emerges in a step-by-step fashion in the learners' grammars.

11.1.3.3 *Relationship with the development of IP*

In the preceding chapter, we saw that under certain hypotheses there should be a relationship between the production of RIs and that of bare NPs. Some argue that both constructions should decrease at about the same time as a result of the development of Number (Hoekstra & Hyams 1998); others claim that maturation should cause D and I to arise at the same time (Radford 1990). Other approaches do not make such developmental links, for instance Rizzi's (2000) Categorial Uniformity Principle which proposes that 'a unique canonical structural realization for a given semantic type' should be assumed. As argued in Section 10.4.3, this principle may not develop simultaneously in the clausal and nominal domains in young children's grammars. Adopting a computational complexity approach to this principle, the computational costs involved in the phrasal and nominal domains may be different, which means that I and D may not start being systematically projected at the same time by children. French bilingual data seem to confirm this prediction. In Anouk's Dutch/French corpus, the incidence of RIs and bare NPs is 20% and 70% respectively between the ages of 2;3.13 and 2;7.5. Later on, between 2;7.28 and 3;1.4, the incidence of RIs is about the same (24%), but the ratio of bare NPs has plunged by half (32%). In Anne's Swedish/French data, the incidence of RIs increases between ages 2;3 and 2;6 (from 0% to 20%), while that of bare nouns decreases during the same period (from 76% to 30%). Jean is the one learner showing a different tendency: the incidence of his bare nouns and root infinitives is about the same initially (between 50% and 80%), and both constructions start dropping dramatically at the same time, at age 2;4. Although this development pattern is compatible with Hoekstra & Hyams' approach, it neither supports nor argues against Rizzi's view. Under the latter approach, RIs and bare nouns may display similar developmental trends without being in any kind of principled relationship.

11.1.3.4 *Relationship between the development of determiners and object clitics*

In acquisition of French by monolinguals, we saw that object clitics are delayed and appear later than determiners. Similar trends obtain in the acquisition of French by bilingual children. Comparing the ages at which determiners and object clitics develop (comparing Table 1 above to Table 3 in Section 7.1.1.2) shows that although the incidence of both full DPs and object clitics is quite low initially, definite determiners emerge earlier than object clitics. For example, in Anouk's data, definite articles are productively used as of age 2;4.17, whereas only two object clitics appear during the first phase (age 2;3.13–2;7.5) and three thereafter. In Céline's data, object clitics don't emerge until age 3;4.9, at which time determiners have already reached the 90% production ratio in obligatory contexts. The same trend is observed in German/French child Ivar (Müller 1994a; Müller & Hulk 2001). These findings disconfirm Schaeffer's (2000) hypothesis according to which specificity is underspecified in the very first grammars. Since definite articles and object clitics both involve specificity, they should develop in parallel and emerge at the same time under Schaeffer's analysis, which clearly they do not.

11.1.4 Conclusion

In bilingual French, we saw that there exists an initial period during which determiners are optionally produced. Obligatory use of determiners is eventually mastered, sometimes only after a long time. Although the delay is not clearly attributable to cross-linguistic influence or language dominance in the children studied to date, no firm conclusion can be drawn because most of the children were learning French along with a Germanic language. Germanic languages allow bare NPs in more contexts that does French, which may have influenced the children to allow bare NPs in French. Other studies combining different languages, for example French and another Romance language in which the occurrence of bare NPs is more constrained than in Germanic languages, would shed light on whether and to what extent the other language being learned influences the acquisition of determiners in French.

From a theoretical standpoint, the findings reported so far point to the availability of D in initial IL grammars. Some children are observed to use placeholders in the early stages of acquisition. Moreover, the degree of omission depends on the status of the NP, predicate or argument, with lower omission in the case of arguments. Finally, determiners are treated as clitics from the moment they start being produced. These observations also call for more fine-grained analyses of the phenomenon of determiner omission in young bilingual children.

Bilingual children acquire different aspects of number and gender at different times. For example, quantifiers and numerals emerge before plural determiners, the masculine gender seems to be overgeneralized initially, and indefinite determiners seem to cause more problems than definite ones. Some of the explanations provided to account for these findings, such as the delayed development of definiteness, do not seem to be strongly supported by the data. All the data analysed so far come from spontaneous production protocols. Research involving other means of data collection, such as elicited production and comprehension tasks, would give us more insight into the development of determiners in general, and of gender and number in particular. The same is true for knowledge of definiteness, which has not been investigated much in French bilinguals.

Finally, the bilingual data available so far do not show any strong parallel between the development of determiners and that of finiteness and object clitics. This trend is similar to what is observed in the acquisition of French by monolinguals, and is likewise a challenge to approaches such as the initial underspecification of Number (Hoekstra & Hyams 1998) and specificity (Schaeffer 2000).

Bilingual children learning French seem to have an early developmental phase during which nouns appear after adjectives. The adjectives they produce at this stage, however, are those that tend to occur prenominally in adult French, such as *petit(e)*, *grand(e)*, and *gros(se)*. In later phases, some errors in noun placement are reported, involving adjectives that are postnominal in the target language but that are used prenominally by the children. However, the other language being learned in the studies reporting such errors only have prenominal adjectives. It is therefore difficult to know whether the late development of target-like adjective placement in French is due to cross-linguistic influence or whether it is systematically delayed in bilinguals. Further studies involving bilinguals learning French and another Romance language with similar adjective placement would help to resolve the issue.

11.2 The acquisition of French DPs by children with SLI

In contrast to tense and object clitics, determiners do not seem to pose particular problems to children with SLI. Although bare NPs may be observed at first, as in typical development, determiner omission seems to be rapidly resolved. Likewise, number and noun placement with respect to adjectives do not appear to be affected by the children's condition, although little research has been carried out in these topics. Gender, on the other hand, can be the source of some problems in children with SLI without, however, reaching the level of difficulty posed by object clitics.

11.2.1 Development of French determiners in children with SLI

The development of determiners in children with SLI seems to be normal, contrary to other aspects of the language, such as tense (see Section 3.2) and object pronouns (see Section 7.2). Jakubowicz et al. (1998) administered an elicited production task to 13 children with SLI (age 5;7–13;1; mean: 8;11) and 20 typically developing children learning L1 French (age 5;6–5;11; mean: 5;7). Elicitation was obtained by presenting pictures to the children and asking them questions about the actions they depicted. Targeted conditions were determiners *le/la*, object clitics *le/la*, object reflexive clitic *se*, and subject clitics *il/elle* (see Section 7.2.1). In general, there was no difference between the SLI and TD children with respect to the production of determiners: they both produced articles in at least 90% of obligatory contexts. Cross-sectional studies based on spontaneous production data yield similar results. Paradis and Crago (2004) found that the production of overt determiners in obligatory contexts was above 90% in a group of 10 children with SLI (mean age 7;6). A study combining elicited and spontaneous production data reaches similar conclusions: for the five children over five years old (among the 11 children with SLI recruited for the experiment), determiner drop was extremely low (Hamann 2003).

Data from younger children with SLI suggest that, as in normal development, the incidence of bare NPs may be quite high in the initial stages of acquisition. However, this may not obtain in all children. A study by Hamann et al. (2002) investigated determiner drop in longitudinal data from two children with SLI, Rafaelle (age 3;10–4;8) and Loris (4;7–5;6). Opposite patterns of early development are reported in the two children. In Rafaelle's data, the incidence of null determiners is relatively low throughout: at most 15.2% at age 3;10 and below 10% thereafter. In contrast, the rate of determiner omission is rather high in Loris' data. It is 41.6% in the first sample (age 4;7) and only starts seriously decreasing as of age 5;0 (where the rate of null determiners is still over 30%). It drops below 10% at around 5;3. Despite this difference, one should note that overt determiners were produced from the first sample on by both children. They were used in a variety of contexts, including complement DPs, isolated nouns, and dislocated

DPs. In addition, both definite and indefinite articles were correctly used from the first recording. This further confirms that although determiners may be omitted in the early stages, they can be successfully acquired by children with SLI.

Although the consensus seems to be that children with SLI have less difficulty with determiners than other aspects of morphosyntax, they are sometimes reported to omit more determiners than younger TD children. However, this may be due to methodological considerations. In a series of studies investigating the development of gender in children with SLI (see Section 11.2.2), a relatively high ratio of determiner omission (17.7%) is reported in Det+N sequences elicited from 18 children with SLI (mean age 8;9) compared to error-free performance by 18 TD six-year olds (Roulet 2007), whereas no determiner omission was found in the elicitation of Det+Adj-N sequences in 14 children with SLI (mean age 9;5) (Roulet-Amiot & Jakubowicz 2006) (see Table 4 below). These two studies did not use the same elicitation techniques, however. In the first one, children were asked to describe what they saw in a series of pictures, which may have led them to answer with bare nouns (*Qu'est-ce que tu vois sur cette image?* 'What can you see in this picture?'). In the second experiment the test was a sentence completion task, also based on pictures, in which children were instructed to provide the end of a sentence whose subject and verb were given by the experimenter, as in *Ici, l'éléphant porte…* 'Here the elephant is wearing…'. In this case, the expected answer had to start with a determiner (e.g. *une chemise verte* 'a green shirt').

11.2.2 Development of number, gender, and noun placement in children with SLI learning French

Most studies on knowledge of determiners in children with SLI have focused on the incidence of determiner omission and gender. Few have investigated in detail the issues of number and noun placement with respect to adjectives. Studies that have looked at the latter properties report that neither number nor noun placement seem to pose any particular difficulties to children with SLI. In a study involving ten children with SLI (mean age 7;6), Paradis & Crago (2004) report that production of plural articles was 100% correct. Noun placement was also largely correct in the data collected. A total of 76 adjectives were produced by the ten participants, of which 64 are generally prenominal in adult French. Those were all correctly placed in front of the noun. Of the remaining 12 adjectives, that are usually postnominal in the target language, ten appeared correctly after the noun. These results suggest that noun movement is acquired quite early by children with SLI. Note, however, that the number of tokens is quite low, so some caution is warranted in interpreting the conclusions reached by this study.

Gender seems to pose some problems to children with SLI, but the extent of their difficulties does not appear to reach that posed by object clitics. In Paradis and Crago's (2004) study, although there was no significant difference between the choice of feminine versus masculine determiners, the incidence of correct feminine articles was lower than their masculine counterparts (86% vs. 97.2%). Note, however, that the rates of correct use are quite high in both cases. Studies based on elicited production techniques report more frequent gender errors in children with SLI than with younger TD children. In Roulet's (2007) study, the ratio of gender errors is 7% in the SLI group (mean age 8;9) versus 0% in the comparative TD group of six-year-old children (see Table 4). In terms of distribution, more errors occur with feminine nouns than with masculine ones, that is, masculine determiners tend to be used instead of feminine determiners and not vice-versa. Interestingly, the ending of the noun seems to play an important role in the distribution of errors: the error rate is higher when the ending is not associated with a particular gender in French (e.g. [e], as in *café* 'coffee+MASC' and *épée* 'sword+FEM') than with endings with a highly predicative gender value (e.g. [al], as in *cheval* 'horse+MASC'). Similarly, in the study eliciting Det+Adj+N sequences mentioned in the preceding section, there are more gender errors in children with SLI (mean age 9;5) than in groups of younger TD children (four- and six-year olds) and adults (Roulet-Amiot & Jakubowicz 2006). In this case, as shown in Table 4, the percentage of errors is higher than what is reported in Det+N by Roulet (2007): 27.2% in the children with SLI, 18.5% in the TD four-year olds, and 5.2% in the TD six-year olds. Most errors are found in feminine DPs, where the adjective often appears unmarked for the feminine (e.g. **une grand casserole* 'a.FEM large+MASC saucepan+FEM').

Table 4. Percentage of gender errors in elicitation of Det+N and Det+Adj+N sequences (from Roulet 2007 and Roulet-Amiot & Jakubowicz 2006)

Group	Det+N[a]	Det+Adj+N[b]			
	Gender error on Det	Gender errors on Det	Gender errors on Adj	Gender errors on Det and Adj	Total
SLI	7%	1.5%	22%	3.7%	27.2%
TD4	–	0.3%	17.1%	1.1%	18.5%
TD6	0%	0.3%	4.6%	0.3%	5.2%

a. Roulet (2007): SLI group: n =18, age range 6;11–11;3, mean 8;9; TD6 group: n=18, age range 6;5–6;7, mean 6;6.

b. Roulet-Amiot & Jakubowicz (2006): SLI group: n=14, age range 6;10–12;6, mean 9;5; TD6 group: n=14, age range 6;4–6;11, mean 6;7; TD4 group: n=14, age range 4;4–4;11, mean 4;8.

Interestingly, error rates also depend on the position of the adjective. The elicitation task designed by Roulet-Amiot and Jakubowicz involved the production of postnominal and prenominal adjectives. The incidence of gender errors was significantly higher when the adjective was placed in a postnominal position in all children's groups.

It must be pointed out, however, that few adjectives produced by the children were prenominal (10% in all), so the results should be interpreted with caution and should be completed by more data.

Results on perception tasks suggest that children with SLI do have knowledge of gender. In a study measuring reaction time and response accuracy, children were asked whether particular DPs belonged or not to a semantic category identified by the experimenter (e.g. *Dis-moi si ce que tu entends peut se manger* 'Tell me whether what you hear is edible or not') (Roulet 2007). The DPs contained a determiner and a noun, with either concordant gender (e.g. *le bonbon* 'the+MASC candy+MASC' and *la banane* 'the+FEM banana+FEM') or discordant gender (e.g. **la bonbon* 'the+FEM candy+MASC' and **le banane* 'the+MASC banana+FEM'). The children used a mouse attached to a computer to give their answer (yes or no) and the time taken to respond was measured.

Table 5. Mean reaction time on concordant and discordant gender in Det+N sequences (from Roulet 2007)

Group	Concordant gender	Discordant gender
SLI (n=18)	1509.7 ms	1420.4 ms
TD6 (n=18)	1833.6 ms	1713.9 ms

Table 5 shows that it took more time for the children with SLI (mean age 8;9) and a comparative group of TD six-year olds to respond in the discordant gender condition than in the concordant gender condition, although the differences were not statistically significant.[152] Similarly, categorization errors were more frequent in the discordant gender condition (3.7 in the SLI group and 3.4 in the TD group) than in the concordant gender condition (2.4 in the SLI group and 2.3 in the TD group), although no statistical differences were found. Despite the lack of statistical significance, the results suggest that the children can tell between discordant gender and concordant gender. With Det+Adj+N DPs, the same methodology was used, but with two discordant gender conditions, one on the determiner (e.g. **un grande cuillière* 'a+MASC large.FEM spoon+FEM') and one on the adjective (**une grand cuillière* 'a.FEM large+MASC spoon+FEM') (Roulet-Amiot & Jakubowicz 2006).

152. The children with SLI were also faster at giving their responses than the TD six-year olds, which suggests that SLI development is not globally delayed. The same remark applies to the study reported below, in which number concordance/discordance was investigated in Det+Adj+N sequences.

Table 6. Mean reaction time on concordant and discordant gender on determiners and adjectives in Det+Adj+N sequences (from Roulet-Amiot & Jakubowicz 2006)

Group	Determiner		Adjective	
	Concordant gender	Discordant gender	Concordant gender	Discordant gender
SLI (n=14)	1019.5 ms*	1143.3 ms	1060.5 ms	1092.7 ms
TD6 (n=14)	1297.3 ms*	1555.6 ms	1329 ms	1383.8 ms
Adults (n=7)	493.6 ms*	572.1 ms	493.5 ms	594.5 ms

* significant difference between concordant and discordant gender

As indicated in Table 6, reaction time was significantly lower with concordant gender than with discordant gender in all groups. This suggests that children are sensitive to correct and incorrect gender. In the children with SLI, when the source of gender discordance was the determiner, they were significantly faster to react in the concordance condition than in the discordance condition; however, when the adjective was the cause for gender discordance, there was no reaction time difference between the two conditions. In the TD6 group, both the determiner and the adjective led to significant differences between the concordant and discordant conditions. Importantly, there was no gender effect with postnominal adjectives, meaning that reaction times were similar with concordant or discordant gender (around 1100 ms). With prenominal adjectives, however, reaction time was significantly higher in the gender discordance condition (+100 ms). With respect to categorization, few errors were found (less than 10%). Finally, no correlation was observed between gender discordance and production. That is, the children who failed to perceive gender discordance were not the ones who made most gender errors in production.

To summarize, children with SLI lay behind TD children only in production of gender. In perception, their performance is either better (in reaction time) or similar (in categorization). This suggests that the grammar itself is not deficient (in other words, there is no deficit in the operation Agree), and what is affected is the production system. We also saw that postnominal adjectives lead to more errors in production and to a lower sensitivity to gender discordance. This is expected under a CCH account and Jakubowicz's (2005) Derivational Complexity Metric according to which derivational complexity is affected by the number of Merge operations (recall Section 6.2.2.2; see also Section 14.1.6). Given that Det+N+Adj sequences involve one extra (internal) Merge operation due to overt noun movement, the derivation is more complex than the derivation underlying sequences with prenominal adjectives. Finally, Roulet & Jakubowicz (2006) appeal to frequency to explain why there should be more gender errors with adjectives than with determiners in Det+Adj+Noun sequences. Determiners are obligatory in French (except in few cases) while adjectives are optional. Their lower frequency would therefore lead to more errors.[153]

11.2.3 Comparison with the development of object pronouns in children with SL1 learning French

We saw in Section 7.2 that children with SLI have problems with object clitics. They do not seem to have similar problem with determiners, although determiners and object clitics share the same forms, *le, la,* and *les.* Therefore, there does not seem to be any connection between the development of clitic pronouns and the development of determiners in children with SLI. In Jakubowicz et al.' s (1998) study, we saw that children with SLI produced object pronouns in only 25% of obligatory contexts (see Section 7.2.1). The incidence of determiners *le* and *la* was significantly higher (90%) than the incidence of object clitics *le* and *la* for 12 of the 13 children with SLI (one child did not produce any clitics or determiners). Instead of clitic pronouns, the children either produced DPs, possessors, or strong pronouns, or dropped the object altogether. The findings were replicated in Jakubowicz et al. (2001) in a study involving 12 children with SLI (mean age 6;4) and 12 TD children (mean age 3;3). The children were tested twice with a 13 months gap (20 months for five children with SLI). Using the same methodology as in Jakubowicz et al. (1998), the authors found a very high rate of overt determiners in the children with SLI at both testing times in the children with SLI (81.8% and 98.1% respectively), compared to a very low rate of accusative clitics (6% and 16%). Finally, Hamann et al. (2002) report that at the first recording session, clitic omission for Rafaelle was close to 50%, compared to about 15% for determiner drop; for Loris, clitic drop was lower than Rafaelle (21%) at age 4;7, but it also appeared to be disconnected from the development of determiners, for which a high omission rate of 41% was observed.

Interestingly, a similar dichotomy between determiner drop and clitic omission is reported in adults suffering from agrammatic aphasia. In a study by Jarema & Friederici (1994), a sentence-picture matching task was administered to five agrammatics (mean age = 40) and five controls. The task targeted comprehension of determiners, object clitics, and gender. It involved 16 homophonous nouns only distinguishable by their gender, such as *le poste* 'the+MASC station' and *la poste* 'the+FEM post office', appearing as the object in 32 sentences. They were presented either as a full DP, as in (15a), or an object clitic, as in (15b). The participants were presented with pairs of

153. Another explanation rests on the fact that masculine and feminine determiners are lexical items while gender in adjectives is rule-derived. The higher error rate with adjectives could therefore stem from difficulties children with SLI seem to have with inflectional rules in comparison to suppletion (see Section 3.2.1.1).

pictures corresponding to sentences contrasting in the gender of the object (so, for (15a–b), a picture of a soldier leaving his post and a picture of a soldier leaving the post office). Each sentence had to be matched to a particular picture.

(15) a. Le soldat quitte le poste / la poste.
the soldier leaves the+MASC post the+FEM post office
'The soldier is leaving the post/post office.'

b. Le soldat le / la quitte.
the soldier it+MASC it+FEM leaves
'The soldier is leaving it.'

Many more errors were obtained with object clitics (35%) than with determiners (13.1%). Significant differences were found for four of the five patients, while the controls' performance was perfect. However, errors did not occur with all pronouns: differences only arose with grammatical gender. There was no significant difference between pronouns and determiners when natural gender was considered. It would be interesting to know if similar behavior also characterizes children with SLI.

11.2.4 Relationship with the development of RIs in children with SL1 learning French

In typically developing children, we saw that there may not be a point at which the rates of both null determiners and RIs start decreasing simultaneously. Moreover, the rate of null determiners is almost always higher than that of RIs. The picture is slightly different in children with SLI. Although, as with TD children, no particular relationship appears to exist between the development of determiners and the end of the RI period, the ratio of RIs may surpass that of determiner omission in children with SLI. As reported in Hamann (2003), in Rafaelle's data, the rate of RIs is quite high in the first sample (70%), and steadily decreases thereafter. It reaches the 10% mark at around age 4;7. During the same period, the incidence of null determiners is very low (usually below 10% and never higher than 15.2%). The opposite picture obtains with Loris: the ratio of RIs is rather low throughout his data (he is reported to use *passé composé* and *imparfait* forms correctly and the highest RI rate is found in the first sample – 13.3%), but his incidence of determiner omission is high (41%). Cross-sectional studies confirm these results. As seen above, Paradis & Crago (2004) report that, for the 10 children with SLI they investigated, all plural determiners produced correctly appeared in plural contexts, which suggests target-like knowledge of number. This is to be compared to the 74% ratio of past tense morphology reported in Paradis & Crago (2000).

11.2.5 Theoretical implications

The fact that determiners seem to be easily acquired by children with SLI suggests that the functional category D is part of their grammar. This goes against the Functional

Deficit Hypothesis (e.g. Gopnik 1990), according to which SLI grammars lack functional projections. Moreover, the correct noun placement with respect to adjectives reported by Paradis & Crago (2004) suggests that noun raising does not pose any particular problems for children with SLI, which argues against the view that children with SLI have difficulties with structure-dependent operations, such as movement (van der Lely 1998). Despite these findings, more research on noun placement is needed.

The observed differences in the acquisition of determiners and object clitics argues against the predictions of yet another major hypothesis accounting for the difficulties experienced by children with SLI, namely the Surface Hypothesis (e.g. Leonard 1998) according to which errors arise due to processing deficits (related to production or perception). Under this analysis, it is predicted that (definite) determiners and clitics should be equally problematic for SLI children because both definite determiners and clitics are phonologically weak elements (in fact, they are all considered clitics, and they have the same form). Clearly, the French acquisition facts do not confirm this prediction.

In contrast, the results are consistent with Jakubowicz & Nash's (2001) Computational Complexity Hypothesis (CCH). According to the CCH, syntactic computation in a given language is less complex when a merged functional category must be present in every clause. Such is the case of D in the nominal domain since D provides referential properties to the NP it selects. Determiners are not computationally complex and are therefore acquired early.[154] Likewise, Infl is required in verbal clauses as an expression of finiteness. Conversely, syntactic computation is assumed to be more complex when merging takes place only occasionally, as is the case for example with the functional category assumed to underlie past tense (see Section 3.2.2). Computational complexity is also held to arise when an argument is non-canonically merged with a functional category (that is, merged in the functional domain). Such is the case of accusative clitics which appear preverbally in French, as this is a non-canonical position for object arguments (see Section 7.2.1). Clitics, therefore, involve more computational complexity and develop later. In short, under the CCH, production errors are due to the application of economy strategies by immature or deficient production systems, not to a deficient grammar.

In order to account for the use of default masculine determiners, Jakubowicz & Roulet (2008) assume that *le* is not specified for gender in French, in contrast to *la*, which is [+feminine]. Once the operation Agree (which is not deficient) between a [+feminine] noun and D has occurred, with checking of the uninterpretable gender

154. For Jakubowicz & Roulet (2008), the few cases of determinerless DPs result from the application of an omission strategy aimed at reducing processing load, since omission involves less phonological encoding and fewer articulatory gestures than overt production.

feature of D, a feature deletion operation (Impoverishment, according to Distributed Morphology) applies on D post-syntactically. No gender feature is therefore associated with D any longer, which leads to the insertion of the default determiner *le*. Insertion of *la*, which is [+ feminine], would be impossible according to DM, because no matching feature appears on the host head. Feature deletion is taken to be an economy strategy since it leads, among other things, to a searching operation over fewer Vocabulary items.

The data on the production of determiners and verbal morphology by children with SLI learning French further suggest that the development of D and the development of Infl are unrelated in the acquisition of French. Interestingly, the data reported for children with SLI generally echo what is observed in TD child French (modulo some TD children who appear to acquire both D and Infl simultaneously). These data tend to support the argument that the nature of linguistic development is similar in TD and children with SLI, only slower in the case of children with SLI (Hamann 2003; Jakubowicz & Nash 2001). If this hypothesis is correct, then the SLI data suggest that the two domains are generally acquired independently of each other, and that the apparently simultaneous development of D and I observed in some TD children is only an artifact of the rapidity of L1 development and not evidence of a fundamental connection between the two domains.

11.2.6 Conclusion

Children with SLI acquire the properties of DPs with no apparent difficulties. In particular, they demonstrate target-like knowledge of determiners, number, gender, and noun placement at an age when they otherwise display tremendous difficulties with tense and object clitics. Theoretically speaking, these findings strongly argue against the parallel development of the nominal and verbal domains in children with SLI. They also argue against accounts of SLI relying on processing difficulties, given that determiners, much like object clitics, are phonologically weak elements. In contrast, they are compatible with Jakubowicz et al.'s (1998) Computational Complexity Hypothesis since D must be obligatorily merged in the representation of noun phrases.

Although the data on DPs are extremely helpful in pinpointing the linguistic shortcomings of children with SLI, more data should be gathered on SLI children's knowledge of number and gender, which has been only recently touched on in French. Moreover, studies looking at the development of definiteness are needed, as they are virtually absent from SLI research on French so far.

CHAPTER 12

Determiner phrases in L2 French acquisition

The last two chapters focused on the development of various aspects of DPs in L1 acquisition and in French bilinguals. This chapter addresses the development of these properties in child and adult L2 French. In these learning contexts, we will see that acquisition can be facilitated when the L1 grammar already contains D as well as features pertaining to definiteness, gender, and number. We will also see how, in contrast to monolinguals and bilinguals, both child and adult L2 learners of French tend to use determiners productively from the early stages on and struggle with gender. Number seems to cause fewer problems to French L2 learners, but again, L1 properties play an important role in the learning process. Finally, adjective placement with respect to nouns has been the subject of several studies in L2 French. In general, these studies show that target properties can be acquired, as can the semantic correlates of adjective placement, which constitutes a strong case for the availability of UG in L2 acquisition.

12.1 DPs in child L2 French

Few studies have looked at the development of DPs in child L2 French. So far, early production of determiners has been reported, and accuracy in gender seems to be lower than in number.

12.1.1 Development of determiners in child L2 French

In contrast to child L1 acquisition, determiners are very productive from the outset in child L2 French. However, since the studies undertaken so far involve an L1 that also has determiners, one cannot discard potential L1 effects in that domain. Grondin & White (1996) report early and regular production of determiners in two anglophone children (Kenny and Greg; see Section 4.1.1.1), including definite, indefinite, masculine, feminine, plural, and possessive determiners, as illustrated in (1) and (2). In Greg's data, production of determiners in obligatory contexts reaches 86% (24/28) at month 5, and it is above 90% as of month 9 (47/51). For Kenny, the ratio is 67% (4/6) at month 2, it is already above 90% at month 3 (18/20), and it never goes below that mark thereafter.

(1)	a.	C'est	pas	ma	maman.			(Kenny, L1=English, month 2)
		it is	not	my+FEM	mother			
	b.	C'était	toute	la	famille.			(Kenny, L1=English, month 3)
		it was	all	the+FEM	family			
(2)	a.	Le	lion	mange	les	girafes.		(Greg, L1=English, month 5)
		the+MASC	lion	eats	the+PL	giraffes		
	b.	Regarde	mon	dessin.				(Greg, L1=English, month 5)
		look+at	my+MASC	drawing				

In their study comparing SLI and L2 grammars in child French, Paradis & Crago (2004) report a 96% production rate of determiners in obligatory contexts by 15 anglophone children (average age 6;10). These children had been exposed to French for two years prior to being interviewed.

It is unclear whether determiners are considered clitics by L2 child learners. Carroll (1989) does not seem to think so, as she reports that English-speaking children learning French in immersion contexts tend to produce stressed articles and to leave pauses between an article and the following noun. This is a preliminary result only which needs to be further investigated and complemented by other data on elision and contraction.

12.1.2 Development of number and gender in child L2 French

Grondin & White (1996) found that on average 20% of the DPs produced by the children displayed the wrong gender, as illustrated in (3). This is observed in each child throughout the observation period. In contrast, very few errors involving number were observed.

(3)	C'est	une	grosse	accident	(Kenny, L1=English, month 2)
	it is	a.FEM	big.FEM	accident+MASC	

In their study, Paradis & Crago (2004) report that children were significantly less accurate on gender than L1 French monolinguals: accuracy rate for the L2 learners was 89.6% versus 97.1% for the 10 monolinguals aged 3;3 and 99.1% for the 10 monolinguals aged 7;3. In addition, the L2 learners were slightly less accurate on masculine than feminine determiners, meaning that when they produced a feminine determiner they almost always used it with a feminine noun in French. Nonetheless, accuracy rates were quite high for both determiners.

12.1.3 Theoretical implications

The data reviewed above suggest the early availability of D in early child L2 French, which argues against a lexical approach to initial IL grammars (Vainikka & Young-Scholten 2005). However, as previously mentioned, D is also instantiated in the L1s involved, so one cannot discount the potential influence of the L1. Further evidence for the early projection of DPs includes the production of the Case-marking preposition *de* 'of' in front of a nominal by Kenny and Greg (Grondin & White 1996), as in (4a–c). Since every DP must receive

Case, the appearance of *de* in front of a nominal suggests that the nominal is considered a DP by the learners; very few errors of N-N juxtapositions (4d) are reported in the data.

(4) a. Fête de Halloween. (Kenny, L1=English, month 2)
party of Halloween

b. Ça c'est de toi? (Kenny, L1=English, month 2)
this it is of you

c. Où l' autre des jaunes? (Greg, L1=English, month 9)
where the other of+the.PL yellow

d. Sporty est pas le nom chat. (Greg, L1=English, month 9)
Sporty is not the name cat

Apart from the early availability of D, little is known about the development of other properties of nominals, such as gender, number, and definiteness. Although accuracy in gender seems to be lower than in number, little is known as to the actual development of gender in L2 child French. Do the learners use a default gender for a while? Do children rely on morphophonological cues when attributing gender to a noun? How does acquisition of gender proceed in L2 French when the L1 already has gender versus when it does not? For number, what are its developmental characteristics when the L1 does not instantiate the uninterpretable [*u*number] feature, such as Chinese? Finally, little has been done on the acquisition of noun placement in child L2 French. Is it delayed or does it take place rapidly? What is the role played by the L1 in the acquisition process? All these issues should be addressed by future research.

12.2 DPs in adult L2 French

In adult L2 acquisition, early production of determiners very much depends on properties of previously learned languages. If D is instantiated in the L1 (or the L2, if French is the L3), productive use of determiners is observed; if it is not, the incidence of determiners is much lower. However, early production of determiners does not guarantee knowledge of their properties, especially their status as clitics. For noun placement with respect to adjectives, on the other hand, the target order can eventually be achieved, even if the L1 exhibits a different parametric value. Research on phenomena at the syntax/semantics interface (including some of the semantic consequences of adjective placement in L2 French) also suggests that native-like knowledge can be attained.

12.2.1 Development of determiners, definiteness, number, and gender in adult L2 French

12.2.1.1 *The production of determiners by adult L2 French learners*

Among the studies that have looked at the development of DPs in IL grammars, two involve an L1 in which D is active, namely Swedish and English. Granfeldt (2003) investigated determiners in spontaneous production data from eight Swedish learners of French at different levels of proficiency. Most of the learners (six) were learning French in an informal setting, whereas two where taking French courses. Granfeldt reports that in the 21 samples he looked at, determiners were produced in at least 82% of obligatory contexts. This includes samples from the three learners with the lowest proficiency level, Henry, Petra and Sara, who were learning French in an informal setting (Table 1).

Table 1. Production of determiners in Swedish-French beginner learners (informal setting) (from Granfeldt 2003)

Learner and recording	Months of exposure	Det + N	0 + N	% Det+N
Henry 1	less than 3	117	23	84%
Henry 2	less than 3	128	5	96%
Petra 1	3	140	11	93%
Petra 2	5	109	8	93%
Sara 1	5	124	18	87%
Sara 2	7	84	9	90%

Gess & Herschensohn (2001) administered a written sentence-completion task to 85 English-speaking learners of French at five different levels, including 14 beginners. The participants were instructed to provide a full-fledged DP (including an adjective) in the 30 sentences of the test. Results show that for 8 of the 14 beginners the incidence of determiners was 77%, as can be seen in Table 2. The authors note that even the beginner learners managed to provide determiners in contexts where a bare NP is allowed in their L1, although no example is provided. At the next level, the incidence rate for determiners reaches 90%. Gess & Herschensohn (2001), on the other hand, report that for six beginners, only 6% of the nouns they produced occurred with a determiner. However, the authors argue against a bare noun stage for these learners, given that they produced N-Adj sequences (see Section 12.2.2), which suggests that noun movement was allowed in their IL grammar and thus that at least one functional category was available to them (in the nominal domain).

Table 2. Production of determiners in adult L2 French (L1=English) (from Gess & Herschensohn 2001)

Proficiency level	Number of participants	% Det+N
Level 1a	6	6%
Level 1b	8	77%
Level 2	29	92%
Level 3	14	100%
Level 4	20	99%
Level 5	7	100%

Other studies have looked at the production of determiners by learners in whose L1 D is not instantiated. Leung (2002) investigated the acquisition of various aspects of French DPs by native speakers of Vietnamese and Chinese (Cantonese). The Chinese learners had reached an advanced proficiency in English prior to learning French, while the Vietnamese learners had no prior knowledge of English (see Section 4.2.1.1). The two groups will be referred to as the L3 and L2 groups, respectively. Neither Vietnamese nor Chinese have overt determiners, gender, overt plural marking on nouns, or number agreement between nouns and adjectives. Rather, nouns may be preceded by so-called classifiers and numerals. In these languages, noun phrases are assumed to be projections of NumeralP whose head takes a ClassifierP complement, as in the following hierarchy: NumeralP > ClassifierP > NP (see Cheng & Sybesma 1999). The head of ClassifierP is held to be associated with uninterpretable [±specific] features, which are deemed to be strong in Vietnamese and weak in Chinese (Leung 2002). Uninterpretable [±definite] and [±singular] features are assumed not to be instantiated in either language. Results of an elicited oral production task based on pictures are presented in Table 3. They show that while the incidence of determiners was target-like in the L3 learners, even at the beginner level, the performance of the L2 learners was significantly lower. The L3 learners may have transferred the D category from their L2 English grammar.

Table 3. Production of determiners in adult L2/L3 French (L1 = Vietnamese and Chinese) (from Leung 2002)

Group	**L1**	**Number of obligatory contexts for determiners**	**Number of determiners**	**% Determiners**
L2 French Beginn (n=16)	Vietnamese	994	706	71%
L3 French Beginn (n=41)	Chinese	1619	1478	91.3%
L3 French Interm (n=27)	Chinese	764	718	94%
L3 French Adv (n=13)	Chinese	330	311	94.2%

The learners were also administered a preference task focusing on demonstratives and possessives. In each pair of sentences, these elements appeared either directly before the noun (as in *ce/ton crayon* 'this/your pencil'), or followed by a determiner, which is ungrammatical in French (e.g. **ce/ton le crayon*). In the learners' L1s, the sequence demonstrative/possessive + Classifier + Noun is grammatical. The results show that while the L3 group strongly rejected the ungrammatical sentences from the beginner level on, the L2 learners' performance was at around chance level. In other words, the Vietnamese learners, who had no previous knowledge of a language without classifiers, treated French determiners as classifiers, in contrast to the Chinese learners, who had been exposed to English, a language that, like French, lacks classifiers. This strongly suggests that the Chinese learners were able to tap into their experience with a previous L2 to influence their learning of L3 French.

12.2.1.2 *Development of definiteness in adult L2 French*

Although determiners are often used productively by adult L2 learners, they may not always be used correctly. For instance, accuracy is higher on definites than on indefinites, a difference also often observed with monolinguals. Granfeldt (2003) reports a 75% to 79% accuracy rate on definites *le* and *la* versus 65% to 69% on *un* and *une* in his Swedish/French data. Despite this fact, adult L2 learners whose L1 instantiates definiteness features seem to have early knowledge of the [±definite] features. Granfeldt mentions that even for the least proficient learners newly mentioned nouns are almost always introduced with an indefinite determiner, and are later on repeated with a definite one, as illustrated by the two occurrences of the word *film* during the same interview in (5).

(5) a. Non oui eh hier je j'ai été vu eh une film eh de
no yes yesterday I I have been seen a film of
theatre de soleil.
theatre of sun

b. Le film c'est quatre heures... (Sara 1, L1=Swedish)
the film it is four hours

When the L1 does not instantiate definiteness features, performance is lower, especially in the early stages of acquisition. Table 4 tracks the behavior of Vietnamese and Chinese learners of French on definite and indefinite determiners in the elicited oral production task administered by Leung (2002) (see above). The results show a tendency, especially on the part of the beginner learners, to overgeneralize indefinite articles. In contrast, when definite articles are used, they are found in correct environments. Moreover, indefinites seemed to cause more problems for the (beginner) L2 learners, who showed a 40% omission rate for indefinites, than for the beginner L3 learners, who only omitted them 12% of the time. Definite articles were only rarely omitted by either group.

Table 4. Percentage of correct use, substitution and omission of definite and indefinite determiners in adult L2/L3 French (L1 = Vietnamese and Chinese) (from Leung 2002)

Group	L1	Correct use		Substitution		Omission	
		Def	Indef	Def	Indef	Def	Indef
L2 French Beginn (n=16)	Viet.	49%	59.4%	43.7%	0.3%	7.3%	40.3%
L3 French Beginn (n=41)	Chin.	58.6%	87.8%	39%	0.4%	2.4%	11.9%
L3 French Interm (n=27)	Chin.	77.2%	92.8%	17.8%	0.8%	5%	6.4%
L3 French Adv (n=13)	Chin.	82.3%	94.7%	13.7%	0.9%	4%	4.4%

However, in a multiple choice task administered to other Vietnamese and Cantonese learners of French, Leung (2002) reports a much higher accuracy rate for all groups, including the beginners. As shown in Table 5, the performance of the beginner L3 learners was at least 80% accurate on both definite and indefinite determiners, presumably as a result of transfer from English. In contrast, the results of the L2 learners, albeit higher than on the production task, were at around chance level or slightly above it. This may be due to L1 influence.

Table 5. Accuracy on definite and indefinite determiners in a multiple choice task by adult Vietnamese- and Chinese-speaking learners of French (from Leung 2002)

Group	L1	Definite (and specific)	Indefinite (and specific)	Indefinite (and non-specific)
L2 French Beginn (n=12)	Vietnamese	66.6%	53.8%	56.2%
L3 French Beginn (n=44)	Chinese	93.6%	89%	79.8%
L3 French Interm (n=27)	Chinese	97.1%	94.5%	90.9%
L3 French Adv (n=13)	Chinese	99%	92%	99%
Controls (n=12)	French	99%	99.3%	99%

12.2.1.3 *The clitic status of determiners in adult L2 French*

In contrast to child learners of French, adult learners do not seem to treat determiners as clitics in the early stages of acquisition, as shown by their poor performance on elision and contraction. First, elision is not mastered until late by adult learners. Instead, the least proficient learners use full determiners in contexts where elision is required, as illustrated in (6) (from Granfeldt 2003).

(6) a. Eh le le autre chien vient. (Petra 1, L1=Swedish)
the+MASC the+MASC other dog comes

b. Et, mais, le l la histoire c'est vrai! (Henry 1, L1=Swedish)
and but the+MASC the+FEM story it is true

Granfeldt reports an elision rate below 50% for the three Swedish-French learners at the lowest proficiency level (Henry, Petra, and Sara). At this stage, the incidence of determiner doubling (such as *la l'école* 'the+FEM the school') is quite low, which differs from what is observed in bilingual French (recall Section 11.1.1). The next stage is characterized by variability in the production of elided and non-elided determiners. This is also the period during which determiner doubling occurs the most. In general, the rate of non-elided determiners and of determiner doubling decreases with proficiency, and elided articles occur in at least 90% of obligatory contexts in the most advanced learners (Knut and Sama).[155] Interestingly, Swedish has clitic determiners,

155. According to Granfeldt, elided determiners would first appear within PPs, and would then increasingly be used in regular DPs.

such as *-en* 'the' in *lingvisten* 'the linguist' (Delsing 1993). Although they are enclitics, rather than proclitics as in French, the fact that they can cliticize might have led us to expect that the clitic status of French determiners would be easy for Swedish learners to acquire. However, this does not seem to be the case.

Second, definite articles fail to systematically occur as contracted forms with the prepositions *de* 'of' and *à* 'at'. Instead of target forms *du* 'of+the' and *au* 'at+the', beginner learners use either *de le* (or *à le*) or leave out both the preposition and the determiner (Ø), as in (7). Contracted forms are found in subsequent stages, but they alternate with non-contracted forms. Finally, at the advanced stage, contracted forms are used in contexts where they are expected to occur.

(7) a. Exercice # # et après je viens à le maison # pour manger.
exercise and then I come to the house to eat
(Sara 1, L1=Swedish)

b. Eh si il fait beau je reste quand avoir Ø soleil he he.
if it makes beautiful I stay when have sun
'If the weather is fine, I stay when the sun shines.'
(Petra1, L1=Swedish)

A final argument suggesting that L2 adult learners of French treat determiners differently from native speakers has to do with the potential repetition of a determiner if a pause immediately follows it. As shown by Candea (1998, 2000), native speakers of French have a strong tendency to repeat the determiner after a pause, as in (8), which confirms the clitic status of determiners in the target language. In contrast, adult learners tend to carry on with the noun without repeating the determiner, as in (9).

(8) a. C'est que : le:: le serviteur s'en va dans : dans la forêt.
It is that the the servant is going to to the forest

b. Oh: mon ::: # mon caf est trop chaud et puis…
Oh my my coffee is too hot and then
(examples from Candea (1998) as cited in Granfeldt (2003))

(9) a. Des deux fois le # eh restaurant Canari. (Henri 1, L1=Swedish)
of+the two times the restaurant Canari

b. C'est la # idée. (Henry 2, L1=Swedish)
it is the idea

12.2.1.4 *Development of gender in adult L2 French*

In adult learners of French, gender gradually becomes accurate, although errors may continue into the advanced stages (Andersen 1984; Bartning 2000; Carroll 1989;

Dewaele & Veronique 2001; Harley 1992; Hawkins 1998; Towell 1987). Most learners make use of default determiners at least sometimes, often the masculine form, although the gender of the default form may sometimes differ in definite and indefinite contexts (e.g. it may be *le* for definite determiners and *une* for indefinites). Default forms are also reported in gender agreement with adjectives (which in general seems to be more difficult, even for advanced learners, than selection of the correct determiner).

In the early stages of Swedish speakers' L2 French, Granfeldt (2003) reports that gender errors range from 20% to 30%, including the least proficient learners. The error rate decreases with proficiency, but remains at 16% even for the most proficient. Errors with definite articles usually involve overgeneralization of *le*: in the 15 samples in which errors are reported, *le* is oversupplied in 11. In general, *la* is correctly used more often than *le*: 79% vs. 75%. Note that overgeneralization of the masculine form is reported in L2 Spanish as well (Bruhn de Garavito & White 2002; Franceschina 2001). For indefinites, *une* is the chief source of errors in 10 of 16 samples. Accuracy with *une* is 65%, which is lower than accuracy on its masculine counterpart *un* (69%). Granfeldt's data also shows that accuracy is higher with indefinites than with definites, a tendency reported for other Swedish learners of French (Bartning 2000).

At the advanced level, gender accuracy is above 90%, as shown by several studies investigating gender in spontaneous production data (summarized in Table 6). At this level, the few errors recorded tend to result from overgeneralization of the masculine form. For instance, Dewaele and Véronique (2001) report that, in the data they looked at, 22 of the 28 nouns that induced most errors (including the top 9 nouns) are feminine, including *politique* 'politics', *chose* 'thing', and *année* 'year'. Among the

Table 6. Summary of studies investigating knowledge of gender in highly proficient adult L2 learners of French

Study	Learners	L1	Gender accuracy on determiners	Gender accuracy on adjectives	Overgeneralized gender
Dewaele and Véronique (2001)	27 adv and preadv	Dutch	Around 95%	Around 91%	Masculine
Bartning (2000)	6 adv and 9 preadv	Swedish	Advanced: 90% Preadvanced: 74%	Adv: 81% Preadv: 80%	Adv: MASC (only with definites) Pre-adv: MASC or FEM
Hawkins (1998)	2 groups of 10 Adv	English	93% and 89% (on definite articles)	NA	Masculine or feminine
Gess and Herschensohn (2001)	7 Adv	English	100%	98%	NA

Adv = advanced; Preadv = preadvanced

22 are nouns with natural feminine gender, such as *femme* 'woman' and *mère* 'mother'. However, Hawkins (1998) reports that the form that is overgeneralized is not the same across learners: it may be *le* for some learners and *la* for others. The learners may also overgeneralize one gender for definite determiners and the other for indefinites. Note also that use of default determiners is not always found. For example, at the preadvanced level, Bartning (2000) did not find any particular default form in the Swedish/French data she investigated.

Accuracy in gender agreement with adjectives is generally lower than with determiners, even at the advanced level, as shown in Table 6. This is also reported in L2 acquisition of other Romance languages, such as Italian (Chini 1995) and Spanish (Bruhn de Garavito & White 2002). Adult learners can nevertheless eventually reach relatively high levels of accuracy with gender on adjectives.[156] Accuracy may also depend on the position of the adjective. In particular, the gender of prenominal and predicative adjectives tends to be less target-like than that of postnominal adjectives. This is reported by Bartning (2000) in her study of Swedish/French learners (Table 7). Interestingly, errors in gender agreement with adjectives are overwhelmingly due to the lack of overt agreement in the feminine. The same tendencies are also reported in English/French data by Dewaele & Véronique (2001), although the difference in rate of accuracy between prenominal, postnominal, and predicative adjectives was not statistically significant in that study.[157]

Table 7. Gender accuracy on prenominal, postnominal, and predicative adjectives in adult L2 French (L1 Swedish) (from Bartning 2000)

Learners	Prenominal		Postnominal		Predicative		Total	
	Masc	Fem	Masc	Fem	Masc	Fem	Masc	Fem
Preadvanced (n=9)	27/28 (96%)	4/11 (36%)	8/9 (89%)	7/9 (78%)	25/26 (96%)	9/18 (50%)	60/63 (95%)	20/38 (53%)
Advanced (n=6)	64/72 (88%)	25/48 (52%)	40/44 (90%)	27/36 (75%)	150/161 (93%)	16/37 (43%)	254/277 (92%)	68/121 (56%)

156. Granfeldt (2003) also observes a tendency on the part of the least proficient learners not to take into account the gender of the determiner when using an adjective.

157. In Granfeldt's (2003) Swedish/French data, one can also observe a difference between masculine and feminine marking accuracy on prenominal adjectives, but it is much less spectacular than what is reported by Bartning. From his Table 6–23 (p. 239), one can infer that there is correct adjective-noun agreement with 115 masculine nouns out of 146 (78.8%) and with 53 feminine nouns out of 78 (67.9%).

Experimental studies of how adult learners attribute gender in French have investigated potential phonological, morphological, and semantic cues. In Carroll's (1999) study, 88 native speakers of English with little or no knowledge of French were divided into four input groups: phonological, morphological, semantic, and 'comparison'. The experiment comprised two parts: a learning part and a guessing part. In the learning part, the participants were presented orally with a list of 10 words whose gender they were expected to learn. Once they had learned the gender of these words, they were presented with a new list of 16 words for which they were asked to guess the gender. The two lists formed List One set. This procedure was repeated with two new lists – List Two set. One of the two list sets followed 'natural' generalizations about gender attribution in French, whereas the other list set did not (the nonnatural list). Depending on the groups, the 'natural' generalizations were based either on the sound shape of the final stressed syllable endings (phonological cues), the segmentation of the words into morphemes (morphological cues), or the sex of the referent of the word (semantic cues). In the 'comparison' group, the lists contained items from all the other lists. For each word presented to the participants, an English translation was provided. The results of the guessing part of the experiment (Table 8) show that the groups generally performed better on the natural lists than on the nonnatural lists. The semantic group performed best on both lists, and best overall. The morphological group came second on the natural lists. As to the phonological group, it performed equally on natural and nonnatural lists (10.2 and 10.4, out of 16), suggesting that phonological endings are not readily used as cues for generalizations of gender attribution. This is to be compared to the morphological group which performed significantly better on the natural lists than on the nonnatural lists (12.3 and 8.4, out of 16 respectively), which shows that generalizations were made based on the segmentation of words into different morphological entities. Taken together, Carroll argues, the results show that cues for the acquisition of gender are not all equal and that what seems to play the most important role in such a task is the mediation of some kind of conceptual representation, as advocated by UG-based models of acquisition, and not the mere recognition of objective patterns in the input (in which case the learners should have obtained similar results on all conditions). In other words, the learners are in some way 'prepared' to make sense of the input.

Table 8. Correct scores for the guessing of gender in adult L2 French (L1=English) (adapted from Carroll 1999)

Lists	Phonological (n=22)	Morphological (n=22)	Semantic (n=22)	Comparison (n=22)
Natural (n=16)	10.2	12.3	15.2	10.9
Nonnatural (n=16)	10.4	8.4	14.3	8.7
Mean	10.3	10.3	14.7	9.8

12.2.1.5 *Development of number in adult L2 French*

As with definiteness, acquisition of number in L2 French seems to be influenced by the properties of the L1. Native speakers of a language which instantiates number use plural determiners in L2 French right from the outset. This is true of the Swedish/French learners investigated by Granfeldt (2003). Even the ones at the lowest proficiency level were found to use several types of plural determiners. At least 87% of their plural nouns were used with an appropriate plural determiner. In a learning situation involving an L1 from which uninterpretable [±singular] features are absent, on the other hand, performance on plural determiners can be quite low in the early stages of acquisition. This is the case of the Vietnamese learners investigated by Leung (2002) whose results on a picture identification task focusing on number were at chance level (see Table 9). In contrast, the performance of the Chinese learners was much more accurate, even on the part of the beginners, presumably thanks to the prior acquisition of the relevant features in English.

Table 9. Accuracy rate on number in a multiple choice task by adult Vietnamese- and Chinese-speaking learners of French (from Leung 2002)

Group	L1	Singular	Plural	Overall
L2 French Beginn (n=16)	Vietnamese	96.1%	53.5%	74.8%
L3 French Beginn (n=41)	Chinese	96.3%	98.8%	97.6%
L3 French Interm (n=27)	Chinese	100%	96.1%	98.1%
L3 French Adv (n=13)	Chinese	100%	100%	100%
Controls (n=22)	French	100%	98.9%	99.4%

12.2.1.6 *Theoretical implications*

12.2.1.6.1 Knowledge of D

We saw that if the learners' L1 possesses determiners (and therefore the D category), use of determiners is productive from the outset of L2 acquisition, which suggests that DP is available from the earliest stages, presumably via transfer from the L1. This finding argues against the existence of an initial lexical stage in L2 acquisition (Vainikka & Young-Scholten 1996, 2005, for example). Evidence from L3 French suggests that early knowledge of D may also result from transfer from the L2. The early availability of D in adult IL grammars is similar to what is observed in the case of child learners.

However, in contrast to child L2 acquisition, adult learners may start out analysing definite determiners not as heads, but as XPs (much like demonstratives) since, as we have seen, adult learners initially fail to appropriately elide and contract these articles. This analysis seems to be supported by Granfeldt's observation that adult learners may leave a pause between a determiner and the following noun. To account for these facts, Granfeldt (2003) proposes that determiners are spell-outs of the definite feature and that they occur in the specifier of DP in the early stages of adult L2 French, as shown in (10).[158] Note that this obtains even in learning situations where the L1 has determiners, such as Swedish.

(10)

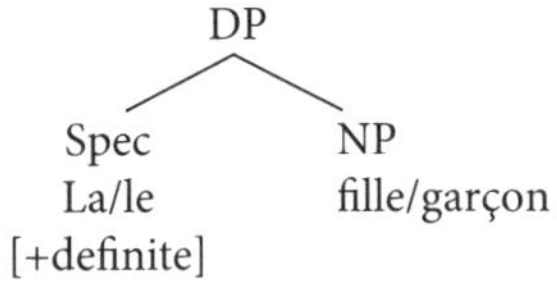

The way adult L2 learners treat definite determiners seems similar to the way they treat pronominal clitics in the early stages of acquisition (see Section 8.1.2.1). In both cases, clitics seem to be initially analysed as XPs by the learners. According to Granfeldt (2003), this can be explained if adult L2 learners follow a universal principle of Categorial Uniformity which leads them to assume a unique canonical structure for a given semantic type, nominals in this case (see Rizzi 2000). In contrast, he argues, children follow the principle of Structural Economy, which is why it takes them so little time to acquire the clitic status of definite determiners in French. This parallels the discussion in Section 4.2.1.4 with respect to root infinitives in child and adult L2 French: children, guided by Structural Economy, project VP roots, whereas adults follow Categorial Uniformity, which means that functional categories are part of the underlying representations of their declarative utterances, including RIs.

When D is not instantiated in the L1, as in Vietnamese and Chinese, we saw that beginner learners may first consider determiners not as determiners, but as classifiers. The D category may be acquired later on, although data from advanced adult learners of French (with no previous L2 experience) are lacking. This developmental scenario is compatible with Schwartz and Sprouse's (1996) Full Transfer/Full Access hypothesis.

12.2.1.6.2 Knowledge of gender

Gender is problematic to many adult L2 learners, and recourse to default gender, often masculine, has been reported in several studies. The difficulties posed by the acquisition of gender raise the issue of whether gender features can ever be acquired if they are not activated in the learners' L1. At stake is whether or not interlanguage grammars can ever become native-like, and whether or not they are deficient (see Meisel 1997). According to Hawkins (1998), L2 learners whose L1 does not make gender distinctions use morphophonological cues in order to decide about the gender of nouns, much as monolingual French children do before age 6 (see Section 10.3). For Hawkins & Franceschina

158. In Granfeldt's (2003) hypothesis, it is not clear what should be the head of DP. If this position is empty, we may also wonder why it is DP, and not NP, that projects above NP. In other words, why should the learners assume that there is a DP anyway?

(2004), this reliance on morphophonological cues suggests that there is no underlying [*u*gender] feature in Num in IL French grammars. Recourse to default forms is triggered whenever the learners are not sure of the gender of the word, namely when the morphophonological ending of the noun does not give them any clear gender cue. In spite of this analysis, the accuracy rates on gender reported by Hawkins (1998) are quite high: 93% on definite articles for one group, and 89% for the other. If indeed IL grammars lack the [*u*gender] feature, why are these learners assigning gender so accurately? Hawkins argues that the learners' long exposure to French has allowed them to learn a list of exceptions to their default forms. So, at one point a learner may produce *le village* 'the village', *le ville* 'the city', and *le forêt* 'the forest', using *le* as a default determiner, and later on learn that *forêt* is an exception and that it should be used in the feminine. This would explain why *forêt* may be correctly used with a (non-default) feminine determiner thereafter. In short, for Hawkins, high accuracy rates in gender on the part of English-speaking learners do not mean that [*u*gender] has been acquired. In fact, he assumes that acquisition of [*u*gender] is impossible if [*u*gender] is not activated in the L1 (as it is not in English) and if acquisition begins after puberty, regardless of the type of input received. This is reminiscent of Tsimpli (2003)'s idea that uninterpretable features cannot be acquired by adult L2 learners.

Hawkins' position seems very difficult to maintain in view of the almost perfect scores reported in the literature on the acquisition of gender by English-speaking learners of French. Gess & Herschensohn (2001), for instance, found a 98% accuracy rate on gender (and number) agreement in their study of written samples by advanced learners. This strongly suggests that these learners have acquired gender features and that L2 learners can acquire target features, even when they are not active in the L1. At this point, however, it may be necessary to take some distance with respect to the significance of accuracy rates in the discussion of the acquisition of gender. Granted, almost perfect scores, such as the ones reported by Gess & Herschensohn, are strongly suggestive of the acquisition of underlying properties, but what about lower accuracy rates, such as 90%, 80%, or even less? That they are lower means that errors are being made with respect to the target language, but does this necessarily mean that the learners' IL grammars lack gender? It could be the case that the learners, especially at the advanced stages, have acquired the notion of gender, and that their grammars have the [*u*gender] feature, but that they sometimes assign the *wrong* gender to the noun. Under this scenario, the 'wrong' (interpretable) gender feature of the noun would check the [*u*gender] feature of the article, which would yield an error with respect to the target language. The 93% and 89% accuracy rates posted by Hawkins (1998) could very well be analysed in this way.

Another argument against Hawkins' (1998) and Hawkins & Franceschina's (2004) views is that it is not clear that adult learners pay that much attention to morphophonological cues for gender assignment in French. Indeed, adult L2 learners sometimes even produce the wrong gender with nouns whose ending is almost always associated with a specific gender in the target language, such as masculine /m/ and feminine /e/ (Dewaele & Véronique 2001; Granfeldt 2003). This is illustrated in (11). Carroll (1999) has also shown that in contrast to children learning French as their L1, adult L2 French learners do not rely strongly on the phonological ending of words; rather, they are much more sensitive to semantic and morphological cues in the input, which suggests that they are guided by conceptual and structural representations in their learning process.

(11) a. La atome. (Karl, L1=Swedish)
the+FEM atom+MASC

b. Euh monsieur De Benedetti a le
Mister De Benedetti has the+MASC
possibilité de de dire non. (Johan, L1=Dutch)
possibility+FEM to to say no

Under Granfeldt's analysis, the fact that determiners are considered XPs by adult learners means that they are structurally far from the noun at both the syntactic and prosodic levels, and this distance prevents learners from using the morphophonological properties of the noun for gender assignment. We also saw that adult L2 learners may use different gender default forms with definite and indefinite determiners. For Granfeldt, this lack of consistency in the gender of default forms suggests that initial adult IL grammars of French lack the gender feature. But this should by no means suggest that this feature can never be acquired by L2 learners. In fact, Granfeldt claims that the decline of default determiner forms should be associated with the emergence of the gender feature.

Learners' use of default determiners, specifically the fact that the masculine form is often used for the feminine by adult learners but not vice versa, argues against the idea that their IL grammars are deficient. If IL systems were deficient, in the sense of Meisel (1997), errors would not be expected to mostly go into one direction. Moreover, non-target gender assignment seems to be systematic for a given noun. In other words, it is not the case that nouns may appear either with a feminine or a masculine determiner in adult learners' speech. Dewaele & Véronique (2001) observe that such errors, which they call temporary word gender assignment, account for only 13.3% of the total number of gender errors identified in their data (69/519).[159] In (12), the

159. Dewaele & Véronique also talk about non-systematic gender agreement. Included in this category of errors are cases of hesitation and slips of the tongue where the noun is preceded by two determiners of different genders, such as *le la politique* 'the+MASC the+FEM politics'. For the authors, these arise as a result of conscious monitoring.

feminine noun *région* 'region' is used in both the feminine and the masculine by a learner during the course of the same interview.

(12) a. Un petit region / ce petit region. / et
a+MASC small region this+MASC small region and

le petit region
the+MASC small region

b. ... de la region...
of the+FEM region

Rather, in the majority of cases (294/519 = 56.6%), erroneous gender assignment is systematic. As an example, Dewaele & Véronique mention the systematic use of the feminine noun *bête* 'beast' with a masculine determiner by Filip, a preadvanced learner. In other words, errors are not observed across the board, contrary to what a deficient approach to IL grammars would predict. Interestingly, we have seen that while L2 learners use some determiners as default forms, they also produce determiners in appropriate contexts, namely with masculine and feminine nouns. One way to account for this difference is to consider default determiners to be underspecified for gender, in the same way that infinitival forms are underspecified for finiteness (Prévost & White 2000b; see Section 4.2.1.4). As to appropriately used determiners, they are fully specified for gender. Under this account, default determiners *le* and *un* are [0 masculine], whereas *la* and *une* are [−masculine]. If feminine forms *la* and *une* are used as defaults, then they are [0 masculine] (or [0 feminine], depending on one's view of how gender features should be represented), whereas *le* and *un* are [+masculine].

Another issue in the L2 acquisition of gender in French is that of L1 influence. Do gender properties of the L1 affect the way gender is acquired in French? For Carroll (1989), they do. Based on the difficulty that English-speaking learners have with gender in French, she argues that there is transfer of the N category (with no gender feature) from English. Determiners are then learned as independent phonological units, in contrast to what happens in child L1 French acquisition where, she claims, they are learned as part of the noun. Adult L2 French learners resort to guessing mechanisms for the gender of nouns, trying to come up with generalizations or rules. When overgeneralizations are made, the masculine is used. In contrast, Granfeldt (2003) believes that L1 gender is not transferred to French IL. In particular, although there are two genders in Swedish, common and neuter, Swedish learners of French do not seem to be sensitive to gender in French, at least in the initial stages of acquisition. For instance, we saw that they may resort to two different default genders with definites and indefinites. Likewise, White, Valenzuela, Macgregor, and Leung (2004) found that English- and French-speaking learners of Spanish at either the intermediate or advanced level showed similar gender accuracy in a picture identification task. If the L1 influenced acquisition of gender in the L2, we would expect the French-speaking learners to perform better than the English speakers, since French has similar gender properties to Spanish.[160] More studies investigating the potential influence of the L1 in the development of knowledge of gender in L2 French are needed. In particular, a series of comparative studies involving L1s with no gender, such as Vietnamese and Chinese, L1s with similar gender systems similar to that of French, such as Spanish and Italian, and L1s with a different gender system, such as German, would offer a comprehensive picture of the influence of the L1 on gender acquisition.

Finally, we saw that gender agreement accuracy was lower with adjectives than with determiners. Dewaele & Véronique (2001) argue that accuracy with determiners is higher due to frequency effects: there are fewer types of determiners than of adjectives, and determiners are more frequent and shorter than adjectives. According to Granfeldt (2003), however, the frequency account makes the wrong prediction with respect to gender marking on prenominal adjectives. In Section 9.1.4, we saw that the list of adjectives occurring mainly in this position is finite in French. Moreover, most of them are monosyllabic and they are quite frequent in the language. If accuracy in gender assignment were related to frequency, one would therefore expect gender to start being more accurate on these adjectives than on adjectives appearing in a postnominal or predicative position. As shown in Table 7, however, this is not the case. In adult L2 French, gender is more accurate on postnominal adjectives.

12.2.1.6.3 Knowledge of definiteness and number

With respect to definiteness and number, we saw that the properties of the L1 seem to have a strong influence over the content of initial IL grammars. In particular, if the L1 does not instantiate the relevant features, as Vietnamese, performance is low in the initial stages of L2 French (Leung 2002). However, native-like command of definite and indefinite determiners, as well as plural articles, can be achieved. This suggests that the associated features can be acquired, which argues against Hawkins & Franceschina's (2004) view (see also Hawkins (1998) and Hawkins & Chan (1997)). Leung's (2002) findings, however, need confirmation. Her Vietnamese learners were at the beginner level and her Chinese learners had already acquired command of another language, English, which possesses the features in question. To accurately assess the question of the influence of the L1 on the acquisition of definiteness and number in L2 French, data from intermediate and advanced learners whose L1 does not instantiate the relevant features, and who have not acquired any other language where such features are present, is needed.

Systematic research on the development of definiteness features in L2 French for learners whose L1 does include definiteness features is also lacking. Research so far suggests rapid development in this learning context, but this is mainly based on spontaneous production data. Moreover, detailed figures are not always provided.

160. However, the authors acknowledge that their learners may not have been true beginners, which leaves open the possibility of L1 influence in the initial stages of acquisition.

Future studies that integrate more experimental paradigms would help clarify the development of definiteness in adult L2 French.

12.2.2 Noun placement in adult L2 French

Knowledge of noun placement with respect to adjectives in French can be investigated from two different angles: the purely syntactic order of nouns and adjectives, and the semantic consequences of adjective placement. This section addresses the first kind of knowledge; the second is dealt with in Section 12.2.3.1.

Recent studies show that, although L1 influence is evident in the early stages of acquisition, adult learners of French are able to acquire the fact that for most adjectives, in most contexts, the noun precedes the adjective in French DP, even if their L1 does not exhibit this word order.[161] Hawkins (1998) reports almost no errors on the part of his (advanced) English-speaking participants: the noun almost always appears in front of the adjective. In Gess & Herschensohn's (2001) study, a 90% accuracy rate in N-Adj was obtained with 8 beginner learners (native speakers of English) who used determiners productively in a written production task (recall Section 12.2.1.1) (see Table 10).[162] More proficient learners performed at a rate higher than 90%.

Table 10. Results on adjective placement by adult English-learners of French (adapted from Gess & Herschensohn 2001)

Proficiency level	Number of participants	% N+Adj
Level 1a	6	34%
Level 1b	8	91%
Level 2	29	93%
Level 3	14	99%
Level 4	20	100%
Level 5	7	100%

Leung (2002) administered a grammaticality judgment task to the Vietnamese and Chinese learners in her study, and found that the Vietnamese speakers performed better than the Chinese speakers on ungrammatical Adj-N sequences (Table 11). In Vietnamese, the default order of adjectives and nouns mirrors that of French, namely

161. Recall that some adjectives in French tend to occur prenominally, such as *grand* 'big' and *petit* 'small'. The results reported by the studies mentioned here are based on the positioning of adjectives that are supposed to appear after the noun in the target language.

162. The other six beginner learners who participated in the study performed at 66% accuracy on target noun placement. Although their results are lower than those of the other beginners, their behaviour does not fit with an L1-derived grammar. These learners were presumably in the midst of acquiring the target placement of nouns, since they had already acquired the fact that adjectives may appear postnomally in French.

N-Adj. Leung assumes that this is due to strong specificity features located in the head of ClassifierP, which force overt noun movement across the adjective. In Chinese, where adjectives typically precede the noun, as in English, Leung takes the specificity features of Classifier to be weak, which means that the noun will not raise until LF. This is similar to the typical analysis for English, except that covert noun movement in English is due to the weak nature of number features in Num. Leung's results (Table 11) suggest that the Vietnamese learners have transferred their strong specificity features into their IL grammar. The behavior of the Chinese learners show more variability: while they accept the French N-Adj order, which is disallowed in both their L1 and their L2, they still seem to have problems rejecting the order typical of their L1 and L2. In a sense, these results are similar to the ones reported for verb placement with respect to adverbs. Note that although the Vietnamese learners' performance on ungrammatical sentences is also not perfect (at 67.8%), their performance in production is better: in a production task administered to the learners, accuracy in noun placement climbs to 95.7% for the Vietnamese participants, compared to 75.2% for the beginner L3 French learners.

Table 11. Accuracy at accepting and rejecting grammatical and ungrammatical noun placement with respect to adjectives by adult Vietnamese- and Chinese-speaking learners of French (from Leung 2002)

Group	L1	N-Adj	*Adj-N
L2 French (n=16)	Vietnamese	100%	67.8%
L3 French Beginn (n=41)	Chinese	96.2%	33.8%
L3 French Interm (n=27)	Chinese	97.3%	61.1%
L3 French Adv (n=13)	Chinese	100%	87.5%
Controls (n=22)	French	98.7%	95.4%

While these studies offer insight into learners' behaviour with respect to canonical postnominal placement of adjectives, they provide only an incomplete picture as far as general knowledge of adjective placement in L2 (and L3) French is concerned. As mentioned above, some adjectives can occur before or after the noun, with important semantic consequences. Learners' knowledge of interpretation with these adjectives is discussed in Section 12.2.3.1.

12.2.3 The nominal domain and the syntax/semantics interface in adult L2 French

In recent years, SLA researchers have been increasingly interested in the acquisition of phenomena at the syntax/semantics interface as a way to investigate whether UG is available to adult learners. In many cases, the phenomena in question are associated with subtle interpretational distinctions that native speakers and language instructors are generally not conscious of, which means that L2 learners do not receive specific instruction in these areas. If, in addition, such phenomena are absent from the L1, their acquisition in the L2 involves a true poverty-of-the-stimulus issue. Successful acquisition of interpretational distinctions thus represents a very strong argument in favour of the availability of UG in adult L2 acquisition. Several experiments focusing on phenomena at the syntax/semantics interface, which were mainly designed by Laurent Dekydtspotter, Rex Sprouse, and their colleagues, are reviewed in this book (see in particular Section 16.2.5). Below we discuss adjective placement and quantified nominals.

12.2.3.1 *The semantic interpretation of adjective placement in adult L2 French*

Investigating the potential resetting of the noun movement parameter should not only focus on whether learners can acquire target-like noun placement with respect to adjectives (and learn to reject non-target-like placement); it should also entail a detailed examination of more subtle properties associated with noun movement, such as the semantic consequences of adjective placement. As seen in Section 9.1.4, postnominal adjectives enter into a predicative relationship with the noun they modify. It is as if the adjective identifies or 'picks out' the referent denoted by the noun from a set of potential referents. For example, in the phrase *le type sale* 'the dirty man', the postnominal position of *sale* suggests that there is a group of men, some of whom are not dirty, and that the man who is dirty is being singled out. The postnominal position is said to be restrictive or intersective in the sense that the domain of N-Adj (the man who is dirty) corresponds to the intersection of the domain of N (men) and the domain of A (dirty). Moreover, given the intersective nature of the postnominal position, it follows that N-Adj sequences can appear in contexts where several other possible referents for the noun are present (for example, a group of men, of which one is dirty). This is impossible in the case of prenominal adjectives. These adjectives do not have a predicative relationship with the noun, and there is no presupposition of a larger set of Ns. In *le sale type* 'the dirty man', no particular individual is being singled out from a set of individuals; rather, a single individual is being referred to, to whom a description is applied. In other words, *le sale type* has a unique noun referent. The meaning of the adjective is defined with respect to the noun, and not independently of it, as is the case with *le type sale*. In Wilmet's (1981) terms, the domain of Adj-N is a subset of N.[163] If parameter resetting is possible in adult L2 acquisition, then, not

---

163. Similar effects obtain in English. In the sentence *Dumbo is a gray elephant,* the phrase *gray elephant* entails that Dumbo is a gray animal. The interpretation is intersective. In contrast, in *Dumbo is a small elephant,* the NP *small elephant* does not entail that Dumbo is a small animal; after all, Dumbo is still an elephant, by definition a large mammal. The interpretation is therefore non-intersective (Anderson 2002: 122–124). The two adjectives are assumed to occupy two different positions in the representation: *small* is in the specifier of NumP and *gray* is in the specifier of NP.

only should the learners acquire noun movement in French, they should also reject a non-intersective reading of the N-Adj order, and they should reject intersective interpretations of Adj-N. Moreover, they should only accept non-unique noun reference when the adjective is in a postnominal position.

Crucially, the formal input received by learners of French does not usually include instruction on unique/non-unique noun reference, and it does not include information on adjectives that may appear in pre- and post-nominal position without change of translation in English (such *as le sale type* and *le type sale*, which are both translated as 'the dirty man'). Rather, formal instruction on adjective positioning usually focuses on meaning differences that almost always corresponds to different translations in English, such as *la maison ancienne* 'the old house' and *l'ancienne maison* 'the former house'. Since the L1 is not a useful source of information, given that Adj-N is the predominant order in English, the learners are truly facing a poverty-of-the-stimulus situation. Acquisition of the target properties would therefore strongly suggest the availability of UG constraints to the learners.

Anderson (2002, 2008) investigated knowledge of intersective and non-intersective interpretations of adjectives in L2 French. Two acceptability tasks were administered to 100 English-speaking learners at four levels of proficiency, from intermediate to advanced. There were also two control groups: one of native speakers of French and one of native speakers of English (who were administered a literal translation of the test sentences). In the first task, the learners were presented with 32 short scenarios (in English) establishing an intersective or non-intersective interpretation context, as in (13) and (14) below. A sentence in French followed, with either N-Adj or Adj-N, and the learners had to decide whether the sentence was appropriate given the context provided. Eight adjectives were selected for the task.[164] Each adjective appeared in a postnominal and a prenominal position in a context establishing either an intersective or nonintersective interpretation.

---

164. For four of the adjectives, the prenominal and postnominal positions correspond to two different glosses in English, as in (i), whereas for the other four positioning has no effect on the English gloss, as in (ii).

(i) a. cher bijou / bijou cher
'beloved jewel' / 'expensive jewel'

b. ancien roi / roi ancien
'former king' / 'ancient king'

(ii) a. nouveau bâtiment / bâtiment nouveau
'new building' ('additional building' / 'newly built building')

b. nombreuses familles / familles nombreuses
'numerous families' ('many families' / 'families having many members')

(13) *Intersective ('literal meaning') context*
A recent outbreak of malaria has caused many people to come to the emergency room of a small African hospital. Surprisingly, each case of the illness was distinct in its symptoms: one patient could hardly breathe, another lost feeling in her arms and legs, still another patient had severe headaches. The traditional medication didn't seem to be working, and the doctors at the hospital didn't know how to treat them.

a. *L'hôpital ne savait pas soigner les différents cas de cette maladie.
'The hospital didn't know to treat the different cases of this illness.'

b. √ L'hôpital ne savait pas soigner les cas différents de cette maladie.

(14) *Non-intersective ('figurative meaning') context*
The emergency room of a small community hospital had a very busy day today. One patient came in complaining that he could not stop vomiting and was losing all feeling in his arms and legs. Then, another person came in an hour later complaining of the exact same symptoms. Then another person! The doctors at the hospital had no idea what could have caused this illness, and didn't know how to treat (=*soigner*) these cases (=*cas*). The patients were sent to a larger hospital for testing.

a. √ L'hôpital ne savait pas soigner les différents cas de cette maladie.
'The hospital didn't know to treat the different cases of this illness'

b. *L'hôpital ne savait pas soigner les cas différents de cette maladie.

As can be seen in Table 12, French native speakers performed as expected. With prenominal adjectives, acceptance of nonintersective readings was significantly higher than acceptance of intersective interpretations, while the opposite results obtained with adjectives in postnominal position. In English, adjectives are prenominal, so both interpretations should be equally accepted by the anglophone native speakers, and they should be equally rejected with postnominal adjectives. Results summarized in

Table 12. Response rates on intersective/nonintersective interpretations (from Anderson 2002, 2008)

Participants	**Prenominal order (Adj-N)**		**Postnominal order (N-Adj)**	
	Nonintersective (n=8)	**Intersective (n=8)**	**Nonintersective (n=8)**	**Intersective (n=8)**
French NSs (n=27)	74.5%***	47.2%	13.9%	58.8%***
English NSs (n=30)	79.3%	79.3%	8.4%	11.7%
Learners Level 1 (n=29)	55.4%	63.7%	56%	60.3%
Learners Level 2 (n=24)	57.4%	63.5%	50.7%	56%
Learners Level 3 (n=27)	58.6%	51.8%	38.9%	69.8%***
Learners Level 4 (n=20)	81.9%***	35.6%	12%	76.2%***

*** significant difference between Nonintersective and Intersective ($p < .001$).

Table 12 show that this was indeed the case. As for the L2 groups, we can see that lower proficient learners accepted both interpretations to a somewhat similar extent for both prenominal and postnominal adjectives. However, native-like distinctions were observed as of Level 3 with postnominal adjectives (where the intersective intersection was strongly preferred) and at Level 4 for prenominal adjectives (for which a nonintersective interpretation was preferred). These results strongly show not only that N-Adj was accepted by English-speaking learners of French, but also that the appropriate semantic interpretations can be acquired.

The second task was designed around the same methodology as the first. This time, the interpretation involved a unique versus non-unique noun referent context (for an example of a non-unique referent context, see ft 165). Recall that in French, N-Adj sequences are compatible with either; however, the Adj-N sequence is compatible only with unique noun referent contexts. Note also that the change in adjective position does not affect the English translation (e.g. *la valise lourde* and *la lourde valise* 'the heavy suitcase').

Table 13. Response rates on unique/non-unique noun referent interpretations (from Anderson 2002, 2007)

Participants	**Prenominal order (Adj-N)**		**Postnominal order (N-Adj)**	
	Unique (n=8)	**Non-unique (n=8)**	**Unique (n=8)**	**Non-unique (n=8)**
French NSs (n=27)	74.1%***	48.7%	51.8%**	36.5%
English NSs (n=30)	95.2%***	84.8%	10.9%*	6.2%
Learners Level 1 (n=29)	62.3%	57.6%	78.3%**	65%
Learners Level 2 (n=24)	62.5%***	38.1%	86.5%***	60.3%
Learners Level 3 (n=27)	50.5%**	35.2%	83%**	68.2%
Learners Level 4 (n=20)	51.4%**	33.6%	76.4%	67.1%

significant difference between Unique and Nonunique: * $p < .05$; ** $p < .01$; *** $p < .001$.

Table 13 shows that the L2 French learners managed to acquire the relevant distinctions: they accepted Adj-N in unique noun referent contexts significantly more often than in non-unique noun referent contexts as of level 2. At the same time, they accepted N-Adj in non-unique referent contexts over 60% of the time (as of level 1). There was no difference in the acceptance rate of N-Adj between the two contexts at level 4. As expected, the English native speakers strongly accepted Adj-N and strongly rejected N-Adj regardless of whether the referent was unique or not, although significant differences were found. The behaviour of the French controls was not quite as expected. They displayed a strong bias against nonunique noun referent contexts for Adj-N sequences, which was expected, but they displayed a similar bias against nonunique noun referent contexts for N-Adj sequences, which was not expected. Anderson argues that this is due to a pragmatic bias on the part of the controls. In the scenarios establishing non-unique noun referent contexts, N-Adj is semantically appropriate but pragmatically incompatible with the situation depicted.[165] Anderson argues that such a pragmatic bias does not affect the judgments of the L2 learners.

Dekydtspotter, Sprouse & Anderson (1997) investigated knowledge of noun movement in French via one of its syntactic consequences — the possibility of multiple *de*-arguments in dyadic nominals (that is, nominals with two arguments). Consider the pairs of sentences in (15) and (16).

(15) a. La destruction de la ville par Godzilla
the destruction of the city by Godzilla
'Godzilla's destruction of the city' / 'The destruction of the city by Godzilla'

b. *La destruction de la ville de Godzilla
the destruction of the city of Godzilla

(16) a. La version de la 9e par Karajan
the version of the 9th by Karajan
'Karajan's version of the 9th' / 'The version of the 9th by Karajan'

b. La version de la 9e de Karajan
the version of the 9th of Karajan

The difference in acceptability between the NPs in (15) and those in (16) is argued to result from the different 'types' of nominals that head them. The head of the NPs in (15), *destruction*, is a process nominal that describes an ongoing event, whereas

165. Consider the following scenario and the two related sentences in (i) (Anderson 2002: 200): 'At the airport, an airline agent tells Pierre that his plane to Florida has reached maximum weight. He must leave all his suitcases at the airport. They will be put on the next flight out, and delivered to him at his hotel in Florida. He isn't bothered too much by having to leave his suitcases: though most are small and easy to carry (being filled with summer clothing), one of the suitcases is so loaded down with books, sports equipment, and gifts for his friends that he can hardly lift it!'

(i) a. *Pierre doit laisser la lourde valise à l'aéroport.

b. √ Pierre doit laisser la valise lourde à l'aéroport.
'Peter must leave its heavy suitcase with his friend at the airport'

According to the context, Pierre must leave all his suitcases behind, of which one is heavy, and not only one, as implied by the presence of the definite determiner *la*. Option (ib) is correct semantically because the order N-Adj establishes that there is a suitcase which is heavy among a group of suitcases, but it is pragmatically odd given that all suitcases, and not just the heavy one, must be left at the airport. This may have prompted the French native speakers not to entertain this answer. Option (ia) is wrong both semantically (since the presence of a prenominal adjective presupposes that there is only one suitcase in the context) and pragmatically (because of the presence of *la*, as seen above).

the head of the NPs in (16), *version*, is a result nominal that names 'the output of a process or an element associated with a process' (Grimshaw 1990). With both types of nominals, the internal argument, *ville* in (15) and *9e* in (16), can appear in a PP headed by *de* 'of'. In addition, the agent, *Godzilla* in (15a) and *Karajan* in (16a), can occur with the preposition *par* 'by'. The difference between the two types of nominals is that, for process nominals, the agent could instead be preceded by *de* (16b), in which case multiple *de*-arguments appear in the DP. Such a possibility is not available with result nominals, as can be seen by the ungrammaticality of (15b). In English, the agent of both process and result nominals can be expressed via a genitive or the preposition *by*, as illustrated in the gloss of sentences (15a) and (16a), but not via the preposition *of*, as shown in (17).

(17) a. *The destruction of the city of Godzilla
b. *The version of the 9th of Karajan

The possibility of having multiple *de*-arguments in French is argued to relate to overt noun raising. According to Dekydtspotter et al. (1997), noun movement to Num means that the noun c-commands its agent, which in turns allows case-assignment (via *de*-insertion). In contrast, noun movement is not overt in English, which means that the noun does not c-command its agent. Case-assignment cannot therefore take place via *of*-insertion. In terms of acquisition, English-speaking learners of French not only have to acquire the fact that agents can be introduced by *de* in French (as a result of noun movement), they also have to learn the restrictions on such marking (the fact that multiple *de*-arguments are prohibited with result nominals). This learning situation represents another clear example of the poverty-of-the stimulus problem given the rarity of dyadic nominals in classroom input. Furthermore, L2 learners are not taught about the kinds of restrictions on agentive PPs discussed above.

The methodology in Dekydtspotter et al.'s (1997) investigation of English-speaking learners' competence with such multiple *de*-arguments is similar to that of Anderson's (2002) experiment on the interpretation of adjective placement. There were 22 scenarios establishing the status of the nominal, either process or result. Each scenario was then followed by a sentence including either a result and or a process nominal introduced by *de*. For each context-sentence pairing, the participants had to decide whether the sentence sounded *fine* or *odd*. The results are summarized in Table 14. The French controls accepted *de*-marked agents significantly more often with result nominals than with process nominals,[166] and the English controls accepted *de*-marked

166. The acceptance rate of *de*-marked agents with result nominals was relatively low (45%). Dekydtspotter et al. (1997) argue that this is due to the fact that multiple complements with a *de*-marked agent, albeit grammatical, is often stylistically awkward in French (in comparison to multiple complements with a *par*-marked agent). Nonetheless, the difference between the two types of nominals was clearly made by the French NSs when it came to *de*-marked agents.

agents to a much lower extent than did the French control group. Therefore, native speakers behaved as expected. What about the L2 French learners? The difference between result and process nominals with respect to *de*-marked agents was established as of the lowest level, and increased with proficiency. The advanced learners accepted agents' occurrence with *de* only about 25% of the time. In general, then, the adult learners appeared to have acquired the fact that multiple *de*-agents can occur with dyadic nominals, which suggests that they had acquired noun movement in French. In addition, they had acquired the fact that such a possibility is restricted to nominals denoting a result interpretation.

Table 14. Acceptance rates on Result and Process interpretations of *de*-marked agents (from Dekydtspotter et al. 1997)

Participants	Result (n=10)	Process (n=12)
French NSs (n=48)	50.42%	15.65%***
English NSs (n=24)	22.08%	10.53%*
Beginners (n=38)	69.21%	53.51%**
Intermediates (n=32)	71.56%	48.96%**
Advanced (n=20)	63.5%	24.17%***

significant difference between Result and Process: * $p < .05$ ** $p < .01$; *** $p < .001$.

These results are duplicated in Anderson (2002, 2007) who also incorporated *par*-agents with result and process nominals in his study. All participants, including French and English NSs, and L2 French learners, strongly accepted *par*-agents with both types of nominals.

12.2.3.2 *Acquisition of quantified expressions by adult L2 French learners*

In French, in quantified object nominals involving quantifiers such as *beaucoup* 'much/many', *trop* 'too much/too many', or *peu* 'little/few', the quantifier may appear either together with the NP that it modifies, as in (18a), or distanced from it, as in (18b). The latter construction is referred to as a quantifier at a distance (QAD) construction, the former, a non-QAD construction. In QAD sentences, the quantifier is assumed to bind a variable within the NP (Obenauer 1983, 1984/1985).

(18) a. Il a trouvé $[_{NP}$ $[_{QP}$ beaucoup] de pièces d'or].
he has found many of coins of gold

b. Il a $[_{QP}$ beaucoup$_i$] trouvé $[_{NP}$ $[_{QP}$ ec$_i$] de pièces d'or].
'He found many gold coins.'

The two sentences in (18) may not receive the same interpretation. In particular, a QAD construction is only possible if the event which it denotes can be subdivided into multiple events, as illustrated in (19a); it cannot be used for an event that can be viewed as a single point, as shown in (19b). In contrast, non-QAD constructions are possible in either multiple event or single event contexts, as shown in (20a) and (20b).

(19) a. En cherchant partout, il a beaucoup trouvé de pièces d'or.
while searching everywhere he has many found of coins of gold
'(By) searching everywhere, he found many gold coins.'

b. * En une seule fois, il a beaucoup trouvé de pièces d'or.
in one single time he has many found of coins of gold

(20) a. En cherchant partout, il a trouvé beaucoup de pièces d'or.
while searching everywhere he has found many of coins of gold
'(By) searching everywhere, he found many gold coins.'

b. En une seule fois, il a trouvé beaucoup de pièces d'or.
in one single time he has found many of coins of gold
'In a single time, he found many gold coins.'

The impossibility of single event reading of QAD constructions obtains via a complex relationship involving the syntactic representation of these constructions and the semantic representation of event-related interpretations (see Dekydtspotter, Sprouse & Thyre 1999/2000). The details of this relationship are not relevant to the discussion here. What is relevant is that if this representational apparatus is unavailable to L2 French learners, they should not be able to acquire the target semantic restrictions on QAD constructions (further assuming that such constructions are not possible in the L1). These restrictions are typically not taught in French language classrooms, and native speakers, including language instructors, are usually unaware of them.

To investigate L2 learners' knowledge of these semantic restrictions, Dekydtspotter et al. (1999/2000) administered a truth-value task similar in nature to the ones described in the previous section. The participants were given a series of scenarios establishing an event as either a single event or an iterative event. Each scenario was then followed by a sentence containing either a QAD construction (which either matched the scenario given or did not) or a non-QAD scenario (which could match either possibility). The learners were native speakers of English, a language that does not allow QAD constructions. Two experiments were carried out. The first one only involved English-speaking learners (n=46), whose level of French was assessed as advanced. The results are presented in Table 15.

Table 15. Percentage of yes answers on non-QAD and QAD constructions (Experiment 1) (adapted from Dekydtspotter et al. (1999/2000))

Interpretation	Non-QAD	QAD
Multiple event	88.7%	70.2%*
Single event	90.2%	60.3%

* Significant difference between Multiple event and Single event interpretations ($p = .001$)

The learners clearly distinguished between a multiple event reading of QAD constructions and a single event interpretation, which they accepted to a significantly lower extent. In contrast, no distinction was made between the two readings in non-QAD constructions: acceptance of both interpretations was equally high. As explained by the authors, the results are compatible with either the construction of an IL system similar to that of French NSs (although no NSs were tested in the first experiment) or with the interpretation of the QAD construction as meaning *beaucoup de fois* 'many times'. This could happen if the learners interpret QAD sentences as involving a series of recurrent events rather than a distribution of the event over several subevents. The distinction can be seen in (21), where (21b) can only be true if there have been several explosions.

(21) a. L' explosion a beaucoup brisé de vitres.
the explosion has many broken of windows
'The explosion broke many windows.'

b. L' explosion a brisé des vitres beaucoup de fois.
the explosion has broken some windows many of times
'The explosion has broken some windows many times.'

A second experiment was therefore designed to test L2 learners' knowledge of the interpretation of QAD versus *beaucoup de fois*. The same methodology was used as in the first experiment, with test scenarios establishing either a multiple event or single event context. Two groups of native speakers were also involved: French NSs and English NSs (who were administered a literal translation of the test sentences). The results replicate those obtained in the first experiment, with a multiple event reading of QAD being significantly preferred over a single event interpretation (Table 16). This is true for both the learners and the French NSs. These participants also widely accepted the multiple event interpretation of *beaucoup de fois* sentences. Crucially, however, the single event reading of these sentences was almost never selected. This differs significantly from the acceptance rate of the single event interpretation in QAD, which suggests that the learners did not treat QAD as *beaucoup de fois*. The English-speaking controls did not show any significant difference between the two readings of QAD.

Table 16. Percentage of True answers in QAD and *beaucoup de fois* constructions (adapted from Dekydtspotter et al. (1999/2000)

Group	QAD		*beaucoup de fois*	
	Multiple events	Single events	Multiple events	Single events
French controls (n=24)	63.9%*	38.7%	59.3%*	1%
English controls (n=11)	56.6%	46%	–	–
Learners (n=72)	92.7%*	63.8%	95%*	9.6%

* Significant difference between Multiple event and Single event interpretations

12.2.4 Theoretical implications

Results from production and grammaticality judgments suggest that L2 learners can acquire the target strength of the number feature. Beginner learners have been found to produce and allow N-Adj orders (although not to the extent of native speakers or advanced learners), even when their L1 disallows such sequences. This suggests that even the grammars of beginner learners have a Number head to which the noun can move. The native-like performance on noun placement on the part of advanced learners suggests that these learners have acquired the strong value of French Num. Since the learners involved in the studies reviewed above have a Germanic language as L1, where the Num feature is weak, these results suggest that parameter resetting is possible in L2 acquisition. This contradicts proposals according to which acquisition of target parametric values cannot be achieved when the L2 values differ from the values instantiated in the L1 (Tsimpli & Roussou 1991, for example). Nonetheless, some of the results should be interpreted with caution. In particular, written elicited production tasks may not tap the learners' instinct about noun movement; rather, the results obtained on such tasks may reflect metalinguistic knowledge of adjective placement based on explicit instruction. Alternative methods of collecting data on adjective placement should be developed, such as (on-line) judgment tasks.

Subtle semantic consequences of adjective placement, as well as syntactic consequences of noun movement and the interpretation of QAD constructions, have also been investigated. Since these properties are generally not taught and are quite difficult to discern from the input, learning them is a true poverty-of-the-stimulus problem. By and large, results from learners in whose L1 noun movement is not overt show that learning is possible and that linguistic intuitions similar to those of French native speakers can be attained. The same can be said of the interpretation of QAD constructions, which are most often associated with a multiple event reading, despite the lack of QAD in the learners' L1. These results strongly suggest that UG is available in post-puberty L2 acquisition (contra Bley-Vroman 1990; Clahsen 1988; Meisel 1997, and others who argue that there is a critical period for language acquisition). UG access guarantees that parameter resetting can be achieved in L2 learning and that native-like grammars can be constructed by L2 learners (contra Coppieters 1987).

12.3 Conclusion

This chapter has highlighted the role of the L1 in the acquisition of various properties of DPs in L2 French and shown that acquisition is facilitated when the mother tongue possesses the categories and features that are activated in French. For instance, initial production of determiners can be quite high, and early knowledge of definiteness and number can be observed. This suggests that functional categories and features are present in initial IL grammars, and argues against proposals advocating the existence of a lexical stage in adult L2 acquisition (Vainikka & Young-Scholten 1996, 2005). However, that acquisition is facilitated does not mean that there is target-like knowledge of D-properties from the outset. For instance, adult L2 learners do not necessarily treat determiners as clitics at first, even if their L1 contains clitic-like determiners. This ties in with findings in other linguistic domains, such as verbal inflection and object pronouns, suggesting that adult learners follow Rizzi's (2000) Categorial Uniformity Principle, but more studies of adult learners of French whose L1 has prenominal determiners that are clitics, such as Spanish and Italian, are needed. If Categorial Uniformity holds, then elision and contraction should be rare in early production. The acquisition of the clitic status of determiners in child L2 French is another understudied area.

When the L1 does not instantiate the relevant D-features, such as Vietnamese, acquisition of determiners by L2 learners follows a different path. For instance, these learners may produce determiners initially but seem to consider them classifiers, and they may have difficulty with definiteness and number. This tends to support Schwartz & Sprouse's (1996) FTFA hypothesis, although more data should be obtained from more proficient learners. The FTFA model claims that restructuration of IL grammars is possible with time and exposure to relevant input, which suggests that determiners should stop being considered classifiers and that definiteness and number can eventually be acquired. To date, however, only beginner L2 learners of French (with Vietnamese as their L1) have been tested (Leung 2002).

Although results reported in the literature clearly suggest that the L1 has a strong influence over the construction of early L2 French grammars, specific details and statistical evidence of learners' performance are often lacking, particularly in the area of definiteness. Further research addressing the development of French D-features in more detail, with both child and adult L2 learners, and going beyond the analysis of spontaneous production data would be helpful. Perhaps some of the experimental designs developed in L1 acquisition (see Chapter 10) could be adapted for more detailed research with L2 learners.

Research into the L2 acquisition of gender suggests gradual development, including the use of default determiners that may differ with definites and indefinites. Eventually, L2 learners can reach high levels of accuracy, even when the L1 does not have gender. This suggests that the relevant uninterpretable features can be acquired, in contrast to proposals by Hawkins & Franceschina (2004).

A number of different proposals have been made about the cues that learners use in their acquisition of gender in French. Some researchers argue that morphophonological cues are primary (e.g. Hawkins & Franceschina 2004), while others have proposed that cues use is mainly semantic (e.g. Carroll 1999). Likewise, different views exist as to L1 influence over gender acquisition. For Carroll (1989), the difficulty encountered by English-speaking learners with the acquisition of gender is due to the fact that there is no gender in their L1; for Granfeldt (2003), L1 gender properties are not transferred to French IL grammars, even when the L1 makes gender distinctions. More research is clearly needed on the development of gender in French, and as in the case of bilingual acquisition, research on a variety of learning situations, with a variety of L1s in which gender is instantiated (e.g. Italian, Spanish, and German), would be particularly revealing.

The last aspect of the acquisition of DP structure that was looked at in this chapter was noun placement. Research shows that target noun placement can be acquired by adult L2 learners of French, although here again L1 influence is observable. Target-like knowledge of noun placement in French is also shown by the results of the investigation of subtle properties at the semantic/syntactic interface (such as the interpretation of adjectives), which are not immediately obvious in the input and are rarely taught. The target-like performance reported in such poverty-of-the-stimulus situations is very important as it strongly suggests that parameter resetting can be achieved in adult L2 acquisition, presumably via the availability of UG, contra proposals by Bley-Vroman (1990), Clahsen (1988), and Tsimpli & Roussou (1991). These results are important in understanding L2 learners' acquisition of the properties of DP, but do not represent a complete picture of the acquisition of noun placement in L2 French. More research is required, particularly in child L2 French. Future research should look at different ways of eliciting data on this property, trying as much as possible to prevent recourse to metalinguistic knowledge.

PART IV

Questions and embedded clauses

CHAPTER 13

Questions and embedded clauses in French

Facts and analyses

This chapter explores the properties of questions and other complex structures in French, such as embedded declaratives, embedded questions, and relative clauses. Such constructions are of interest to acquisition researchers since they involve the projection of the functional category C and its associated features, such as [±wh]. As with other functional categories, one question is whether C is present in initial underlying grammars, or whether it develops later on, for example after the acquisition of I. In L2 acquisition, we may additionally wonder whether or not the L1 characteristics of C influence the development of C in the target language. Moreover, CP-clauses involve a certain degree of complexity, for instance in terms of movement or degree of embedding. The question therefore arises as to whether or not language learners tend to start off with less complex derivations.

Some of the constructions discussed in this chapter involve a relatively high degree of variability in French. For example, in root wh-questions, the wh-word may appear at the front of the question (as *qui* 'who' in *Qui connais-tu?* 'Who do you know?') or remain in its underlying position (in situ) (*Tu connais qui?* lit. 'You know who?'). The verb may also appear in two positions, either before the subject (as *connais* 'know' in *Qui connais-tu?)* or after it (*Qui tu connais?).* Other constructions, such as embedded questions, allow much less variability. One goal of this chapter is to describe the extent of allowable variability in these constructions and the constraints underlying it. As we have seen, acquisition data tend to contain a high degree of variability, so it is important to understand the acceptable variability in the adult language before proposing analyses of language learners' data.

13.1 Root interrogatives

Two of the main characteristics of French matrix questions are the placement of the wh-word and the possibility of subject/verb inversion. Both exhibit a fair degree of variability.

13.1.1 Wh-word placement

In French wh-questions, the wh-word may appear at the front of the interrogative sentence, as in (1a), or it can remain in situ, namely in its base-generated position, as in (1b).

The latter option is mainly found in colloquial French.[167] Note that wh-questions can also be formed with the periphrastic expression *est-ce que*, which will be discussed in Section 13.1.5

(1) a. Où vas- tu?
where go you
'Where are you going?'

b. Tu vas où?

Although most wh-pronouns retain the same form regardless of whether they are preposed or in situ, *quoi* 'what' does not. *Quoi* changes to *que* when fronted (the so-called *que/quoi* alternation), as illustrated in (2).

(2) a. Tu fais quoi?
you do what

b. Que fais-tu?
what do you
'What are you doing?'

However, if a preposition is involved, then *quoi* is obligatory, as in *Avec quoi tu vas faire ça?* 'With what are you going to do that?'.[168]

Finally, when the wh-word is part of a prepositional phrase, as in *à qui* 'to whom' in (3), the whole PP must appear at the front of the sentence (3a); preposition stranding is ungrammatical in French (3b). This differs from English, as can be seen in the gloss of (3a). Note that the whole PP may also be left in situ, as illustrated in (3c).

---

167. For some researchers, questions with fronted wh-words should not be considered equivalent to questions with wh-words in situ. Questions with wh-words in situ are said to be associated with a 'strongly presupposed context' (Chang 1997; Cheng & Rooryck 2000; but see Mathieu 2004). Thus, a question such as *Marie a acheté quoi?* 'Marie bought what?' would only be possible under the speaker's presupposition that Mary bought something. When the wh-word is fronted, there would not be such a presupposition. However, since the proposed difference is far from being established and has not been investigated in the acquisition of French, I will not pursue the issue any further.

168. Another property of *que* and *quoi* is that neither of them can stand for the subject, as is the case with psych-verbs such as *effrayer* 'frighten' (see (ia)). In these cases a periphrastic question must be used, as illustrated in (ib).

(i) a. *Que/*quoi effraie Jean?
what frightens John

b. Qu'est-ce qui effraie John?
what ESK frightens John
'What frightens John?'

(3) a. À qui as- tu parlé?
to whom have you talked
'To whom did you talk?' or 'Who(m) did you talk to?'

b. *Qui as-tu parlé $[_{PP}$ à __] ?

c. Tu as parlé $[_{PP}$ à qui]?

13.1.2 Inversion

Wh- and yes/no-questions may or may not exhibit subject/verb inversion. Three types of inversion are discussed in the literature: inversion of the subject clitic and the verb, complex inversion, and stylistic inversion.

13.1.2.1 *Clitic/verb inversion*

In clitic/verb inversion, the pronoun appears after the verb, whether it is a lexical verb or a light verb (an auxiliary or the copula *être*). Inversion of the subject clitic and the verb can occur in both yes-no questions (4) and wh-questions (5).[169]

(4) a. Pars-tu demain?
leave you tomorrow
'Are you leaving tomorrow?'

b. As- tu appelé hier?
have you called yesterday
'Did you called yesterday?'

c. Vont-ils voter?
go they vote
'Are they going to vote?'

d. Est-il bleu?
is it blue
'Is it blue?'

169. Clitic/verb inversion and complex inversion (see Section 13.1.2.2) are also found in other constructions not discussed in detail in this book. These constructions involve modal adverbs such as *peut-être* 'perhaps', as in (i), and conditional clauses, as in (ii). Such conditional clauses are principally used in formal speech.

(i) Peut-être (Pierre) est-il arrivé à l'heure.
perhaps Peter is he arrived on time
'Perhaps Peter/he arrived on time.'

(ii) (Jean) aurait -il fait ses devoirs, il aurait reçu
John have.COND.3SG he done his homework he have.COND.3SG received
une meilleure note.
a better grade
'Had John/he done his homework, he would have received a better grade.'

(5) a. Où vas-tu?
where go you
'Where are you going?'

b. Quand as- tu appelé?
when have you called
'When did you call?'

c. Dans quel état vont-elles terminer la course?
in what state go they finish the race
'In what state are they going to finish the race?'

d. Pourquoi est- il sale?
why is it dirty
'Why is it dirty?'

Clitic/verb inversion is not obligatory, except with the wh-word *que* 'what' (see (8)), especially in colloquial registers and French varieties such as Quebec French. It is usually considered to be characteristic of formal (written) language (see, e.g. Vinet 2001).[170] When clitic/verb inversion does not occur, interrogation is signaled by rising intonation.

(6) a. Tu pars demain?
b. Tu as appelé hier?
c. Ils vont voter?
d. Il est bleu?

(7) a. Où tu vas?
b. Quand tu as appelé?
c. Dans quel état elles vont terminer la course?
d. Pourquoi il est sale?

(8) a. Que fais-tu?
what do you
'What are you doing?'

b. *Que tu fais?

In wh-questions with clitic/verb inversion, the wh-word must be fronted; it cannot remain in situ: **Vas-tu où?* Finally, in very colloquial registers, the complementizer *que* 'that' may intervene between the wh-word and the non-inverted subject, as in *Où que tu vas?* lit. 'Where that you go?' and *Quand que tu as appelé?* lit. 'When that you called?'.

If the subject is a full lexical DP, subject/verb inversion is ungrammatical, as in (9) and (10). In particular, a full lexical DP subject cannot appear between an auxiliary and a verb, or between a modal and a verb, in contrast to subject clitics. For grammatical

170. The lack of inversion seems to be most acceptable when the fronted wh-word is adverbial or within a PP. It is less natural with argumental wh-pronouns, as in *?Qui tu admires?* 'Who do you admire?' or *?Quel disque tu as acheté?* 'Which cd did you buy?'.

cases of inversion involving a full DP (e.g. *Où va Jean?* 'Where is John going?' and *Où est allé Jean?* 'Where did John go?'), see Section 13.1.2.3.

(9) a. *Part Jean demain?
leaves John tomorrow

b. *A Jean appelé hier?
has John called yesterday

c. *Vont les gens voter?
go the people vote

d. *Est le sac bleu?
is the bag blue

(10) a. *Quand a Jean appelé?
when has John called

b. *Dans quel état vont les coureuses terminer la course?
in what state go the runners finish the race
'In what state are the runners going to finish the race?'

c. *Pourquoi est le sac sale?
why is the bag dirty

13.1.2.2 *Complex inversion*

Complex inversion involves both a full DP subject and a co-referring clitic, with the finite verb and the clitic being inverted, as illustrated in (11) and (12). As with (simple) clitic/verb inversion, complex inversion is found in both yes/no questions and wh-questions.[171]

(11) a. Jean part-il demain?
John leaves he tomorrow
'Is John leaving tomorrow?'

b. Jean a-t-il appelé hier?
John has he called yesterday
'Did John call yesterday?'

c. Les gens vont-ils voter?
the people go they vote
'Are the people going to vote?'

d. Le sac est-il bleu?
the bag is it blue
'Is the bag blue?'

171. Complex inversion is impossible with a fronted *que*: **Que Jean a-t-il acheté?* 'What did John buy?', which is an instantiation of the general prohibition against anything intervening between *que* and the verb (compare *Quand, d'après toi, arrivera Jean?* 'When, according to you, will John arrive?' with **Que, d'après toi, fera Jean?* 'What, according to you, will John do?'). Arguably, *que* is a clitic (the clitic counterpart of *quoi*) which attaches to the verb in C (e.g. *Que fera-t-il?* 'What will he do?'). See Footnote 175.

(12) a. Où Jean va-t-il?
where John goes he
'Where is John going?'

b. Quand Jean a-t-il appelé?
when John has he called
'When did John call?'

c. Dans quel état les coureuses vont-elles terminer la course?
in what state the runners.FEM go they+FEM finish the race
'In what state are the runners going to finish the race?'

d. Pourquoi le sac est-il sale?
why the bag is it dirty
'Why is the bag dirty?'

13.1.2.3 *Stylistic inversion*

In stylistic inversion, the full DP subject occurs after the verb or after the second verb in constructions involving complex tenses or a modal followed by another verb. This is different from clitic/verb inversion, in which the clitic always follows the first verb if there are multiple verbs.[172,173]

(13) a. Où va Jean?
where goes John
'Where is John going?'

b. À quelle heure a appelé Jean?
at what time has called John
'At what time did John call?'

c. Dans quelle voiture vont arriver les invités?
in which car go arrive the guests
'In which car are the guests going to arrive?'

---

172. Note that stylistic inversion cannot occur with *pourquoi* 'why', presumably because no wh-movement is involved here: **Pourquoi a téléphoné Jean?* lit. 'Why has called John?'.

173. Stylistic inversion can also be found in exclamatives, as in (i), and with preposed adverbials, as in (ii) (examples from Jones 1996).

(i) Quelle chance a eue Pierre!
what luck has had Peter
'How lucky Peter has been!'

(ii) Sur la table se trouvait un magnétophone.
on the table self found a tape recorder
'On the table was a tape-recorder'

d. Que fait Martin?
what does Martin
'What is Martin doing?'

e. Où est Martin?
where is Martin
'Where is Martin?'

Note that stylistic inversion cannot apply in the presence of certain verb complements, such as direct objects, as illustrated in (14).[174]

(14) a. *À qui a prêté ce livre Pierre?
to whom has loaned this book Peter

b. *À qui a prêté Pierre ce livre?
to whom has loaned Peter this book

Another difference with clitic/verb inversion is that stylistic inversion is restricted to wh-questions; it cannot occur in yes/no questions, as shown in (15).

(15) a. *Part Jean?
leaves John

b. *A appelé Jean?
has called John

c. *Vont arriver les invités?
go arrive the guests

d. *Est Martin dans sa chambre? / est dans sa chambre Martin?
is Martin in his room is in his room Martin

13.1.3 Infinitival questions

The main verb of a matrix question may be in the infinitive in French, but almost only with wh-questions (16a–c) — and not when the interrogative questions the subject (16d).

174. However, the presence of a complement does not systematically block stylistic inversion. In (ia), the wh-word stands for the direct object and the indirect object appears within VP; yet, the sentence is grammatical. Note that in this case, adjacency between the verb and the subject must be respected. If the indirect object intervenes between the two, the sentence is ungrammatical, as in (ib).

(i) a. Qu' a prêté Pierre à ses parents?
what has loaned Peter to his parents
'What did Peter loan to his parents?'

b. *Qu'a prêté à ses parents Pierre?

(16) a. Où aller?
where go.INF

b. Que faire?
what do.INF

c. Comment lui faire comprendre?
how him+DAT make understand

d. *Qui partir?
who leave.INF

The subject in infinitival questions is systematically null and is assumed to be PRO. In addition, infinitivals have a modal reading. In (16a) and (16b), the speaker wonders where he/she should go and what he/she should do. In (16c), the question refers to some kind of capacity (How can I tap into the person's capacity for understanding?). Such questions cannot have a simple information-seeking interpretation. For instance (16a) and (16b) cannot mean 'Where are we going?' and 'What are we doing?'. Such readings must be conveyed via a finite form, such as *On va où?* and *Qu'est-ce qu'on fait?*

Infinitival yes/no questions are largely impossible, as shown in (17). Only counterfactuals can be grammatical, as illustrated in (18).

(17) a. *Partir à 5pm?
leave.INF at 5pm

b. *Aller en Espagne?
go.INF to Spain

c. *Faire un dessin?
do.INF a drawing

(18) Lui venir avec nous? Absolument pas!
him come.INF with us absolutely not
'Him come with us? Absolutely not!'

13.1.4 Theoretical accounts

Let us start by assuming that the structure of interrogatives generally involves the CP node (see Rizzi 1997 for an extended approach to the left periphery). In wh-questions, the wh-word may move to the front of the interrogative sentence, to the specifier of CP, as illustrated in (19a), which also shows clitic/verb inversion, and (19b), which does not.

(19) a. $[_{CP}$ Où$_i$ vas$_j$ $[_{IP}$ tu t_j $[_{VP}$ t_j t_i]]]?
where go you

b. $[_{CP}$ Où$_i$ $[_{IP}$ tu vas$_j$ $[_{VP}$ t_j t_i]]]?
'Where are you going?'

According to Rizzi's (1991) Wh-Criterion, a wh-operator must be in a specifier-head configuration with a [+wh] head and vice versa. This explains cases of clitic/verb inversion, as in (19a), quite straightforwardly. The wh-word has moved into the specifier position of CP whose head is occupied by the verbal element *vas* 'go'. This element has itself moved from I, where the [+wh] feature is assumed to be generated. I-to-C movement ensures that the [+wh] feature ends up in C, thereby satisfying the Wh-Criterion. The tree representation is given in (20).

(20)

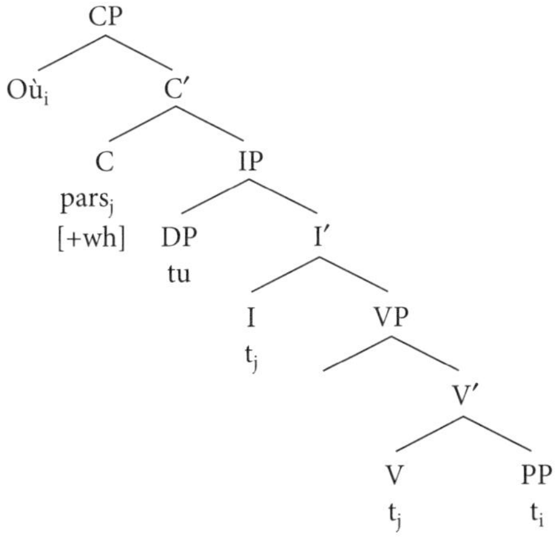

To account for cases where there is no clitic/verb inversion, as in (19b), Rizzi assumes that French wh-operators are able to 'pass on' their wh-features to C, which again satisfies the Wh-Criterion. This operation, labeled Dynamic Agreement, is not allowed in languages such as Dutch, English, and German, in which subject/verb inversion is required.[175]

In Minimalist terms, the fact that wh-movement can be overt in French suggests that uninterpretable wh-features are strong in French (as they are in English), in contrast to Chinese, where the wh-word systematically remains in situ. Assuming that the [+wh] feature is specified on I (or T), checking cannot take place within IP if the wh-question is a non-subject interrogative, as in (19a). Indeed, movement of the subject into SpecIP will not result in the checking of the [+wh] feature. I-to-C movement is therefore necessary for feature-checking to take place. That wh-features are strong in French is further shown by the fact that wh-words are fronted in embedded questions; they cannot remain in their base-generated positions (see Section 13.2.1).

175. With respect to the *que/quoi* alternation, we saw that *que* cannot appear in situ; rather, it must be preposed and followed by the verb. One possible analysis is that *que* is the weak version of *quoi*, much like pronominal clitics are the weak version of strong pronouns. Accordingly, *que* must appear in SpecCP and then cliticize onto the verb. As the strong counterpart of *que*, *quoi* can occur on its own (as in *quoi?* 'what?'), it may appear in situ and in PPs. Crucially, it can be followed by a non-verbal element (e.g. *Sur quoi Pierre est-il assis?* 'On what is Pierre sitting?'), which is impossible with *que*.

In cases where there is overt wh-movement but no inversion, as in (19b), a Minimalist alternative to Dynamic Agreement would be to assume that the [+wh] feature is directly assigned to C, hence rendering I-to-C movement unnecessary (Plunkett 2000). In such cases, movement of the wh-word to SpecCP would be forced for feature-checking purposes.

If the uninterpretable [+wh] feature is strong in French, as suggested by the fact that wh-movement can be overt, then why can wh-phrases sometimes remain in situ, as in *Tu vas où?* lit. 'You're going where?' In other words, if wh-features are strong in French, shouldn't wh-movement be systematic? One possibility is that in questions where the wh-word remains in situ, there is no uninterpretable wh-feature present in the representation (see Plunkett 2000; Rizzi 1991). If there is no feature to be checked, no wh-movement is required. According to Plunkett (2000), the sentence can still be interpreted as a question because of the presence of an interpretable wh-feature (on the wh-word itself), which is sufficient for it to be assigned scope and for the clause containing it to be considered interrogative.[176] Alternatively, the wh-word left in situ may be bound by a question morpheme Q in the C domain, as in (21). This morpheme can be thought of as a phonological morpheme merged in C and spelled out as rising intonation (Cheng & Rooryck 2000).[177] Merging the Q morpheme would also check the [+wh] feature of C.

(21) $[_{CP}$ Q_i $[_{IP}$ tu vas $où_i]$?

In yes/no questions, it is usually assumed that an abstract question marker occupies the specifier position of CP, from which it can have scope over the rest of the sentence, as in (22). This marker allows the sentence to be interpreted as a question at LF, regardless of whether clitic/verb inversion has occurred.

(22) a. $[_{CP}$ Q $[_{IP}$ Tu pars demain]]?
you leave tomorrow
'Are you leaving tomorrow?'

b. $[_{CP}$ Q $Pars_i$ $[_{IP}$ tu t_i demain]]?]

176. For Plunkett (2004a), wh-questions exhibiting clitic/verb inversion do not involve the CP node. Rather, Plunkett assumes that T, equipped with the [+wh] feature, moves and adjoins to its own projection, as in (i). This yields the projection of a new specifier position to which the wh-phrase raises, which allows the feature to be checked.

(i) $[_{TP}$ $Wh\text{-}phrase_j$ $[_{TP}$ T_i $[_{TP}$ DP t_i $[_{VP}$ $\ldots t_j$]]]]
+Wh +Nom

177. For Mathieu (2002), the Q element is an operator that has moved to SpecCP to check the [+wh] feature of C, as in (i):

(i) $[_{CP}$ OP_i $[_{IP}$ Tu vois $[_{DP}$ t_i qui_i]] ce soir]] ?

This account is based on a split DP analysis and it assumes that wh-phrases such as *qui* and *quoi* are not specified as [+Q].

We will further assume that the Q-marker is also involved in the representation of periphrastic yes/no questions of the type *Est-ce que tu viens demain?* lit. 'Is it that you are coming tomorrow?' (see Section 13.1.5).

With this theoretical background, it is now possible to discuss in detail the three types of inversion: clitic/verb inversion, complex inversion, and stylistic inversion. We have already seen how to account for the optionality of clitic/verb inversion. Given that subject clitics are associated with the IP node, clitic/verb inversion is usually taken to involve verb movement to C, with the clitic remaining within IP, as illustrated in (20). The verb thus undergoes a double movement in such cases: first from V to I, and then from I to C. Note that clitic/verb inversion is incompatible with the idea that subject clitics are agreement prefixes (see Section 5.1.2.2). If they were, the verb would not be able to move without its prefix attached to it. Instead, the V-cl order in clitic/verb inversion suggests that the clitic occupies SpecIP and that cliticization to the verb occurs once the verb has raised to C. The question then is: why are full DP subjects ruled out in such constructions? In other words, why can't a full DP subject occur in SpecIP with the finite verb in C, as in **Où est Jean allé?* 'Where did John go?' One analysis is that French C is not able to assign Case to the specifier position of IP, in contrast to languages such as Dutch, English, and German. The subject DP is therefore left without Case, and the derivation crashes. The problem does not arise with subject pronouns, as they can incorporate into the finite verb via cliticization.

In complex inversion (e.g. *Où Jean est-il parti?* 'Where did John go?'), the verb raises to C, as in cases of clitic/verb inversion, and the subject DP adjoins to C' (Rizzi & Roberts 1989). This is illustrated in (23).

(23)

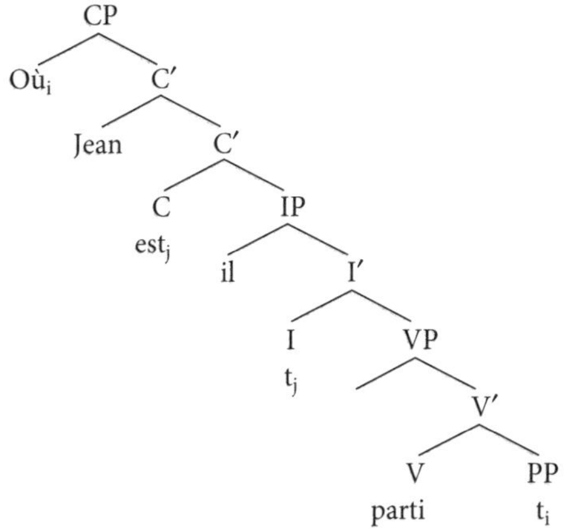

In stylistic inversion (e.g. *Où va Jean?* Where is John going?'), the verb moves to I, but not to C, in contrast to the two other types of inverted constructions seen so far. In addition, the subject remains within VP, as shown in (24). A null expletive *pro* appears in SpecIP in order to satisfy the Extended Projection Principle, according to which all sentences must have a subject. It is licensed by C associated with wh-features (presumably as a result of Dynamic Agreement under Rizzi's (1991) account).[178] The DP subject then adjoins to *pro* at LF in order to check its Case feature and to keep the expletive *pro* from violating the Principle of Full Interpretation (an expletive cannot receive a coherent interpretation at LF).[179]

(24)

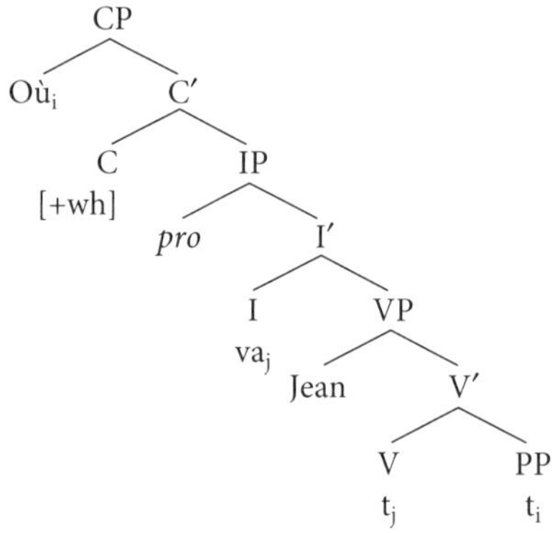

This account of stylistic inversion, in which the subject remains within VP, explains why stylistic inversion involves DP subjects but not clitics: clitics cannot stay within VP (see Chapter 5). Moreover, the fact that the expletive *pro* is licensed by the wh-features of C can account for the fact that stylistic inversion is not found in yes/no questions where no such features are involved.

13.1.5 *Est-ce que* questions

Matrix questions may include the sequence *est-ce que* (lit. 'is it that'), as in *Est-ce que tu viens?* 'Are you coming?' and *Qu'est-ce que tu fais?* 'What are you doing?'. The nature of *est-ce que* is disputed in the literature: it may be a simple unanalysed question marker (ESK, under C), as in $[_{CP}$ ESK $[_{IP}$ tu viens]]?, or a complex construction involving the inversion of *ce* 'it' and *est* 'is' and an embedded clause introduced by the complementizer *que* 'that', as in (25c).[180]

---

178. An alternative account has been proposed by Kayne & Pollock (2001) according to which two main movements are involved: movement of the subject to the specifier of a functional category (F in (i) below) followed by movement of the TP (which includes the trace of the subject and the verb) to the left periphery (to a position labeled G in (i)) (see also Lahousse 2004):

(i) $[_{GP} [_{TP}\ t_{subject} [_{T^{\circ}}\ verb]]]\ [_{G^{\circ}}]\ [_{FP}\ subject\ [_{F^{\circ}}]\ t_{TP}]]$

179. For Friedemann (1997), the representation in (24) includes a right-branching SpecVP (see also Section 2.3.2). This could explain why the lexical subject appears after the verb in stylistic inversion with complex tenses, as in *Où est allé Jean*? 'Where did John go?'.

180. Arguments in favour of the question marker approach to *est-ce que* are that *est-ce que* does not appear in other tenses, such as *imparfait* (**était-ce que...*) or future (**sera-ce que...*),

(25) a. C'est que tu viens.
it is that you come
'It is that you're coming'

b. Est-ce que tu viens?

c. $[_{CP}$ Q est$_{t}$ $[_{IP}$ ce t$_{t}$ $[_{CP}$ que tu viens]]]?

Note that in *est-ce que* questions, clitic/verb inversion is impossible, since *est-ce que* or *que* (depending on the analysis of the *est-ce que* sequence) occupies the C position: **Est-ce qu'est-il arrivé?*, **Où est-ce que vas-tu?* Finally, *est-ce que* cannot be used in wh-questions if the wh-pronoun has not been fronted, as in **Est-ce que tu vas où?* Assumming that *est-ce que* is a question marker merged in C, this suggests that checking of the [+wh] feature must take place via overt wh-movement.

13.2 Embedded clauses

13.2.1 Embedded questions

In embedded wh-questions, the wh-word must be fronted. If it remains in situ, the sentence is ungrammatical, in contrast to matrix questions:[181,182]

(26) a. Je me demande où tu vas.
I myself ask where you go
'I wonder where you're going.'

b. *Je me demande tu vas où.

Only one type of inversion can be found in embedded wh-questions, namely, stylistic inversion.

(27) a. Je me demande où va Jean.
I myself wonder where goes John
'I wonder where John is going.'

---

and that it cannot be modified by an adverb, such as *peut-être* 'perhaps': **est-ce peut-être que...* This contrasts with the declarative construction *c'est que*, which can be found in other tenses (*c'était que..., ce sera que...*) and can be modified by an adverb (*c'est peut-être que...*). Arguments in favour of a derivational approach to *est-ce que* mainly rest on the fact that *que* changes into *qui* in interrogatives questioning the subject, as *Qui est-ce qui a téléphoné?* 'Who called?'), which suggests that *est-ce que* is not a fixed expression (see Jones 1996; Plunkett 2004a).

181. According to Mathieu (2004), embedded wh-words in situ are possible, albeit in a very limited way, in some variants of French, as in *Je sais pas c'est où* 'I don't know where it is'.

182. Note that *quoi* and *que* 'what' cannot stand for the subject or the object in embedded questions. Instead, *ce qui* (subject) and *ce que* (object) are used, as in *Je me demande *quoi/*que/ce qui effraie Jean* 'I wonder what frightens John' and *Je me demande *quoi/*que/ce que Jean veut* 'I wonder what John wants'.

b. Je me demande à quelle heure a appelé Jean.
I myself wonder at what time has called John
'I wonder at what time John called.'

c. Je me demande dans quelle voiture vont arriver les invités.
I myself wonder in which car go arrive the guests
'I wonder in which car the guests are going to arrive.'

d. Je me demande ce que fait Martin.
I myself wonder what does Martin
'I wonder what Martin is doing?'

Clitic/verb inversion and complex inversion are impossible in embedded wh-questions:

(28) a. *Je me demande où va-t- il.
I wonder where goes he

b. *Je ne sais pas à quelle heure Jean part il.
I NEG know not at what time John leaves he

This is also true of embedded yes/no questions, which in French are introduced by *si* 'if', as in (29).

(29) a. *Je me demande si part- il ce soir.
I myself ask if leaves he this evening

b. *Je me demande si Jean part- il ce soir.
I myself ask if John leaves he this evening

Additionally, embedded yes/no questions cannot involve stylistic inversion (in contrast to embedded wh-questions, as shown above):

(30) *Je me demande si part Jean ce soir.
I myself ask if leaves John this evening

Note that the *est-ce que* construction can be found in embedded wh-questions (in informal speech registers) but not in embedded yes/no questions.[183]

(31) a. Je me demande où est- ce que va Jean.
I myself ask where ESK goes John
'I wonder where John is going.'

b. *Je me demande si est- ce que Jean a téléphoné.
I myself ask if ESK John has called

13.2.2 Embedded declaratives

In embedded declaratives, for instance those introduced by *que* 'that' (see below), none of the three types of inversion discussed above is typically allowed, as shown in (32b–d).[184]

---

183. In particular, embedded wh-questions with *est-ce que* are very frequent in Quebec French (see Plunkett 2004a).

184. However, with embedded subjunctive, stylistic inversion is acceptable, especially in the passive voice:

(32) a. Je pense que Jean/il part ce soir.
I think that John he leaves this evening
'I wonder whether John is leaving tonight'

b. *Je pense que part- il ce soir.
I think that leaves he this evening

c. *Je pense que Jean part- il ce soir.
I think that John leaves he this evening

d. *Je pense que part Jean ce soir.
I think that leaves John this evening

13.2.3 Embedded infinitival clauses

Embedded infinitival wh-questions have the same properties as their matrix counterparts: they are derived via wh-movement, the subject is null, and embedded questions referring to the subject are ungrammatical. Moreover *si* embedded infinitival questions are impossible, much like matrix infinitival yes/no questions.

(33) a. Je me demande où aller.
I myself ask where go.INF

b. Je me demande quoi faire.[185]
I myself ask what do.INF

c. Je me demande comment lui faire comprendre.
I myself ask how him+DAT make understand

d. *Je me demande qui partir.
I myself ask who leave.INF

(34) a. *Je me demande si partir à 5 p.m.
I myself ask if leave.INF at 5 p.m.

b. *Je me demande si aller en Espagne.
I myself ask if go.INF to Spain

c. *Je me demande si faire un dessin.
I myself ask if do.INF a drawing

As to infinitival embedded declaratives, they can be introduced by a preposition, such as *de* and *à*, or they may not involve any complementizer, as in the following examples.

(i) Je refuse que soit interrompu mon discours.
I refuse that be.SUBJ.3SG interrupted my speech
'I refuse that my speech be interrupted.'

185. Note that in contrast to matrix questions, embedded interrogatives questioning a non-human object are introduced by *quoi* and not *que*, except in formal registers (e.g. *Je ne sais pas que faire* 'I don't know what to do').

(35) a. J'apprends à parler le japonais.
I learn to speak.INF the Japanese

b. J'ai envie d' aller en Espagne cet été.
I have desire to go.INF in Spain this year

c. Je pense aller en Espagne cet été.
I think go.INF in Spain this summer

13.2.4 Theoretical account

Like matrix interrogatives, embedded wh-questions involve wh-movement, in this case, to the specifier of the embedded CP node. However, in contrast to matrix questions, such movement is obligatory. Moreover, both clitic/verb inversion and complex inversion are impossible in embedded interrogatives, which suggests that verb movement to C cannot take place, or rather, as we will see, need not take place. It is generally assumed that the embedded C, along with its [+wh] specification, is selected by the higher verb, e.g. *se demander* 'wonder'. Since the (strong) [+wh] feature is directly generated on C, there is no need for verb movement; only the wh-word needs to raise for feature-checking purposes. A sample representation is given in (36). In embedded yes/no questions and embedded declarative clauses, C is occupied by a complementizer (*si* or *que*), which makes this position unavailable as a host for verb movement.

(36)

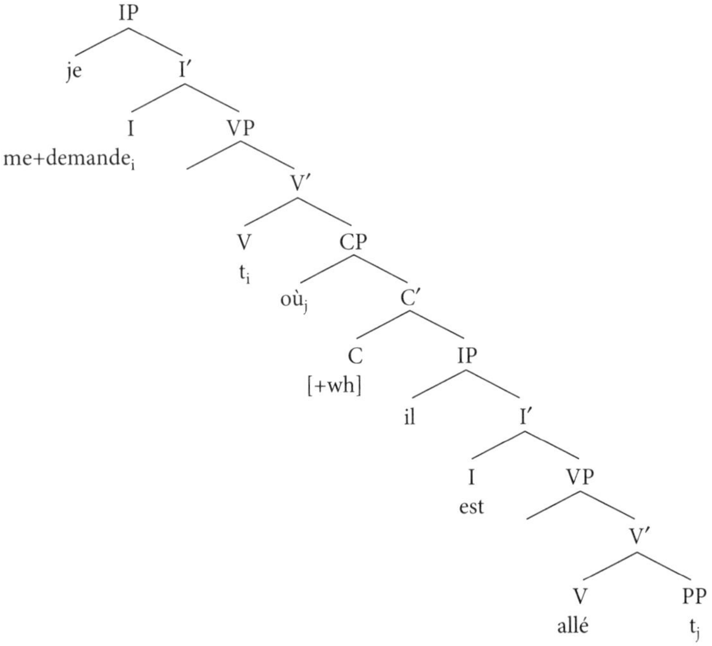

Stylistic inversion is the only type of inversion that can be found in an embedded context. As in matrix questions, stylistic inversion in embedded contexts is restricted to wh-environments, in which the wh-feature of C licenses an expletive *pro* in SpecIP. Its representation is thus similar to the one given in (24), with the subject appearing within VP. Stylistic inversion is ungrammatical in embedded yes/no questions and embedded declaratives, which do not involve wh-features.

Finally, when no overt complementizer is involved, the higher verb selects a CP with a null complementizer, as in (37a). When the infinitival clause is introduced by a preposition, the preposition is assumed to be in C (37b).

(37) a. Je$_i$ pense [$_{CP}$ [$_{C°}$ Ø] [$_{IP}$ PRO$_i$ aller en Espagne cet été]].
I think go.INF in Spain this summer

b. J$_i$'apprends [$_{CP}$ [$_{C°}$ à] [$_{IP}$ PRO$_i$ parler le japonais]].
I learn to speak.INF the Japanese

13.3 Relative clauses

Like embedded wh-questions, relative clauses involve a strong [+wh] feature in C and obligatory wh-movement. There is also coindexation between the head of the NP to which the relative clause applies and the wh-word in SpecCP, so that the predicate status of the relative can be established. This is illustrated in (38).

(38) a. La rue où Jean habite.
the street where John lives
'The street where John lives'

b.

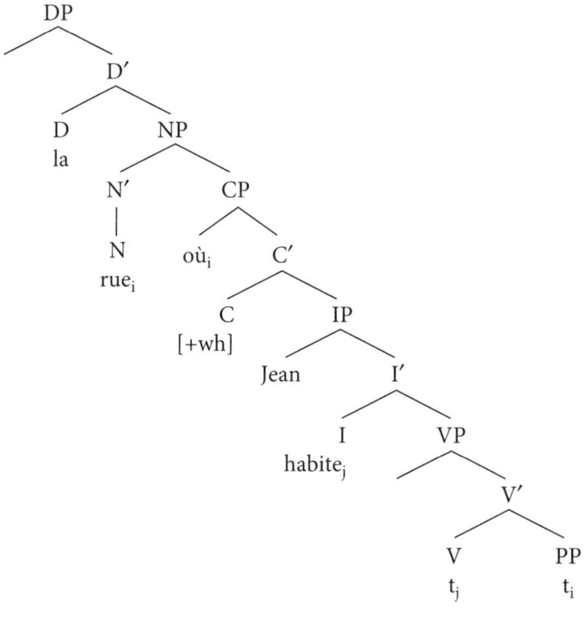

Stylistic inversion can also be found in such constructions, since there is a wh-environment. As expected, no other types of inversion are possible since C is assumed to be specified as [+wh]:

(39) a. La rue où habite Jean.
b. *La rue où habite-t-il.
c. *La rue où Jean habite-t-il.

In object and subject relatives, there is no wh-word. Rather, relativization is expressed by the complementizers *que* and *qui*.[186] This is similar to the use of *that* in English relatives (e.g. *the man that I saw* and *the man that saw you*).

(40) a. La femme que Jean connaît __.
the woman that John knows
'The woman that John knows.'

b. La femme qui __ connaît Jean.
the woman who knows John
'The woman who knows John.'

In such cases, it is assumed that the complementizer *que* is base-generated in C and that there is a null operator (OP) in the gap. This operator is equipped with an interpretable [+wh] feature and raises to SpecCP for feature-checking purposes, as in (41a) and (41b). In the case of subject relatives, the specifier/head (agreement) relationship between the nominative null operator and *que* yields nominative *qui* (Rizzi 1990).[187] *Qui* is therefore *que* + Agr, which allows it to govern the trace of the operator in SpecIP.

(41) a. La femme$_i$ [$_{CP}$ OP$_i$ que [$_{IP}$ Jean$_j$ connaît$_k$ [$_{VP}$ t$_j$ t$_k$ t$_i$]]]
the woman that John knows

b. La femme$_i$ [$_{CP}$ OP$_i$ qui$_i$ [$_{IP}$ t$_i$ connaît$_j$ [$_{VP}$ t$_i$ t$_j$ Jean]]]

This raises the question of how to distinguish between the complementizer *qui* (in relative clauses) and the wh-pronoun *qui* found in questions. One of the main differences is that wh-*qui* only refers to humans, as shown in (42a). In contrast, the occurrence of *qui* as the 'subject' of a relative clause is purely grammatical (it expresses a subject function) and is unrelated to whether its referent is human or not. Indeed, it can stand for non-human items, as in (42b).

186. In Section 14.3.1, we will see that in informal varieties of French, *que* tends to be used in all kinds of relative clauses (Zribi-Hertz 1984).

187. In Section 14.3.2, another account of relative clauses will be presented according to which CP is the sister of D, and the head of the relative moves to SpecCP (Kayne 1994).

(42) a. Qui est- ce que Jean a vu? Pierre/*une vache/*une table.
Who ESK John has seen Peter a cow a table
'Who did John see? Peter'

b. Voici la chose / le chien qui effraie Jean...
here+is the thing the dog that frightens John
'Here is the thing/the dog that frightens John'

Moreover, if both *qui* elements were the same, one would expect wh-*qui* to appear in relative clauses when referring to a human antecedent, *regardless* of its function. In other words, one should find (human) *qui* introducing object relative clauses, contrary to fact:

(43) a. La femme que Jean connaît.
the woman that John knows
'The woman that John knows.'

b. *La femme qui Jean connaît.

Thus, we must assume that wh-*qui* and relative clause *qui* are merely homophones.

Another fact of French relative clauses is that when the wh-word is in a PP, the whole PP must move to the front of the clause (44a), as in wh-questions; preposition stranding is ungrammatical, as shown in (44b).

(44) a. L'homme $[_{CP}$ $[_{PP}$ avec qui$]_i$ $[_{IP}$ Pierre a parlé $t_i]$.
the man with whom Peter has talked
'The man with whom Peter talked.'

b. *L'homme $[_{CP}$ qui$_i$ $[_{IP}$ Pierre a parlé $[_{PP}$ avec $t_i]]$.

Note that wh-words preceded by the preposition *de* 'of' (e.g, *de quoi* 'of what', *de qui* 'of whom', *duquel* 'of which') very often change to *dont*, as shown below. This rule is optional, however, since it is common to use *de*+wh-word sequences (e.g. *l'enfant de qui il est fier* 'the child of whom he is proud').[188]

(45) a. L'enfant dont il est fier
the child of whom he is proud
'The child he is proud of'

b. Le livre dont tu m' as parlé
the book of which you me have talked
'The book you told me about'

188. This rule does not apply to *d'où* 'of where' (e.g. **la salle dont je sortais* 'the room from where I was leaving').

In the upcoming chapters, it will be shown that learners of French struggle with complementizers introducing relative clauses and with pied-piping. In particular, they tend to first use *que* as a default complementizer.

13.4 Constraints on wh-movement

As in other languages, wh-movement is severely constrained in French. In particular, although a wh-word can move from an embedded clause into the SpecCP of the higher clause, as in (46), long-distance wh-movement cannot always occur in such a context. One of the constraints long-distance movement must obey is cyclicity, which ensures that wh-movement occurs locally. This is illustrated in (46a–b) where the low wh-phrase first stops in the empty SpecCP position of the lower clause on its way to its final destination.

(46) a. [$_{CP}$ Qu'$_i$ as- tu admis [$_{CP}$ t_i que [$_{IP}$ tu as offert à Jean t_i]]]] ?
what have you admitted that you have offered to John
'What did you admit that you offered to John?'

b. [$_{CP}$ Qu'$_i$ as- tu admis [$_{CP}$ t_i Ø [$_{IP}$ avoir offert à Jean t_i]]]] ?
what have you admitted have.INF offered to John
'What did you admit to having offered to John?'

A useful way of describing these restrictions is the barriers framework first elaborated in Chomsky (1986), according to which some nodes, called bounding nodes, act as barriers for wh-movement. Different nodes can be bounding nodes in different languages, but across languages wh-movement cannot cross more than one bounding node at a time. In French, the bounding nodes are DP, PP, and (finite) IP. In (47), the wh-word *à qui* 'to whom' occupies the specifier position of the lower CP. This means that the other wh-word *que* 'what' cannot stop in that position on its way to the upper CP, in contrast to what we saw in (46a–b). As a result, it must cross both the lower and the higher IPs (therefore two bounding nodes) in one hop. This movement is ruled out and the sentence is ungrammatical.

(47) *[$_{CP}$ Qu'$_i$ as-[$_{IP}$ tu dit [$_{CP}$ à qui$_j$ [$_{IP}$ tu as offert t_i t_j]]]]?
what have you said to whom you have offered

Only finite Infl is assumed to be a bounding node in French, so when Infl is nonfinite, long-distance movement is allowed across both the higher and lower higher IPs (and the CP, which is not assumed to be a bounding node), as in (48).

(48) [$_{CP}$ Que$_i$ te demandes-tu [$_{CP}$ à qui$_j$ [$_{IP}$ offrir t_i t_j]]]] ?
what yourself ask you to whom offer.INF
'What do you consider offering to whom?'

Wh-movement out of so-called complex NP constructions is also blocked, since the wh-word would have to cross both DP and the higher (finite) IP in one shot, which is ruled out:

(49) $*[_{CP}$ Qu$_i$' $[_{IP}$ appuies- tu $[_{DP}$ l' idée $[_{CP}$ t_i que le
what support you the idea that the
président n' a pas gagné t_i]]] ?
president NEG has not won

In PP contexts, a wh-word cannot be extracted from within the selected DP, as in (50), because both the DP and the PP are bounding nodes to movement.

(50) $*[_{CP}$ De qui$_i$ est-il fier $[_{PP}$ de $[_{DP}$ la fille t_i]]]?
of whom is he proud of the daughter

A wh-word also cannot move out of a clausal subject. Under the assumption that clausal subjects are DPs, wh-movement would cross two bounding nodes, namely DP and the higher IP:

(51) $*[_{CP}$ À qui$_i$ $[_{IP}$ $[_{DP}$ $[_{CP}$ t_i que Jean ait parlé t_i]] te plaît-il]]?
to whom that John has spoken you like it

Finally, extraction is impossible out of direct quotations. In (52), moving the wh-word *Que* 'what' out of the direct quotation of the words spoken by someone yields ungrammaticality. In contrast, as seen in (46a), wh-movement is possible if the words are quoted indirectly. In that case, the quotation is (obligatorily) introduced by the complementizer *que*, which means that there is an escape hatch in the lower SpecCP for the raising wh-word. In contrast, there is no CP present with embedded direct quotations.

(52) *Qu'$_i$ as- tu dit: "J'ai offert à Jean t_i"?
what have you said I have offered to John

13.5 Questions for acquisition

As discussed in the introduction to this chapter, one of the main interests in looking at questions and subordinates in language acquisition is to determine how C and its associated features develop in underlying grammars. In particular, issues of interest are whether children produce questions and embedded clauses early on in L1 acquisition, and if they do, whether they implement wh-movement and clitic/verb inversion in the earliest phases of acquisition. Another investigation issue concerns the concept of derivational complexity. Since wh-questions may involve several overt movements, such as wh-movement and V-to-C raising, the question arises as to whether children tend to avoid such complex structures at first and start off with interrogatives with no overt movement. The issue of initial avoidance of complexity also concerns embedded clauses involving the projection of complex multiclausal structures, which in the case of embedded wh-questions and relative clauses is coupled with wh-movement. Finally, do children respect the constraints on wh-movement of the adult grammar? In other words, do they know what kinds of interrogatives not to ask from a syntactic point of view, and do they know this right from the start or do they initially have different or more lax constraints?

Similar questions can be asked in other language learning situations by young children, such as bilingualism and acquisition by children with SLI. With bilingual children, the question can be investigated of whether (and to what extent) the characteristics of the other language being learned influence the development of questions and embedded clauses in French. In SLI development, the question is whether or not C is affected by the children's condition. In particular, is the development of C delayed in comparison to typically developing children? We may also wonder to what extent derivational complexity can account for any observed developmental delay or deviance in SLI when compared to TD development.

In L2 acquisition, as for I and D, we will want to know whether C is available in the initial stages and whether the L1 properties of C influence the development of questions and embedded clauses in L2 French. For example, if the [+wh] feature is weak in the L1, is this strength first adopted in French IL grammars? This can be measured by the extent of wh-movement and inversion practiced (or accepted) in early stages of acquisition. Finally, in considering the influence of L1 properties on L2 learners, it is interesting to ask whether L2 learners can ever acquire the appropriate setting for the strength of [+wh] in French (strong), especially if their L1 instantiates the weak value. In the upcoming chapters, we will examine each of these questions in detail.

CHAPTER 14

Questions and embedded clauses in child L1 French

This chapter looks at the acquisition of CP-related constructions in child L1 French and shows that although these clauses may appear relatively early in spontaneous speech, the acquisition of their properties may take some time. For example, while wh-questions are reported to appear at around the age of two, only predicative questions are used at this age. Argumental wh-questions are found much later, with subject questions appearing last. With respect to relative clauses (RCs), *qui* and *que* constructions develop relatively early, but overgeneralization of *que* can be quite high. In addition, prepositional RCs, which involve pied-piping of the preposition, are not mastered until the age of six. The fact that CP-related properties may take so much time to develop has prompted some researchers to propose that C is not available in early child grammars of French. However, as we will see, computational complexity involved in CP-clauses, especially wh-questions and relative clauses, can explain some of the difficulties experienced by children with such constructions.

The first section of the chapter investigates the acquisition of matrix interrogatives, with particular focus on wh-questions. The acquisition of embedded clauses is then addressed; embedded questions and declaratives are examined in the second section, and relative clauses are dealt with in the third. Finally, the last section of the chapter focuses on children's knowledge of the constraints on wh-movement.

14.1 Development of matrix questions in child L1 French

The development of main interrogatives takes place in several stages. The first wh-questions are predicative, as in child L1 English, with preposed wh-words such as *où* 'where'. There is no clitic/verb inversion in early questions. Later on, lexical verbs start appearing in interrogatives, the number of wh-words increases, and inversion is observed.

14.1.1 The first questions in child L1 French

Wh-questions are reported to emerge quite early in some children learning L1 French, at around the age of two, although there is tremendous individual variation. The first instances of wh-questions are predicative, and they mostly include *où* 'where' and the copula form *est* 'is', as in (1).[189] The sequence *où est* 'where is' is very common, and it is not clear that this sequence is fully analysed by the children in the early stages. Sometimes, the wh-word is used with only an NP (e.g. *Où la mer?* 'Where the sea?' (Anne 1;11.13), *Qui ça?* 'Who this?' (Max, 1;11.00)).[190]

(1) a. Où il est le fil? (Philippe, 2;1.19)
where it is the thread

b. Où il est chausson? (Grégoire, 1;9.18)
where it is slipper

c. Est où maman? (Augustin, 2;6.16)
is where mommy

d. Où il est canard? (Marie, 2;1.28)
where it is duck

e. Où est-elle le marteau? (Edm., 2;0)
where is she the hammer

Other frequent wh-pronouns in the early stages are *que* and *quoi* 'what', but as with *où*, they are almost always used in a predicative way (but see (2c)).

(2) a. Qu'est-ce c'est dedans? (Philippe, 2;1.19)
what is it it is inside

b. C'est quoi? (Max, 2;0.28)
this is what

c. e fait quoi? (Anne, 1;11.13) (Plunkett 2004b)
he does what

Although wh-questions appear early in the speech of some children, they may not be very productive at first. In Marie's data (1;8.26–2;3.3), for example, Hamann (2000a) found 12 wh-questions during the first recordings, but only two in the next five sessions (to age 2;1.7). The number of wh-questions then increases to 16 in the last two files (2;1.28–2;3.3). In other children, wh-questions are quite slow to emerge. For instance, they first appear relatively late in Augustin's data (after two months of recording, at age 2;2.13) and become productive even later (at month 2;4.1). The Belgian child Léa (2;8.22 – 4;4.5) is reported to have started using wh-questions only one month before

189. Plunkett (2004b) reports that over 80% of the wh-questions produced by Anne (2;0.14 – 3;0.02) and Max (1;11.13 – 2;9.12) from the York corpus include a copula, as compared to around 20% of their yes/no questions.

190. However, copula omission is much less frequent than what has been reported in the L1 acquisition of other languages, such as English.

the first recording, at around 2;8. Finally, in Grégoire's recordings (1;9.18–2;5.27), there are only 31 wh-questions (Plunkett 1999).

It is also interesting to observe that the first questions constructed by children sometimes lack the wh-word, as in (3). This is particularly true of *que*-questions, which often appear without *que* initially, as in (3b–d). Similar findings are reported in child L1 German, Swiss German, and Dutch (Clahsen et al. 1995; Penner 1994; Tracy 1994; van Kampen 1997).

(3) a. (Où) il est l' autre de maman? (1;10) (from Guillaume 1927)
(where) it is the other of mommy

b. Elle cherche (quoi) maman? (Philippe, 2;2.10)
she looks+for (what) mommy

c. (Qu' est-ce) que c' est? (Grégoire, 2;5.13)
(what is it) that it is

d. (Qu' est-ce que tu) e apporté, toi? (Max, 2;0.28)
(what ESK you) brought you

As noted earlier, the vast majority of the first questions produced by children are predicative. Lexical verbs are rarely part of early child interrogatives. Non-predicative questions develop later, first with adverbial wh-words such as *comment* 'how', and then in argumental questions. The first lexical verbs used in questions are often *faire* 'do' and *aller* 'go'.

(4) Comment on fait pour casser les maisons? (Philippe, 2;1.26)
how one does to break the houses

Among argumental questions, it is often reported that object questions develop before subject interrogatives, a claim discussed in more detail in Section 14.1.3 below.

14.1.2 Development of wh-word placement in child L1 French

From the very first wh-questions they produce, children may either front the wh-word, as shown in the examples in (1) and (4) above, or leave the wh-word in situ. Some children seem to choose only one of the two options for question formation, as illustrated in Table 1. In Philippe's initial recordings, for example, there are almost no wh-words in situ. Of the 114 wh-questions that he produced between 2;1.19 and 2;3.21, only one has the wh-word in its base-generated position (Hamann 2000a); the rest have a fronted wh-word. Similar results are reported for other children, such as Grégoire (1;9–2;3) (Déprez 1994) and Stéphane (2;3 – 4;9) (Plunkett 1999) and the Belgian child Tom (2;1.11 – 2;10.7) (De Cat 2002). The next stage in Philippe's data (2;6.13 – 2;7.18) shows a sharp increase in questions with the wh-word in situ (81/199 = 41%). Other children, such as Augustin and Marie, favour wh-in situ from the beginning. Questions with a fronted wh-word represent only about 10% of their wh-questions. It is only later that these children use both strategies. The wh-in situ strategy is also found early in Max and Anne, two children learning different varieties of French, namely, Canadian French and Parisian French (see Plunkett 1999).

Table 1. Incidence of wh-questions with fronted wh-words and wh-in situ in early L1 child French

Child	Age	Emergence of wh-questions	Fronted wh	Wh-in situ	Total wh-questions
Philippe	2;1.19–2;7.18	2;1.19	231	82	313
Augustin	2;0.2–2;9.30	2;2.13	8	86	94
Marie	1;8.26–2;3.3	1;8.26	3	27	30

Some children, like the Belgian child Léa, use both strategies from the outset (Plunkett 1999).[191] Interestingly, most wh-in situ questions appear with the copula in Léa's data, while interrogatives with a preposed wh-phrase tend to involve a lexical verb. Moreover, many of her wh-in situ questions involve a cleft construction, or copular clause, as in *C'est quoi que t'as fait, Mamy?* 'It is what that you did, Granny?' (Léa, 2;9.05). According to Plunkett (1999), the use of cleft questions is a simplification strategy allowing children to use subject and object wh-questions, which are new to them, while maintaining the wh-word in a predicative position, with which they are familiar. It would be interesting to determine whether there is a similar relationship between the nature of the verb (copular or non-copular) and the position of the wh-phrase (preposed or in situ) in other children.

In an elicitation task administered to somewhat older children (4;0–5;9 – mean: 4;7), Hulk & Zuckermann (2000) report few interrogatives with the wh-word in situ (57/881 = 6%); the children almost always used fronted wh-words (784/881 = 89%). Interestingly, the same task administered to adult speakers (most of them the children's parents) yielded a similarly low incidence of wh-words in situ (32/688 = 5%). However, when only the children and their parents are considered, a significant difference between the two groups arises, with a significantly lower incidence of wh-in situ in the adults (1%) than in the children (8%). In other words, there is a (slight) tendency, on the part of the children, to use the in situ strategy, despite the fact that most wh-words are fronted in the input they receive from their parents. The authors further report a significant correlation between wh-fronting in the adults and wh-in situ in the children (the wh-words appearing in a preposed position in the parents' questions tend to remain in situ in the children's).

191. Léa's first recording was obtained quite late, after the age of 2;8, so it is possible that her initial behaviour was different.

It is important to point out that the low incidence of wh-in situ reported in this study may have been influenced by the stimulus used to elicit wh-questions. In the task developed by the authors, which was adapted from Crain and Thornton (1996), the experimenter urged children to ask questions to a puppet, targeting different wh-words. The experimenter would introduce a wh-question in an embedded clause (e.g. *Je veux savoir où il est allé* 'I want to know where he (the puppet) went') and expect the child to ask the puppet a question including a main wh-interrogative (e.g. *Où es-tu allé?* 'Where did you go?'). As can be seen, the stimulus itself included a preposed wh-word, which may have led the participants to use a similar strategy in their questions.[192] An alternative prompting cue would be to include the wh-word in a monoclausal utterance, as in *Il est allé quelque part; demande-moi où.* 'He went somewhere; ask me where'. This is exactly what Strik (2007) did in an elicitation task administered to three groups of 12 children aged in average 3;5, 4;2, and 6;6 respectively, and a group of 12 adults. Strik reports a high incidence of wh-words in situ in object interrogatives in the youngest group (about 50%), and a lower proportion of wh-in situ in the other child groups (between 25% and 30%). No significant difference was found between wh-fronting and wh-in situ in object wh-questions in the three-year olds, whereas the proportion of wh-fronting was significantly higher than that of wh-in situ in all the other groups.

14.1.3 Development of inversion and *est-ce que* questions in child L1 French

One characteristic of the first questions produced by children learning French is that they lack clitic/verb inversion, as can be clearly seen in most of the examples cited so far. In the case of yes/no questions, this means that the interrogative is marked by intonation only. The fact that the first questions produced by children do not display clitic/verb inversion is not necessarily surprising, given that it is not obligatory in spoken French.[193] In their investigation of older children (4;7), however, Hulk and Zuckermann (2000) report a significant difference between the children and the adults in their use of inversion (see above). While the incidence of inversion was quite low in the children (40/881 = 5%), it was much higher in the case of the adults (412/668 = 62%) – mostly clitic/verb inversion. This differs from the pattern observed with wh-preposing, where performance of both groups was similarly high (see above). Focusing on the children and their parents who participated in the study, the authors noted that in addition to the fact observed above, namely that wh-words appearing in a fronted position in the parents' wh-questions tended to remain in situ in the children's, if subject/verb inversion

192. Similarly, Strik (2008) reports a low ratio of wh-words in situ in an elicitation task administered to three groups of children (aged 3, 4, and 6) and a group of adults. As in Hulk and Zuckermann (2000), stimulus sentences involved fronted wh-words.

193. However, Plunkett (1999) reports that non-inverted subject clitic/verb questions account for only 5% of the wh-questions used by Léa's mother and grandmother.

was also present in the parents' wh-questions, the wh-word tended to be fronted in the children's.

Another finding is that *est-ce que* questions emerge late in child French. Under a complex analysis of such periphrastic questions (in which *est-ce que* signals a biclausal structure), there is inversion between the verb *est* 'is' and the clitic subject *ce* 'it'. The fact that such questions are delayed suggests that inversion is initially lacking. Reviewing data from Léa (see above), Plunkett (1999) reports that the first *est-ce que* wh-questions appear at 2;9.5, as shown in (5). At first, *est-ce que* only appears with *que* 'what', although it soon occurs with other wh-words as well, such as *pourquoi* 'why'.

(5) a. Qu'est-ce que tu as dit? (Léa, 2;9.5)
what ESK you have said

b. Minnie, qu' est-ce que tu fais? (Léa, 2;10.7)
Minnie what ESK you do

c. Pourquoi est-ce que je ne peux pas fermer? (Léa, 3;0.5)
why ESK I NEG can not close

In all, Léa produced 115 full wh-questions by age 3;5.17, of which only 12 displayed *est-ce que*. After age 3;5.17, *est-ce que* was present in 25% of her wh-questions.[194] The late development of periphrastic questions is confirmed in other child data: Stéphane (2;3–4;9), Anne (1;10.12–3;1.15), Grégoire (1;19.28–2;5.27), Max (1;9.19–2;10.24), and Tom (2;1.11–2 ;10.7).[195] This slow development does not seem to be related to the input, given that interrogatives of this type are used productively by adults. A survey of Léa's mother's and grandmother's speech reveals that *est-ce-que* is used in 30% of their wh-questions (Plunkett 1999). Instead, the presence of *est-ce que* appears to increase the derivational complexity of wh-questions, which would explain their delayed emergence in child speech.

In fact, it seems that periphrastic questions are not produced until other complex constructions, such as embedded questions, are in place. In data from Max and Tom, embedded questions are reported to appear at ages 2;5.1 and 2;3.22, respectively, while *est-ce que* questions are found at 2;8.0 and 2;6.12 (De Cat 2002). In Léa's data, embedded questions and *est-ce que* interrogatives occur at around the same age (2;9), but adult-like incidence of periphrastic interrogatives is not found until 3;5.17. In some cases, inversion also emerges before *est-ce que* questions, as with Anne (2;7.16 versus 2;8.20) and

194. Note that *est-ce que* appears slightly earlier in yes/no questions than in wh-interrogatives.

195. The one exception to this developmental pattern seems to be Philippe (2;1.19–3;3.12), who uses *est-ce que* wh-questions much earlier (at age 2;1.19). However, all of these questions are of the form *qu'est-ce...*, that is, without the following complementizer *que*. Since Philippe rarely uses *que* in other contexts, for instance in embedded clauses, these sequences could therefore be considered routines. In other words, he seems to be treating *qu'est-ce* as a variant of the wh-word *que*.

Max (2;3.20 versus 2;6.12). In Léa's case, adult-like use of *est-ce que* questions is also preceded by inversion, which is reported to emerge at around 2;10 (see (6)).

(6)	Que	fais-tu	là,	Minnie?	(Léa, 2;10.07)
	what	do you	here	Minnie	

The delayed development of *est-ce que* questions may explain another finding reported in the literature on child L1 French, namely, that object questions develop before subject questions. This may be due to the fact that children tend to use periphrastic or cleft constructions to question the subject, as in (7).

(7) a. Que c' est ça fait du bruit? (Philippe, 2;3.07)
what this is that makes some noise

b. Qui c'est va tomber? (Philippe, 2;3.21)
who this is go fall.INF

14.1.4 Long distance (LD) wh-questions in child L1 French

Extraction of the wh-word from a lower clause can be difficult for children for quite a long time. In an elicited production task, Strik (2003) compared the number and types of monoclausal and biclausal wh-questions used by three groups of children aged 3;4 (3;1–3;6), 4;3 (4;0–4;6) and 6;6 (6;4–6;8), and a group of adult controls. The experiment involved a little plastic robot named Tommy to whom children were trained to ask questions. An example of a stimulus designed to elicit LD questions is given in (8a); expected answers are listed in (8b).

(8) a. Experimenter: Voyons ce que Tommy croit que tu bois. Demande-lui.
'Let's see what Tommy thinks you're drinking. Ask him.'

b. Child (expected answers):
b′. Qu'est-ce que tu crois que je bois ?
what ESK you think that I drink
b″. Que crois-tu que je bois ?
what think you that I drink
b‴. Tu crois que je bois quoi ?
you think that I drink what
'What do you think I'm drinking ?'

While the percentage of target monoclausal wh-questions was very high for every group (88.9% for the youngest group and higher for the others), the ratio of target LD wh-interrogatives was quite low for the children (12.5% for the three-year olds and below 40% even for the six-year olds), in contrast to the adults (84.1%). In addition, only half of the children produced any LD questions (and only 3/10 in the youngest group). Instead of LD wh-questions, children used monoclausal questions, embedded yes/no questions, or simply answered the questions asked by the experimenter. Further differences between the four groups were observed in the properties of the LD questions produced, as shown Table 2. In particular, the children almost never used inversion, in contrast to the adults. This difference was also observed in the wh-monoclausals. The children also produced a high proportion (about 25%) of interrogatives with the wh-word in a medial position, instead of placing it at the front of the utterance, as in *Tu penses quoi que je lis?* lit. 'You think what that I read?'. The adults did this only rarely (about 3%). However, the LD questions used by the children and the adults also displayed similar properties in that they overwhelmingly exhibited a preposed wh-word and few wh-words in situ.[196]

Table 2. Types and number of biclausal wh-questions produced by children and adults (from Strik 2003)

Group	**Preposed wh**			**Medial wh**	**Wh-in situ**	**Total**
	Invers.	**No invers.**	**Reinforced/cleft**[a]			
3-years (n=10)	2	10	2	5	1	20
4-years (n=12)	0	10	20	14	8	52
6-years (n=10)	0	18	24	14	2	58
Adults (n=22)	140	18	110	10	18	296

a. These possibilities correspond to sentences such as *Wh-word est-ce que…* and *C'est wh-word que …* respectively.

Oiry & Demirdache (2006), based on a protocol similar to the one used in the previous study, report a higher ratio of expected LD questions than Strik (2003) (87/144 = 60%). The elicited production task was administered to 20 children aged 3;02–5;11. As Strik, however, Oiry & Demirdache found few instances of wh-in situ (2%) and a on negligible ratio of medial-wh questions (8%).

14.1.5 Other properties of matrix interrogatives in child L1 French

As seen in Section 2.2, children's early questions are almost always finite, even though their main declaratives may contain a high ratio of nonfinite forms.[197] The fact that the majority of their wh-questions involve the copula may explain the lack of nonfinite verbs in such constructions (see Phillips 1995), but this cannot be the whole story because the lexical verbs that do appear in wh-questions are also systematically finite (see Hamaan 2000a). Moreover, nonfinite verbs are also rare in yes/no questions, where the incidence of the copula is much lower than in wh-questions.

196. These results were confirmed in Strik (2007).

197. Properties of children's matrix questions are also discussed in Sections 2.1.

Children's early questions also differ from their early declaratives is in that they rarely exhibit a null subject (see Section 6.2.1.2). This is particularly true of wh-questions, especially those with a fronted wh-word. In contrast, the incidence of null subjects can be relatively high in root declaratives, including finite ones. The few null subjects that are found in interrogatives tend to appear in yes/no questions, and in wh-questions where the wh-word has remained in situ (e.g. *Est où?* lit 'Is where?') and where *pourquoi* 'why' appears in a fronted position (e.g. *Pourquoi coupe le bois?* lit 'Why cut the wood?'). Here again, the global low ratio of subjectless interrogatives could be related to the high incidence of the copula in such constructions, especially wh-questions. However, null subjects may be found in finite root declaratives involving the copula, as seen in Section 6.2.1.2. The question is therefore why null subjects may appear in copular declaratives and not in copular (wh-)questions.

14.1.6 Theoretical implications

How children learn interrogatives has been argued to support various hypotheses about the more general question of the representation of early child grammars. We will examine these in turn and see what data they can account for and what data pose more of a challenge.

As seen in previous chapters, some researchers argue for the Weak Continuity Hypothesis, according to which functional categories are initially absent from child grammars and develop after lexical categories, either through maturation or lexical learning. Proponents of lexically driven development assume an incremental emergence of functional categories, with C developing after I. With respect to the acquisition of question formation, the delayed development of clitic/verb inversion could be argued to illustrate this incremental emergence: inversion is not enforced at first due to the early unavailability of C in child grammars. Labelle (1990), for instance, argues that the CP node is not activated before the age of three. This could further explain the occasional omission of wh-words in the early stages of acquisition. Hulk & Zuckermann (2000) also favour a developmental approach. They assume that children start out with the in situ strategy, which they argue is the most economical option in terms of the representation since it (apparently) does not involve movement (see also below for more discussion on computational costs). Development is then assumed to involve a subtle interaction between economy principles and the input: children will only start fronting wh-words if wh-words are used in inverted questions by their parents, but if wh-words are preposed in the parents' interrogatives (without inversion), the children will leave their own wh-words in situ. It is as if acquisition of wh-questions followed a three-point markedness scale, with the in situ strategy as the least marked option, i.e. in situ > fronting > inversion. While interesting, this proposal is contradicted by the fact that very few questions with wh-words in situ were produced by the children in Hulk & Zuckermann's study (at most 8% depending on the group considered). We saw that this may be related to the stimulus sentences used by the experimenters, where the wh-words appeared in a preposed position.

Under the developmental assumption that C is absent from initial grammars, the question then arises as to the exact position of the fronted wh-word in some of the early wh-questions produced by children. One obvious possibility is SpecIP. Hulk (1995) looked at production data from Philippe (between 2;01.19 and 3;03.12) and noticed that in all his questions involving a preposed wh-word, the subject is a clitic, as in (9).

(9)	a.	Pourquoi	il	met	du	sucre	dedans?	(Philippe, 2; 07.11)
		why	he	put.FIN	some	sugar	inside	
	b.	Lequel	il	marche	pas?			(Philippe, 3;02.03)
		which one	it	walk.FIN	not			

In such utterances, Hulk concludes, the clitic and the finite verb are in I, which means that subject clitics are treated as agreement prefixes and that the wh-word occupies the specifier position. This analysis is also argued to hold in the few instances of subjectless wh-questions such as (10). In such cases, it is assumed that there is a null clitic under I (with the verb) and that the wh-word is in SpecIP (see (31) in Section 6.2.1.2).

(10) $[_{IP}$ Pourquoi $[_{I}$ *pro*+coupe] le bois]?
why cut.FIN the wood

Note that if this analysis is correct, then at this stage one should not find wh-questions with a preposed wh-word followed by a full lexical subject, as in **Quand Jean part?* lit. 'When John leaves?'. This remains to be further investigated.

In a similar vein, for Plunkett (1999), the fact that children produce fronted wh-words does not mean that these pronouns are in SpecCP.[198] She argues that children learning L1 French do not know where the wh-pronoun should go at first, as witnessed by the lack of inverted interrogatives. Plunkett further claims that embedded wh-questions, in which the order is Wh-Subject-Verb, provide children with the necessary evidence. These constructions force children to assume that the wh-word is located higher than the subject in SpecIP, namely in SpecCP. Once they have established the CP > IP hierarchy based on embedded questions, they adopt the same hierarchical pattern for main wh-questions.

198. For wh-questions displaying a preposed wh-word and an omitted copula, such as *Qui ça?* 'Who that?' (Max, 1;11.00) Plunkett (1999) argues that they are cases of dislocation with an empty resumptive pronoun and should be interpreted as *(C'est) qui, ça?* '(This is) who, that?' (see Labelle & Valois 1996). According to this view, the wh-word does not occupy a preposed position but remains in situ.

This in turn makes C available as a host of verb movement, and inversion can then become productive.

In contrast to the Weak Continuity view, other researchers such as Hamann (2000a) argue that the first questions produced by children are full-fledged CPs, although inversion is not initially in place. The idea is that the presence of a wh-word in the sentence, whether fronted or in situ, forces an interrogative interpretation, which entails the presence of a question marker in SpecCP (whether null or overt). A similar argument is used to account for wh-questions from which wh-words are missing. For example, Yamakoshi (1999) argues that children initially resort to null operators rather than wh-words, as part of a general preference for null over realized elements on the part of children, due to performance constraints. According to this analysis, the null operator moves from its base-generated position to the front of the sentence (SpecCP). Such wh-questions are clearly meant as questions by the children, and they have the same meaning as mature questions with an overt wh-pronoun. A question marker is therefore assumed to be present at some level. Another argument that children's early grammars do contain C is that the incidence of wh-word omission is very low in child L1 French. If CP were absent from early systems, the omission rate would be expected to be much higher.

Under the assumption that functional categories (including C) are available to children from the outset, it remains to be explained why children do not initially produce adult-like questions. As suggested for other complex structures, one possibility is that children have computational difficulties in systematically implementing wh-movement and inversion at first. According to this hypothesis, children seek to use the fewest operations (the least complex option) in the early stages of acquisition and slowly become capable of performing more complex computations (see Hamann 2006; Jakubowicz 2004, 2005). This is what Jakubowicz (2005) captures in her Derivational Complexity Metric:

(11) a. Merging α_i n times is less complex than merging α_i (n+1) times.
b. Internal Merge of α gives rise to a less complex derivation than Internal Merge of $\alpha + \beta$.

According to this metric, leaving the wh-word in situ is the least complex (most economical) strategy, which can explain why children adopt it initially (see also Hulk and Zuckumann 2000). Conversely, inversion would be implemented later as it also requires wh-fronting. Two overt movements are therefore required, which is computationally costly, as expressed in (11b). The delayed development of *est-ce que* questions can also be accounted for by computational complexity considerations since an extra Merge operation is needed for the appearance of the question marker. Moreover, derivational complexity as described in (11a) can explain the delayed and staggered development of LD wh-extraction observed by Strik (2003, 2007). Children would start by placing the wh-word in a medial position, which represents one instance of wh-movement (to the lower SpecCP), and as they become able to handle more complex structure, proceed to further move the wh-word to a preposed position, namely the higher SpecCP.[199]

The availability of functional categories initially, combined with the Truncation approach to early child grammar, can also explain why the rate of subjectless and non-finite matrix interrogatives is low in child L1 French – at the same time as RIs and subjectless finite root declaratives are produced (Rizzi 1993/1994, 1998, 2000). According to Truncation, when the CP node is projected, so are the other functional categories below it, which explains why the vast majority of questions are finite in child L1 French. Moreover, null constants, which are argued to underlie null subjects found in the speech of children learning non-*pro*-drop languages such as French, can only appear in the specifier of the root, IP or VP, for identification purposes. When CP is projected, IP is no longer the root, so a null constant in SpecIP is not in the specifier of the root and cannot be identified, hence the very low rate of subjectless interrogatives in child L1 French data. The correlation between the low rate of subjectless and nonfinite matrix interrogatives on the one hand, and the production of RIs and subjectless finite root declaratives on the other hand, cannot be explained by the Weak Continuity approach.

---

199. For Oiry & Demirdache (2006), however, the development of LD wh-questions is not related to computational complexity, but to alternative wh-scope marking strategies available in natural languages. For LD questions displaying the wh-word in situ or in a medial position, which they call the direct strategy, a Q morpheme binding the wh-word is argued to merge in the matrix SpecCP, as in (ia–b) (see Cheng & Rooryck (2000) and Mathieu (2002) for wh-in situ in French root interrogatives). The Q morpheme is assumed to check the [+wh] feature of the wh-word via Agree, and there is no subsequent covert movement of the wh-word.

(i) a. $[_{CP}$ Q_i $[_{IP}$ tu penses $[_{CP}$ $quoi_i$ [que [je lis t_i]?
you think what that I read

b. $[_{CP}$ Q_i $[_{IP}$ tu penses $[_{CP}$ [que [je lis $quoi_i$]?

In cases where a wh-word is found in both the root clause and the embedded clause, as in (iia), Oiry & Demirdache (2006) argue that there are two juxtaposed matrix questions, as in (iib), a construction found in languages such as Hindi (Dayal 2000). Semantically, the wh-phrase in CP1 quantifies over the set of propositions restricted by the wh-question with which it is coindexed (Oiry & Demirdache 2006: 305). This is the indirect strategy.

(ii) a. Tu crois quoi Lala elle aime bien quoi?
you think what Lala she likes well what
'What do you think Lala likes?'

b. $[_{CP1}$ Tu crois $quoi_i$] $[_{CP2i}$ Lala elle aime bien $quoi_j$]?

Developmentally, Oiry & Demirdache propose that children first adopt the indirect strategy, scope-marking via a wh-word in an argument position, then the direct strategy, scope-marking via a Q-morpheme in an A' position, then target LD-movement. It is further suggested that the shift from the indirect strategy to the direct strategy could be correlated with the acquisition of subordination. These proposals await further confirmation.

Under this view, RIs are considered VPs, which means that CP should not be available yet. The production of matrix interrogatives clearly disconfirms this prediction.

Now, it is not entirely true that early interrogatives always include an overt subject. The few subjectless questions that are observed are yes/no questions, wh-questions with the wh-phrase in situ or with a preposed *pourquoi* 'why'. If such constructions are assumed not to involve the projection of a CP, which is in line with Structural Economy, then null constants can be identified. Adopting an extended representation of the left periphery à la Rizzi (1997) (ForceP > Int(errogative)P > ReasonP > TopP > Foc/WhP > TopP > IP > VP), Hamann (2006) proposes essentially that. She argues that the root of wh-questions with a wh-word in situ is WhP, as a result of truncation. A Q-head occupies the head of this category (Wh°) and is in an Agree relation with the wh-word in situ. Crucially, the specifier of WhP is empty. WhP being the root, a null subject is allowed to appear in that position; in contrast, in preposed wh-questions, SpecWhP is occupied by the wh-word, which prevents the occurrence of an empty subject. As for *pourquoi*, it is assumed to be based-generated in the specifier position of a Reason phrase, higher than WhP (see also Rizzi 1997).[200] In adult French, *pourquoi* is further held to move to IntP. Assuming that truncation takes place in early child grammars, Hamann proposes that *pourquoi* questions with null subjects are instances of IntP where *pourquoi* has remained in situ in SpecReasonP. A Q-head occupies the head of IntP, and the null subject occupies the specifier position of IntP, which is the specifier of the root, satisfying the need for identification of the null constant.

14.2 Development of embedded clauses in child L1 French

14.2.1 The findings

Few studies have looked at the development of embedded declaratives and embedded questions in L1 French, but research so far reports that infinitival embedded clauses, as shown in (12) (from De Cat 2002), are among the first instances of embedding in child L1 French and are produced relatively early.

---

200. In particular, Hamann (2006) argues that *pourquoi* can precede focused constituents, in contrast to other wh-words in French, as shown in (i) and (ii).

(i) a. Pourquoi MON LIVRE t' as donné à Jean, pas le tien?
why my book you have given to John not yours
'Why did you give MY BOOK to John, not yours?'

b. *Quand MON LIVRE t' as donné à Jean, pas le tien?
when my book you have given to John not yours
'When did you give MY BOOK to John, not yours?'

(12) a. Viens voir! (Anne, 1;11.13)
come see.INF

b. Je veux fermer. (Anne, 2;1.19)
(I) want close.INF

c. xx, moi, (je) (suis) pas capable@d # de l'ouvrir. (Max, 2;0.28)
me I am not able to it open.INF

In addition, early infinitival clauses may be introduced by a preposition, such as *pour* 'for'. There are 31 such constructions in Philippe's data. In the York corpus, De Cat (2002) reports that *pour* is used before true nonfinite complementizers, such as *de*.

(13) a. C' est dur il rentre - pour rentrer là la voiture
this is hard he goes+in to go+in.INF there the car
(Philippe, 2;2.3)

b. euh pour donner. (Tom 2 ;3.22) (De Cat 2002)
to give.INF

(14) a. pour manger. (Anne, 2 ;4.20)
to eat.INF

b. C'est qui, en train de tomber ? (Anne, 2 ;8.20)
it is who in process of fall.INF

Early finite embedded clauses tend to first consist of adjoined clauses, sometimes lacking an overt complementizer, as in (15). Similar findings are reported in L1 German (Müller & Penner 1996).

(15) a. (Si) il pleut comme ça peux pas promener.
if it rains like that can not walk

b. C'est Myriam (qui) a cassé le tracteur. (Jérôme, 2;1) (Cohen 1968)
it is Myriam who has broken the tractor

Overt complementizers start being produced at around the age of 2;6, after the first questions. The first conjunction tends to be *parce que* 'because' (see (16)), quickly followed by *quand* 'when' and *si* 'if'.

(16) Fermer capote parce qu' il pleut. (JB 2;4)
close.INF hood because it is+raining

Dummy placeholders, such as *y* and *là*, are also produced instead of target-like complementizers at first, as in (17).

(17) Monté sur le petit manège y a des chevaux.
climbed on the little merry-go-round *ph* some horses
(Philippe, 2;3,7)
(from Müller & Penner 1996)

The first selected embedded clauses may also involve a missing complementizer, as illustrated in (18).

(18) a. Et on voit (que) le chat est dans la barrière.
and one sees (that) the cat is in the fence
(Anne, 2;6.2) (De Cat 2002)

b. je veux (que) tu ouvres le couvercle. (Tom, 2;5.24)
I want (that) you open.FIN the lid

In Philippe's data (2;1.09 – 3;3.12), for instance, Müller & Penner (1996) found 17 non-target-like subordinate clauses before age 2;6. Of these, 15 occur without a complementizer, and two appear with a dummy placeholder. Note that there is a transition period during which placeholders and target-like complementizers coexist. In Philippe's data, placeholders disappear at age 2;8.8.

14.2.2 Theoretical implications

Although complementizers take some time to develop, this is not necessarily evidence for the early unavailability of C. Once again, this is an area of debate in the literature. Some researchers argue that the fact that children resort to dummy placeholders for a while tends to suggest that they do project C. In other words, the position is there although target-like complementizers are not produced yet, presumably for some other reason. Children also tend to omit complementizers initially, but clearly they can express the semantic relation that corresponds to the missing complementizer (such as *si* 'if' in (15a)) before they are able to use the relevant linguistic expression. In other words, just because children are not yet able to produce target-like complementizers does not mean that they have no knowledge of the corresponding semantics and that they are not able to produce multiclausal utterances. Children apparently need time to acquire the paradigm of complementizers. According to Müller & Penner (1996), these facts suggest that CP is present in underlying grammars from the outset but C is underspecified. The subordinate clause relationship is signaled by default markers: dummy placeholders and gaps. Crucially, Müller & Penner do not consider early non-target-like subordinates to be IPs.

Other researchers, for whom the lack of complementizers in early production is evidence for the unavailability of C, take the opposite view (e.g. Pierce 1992). Under this approach, the development of the CP layer is triggered by the acquisition of the complementizers themselves, an instance of lexical learning. Until then, Infl is assumed to be the only functional category in child grammars, and complementizer-less subordinate clauses are taken to be instances of IP. For example, the sentence in (15b) is considered to be monoclausal: *c'est Myriam* 'this is Myriam' is analysed as a chunk (i.e. *c'est* NP 'it is NP') adjoined to IP, the subject of which is null:

(19) [$_{IP}$ C'est Myriam [$_{IP}$ *pro* a cassé le tracteur]].
this is Myriam has broken the tractor

As seen in other areas of the grammar throughout this book, however, the simple absence of particular items from production cannot be taken as evidence of the unavailability of underlying structure. Moreover, in order to conclude about the status of particular projections in developing grammars, different kinds of evidence must be taken into account —not only the production or the non-production of morphological items. In the case of C, the fact that children are able to construct complex sentences, although they fail to use complementizers overtly strongly argues for its early availability. This ties in with other evidence presented in this chapter in favour of the presence of C in initial grammars.

14.3 Development of relative clauses in child L1 French

14.3.1 The findings

The first relative clauses appear at around age 2;6 in spontaneous production, as shown below, but children are reported to struggle with these constructions for some time after their initial appearance.

(20) a. Un bateau qui siffle. (Ch., 2;4)
a boat that whistles

b. C'est un petit oiseau qui s' appelle corbeau. (FC, 2;6)
this is a little bird that itself calls blackbird

In particular, *que* 'that' seems to act as an all-purpose marker of subordinate clauses for quite a while, for both subject and object relatives. Resumptive pronouns also tend to be used in relative clauses early on. This is illustrated in (21).

(21) …C'est moi que je les ai fermées. (Léa, 2;8.22) (De Cat 2002)
it is me that I them have closed

Labelle (1990) investigated over 1,300 relative clauses elicited from 108 children aged three to six years. The elicitation task involved picture cues intended to make the children produce relative clauses. Each child was presented with pairs of pictures depicting the same character or object involved in different activities. The child was then asked a question the answer to which required a relative clause. He/she was also given a sticker and instructed to place it on the picture corresponding to the answer. Five types of relative clauses were tested, targeting the subject, the direct object, the indirect object (where pied-piping is obligatory – with *à qui* 'to whom'), the genitive object (with *dont* 'whose'), and the locative (with *dans lequel* in 'which' and *où* 'where'). Most of the relative clauses produced by the children included the complementizer *que* 'that', which Labelle (1990) chose to focus on. Note however, that some relatives produced by the children included a wh-phrase, such as *où* 'where' and *quand* 'when' (see below).

Labelle suggests that children use two main strategies in forming relative clauses: the resumptive strategy and the gapping strategy. In the resumptive strategy, children use a resumptive pronoun (22a), a resumptive NP (22b), or a resumptive preposition (22c) coindexed with the main noun. This strategy is also used in subject relatives, as shown in (22d) where the lower clause subject is feminine.

(22) a. Sur la balle qu' i(l) l' attrape. (LE, 3;08)
on the ball that he it catches

b. Sur la balle qu' i(l) lance la balle. (M, 5;0)
on the ball that he throws the ball

c. Sur la boîte que le camion rentre dedans. (S, 4;08)
on the box that the truck goes into

d. C'est la celle qu' a dessine. (A, 3;04)
it is the this+one that she draws

Resumptive pronouns are not grammatical in relative clauses and wh-questions in standard French, as shown in (23).

(23) a. * La balle qu' il la lance.
the ball that he it throws

b. * Quelle balle il la lance?
what ball he it throws

In the gap strategy, children produce relative clauses that do not contain any overt element coindexed with the antecedent, as in non-subject relative clauses in (24). These utterances are all ungrammatical in standard French.[201]

(24) a. Sur la petite fille que le monsieur i(l) montre un dessin __
on the little girl that the man he shows a drawing
(MJ, 3;06)

b. Sur le petit garçon que le chien i(l) est assis __. (M, 5;01)
on the little boy that the dog he is sit

201. These two examples require pied-piping in standard French (*à qui* 'to whom' in (ia) and *sur lequel* 'on which' in (ib)):

(i) a. La petite fille à qui le monsieur montre un dessin
the little girl to whom the man shows a drawing

b. Le petit garçon sur lequel le chien est assis
the little boy on which the dog is sit

Interestingly, there is no evidence of pied-piping in the relative clauses analysed by Labelle, although pied-piping seems to be mastered quite early in wh-questions, as in (ii). This suggests that the errors in (24) are not due to some kind of complexity associated with the pied-piping operation.

(ii) Sur quoi on pèse? (JF, 2;0)
on what one pushes

Children also behave differently according to the type of RCs. For instance, they are more prone to produce erroneous indirect object relatives than erroneous subject relatives. This was shown by Fragman (2000), who administered an elicited production task to 25 children (aged 4–7) and 25 adults. In the task, the experimenter produced a stimulus sentence, followed by a question designed to elicit a relative clause with a subject, a direct object, or an indirect object gap. Some stimulus sentences are illustrated in (25).

(25) a. Une fille s'amuse avec un chat et une autre
a girl plays with a cat and a other
fille court après un chien.
girl runs after a dog

b. Une maman embrasse sa fille et une autre
a mom kisses her daughter and a other
maman chatouille sa fille.
mom tickles her daughter

c. Un papa téléphone à sa fille et un autre papa
a dad calls to his daughter and a other dad
donne un dessin à sa fille.
gives a drawing to his daughter

After each stimulus sentence, the experimenter asked the participant which little girl he or she would like to be, hoping to elicit answers such as the following:

(26) a. La fille qui s'amuse avec un chat.
the girl who plays with a cat

b. La fille que la maman chatouille.
the girl that the mother tickles

c. La fille à qui le papa téléphone.
the girl to whom the daddy telephones

Each response was graded on an 8-point scale, where 8 was the maximum.[202] The results are reported in Table 3. Note that the children's performance was not affected by age.

Table 3. Mean scores on different types of RCs in child L1 French (max = 8) (from Fragman 2000)

Participants	Subject	Direct object	Indirect object	Total
Children	6.76	5.40*	5.20*	5.79*
Adults	7.39	6.92	6.73	7.01

* significant difference between the children and the adults

202. The highest grade corresponds to an answer exhibiting a structure which is restrictive, relative, grammatical, in accordance with the information presented in the stimulus, and with the same function as the element targeted in the stimulus.

Interestingly, both groups of participants showed the same pattern of responses, namely they all produced non-optimal relatives in the same contexts, although there were significant differences between the two groups. Performance on subject relatives was the highest. Performance on direct object relatives was lower than on subject relatives in both groups; it was even lower on indirect object relatives. In many cases, the participants failed to produce object relatives; instead, they came up with subject RCs. For example, answers such as (27a) and (27b) were obtained for questions about statements (25b) and (25c), respectively. These answers involve the use of the passive voice (27a) and a change of predicate (from *téléphoner* 'to phone' in the stimulus sentence to *recevoir un coup de téléphone* 'to receive a phone call') (27b). Note that some of the subject RCs produced by the children did not correspond to the statement provided.

(27) a. La fille qui est embrassée par la maman.
the girl who is kissed by the mom

b. La fille qui reçoit un coup de téléphone.
the girl who receives a telephone call

Similar results were obtained by Guasti & Cardinaletti (2003) on an elicited task administered to 17 children learning French (4;5 – 7;3). As with Fragman, the best results were obtained on subject relative clauses, which were almost always introduced by *qui*, and almost never included any resumptive pronoun. Direct object RCs were either introduced by *que* or by *où*. When they were introduced by *où*, resumptive pronouns were frequently used as well. In indirect object and genitive RCs, the target forms (*à qui* and *dont*) were almost never produced, and resumptive pronouns were used in about one third of the cases. Finally, the relative pronoun *où* was mostly correctly used in locative RCs, and again the incidence of resumptive pronouns was relatively high, around 33%.

14.3.2 Theoretical implications

As shown in Section 13.3, relative clauses involve wh-movement of either an overt wh-word or a null [+wh] operator. For some researchers, the many errors produced by children with respect to relative clauses (such as the use of resumptive pronouns and gapping) indicate that wh-movement does not take place in these clauses initially. Labelle (1990) argues that wh-movement is evident at age four in the case of wh-questions (recall that at the time of testing, the children had knowledge of wh-movement in questions), but that it does not apply until six in relative clauses. Instead, Labelle proposes that children consider relatives as predicative clauses, based on the frequency in the input that they receive of non-restrictive relatives and clefts in which there is no overt wh-movement. Indeed, such clauses only exhibit *qui* or *que*. In the case of non-restrictive relatives, they are extremely frequent in presentational constructions such as (28).

(28) a. (What's this noise?)
C' est Marie qui arrive.
this is Marie who arrives
'It's Marie who is arriving.'

b. C' est Marie qui arrive (et non Pierre).
this is Marie who arrives and not Pierre
'It is Marie who is arriving (and not Pierre).'

These constructions are acquired quite early by children (as early as 2;0), much earlier than the first instances of (restrictive) RCs, as shown in (29).

(29) a. C'est ça qui va là. (JF, 2;0)
this is that that goes there

b. Tit frère qui pleure. (Ch, 2;1)
little brother that is crying

Labelle claims that the relation of predication in early relative clauses is established via coindexation between the resumptive pronoun or NP and the antecedent, as in (30). According to Labelle, then, there is no reason to believe that a null wh-word has moved to SpecCP, with its trace spelled out as a resumptive element.

(30) Sur [la balle]$_i$ [qu' i(l) lance [la balle]$_i$] (M, 5;0)
on the ball that he catches the ball

For Labelle, the same rationale applies in gapping cases: these constructions involve an empty element coindexed with the antecedent, which establishes predication, as in (31). Once again, there is no reason to assume movement of an empty wh-word. Even for relative clauses introduced by *qui* the occurrence of wh-movement is not clear: clauses could involve *que* followed by an empty subject.

(31) Sur [la petite fille]$_i$ [que le monsieur i(l) montre un dessin ec$_i$] (MJ, 3;06)
on the little girl that the man he shows a drawing

Finally, Labelle (1996) argues that overextension of *où* to non-locative relatives suggests that *où* may not be analysed as a wh-operator by children in the early stages of acquisition.

Although Labelle's account seems quite appealing, it leaves unexplained why children who have knowledge of wh-movement would only apply it in root questions and not in relative clauses. Moreover, they do produce relative clauses introduced by wh-words. Labelle mentions that the children she looked at produced 83 relatives with *où*, some of them perfectly grammatical, as in (32), and four with *quand* 'when'.

(32) La boîte où la voiture rentre. (M, 4;08)
the box where the car goes

In many cases, however, the wh-word is not coreferential with the antecedent, as in (33), and does not seem to participate in the prediction relationship between the antecedent and the relative clause.

(33) La petite fille où le garçon lui dit bonjour. (J, 5;07)
the little girl where the boy to+her says hello

In contrast to Labelle, the fact that early relative clauses are built with *que* (as in (22)) and *où* (as in (33)) may be due to lack of knowledge of relative operators, and the difficulty children experience with relative clauses may not be related to the unavailability of wh-movement in early child grammars, as argued by Guasti & Shlonsky (1995) and Guasti & Cardinaletti (2003). Guasti & Shlonsky adopt Kayne's (1994) representation of relative clauses, in which CP is the sister of D, and the head of the relative moves to SpecCP from the lower clause, as in (34b).

(34) a. L'homme que je rencontre aujourd'hui.
the man that I meet today
'The man that I'm meeting today.'

b. $[_{DP}$ $[_{D'}$ le $[_{CP}$ homme$_i$ que $[_{IP}$ je rencontre t_i aujourd'hui]]]]

If there is an overt wh-word, an additional CP layer is posited. The top CP layer acts as a host for the head of the relative, while the second (lower) CP receives the moved wh-word. This is illustrated in (35). In this sentence, the [+wh] PP moves to the lower CP, and the head of the relative is then extracted from the moved PP into the second CP layer. According to this account, only relatives with pied-piping contain a relative operator.

(35) a. La femme avec qui j'ai soupé hier soir.
the woman with who I have had+dinner yesterday evening
'The woman with whom I had dinner last night.'

b. $[_{DP}$ $[_{D'}$ la $[_{CP}$ femme$_i$ $[_{CP}$ [avec qui t_i]$_j$ $[_{IP}$ j'ai soupé t_j hier soir]]]]

For Guasti & Shlonsky, children first analyse relative clauses as in (34b), overgeneralizing this structure to all types of relatives. It is only after relative operators mature that children will adopt a representation such as (35b) and produce relative clauses with pied-piping. Note that this allows for a straightforward account of why pied-piping does not occur in early relative clauses despite its relatively early development in wh-questions. The following relative clause, which Labelle argues to result from a gapping strategy, would therefore be analysed as in (36b) under Guasti & Shlonsky's account.

(36) a. Sur la petite fille que le monsieur i(l) montre un dessin.
on the little girl that the man he shows a drawing
(J, 3;06)

b. $[_{PP}$ Sur $[_{DP}$ $[_{D'}$ la $[_{CP}$ petite fille$_i$ que $[_{IP}$ le monsieur i(l) montre un dessin t_i]]]]

To account for the presence of resumptive elements in the relative clause, Guasti & Shlonsky suggest that they are in situ, while the head of the relative is in CP. They argue that children's production of resumptive elements stems from an overgeneralization of the in situ option in wh-interrogatives. The head of the relative clause and the element in situ are coindexed so as to establish a predicative relation, as illustrated in (37). Note that the resumptive element is assumed to move to SpecCP at LF and replace the head of the relative clause which, for Guasti & Shlonsky, functions as a pleonastic element.

(37) a. Sur la balle qu'i(l) lance la balle. (M, 5;0)
on the ball that he throws the ball

b. $[_{PP}$ Sur $[_{DP}$ $[_{D'}$ la $[_{CP}$ balle$_i$ que $[_{IP}$ i(l) lance la balle$_i$]]]]]

In Guasti & Cardinaletti's (2003) study, resumptive pronouns, when they occur, are found with (non-object) *que* and *où*, but almost never with *qui* and object *que*, which they argue suggests that the children can distinguish between the different types of relative clauses. In *qui*- and object *que*-RCs, there is wh-movement of a null operator to SpecCP; in the other RCs, a wh-word, including a null operator, is based-generated in SpecCP and coindexed with the resumptive pronoun. As to *où*, it might be overgeneralized to relatives with extraction from different grammatical functions, or it might be based-generated in SpecCP with a coindexed resumptive pronoun. The fact that the same element introducing RCs can be found with a gap and a resumptive pronoun in child grammars does not differ significantly from what occurs in natural languages, they argue, citing the example of *she* in Hebrew (Shlonsky 1992). Moreover, in some languages, such as Swiss German, the equivalent of *où* can be used to introduce different types of RCs, including non-locative ones. This leaves the question of why preposition stranding is acquired late in RCs. Guasti & Cardinaletti argue that such constructions are part of a standard or formal variety of the language, and that children first tend to learn the properties of non-standard varieties. In spoken and informal varieties of French, RCs may be introduced by *que*, including indirect object, genitive, prepositional, and direct object RCs, as in (38a–d). In addition, RCs may or may not contain a resumptive pronoun (see Zribi-Hertz 1984).[203]

203. In colloquial Italian (spoken in Emilia), Berruto (1980), quoted by Guasti & Cardinaletti (2003), reports the following ratios of resumptive pronoun in different types of RCs: 30% in object RCs, 53% in locative RCs, and 79% in indirect object RCs.

(38) a.

Voici	l'homme	que	Marie	lui	a	parlé.
here+is	the man	that	Mary	to+him	has	talked

'Here is the man to whom Mary talked.'

b.

Voici	la	femme	que	son	mari	est	mort	hier.
here+is	the	oman	that	her	husband	is	dead	yesterday

'Here is the woman whose husband died yesterday.'

c.

Voici	la	maison	que	Marie	y	pense	encore.
here+is	the	house	that	Marie	about+it	thinks	still

'The house about which Mary still thinks.'

d.

Voici	l'	homme	que	je	le	regarde.
here+is	the	man	that	I	him	watch

'Here is the man I'm watching.'

According to Guasti & Cardinaletti (2003), children will learn pied-piping in RCs once they start going to school and are exposed to standard French.

Yet another potential explanation for the problem that young children have in producing target-like relative clauses appeals to computational costs. As argued by Fragman (2000), it could be that the global cost of producing relative clauses exceeds that of forming wh-questions. For instance, indirect object RCs and wh-questions may involve different computational costs, although both are introduced by the same wh-word *à qui* 'to whom'. The depth of embedding of RCs, which are inserted within a DP, can be argued to increase computational costs, in comparison to matrix wh-questions (see Delage Monjauze, Hamann & Tuller 2007; see also Section 15.2). Moreover, the computational cost may differ according to the type of RC; for instance, subject relatives may be less costly than indirect object ones. This would explain the main results of Fragman's study, which showed that indirect object relatives yielded the lowest proportion of responses matching the target. Interestingly, this was observed not only for the child learners, but for the adults as well. Indeed, almost half of the adult participants did not produce the targeted indirect object relatives. This corroborates findings in processing studies focusing on adults which show that it is more difficult for adults to process object RCs than subject RCs (see, e.g., Gibson 1998, 2000). The difference has to do with the notion of distance between the antecedent and the gap, where distance is measured by the number of referential expressions intervening between them (see also Section 15.2.2.). It is shorter in the case of subject RCs than in object RCs.[204]

204. Asymmetries between subject and object relatives of the kinds discussed in this section are also reported in comprehension studies carried out on TD children and children with SLI (see Friedmann & Novogorodsky (2004) on Hebrew). See Section 15.2.2.

In addition, Fragman found that children produced resumptive pronouns in their relatives (in contrast, almost all the relatives produced by the adults were correct), and that the incidence of resumptive elements and gapping differed according to the type of RC produced. In response to a subject stimulus, the children did not produce a single resumptive element. In the relative object relatives produced in response to a direct object stimulus, the ratio of resumptive pronouns (44%) was much higher than that of resumptive NPs (19%). The pattern of responses to indirect object stimulus was different yet again: the incidence of resumptive pronouns and resumptive NPs was almost the same (44% and 50%). This is not expected under Labelle's account, which treats all non-standard relative clauses the same.

As noted above, Fragman's data show that children do not behave in the same fashion when dealing with a subject stimulus and a direct object stimulus. Their responses to subject stimulus were very often target-like and their performance was close to that of the adults. Their performance on direct object stimulus was much lower. Indeed, half of the children chose to produce subject relatives instead of direct object ones. This difference seems to be unexpected for Guasti & Shlonsky (1995) under whose model object relatives should pose no problem for children. In fact, the pattern of responses to direct object stimulus is similar to that obtained for indirect object stimulus, such as use of resumptive pronouns and of subject relatives that did not exactly match stimulus sentences (recall (27) for example). So, children seem to face similar problems when dealing with direct and indirect objects. This again is not predicted by Guasti & Shlonsky's analysis. According to Fragman (2000), the fact that children produce subject relatives in the appropriate contexts suggests that errors related to other relative clauses are not due to a deficit in the grammar. Instead, they may be stem from limited cognitive resources and insufficient working memory capacity. The recourse to resumptive pronouns may be a strategy used to reduce the costs of having to form a chain between the wh-word or operator and its trace.

14.4 Knowledge of constraints on wh-movement by child L1 French learners

Children learning L1 French seem to have early knowledge of long distance wh-movement (from either a finite or nonfinite embedded clause) and of the constraints applying to wh-movement, such as wh-islands. As shown by Weissenborn, Roeper & de Villiers (1995), when presented with a question with two potentially licit gaps, one in the higher clause and one in the lower clause, such as (39) and (40), children as young as three years of age provide answers showing they can interpret the wh-word as relating to either the higher or the lower clause (although there is a slight preference for extraction from the higher clause). That is, the wh-word is taken to originate from either position, as shown in Table 4, which summarizes the results from 42 children aged 3;3–6;1. The children were told 13 stories with accompanying pictures. After each story, the children were asked a biclausal question for which two answers were possible, one for the upper and one for the lower clause (see de Villiers, Roeper & Vainikka 1990).[205]

(39) a. Comment est-ce que le clown a dit __ avoir attrapé le ballon __?
how ESK the clown has said have.INF caught the balloon
'How did the clown say that he caught the balloon?'

b. Quand est-ce que le garcon a dit __ qu'il s' est fait mal __?
when ESK the boy has said that he REFL is done harm
'When did the boy say that he hurt himself?'

Table 4. Percentages of answers pertaining to the higher or lower clause in licit and illicit extraction contexts (from Weissenborn et al. 1995)

Violation or not	Clause type	Type of extraction	Higher clause	Lower clause
No violation	Subordinate (finite)	Extraction of argument	53	33
		Extraction of adjunct	44 [a]	36
	Subordinate (nonfinite)	Extraction of argument	67	26
		Extraction of adjunct	32 [a]	63
Violation	Wh-island	Adjunct over argument	55	2
		Adjunct over adjunct	47 [a]	9
	Direct quotation	Extraction of adjunct	59 [a]	37

a. In some cases, the extracted adjunct (e.g. *comment* 'how' and *où* 'where') was confused with an argument, i.e. *à qui* 'to whom'.

For questions with a wh-word that appeared to have been extracted from the lower clause and moved over a (wh-) argument, as in (40a), or over another (wh-) adjunct, as in (40b), the children clearly preferred extraction from the higher clause.

(40) a. Comment est-ce que le canard demande __
how ESK the duck asks

qui il peut appeler au téléphone __?
whom he can call at+the telephone

'How does the duck ask whom he can call?'

b. Où est-ce que la maman raconte __ comment
where ESK the mother tells how

le petit garcon a fait du cheval __?
the little boy has done some horse

'Where does the mother recount how the little boy had been riding?'

205. Note that the children were shown to provide the correct interpretation when the wh-word (adjunct or argument) was left in situ in the lower clause.

This strongly suggests that long distance movement is blocked by the intervening wh-word. Crucially, this result does not stem from any incapacity on the part of the children to apply long distance wh-movement, since, as we have seen, they allow movement in contexts where no violation is involved. Curiously, knowledge of the limitation of wh-movement does not seem to apply to all barriers. In particular, children allowed extraction from the lower clause in cases of direct quotation, as in (41), which is considered a strong barrier in French (see Section 13.4). Weissenborn et al. (1995) report that children equally accepted extraction from a direct quotation and an indirect quotation introduced by *que* 'that' (grammatical in French), as in (39b) above.

(41) Comment est-ce que le garcon a dit __"La jeune
how ESK the boy has said the young
fille va jouer du tambour __?"
girl go play.INF some drum
'How did the boy say, "the girl is going to play the drums"?'

In order to explain this finding, Weissenborn et al. (1995) suggest that young children may not recognize quotations at this stage of acquisition and that they assume complementizers may be deleted in French (just as they are in English: *I think Ø/that I'm tall*). In fact, the existence of quotations in the input may be interpreted as evidence for deletable complementizers. In short, Weissenborn et al. argue, children may consider sentences like (41) to be regular subordinate clauses. To get past this stage, they need to acquire the concept of quotation and the fact that complementizers are obligatorily overt in French.

This study argues in favour of early knowledge of the restrictions on wh-movement — and thus in favour of the application of wh-movement in early child grammars — but the results are not broken down by age. In particular, we do not know how the youngest children responded in comparison to the older ones, which leaves open the possibility that in the earliest grammars, wh-movement is not available.[206]

206. Weissenborn et al. (1995) also report that extraction of argument wh-phrases over adjunct wh-items is allowed. In (i), 21% of the responses pertain to the lower clause (and 55% to the higher one):

(i) À qui le canard demande __ comment il peut donner un coup de main __ ?
to whom the duck asks how it can give a help

This can be accounted for since arguments are lexically licensed by the verb.

14.5 Conclusion

In this chapter, we saw that wh-questions are predicative at first (and usually include *où*) and that they do not exhibit clitic/verb inversion or *est-ce que*. In these first wh-questions, the wh-word may either be preposed or appear in situ; in some cases, it is left out altogether. Moreover, as seen in earlier chapters, wh-questions are almost always finite and they rarely contain a null subject. Embedded clauses are also reported to occur rather early, appearing first in the form of embedded infinitives. Finite embedded clauses develop later on, often without any complementizer. Dummy complementizers are also reported.

For some researchers, C is not instantiated in early child grammars. This would account, among other things, for the lack of inversion in initial questions, the delayed development of finite embedded clauses, and the occasional omission of wh-words and complementizers. According to this view, early preposed wh-phrases are in SpecIP, (see Hulk 1995; Pierce 1992; Plunkett 1999; see also Section 6.2.1.2) and early embedded clauses are IPs instead of CPs. In contrast, other researchers argue in favour of the early availability of C, based principally on the fact that wh-questions are indeed produced early on and that these constructions require a [+wh] feature and the C category in the adult language (Hamann 2000a). Moreover, the fact that some children produce dummy complementizers early on is argued to support the early availability of C. Economy considerations, whereby fewer syntactic operations are favoured at first, are argued to explain the lack of inversion in the first questions, the difficulty with LD wh-extraction (and the production of wh-words in a medial position), and why wh-words are initially left in situ by some children. (Hamann 2006; Jakubowicz 2004, 2005; Strik 2003, 2007)

With respect to relative clauses, acquisition is gradual and can take quite some time, especially as far as prepositional RCs are concerned. Children seem to overgeneralize *que* and *où* at first, and use resumptive pronouns where gaps are required in standard French. In line with those who hold that C is absent from early child grammars, the findings may be analysed in terms of the early unavailability of wh-movement (Labelle 1990). Instead, early RCs may be derived via a predication relationship with the head noun. From the opposite viewpoint, early RCs are assumed to involve wh-movement, given that resumptive pronouns may be found in RCs in nonstandard French and that these pronouns do not occur in all RCs produced by children (particularly in subject and direct object RCs) (Guasti & Cardinalltti 2003). The fact that subject RCs emerge earlier than object RCs and RCs involving pied-piping of the preposition can be explained by computational complexity, assuming that the distance between the antecedent and the gap is shorter in subject RCs than in the other types of RCs. (Fragman 2000; see also Delage et al. 2007)

Finally, preliminary research on acquisition of constraints on wh-movement so far shows that knowledge of such restrictions is in place relatively early (Weissenborn et al. 1995). Children seem to have early knowledge of when wh-movement cannot apply from embedded clauses (although at the same time they may have difficulty producing long distance wh-questions). This suggests not only that early child grammars are UG-constrained, but also that that there is early knowledge of wh-movement, which may be extended to early knowledge of C. However, little attention has generally been paid to the development of constraints on movement in early French. More research, in particular on young children, is needed in this area before the preliminary findings can be accepted with any certainty. More restrictions should also be tested, such as extraction out of relative clauses and complex NPs.

CHAPTER 15

The development of questions and embedded clauses in French bilingual acquisition and in children with SLI learning French

Research on the development of CP-clauses is scarce in bilingual French acquisition. Similarities between bilingual acquisition and monolingual development have been reported, but not all constructions have been investigated. Relative clauses, for example, have not been studied much. Similarly, no studies have looked at early knowledge of wh-constraints in French bilinguals. In children with SLI, derivational complexity seems to affect the emergence of the various constructions related to the C-domain, those constructions involving less complexity (such as subject relatives and wh-questions with the wh-word in situ) developing before more complex ones (such as object relatives and wh-questions with clitic/verb inversion).

15.1 CP-clauses in French bilingual acquisition

As with the verbal and nominal domains, the development of constructions related to CP in bilingual French children is similar to what is observed in monolinguals. In particular, the first wh-interrogatives are predicative, and there is no clitic/verb inversion. Embedded clauses appear after the emergence of interrogatives, and in many cases, either the complementizer is omitted or it takes the form of a dummy item in the early phases.

15.1.1 Development of matrix questions in French bilingual acquisition

As in acquisition by monolinguals, *où* 'where' is the first wh-word used by French bilinguals, as illustrated in (1). Other wh-phrases develop later. Analysing data from the German/French child Ivar (2;4–3;5), Müller et al. (1996) report that *où* is used in the first recordings (see (1a)) and that it is the only wh-word used until age 2;11. Other wh-words start being used productively as of 3;1.

(1) a. Où il est baguette? (Ivar, German/French, 2;05.7)
where it is stick
b. Où il est le papa? (Pascal, German/French, 2;04.7)
where he is the daddy
c. Où l' est le papier? (Caroline, German/French, 2;05.8)
where it is the paper

No inversion is found in the first questions produced by the German/French children investigated. In Ivar's case, subject/verb inversion emerges at the same time as the first target-like complementizer, at age 2;11.[206] The first embedded questions are also observed at this time.[207]

15.1.2 Development of embedded clauses in French bilingual acquisition

The emergence of complementizers is delayed, and as in monolinguals, they are initially not used systematically once they have emerged. Dummy placeholders are also used in the early stages of bilingual acquisition. In Ivar's data, complementizers are observed at age 2;11 for the first time, as illustrated in (2). In data from the Dutch/French child Anouk, the first complementizer is found at 3;3.17 (along with her first relative clauses) (Müller & Hulk 2001). In data from two other German/French children, Caroline and Pascal, the first complementizers are found earlier, at around the age of 2;6. Interestingly, complementizers are reported to develop earlier in French than in German for these two children (2;6 and 3;1, respectively, for Caroline, and 2;5 and 2;9 for Pascal) (Müller 1994b). As in monolinguals, *parce que* and *quand* are the first complementizers to emerge; *que* and *si* develop later (3;1 for Ivar, 3;3.17 for Anouk).

(2) Parce que une piqûre on va, une piqûre.
because an injection one will an injection
(Ivar, German/French, 2;11.21)

Before target-like complementizers develop, bilingual children do produce complex sentences, just as monolinguals do. Müller (1994b) calls these preconjunctional subordinate clauses and notes that among their characteristics are complementizer omission, as in (3), and the use of dummy placeholders, such as the clitic *y* 'there' and the adverbial *là* 'there', as illustrated in (4a).

206. In Ivar's German, the first target complementizers coincide with the emergence of object topicalization. Prior to that point, the application of V2 is limited (Müller 1994).

207. The first embedded wh-questions frequently lack a wh-word, although children are otherwise able to produce wh-words in matrix questions.

(3) a. Et maintenant c'est moi (qui) fais une piqûre.
and now it is me (who) make an injection
(Ivar, German/French, 2;9.5)

b. (Si il) est pas gentil il va il va dans le sac.
(if it) is not nice it goes it goes in the bag
(Ivar, German/French, 2;9.18)

(4) Demander maman là il est. (Ivar, German/French, 2;6.6)
ask.INF mummy *ph* it is

Of the 27 preconjunctional subordinate clauses in Ivar's French utterances to age 2;11, 18 appear without any overt complementizer, and 9 are found with a dummy place-holder (Müller & Penner 1996). Such clauses are also observed in his German data. Note that dummies do not immediately disappear once overt complementizers start being used: the two coexist for a while (between 2;11 and 3;5.28 for Ivar).

15.1.3 Theoretical implications

The fact that elements related to C emerge later than the productive use of Infl-related elements such as clitic subjects, verbal inflection, and auxiliaries, coupled with the fact that subject/verb inversion is initially absent in French bilingual data, could mean that C is not present in the earliest French grammars constructed by bilingual children (see, for example, Müller & Hulk 2001). According to Meisel & Müller (1992), development of C occurs between ages 2;6 and 3 in bilinguals. Interrogatives produced before that age are IPs, with wh-features in Infl and wh-phrases in SpecIP. In other words, bilingual children are able to produce main clause wh-questions, but they are not CPs, and they are not selected wh-questions. According to Meisel and Müller (1992) and Müller (1994b), only Infl is projected above AgrP initially. Additionally, they assume that Infl is specified for non-selected [+wh], [+Finiteness], and modality in both languages. Finally, Müller (1994b) takes SpecIP to be an A-position in French and either an A- or A'- position in German. In German, therefore, SpecIP can be the landing site for the subject or a wh-phrase. In French, where SpecIP can only host the subject, A'-movement can only result in adjunction to IP. In accordance with a Weak Continuity approach to language acquisition, C is assumed to emerge later, once the forms of complementizers are acquired. Only then will bilingual children associate this 'new' meaning (selected [+wh]) with a new position (C) and start using them in embedded clauses.

The delayed development of embedded clauses does not seem to stem from performance limitations on the part of the children. They are able to build complex sentences early on using preconjunctional subordinate clauses as well as coordinating conjunctions, such as *et* 'and'. Moreover, the absence of complementizers does not seem to stem from semantic difficulties. All bilingual children use adverbs and prepositions that express semantic relations similar to those expressed by complementizers (e.g. *après* 'after', *pour* 'for'). In short, the initial lack of complementizers in production data cannot be explained by any cognitive or semantic problems.

As discussed throughout this book, the fact that children do not produce a particular element does not necessarily mean that the category underlying that element is lacking. The fact that bilingual children omit complementizers or that it may take them some time to learn the exact forms of complementizers, therefore, does not necessarily imply that C is absent from initial grammars. Evidence for the loose connection between underlying syntactic knowledge and the production of target forms comes from the fact that bilingual children produce dummy placeholders for a while in the early stages of acquisition. Although not all children use dummies, the fact that some of them do suggests that children have knowledge of the underlying position before they start using the target-like elements associated with that position. Dummy placeholders may have no feature specification, or they may be underspecified with respect to the features associated with C, as argued by Müller & Penner (1996), but their presence suggests that C is not altogether unavailable. In other words, CP is likely to be present in the very first child grammars, in accordance with the hypothesis of Strong Continuity in language development, but C is un(der)specified and the specification of its features is achieved gradually. Further evidence that the first complex sentences likely involve CP comes from word order in the other language used by bilingual children. In particular, when the other language is German, it is reported that early complementizerless embedded clauses have the verb in final position, thus conforming to the requirements of the target language.

15.1.4 Conclusion

The few studies on the acquisition of questions and embedded questions in bilingual French suggest that the developmental pattern is similar to that observed in monolingual French, with predicative questions being used first and inversion appearing later, and target-like embedded clauses appearing only after the first questions. As is the case in monolingual French, the acquisition pattern appears to be compatible with two conflicting interpretations: either C is absent from early grammars and only develops with the acquisition of the specific forms of the complementizers (in accordance with the Weak Continuity approach), or C is present from the beginning (following the Strong Continuity Hypothesis) but the target lexical forms are not produced for some other reason. As seen before, that lexical forms are not produced should not be used as evidence for the absence of underlying categories. The fact that dummy placeholders are used by some children and that target word order is found in embedded clauses early on favour Strong Continuity. Unfortunately, few studies have been investigating the C-domain in French bilinguals, and those that have been carried out, mainly on the development of wh-questions, often fail to provide a detailed account of the development of inversion and the placement of wh-phrases in early interrogatives. Research involving more children and investigating various language combinations is therefore required. Ideally, research should also focus on the development of relative clauses and knowledge of constraints on wh-movement, and should combine, when possible, production and comprehension tasks.

15.2 CP-clauses in the acquisition of French by children with SLI

Researchers investigating language acquisition by French-speaking children with SLI have only recently begun to examine the development of the CP-domain, mostly focusing on production. It is reported that computational complexity plays a major role in their performance, as reflected by the high ratio of wh-in situ in their wh-questions and their tendency to commit more errors as the level of depth of embedding increases.

15.2.1 The findings

The questions produced by children with SLI exhibit the same properties as those initially produced by typically developing children: clitic/verb inversion and *est-ce que* are very rare, and there is a strong tendency to leave the wh-word in situ. As in other domains, these properties persist longer for children with SLI than for TD children. Nonfinite verbs are also quite rare in the questions produced by French children with SLI, which is the same as TD children learning French, but different from SLI children learning other languages, such as German (Hamann, Penner, & Lindner 1998). Finally, differences from TD children are also reported, especially with respect to subject omission in questions containing a preposed wh-word.

It is clear that children with SLI, even very young children, can produce questions, but they may not produce very many. Hamann (2006), for example, investigated spontaneous production data of 11 children with SLI learning French and found a total of 29 interrogatives in the youngest child (between 3;10 and 5;1).[208] Some of the other children used very few interrogatives. For instance, in a selection of recordings of six other children, Hamann found only 40 interrogatives in total. In other cases, however, a large number of questions were observed, included in the youngest children (for example, almost 90 were found in the second youngest child between ages 4;2 and 5;6).

208. The children ranged in age from 3;10 to 7;11 when they were recorded for the first time. They were followed for about two and a half years. In this paper, Hamann (2006) looked at the first five or six recordings (age range: 3;10 – 9;1).

Questions produced by children with SLI learning French also rarely show inversion or *est-ce que*/*qu'est-ce que*, and they tend to have the wh-word in situ. Looking at the same data, Cronel-Ohayon (2004) found a total of 853 questions, of which only four displayed inversion (0.5%) and 19 *est-ce que* or *qu'est-ce que* (2.2%). Hamann (2006) further reports that at least 66% of the wh-questions contain the wh-word in situ, with a percentage of over 80% in five cases (see also Baranzini 2003).[209]

The findings in spontaneous production are confirmed in Cronel-Ohayon's (2004) three elicited production experiments involving the same children (they were aged between 5;4 and 9;7 at the time of the experiments) and 11 TD children (mean age: 5;1; range: 4–6), which are reviewed in Hamann (2006). The first experiment targeted yes/no questions only, while the two other experiments focused on both yes/no questions and wh-questions. In experiment 1, the children were invited to ask questions about cards on which different characters appeared. They were instructed either to ask any questions they wanted, or to start their questions with *est-ce que* or *a-t-il* (lit: 'has he'). The children with SLI had more difficulties than the controls asking questions with *est-ce que* and even more trouble with *a-t-il*. For questions with *a-t-il*, their ratio of inversion was 50% versus almost 80% for TD children. Their most frequent error was the use of a full SVO clause following *a-t-il*, as in *A-t-il il a un chapeau?* lit. 'Has he he has a hat?', suggesting, as argued by Hamann (2006), that the children with SLI were using *a-t-il* as a question marker and not as a genuine case of inversion.

In the second experiment, the children were prompted to ask questions to a puppet, both as yes/no questions, as in (5a), and wh-questions, as in (5b–c) (see also Hulk & Zuckermann 2000). For the wh-questions, the experimenter prompted the children with a wh-word only (5b) or with a complete embedded questions (5c).

(5) a. Je sais qu' il aime jouer au Gameboy. Demande- lui s'il
'I know that he likes to play Gameboy. Ask him if he
aime aussi regarder la télé.
also likes to watch TV.'

b. Ce matin, il est allé à l'école. Demande- lui comment.
'This morning he went to school. Ask him how.'

c. Demande- lui où il habite.
'Ask him where he lives.'

---

209. This tendency to leave the wh-word in situ is quite different from what has been observed in children with SLI learning German, a language which, in contrast to French, does not allow wh-words in situ. Reviewing six corpora of spontaneous production data obtained from a total of 36 German children with SLI (age 3;2 – 10;3), Hamann et al. (1998) report that close to 70% of the wh-questions produced by the children were target-inconsistent, but none displayed the wh-word in situ.

The children with SLI showed a strong tendency to use wh-words in situ, compared to TD children (Table 1), even when the experimenter's lead-in sentence involved a complete embedded question with a preposed element, which could have prompted a fronted wh-word.

Table 1. Ratio of questions with wh-in situ vs. fronted wh-words in elicited production (Experiment 2) (from Hamann 2006)

Children	Age range	Fronted wh	Wh-in situ
TD children (n=11)	4–6	64.6%	24.2%
SLI children (n=11)	5;4–9;7	50.4%	40.4%

In the third experiment, the children were simply asked to repeat yes/no and wh-questions. Two types of yes/no questions were used: questions with inversion and questions starting with *est-ce que*. In the wh-questions, the wh-word was either preposed or left in situ. Some questions with a preposed wh-word exhibited inversion and some did not. In general, children with SLI had problems with inversion. In the yes/no question condition, nine of the questions were (incorrectly) repeated with SVO, compared to only two for the TD children. In the wh-question condition, the SLI children's accuracy rate was 37.9%, versus 79.5% for the controls, when the question displayed both a preposed wh-word and inversion. That the problem stemmed from inversion and not from wh-movement is shown by the fact that the SLI children's accuracy rate reached 90% when there was wh-fronting but no inversion. Interestingly, nine cases of subject omission were also reported for the SLI children in the repetition of wh-questions with both wh-preposing and inversion, as compared to only one for the TD group.

Apart from the issue of question formation (which concerns wh-word placement and subject/verb inversion, for example), the questions produced by children with SLI display some properties that are both similar to, and different from what is found in TD development. Similarities have to do with the use of finiteness. Recall that in TD children learning French, nonfinite verbs are almost nonexistent in questions. Likewise, the incidence of nonfinite wh-questions is generally low in the 11 French SLI children's spontaneous data examined by Hamann (2006). In the younger group of children (age range 3;10 – 6;1), less than 3% of their wh-questions are nonfinite, regardless of whether the wh-word is preposed or in situ (versus 6.3% of their main declaratives).[210] In contrast, children with SLI and TD children differ in the extent to which they produce

210. This contrasts with the findings reported by Hamann et al. (1998) for German children with SLI, whose use of nonfinite forms was identified as one of four main patterns of errors in wh-questions.

subjectless questions. In questions used by TD children, null subjects are quite rare. Any null subjects that are found tend to appear either in yes/no questions or in wh-questions with the wh-word in situ, but not in wh-questions with a preposed wh-word (except for *pourquoi* 'why' wh-questions) (see Section 6.2.1.2). In all SLI groups involved in Hamann's (2006) study, production of subjectless wh- and yes/no questions was observed. Interestingly, subject omission was found in wh-questions with a preposed wh-word, unlike what happens in TD children. In two of the children, the ratio of subject omission in wh-questions with a preposed wh-word ranged from 25% to as high as 60%.

Preliminary results on comprehension of non-subject wh-questions suggest that children with SLI have no problem understanding interrogatives with wh-fronting in French, although they may not produce them systematically. Haiden, Prévost, Tuller, Ferré & Scheidnes (2009) compared production and comprehension of wh-questions in French by TD monolinguals at different ages, monolinguals with SLI, and English-speaking children learning French. The production task involved 54 items and the comprehension test, 72.[211] Table 2 shows that while the ratio of production of wh-in situ was higher in the children with SLI (and in the child L2ers) than in the TD children and adults, their comprehension of questions with wh-fronting was target-like.

Table 2. Production and comprehension of non-subject wh-questions by TD monolinguals, monolinguals with SLI and child L2ers (adapted from Haiden et al. 2009)

Group	Age	Production		Comprehension	
		Wh-in situ	Wh-fronting	Wh-in situ	Wh-fronting
TD4 (n=17)	4;0 – 4;5 (*M*=4;2)	21.8%	78.2%	96.6%	87.3%
TD6 (n=12)	6;2 – 6;8 (*M*=6;5)	2.7%	97.3%	97.9%	95.1%
TD Adults (n=12)	19;4 – 24;3 (*M*=22;0)	0%	100%	100%	100%
SLI (n=13)	6;6 – 12;11 (*M*=9;4)	59.1%	40.9%	98.7%	94.9%
L2 (n=19)	6;8 – 12;7[a] (*M*=9;9)	40.9%	51.9%	97.1%	99.2%

a. The age of first exposure to French ranged from 4;3 to 9;10 (*M*=6;11) and the length of exposure to French ranged from 0;11 to 4;6 (*M*=2;10).

211. Both tasked were picture-based. Design materials were initially provided by Na'ama Friedmann and adapted by Jakubowicz (2005). In the elicited production task, stimulus sentences did not involve wh-fronting, e.g. *Le lapin pousse quelqu'un mais on ne voit pas qui; demande-lui* 'The rabbit is pushing someone, but we can't see who; ask him'. In the comprehension task the children were presented with pictures displaying three different characters

Comprehension was the lowest on wh-questions with wh-fronting and stylistic inversion (TD4: 37.2%; TD6: 54.2%; TD adults: 81.9%; SLI: 44.9%; L2ers: 25%), and no such questions, which were deemed the most complex by the authors, were produced by the children.

Children with SLI also differ from TD children in their use of embedded clauses. In particular, they tend to commit more errors than TD children when producing an embedded clause, and they tend to produce subordinates which arguably involve a low level of derivational complexity. In spontaneous data collected from 10 children with SLI aged 5;10 to 10;5 (mean 8;0) and three groups of TD children (with mean ages of 6;4, 8;2, and 11;4 respectively), Hamann, Tuller, Monjauze, Delage & Henry (2007) found that over 33% of the complex clauses produced by the children with SLI were erroneous (a ratio close to 50% in the case of finite complement clauses). The difference between the children with SLI and the TD children is particularly striking when looking at error rates in utterances containing relative clauses: in the SLI group, the percentage of erroneous utterances was between 4 and 10 times higher than in the TD groups (see also below).[212] A higher number of alternative strategies for the production of subordinate clauses were also used by the children with SLI than the TD children, as shown in Table 3. These concerned attempts at subordination, such as juxtaposition of matrix clauses (6a) and self interruptions (6b), and use of grammatical complementizer omission, as in (7).[213] All examples in (6) and (7) were produced by children with SLI (Hamann et al. 2007).

---

performing the same action over each other, for instance filming. Subject and object questions were asked about the central character (e.g. *Qui filme le roi?* 'Who is filming the king?' and *Qui le roi filme?* 'Who is the king filming?'), and the children were instructed to give their answers by pointing.

212. Interestingly, the ratio of complex utterances may not increase with age in children with SLI; however, the error rate does. Hamann et al. (2007) investigated spontaneous production of 18 adolescents with SLI (aged 11 to 16). They report that the percentage of complex utterances (22.5%) did not differ significantly from that found in the younger SLI group (17.5%). In particular, for six of the teenagers, the error rate was under 10%, but these subjects were found to avoid complexity either by producing few embedded clauses, or by avoiding more complex embedding, such as finite subordinate clauses, which involve different kinds of dependencies, such as Complementizer-Tense agreement and subject-verb agreement (see Hamann et al. 2007).

213. Complementizer omission can be grammatical in colloquial French, as in (7); however, it is not always allowed, as shown by Hamann et al. (2007). Interestingly, ungrammatical complementizer omission was also found in the children with SLI, which corroborates findings in children with SLI learning German (Hamann et al. 1998). In their study, Hamann et al. found that over 80% of the embedded clauses produced by 35 children with SLI were erroneous with respect to the target language (range 57%–100%).

(6) a. Non [j'ai fait avec ma maîtresse] *(qui) [il s' appelle Doris]
no I did with my teacher (who) he's REFL called Doris

b. Après on attend [qu' ils applau…]
after one waits that they applau(d)

(7) Je pense (qu') on va faire des jeux.
I think (that) we will do some games
'I think we're going to play games.'

Table 3. Attempts at subordination and use of grammatical complementizer omission by children with SLI and TD children (adapted from Hamann et al. 2007)

Strategy	SLI (8;0 yrs)	TD-6 (6;4 yrs)	TD-8 (8;2 yrs)
Attempts at subordination	31.2%	8.6%	3.6%
Grammatical complementizer omission	15%	0.5%	0%

Delage, Monjauze, Hamann & Tuller (2007) analysed the use of relative clauses in spontaneous production from 21 children with SLI aged 9;2 –13;7 (mean: 11;6) and from three groups of typically developing children (mean ages 6;4, 8;2, and 11;7).[214] The performance of the children with SLI was systematically lower than that of the age-matched TD-11 children on five counts, and almost always lower than that of the youngest TD-6 children. As summarized in Table 4, the comparisons addressed the percentage of relatives (which was the lowest for the children with SLI), the mean number of non-subject RCs (which increased with age, with the SLI children scoring twice as low as the TD-11 children), the percentage of pseudo relatives based on the use of presentational *y'a* clauses, as in (8) (which was over three times higher for children with SLI than for TD-11 children), the percentage of so-called genuine RCs (see below) (which was twice as low for the children with SLI as TD-8 and TD-11 children), and the percentage of errors found in RCs (which was close to 40% for children with SLI versus less than 10% for the TD groups). Note that few cases of resumptive pronouns were observed by Delage et al. (5% at most).

(8) Y a des bonhommes qui nous parlent (RE 11;2)
there are some guys who us+DAT talk
'There are some guys who are talking to us'

214. The study also involved 21 children with mild-to-moderate hearing loss (9;3–13;3, mean 6.7) and 11 children with Rolandic epilepsy (9;1–13;11, mean 7.9). The tendencies reported in these groups were generally similar to what was observed in the children with SLI.

Table 4. Characteristics of relative clauses in spontaneous production in children with SLI and TD children (adapted from Delage et al. 2007)

RC characteristics	SLI (11;6 yrs)	TD-6 (6;4 yrs)	TD-8 (8;2 yrs)	TD-11 (11;7 yrs)
Mean N relatives / N utterances	4.1%	5.1%	5.4%	6.5%
Mean N of non-subject relatives	1.4	1.4	1.3	2.9
Mean N presentational *y'a* / N relatives	44.3%	32.5%	22.2%	12.9%
Mean N genuine relatives / N relatives	20.9%	17.2%	42.1%	49.8%
Mean N errors / N relatives	38.4%	6.2%	9.2%	1.2%

15.2.2 Theoretical implications

The development of interrogatives and RCs in French children with SLI is compatible with economy considerations, as proposed under the Computational Complexity Hypothesis (Jakubowicz et al. 1998) and more recently by Jakubowicz (2004, 2005). Under this account, children with SLI have a limited working memory capacity, which constrains their ability to perform operations that are too complex. More precisely, under the assumption that a derivation requiring *n* chains is less complex than a derivation requiring *n*+1 chains, children with SLI will tend to prefer fewer movements or no movement at all. With respect to interrogatives, this translates into a strong tendency on the part of children with SLI to use wh-words in situ rather than wh-fronting, and not to perform clitic/verb inversion. These characteristics, we saw, are also typical of the interrogatives used by some TD children. The difference is that in the case of children with SLI, they are observed more systematically and over a longer period of time, presumably due to more limited computational capacities. This suggests once again that the development of children with SLI is similar to that of TD children, albeit delayed. In future research, it would be interesting to obtain data from older children with SLI in order to draw further comparisons with normal development; for example, it would be interesting to know whether adolescents with SLI also tend to produce a high percentage of wh-questions with the wh-word in situ.

With respect to the development of RCs, which also involve movement, we saw that children with SLI tend to use pseudo-relatives rather than genuine RCs. The two types differ in the level of embedding they involve: while genuine RCs are embedded within a DP which is itself embedded within an IP, as in (9a), pseudo-relatives can be argued to involve a level of embedding which is less deep. In presentational *y'a* constructions, the DP following *y'a* can be said to be within the Specifier of CP, as in (9b) (see Delage et al. 2007). In other words, as originally proposed by Lambrecht (1988), presentational *y'a* constructions do not involve a relative clause modifying an NP.

(9) a. $[_{IP}$ Je connais $[_{DP}$ le gars$_i$ $[_C$ OP$_i$ qui $[_{IP}$ t$_i$ $[_{VP}$ est venu]]]]].
b. Y' a $[_{CP}$ un gars$_i$ $[_C$ qui $[_{IP}$ t$_i$ $[_{VP}$ est venu]]]].
there is a guy who came
'There's a guy who came'

Assuming that constructions that are less deeply embedded are less complex computationally, the fact that children favour *y'a* constructions to genuine RCs can be explained by the CCH. The children with SLI also used significantly fewer RCs than aged-matched TD children, and produced many more erroneous RCs than the TD children. Finally, the incidence of subject relatives was higher than that of non-subject RCs in the speech of children with SLI. The fact that the distance between the antecedent and the gap is longer in object relatives than in subject relatives (see Gibson 1998, 2000 for the notion of distance; see also Section 14.3.2) suggests that subject relatives are less complex than their non-subject counterparts, which is consistent with the CCH (see also Fragman 2000 for L1 acquisition by TD children). Computational complexity of object RCs is such that asymmetries between subject and object RCs are also found in comprehension. Although this is observed in young TD children, it is particularly striking in children with SLI (see Friedmann & Novogorodsky (2004) on Hebrew).[215]

That children with SLI may have problems with more complex computations in interrogatives and RCs does not mean that their grammar lacks the relevant functional layers, in particular C (contra Gopnik 1990). Indeed, it is not the case that wh-movement is altogether absent from the speech of children with SLI. We saw that wh-raising can be easily elicited from these children, although they maintain a stronger tendency to use wh-words in situ than TD children. Comprehension of questions with wh-fronting is also extremely high. The underlying grammar of children with SLI is therefore not deficient, as argued in other places in this book. In particular, that wh-movement occurs in children with SLI also goes against van der Lely's (1998) hypothesis that obligatory movement for feature checking purposes is missing from SLI grammars. In an elicited production task administered to an English-speaking adolescent with SLI (AZ, aged 15;6), van der Lely (1998) found many errors with object wh-questions. Of 18 object wh-questions, only three (16%) were target-consistent.[216] Although the wh-word was systematically preposed in AZ's wh-questions, van der Lely assumes no wh-movement

216. For a more recent analysis, see Friedmann, Belletti & Rizzi (2009).

217. Of the 15 erroneous object questions, five concerned the construction of the interrogatives themselves. Some of the observed errors involved a resumptive NP (e.g. *What did Mrs Brown broke something?*) and the production of a subject question instead of the targeted

is present; instead, she assumes that preposed operators are base-generated in their clause-initial position. However, if movement is not obligatory in SLI grammars, why aren't wh-words found in situ in AZ's interrogatives? For van der Lely, this is explained by the fact that AZ had been undergoing speech therapy and that, once in therapy, children with SLI are explicitly instructed to form questions with a preposed wh-word. However, we saw that wh-words may be preposed in children with SLI who are much younger than AZ, and therefore presumably in therapy for a much shorter period of time, which calls van der Lely's analysis into question.

An alternative idea is that children make use of economy strategies made available by the language that they are learning. In adult French, wh-in situ is grammatical, as well as wh-fronting without subject/verb inversion. Therefore, children with SLI, and young TD children, exploit these possibilities, which involve less derivational complexity, before producing wh-questions with wh-preposing and inversion, which are more complex. In contrast, children learning English or German, where wh-movement and inversion between the subject and the auxiliary or the verb is obligatory, do not entertain the wh-in situ option. This would apply to SLI development as well (see Hamann et al. 1998 for the acquisition of German by children with SLI). Other economy strategies could be used by these children, such as nonfinite wh-questions (see Hamann et al. 1998).[217] Such constructions are not found in children with SLI learning French. Finally, it is worth pointing out that problems with derivational complexity is not only observed in production; low performance in comprehension can also be obtained in the highest cases of derivational complexity, as with questions involving wh-fronting and stylistic inversion (under Kayne & Pollock's (2001) analysis, for example). However, not much is known about the development of stylistic inversion, so more research should address the development of

object interrogative (e.g. *Who passed Colonal Mustard?* instead of *Who did Colonel Mustard pass?*). Other errors pertained to tense and *do*-support omission.

218. For Hamann et al. (1998), the grammatical systems constructed by children with SLI are instances of Minimal Default Grammars (MDGs) (see Roeper 1999). An MDG is a set of defaults made available by UG. By definition, it contains a subset of formal features required by the target adult language. Moreover, the basic mechanism of structure building, provided by UG, is Merge. In wh-questions produced by children with SLI, it is assumed that there is no feature-checking mechanism. Instead, the wh-word is merged with the rest of the clause, which is referred to as the 'event'. In other words, the structure does not involve a CP subcategorizing for an IP node. Although the MDG account and the analysis of the interrogatives produced by French children with SLI share similar preoccupations with respect to economy of derivation, it is not immediately clear how the two approaches can be reconciled. In particular, if the MDG account is correct, nonfinite CPs should be found in French children with SLI, a prediction not borne out by the facts.

this phenomenon, perhaps comparing it to other types of inversion, such as clitic/verb inversion.

Although most results reported for French children with SLI match what has been found in TD children with respect to the development of interrogatives, some differences were also found, for example with respect to subject omission in questions with preposed wh-words. Such omissions were found in children with SLI, but not in TD children, although the extent of this phenomenon remains to be established. In the data reported by Hamann (2006), this was particularly observed in two of the 11 children investigated. Unfortunately, a number of children produced few wh-questions, which prevented further analyses. We saw that with TD children, subjectless wh-questions strongly tend to occur when the wh-word is in situ. In Section 14.1.6, an account of such interrogatives proposed by Hamann (2006) was presented, in which the root of such questions is WhP, with a Q-head in Wh° in an Agree relation with the wh-word in situ and a null subject in the specifier of WhP. In preposed wh-questions, since the specifier of WhP is taken by the wh-word, no empty subject can appear there. For children with SLI, Hamann (2006) proposes that in preposed wh-questions, the wh-word may be misanalysed as a Q-head. This element would therefore not occupy the specifier position of WhP but that of the head, thus freeing the specifier of the root for a null subject to occur. For Hamann (2006), the fact that inversion does not occur in wh-questions should be taken as evidence that the head-position of Wh is already filled by an interrogative element.

15.2.3 Conclusion

Research on the development of interrogatives in children with SLI learning French reveals characteristics that are similar to early normal development, such as wh-words in situ and lack of clitic/verb inversion, as well as some wh-movement. These properties suggest that children with SLI have computational or working memory capacities that are more limited than TD children, rather than a functional deficit (in the left periphery) or a problem with movement (in contrast to proposals by Gopnik (1990) and van der Lely (1998), respectively). Presumably, the similarities in development arise because computational limitations in both children with SLI and young TD children lead them to prefer economical structures and derivations, that is, those that involve fewer and shorter dependencies than would be required in the adult language. A similar explanation in terms of computational complexity can also be used to account for the development of relative clauses in children with SLI: spontaneous production data suggest that they prefer constructions that are less computationally costly (e.g. pseudo-relatives and subject RCs) to more complex constructions, such as genuine and non-subject RCs.

Differences in behaviour between children with SLI and TD children were also uncovered: children with SLI sometimes omit the subject in interrogatives in which the wh-word has been preposed, whereas TD children rarely do so. Following Hamann (2006), this can be explained in terms of economy considerations as well, involving structural economy, long distance Agree, and a misanalysis of wh-words as heads. Further research is needed, examining in particular the extent of the phenomenon of subject drop in questions with preposed wh-words.

As previously mentioned research in the CP-domain in French children with SLI is relatively recent. Ideally, new studies should collect both spontaneous and elicited production data, and should investigate comprehension as well as production.

CHAPTER 16

Questions and embedded clauses in L2 French acquisition

Few studies have focused on the development of questions and embedded clauses in L2 acquisition of French. For example, little is known about the development of relative clauses in child learners, and no studies have looked at knowledge of constraints on wh-movement in either child or adult L2 French. This chapter reviews some of the few studies existing to date, occasionally pointing out serious needs for further research. Despite these shortcomings, as in the case of adjective placement (see Chapter 12), interesting research has been conducted on the interface between syntax and semantics with wh-questions (see Section 16.2.5). Interface domains offer an extremely promising perspective in tackling the issue of UG-accessibility in (adult) L2 acquisition, which has been keeping scholars busy for the last 20 years or so.

16.1 CP-clauses in child L2 French

Given the paucity of research in the development of CP-related constructions in child L2 French generalizations about child L2 development and comparisons with child L1 French are difficult to establish. Data reported so far point to earlier appearance of matrix questions than of embedded questions. Moreover, a difference is found between spontaneous and elicited data: while the incidence of wh-in situ is low in spontaneous production, it is much higher in elicited speech. Further detail will be given on the development of relative clauses and some properties of embedded clauses (concerning finiteness and overt subjects). The data will then be analysed in terms of the development of C in child interlanguage grammars.

16.1.1 Development of matrix questions in child L2 French

Two main studies have looked at the development of questions and embedded clauses in spontaneous production in child L2 French. The first one is Grondin & White's (1996) investigation of Kenny and Greg, two anglophone children after little exposure to the language (see Section 4.1.1.1). The second one report on two children, Elisa (L1 German) and Lorenzo (LI Italian), who had been exposed to French for a longer period than Kenny and Greg at the time of their first recording sessions (Belletti & Hamann 2004) (see Section 4.1.1.2). Matrix yes/no questions and wh-questions emerge early in Kenny and Greg: they appear at month 3 for Kenny and month 5 for Greg. In data from Elisa and Lorenzo, wh-questions are also reported to appear in the earliest recordings, but, as mentioned above, the two children had had a longer exposure period to French than Kenny and Greg when they started being investigated.

As in child L1 French, the first questions are largely uninverted. This is particularly the case in Kenny's and Greg's yes/no questions, as shown in Table 1. The majority of the inverted yes/no questions in their data are found in later recordings (after month 20), but their incidence remains very low. Examples are given in (1) and (2).

Table 1. Formation of matrix questions in child L2 French (L1=English) (from Grondin & White 1996)

Child	Yes/no questions		Wh-questions		
	Inverted	Non-inverted	Inverted	Non-inverted	In situ
Kenny	7	95	131	97	8
Greg	6	141	115	111	57

(1) a. Ça, c' est une giraffe? (Greg, L1=English, month 5)
that this is a giraffe

b. Ça c' est de toi? (Kenny, L1=English, month 3)
that this is of you

(2) a. Veux-tu faire de le dessin? (Greg, L1=English, month 20)
want you make.INF of the drawing

b. Peux-tu enlever ça? (Kenny, L1=English, month 20)
can you remove.INF this

Wh-questions, on the other hand, involve inversion right from the outset. The incidence of inversion is high in the data from Kenny and Greg: it is found in half of Kenny's wh-questions (131/236 = 51.2%) and 40.6% of Greg's. Most inverted questions are predicative and include the sequence *où est* 'where is', as in child L1 French. Note that little is known about the development of clitic/verb inversion in the children's corpus.

(3) a. Qui est ça? (Greg, L1=English, month 5)
who is that

b. Où est le rouge? (Kenny, L1=English, month 3)
where is the red

When there is no inversion, the wh-phrase is very likely to be preposed, as in (4). There are few instances of wh-words in situ, especially in Kenny's data. More can be found in Greg's speech, but only in later recordings, as of month 20. The examples in (5), with the wh-word in situ and no inversion, are extremely rare in these children's data. Finally, all wh-questions exhibit an overt wh-word, in contrast to child L1 questions where the omission of the wh-phrase is not uncommon.

(4) a. Où ça va? (Greg, L1=English, month 10)
where this go.FIN

b. Pourquoi i' pleure? (Kenny, L1=English, month 3)
why he cry.FIN

(5) a. C' est où? (Greg, L1=English, month 10)
it is where

b. Le lion est où? (Kenny, L1=English, month 8)
the lion is where

In child L1 French, we saw that wh-words are either preposed or left in situ. A different tendency seems therefore to be found in early child L2 French. Naturally, this would need to be confirmed with data from other child learners. With more exposure, children start using wh-words in situ, as evidenced by the wh-questions produced by Elisa and Lorenzo (Belletti & Hamann 2004). Note that in Italian (Lorenzo's L1), unlike in French, wh-questions with the wh-word in situ are ungrammatical.[219]

(6) a. Ça va par où? (Elisa, L1=German, rec 1)
that goes to where

b. Il est où l' autre? (Lorenzo, L1= Italian, rec 1)
he is where the other one

In elicited production of wh-questions, very different results are reported. In particular, we saw in Section 15.2.1 that English-speaking learners of French tend to frequently use wh-in situ in French, much like French monolinguals with SLI (Haiden et al. 2009). In the data elicited from 19 British children (mean age 9;9 and mean length of exposure 2;10) who had immigrated to France with their parents and from comparative groups of children with SLI and TD children, Haiden et al. found that the ratio of wh-in situ was around 40% for the L2ers and around 60% in the age-matched children with SLI, compared to 22% and 3% for TD monolinguals aged four and six respectively (see Section 15.2.1,

219. In the case of Lorenzo, it is further shown that *quoi* is always correctly left in situ, as shown in (i). All of his 20 *quoi*-questions display the wh-word in its base-generated position.

(i) a. C' est quoi? (Lorenzo, L1= Italian, rec 2)
It is what

b. Ça veut dire quoi, golf? (Lorenzo, L1= Italian, rec 4)
that wants say what golf

Table 2). Low rates of clitic/verb inversion are also reported in the child L2ers (16%, compared to 21.1% for the TD6 children and 75.2% for adult French native speakers, the children with SLI scoring at 7.9% and the TD4 children at 0%). These findings are interesting from the point of view of L1 influence given than in the children's mother tongue, both wh-fronting and inversion (between the subject and the auxiliary) are obligatory. Importantly, Haiden et al. report no correlation between the incidence of wh-in situ and age, length of exposure, or age of first contact with French. Finally, comprehension of wh-questions with wh-fronting and wh-in situ was native-like (above 97%), but that of interrogatives with wh-fronting and stylistic inversion was much lower, at 25%.

16.1.2 Development of embedded clauses in child L2 French

In contrast to matrix questions, subordinate clauses are delayed in Kenny and Greg's data. Embedded clauses emerge at month 10 for Kenny and at month 14 for Greg. Subordinates are reported in the first samples of Lorenzo's and Elisa's data, but again the children had had more exposure to French than Kenny and Greg when recording began and might have previously passed through a stage without subordinate clauses.

(7) a. Je crois qu' il est cassé. (Greg, L1=English, month 18)
I think that it is broken

b. Regarde qu' est-ce que la marionnette fait.
look what ESK the puppet does
(Kenny, L1=English, month 10)

c. Quand on a pas les mêmes… (Elisa, L1=German, rec 2)
when one has not the same ones…

d. Regard, qu' est-ce que le petite a fait.
look, what ESK the small+one has done
(Elisa, L1=German, rec 2)
'Look what the small one has done.'

Infinitival clauses, such as those introduced by *de*, are rarely investigated in detail in child L2 French. However, what evidence there is suggests that they develop late. In Kenny and Greg's corpus, they are not productively used until after month 25, as in (8).

(8) Veux- tu arrête de lancer. (Greg, L1=English, month 25)
would you stop.FIN to throw.INF

Once embedded clauses start to appear, they almost always include complementizers. This is particularly interesting in Kenny's and Greg's cases since their L1 allows null complementizers. Out of the 137 embedded clauses produced by Kenny, only three are complementizerless (2.2%); for Greg, the ratio is 16/112 (14.3%). It is as if the children quickly learned that complementizers must be overtly expressed in French, in contrast to their L1. Note that some complementizerless embedded clauses are found in the late recordings. Interestingly, no dummy complementizers are reported in the data.

Finally, in embedded wh-questions, it has been shown that the wh-word is correctly fronted, as illustrated in (9). However, more data should be analysed to confirm this tendency.

(9) Tu sais où j' ai mis les crayons? (Lorenzo, L1=Italian, rec 5)
you know where I have put the crayons?

16.1.3 Development of relative clauses in child L2 French

The development of relative clauses in child L2 French is not well documented. The existing data indicate few errors in the *que/qui* alternation, even on the part of children whose L1 lacks this property, such as Lorenzo. Correct use of *qui* and *que* on his part is illustrated in (10) and (11), respectively. Examples (10b) and (11) further show that the alternation is not driven by the animacy characteristics of the head noun of the relative clause since in these cases a non-animate item is referred to.

(10) a. Non, c' est pas moi qui devrais l'amener. (Lorenzo, L1=Italian, rec 1)
no it is not me who should it take.INF

b. Non, j' ai pas vu des voitures qui font comme ça.
no I have not seen any cars which make like that
(Lorenzo, L1=Ital., rec 2)

(11) a. C'est la maison que je habite. (Lorenzo, L1=Italian, rec 2)
that is the house that I live

b. Non, c'est un outil qu' on utilise, là. (Lorenzo, L1 =Italian, rec 5)
no it's a tool which we use there

16.1.4 Other properties of the first questions and embedded clauses in child L2 French

In Sections 4.1.1.2 and 8.2.1, we saw that much like in child L1 French, interrogatives and subordinates strongly tend to be finite and contain overt subjects in Grondin & White's (1996) English/French corpus. We saw that at most 6% of the questions and embedded clauses produced by Kenny and Greg had a nonfinite verb. In contrast, RIs represented more than 10% of their main declaratives until the 18th month of acquisition. That this behaviour can be generalized to all child L2 French learners is challenged by Belletti & Hamann (2004) who report nonfinite forms in questions and embedded clauses produced by Elisa, as illustrated in (12).

(12) a. Quoi… faire… la maman? (Elisa, L1=German, rec 2)
what do.INF the mommy

b. Si elle te couper une pomme. (Elisa, L1=German, rec 5)
if she you+DAT cut.INF an apple

In all, there are five nonfinite verbs in the 48 questions and embedded clauses produced by Elisa (10.4%). By comparison, only one RI occurs in her 368 main declaratives (<1%).

With respect to null subjects, we saw that their incidence is significantly lower in interrogatives and subordinates than in main declaratives. In Kenny's and Greg's data, they represent at most 5.5% of all subjects in questions and embedded clauses compared to at least 10% of subjects in finite root declaratives (20% in Kenny's case) and 30% in RIs (53% in Greg's case).

16.1.5 Theoretical implications

The fact that matrix questions are produced early on by child L2 French learners, along with the low omission rate of wh-words, suggests that C is available in early child interlanguage grammars. This is corroborated by the fact that wh-questions are very well understood. This argues against an approach to child L2 development that assumes early stages of L2 acquisition are lexical in nature (Vainikka & Young-Scholten 2005). Child L2 learners' early knowledge of C could stem from transfer from the L1.

In spontaneous production, the vast majority of wh-questions produced by the child L2 learners investigated so far have preposed wh-words, as is also the case in their respective L1s, namely, English, German, and Italian; in situ wh-words are found only in later recordings. Among the child L2 learners studied so far, and as in L1 acquisition, predicative wh-questions are the most common type of interrogative at first. As with any complex expressions used early by child learners, it is not easy to determine the status of these first wh-questions. They could be formulaic expressions, such as *Qu'est-ce que c'est?* and *Qu'est-ce que c'est que ça?*, whose incidence is high in Kenny's and Greg's data. On the other hand, Kenny and Greg produced many other questions that do not seem to be routines (as Grondin & White (1996) have pointed out). The observed early cases of inversion may also not be evidence of C, but simply translations of their L1 equivalents (e.g. *where is* and *who is*). More data should be collected from children in whose L1 wh-movement is not instantiated, such as Chinese, starting as close to the beginning of their exposure to French as possible, to help determine whether and to what extent the L1 is influencing acquisition of wh-fronting in L2 French.

In elicited data, the incidence of wh-fronting and clitic/verb inversion is much lower than what is found in French TD monolinguals. In such tasks, the questions used by the children cannot be considered formulaic. As in the case of children with SLI, the L2ers seem to favour constructions that involve little computational complexity, such as wh-in situ. This does not mean that transfer does not occur in the initial stage of child L2 acquisition. As far as the development of questions is concerned, English-speaking children may transfer wh-movement and inversion from their L1, but their limited computational capacities may prevent them from performing these operations systematically. Longitudinal studies of elicited production data should tell us whether the incidence of wh-fronting and inversion increases with time, presumably due to developing WM capacities (see Konhert et al. 2009; see also Section 4.1.3). Note that in comprehension, results are low for the construction deemed to be the most complex one in the experiment by Haiden et al. (2009), that involving wh-fronting and stylistic inversion. However, it is not clear whether this is indeed due to the high complexity of the construction or to the fact that stylistic inversion does not exist in the children's L1.

If C is available in early child L2 grammars, as suggested by the presence of matrix questions, why do embedded clauses only develop later? One possibility is that the appropriate contexts for complementizers are lacking in the earliest productions. In Kenny's and Greg's data, Grondin & White (1996) report that there are no appropriate contexts for complementizers before the moment these elements emerge, but that once such contexts arise, the incidence of complementizers is high. Alternatively, the two children did not know how to use these elements. Another explanation for the early lack of complementizers may be the rate at which vocabulary is acquired. Indeed, learners must learn the forms of the complementizers and the verbs that require a CP complement, which may take some time. Given the current lack of data, all of these scenarios are plausible. Looking at comprehension data may give us more detailed insight into knowledge of subordination in the early stages of child L2 French.

We saw above that once complementizers emerge, they are almost always overt; very few cases of omission are reported. For example, in Kenny's data, overt complementizers appear in well over 90% (134/137) of appropriate contexts, and in Greg's data, they appear in over 85% (96/112 = 85.7%) of appropriate contexts. This is much higher than what is reported in the acquisition of L2 English by Spanish-speaking learners (Lakshamanan & Selinker 1994). This asymmetry suggests that children are sensitive to the obligatory or optional status of complementizers in the target language. Complementizers are optional in English in contrast to French. If the children investigated by Lakshamanan & Selinker have acquired the optionality property in English, this can explain their lower production rate. The reverse can be said of Kenny and Greg who showed command of the target property as soon as they started using complementizers.

Other properties of interrogatives and subordinates, such as the low incidence of nonfinite verbs and null subjects, are consistent with a Truncation or Structural Economy analysis of early child IL grammars of French, as argued in Section 8.2.1.1. Although the data from Elisa (Belletti & Hamann 2004) seem to challenge this analysis, since over 10% of her embedded clauses and questions contain a nonfinite verb, recall that she had been exposed to French for much longer prior to data collection, as compared to Kenny and Greg. Investigation of earlier declaratives, interrogatives, and subordinates is necessary before significant comparisons with the English/French data can be drawn.

With respect to relative clauses, we saw that children can learn the *qui/que* alternation quite rapidly, although more data should be gathered from earlier stages of acquisition. Examining earlier data would perhaps allow us to identify potential cases of overgeneralization of one complementizer over the other, as seen in child L1 French. In the Italian/French data, the alternation is in place relatively early, which suggests, as pointed out by Belletti & Hamann (2004), that the child has acquired the fact that French is not a null subject language. Indeed, in Section 8.2.1 we saw that Lorenzo used almost no null subjects in his French utterances (only 4/601). In a non-*pro*-drop language such as French, the appearance of agreeing *qui* is required in order to license the empty subject position of the relative clause. Without the *qui*, that empty position is not allowed in French, in contrast to Italian. If Lorenzo assumed that subject *pro* was possible in French, just like in his L1, he would overextend the use of *que* in subject relative contexts, contrary to fact.

16.2 CP-clauses in adult L2 French

As with child learners, adult learners use questions and embedded clauses quite early in their acquisition process. However, according to some researchers, it is not entirely clear that the first interrogatives are fully analysed by the learners, especially when learning is mostly taking place in formal settings. Learners are reported to struggle more with wh-questions that involve a deeply embedded wh-phrase than with other types of questions. Finally, inversion may also cause problems for adult L2 French learners.

16.2.1 Development of matrix interrogatives in adult L2 French

Studies based on production data show that wh-questions are sometimes produced even by adult learners whose proficiency level is deemed to be quite low. Prévost (1997) reports early questions for some of the immigrant workers living in France who were interviewed as part of the European Science Foundation project on L2 acquisition (Perdue 1984). Although these learners had been in France for a year or so before they were recorded for the first time, they were reported to have had little contact with French. It can therefore be assumed that the data reflect the very early stages of acquisition. Prévost (1997) analysed the production data of two of these workers, Abdelmalek and Zahra, both native speakers of Moroccan Arabic (MA), and reported that questions are productively used in the earliest recording samples. Other studies also show early use of interrogatives. For example, of the nine English-speaking learners at the beginner level interviewed by Prévost (2003a, 2004), eight produced interrogatives, as illustrated in (13). Since question formation was not the focus of investigation of this study, specific details of the acquisition of questions are not available.

(13) a. Je poser une question? (Morgan, L1=English, Beginner)
I ask.INF a question

b. Vous conduire? (Frank 1, L1=English, Beginner)
you drive.INF

Importantly, the learners were interviewed only one to two months after taking a placement test that established their status as beginner learners. Thus, they were in the very early stages of acquisition and were producing interrogatives within a couple of months of the beginning of formal instruction. These learners lived in a francophone community, so they had access to French outside the classroom, which may have sped up the acquisition process.

Some researchers challenge the productivity of the first questions used by L2 learners. Myles, Mitchell & Hooper (1999) looked at the acquisition of questions in L2 French by 16 English-speaking adolescents over the first two years of their exposure to the target language. Acquisition was taking place in a classroom setting within a non-francophone community. At first, students learned a small set of questions that they used routinely regardless of their appropriateness to the context. These may be called 'routine' questions or chunks. In their experiments, the authors paired their informants and asked them to engage in semi-spontaneous dialogues based on information-gap tasks and family photographs. Recordings took place six times over two years. Three types of questions were used by the learners: routines, as in (14), verbless questions (15), and verbal questions (16), in which the verb was either finite or nonfinite. The incidence of each question type is given in Table 2.

(14) a. Quel âge as- tu that one? (Pupil 24, L1=English, rec 2)
what age have you that one
'How old is that one?'

b. Mon petit garçon euh où habites-tu? (Pupil 45, L1=English, rec 2)
my little boy umm where live you
'Where does your little boy live?'

c. Comment t' appelles-tu la fille? (Pupil 51, L1=English, rec 5)
how yourself call you the girl
'What's the girl's name?'

(15) a. Où la plage? (Pupil 24, L1=English, rec 4)
where the beach

b. Jaune? (Pupil 27, L1=English, rec 3)
yellow

c. La dame à la stade? (Pupil 51, L1=English, rec 5)
the woman at the stadium

(16) a. Je manger douze heures? (Pupil 2, L1=English, rec 4)
I eat.INF twelve o'clock

b. Tu et moi visiter le cinéma? (Pupil 2, L1=English, rec 6)
you and me visit.INF the cinema

c. La mère regarde euh lire euh la petite frère
the mother look.FIN read.INF the little brother

et soeur euh fêchent (=pêchent)? (Pupil 38, rec 6)
and sister fish.FIN

Table 2. Question formation in L2 French (L1=English) (from Myles et al. 1999)

Interrogative type	Sample 1	Sample 6
Verbal chunks	77%	15%
Verbless questions	22%	69%
Verbal questions (creative)	1%	16%

Myles et al. argue that at first, questions are untensed: they either contain no verb or they are routines. At sample 6, the incidence of verbal questions has increased, although many verbs appear in the infinitive. The incidence of routine questions has gone down, but verbless questions are on the rise. This is taken as an indication that the learners appeal less and less to formulaic expressions; in other words, they are more and more creative. For Myles et al. the L2 acquisition of questions in French proceeds as follows: (a) verbless questions, (b) nonfinite questions, and (c) finite questions. To this development, an initial stage of routine questions must be added (see also Myles 2004).

One factor that seems to cause difficulty in the L2 acquisition of questions is the level of embedding of the wh-phrase. It seems that the deeper the level of embedding, the more difficult it is for learners to process questions. Myles (1995) administered a repetition task to 78 first-year undergraduates who had studied French for seven years in the UK. The test consisted in 20 sentences differing in the level of embedding of the wh-phrase, from level 1 (least embedded) to level 4 (most embedded), as illustrated in (17).

(17) a. Level 1: Dans quel livre Zola dépeint-il la vie des mineurs __?
'In which book does Zola describe minors' life?'

b. Level 2: À quoi les publicitaires attachent une grande importance __?
'To what do advertisors grant importance?'

c. Level 3: Dans la maison de qui les adolescents du quartier se réfugient-ils __?
'In whose house do local teenagers find refuge?'

d. Level 4: De la maîtresse de qui Cécile provoque-t-elle le suicide __?
'Of whose lover does Cecile cause the suicide?'

The results show that the learners were more prone to commit errors in their repetitions as the level of embedding increased. In particular, they tended to omit the subject of the question (*Cécile* in (17d)) significantly more often in level 4 interrogatives than in any other questions. A significant difference was also observed between level 3 on the one hand, and levels 1 and 2 on the other. This is summarized in Table 3.

Table 3. Percentage of omitted subjects in wh-questions according to the level of embedding of the wh-phrase across 78 L2 French learners (from Myles 1995)

Level of embedding	Subject omission
1	10.43%
2	9.78%
3	17.39%
4 or more	51.30%

Interestingly, significant differences were obtained on questions in which the wh-word has similar syntactic functions. In (17c) and (17d), for instance, the wh-phrase is genitive, but it appears at two different levels of embedding. The difference in the answer patterns suggests that the source of the difficulty is not the nature of the question type, but the level of embedding of the wh-phrase. Note that the results cannot be attributed to sentence length either, given that level 4 questions were in general shorter than level 3 questions.

Another aspect of questions that may cause problems to L2 French learners is inversion. As seen in Section 13.1.2, there are different types of inversion in French, which may be confusing to the learners. Hulk (1996) investigated knowledge of inversion in L2 French among native speakers of Dutch. Dutch is a V2 language, in which the verb must occupy the second position in root clauses (see Section 4.2.2.2). In non-subject interrogatives, this means that the tensed verbal element (the main verb or the auxiliary) appears in second position, in front of the subject. In other words, inversion between the tensed verb and the subject is systematic in Dutch non-subject interrogatives, as illustrated in (18).

(18) a. Was lust Jan niet?
what likes John not
'What doesn't John like?'

b. Wanneer heeft Jan aardbeien gegeten?
when has John strawberries eaten
'When did John eat strawberries?'

In non-V2 languages, such as French, there is no V2 requirement. In non-subject wh-questions, for instance, the verb may appear in front of the subject (which is a V2 order), as in cases of clitic/verb inversion, but it does not have to. Finally, as seen in Section 13.1.2.3, French wh-questions may also display stylistic inversion. In such cases, the subject remains in the VP (but see Kayne & Pollock (2001) for an alternative proposal). The 20 L2 French learners who participated in Hulk's (1996) study were at the advanced level (after 5 or 6 years of French at school). Their knowledge of the [-V2] property of French was investigated via a grammaticality judgment task containing several types of wh-questions:

(19) a. Inversion with lexical subjects:

*Quand écoute Jean la radio?
when listens+to John the radio

b. No inversion:

Pourquoi Jean a mangé les fraises?
why John has eaten the strawberries

c. Stylistic inversion:

Quand est parti le train?
when is left the train

d. Inversion with subject clitics:

Quand avons-nous regardé la télévision?
when have we watched television

e. Complex inversion:

Pourquoi Jean a-t-il regardé la télévision?
why John has he watched the television

The results are reported in Table 4. The learners made different judgments on inversion with a full DP and with a clitic subject, clearly preferring inversion with a clitic, which suggests some movement towards the grammaticality judgments of the target language. That said, most learners did still accept the (ungrammatical) wh-V-DP order, a result that may be influenced by the V-DP order found in the target language with stylistic inversion. The low performance on questions without inversion (40%) suggests that the learners preferred inversion. Similarly, low performance on stylistic inversion (40%) suggests that the learners have not yet abandoned the V2 property of their L1.

Table 4. Acceptance rates of different types of inversion in wh-questions in adult L2 French (L1=Dutch) (from Hulk 1996)

Inversion type	Acceptance rate
*Inversion with nominal subjects	60%
Inversion with clitics	100%
No inversion	40%
Stylistic inversion	40%
Complex inversion	100%

*Ungrammatical in French

16.2.2 Development of embedded clauses and relative clauses in adult L2 French

Like wh-questions, embedded clauses are reported to develop relatively early in adult L2 French. While the first complex utterances involve juxtapositions with connectors such as *et* 'and', *mais* 'but', and *puis* 'then', subordinate clauses emerge rapidly. They are first introduced by causal and temporal complementizers such as *parce que* 'because' and *quand* 'when' (see Bartning & Schlyter 2004). Relative clauses are also among the first biclausals; they are introduced by *que* and *qui*.

(20) a. eh eh quand il euh prend les ballons il descenD…
when he takes the balloons he goes+down
(Carin, L1=Swedish)

b. J' étudier avec un homme qui s' appelle NN.
I study.INF with a man who himself calls NN
(Pelle, Int 2, L1=Swedish)

Bartning & Schlyter (2004) further state that complementizer *si* 'if' and embedded clauses introduced by *que* 'that' emerge later on. This developmental trend needs further investigation involving different combinations of languages.

Hawkins (1989) looked at English-speaking learners' acquisition of French restrictive relative clauses. In particular, he looked at knowledge of the morphology of relative pronouns (*que, qui,* and *dont*) in relation to the animacy of the head noun, and at the extraction site, given the possibility of stylistic inversion in French (see (21a) and (21b)) and the fact that genitive *dont* can be used with nouns in subject and object position, as in (22a) and (22b).

(21) a. L'homme [que Jean connaît __].
the man that John knows

b. L'homme [que connaît __ Jean].
'The man that John knows.'

(22) a. L'homme [dont le nom __ m'échappe].
the man whose the name me eludes
'The man whose name eludes me.'

b. L'homme [dont j'ai oublié le nom __].
the man whose I have forgotten the name
'The name whose name I have forgotten.'

The idea is that if L2 learners are guided by superficial mechanisms, they should find it more difficult to process sentences with a long distance between the relative pronoun and the gap, as in (22b), than those with a short one, as in (22a). They should also find it easier to process subject RCs (with *qui*) than object RCs (with *que*). Furthermore, selection of the relative pronoun should be affected by distance. Specifically, in object RCs displaying stylistic inversion, as in (21b), learners should tend (incorrectly) to use *qui* rather than *que* since the relative pronoun is close to the verb, as in subject RCs. This should not occur in object RCs displaying SV, as in (21a), since the subject intervenes between the relative pronoun and the verb. Learners should thus select *que* in this context. If, on the other hand, learning is guided by considerations of grammatical relations, the distance should not cause the learners any difficulty, since the same grammatical relation is found in both pairs of sentences, direct object in (21a–b) and genitive complement in (22a–b). The learners were native speakers of English, where there is no *qui/que* alternation and no stylistic inversion, and where the genitive relative pronoun cannot be extracted from its NP (e.g. **The man whose I forgot the name__*). A written elicited production task forcing the production of relative pronouns was administered to 119 learners divided into three groups depending on their numbers of years of formal instruction in French. The results in Table 5 show that accuracy was highest on *qui*, followed by *que*, and then *dont*. The lower performance on *qui* by the least proficient learners is explained by a tendency restricting the use of *qui* to animate head nouns. This strategy disappears as of Group 2.

Table 5. Accuracy rate at providing target-like relative pronouns in adult L2 French (L1=English) (from Hawkins 1989)

Relative clause	**Group 1** (5 years) (n=25)	**Group 2** (7 years) (n=50)	**Group 3** (8 years) (n=44)
Subject (*qui*) (n=13)	35.7%	92.5%	95.1%
Direct object (*que*) (n=22)	44.2%	74.6%	82.5%
Genitive (*dont*) (n=16)	30.3%	59.8%	60.4%

Table 6 shows that all learners were sensitive to the distance between the gap and the relative pronoun. With *dont*, the shorter the distance, the better the performance, which is reminiscent of the findings in child L1 French (see Section 14.3). With *que*, performance was higher when the object gap occurred after the SV sequence. Interestingly, performance on *que* increased with proficiency in the stylistic inversion context, and Hawkins also reports an animacy effect: accuracy was much higher with inanimate head nouns than with animate ones.

Table 6. Accuracy rate at providing target-like relative pronouns according to the distance between the extraction site and the relative pronoun in adult L2 French (L1=English) (from Hawkins 1989)

Relative clause		**Group 1** (5 years) (n=25)	**Group 2** (7 years) (n=50)	**Group 3** (8 years) (n=44)
que	No inversion (n=22)	44.2%	74.6%	82.5%
	Styl. Inversion (n= 8)	30.5%	39%	47.4%
dont	Subject (n=8)	32.5%	67.8%	71.3%
	Object (n=8)	28%	51.8%	49.9%

Although accuracy at providing the target relative pronouns according to the distance between the gap and the relative pronoun stems from a combination of grammatical effects (to the extent that performance with inanimate head nouns is high) and non-grammatical ones (since learners seem to prefer a shorter distance between the relative pronoun and the gap), it would be useful to supplement these findings with results from other tasks, such as comprehension tasks and on-line reading tests (see Juffs & Harrington 1995, 1996; Papadopoulou & Clahsen 2003). The tests should also be administered to native speakers of French, which Hawkins did not do in his study.

16.2.3 Other properties of interrogatives and subordinates in adult L2 French

In contrast to what we saw with child L2 French, adults frequently produce nonfinite verbs in questions and embedded clauses. This tendency is reported in various learning contexts, such as English/French, MA/French, and Swedish/French (Bartning & Schlyter 2004; Prévost 1997; Prévost & White 2000a,b). This is illustrated in the examples in (13) and (16a–b) above, and in (23) below.

(23) a. parce qu'il trouver le sable rapide. (Jane 6, L1=English)
because he find.INF the sand quick

b. … quand ils ouvrir les cadeaux. (Kate, L1=English, Int 2)
when they open.INF the presents

c. Des artistes qui faire des choses musicales.
some artists who do.INF some things musical
(Dorothy, L1=English, Int 4)

d. combien tu rester ici? (Abdelmalek, L1=MA, month 24)
how (long) you stay-INF here

e. et Malika, pourquoi téléphoner à toi à la maison?
and Malika why call-INF to you at the house
(Zahra, L1=MA, mth 38.5)

The other difference between child and adult learners of L2 French with respect to questions and embedded clauses is that adults produce clauses with null subjects whereas children rarely do so. The possibility of null subjects in the adult data seems to be related to properties of the L1, particularly the *pro*-drop property. In Section 8.2.2.1, we saw that null subjects were more frequent in the speech of MA-speaking learners than in that of English-speaking learners. This is illustrated in (24). Confirmation of this finding should be investigated in other language combinations.

(24) quand toujours dort (Zahra, L1=MA, month 21.7)
when always sleep.FIN

In child data, null subjects are rarely found in questions or embedded clauses, even when the L1 is a null subject language such as Italian (see Belletti & Hamann 2004). However, it could be the case that the child investigated by Belletti and Hamann was too advanced at the time of his first interview. More research is therefore necessary with children whose L1 allows null subjects, and have had little prior exposure to French.

16.2.4 Theoretical implications

The debate concerning the early presence of C in IL grammars constructed by adult learners is fierce. On the one hand, early production of questions and embedded clauses suggests to some researchers that knowledge of the CP system is present in early L2 French, possibly caused by transfer from the L1. On the other hand, the fact that some of the early questions may be simple routines or chunks is enough to challenge this conclusion for other researchers. As seen in Section 4.2.1.4, Myles (2004) proposes that, at least initially, chunks have no syntactic representations; rather, they are simple mappings between semantic representations and phonological strings, for instance [ask name] = [*Comment t'appelles-tu?* lit. 'How refl+2SG call you?'] regardless of whether the person whose name is being asked is the interlocutor (in which case the sentence is correctly formed) or not (in which case the reflexive pronoun and the subject are wrongly used). Myles et al. (1999) argue that the use of chunks may change over time. They may first be inappropriately used and overextended, as described above and in (14c) (where target-like *Comment s'appelle-t-elle?* lit. 'How refl+3SG call she?' should be produced), and then gradually be modified to more closely resemble the target utterance. For instance, the learner may first add an NP (e.g. *Comment t'appelles-tu la fille?* lit. 'How refl+2SG call you the girl?') to indicate that the question is not directed at the interlocutor, then omit the inadequate subject, and finally produce the target-like utterance. The problem is that while this developmental sequence may well exist, it is difficult to situate it with respect to the development of phrase structure proposed by Myles (2004) (VP > IP > CP). Does the breaking down of chunks precede the development of phrase structure or does it happen in parallel? It is difficult to see how to reconcile the breaking down of chunks such as *Comment t'appelles-tu?* with the four stages proposed by Myles et al.: (a) routines, (b) verbless questions, (c) nonfinite questions, and (d) finite questions.

The debate often turns on the definition of routines and the theoretical use one wants to make of them. For example, the questions in (14) are all correctly formed from the perspective of the target language: some of them involve wh-movement and clitic/verb inversion. It could very well be, and frequently is, the case that such questions are used in the wrong context, a criterion normally used to determine whether an interrogative can be considered a routine. But although they may be wrongly used, they still are questions displaying a preposed wh-word and they are clearly used with an interrogative intention. Should they therefore be utterly dismissed in the discussion of early knowledge of C? Or should they be considered evidence for the projection of C?

Another area of debate in the literature is the assumption that initial IL grammars only contain lexical categories (via transfer from the L1, as argued in Vainikka & Young-Scholten (1994), for example) and that functional categories develop only later. Some researchers have questioned why, in principle, lexical categories should be the only ones transferring to the L1. To Schwartz and Sprouse (1996), for example, this seems cognitively implausible:

> 'Moreover, consider the idea that structures, such as VP (cf. Vainikka & Young-Scholten [1994, 1996]) and IP (cf. Eubank [1993, 1994]), are the results of module interactions – i.e. in the words of Chomsky and Lasnik (1993: 513), they are 'descriptive artifacts'; from such a vantage point, it does not seem to be plausible, in cognitive terms, that these structures could be 'excerpted' from the cognitive state, namely, from the L1 grammar. Indeed, it is difficult to imagine what sort of cognitive mechanism would be involved in extracting a proper subpart from the L1 grammar and using that proper subpart as the basis of a new cognitive state' (p. 66).

Syntax theory and computation considerations may also account for the development of wh-questions and relative clauses. We saw that the level of embedding of the wh-phrase could affect performance in the production of wh-questions. Myles (1995) argues that beginner learners can only deal with low-level processes, presumably because of constraints on short-term memory operations. Therefore, they have difficulties establishing a chain between a wh-phrase and its trace, regardless of the syntactic role of the phrase in the sentence. As competence increases and operations become more automatic, learners are able to establish chains involving deeper levels of embedding; that is, they can process more complex operations. In Hawkins' (1989) study of L2 acquisition of French relative clauses, learning combines innate knowledge of grammatical relations, such as subject and object, movement, and binding, and increasing processing capacities. L2 learners need to figure out, among other things, from which positions relativization takes place in the target language. According to Hawkins' account, parsing first involves the most adjacent category, and relates nonadjacent categories only later on. Many studies discussed throughout this book have appealed to the weight of the processing load to account for learners' behaviour – crucially without denying knowledge of underlying properties. However, Myles' and Hawkins' studies suffer from important methodological shortcomings. In Myles' (1995) study, the data were elicited via imitation, which has often been criticized in the literature because it is not clear what this technique truly tests: linguistic competence or memory ability. Moreover, no control group of native speakers was tested in either Myles' or Hawkins' studies, so there is no baseline against which to truly evaluate the learners' performance. The relationship between processing load and the acquisition of wh-questions and relative clauses in French L2 acquisition thus awaits further investigation.

Finally, the occurrence of nonfinite CP-clauses in adult L2 data are compatible with a Missing Surface Inflection approach to root infinitives, but not with a Truncation analysis. According to the Missing Surface Inflection Hypothesis, L2 learners have difficulty accessing inflectional morphology or mapping syntax and morphology, which results in the production of default verbal forms that frequently take the shape of infinitival verbs. Under this analysis, there is in principle no restriction on the type of clause in which this problem should occur: it could be found in root declaratives, as well as in root interrogatives and embedded clauses. This is not true of the Truncation approach, according to which the erroneous occurrence of nonfinite forms is related to the projection of a reduced representation, specifically a representation from which the functional projections underlying finiteness are missing. This approach also holds that all projections located below the root should be part of the representation. In particular, if CP is the root, AgrP and TP should be projected, which should prevent the occurrence of nonfinite forms in such clauses. Although the data from child L2 acquisition support this hypothesis, the data from adult L2 French acquisition presented earlier in this chapter do not: nonfinite forms occur in CP clauses in adult L2 French, thus contradicting the predictions of the Truncation approach.

In addition to the general question of the presence of functional categories in initial L2 grammars, there is the question of the acquisition of their features, given that languages may display parametric differences with respect to these properties. At stake is whether parametric values may be reset in adult L2 acquisition or not. One of the parameters related to the properties of C that has been investigated in L2 acquisition of French is the V2 parameter. According to this parameter, languages differ in whether or not C possesses Infl characteristics. When C possesses Infl characteristics, as in languages such as Dutch and German, verb movement to C is obligatory (in root declaratives and in non-subject wh-questions); when it does not, as in French, verb movement may stop in I. Another characteristic of French C is that it cannot assign Case to lexical subjects, in contrast to Dutch. We saw that in Hulk's (1996) study, Dutch learners of French strongly prefer inversion with a subject clitic over inversion with a lexical NP. This suggests that the learners do not apply V2 systematically. It also suggests that they make the distinction between the two types of elements as far as Case assignment is concerned. In other words, they have acquired the Case assignment restrictions in French. That these learners have knowledge of the non-V2 property of French is reinforced by Hulk's (1991) study involving the same advanced learners who were tested on knowledge of topicalization in French (see Section 4.2.2.2). In Dutch, topicalization involves movement of the topicalized element to SpecCP and movement of the verb to C (hence V2); in French, topicalization can be achieved via adjunction to IP, with the verb moving to I and the subject appearing in SpecIP (hence V3). As seen in Section 4.2.2.2, the results of Hulk's (1991) study show that the V3 order is largely accepted by the more advanced learners, which suggests that parameter resetting is possible in L2 acquisition, contra Hawkins & Chan (1997) and Tsimpli & Roussou (1991). Returning to Hulk's investigation of knowledge of inversion in French wh-questions, we saw that some learners do allow verb movement to C when the subject is a lexical NP. Assuming Rizzi's (1991) Wh-Criterion for the derivation of questions (see Section 13.1.4), Hulk concludes that these learners may think that V2 is the only way to satisfy this criterion in French. This would also explain the low performance on non-inverted questions. In other words, these learners have not yet acquired the fact that the Wh-Criterion may be satisfied via other means in French, in particular via Dynamic Agreement.

16.2.5 The syntax/semantics interface in adult L2 French

Knowledge of rules underlying question formation, such as wh-movement, can also be investigated via their semantic consequences. Consider, for example, interrogatives including the sequence *qui de* 'who of' followed by an adjectival phrase. Such a sequence can appear as a continuous or discontinuous stretch, as in (25a) and (25b). When the sequence is discontinuous, the verb intervenes between the wh-phrase and the sequence *de*+AP.

(25)	a.	Qui	de	célèbre	fumait	au	bistro	dans	les	années	60?
		who	of	famous	smoked	in+the	bar	in	the	years	60's
	b.	Qui	fumait	de	célèbre	au	bistro	dans	les	années	60?
		who	smoked	of	famous	in+the	bar	in	the	years	60's
		'Which famous person/people smoked in bars in the 60's?'									

The questions in (25a) and (25b) have different interpretations, as explained by Dekydtspotter & Sprouse (2001). In (25a), the adjective *célèbre* refers to either the set of individuals famous at the time of speech or the set of individuals famous in the past, namely in the 60's. In (25b), *célèbre* can only refer to the set of individuals famous in the past; its interpretation cannot include those individuals famous at the time of speech (unless they were also famous in the past). The difference in interpretation stems from the structure of the interrogatives and in particular from the movements that have occurred. In (25a), the whole sequence *qui de célèbre* has moved from a VP internal position to the specifier of CP. It therefore has scope over the whole sentence. Crucially, *célèbre* is not within the scope of (past) T, so the restriction can be interpreted either over or under T. Hence, the question can refer to individuals in the past or at the speech time. In (25b), only *qui* has been extracted from the VP and has moved to SpecCP; *célèbre* is left in the VP, within the scope of T. The restriction can therefore only be interpreted under T, which means that only individuals famous in the past can be referred to.

In Section 12.2.2, where we looked at the L2 acquisition of the semantic consequences of adjective placement, we saw that this constitutes a poverty-of-the-stimulus learning phenomenon which offers direct insight into the availability of UG in L2 acquisition. The same can be said of the acquisition of *qui de AP* questions: not only are these types of questions ungrammatical in English, as shown in (26), they are also not taught in French classrooms, and instructors are generally quite unaware of the interpretational properties of continuous versus discontinuous interrogatives.

(26) a. *Who of famous smoked in bars in the 60's?

b. *Who smoked of famous in bars in the 60's?

If English-speaking learners of French show sensitivity to the different interpretation of continuous versus discontinuous *qui de AP* interrogatives, then this cannot stem from knowledge acquired through instruction or from the L1. Presumably, it can only have come from UG.

Dekydtspotter & Sprouse (2001) administered a truth-value interpretation task similar to the one discussed in Section 12.2.2 to 47 intermediate and 11 advanced learners of French, as well as to two control groups. The learners were all native speakers of English. The task contained a series of scenarios in English meant to establish the time reference of the adjective (past time or speech time). Each scenario was followed by either a continuous or a discontinuous *qui de AP* interrogative asked by a fictive character, Mme Goyette (a teacher). An answer to this question then appeared, provided by a pupil. The participants had to decide whether the answer was correct or not (answering either 'yes' or 'no'), given the scenario provided. An example is given in (27). Two characters are introduced in the scenario: one famous in the past (Herman the Hermit) and one famous in the present (Linda Tripp). In (27), the question is continuous. Therefore, the adjective *célèbre* can apply to either character. The answer provided by the pupil – *Herman the Hermit* – is correct; *Linda Tripp* would also have been correct.

(27) Attitudes toward smoking have changed drastically since the 1960s. In the 1960s many people would go to bars and smoke every night. For example, Herman the Hermit was a famous rock star in those days and was often seen at bars smoking with Linda Tripp, who was then totally unknown. How times have changed! It is Linda Tripp who is famous, and neither of them smokes any more.
Mrs. Goyette: Qui de célèbre fumait au bistro durant les années 60?
Pupil: Herman the Hermit

The same scenario can be used with a discontinuous interrogative, as in (28), where the adjective can only refer to the character famous in the past, i.e. *Herman the Hermit*. Hence, the answer given by the pupil in (28), *Linda Tripp*, is incorrect.

(28) Mrs. Goyette: Qui fumait de célèbre au bistro durant les années 60?
Pupil: Linda Tripp

There were a total of 32 test items: eight scenarios which each appeared four times in the test, twice associated with a continuous interrogative, and twice with a discontinuous interrogative, and each question was paired with either a speech time answer or a past time answer. The results on the test items are presented in Table 7.

Table 7. Percentage of 'Yes' answers on speech time and past time interpretations of discontinuous vs. continuous interrogatives provided by each group (from Dekydtspotter & Sprouse 2001)

Group	**Interrogative**	**Speech time interpretation**	**Past time interpretation**
Intermediate (n= 47)	Continuous	41.22%*	90.69%
	Discontinuous	25%	90.69%
Advanced (n=11)	Continuous	46.59%*	79.55%
	Discontinuous	15.90%	90.90%
French Controls (n=30)	Continuous	12.50%	88.75%*
	Discontinuous	5%	96.25%
English Controls (n=23)	Continuous	30.98%	86.95%
	Discontinuous	22.28%	86.95%

* Significant difference between continous and discontinous interrogatives

As far as acceptance of past time answers is concerned, there were no significant differences between continuous and discontinuous interrogatives for the learners. However, the learners showed a significant preference for speech time answers with continuous interrogatives compared to discontinuous ones. This difference seems to be established quite early, given that it is observed in the intermediates (although it is more pronounced in the advanced group). The French controls' performance was slightly different from the learners'. In particular, there was no significant difference between continuous and discontinuous interrogatives for speech time answers in the French native speakers, although the results point toward a preference for the continuous option. This result suggests that the evidence the learners may have had from the input in order to develop their intuitions was quite weak. A significant difference within the French controls was observed with the past time interpretation answer, however; they showed a significant preference for discontinuous questions. In the English-speaking control group (who were administered a literal translation of the test) no statistically significant differences were found between continuous and discontinuous interrogatives with either interpretation. Particularly revealing is the fact that no significant difference was observed with speech time answers. This suggests that the learners' performance was not influenced by their L1. Altogether, the results demonstrate target-like knowledge of the semantic consequences of continuous versus discontinuous *qui de + AP* questions, which strongly suggests that UG is still active in adult L2 acquisition.[220]

16.3 Conclusion

Both child and adult L2 learners of French produce interrogatives in the early phases of acquisition. In child data, the first questions are often predicative, as is the case in L1 child French. Wh-words are almost never omitted and are largely preposed initially. This suggests that C is available to child L2 learners, possibly as a result of transfer from the L1. However, many of these first questions could be formulaic and be literal translations of L1 questions. In elicited production, wh-fronting and clitic/verb inversion are not very frequent, which suggests that L2 children are sensitive to computational complexity, regardless of the properties of their L1.

The fact that embedded clauses seem to be delayed with respect to interrogatives, as is the case in child L1 French, does not necessarily call early knowledge of C into question, as the appropriate contexts for complement clauses, as well as the different forms of complementizers, must be learned. The delay may therefore arise from something independent of the appropriate functional apparatus. This should be investigated with further research. Another area requiring further research is the development of relative clauses, about which very little is known. Current data only deals with the

220. Native-like judgments were also obtained from English-speaking learners of French in a similar truth-value judgment task focusing on another construction involving wh-movement and scope interpretation (Dekydtspotter, Sprouse & Swanson 2001). These constructions display *combien* 'how much/many' extraction. Compare (i) and (ii), which have a quantified object. In (i), the whole object has been preposed, presumably to SpecCP; in (ii), only *combien* has been preposed with the rest of object remaining in its base-generated position.

(i) [$_{DP}$ Combien de livres]$_i$ les étudiants ont- ils tous acheté t$_i$?
how+many of books the students have they all bought
'How many books did all the students buy?'

(ii) [$_{QP}$ Combien$_i$] les étudiants ont- ils tous acheté [$_{DP}$ t$_i$ de livres]?
how+many the students have they all bought of books
'How many books did all the students buy?'

In French, both narrow and wide scope interpretations can obtain with continuous *combien* extraction, but only wide scope can obtain with its discontinuous counterpart. In English, only continuous extraction is allowed (compare the gloss in (i) to the ungrammaticality of **How many did all the students buy of books?*). Dekydtspotter et al. (2001) show that the L2 learners accepted wide scope to a significantly higher extent with continuous *combien* extraction than with the discontinuous version.

apparent success in learning the *qui/que* alternation, but there is little information about the actual development process of the clauses in which it appears.

Interestingly, very few nonfinite verbs and null subjects are found in the interrogative and embedded clauses produced by child L2 French learners, in contrast to what is observed in their main declaratives. This difference, we saw, tends to support the analysis of child IL grammars in terms of Truncation or Structural Economy.

The presence of C in early adult L2 grammars can also be argued for, based not only on adult learners' use of interrogatives, but also on their early production of embedded clauses. However, the early availability of C in adult L2 learners' initial underlying IL grammars is challenged by the interpretation of their first interrogatives as formulaic expressions without any syntactic structure. Under this view, adult learners' first interrogatives are assumed to be phonological strings mapped to particular semantic representations, such as [ask name] = [*Comment tu t'appelles?*]. Although such utterances may be incorrect from the perspective of the target language and may truly represent learners' initial efforts to break into a communicative mode, they could still be analysed as projections of CPs that are used in a deviant manner from the perspective of the target language. The extent to which apparent routines are used should be further investigated, in particular in child L2 learning, to see whether there are differences between child and adult learners. The incidence of such utterances may also depend on the learning context and could be lower when learning takes place within a francophone environment than when French is not the language of the community.

Another property of adult interrogatives and embedded clauses is that also different from child L2 learners they may involve nonfinite forms. This suggests that adult IL grammars are not organized according to Truncation (or Structural Economy); rather, as previously seen in this book, the most likely hypothesis for adult grammars is Categorial Uniformity. The use of nonfinite forms by adult learners is in fact consistent with the Missing Surface Inflection Hypothesis according to which underlying functional categories are present in IL grammars even though target-like inflectional morphology may not be systematically used.

Finally, we saw that research on the acquisition of wh-questions in L2 French can provide evidence for the availability of UG in adult L2 acquisition. This is made clear in the research on parameter resetting, as in the case of knowledge of inversion by Dutch native speakers, and on knowledge of semantic interpretation of particular interrogatives (such as *qui de AP...?* questions). Such syntax/semantics interface phenomena represent true poverty-of-the-stimulus situations, in which the L2 learners' knowledge stems neither from the L1 nor from explicit teaching. Research on such learning situations should be pursued, as advocated by Schwartz & Sprouse (2000).

Conclusion

This book has looked at the development of French acquisition in different learning situations: L1 French by typically developing monolingual children, bilingual children, and children with SLI, and L2 French by children and adults. In so doing, it has explored the content of the grammars constructed by the learners during the acquisition process in four main domains: the verbal domain, the pronominal domain, the nominal domain, and the CP domain. Some of the questions raised are common to all these areas, such as the status of functional categories and their features in developing grammars, while others are specific to one domain, such as knowledge of constraints on wh-movement and knowledge of binding. Some of the questions raised also apply to all learning situations, while others are specific to a particular context in which acquisition is taking place. For example, whether developing grammars are UG-constrained is a question for debate in L2 acquisition but it is taken for granted in L1 acquisition, and the issue of language dominance is specific to bilingual acquisition contexts. This concluding chapter begins by identifying some of the main contributions of the research on the acquisition of French to the general field of language acquisition, then compares the research on the different learning situations within the four domains investigated, occasionally identifying remaining problems that should be resolved by further investigation, and finally, explores general avenues for future research in the acquisition of French.

Some of the main contributions of the studies on the acquisition of French

By and large, studies on the acquisition of French show that functional categories are available to learners initially (in contrast to proposals for L1 acquisition, such as Radford (1990), or for second language acquisition, such as Vainikka & Young-Scholten (1994, 1996, 2005), although, among the different categories, the status of C is the most difficult to establish in early grammars. There is also evidence that underlying grammars are constrained by UG principles, as evidenced, in the case of children, by early knowledge of the constraints underlying wh-movement and binding. In general, then, the findings support the Strong Continuity Hypothesis for language development.

The data also suggest that UG remains accessible to adult L2 learners, in contrast to Bley-Vroman (1990), Clahsen (1988), and Meisel (1997), among others. This is particularly evident in the studies showing that properties at the interface between syntax and semantics can be acquired, such as *qui de AP* questions and the semantic consequence of adjective placement, which are not explicitly taught and are absent from the L1. In addition, studies of very advanced learners suggest that parameter resetting is possible (contra Hawkins et al. 1993; Smith & Tsimpli 1995; Tsimpli & Roussou 1991), as in the case of the verb movement parameter despite early struggles with adverbs and quantifiers. The same can be said of the acquisition of noun movement and subject/verb inversion in French (by Dutch speakers). Finally, target-like behavior with respect to gender can be reached. All this suggests that parameter resetting can be achieved in adult L2 acquisition, and that (uninterpretable) features only activated in the L2 can be acquired, in contrast to proposals by Hawkins & Liszka (2003) and Hawkins & Hattori (2006).

Research on early development in child learners suggests that the processes of language acquisition in monolinguals, bilinguals, SLI children, and child L2 learners are all very similar. In particular, computational complexity seems to play an important role initially for children in the different acquisition contexts, which may explain why root infinitives are produced despite early knowledge of functional categories, and why object clitics are delayed with respect to nominative pronouns. Children seem to adopt Rizzi's (2000) Structural Economy Principle early on, according to which the least amount of structure should be projected. This principle may be related to computational limitations or to restricted working memory capacity. In more recent proposals, structural economy has been defined in terms of the number of chains that a derivation involves; specifically, a derivation requiring *n* chains is assumed to be less complex than a derivation requiring *n*+1 chains. Moreover, merging an element *n* times (externally or internally) is less complex than merging an element (*n*+1) times (see Jakubowicz 2004, 2005; Jakubowicz & Nash 2001). Complexity of derivation has been argued to be most challenging for children with SLI, whose problems with acquisition are similar to those of TD children but persist for a longer time. Structural Economy seems also to be an active principle in child L2 acquisition, although perhaps to a lesser extent.

Research on acquisition of French has also helped to disconfirm some hypotheses on early development. For example, the fact that nonfinite verbs rarely appear in CP-clauses in TD monolinguals and bilinguals is a challenge to Wexler's (1998) Unique Checking Constraint hypothesis. In addition, the lack of any strong link between the development of determiners, finiteness, and object clitics, while compatible with Structural Economy, is difficult to explain with hypotheses such as the underspecification of Number (Hoekstra & Hyams 1998) or the underspecification of specificity (Schaeffer 1997, 2000). In the case of children with SLI, the French data suggests that impairment does not stem from an absence of functional categories in their grammar (contra Gopnik 1990), from inherent difficulties with movement (contra van der Lely 1998), or from perception difficulties (contra Leonard 1998). Additionally, there is no relationship between the appearance of object clitics and the end of the RI period in this population, which again argues against the UCC. Research on bilingual children learning French strongly suggests that each language has its own system from the outset, which clashes with proposals by Volterra & Taeschner (1978). Whether production in French is target-like or non-target-like seems to be independent of the properties of the other language being used, which does not mean that cross-linguistic influence is ruled out. Interestingly, cross-linguistic influence is not necessarily related to language dominance (contra Schlyter 1997), as in the case of object drop.

Finally, French L2 data show interesting differences between child and adult learners (see also Schwartz 2003). For example, adult learners seem to follow the Categorial Uniformity Principle (Rizzi 2000), according to which a unique canonical structural realization is assumed for a given semantic type. This is particularly obvious in their treatment of RIs, clitics, and determiners. In other words, they do not seem to adopt Structural Economy, in contrast to child L2 learners. Adult L2 production data are also compatible with the Missing Surface Inflection Hypothesis, according to which adult L2 learners may have problems mapping syntax and morphology or accessing the relevant morphology (Epstein et al. 1996; Lardiere 1998, 2000; Prévost & White 20001b; Schwartz & Sprouse 1996). This means that their RIs are finite, in contrast to child RIs which have nonfinite properties. Crucially, the fact that adult L2 learners produce RIs should not be equated with the lack of relevant functional categories or impaired grammars (contra Beck 1998; Meisel 1997). In other words, the fact that adults display acquisition behaviours different from children's does not necessarily mean that adult learners no longer have access to UG.

General findings by domain

The verbal domain

In the investigation of inflectional morphology, we have seen that although finite markers are not always provided, when they are provided, they are largely correct. This applies not only to child learners, but also to adults. Moreover, in acquisition by children (including L2, L1, and bilingual acquisition), inflectional morphology develops rapidly (with early verbal (default) inflection being largely in the present and third person singular). Subject clitics are also used very early. Furthermore, all learners have been found to produce RIs instead of target finite forms. In children, RIs seem to share particular properties, such as the lack of subject clitics, the presence of strong pronoun subjects, a modal reading (although this remains to be confirmed in bilingual children), and the lack of nonfinite CP-clauses. All this suggests that the distribution of nonfinite forms in children is structure dependant; in other words, RIs are truly nonfinite. Finally, verb placement is largely correct from the outset with respect to negation: finite verbs appear to the left of negation *pas*, and nonfinite verbs to its right.

The extent of the errors produced differs across learning contexts. For example, bilinguals seem to use RIs for longer than monolinguals, and children with SLI experience long-lasting problems with past tense, using RIs and present tense instead (although the rate of RIs reported varies across the literature). In adult L2 French, the RI stage tends to last for a long time as well; longer than in child L2 learners. In fact, the properties of adult RIs are different from those of other learners in that they can be found with subject clitics, the nonfinite verb may precede a negative adverb, and nonfinite forms can be found in interrogatives and embedded clauses. Finally, with respect to verb placement, we saw that adverbs and floating quantifiers pose tremendous problems for adult learners, especially in pre-advanced stages. Interestingly, we do not know whether the same is true in acquisition by children, as few adverbs are used in spontaneous speech. This should be further investigated, especially through methodologies other than spontaneous production.

From the standpoint of theory, the findings show that there is early knowledge of finiteness, even in the case of adult learners, which is compatible with the idea that at least one functional category is available to learners initially, whether or not subject clitics are considered agreement markers in French. We saw that, when used, finite inflection is largely correct and that finite forms are restricted to finite positions (except for L1 English speakers). Nonetheless, it is not always easy to distinguish formulaic expressions from genuine creativity. Finally, as said above, the findings in acquisition by children favour an analysis of early projections in terms of Structural Economy, presumably due to computational limitations, which means that their RIs are VP roots (and have nonfinite properties). This analysis could be extended to explain why children with SLI struggle with past tense if past tense involves the projection of an extra functional layer, in contrast to the present tense. In the case of L2 acquisition, early knowledge of functional categories may result from transfer from the L1 grammar. They could also have developed from direct access to UG. In any case, the mere fact that functional categories may be present in early grammars argues against the existence of an initial strictly lexical stage. As already noted, the adult data are compatible with the Missing Surface Inflection Hypothesis in the sense that nonfinite forms tend to be used as substitutes for finite verbs. This further suggests that nonfinite forms are underspecified for (non)finiteness in adult L2 grammars.

The pronominal domain

Within the pronominal domain, we saw that not only do subject clitics emerge early (although delayed emergence is observed with some bilinguals), they also become productive very quickly. Learners make an early distinction between clitics and strong pronouns: with children, subject clitics are generally appropriately positioned (e.g.

they only appear with finite verbs); with adults, strong pronouns are never used as subjects. In all learning contexts, the development of object clitics is delayed with respect to subject clitics, and even with respect to their reflexive counterparts (although this needs further investigation in child and adult L2 acquisition). This is particularly true of children with SLI: so much so that the delayed emergence of object clitics could be used as a clinical diagnosis for their condition (Paradis & Crago 2003), along with the delayed development of past tense. Despite their delayed development, object clitics are used in target-like positions, especially in acquisition by TD monolinguals and by children with SLI. In bilingual and L2 data, errors of clitic placement are reported, which could be explained by crosslinguistic influence. The role of crosslinguistic influence in this area should be explored through other language combinations, particularly with languages exhibiting preverbal object clitics, as is the case in French. Despite this difficulty for bilingual and L2 learners, clitic placement is by and large correct in acquisition by children from the moment these elements emerge, suggesting that they are considered clitics from the very beginning. This greatly differs from what is observed in adult L2 learners. For instance, adults use subject clitics with non-finite forms and do not always perform elision in obligatory contexts. Taken together, these differences indicate that clitics are not treated as clitics in adult L2 French. A four-stage developmental path for object clitics has been proposed for these learners: postverbal placement, omission, intermediary positioning, and target-like placement. This proposal needs to be further examined. Note that object clitic placement may remain problematic for some learners, for instance in restructuring contexts in the case of adult Spanish speakers learning French (note that this has been little investigated in child L2 French).

Research on the development of pronouns has reported that TD children and children with SLI have early knowledge of binding, based on the fact that errors involving pronouns are typically gender and Case errors, not binding ones. This is particularly interesting in the case of children with SLI since it suggests that their grammars are UG-consistent and not deficient. However, knowledge of binding has not been fully investigated in all domains of French acquisition research (for example in bilingual French and in L2 French), so understanding of this phenomenon is limited.

We have also seen that null arguments are reported in all learning contexts. Null subjects are largely restricted to main declaratives in monolingual, bilingual, and child L2 French acquisition (note that in the studies on bilingual and L2 French, the other language rarely allows null subjects). Moreover, in L1 and L2 French, the incidence of null subjects in finite main clauses declines sharply at the same time as RIs. This does not seem to be the case in children with SLI, and may or may not be the case for bilinguals (more research is needed, however). In adult learners, the use of null subjects is strongly related to the *pro*-drop properties of the L1. In particular, null subjects are found in CP-clauses, where their incidence is rather low in child data, if null subjects are allowed in the adults' L1. Object omission is slightly more delicate to investigate than subject omission since null objects are not impossible in French. When illicit contexts of omission are taken into account, which can be manipulated via elicited production tasks, the ratio of null objects can be quite high. Furthermore, object drop has often been reported to be more common in bilinguals than in monolinguals, especially if null objects are allowed in the other language being learned (e.g. German). However, recent studies on bilingual learning situations involving a language where objects are not as easily dropped, such as English, suggests otherwise. This kind of comparative research should clearly be pursued. In L2 acquisition, the incidence of null objects has mainly been investigated within the general context of the acquisition of object clitics. However, in one of the few studies focusing on object drop in child L2 French it was found that illicit object omission and RIs end at about the same time (Prévost 2006a). New studies should tell us whether the same obtains in other children.

The fact that subject clitics are produced from the outset reinforces the idea that functional projections are available in the earliest stages of acquisition. The delayed emergence of object clitics could be accounted for by the fact that these elements do not occupy the canonical object position in French. In particular, it is possible that the preverbal position of object clitics in French poses computational problems for children, as proposed by Jakubowicz et. al (1998) (see also Chillier-Zesiger et al. 2006; Grüter 2006). The fact that child learners treat clitic as clitics, that is, as heads, from early on is also compatible with Structural Economy. Again, adult learners seem to behave differently from children insofar as they follow Categorial Uniformity and treat clitics as XPs, presumably assuming that clitics belong to the general category of nominals and should therefore have a phrasal status. The development of object clitics in adults requires more study, ideally including both production and comprehension; methodologies similar to the ones developed in child L1 and L2 French (see Grüter 2005, 2006; Jakubowicz et. al 1998; van der Velde 2003), such as elicited production tasks (based on questions such as 'What does X do to Y?') and picture identification tasks (based on instructions such as 'Show me the picture where X says that Y does something to Z'), would undoubtedly be helpful.

The nominal domain

In French L1 acquisition by monolinguals and bilinguals, determiners seem to follow a threefold developmental path: omission, optionality, and target-like use. However, not all children drop determiners altogether and some use placeholders or filler syllables in the early stage. Once determiners emerge, children seem to recognize that they are clitics and treat them appropriately, as evidenced by their use of elision. Among the other properties associated with D, number develops first, followed by gender, a sequence that seems to hold in both L1 acquisition and L2 acquisition by children and adults. Gender errors tend to involve overgeneralization of one gender, usually the masculine, but may affect definite and indefinite markers differently. Various studies have come to opposite conclusions on this question, although the data on adult L2 acquisition seem to suggest that both definite and indefinite determiners are affected. Definiteness seems to be acquired last, although this is not certain for children with SLI as the development of definiteness has been virtually unstudied with this population. Interestingly, acquisition of the properties of D, along with number and noun placement, does not seem to be significantly more challenging for children with SLI than for TD children, although more systematic research should be undertaken on this question, especially with respect to the last two properties. Problems with gender are reported in SLI development, however, but they do not seem to be as severe as what is observed with tense and object clitics. Finally, there does not seem to be any strong relationship between the development of determiners, finiteness, and object clitics in child L1 French. In L2 acquisition, L1 influence appears to play an important role in the acquisition of the properties of D in French. For example, production of determiners can be quite high early on if D is instantiated in the L1, and acquisition of definiteness is facilitated when it is overtly marked in the L1. Conversely, when the relevant D-features are not instantiated in the learners' mother tongue, performance is poorer in the initial stages. It should be noted that no study has looked in detail at the development of the D-domain in child L2 learners of French, especially from the point of view of children whose L1 does not have determiners (such as Chinese). Regardless of whether the L1 has determiners or not, adult learners' early production of determiners suggests that these elements are not initially treated as clitics (even though their L1 may contain clitic-like determiners as well). Finally, although adult learners struggle with the various properties of D in the early stages of acquisition, whether or not this is due to influence from their L1, high levels of accuracy can be eventually reached, as shown in research on L2 acquisition of gender.

Within the D-domain, learners must also acquire the correct placement of nouns with respect to adjectives. Some research on monolingual French acquisition suggests that only one element, either be an adjective or a determiner, can appear before the noun in the earliest stages. In acquisition by bilinguals, and in child L2 French, there seems to be an early developmental phase during which adjectives only appear before nouns, which is not the canonical order for the majority of adjectives in French. However, the adjectives reported to be produced at this stage are those that do tend to occur prenominally in French (such as *petit* 'small' and *grand* 'big/tall'). In later phases, some errors in noun placement are reported, involving adjectives that are postnominal in the target language but that are used prenominally by the children. However, the other languages being learned in the studies reporting such errors only have prenominal adjectives. It is therefore difficult to know if the late development of target-like noun placement in French is due to cross-linguistic influence. In L2 acquisition by adults, in spite of initial L1 influence, it seems that target properties of noun placement can be acquired, including knowledge of properties at the semantic/syntactic interface (e.g. interpretation of adjectives).

Structural Economy may explain the optionality of determiners in the early stages of child L1 acquisition, without calling into question the early availability of D. For children with SLI, presumably determiners do not represent any major source of difficulty because D must be obligatorily merged in the representation of noun phrases, following Jakubowicz et al.'s (1998) proposal that obligatory merging is less computationally costly than non-obligatory merging. However, more fine-grained analyses of the phenomenon of determiner omission in all learning situations are needed. For instance, does the predicate or argument status of the NP influence determiner omission, with lower omission for predicate NPs? The availability of D is also evidenced by the use of default forms, such as masculine determiners. Such forms could be underspecified for some particular features, such as gender, and feature deletion on the hosting head may take place before Vocabulary insertion. This operation could be thought of as an economy strategy designed to decrease the computational load (Jakubowicz and Roulet 2008). Research on use of default determiners should be extended to definiteness, which has been understudied in the acquisition of French. Definiteness errors are frequently reported in early child French, with definite markers apparently overgeneralized to indefinite contexts, but further investigation of this phenomenon is needed in the different learning contexts. More systematic exploration of the development of gender in French is also needed. For example, gender concord errors are reported to be quite frequent in early child French (e.g. *gros porte* 'big+MASC door+FEM' instead of *grosse porte* 'big.FEM door+FEM' (Clark 1985), but studies on this topic are rare. Exploration of this phenomenon should ideally be done via elicited production tasks which would force the learners to use adjectives with a variety of masculine and feminine nouns. Prenominal and postnominal adjectives should also be used in order to compare error rates in these two types.

The CP domain

In acquisition by children, the first wh-questions are predicative (usually with *où*) and they do not exhibit clitic/verb inversion or *est-ce que*. In monolinguals the wh-word may either be preposed or appear in situ; in some cases, it is left out altogether. In children with SLI, the wh-in situ option seems to be strongly favoured at first. The same obtains in elicited production from child L2 French. In L2 spontaneous speech, however, wh-words are almost never omitted and are generally preposed initially, although this may be due to use of routine expressions. Finally, nonfinite verbs rarely appear in children's wh-questions, but they are observed in adult L2 French. The development of finite embedded clauses is delayed in monolinguals and bilinguals, and in child L2 French (not much is known about the development of subordinate clauses in children with SLI). Finite embedded clauses tend to appear after the emergence of wh-questions. Complementizers are often omitted at first (interestingly, except in child L2 French, even when omission is allowed in the L1, such as English). The acquisition of relative clauses is gradual and can take quite some time (especially prepositional RCs) in monolinguals. Overgeneralization of *que* and *où* is observed at first and resumptive pronouns are also used. Relative clauses have not been investigated in detail in bilinguals or in children learning L2 French. In adult learners, early production of interrogatives and embedded clauses is reported, although arguably initial use of some wh-questions is formulaic. Target-like knowledge of semantic interpretation of particular wh-questions, such as *qui de AP* questions, can also be reached, which is a strong argument in favour of the availability of UG in second language acquisition.

Whether C is present in initial grammars is a question of relevance to linguistic theory. Some researchers assume that C is not available initially, and consider the first wh-questions and embedded clauses to be IPs. Others argue that since the first questions used by children are indeed questions, they should be treated as instances of CP like any other interrogatives. For this camp, children's early tendency to maintain the wh-word in situ and not to perform inversion is assumed to stem from their computational limitations. This leads them to favour less costly options with fewer operations. Children with SLI are assumed to have the most limited capacities, so they favour least costly options more often and for longer than TD children. Child L2 learners may experience similar computational problems, as they do not systematically perform wh-movement in elicited production. In addition, like other child learners, child L2 learners appear to disfavour inversion to a great extent initially, even if it is present in their L1. The delayed development of embedded clauses has also been argued to suggest that children initially lack the appropriate functional structure for them. However, both the appropriate contexts for complement clauses and the different forms of complementizers must be learned, so their delayed emergence may not be due to the lack of the appropriate functional layer, but simply to the time this learning requires. Moreover, most child data have been obtained via spontaneous production tasks, and we know that there may not be systematic correspondence between lack of production (in this case, omitting the complementizer) and lack of underlying projection. Other methodologies should be used in order to further investigate the development of interrogatives and embedded clauses in children. In adult L2 French, C seems to be attested early, which could be the result of transfer from the L1. The degree to which learners use formulaic interrogatives may be related to the contexts in which acquisition is taking place. Those learning within a

French-speaking community seem much less likely to use such formulaic expressions than those who are not.

Possible avenues for future research

Many studies in L1 and L2 French rely on spontaneous production. As advocated throughout this book, supplementing such studies research using other methodologies, such as elicited production and comprehension tasks, would allow for a more fine-grained account of development. In bilingual and L2 French acquisition, it would also be extremely useful to vary language combinations so as to obtain a greater insight into the influence of the other language and, in the case of bilingualism, of language dominance over the development of French. Finally, increasing cross-populations studies should be carried out, in particular studies involving different pathologies.

A largely understudied area in child L1 French is the acquisition of argument structure. Some authors have reported errors of the kind found in L1 English (Bowerman 1982; Pinker 1989), such as the use of intransitive verbs, like *tomber* 'fall', with objects (see Barrière & Lorch 2006; Barrière, Lorch & Le Normand 2000, 2001). In French, some transitive verbs alternate with an intransitive use. Sometimes the intransitivity is marked by *se* 'self' (e.g. *Le vent a cassé la branche* 'The wind broke the branch' and *La branche s'est cassée* 'The branch broke'), but this is not systematic (e.g. *Le soleil a fondu la neige* 'The sun melted the snow' and *La neige a fondu* 'The snow melted') (see Jones 1996; Ruwet 1972, among others). Erroneous cases of *se* 'self' affixation and *se* omission have been reported in child L1 French, such as *se fondre* 'melt itself' on the one hand, and *envoler* 'fly away' on the other. More research is needed to better understand these errors, and it should also be extended to other learning contexts.

Among the different domains reviewed in this book, the CP domain has received the least attention by researchers, especially in learning contexts other than acquisition by TD monolinguals. For instance, no work has targeted the development of stylistic inversion, and more needs to be done on the development of wh-questions and relative clauses, including in learners with little exposure to the language in order to track down development from the earliest stages. Such work could be tied in with research questions on interface phenomena connecting syntax and pragmatics, as argued below.

Interface phenomena, where syntactic knowledge interacts with other areas of the grammar (such as semantics and pragmatics), have caught researchers' attention in the last few years. They represent one of the most significant areas for future research in the different kinds of acquisition contexts reviewed in this book. Such phenomena are argued to be inherently more difficult to acquire than purely syntactic phenomena (see Sorace (2003) for a general presentation of the issues at stake). This additional level of difficulty is argued to be evident in all learning situations, but while simple delays may be observed in acquisition by children, serious difficulties may be observed in acquisition with adults, resulting in fossilization, incomplete, or so-called residual optionality (Montrul 2002, 2004; Serratrice, Sorace & Paoli 2004; Sorace 2004, 2005; Tsimpli, Sorace, Heycock & Filiaci 2004). At stake is whether adult IL grammars can ever attain native-like levels. It also has recently been proposed that not all interfaces are equal in terms of 'ease of acquisition'; some phenomena are more difficult than others, which presumably results in longer-lasting optionality (Tsimpli & Sorace 2006). This is argued to be true of the syntax/pragmatic interface, for example, as compared to syntax/semantic phenomena (see, for example, the work of Dekydtspotter, Sprouse, and their colleagues discussed in Sections 12.2.3.2 and 16.2.5). Much of the research on these issues has been carried out on languages such as Spanish and Italian, but very little has been done in French. For example, little is known, from the perspective of generative grammar, about the late development of properties such as aspect (e.g. *imparfait*) and mood (e.g. the subjunctive). The marking of aspect and mood may depend on semantic notions such as presupposition, so researching these properties would help us understand how interface phenomena develop (see Borgonovo, Bruhn de Garavito & Prévost (2006) on the acquisition of mood marking in L2 Spanish). Additionally research on syntax/semantics interface phenomena should be pursued, as advocated by Schwartz & Sprouse (2000), because such properties represent genuine poverty-of-the-stimulus situations, with important implications for the potential role of UG in adult L2 acquisition.

More research should also be undertaken on the interface between the development of inflectional morphology and phonology, on prosodification issues in particular, in all learning contexts addressed in this book. We have already seen how the acquisition of prosodic constraints could be integrated into the investigation of the development of determiners in monolinguals (see Section 10.4.1) (Demuth & Tremblay 2008; Veneziano & Sinclair 2000). Similar research should be undertaken with bilingual children learning French (see Lleó & Dumuth 1999). It would be interesting to look at bilingual children learning both French and a language with different prosodic constraints and investigate potential effects of crosslinguistic influence. In SLI development, we know that phonology is one of the linguistic domains which can be particularly affected. The interface between phonology and syntax, in particular the interaction between phonological and syntactic complexity, therefore appears as a promising area of research in this learning context (Marshall & van der Lely 2006, 2007; Wauquier-Gravelines 2005). In L2 acquisition, it has been argued that the production of inflectional morphology may be influenced by the prosodic representation of inflectional morphology in the learner's mother tongue (e.g. Goad, White & Steele 2003). This hypothesis should be tested in L2 French, again, by selecting a learning situation involving an L1 whose prosodic representation of morphology differs from French (such as Chinese).

With respect to pronouns, more research should be done on the development of object clitics in children, including examination of later stages of development (beyond the age of four). Object clitics represent a particularly fruitful area of study since they can be tied to research on interfaces, such as discourse/syntax and phonology/syntax. Also, the potential relationship between the decline of RIs and the development of object clitics should be examined. In bilinguals, it remains to be determined if a relationship exists between the end of the null object drop period and the emergence of overt object clitics, as it does in monolinguals. It could be the case that crosslinguistic influence reinforces the kind of difficulty, presumably computational, that child learners seem to have with these elements. Cases of misplacement of clitics (which seem to be the exception rather than the norm) should also be further investigated in bilingual children, as it is not yet clear whether or not such errors should be imputed to cross-linguistic influence.

Finally, as explained in the preface, one of the objectives of this book is to promote cross-population studies of language development. We have seen how such research can help us refine characteristics of linguistic development in each of the populations involved and better understand the process of language acquisition as a whole. This has proven to be particularly illuminating in the case of language acquisition by children suffering from a particular pathology, as comparative work on SLI and child L2 acquisition has shown (Paradis and Crago 2000, 2001; Grüter 2005; Haiden et al. 2009). Not only should this kind of research be pursued, with the goal of identifying clinical markers of pathology, it should also be extended to other kinds of comparisons, and especially comparisons across pathologies. In a review of studies on atypical development of French involving mild-to-moderate hearing loss (Delage 2008) and Rolandic Epilepsy (Monjauze 2007), Jakubowicz and Tuller (2008) show that the linguistic phenomena generating difficulties in these contexts are similar to those reported to be problematic in SLI, such as accusative clitics. Since no neuronal and intellectual deficit were reported in the three populations, the question arises as to whether there are specific areas of the grammar that are particularly sensitive to the effects of pathology and whose development will be impaired regardless of the type of pathology. More comparative research of this kind should be undertaken on other aspects of the grammar, such as verbal morphology and CP-clauses, and factors such as age and degrees of severity of the pathology should be manipulated. Other pathologies should also be investigated, including those where intellectual deficits can be found, such as autism, in order to better assess the impact of the nature of the pathology over linguistic development.

References

Abney, S.P. 1987. The English Noun Phrase in its Sentential Aspect. Ph.D. dissertation, MIT.

Adiv, E. 1984. Language learning strategies: The relationship between L1 operating principles and language transfer in L2 development. In *Second Languages: A Cross-linguistic Perspective,* R. Andersen (ed), 125–142. Rowley MA.: Newbury House.

Andersen, R. (ed.) 1984. *Second Languages: A Cross-linguistic Perspective.* Rowley MA.: Newbury House.

Anderson, B. 2002. The Interpretive Correlates of Adjective Position in Native and Nonnative Grammars of French. Ph.D. dissertation, Indiana University.

Anderson, B. 2007. Learnability and parametric change in the nominal system of L2 French. *Language Acquisition* 14: 165–214.

Anderson, B. 2008. Forms of evidence and grammatical development in the acquisition of adjective position in L2 French. *Studies in Second Language Acquisition* 30: 1–29.

Aoun, J. 1979. On government, case-marking and clitic placement. Ms, MIT.

Auger, J. 1994. Pronominal Clitics in Québec Colloquial French: A Morphological Analysis. Ph.D. dissertation, University of Pennsylvania.

Ayoun, D. 1999. Verb movement in French L2 acquisition. *Bilingualism: Language and cognition* 2: 103–125.

Ayoun, D. 2003. *Parameter Setting in Language Acquisition.* London: Continuum.

Baauw, S. 2000. *Grammatical Features and the Acquisition of Reference. A Comparative Study of Dutch and Spanish.* Utrecht: LOT.

Baltin, M. 1995. FQs, PRO and predication. *Linguistic Inquiry* 26: 199–248.

Baranzini, L. 2003. Le sujet nul, les infinitives racine et les questions wh dans la grammaire des enfants normaux et des enfants SLI francophones. Thèse de DEA, University of Geneva.

Barrière, I. & Lorch, M., 2006. On the acquisition of ambiguous Valency-Marking morphemes: Insights from the acquisition of French SE. In *The Acquisition of Syntax in Romance Languages,* V. Torrens & L. Escobar (eds), 23–50. Amsterdam: John Benjamins.

Barrière, I., Lorch, M. & Le Normand, M.-T. 2000. Argument alternation in French children's speech. In *New Directions in Language Development,* M. Perkins & S. Howard (eds), 139–148. London: Plenum.

Barrière, I., Lorch, M. & Le Normand, M.-T. 2001. La cliticisation en se dans le langage de l'enfant: Sur-généralisation des affixations et des omissions. In *Clitiques et cliticisation: Actes du colloque de Bordeaux, octobre 1998,* C. Muller (ed.), 251–266. Paris: Honoré Champion.

Bartke, S., Marcus, G.F. & Clahsen, H. 1995. Acquiring German noun plurals. In *Proceedings of the 19th Annual Boston University Conference on Language Development,* D. MacLaughlin & S. McEwen (eds), 60–69. Somerville MA.: Cascadilla Press.

Bartning, I. 1997. L'apprenant dit avancé et son acquisition d'une langue étrangère. Tour d'horizon et esquisse d'une caractérisation de la variété avancée. *AILE* 9: 21–50.

Bartning, I. 2000. Gender agreement in L2 French. *Studia Linguistica* 54: 225–238.

Bartning, I. & Schlyter, S. 2004. Itinéraires acquisitionnels et stades de développement en français L2. *Journal of French Language Studies* 14: 281–299.

Bassano, D. 1998. Sémantique et syntaxe dans l'acquisition des classes de mots: L'exemple des noms et des verbes en français. *Langue Française* 118: 26–48.

Bassano, D., I. Maillachon, S. Kampfler & Dressler, W.U. 2001. L'acquisition de la morphologie verbale en français et en allemand autrichien : II. L'épreuve des faits. *Enfance* 2: 117–148.

Beard, R. 1995. *Lexeme-morpheme Base Morphology*. Albany NY: SUNY Press.

Beck, M.-L. 1998. L2 acquisition and obligatory head movement: English-speaking learners of German and the Local Impairment Hypothesis. *Studies in Second Language Acquisition* 20: 311–348.

Belletti, A. 1990. *Generalized Verb Movement: Aspects of Verb Syntax*. Torino: Rosenberg and Sallier.

Belletti, A. 1999. Italian/Romance clitics: Structure and dérivation. In *Clitics in the Languages of Europe,* H. van Riemsdijk (ed.), 543–580. The Hague: Mouton de Gruyter.

Belletti, A. 2001. Agreement projections. In *The Handbook of Contemporary Syntactic Theory,* M. Baltin & C. Collins (eds), 483–510. Oxford: Blackwell.

Belletti, A. & Hamann, C. 2004. On the L2/bilingual acquisition of French by two young children with different source languages. In *The Acquisition of French in Different Contexts: Focus on Functional Categories,* P. Prévost & J. Paradis (eds), 147–176. Amsterdam: John Benjamins.

Berruto, G. 1980. *La variabilità sociale della lingua*. Torino: Loescher.

Berstein, D. 1993. Topics in the Syntax of Nominal Structure across Romance. Ph.D. dissertation, CUNY.

Bhatia, T.K. & Ritchie, W.C. 1996. Bilingual language mixing, Universal Grammar, and second language acquisition. In *Handbook of Second Language Acquisition,* W. Ritchie & T. Bhatia (eds), 627–688. San Diego CA: Academic Press.

Birdsong, D. 1989. *Metalinguistic Performance and Interlinguistic Competence*. New York NY: Spinger.

Birdsong, D. 1992. Ultimate attainment in SLA. *Language* 68: 23–52.

Bley-Vroman, R. 1990. The logical problem of foreign language learning. *Linguistic Analysis* 20: 3–49.

Bloom, P. 1990. Subjectless sentences in child language. *Linguistic Inquiry* 21: 491–504.

Borer, H. 1984. *Parametric Syntax: Case Studies in Semitic and Romance Languages*. Dordrecht: Foris.

Borer, H. & Rohrbacher, B. 2002. Minding the absent: Arguments for the Full Competence Hypothesis. *Language Acquisition* 10: 123–75.

Borer, H. & Wexler, K. 1987. The maturation of syntax. In *Parameter Setting,* T. Roeper & E. Williams (eds), 123–172. Dodrecht: Reidel.

Borgonovo, C., Bruhn de Garavito, J. & Prévost, P. 2006. Is the semantics/syntax interface vulnerable in L2 acquisition? Focus on mood distinctions in relative clauses in L2 Spanish. In *The acquisition of Syntax in Romance Languages,* V. Torrens & L. Escobar (eds), 353–369. Amsterdam: John Benjamins.

Bortolini, U. & Leonard, L. 1996. Phonology and grammatical morphology in specific language impairment: Accounting for individual variation in English and Italian. *Applied Psycholinguistics* 17: 85–104.

Boser, K., Lust, B., Santelmann, L. & Whitmann, J. 1992. The syntax of CP and V2 in early child German (ECG): The Strong Continuity Hypothesis. In *Proceedings of NELS* 23, K. Broderick (ed.), 51–65. Amherst MA: GLSA.

Bottari, P., Cipriani, P. & Chilosi, A.M. 1996. Root Infinitives in Italian SLI Children. In *Proceedings of the 20th Annual Boston University Conference on Language Development,* A. Stringfellow, D. Cahana-Amitay, E. Hughes & A. Zukowski (eds), 75–86. Somerville MA: Cascadilla Press.

Bouchard, D. 1998. The distribution and interpretation of adjectives in French: A consequence of Bare Phrase Structure. *Probus* 10:139–183.

Bowerman, M. 1982. Evaluating competing linguistic models with language acquisition data: Implications of developmental errors with causative verbs. *Quaderni di Semantica* 3: 5–66.

Bowerman, M. 1988. The 'no negative evidence problem': How do children avoid constructing an overly general grammar. In *Explaining Language Universals*, J. Hawkins (ed.), 73–101. Oxford: Blackwell.

Boysson-Bardies, B. de. 1976. *Négation et performance linguistique*. The Hague: Mouton.

Boysson-Bardies, B. de. 1999. *Comment la parole vient aux enfants*. Paris: Éditions Odile Jacob, coll. Opus.

Bromberg, H. & Wexler, K. 1995. Null subjects in wh-questions. *MIT Working Papers in Linguistics* 26: 421–247.

Brousseau, A.-M. & Roberge, Y. 2000. *Syntaxe et sémantique du français*. Saint-Lautent: Fides.

Brown, R. & Hanlon, C. 1970. Derivational complexity and the order of acquisition in child speech. In *Cognition and the Development of Language*, J.R. Hayes (ed.). New York NY: Wiley.

Bruhn de Gavarito, J. & Montrul, S. 1996. Verb movement and clitic placement in French and Spanish as a second language. In *Proceedings of the 20th Annual Boston University Conference on Language Development*, A. Stringfellow, D. Cahana-Amitay, E. Hughes & A. Zukowski (eds), 61–78. Somerville MA: Cascadilla Press.

Bruhn de Gavarito, J. & White, L. 2002. L2 acquisition of Spanish DPs: The status of grammatical features. In *The Acquisition of Spanish Morphosyntax: The L1/L2 Connection*, A.T. Pérez-Leroux & J. Liceras (eds), 164–175. Dordrecht: Kluwer.

Bybee, J. 1995. Regular morphology and the lexicon. *Language and Cognitive Processes* 10: 425–455.

Candea, M. 1998. Contribution à l' étude des pauses silencieuses et des phénomènes dits d' hésitation en français oral spontané. In *Actes du colloque international de Besançon 'Répétition, altération, reformulation'*, 119–130. Annales littéraires de l'Université de Besançon.

Candea, M. 2000. Contribution à l'étude des pauses silencieuses et des phénomènes dits d'hésitation en français oral spontané. Ph.D. dissertation, Université Paris 3.

Caprin, C. & Guasti, M.-T. 2006. A cross-sectional study on the use of "be" in early Italian. In *The Acquisition of Syntax in Romance languages*, V. Torrens & L. Escobar (eds), 117–134. Amsterdam: John Benjamins.

Cardinaletti, A. & Starke, M. 1995. The tripartition of pronouns and its acquisition: Principle B puzzles and ambiguity problems. In *Proceedings of NELS* 25, J. Beckman (ed.), 1–12. Amherst MA: GSLA.

Cardinaletti, A. & Starke, M. 1999. The typology of structural deficiency: A case study of the three classes of pronouns. In *Clitics in the Languages of Europe*, H. van Riemsdijk (ed.), 145–233. Berlin: Mouton de Gruyter.

Cardinaletti, A. & Starke, M. 2000. Overview: The grammar (and acquisition) of clitics. In *The Acquisition of Scrambling and Cliticization*, S. Powers & C. Hamann (eds), 165–186. Dordrecht: Kluwer.

Carroll, S. 1989. Second-language acquisition and the computational paradigm. *Language Learning* 39: 535–594.

Carroll, S. 1999. Input and SLA: Adults' sensitivity to different sorts of cues to French gender. *Language Learning* 49: 37–92.

Carstens, V. 2000. Concord in minimalist theory. *Linguistic Inquiry* 31: 319–355.

Chang, L. 1997. WH-in situ Phenomena in French. MA thesis, University of British Columbia, Vancouver.

Cheng, L. & Rooryck, J. 2000. Licensing Wh-in situ. *Syntax* 3: 1–19.

Cheng, L. & Sybesma, R. 1999. Bare and not-so-bare nouns and the structure of NP. *Linguistic Inquiry* 30: 509–542.

Chien, Y.-C. & Wexler, K. 1990. Children's knowledge of locality conditions in binding as evidence for the modularity of syntax and pragmatics. *Language Acquisition* 1: 225–295.

Chierchia, G., Guasti, T. & Gualmini, A. 2001. Nouns and articles in child grammar and the syntax/semantics map. Ms, University of Milan/University of Siena/University of Maryland, College Park.

Chillier L., Arabatzi, M., Baranzini, L., Cronel-Ohayon, S., Deonna, T., Dubé, S., Franck, J., Frauenfelder, U., Hamann, C., Rizzi, L., Starke, M. & Zesiger, P. 2001. The acquisition of French pronouns in normal children and in children with specific language impairment (SLI), *Proceedings of Early Lexicon Acquisition (ELA)*, CDRom, Lyon, France.

Chillier-Zesiger, L., Arabatzi, M., Baranzini, L., Cronel-Ohayon, S., Franck, J., Frauenfelder, U., Hamann, C., Rizzi, L. & Zesiger, P. 2006. The acquisition and mastery of French pronouns. Unpublished manuscript, University of Geneva.

Chini, M. 1995. Un aspect du syntagme nominal en italien L2: Le genre. *AILE* 5: 115–142.

Chomsky, N. 1981. Principles and parameters in syntactic theory. In *Explanation in Linguistics: the Logical Problem of Language Acquisition*, N. Hornstein & D. Lightfoot (eds), 32–75. London: Longman.

Chomsky, N. 1982. *Some concepts and Consequences of the Theory of Government and Binding*. Cambridge: MIT Press.

Chomsky, N. 1986. *Knowledge of Language*. New York NY: Praeger.

Chomsky, N. 1995. *The Minimalist Program*. Cambridge MA: The MIT Press.

Chomsky, N. 2000. Minimalist inquiries: The framework. In *Step by Step – Essays in Minimalist Syntax in Honor of Howard Lasnik*, R. Martin, D. Michaels & J. Uriagereka (eds), 89–156. Cambridge MA: The MIT Press.

Chomsky, N. 2001. Derivation by phase. In *Ken Hale: A Life in Language*, M. Kenstowicz (ed.), 1–52. Cambridge MA: The MIT Press.

Chomsky, N. 2002. *On Nature and Language*. Cambridge: CUP.

Chomsky, N. & Lasnik, H. 1993. Principles and parameter theory. In *Syntax: An International Handbook of Contemporary Research*, J. Jacobs, A. von Stechow, W. Sternefeld & T. Vennemann (eds), 506–569. Berlin: Walter de Gruyter.

Cinque, G. 1994. On the evidence for partial N-movement in the Romance DP. In *Paths toward Universal Grammar: Studies in Honor of R.S. Kayne*, G. Cinque, J. Koster, J.-Y. Pollock, L. Rizzi & R. Zanuttini (eds), 85–110. Washington DC: Georgetown University Press.

Cinque, G. 1999. *Adverbs and Functional Heads: A Cross-linguistic Perspective*. Oxford: OUP.

Clahsen, H. 1986. Verb inflections in German child language: Acquisition of agreement markings and the functions they encode. *Linguistics* 24: 79–121. Special Issue: *Two Languages. Studies in Bilingual First and Second Language Development*, N. Müller (ed.).

Clahsen, H. 1988. Parameterized grammatical theory and language acquisition: A study of the acquisition of verb placement and inflection by children and adults. In *Linguistic Theory in Second Language Acquisition*, S. Flynn & W. O'Neil (eds), 47–75. Dordrecht: Kluwer.

Clahsen, H., Bartke, S. & Göllner, S. 1997. Formal features in impaired grammars: A comparison of English and German SLI children. *Journal of Neurolinguistics* 10: 151–171.

Clahsen, H., Eisenbeiss, S. & Penke, M. 1996. Lexical learning and early syntactical development. In *Generative Approaches to First and Second Language Acquisition*, H. Clahsen (ed.), 129–159. Amsterdam: John Benjamins.

Clahsen, H., Eisenbeiss, S. & Vainikka, A. 1994. The seeds of structure: A syntactic analysis of the acquisition of case marking. In *Language Acquisition Studies in Generative Grammar,* T. Hoekstra & B. Schwartz (eds), 85–118. Amsterdam: John Benjamin.

Clahsen, H. & Muysken, P. 1986. The availability of UG to adult and child learners: A study of the acquisition of German word order. *Second Language Research* 2: 93–119.

Clark, E. 1985. The acquisition of Romance with special reference to French. In *The Crosslinguistic Study of Language Acquisition,* Vol. 1: *The Data,* D. Slobin (ed.), 687–782. Hillsdale NJ: Lawrence Erlbaum.

Clark, E. 1998. Lexique et syntaxe dans l'acquisition du français. *Langue Française* 118: 49–60.

Cohen, M. 1968. Sur l'étude du langage enfantin. *Enfance* 1: 12–249.

Connors, K. & Nuckle, L. 1986. The morphosyntax of French personal pronouns and the acquisiiton/Learning dichotomy. In *Studies in Romance Linguistics,* O. Jaeggli & C. Silva-Corvalan (eds), 225–242. Dordrecht: Foris.

Coppieters, R. 1987. Competence differences between native and near-native speakers. *Language* 63: 544–573.

Corbett, G.G. 1991. *Gender.* Cambridge: CUP.

Côté, M.-H. 2001. On the status of subject clitics in child French. In *Research on Child Language Acquisition: Proceedings of the 8th Conference of the International Association for the Study of Child Language,* M. Almgren, A. Barreña, M.-J. Ezeizabarrena, I. Idiazabal & B. MacWhinney (eds), 1314–1330. Somerville MA: Cascadilla Press.

Cowper, E. 1994. Intervals and schedules: the English progressive. In *Proceedings of the 1994 Annual Conference of the Canadian Linguistic Association,* P. Koskinen (ed.), 107–118. Toronto: Toronto Working Papers in Linguistics.

Crain, S. & Fodor, J. 1987. Sentence matching and overgeneration. *Cognition* 26: 123–169.

Crain, S. & Thornton, R. 1996. *Investigations in Universal Grammar: A Guide to Experiments on the Acquisition of Syntax and Semantics.* Cambridge MA: The MIT Press.

Crisma, P. 1992. On the acquisition of wh-questions in French. *GenGenP* 0: 115–122.

Cronel-Ohayon, S. 2004. Étude longitudinale d'une population d'enfants dysphasiques. Ph.D. dissertation, University of Geneva.

Cummins, S. & Roberge, Y. 2005. A modular account of null objects in French. *Syntax* 8: 44–64.

Dayal, V. 2000. Scope-marking: cross-linguistic variation in indirect dependency. In *WH-scope Marking,* U. Lutz, G. Müller & A. von Stechow (eds), 157–193. Amsterdam: John Benjamins.

De Cat, C. 2000. Toward a unified analysis of French floating quantifiers. *Journal of French Language Studies* 10: 45–66.

De Cat, C. 2002. French Dislocation. Ph.D. dissertation, University of York, York, UK.

De Cat, C. 2004. A fresh look at how young children encode new referents. *IRAL* 42: 111–127.

De Houwer, A. 1995. Bilingual language acquisition. In *The Handbook of Child Language,* P. Fletcher & B. MacWhinney (eds), 219–250. Oxford : Blackwell.

De Houwer, A. 2005. Early bilingual acquisition: Focus on morphosyntax and the separate development hypothesis. In *The Handbook of Bilingualism,* J. Kroll & A. De Groot (eds), 30–48. Oxford: Oxford University Press.

de Villiers, J., Roeper, T. & Vainikka, A. 1990. The acquisition of long distance rules. In *Language Acquisition and Language Processing,* L. Frazier & J. de Villiers (eds), 257–298. Dordrecht: Kluwer.

Déchaine, R.-M. & Wiltschko, M. 2002. Decomposing pronouns. *Linguistic Inquiry* 33: 409–442.

Dekydtspotter, L. & Sprouse, R. (2001). Mental design and (second) language epistemology: adjectival restrictions of *wh*-quantifiers and tense in English–French interlanguage. *Second Language Research* 17: 1–35.

Dekydtspotter, L., Sprouse, R. & Anderson, B. 1997. The interpretive interface in L2 acquisition: The process-result distinction in English-French interlanguage grammars. *Language Acquisition* 6: 297–332.

Dekydtspotter, L., Sprouse, R. & Swanson, K. 2001. Reflexes of mental architecture in second language acquisition: the interpretation of Combien extractions in English-French interlanguage. *Language Acquisition* 9: 175–228.

Dekydtspotter, L., Sprouse, R. & Thyre, R. 1999/2000. The interpretation of quantification at a distance in English-French interlanguage: Domain specificity and second language acquisition. *Language Acquisition* 8: 265–320.

Delage, H. 2008. Développement du langage dans le contexte d'une surdité moyenne et légère. Ph.D. dissertation. François-Rabelais University, Tours, France.

Delage, H., Monjauze, C., Hamann, C. & Tuller, L. 2007. Relative clauses in atypical acquisition of French. In *Language acquisition and development: Proceedings of GALA 2007,* A. Gavarró & M. João Freitas (eds), 166–176. Newcastle: Cambridge Scholars Publishing.

Delsing, L.-O. 1993. The Internal Structure of Noun Phrases in the Scandinavian Languages: A Comparison Study. Ph.D. dissertation, Lund University.

Demuth, K. 2001. Prosodic constraints on morphological development. In *Approaches to bootstrapping: Phonological, Syntactic and Neurophysiological Aspects of Early Language Acquisition,* J. Weissenborn & B. Höhle (eds), 3–21. Amsterdam: John Benjamins.

Demuth, K. & Tremblay, A. 2008. Prosodically-conditioned variability in children's production of French determiners. *Journal of Child Language* 35: 99–127.

Déprez, V. 1994. Underspecification, functional projections and parameter setting. In *Syntactic Theory and Language Acquisition: Crosslinguistic Perspectives,* B. Lust, J. Whitman & J. Kornfilt (eds), 249–271. Hillsdale NJ: Lawrence Erlbaum.

Déprez, V. & Pierce, A. 1993. Negation and functional projections in early grammar. *Linguistic Inquiry* 24: 25–67.

Devitt, S. 1992. Form and Function in the Developing Verb System of Five Learners of French as a Second Language. Ph.D. dissertation, Trinity College Dublin.

Dewaele, J.-M. & Véronique, D. 2001. Gender assignment and gender agreement in advanced French Interlanguage: A cross-sectional study. *Bilingualism: Language and Cognition* 4: 275–297.

Di Sciullo, A.M. & Williams, E. 1987. *On the Definition of Word.* Cambridge MA: The MIT Press.

Dowty, D. & Brodie, B. 1984. A semantic analysis of floated quantifiers in transformationless grammar. In *Proceedings of the West Coast Conference on Formal Linguistics* 3, 75–90. Standford CA : Standford Linguistics Association.

Duffield, N., White, L., Montrul, S., Bruhn de Garavito, J. & Prévost, P. 2002. Clitic placement in L2 French and Spanish: Evidence from sentence matching. *The Journal of Linguistics* 38: 487–525.

Ellis, R. 1991. Grammaticality judgements and second language acquisition. *Studies in Second Language Acquisition* 13: 161–186.

Epstein, S., Flynn, S. & Martohardjono, G. (1996). Second language acquisition: Theoretical and experimental issues in contemporary research. *Behavorial and Brain Sciences* 19: 677–714.

Eubank, L. 1993/1994. On the transfer of parametric values in L2 development. *Second Language Acquisition* 3: 182–208.

Eubank, L., Bischof, J., Huffstutler, A., Leek, P. & West, C. 1997. 'Tom eats slowly cooked eggs': Thematic-verb raising in L2 knowledge. *Language Acquisition* 6: 171–199.

Eubank, L. & Grace, S. 1996. Where's the mature language? Where's the native language? In *Proceedings of the 20th Annual Boston University Conference on Language Development,*

A. Stringfellow, D. Cahana-Amitay, E. Hughes & A. Zukowski (eds), 189–200. Somerville MA: Cascadilla Press.

Ezeizabarrena, M.J. 1996. *Adquisición de la morfología verbal en euskera y castellano por niños bilingües*. Bilbao: University of the Basque Country.

Felix, S. 1988. UG generated knowledge in adult second language acquisition. In *Linguistic Theory and Second Language Acquisition*, S. Flynn & W. O'Neill (eds), 277–294. Dordrecht: Kluwer.

Ferdinand, A. 1996. *The Develoment of Functional Categories: The Acquisition of the Subject in French*. The Hague: HAG.

Fónagy, I. 1985. J'aime_, je connais_: Verbes transitifs à objet latent. *Revue Romane* 20: 3–35.

Fragman, C. 2000. Grammaire et pouvoir global de computation: deux sources de difficultés possibles dans la production des relatives chez les enfants francophones. *Revue Canadienne de Linguistique* 45: 7–48.

Franceschina, F. 2001. Morphological or syntactic deficits in near-native speakers? An assessment of some current proposals. *Second Language Research* 17: 213–247.

Franck, J., Cronel-Ohayon, S., Chillier, L., Frauenfelder, U, Hamann, C., Rizzi, L. & Zesiger, P. 2004. Normal and pathological development of subject-verb agreement in speech production: A study on French children. *Journal of Neurolinguistics* 17: 147–180.

Freedman, S. & Forster, K. 1985. The psychological status of overgenerated sentences. *Cognition* 19: 101–131.

Friedemann, M.-A. 1993/1994. The underlying position of external arguments in French: A study in adult and child grammar. *Language Acquisition* 3: 209–255.

Friedemann, M.-A. 1997. Inversion stylistique et position de base du sujet. *Revue Canadienne de Linguistique* 42: 379–413.

Friedmann, N., Belletti, A. & Rizzi, L. 2009. Relativized relatives: Types of intervention in the acquisition of A-bar dependencies. *Lingual* 119: 67–88.

Friedmann, N. & Grodzinsky, Y. 2000. Split inflection in neurolinguistics. In *The Acquisition of Syntax*, M.-A. Friedemann & L. Rizzi (eds), 84–104. London: Longman.

Friedmann, N. & Novogorodsky, R. 2004. The acquisition of relative clauses comprehension in Hebrew: A study of SLI and normal development. *Journal of Child Language* 31: 661–681.

Gathercole, S. & Braddeley, A. 1990. Phonological memory deficits in language disordered children: Is there a causal connection? *Journal of Memory and Language* 28: 336–360.

Gawlitzek-Maiwald, I. & Tracy, R. 1996. Bilingual Bootstrapping. *Linguistics* 34: 901–926. Special Issue: *Two Languages. Studies in Bilingual First and Second Language Development*, N. Müller (ed.).

Genesee, F. 1989. Early bilingual development: One language or two? *Journal of Child Language* 6: 161–179.

Genesee, F. 2001. Bilingual first language acquisition: Exploring the limits of the language faculty. In *21st Annual Review of Applied Linguistics*, M. McGroarty (ed.), 153–168. Cambridge: Cambridge University Press.

Genesee, F. & Nicoladis, E. 2006. Bilingual first language acquisition. In *Blackwell Handbook of Language Development*, E. Hoff & M. Shatz (eds), 324–341. Oxford: Blackwell.

Gess, R. & Herschensohn, J. 2001. Shifting the DP parameter: A study of anglophone French L2ers. In *Romance Syntax, Semantics and their L2 Acquisition*, C.R. Wiltshire & J. Camps (eds), 105–119. Amsterdam: John Benjamins.

Gibson, E. 1998. Linguistic complexity: Locality of syntactic dependencies. *Cognition* 68: 1–76.

Gibson, E. 2000. The dependency locality theory: A distance-based theory of linguistic complexity. In *Image, Language, Brain: Papers from the First Mind Articulation Project Symposium*, A. Marantz, Y. Miyashita & W.O'Neil (eds), 95–126. Cambridge MA: The MIT press.

Goad, H., White, L. & Steele, J. 2003. Missing inflection in L2 acquisition: Defective syntax or L1-constrained prosodic representations? *Canadian Journal of Linguistics* 48: 243–263.
Goodluck, H. & Solan, L. 2000. Un effet du Principle C chez l'enfant francophone. *La Revue Canadienne de Linguistique* 45: 49–62.
Gopnik, M. 1990. Feature blindness: A case study. *Language Acquisition* 1: 139–164.
Gopnik, M. & Goad, H. 1997. What underlies infectional pattern errors in genetic dysphasia? *Journal of Neurolinguistics* 10: 109–137.
Granfeldt, J. 2000. The acquisition of the Determiner Phrase in bilingual and second language French. *Bilingualism: Language and Cognition* 3: 263–280.
Granfeldt, J. 2003. L'acquisition des catégories fonctionnelles: Étude comparative du développement du DP français chez des enfants et des apprenants adultes. Ph.D. dissertation, University of Lund.
Granfeldt, J. & Schlyter, S. 2004. Cliticization in the acquisition of French as L1 and L2. In *The Acquisition of French in Different Contexts: Focus on Functional Categories,* P. Prévost & J. Paradis (eds), 333–370. Amsterdam: John Benjamins.
Grévisse, M. 1980. *Le bon usage*. Paris: Duculot.
Grimshaw, J. 1990. *Argument Structure*. Cambridge MA: The MIT Press.
Grodzinsky, Y. & Reinhart, T. 1993. The innateness of binding and of coreference. *Linguistic Inquiry* 24: 69–101.
Grondin, N. & White, L. 1996. Functional categories in child L2 acquisition of French. *Language Acquisition* 5: 1–34.
Grüter, T. 2005. Comprehension and production of French object clitics by child second language learners and children with Specific Language Impairment. *Applied Psycholinguistics* 26: 363–391.
Grüter, T. 2006. Object Clitics and Null Objects in the Acquisition of French. Ph.D. dissertation. McGill University.
Guasti, M.-T. 1993/1994. Verb syntax in Italian child grammar: Finite and nonfinite verbs. *Language Acquisition* 3: 1–40.
Guasti, M.-T. 1996. Semantic restrictions in Romance causatives and the incorporation approach. *Linguistic Inquiry* 27: 294–312.
Guasti, M.-T. 2002. *Language Acquisition: The Growth of Grammar*. Cambridge MA: The MIT Press.
Guasti, T. & Cardinaletti, A. 2003. Relative clause formation in Romance child's production. *Probus* 15: 47–89.
Guasti, M.-T. & Shlonsky, U. 1995. The acquisition of French relative clauses reconsidered. *Language Acquisition* 4: 257–276.
Guéron, J. & Hoekstra, T. 1989. T-chains and the constituent structure of auxiliaries. In *Constituent Structure,* A. Cardinaletti, G. Cinque & G. Guisti (eds), 35–99. Dordrecht: Foris.
Haegeman, L. 1990. Understood subjects in English diaries. *Multilingua* 9: 157–199.
Haegeman, L. 1995. Root infinitives, tense, and truncated structures in Dutch. *Language Acquisition* 4: 205–255.
Haegeman, L. 1996. Root infinitives, clitics and truncated structures. In *Generative Approaches to First and Second Language Acquisition,* H. Clahsen (ed.), 271–307. Amsterdam: John Benjamins.
Haiden, M., Prévost, P., Tuller, L., Ferré, S. & Scheidnes, M. 2009. Production and comprehension of wh-questions in acquisition of French: Comparing L2 children and L1 children with SLI. Paper presented at the Workshop on Production-comprehension asymmetries in child language, Annual Meeting of the German Linguistics Society, University of Osnabrück, Osnabrück, Germany. 3–6 March 2009.

Hale, K. & Keyser, S.J. 2002. *Prolegomenon to a Theory of Argument Structure*. Cambridge MA: The MIT Press.

Halle, M. & Marantz, A. 1993. Distributed morphology and the pieces of inflection. In *The View from Building 20: Essays in Linguistics in Honor of Sylvain Bromberger,* K. Hale & S.J. Keyser (eds), 111–176. Cambridge MA: The MIT Press.

Hamann, C. 2000a. The acquisition of constituent questions and the requirements of interpretation. In *The Acquisition of Syntax: Studies in Comparative Developmental Linguistics,* M.-A. Friedemann & L. Rizzi (eds), 170–201. London: Longman.

Hamann, C. 2000b. Negation, infinitives and heads. In *The Acquisition of Scrambling and Cliticization,* S.M. Powers & C. Hamann (eds), 423–477. Dordrecht: Kluwer.

Hamann, C. 2002. *From Syntax to Discourse. Pronominal Clitics, Null Subjects and Infinitives in Child Language*. Dordrecht: Kluwer.

Hamann, C. 2003. Phenomena in French normal and impaired language acquisition and their implications for hypotheses on language development. *Probus* 15: 91–122.

Hamann, C. 2004. Comparing the development of the nominal and the verbal functional domain in French language impairment. In *The Acquisition of French in Different Contexts: Focus on Functional Categories,* P. Prévost & J. Paradis (eds), 119–144. Amsterdam: John Benjamins.

Hamann, C. 2006. Speculations about early syntax: The production of wh-questions by normally developing French children and French children with SLI. *The Catalan Journal of Linguistics* 5: 143–189.

Hamann, C. 2008. The first language acquisition of French from a generative perspective. In *Studies in French Applied Linguistics,* D. Ayoun (ed), 135–181. Amsterdam: John Benjamins.

Hamann, C., Arabatzi, M., Baranzini, L., Cronel-Ohayon, S., Chillier, L., Dubé, S., Franck, J., Frauenfelder, U., Rizzi, L., Starke, M. & Zesiger, P. 2002. On the dissociation of the nominal and the verbal functional domains in French language impairment. In *Proceedings of the 26th Annual Boston University Conference on Language Development,* B. Skarabela, S. Fish & A.H.-J. Do (eds), 267–277. Somerville MA: Cascadilla Press.

Hamann, C., Kowalski, O. & Philip, W. 1997. The French 'delay of Principle B' effect. In *Proceedings of the 21st Annual Boston University Conference on Language Development,* E. Hughes, M.Hughes & A. Greenhill (eds), 205–219. Somerville MA.: Cascadilla Press.

Hamann, C., Ohayon, S., Dubé, S., Frauenfelder, U.H., Rizzi, L., Starke, M. & Zesiger, P. 2003. Aspects of grammatical development in young French children with SLI. *Developmental Science* 6: 151–158.

Hamann, C., Penner, Z. & Lindner, K. 1998. German impaired grammar: The clause structure revisited. *Language Acquisition* 7: 193–245.

Hamann, C. & Plunkett, K. 1998. Subjectless sentences in child Dutch. *Cognition* 69: 35–72.

Hamann, C., Rizzi, L. & Frauenfelder, U. 1996. On the acquisition of the pronominal system in French. In *Generative Approaches to First and Second Language Acquisition,* H. Clahsen (ed.), 309–334. Amsterdam: John Benjamins.

Hamann, C., Tuller, L., Monjauze, C., Delage, H. & Henry, C. 2007. (Un)successful subordination in French-speaking children and adolescents with SLI. In *Proceedings of the 31st annual Boston University Conference on Language Development,* H. Caunt-Nulton, S. Kulatilake & I. Woo (eds), 286–297. Somerville MA.: Cascadilla Press.

Harley, B. 1989. Functional grammar in French immersion. *Applied Linguistics* 10: 331–359.

Harley, B. 1992. Patterns of second language development in French immersion. *French Language Studies* 2: 159–183.

Haverkort, M. & Weissenborn, J. (1991). Clitic and affix interactions in early Romance. Paper presented at the 16th Annual Boston University Conference on Language Development, Boston University, U.S.A.

Hawkins, R. 1989. Do second language learners acquire restrictive relative clauses on the basis of relational or configural information? The acquisition of French subject, direct object and genitive restrictive relative clauses by second language learners. *Second Language Research* 5: 156–188.

Hawkins, R. 1998. The inaccessibility of formal features of functional categories in second language acquisition. Paper presented at the Pacific Second Language Research Forum. Tokyo, Japan.

Hawkins, R. 2001. *Second Language Syntax: A Generative Introduction*. Oxford: Blackwell.

Hawkins, R. & Chan, C.Y-h. 1997. The partial availibility of Universal Grammar in second language acquisition: The 'failed functional features hypothesis'. *Second Language Research* 13: 187–226.

Hawkins, R. & Franceschina, F. 2004. Explaining the acquisition and non-acquisition of determiner-noun gender concord in French and Spanish. In *The Acquisition of French in Different Contexts: Focus on Functional Categories,* P. Prévost & J. Paradis (eds), 175–206. Amsterdam: John Benjamins.

Hawkins, R. & Hattori, H. 2006. Interpretation of English multiple wh-questions by Japanese speakers: A missing uninterpretable feature account. *Second Language Research* 22: 269–301.

Hawkins, R. & Liszka, S. 2003. Locating the source of defective past tense marking in advanced L2 English speakers. In *The Lexicon-syntax Interface in Second Language Acquisition,* R. van Hout, A. Hulk, F. Kuiken & R. Towell (eds), 21–44. Amsterdam: John Benjamins.

Hawkins, R., Towell, R. & Bazergui, N. 1993. Universal Grammar and the acquisition of French verb-movement by native speakers of English. *Second Language Research* 9: 189–233.

Haznedar, B. & Schwartz, B. 1997. Are there optional infinitives in child L2 acquisition? In *Proceedings of the 21st Boston University Conference on Language Development,* E. Hughes, M. Hughes & A. Greenhill (eds), 257–268. Somerville MA: Cascadilla Press.

Heap, D. & Roberge, Y. 2001. Cliticisation et théorie syntaxique, 1971–2001. *Revue Québécoise de Linguistique* 30: 63–90.

Heinen, S. & Kadow, H. 1990. The acquisition of French by monolingual children. In *Two First Languages: Early Grammatical Development in Bilingual Children,* J. Meisel (ed.), 47–72. Dordrecht: Foris.

Herschensohn, J. 1997. Parametric variation in L2 French speakers. In *Proceedings of the 21st Annual Boston University Conference on Language Development,* E. Hughes, M. Hughes & A. Greenhill (eds), 281–292. Somerville MA: Cascadilla Press.

Herschensohn, J. 1999. Minimalist access to UG in L2 French. In *Formal Perspectives on Romance Linguistics,* M. Authier, B. Bullock & L. Reed (eds), 167–178. Amsterdam: John Benjamins.

Herschensohn, J. 2000. *The Second Time Around: Minimalism and L2 Acquisition*. Amsterdam: John Benjamins.

Herschensohn, J. 2001. Missing inflection in second language French: Accidental infinitives and other verbal deficits. *Second Language Research* 17: 273–305.

Herschensohn, J. 2004. Functional categories and the acquisition of object clitics in L2 French. In *The Acquisition of French in Different Contexts: Focus on Functional Categories,* P. Prévost & J. Paradis (eds), 207–242. Amsterdam: John Benjamins.

Hickmann, M., Hendriks, H., Roland, F. & Liang, J. 1996. The marking of new information in children's narratives: A comparison of English, French, German and Mandarin Chinese. *Journal of Child Language* 23: 591–619.

Hoekstra, T. & Hyams, N. 1998. Aspects of root infinitives. *Lingua* 106: 81–112. Special issue: *Language Acquisition: Knowledge Representation and Processing,* A. Sorace (ed.).
Hoover, M. & Dwivedi, V. (1998). Syntactic processing by skilled bilinguals. *Language Learning* 48: 1–29.
Hu, J., Pan, H. & Xu, L. 2001. Is there a finite vs. nonfinite distinction in Chinese? *Linguistics* 39: 1117–1148.
Huang, C.-T.J. 1984. On the distribution and reference of empty pronouns. *Linguistic Inquiry* 15: 531–574.
Hulk, A. 1987. L'acquisition du français et le paramètre pro-drop. In *Études de linguistique françaises offertes à Robert de Dardel par ses amis et collègues,* B. Kampers-Mahne & C. Vet (eds), 53–61. Amsterdam: Rodopi.
Hulk, A. 1991. Parameter setting and the acquisition of word order in L2 French. *Second Language Research* 7: 1–34.
Hulk, A. 1995. L'acquisition du sujet en français. *Recherches Linguistiques de Vincennes* 24: 33–53.
Hulk, A. 1996. Parameter setting and the acquisition of wh-questions in L2 French. In *Investigating Second Language Acquisition,* P. Jordens & J. Lalleman (eds), 237–259. Berlin: Mouton de Gruyter.
Hulk, A. 1997. The acquisition of French object pronouns by a Dutch/French bilingual child. In *Proceedings of the GALA 1997 Conference on Language Acquisition,* A. Sorace, C. Heycock & R. Shillcock (eds), 521–526. Edinburgh: The University of Edinburgh.
Hulk, A. 2000. L'acquisition des pronoms clitiques français par un enfant bilingue français-néerlandais. *Revue Canadienne de Linguistique* 45: 97–117.
Hulk, A. 2004. The acquisition of the French DP in a bilingual context. In *The Acquisition of French in Different Contexts: Focus on Functional Categories,* P. Prévost & J. Paradis (eds), 243–274. Amsterdam: John Benjamins.
Hulk, A. & Müller, N. 2000. Crosslinguistic influence at the interface between syntax and pragmatics. *Bilingualism: Language and Cognition* 3: 227–244.
Hulk, A. & Zuckerman, S. 2000. The interaction between input and economy: Acquiring optionality in French Wh-questions. In *Proceedings of the 24th Annual Boston University Conference on Language Development,* S.C. Howell, S.A. Fish & T. Keith-Lucas (eds), 438–449. Somerville MA: Cascadilla Press.
Hyams, N. 1986. *Language Acquisition and the Theory of Parameters*. Dordrecht: Reidel.
Hyams, N. 1996. Underspecification of functional categories in early grammars. In *Generative Perspectives on Language Acquisition,* H. Clahsen (ed.), 91–127. Amsterdam: John Benjamins.
Hyams, N. 2001. Now you hear it, now you don't. In *Proceedings of the 25th Annual Boston University Conference on Language Development,* A.H.-J. Do, L. Domínguez & A. Johansen (eds), 34–58. Somerville MA: Cascadilla Press.
Hyams, N. 2007. Aspectual effects on interpretation in early grammar. *Language Acquisition* 14: 231–268.
Hyams, N. & Wexler, K. 1993. On the grammatical basis of null subjects in child language. *Linguistic Inquiry* 24: 421–459.
Iatridou, S. 1990. About Agr(P). *Linguistic Inquiry* 21: 551–577.
Ionin, T. & Wexler, K. 2002. Why is 'is' easier than '-s'? Acquisition of tense/agreement morphology by child second language learners of English. *Second Language Research* 18: 95–136.
Jaeggli, O. 1982. *Topics in Romance Syntax*. Dordrecht: Foris.
Jakubowicz, C. 1991. L'acquisition des anaphores et des pronoms lexicaux en français. In *Grammaire générative et syntaxe comparée,* J. Guéron & J.-Y. Pollock (eds), 229–252. Paris: Éditions du CNRS.

Jakubowicz, C. 1994. Reflexives in French and Danish: Morphology, syntax, and acquisition. In *Syntactic Theory and First Language Acquisition: Crosslinguistic Perspectives*, Vol. 2: *Binding, Dependencies and Learnability*, B. Lust, G. Hermon & J. Kornfilt (eds), 115–144. Hillsdale NJ: Lawrence Erlbaum.

Jakubowicz, C. 2003. Hypothèses psycholinguistiques sur la nature du déficit dysphasique. In *Les dysphasies*, V. Brun & C.L. Gérard (eds), 23–70. Paris: Édition Masson.

Jakubowicz, C. 2004. Question formation in French SLI: Is movement costly? Paper presented at Groningen Workshop on the L1 Acquisition of Tense, Aspect and Questions. June 11, 2004. University of Groningen, The Netherlands.

Jakubowicz, C. 2005. The language faculty: (Ab)normal development and interface constraints. Paper presented at GALA 2005, University of Siena, Italy.

Jakubowicz, C., Müller, N., Riemer, B. & Rigaut, C. 1997. The case of subject and object omissions in French and German. In *Proceedings of the 21st Annual Boston University Conference on Language Development*, E. Hughes, M. Hughes & A. Greenhill (eds), 331–342. Somerville MA: Cascadilla Press.

Jakubowicz, C. & Nash, L. 2001. Functional categories and syntactic operations in (ab)normal language acquisition. *Brain and Language* 77: 321–339.

Jakubowicz, C. & Nash, L. To appear. Why accusative clitics are avoided in normal and impaired children. In *Essays in Syntax, Morphology and Phonology in SLI*, C. Jakubowicz, L. Nash & K. Wexler (eds). Cambridge MA: The MIT Press.

Jakubowicz, C., Nash, L., Rigaut, C. & Gérard, C.-L. 1998. Determiners and clitic pronouns in French-Speaking children with SLI. *Language Acquisition* 8: 113–160.

Jakubowicz, C. & Rigaut, C. 2000. L'acquisition des clitiques nominatifs et des clitiques objets en français. *Revue Canadienne de Linguistique* 45: 119–157.

Jakubowicz, C. & Roulet, L. 2008. Narrow syntax or interface deficit? Gender agreement in French SLI. In *First Language Acquisition of Morphology and Syntax*, P. Guijarro-Fuentes, M.P. Larrañaga & J. Clibbens (eds), 185–225. Amsterdam: John Benjamins.

Jakubowicz, C. & Tuller, L. 2008. Specific language impairment in French. In *Studies in French Applied Linguistics*, D. Ayoun (ed), 97–134. Amsterdam: John Benjamins.

Jarema, G. & Friederici, A.D. 1994. Processing articles and pronouns in agrammatic aphasia: Evidence from French. *Brain and language* 64: 683–694.

Jones, M.A. 1996. *Foundations of French Syntax*. Cambridge: CUP.

Juffs, A. & Harrington, M. 1995. Parsing effects in second language processing: Subject and object asymmetries in wh-extraction. *Studies in Second Language Acquisition* 17: 483–516.

Juffs, A. & Harrington, M. 1996. Garden path sentences and error data in second language sentence processing. *Language Learning* 46: 283–326.

Kaiser, A. 1994. More about INFL-ection and agreement: The acquisition of clitic pronouns in French. In *Bilingual First Language Acquisition: French and German Grammatical Development*, J. Meisel (ed.), 131–159. Amsterdam: John Benjamins.

Karmiloff-Smith, A. 1979. *A Functional Approach to Child Language: A Study of Determiners and Reference*. Cambridge: CUP.

Kayne, R. 1975. *French Syntax*. Cambridge MA: The MIT Press.

Kayne, R. 1989. Null subjects and clitic climbing. In *The Null Subject Parameter*, O. Jaeggli & K. Safir (eds), 239–261. Dordrecht: Kluwer.

Kayne, R. 1994. *The Antisymmetry of Syntax*. Cambridge MA: The MIT Press.

Kayne, R. & Pollock, J.-Y. 2001. New thoughts on stylistic inversion. In *Subject Inversion in Romance and the Theory of Universal Grammar*, A. Hulk & J.-Y. Pollock (eds), 107–161. Oxford: OUP.

Kehayia, E. 1997. Lexical access and representation in individuals with genetic language impairment a cross-linguistic study. *Journal of Neurolinguistics* 10: 139–149.

Kihm, A. 2005. Noun class, gender, and the lexicon-syntax-morphology Interfaces: A comparative study of Niger-Congo and Romance languages. In *The Oxford Handbook of Comparative Syntax,* G. Cinque & R. Kayne (eds), 459–512. Oxford: OUP.

Klein, W. & Perdue, C. 1997. The Basic Variety (or: couldn't natural languages be much simpler?). *Second Language Research* 13: 301–347.

Koehn, C. 1994. The acquisition of gender and number morphology within NP. In *Bilingual First Language Acquisition: French and German Grammatical Development,* J. Meisel (ed.), 29–52. Amsterdam: John Benjamins.

Konhert, K., Windsor, J. & Danahy Ebert, K. 2009. Primary or 'specific' language impairment and children learning a second language. *Brain and Language* 109: 101–111.

Köppe, R. 1994. NP-movement and subject-raising. In *Bilingual First Language Acquisition: French and German Grammatical Development,* J. Meisel (ed.), 209–234. Amsterdam: John Benjamins.

Kupisch, T. 2003. The DP, a vulnerable domain? Evidence from the acquisition of French. In *(In) vulnerable Domains in Multilingualism,* N. Müller (ed.), 1–40. Amsterdam: John Benjamins.

Kupisch, T. 2008. Dominance, mixing and cross-linguistic influence: On their relation in bilingual development. In *First Language Acquisition of Morphology and Syntax,* P. Guijarro-Fuentes, M.P. Larrañaga & J. Clibbens (eds), 209–234. Amsterdam: John Benjamins.

Labelle, M. 1990. Predication, Wh-movement and the development of relative clauses. *Language Acquisition* 1: 95–119.

Labelle, M. 1996. The acquisition of relative clauses: movement or no movement? *Language Acquisition* 5: 65–82.

Labelle, M. 2000. Les infinitifs racines en langage enfantin. *Revue Canadienne de Linguistique* 45: 159–192.

Labelle, M. & Valois, D. 1996. The status of post-verbal subjects in French child language. *Probus* 8: 53–80.

Laenzlinger, C. 2005. French adjective ordering: Perspectives on DP-internal movement types. *Lingua* 115: 645–689.

Lahousse, K. 2004. NP subject inversion in French: Two types, two configurations. *Lingua* 116: 424–461.

Lakshamanan, U. & Selinker, L. 1994. The status of CP and the tensed complementizer *that* in the developing L2 grammar of English. *Second Language Research* 10: 24–48.

Lamarche, J. 1991. Problems for N-movement to NumP. *Probus* 3: 215–236.

Lambrecht, K. 1981. *Topic, Antitopic and Verb Agreement in Non-standard French.* Amsterdam: John Benjamins.

Lambrecht, K. 1988. Presentational cleft constructions in spoken French. In *Clause Combining in Grammar and Discourse,* J. Haiman & S. Thompson (eds), 135–179. Amsterdam: John Benjamins.

Lardiere, D. 1998. Dissociating syntax from morphology in a divergent L2 end-state grammar. *Second Language Research* 14: 359–375.

Lardiere, D. 2000. Mapping syntactic features to forms in second language acquisition. In *Second Language Acquisition and Linguistic Theory,* J. Archibald (ed.), 102–129. Oxford: Blackwell.

Lardiere, D. 2003. Second language knowledge of [±past] vs. [±finite]. In *Proceedings of the 6th Generative Approaches to Second Language Acquisition Conference (GASLA 2002): L2 Links,* J. Liceras, H. Zobl & H. Goodluck (eds), 176–189. Somerville MA: Cascadilla Press.

Lebeaux, D. 1988. Language Acquisition and the Form of Grammar. Ph.D. dissertation, University of Massachussets, Amherst.

Legendre, G, Hagstrom, P., Vainikka, A. & Todorova, M. 2002. Partial constraint ordering in child French syntax. *Language Acquisition* 10: 189–227.

Leonard, L. 1989. Language learnability and specific language impairment in children. *Applied Psycholinguistics* 10: 179–202.

Leonard, L. 1998. *Children with Specific Language Impairment*. Cambridge MA: The MIT Press.

Leonard, L., Bortolini, U., Caselli, M. & McGregor, K. 1992. Morphological deficits in children with specific language impairment: The status of features in underlying grammar. *Language Acquisition* 2: 151–179.

Leonard, L., Sabbadini, L., Leonard, J. & Volterra, V. 1987. Specific language impairment in children: A crosslinguistic study. *Brain and Language* 32: 233–252.

Leung, Y.-k.I. 2002. Functional Categories in Second and Third Language Acquisition: A Cross-linguistic Study of the Acquisition of English and French by Chinese and Vietnamese Speakers. Ph.D. dissertation, McGill University.

Levow, G. 1995. Tense and subject position in interrogatives and negatives in child French: Evidence for and against truncated structures. *MIT Working Papers in Linguistics* 26: 281–304.

Lightbown, P. 1977. Consistency and Variation in the Acquisition of French. Ph.D. dissertation, Columbia University.

Lleó, C. & Demuth, K. 1999. Prosodic constraints on the emergence of grammatical morphemes: Crosslinguistic evidence from Germanic and Romance languages. In *Proceedings of the 23rd Annual Boston University Conference of Language Development,* A. Greenhill, H. Littlefield & C. Tano (eds), 407–418. Somerville MA: Cascadilla Press.

Longobardi, G. 1994. Reference and proper names. *Linguistic Inquiry* 25: 609–665.

Longobardi, G. 1996. The syntax of N-raising: A minimalist theory. *UiL OTS Working Papers in Theoretical Linguistics* 96.

Longobardi, G. 2001. The structure of DPs: Some principles, parameters and problems. In *The Handbook of Contemporary Syntactic Theory,* M. Baltin & C. Collins (eds), 562–603. Oxford: Blackwell.

MacWhinney, B. 2000. *The CHILDES Project: Tools for Analyzing Talk.* Hillsdale NJ: Lawrence Erlbaum.

Marantz, A. 1997. No escape from syntax: Don't try morphological analysis in the privacy of your own lexicon. *U. Penn Working Papers In Linguistics* 4: 201–225.

Marchman, V.A. & Bates, E. 1994. Continuity in lexical and morphological development: A test of the critical mass hypothesis. *Journal of Child Language* 21: 339–366.

Marcus, G.F. 1993. Negative evidence in language acquisition. *Cognition* 46: 53–85.

Marcus, G.F. 1996. Why do children say 'breaked'? *Current Directions in Psychological Science* 5: 81–85.

Marshall, C. & van der Lely, H.K.J. 2006. A challenge to current models of past tense inflection: the impact of phonotactics. *Cognition* 100: 302–320.

Marshall, C. & van der Lely, H.K.J. 2007. The impact of phonological complexity on past tense inflection in children with Grammatical SLI. *Advances in Speech and Language Pathology* 9: 191–203.

Mathieu, E. 2002. The Syntax of Non-canonical Quantification: A Comparative Study. Ph.D. dissertation, University College London.

Mathieu, E. 2004. The mapping of form and interpretation: The case of optional wh-movement in French. *Lingua* 114: 1090–1132.

McDaniel, D., McKee, C. & Smith Cairns, H. (eds). 1996. *Methods for Assessing Children's Syntax*. Cambridge MA: The MIT Press.

Meisel, J. 1990. INFL-ection and subject-verb agreement. In *Two First Languages: Early Development in Bilingual Children,* J. Meisel (ed), 237–297. Dordrecht: Foris.

Meisel, J. 1991. Principles of UG and strategies of language use: On some similarities and differences between first and second language acquisition. In *Point-counterpoint,* L. Eubank (ed.), 231–276. Dodrecht: Kluwer.

Meisel, J. 1994. Getting FAT: Finiteness, agreement and tense in early grammar. In *Bilingual First Language Acquisition: French and German Grammatical Development,* J. Meisel (ed.), 89–130. Amsterdam: John Benjamins.

Meisel, J. 1997. The acquisition of the syntax of negation in French and German: Contrasting first and second language development. *Second Language Research* 13: 227–263.

Meisel, J. 2001. The simultaneous acquisition of two languages: Early differentiation and subsequent developments of grammars. In *Trends in Bilingual Acquisition*, J. Cenoz & F. Genesee (eds), 11–41. Amsterdam: John Benjamins.

Meisel, J. 2004. The bilingual child. In *Handbook of Bilingualism*, T.K. Bathia & W.C. Ritchie (eds), 91–113. Oxford : Blackwell.

Meisel, J. 2007. The weaker language in early bilingualism: Acquiring a first language as a second language? *Applied Psycholinguistics* 28: 495–514.

Meisel, J. & Müller, N. 1992. Finiteness and verb placement in early child grammars: Evidence from simultaneous acquisition of French and German in bilinguals. In *The Acquisition of Verb Movement,* J. Meisel (ed.), 109–138. Dodrecht: Kluwer.

Mertens, P. 1990. Intonation. In *Le français parlé. Études grammaticales,* C. Blanche-Benveniste (ed.), 159–176. Paris: Éditions du CNRS.

Mertens, P. 1993. Accentuation, intonation et morphosyntaxe. *Travaux de Linguistique* 26: 21–69.

Monjauze, C. 2007. Langage et épilepsie à pointes centro-tempoales: Déficits et séquelles. Ph.D. dissertation. François-Rabelais University, Tours, France.

Montrul, S. 2002. Incomplete acquisition and attrition of Spanish tense/aspect distinctions in adult bilinguals. *Bilingualism: Language and Cognition* 5: 39–68.

Montrul, S. 2004. Subject and object expression in Spanish heritage speakers: A case of morphosyntactic convergence. *Bilingualism: Language and Cognition* 7: 125–142.

Morgan, J.L. & Travis, L. 1989. Limits on negative information in language input. *Journal of Child Language* 16: 531–552.

Müller, N. 1990. Developing two gender assignment systems simultaneously. In *Two First Languages: Early Development in Bilingual Children,* J. Meisel (ed.), 193–294. Dordrecht: Foris.

Müller, N. 1994a. Gender and number agreement within DP. In *Bilingual First Language Acquisition: French and German Grammatical Development,* J. Meisel (ed.), 53–88. Amsterdam: John Benjamins.

Müller, N. (1994b). Parameters cannot be reset: Evidence from the development of COMP. In J. Meisel (ed), *Bilingual First Language Acquisition: French and German Grammatical Development* (pp. 235–269). Amsterdam: John Benjamins.

Müller, N. 1998. UG access without parameter fixing: A longitudinal study of (L1 Italian) German as a second language. In *Morphology and its Interfaces in L2 Knowledge,* M. Beck (ed.), 115–164. Amsterdam: John Benjamins.

Müller, N. 2004. Null arguments in bilingual children: French topics. In *The Acquisition of French in Different Contexts: Focus on Functional Categories,* P. Prévost & J. Paradis (eds), 275–304. Amsterdam: John Benjamins.

Müller, N., Crysmann, B. & Kaiser, G. 1996. Interactions between the acquisition of French object drop and the development of the C-system. *Language Acquisition* 5: 35–63.

Müller, N. & Hulk, A. 2001. Crosslinguistic influence in Bilingual Language Acquisition: Italian and French as recipient languages. *Bilingualism: Language and cognition* 4: 1–21.

Müller, N., Hulk, A. & Jakubowicz, C. 1999. Object omissions in bilingual children: Evidence for crosslinguistic influence. In *Proceedings of the 23rd Annual Boston University Conference on Language Development*, A. Greenhill, H. Littlefield & C. Tano (eds), 482–494. Somerville MA: Cascadilla Press.

Müller, N. & Penner, Z. 1996. Early subordination: The acquisition of free morphology in French, German and Swiss German. *Linguistics* 34: 133–165.

Müller, N. & Pillunat, A. 2008. Balanced bilingual children with two weak languages: A French/German case study. In *First Language Acquisition of Morphology and Syntax*, P. Guijarro-Fuentes, M.P. Larrañaga & J. Clibbens (eds), 269–294. Amsterdam: John Benjamins.

Müller, N., Schmitz, K., Cantone, K. & Kupisch, T. 2006. Null arguments in monolingual children: A comparison of Italian and French. In *The Acquisition of Syntax in Romance Languages*, V. Torrens & L. Escobar (eds), 69–94. Amsterdam: John Benjamins.

Murphy, V. 1997. The effect of modality on a grammaticality judgment task. *Second Language Research* 13: 34–65.

Myles, F. 1995. Interaction between linguistic theory and language processing in SLA. *Second Language Research* 11: 235–266.

Myles, F. 2004. From data to theory: The over-representation of linguistic knowledge in SLA. *Transactions of the Philological Society* 102: 139–168.

Myles, F. 2005. The emergence of morpho-syntactic structure in French L2. In *Focus on French as a Foreign Language: Multidisciplinary Approaches*, J.-M. Dewaele (ed.), 88–113. Clevedon: Multilingual Matters.

Myles, F., Hooper, J. & Mitchell, R. 1998. Rote or rule? Exploring the role of formulaic language in classroom foreign language learning. *Language Learning* 48: 323–363.

Myles, F, Mitchell, R. & Hooper, J. 1999. Interrogative chunks in French L2: A basis for creative construction? *Studies in Second Language Acquisition* 21: 49–80.

N'Guyen, D.-H. 1997. *Vietnamese*. Amsterdam: John Benjamins.

Nicoladis, E. 1995. Code-mixing in Young Bilingual Children. Ph.D. dissertation, McGill University.

Obenauer, H.-G. 1983. Une quantification non canonique: La 'quantification à distance'. *Langue Française* 58: 66–88.

Obenauer, H.-G. 1984/1985. On the identification of empty categories. *The Linguistic Review* 4: 153–202.

Oiry, M. & Demirdache, H. 2006. Evidence from L1 acquisition for the syntax of wh-scope marking in French. In *The Acquisition of Romance Languages*, V. Torrens & L. Escobar (eds), 289–315. Amsterdam: John Benjamins.

Papadopoulou, D. & Clahsen, H. 2003. Parsing strategies in L1 and L2 sentence processing: A study of relative clause attachment in Greek. *Studies in Second Language Acquisition* 25: 501–528.

Paradis, J. & Crago, M. 2000. Tense and temporality: A comparison between children learning a second language and children with SLI. *Journal of Speech, Language and Hearing Research* 43: 834–847.

Paradis, J. & Crago, M. 2001. The morphosyntax of specific language impairment in French: An extended optional default account. *Language Acquisition* 9: 269–300.

Paradis, J. & Crago, M. 2003. What can SLI tell us about transfer in SLA? In *Proceedings of the 6th Generative Approaches to Second Language Acquisition conference (GASLA 2002): L2 Links,* J. Liceras, H. Zobl & H. Goodluck (eds), 638–649. Somerville MA: Cascadilla Press.

Paradis, J. & Crago, M. 2004. Comparing L2 and SLI grammars in child French: Focus on DP. In *The Acquisition of French in Different Contexts: Focus on Functional Categories,* P. Prévost & J. Paradis (eds), 89–108. Amsterdam: John Benjamins.

Paradis, J., Crago, M. & Genesee, F. 2003. Object clitics as a clinical marker of SLI in French: Evidence from French-English bilingual children. In *Proceedings of the 27th Annual Boston University Conference on Language Development,* B. Beachley, A. Brown & F. Conlin (eds), 638–649. Somerville MA: Cascadilla Press.

Paradis, J., Crago, M. & Genesee, F. 2005/2006. Domain-general versus domain-specific accounts of Specific LanguageImpairment: Evidence from bilingual children' acquisition of object pronouns. *Language Acquisition* 13: 33–62.

Paradis, J. & Genesee, F. 1996. Syntactic acquisition in bilingual children: Autonomous or interdependent? *Studies in Second Language Acquisition* 18: 1–25.

Paradis, J. & Genesee, F. 1997. On continuity and the emergence of functional catgories in bilingual first-language acquisition. *Language Acquisition* 6: 91–124.

Paradis, J., Le Corre, M. & Genesee, F. 1998. The emergence of tense and agreement in child L2 French. *Second Language Research* 14: 227–257.

Paradis, J., Nicoladis, E. & Genesee, F. 2000. Early emergence of structural constraints on code-mixing: Evidence from French-English bilingual children. *Bilingualism: Language and Cognition* 3: 245–261.

Penner, Z. 1994. Asking questions without CPs? In *Language Acquisition Studies in Generative Grammar,* T. Hoekstra & B. Schwartz (eds), 177–213. Amsterdam: John Benjamins.

Perdue, C. 1984. *Second Language Acquisition by Adult Immigrants: A Field Manual.* Rowley MA: Newbury House.

Pérez-Leroux, A., Pirvulescu, M. & Roberge, Y. 2008. Null objects in child language: Syntax and the lexicon. *Lingua* 118: 370–398.

Pérez-Leroux, A., Pirvulescu, M. & Roberge, Y. 2009. Bilingualism as a window into the language faculty: The acquisition of objects in French-speaking children in bilingual and monolingual contexts. *Bilingualism: Language and Cognition* 12: 97–112.

Philip, W. & Coopmans, P. 1996. The double Dutch delay of Principle B effect. In *Proceedings of the 20th Annual Boston University Conference on Language Development,* A. Stringfellow, D. Cahana-Amitay, E. Hughes & A. Zukowski (eds), 576–587. Somerville MA.: Cascadilla Press.

Phillips, C. 1995. Syntax at age 2: Crosslinguistic differences. *MIT Working Papers in Linguistics* 26: 325–382.

Picallo, C. 1991. Nominals and nominalizations in Catalan. *Probus* 3: 279–316.

Pierce, A. 1992. *Language Acquisition and Syntactic Theory.* Dordrecht: Kluwer.

Pinker, S. 1989. *Learnability and Cognition. The Acquisition of Argument Structure.* Cambridge MA: The MIT Press.

Pinker, S. 1999. *Words and Rules: The Ingredients of Language.* New York NY: Basic Books.

Pirvulescu, M. 2006. The acquisition of object clitic in French L1: spontaneous vs. elicited production. In *Language Acquisition and Development: Proceedings of GALA 2005,* A. Belletti, E. Bennati, C. Chesi, E. Di Domenico & I. Ferrari (eds), 450–462. Newcastle: Cambridge Scholars Press.

Pirvulescu, M. & Belzil, I. 2008. The acquisition of past participle agreement in Québec French. *Language Acquisition* 17: 75–88.

Pirvulescu, M. & Roberge, Y. 2005. Licit and illicit null objects in L1 French. In *Theoretical and Experimental Approaches to Romance Linguistics: Selected Papers from the 34th Linguistic Symposium on Romance Languages (LSRL), Salt Lake City, March 2004,* R.S. Gess & E.J. Rubin (eds), 197–212. Amsterdam: John Benjamins.

Pizzioli, F. & Schelstraete, M.-A. 2008. The argument structure complexity effect in children with Specific Language Impairment : Evidence from the use of grammatical morphemes in French. *Journal of Speech, Language, and Hearing Research* 51: 706–721.

Plunkett, B. 1999. Targeting complex structure in French questions. In *Proceedings of the 23rd Annual Boston University Conference on Language Development,* A. Greenhill, H. Littlefield & C. Tano (eds), 764–775. Somerville MA: Cascadilla Press.

Plunkett, B. 2000. What's 'what' in French questions? *Journal of Linguistics* 36: 511–530.

Plunkett, B. 2004a. Locutionary inversion in modern French. *York Papers in Linguistics* 2: 151–179.

Plunkett, B. 2004b. Early peripheries in the absence of C. In *Peripheries: Syntactic Edges and their Effects,* D. Adger (ed.), 383–405. Dordrecht: Kluwer.

Poeppel, D. & Wexler, K. 1993. The Full Competence Hypothesis of clause structure in early German. *Language* 69: 1–33.

Pollock, J.-Y. 1989. Verb movement, Universal Grammar, and the structure of IP. *Linguistic Inquiry* 20: 365–424.

Prévost, P. 1997. Truncation in Second Language Acquisition. Ph.D. dissertation, McGill University.

Prévost, P. 2001. La variabilité morphologique en français langue seconde. *Langue et Linguistique* 27: 95–124.

Prévost, P. 2003a. On the nature of root infinitives in adult L2 French. In *Romance Linguistics: Theory and Acquisition,* A.-T. Pérez-Leroux & Y. Roberge (eds), 367–384. Amsterdam: John Benjamins.

Prévost, P. 2003b. Verb-types and modality in early child L2 root infinitives. In *Proceedings of the 6th Generative Approaches to Second Language Acquisition Conference (GASLA 2002): L2 Links,* J. Liceras, H. Zobl & H. Goodluck (eds), 238–247. Somerville MA.: Cascadilla Press.

Prévost, P. 2004. Morphological variation in early adult second language French: A cross-sectional study. In *The Eurosla Yearbook* 4, S. Foster-Cohen, M. Sharwood Smith, A. Sorace & M. Ota (eds), 147–175. Amsterdam: John Benjamins.

Prévost, P. 2006a. The phenomenon of object omission in child L2 French. *Bilingualism: Language and Cognition* 9: 263–280.

Prévost, P. 2006b. Morphological variability in the development of L2 French morphosyntax: The issues of impairment and L1 influence. In *Inquiries in Linguistic Development: Studies in Honor of Lydia White*, R. Slabakova, S. Montrul & P. Prévost (eds), 135–156. Amsterdam: John Benjamins.

Prévost, P. 2008. Truncation in child L2 acquisition: Evidence from verbless utterances. In *Current Trends in Child Second Language Acquisition: A Generative Perspective,* B. Haznedar & E. Gavruseva (eds), 177–208. Amsterdam: John Benjamins.

Prévost, P. & White, L. 2000a. Accounting for morphological variability in second language acquisition: Truncation or missing inflection? In *The Acquisition of Syntax*, M.-A. Friedemann & L. Rizzi (eds), 202–235. London: Longman.

Prévost, P. & White, L. 2000b. Missing surface Inflection or impairment in second language acquisition? Evidence from tense and agreement. *Second Language Research* 16: 103–134.

Radford, A. 1990. The syntax of nominal arguments in early child English. *Language Acquisition* 1: 195–223.

Radford, A. 2000. Children in search of perfection: Towards a minimalist model of language acquisition. *Essex Research Reports in Linguistics* 34: 57–74.

Rasetti, L. 2000. Null subjects and root infinitives in the child grammar of French. In *The Acquisition of Syntax*, M.-A. Friedemann & L. Rizzi (eds), 236–268. London: Longman.

Rasetti, L. 2003. Optional Categories in Early French Syntax: A Developmental Study of Root Infinitives and Null Arguments. Ph.D. dissertation, University of Geneva.

Redlinger, W.E. & Park, T. 1980. Language mixing in young bilinguals. *Journal of Child Language* 7: 337–352.

Rice, M., Ruff Noll, K. & Grimm, H. 1997. An extended optional infinitive stage in German-speaking children with Specific Language Impairment. *Language Acquisition* 6: 255–295.

Rice, M., & Wexler, K. 1996. Toward tense as a clinical marker of specific language impairment in English-speaking children. *Journal of Speech and Hearing Research* 39: 1239–1257.

Rice, M., Wexler, K. & Cleave, P. 1995. Specific Language Impairment as a period of extended optional infinitive. *Journal of Speech and Hearing Research* 38: 850–863.

Ritter, E. 1991. Two functional categories in noun phrases: Evidence from Modern Hebrew. In *Syntax and Semantics* 26, S. Rothstein (ed.), 37–62. San Diego CA: Academic Press.

Rizzi, L. 1986. On the status of subject clitics in Romance. In *Studies in Romance Linguistics*, O. Jaeggli & C. Silva-Corvalán (eds), 391–420. Dordrecht: Foris.

Rizzi, L. 1990. *Relativized Minimality*. Cambridge MA: The MIT Press.

Rizzi, L. 1991. Residual verb-second and the Wh-criterion. *Technical Reports on Formal and Computational Linguistics* 2.

Rizzi, L. 1993/1994. Some notes on linguistic theory and language development: The case of root infinitives. *Language Acquisition* 3: 371–393.

Rizzi, L. 1994. Early null subjects and root null subjects. In *Language Acquisition Studies in Generative Grammar*, T. Hoekstra & B. Schwartz (eds), 151–176. Amsterdam: John Benjamins.

Rizzi, L. 1997. The fine structure of the left periphery. In *Elements of Grammar: Handbook of Generative Syntax*, L. Haegeman (ed.), 281–238. Dordrecht: Kluwer.

Rizzi, L. 1998. Remarks on early null subjects. In *Proceedings of the 22nd Annual Boston University Conference on Language Development*, A. Greenhill, M. Hughes, H. Littlefield & H. Walsh (eds), 14–38. Somerville MA: Cascadilla Press.

Rizzi, L. 2000. Remarks on early null subjects. In *The Acquisition of Syntax*, M.-A. Friedemann & L. Rizzi (eds), 269–292. London: Longman.

Rizzi, L. 2006. Grammatically-based target-inconsistencies in child language. In *The Proceedings of the Inaugural Conference on Generative Approaches to Language Acquisition–North America, Honolulu HI* [University of Connecticut Occasional Papers in Linguistics 4]. K.U. Deen, J. Nomura, B. Schulz & B. Schwartz (eds), 19–49.

Rizzi, L. & Roberts, I. 1989. Complex inversion in French. *Probus* 1: 1–39.

Roberge, Y. 1990. *The Syntactic Recoverability of Null Arguments*. Kingston: McGill-Queen's University Press.

Roberts, I. 1997. Restructuring, head movement and locality. *Linguistic Inquiry* 28: 423– 460.

Roeper, T. 1999. Universal bilingualism. *Bilingualism: Language and Cognition* 2: 169–186.

Roeper, T. & Weissenborn, J. 1990. How to make parameters work: Comments on Valian. In *Language Processing and Language Acquisition*, L. Frazier & J. deVilliers (eds), 147–162. Dordrecht: Kluwer.

Romaine, S. 1996. Bilingualism. In *Handbook of Second Language Acquisition*, W. Ritchie & T. Bhatia (eds), 571–604. San Diego CA: Academic Press.

Rondal, J.A. 1985. *Adult-child Interaction and the Process of Language Understanding*. New York NY: Praeger.
Roulet, L. 2007. L'accord grammatical de genre dans la dysphasie de développement. *Psychologie Française* 52: 55–70.
Roulet-Amiot, L. 2008. Traitement de l'accord grammatical chez des enfants atteints d'un trouble spécifique du développement du langage. Ph.D. dissertation, Université Paris Descartes.
Roulet-Amiot, L. & Jakubowicz, C. 2006. Production and perception of gender agreement in French SLI. *Advances in Speech-Language Pathology* 8: 335–346.
Royle, P. 2007. Variable effects of morphology and frequency on inflection patterns in French preschoolers. *The Mental Lexicon* 2: 103–127.
Royle, P., Jarema, G. & Kehayia, E. 2002. Frequency effects on visual word access in developmental language impairment. *Neurolinguistics* 15: 11–41.
Royle, P. & Thordardottir, E.T. 2007. Elicitation of the *passé composé* in French preschoolers with and without Specific Language Impairment. *Applied Psycholinguistics* 29: 341–365.
Rule, S. & Marsden, E. 2006. The acquisition of functional categories in early French second language grammars: The use of finite and non-finite verbs in negative contexts. *Second Language Research* 22: 188–218.
Ruwet, N. 1972. *Théorie syntaxique et syntaxe du français*. Paris: Editions du Seuil.
Sano, T. & Hyams, N. 1994. Agreement, finiteness and the development of null arguments. In *Proceedings of NELS* 24, M. Gonzàlez (ed.), 543–558. Amherst MA: GLSA.
Say, T. & Clahsen, H. 2002. Words, rules and stems in the Italial mental lexicon. In *Storage and Computation in the Language Faculty,* S. Nooteboom, F. Weermman & F. Wijnen (eds), 93–129. Dordrecht: Kluwer.
Schachter, J. 1990. On the issue of completeness in second language acquisition. *Second Language Research* 6: 93–124.
Schaeffer, J. 1997. On the interpretation of (bare) object nouns in child language. In *The Interpretation of Root Infinitives and Bare Nouns in Child Language,* J. Schaeffer (ed.), 92–113. Cambridge MA: The MIT occasional Papers in Linguistics.
Schaeffer, J. 2000. *The Acquisition of Direct Object Scrambling and Clitic Placement: Syntax and Pragmatics*. Amsterdam: John Benjamins.
Schlyter, S. 1993. The weaker language in bilingual Swedish-French children. In *Progression and Regression,* K. Hyltenstam & A. Viberg (eds), 289–308. Cambridge: CUP.
Schlyter, S. 1997. Formes verbales et pronoms objets chez des apprenants adultes de français en milieu naturel. In *Actes du colloque international sur l'acquisition de la syntaxe en langue maternelle et en langue étrangère* [Annales littéraires de l'Université de Franche-Comté 631], C. Martinot (ed.), 273–293. Paris: Les Belles Lettres.
Schlyter, S. 2003. Development of verb morphology and finiteness in children and adults acquiring French. In *Information Structure and Dynamics of Language Acquisition,* C. Dimorth & M. Starren (eds), 15–44. Amsterdam: John Benjamins.
Schmitz, K. & Müller, N. 2008. Strong and clitic pronouns in monolingual and bilingual acquisition of French and Italian. *Bilingualism: Language and Cognition* 11: 19–41.
Schütze, C. 1996. *The Empirical Base of Linguistics: Grammaticality Judgments and Linguistic Methodology*. Cambridge MA: The MIT Press.
Schütze, C. & Wexler, K. 1996. Subject case licensing and English root infinitives. In *Proceedings of the 20th Annual Boston University Conference on Language Development,* A. Stringfellow, D. Cahana-Amitay, E. Hughes & A. Zukowski (eds), 670–681. Somerville MA: Cascadilla Press.

Schütze, C. & Wexler, K. 2000. An elicitation study of young children's knowledge of tense: semantic and syntactic properties of optional infinitives. In *Proceedings of the 24th Annual Boston University Conference on Language Development*, S.C. Howell, S.A. Fish & T. Keith-Lucas (eds), 669–683. Somerville: Cascadilla Press.

Schwartz, B. 1999. Some specs on specs in L2 acquisition. In *Specifiers: Minimalist Approaches,* D. Adger, S. Pintzuk, B. Plunkett & G. Tsoulas (eds), 299–337. Oxford: OUP.

Schwartz, B. 2004. Why child L2 acquisition? In *Proceedings of GALA 2003,* J. van Kampen & S. Baauw (eds), 47–66. Utrecht: LOT.

Schwartz, B. & Sprouse, R. 1994. Word order and nominative case in non-native language acquisition. In *Language Acquisition Studies in Generative Grammar,* T. Hoekstra & B. Schwartz (eds), 317–368. Amsterdam: John Benjamins.

Schwartz, B. & Sprouse, R. 1996. L2 cognitive states and the Full Transfer/Full Access Model. *Second Language Research* 12: 40–72.

Schwartz, B. & Sprouse, R. 2000. When syntactic theories evolve: Consequences for L2 acquisition research. In *Second Language Acquisition and Linguistic Theory,* J. Archibald (ed.), 156–186. Oxford: Blackwell.

Scott, G.-J. 2002. Stacked adjectival modification and the structure of nominal phrases. In *Functional Structure in DP and IP: The Cartography of Syntactic Structures,* Vol. 1, G. Cinque (ed.), 91–121. Oxford: OUP.

Serratrice, L., Sorace, A. & Paoli, S. 2004. Transfer at the syntax-pragmatics interface: Subjects and objects in Italian-English bilingual and monolingual acquisition. *Bilingualism: Language and Cognition* 7: 183–205.

Shapiro, K. & Caramazza, A. 2003. Grammatical processing of nouns and verbs in left frontal cortex. *Neuropsychologia* 41: 1189–1198.

Shapiro, K., Moo, L. & Caramazza, A. 2006. Cortical signatures of noun and verb production. *Proceedings of the National Academy of Science* 103: 1644–1649.

Shlonsky, U. 1992. Resumptive pronouns as last resort. *Linguistic Inquiry* 23: 443–468.

Smith, N. & Tsimpli, I. M. 1995. *The Mind of a Savant.* Oxford: Blackwell.

Sorace, A. 1993. Unaccusativity and auxiliary choice in non-native grammars of Italian and French: Asymmetries and predictable indeterminacy. *Journal of French Language Studies* 3: 71–93.

Sorace, A. 2003. Near-nativeness. In *The Handbook of Second Language Acquisition,* C. Doughty & M. Long (eds), 130–151. Oxford: Blackwell.

Sorace, A. 2004. Native language attrition and developmental instability at the syntax-discourse interface: Data, interpretations and methods. *Bilingualism: Language and Cognition* 7: 143–145.

Sorace, A. 2005. Syntactic optionality at interfaces. In *Syntax and Variation: Reconciling the Biological and the Social,* L. Cornips & K. Corrigan (eds), 46–111. Amsterdam: John Benjamins.

Sportiche, D. 1988. A theory of floating quantifiers and its corollaries for constituent structure. *Linguistic Inquiry* 19: 425–449.

Sportiche, D. 1996. Clitic constructions. In *Phrase Structure and the Lexicon,* J. Rooryck & L. Zaring (eds), 213–276. Dordrecht: Reidel.

Sprouse, R. 1998. Some notes on the relationship between inflectional morphology and parameter setting in first and second language acquisition. In *Morphology and the Interfaces in Second Language Knowledge*, M.-L. Beck (ed.), 41–67. Amsterdam, John Benjamins.

Stowe, L. 1992. The processing implementation of syntactic constraints: The sentence matching debate. In *Island Constraints,* H. Goodluck & M. Rochemont (eds), 419–443. Dordrecht: Kluwer.

Strik, N. 2003. *Où tu as caché ton sac? Qu'est-ce que tu penses que je lis!* Acquisition des questions Wh chez les enfants francophones de 3 à 6 ans. Mémoire de DEA, Universités de Paris V & Paris VIII.

Strik, N. 2007. L'acquisition des phrases interrogatives chez les enfants francophones. *Psychologie Française* 52: 27–39.

Strik, N. 2008. Syntaxe et acquisition des phrases interrogatives en français et en néerlandais: Une étude comparative. Ph.D. dissertation, Université Paris VIII, Saint-Denis.

Suppes, P., Smith, R. & Leveillé, M. 1973. The French syntax of a child's noun phrase. *Archives de Psychologie* 42: 207–279.

Szabolcsi, A. 1983. The possessor that ran away from home. *The Linguistic Review* 3: 89–102.

Szabolcsi, A. 1987. Functional categories in the noun phrase. In *Approaches to Hungarian* 2, I. Kenesei (ed.), 167–189. Szeged: JATE.

Thordardottir, E.T. & Namazi, M. 2007. Specific Language Impairment in French-speaking children: Beyond grammatical morphology. *Journal of Speech, Language, and Hearing Research* 50 : 698–715.

Towell, R. 1987. Variability and progress in the development of advanced learners of a foreign language. In *Second Language Acquisition in Context,* R. Ellis (ed.), 113–127. London: Prentice Hall.

Towell, R. & Hawkins, R. 1994. *Approaches to Second Language Acquisition.* Clevedon: Multilingual Matters.

Tracy, R. 1994. Raising questions: Formal and functional aspects of the acquisition of wh-questions in German. In *How tolerant is Universal Grammar? Essays on Language Learnability and Language Variation,* R. Tracy & E. Lattney (eds), 1–34. Tübingen: Niemeyer.

Trévise, A. & Noyau, C. 1984. Adult native speakers and the acquisition of French negation forms: Individual variation and linguistic awareness. In *Second Languages: A Cross-linguistic Perspective,* R. Andersen (ed.), 165–190. Rowley MA: Newbury House.

Tsimpli, I.M. 2003. Clitics and determiners in L2 Greek. In *Proceedings of the 6th Generative Approaches to Second Language Acquisition Conference,* J.M. Liceras, H. Zobl & H. Goodluck (eds), 331–339. Somerville MA: Cascadilla Press.

Tsimpli, I.M. & A. Roussou. 1991. Parameter resetting in second language acquisition? *UCL Working papers in Linguistics* 3: 149–169.

Tsimpli, I.M. & A. Sorace 2006. Differentiating interfaces: L2 performance in syntax-semantics and syntax-pragmatics phenomena. In *Proceedings of the 30th Annual Boston University Conference on Language Development,* D. Bamman, T. Magmitskaia & C. Zaller (eds), 653–664. Somerville MA: Cascadilla Press.

Tsimpli, I.M., Sorace, A., Heycock, C. & Filiaci, F. 2004. First language attrition and syntactic subjects: A study of Greek and Italian near-native speakers of English. *International Journal of Bilingualism* 8: 257–277.

Tuller, L. 2000. Null objects in deaf French. Ms, University of Tours.

Uriagereka, J. 1995. Aspects of the syntax of clitic placement in Western Romance. *Linguistic Inquiry* 26: 79–123.

Vainikka, A., Legendre, G. & Todorova, M. 1999. PLU stages: an independent measure of early syntactic development. In *Technical Report No JHU-CogSci-99-10.* Baltimore MD: John Hopkins University.

Vainikka, A. & Young-Scholten, M. 1994. Direct access to X'-theory: Evidence from Korean and Turkish adults learning German. In *Language Acquisition Studies in Generative Grammar,* T. Hoekstra & B. Schwartz (eds), 256–316. Amsterdam: John Benjamins.

Vainikka, A. & Young-Scholten, M. 1996. Gradual development of L2 phrase structure. *Second Language Research* 12: 7–39.

Vainikka, A. & Young-Scholten, M. 2005. The roots of syntax and how they grow. Organic grammar, the basic variety and processability theory. In *Paths of Development in L1 and L2 Acquisition,* S. Unsworth, A. Sorace, T. Parodi & M. Young-Scholten (eds), 77–106. Amsterdam: John Benjamins.

Valian, V. 1990. Null subjects: A problem for parameter-setting models of language acquisition. *Cognition* 35: 105–122.

Valois, D. 1991. The Internal Syntax of DP. Ph.D. dissertation, UCLA.

Valois, D. 1997. On French DPs. *La Revue Canadienne de Linguistique* 41: 349–375.

van der Lely, H.K.J. 1998. SLI in children: Movement, economy and decifits in the computational-syntactic system. *Language Acquisition* 7: 161–192.

van der Lely, H.K.J. & Stollwerck, L. 1997. Binding theory and grammatical specific language impairment in children. *Cognition* 62: 245–290.

van der Velde, M. 1998. L'acquisition des clitiques sujets et objets: Une étude sur deux enfants francophones. MA thesis, Universiteit van Amsterdam & CNRS, Paris.

van der Velde, M. 1999. L'acquisition des pronoms et des déterminants en français et en néerlandais. Mémoire de DEA, Université Paris 8, Vincennes – Saint-Denis.

van der Velde, M. 2003. Déterminants et pronoms en néerlandais et en français: Syntaxe et acquisition. Ph.D. dissertation, Université Paris 8, Vincennes – Saint-Denis.

van der Velde, M., Jakubowicz, C. & Rigaut, C. 2002. The acquisition of determiners and pronominal clitics by three French-speaking children. In *The Process of Language Acquisition: Proceedings of the 1999 GALA Conference,* I. Lasser (ed.), 115–132. Frankfurt: Peter Lang.

van Kampen, J. 1997. *First Steps in Wh-movement.* Delf: Eburon.

van Riemsdijk, H. (ed.). 1999. *Clitics in the Languages of Europe.* Berlin: Mouton de Gruyter.

Veneziano, E. & Sinclair, H. 2000. The changing status of 'filler syllables' on the way to grammatical morphemes. *Journal of Child Language* 27: 461–500.

Véronique, D. 1986. L'apprentissage du français par des travailleurs marocains et les processus de pidginations et créolisations. In *Acquisition d'une langue étrangère,* A. Giacomi & D. Véronique (eds), 559–584. Aix-en-Provence: Université de Provence.

Verrips, M. & Weissenborn, J. 1992. Routes to verb placement in early French and German: The independence of finiteness and agreement. In *The Acquisition of Verb Placement,* J. Meisel (ed.), 283–331. Dordrecht: Kluwer.

Vinet, M.-T. 2001. *D'un français à l'autre. La syntaxe de la microvariation.* Saint-Laurent, Québec: Fides.

Volterra, V. & Taeschner, T. 1978. The acquisition and development of language by bilingual children. *Journal of Child Language* 5: 311–326.

Wauquier-Gravelines, S. 2005. *Statut des représentations phonologiques en acquisition, traitement de la parole continue et dysphasie développementale.* Unpublished ms., EHESS, Paris.

Weissenborn, J., Kail, M. & Friederici, A. 1990. Language-particular or language-independent factors in acquisition? Children's comprehension of object pronouns in Dutch, French and German. *First Language* 2: 141–166.

Weissenborn, J., Roeper, T. & de Villiers, J. 1995. Wh-acquisition in French and German: connections between case, wh-features, and unique triggers. *Recherches Linguistiques de Vincennes* 24: 125–155.

Wexler, K. 1994. Optional infinitives, head-movement and the economy of derivations. In *Verb Movement,* D. Lightfoot & N. Horstein (eds), 305–350. Cambridge: CUP.

Wexler, K. 1998. Very early parameter setting and the unique checking constraint: A new explanation of the optional infinitive stage. *Lingua* 106: 23–80. Special issue: *Language Acquisition: Knowledge Representation and Processing*, A. Sorace (ed.).

Wexler, K., Gavarró, A. & Torrens, V. 2004. Feature checking and object clitic omission in child Catalan and Spanish. In *Romance Languages and Linguistic Theory* 2002, R. Bok-Bennema, B. Hollebrandse, B. Kampers-Manhe & P. Sleeman (eds), 253–269. Amsterdam: John Benjamins.

White, L. 1989. *Universal Grammar and Second Language Acquistion*. Amsterdam: John Benjamins.

White, L. 1992. Long and short verb movement in second language acquisition. *Canadian Journal of Linguistics* 37: 273–286.

White, L. 1996. Clitics in child L2 French. In *Generative Approaches to First and Second Language Acquisition*, H. Clahsen (ed.), 335–368. Amsterdam: John Benjamins.

White, L. 2003. *Second Language Acquisition and Universal Grammar*. Cambridge: CUP.

White, L., Valenzuela, E., Kozlowska-Macgregor, M. & Leung, Y.-k. I. 2004. Gender agreement in non-native Spanish: Evidence against failed features. *Applied Psycholinguistics* 25: 105–133.

Wijnen, F. 1998. The temporal interpretation of Dutch children's root infinitivals: The effect of eventivity. *First Language* 18: 379–402.

Wilmet, M. 1981. La place de l'épithète qualificative en français contemporain: Étude grammaticale et stylistique. *Revue de Linguistique Romane* 45: 17–73.

Yamakoshi, K. 1999. The acquisition of wh-questions: Wh-drop in child Swedish, Dutch, German, English, French, Spanish and Japanese. In *Proceedings of the 23rd Annual Boston University Conference on Language Development*, A. Greenhill, H. Littlefield & C. Tano (eds), 720–731. Somerville MA: Cascadilla Press.

Zanuttini, R. 1991. Syntactic Properties of Sentential Negation: A Comparative Study of Romance Languages. Ph.D. dissertation, University of Pennsylvania.

Zribi-Hertz, A. 1984. Prépositions orphelines et pronoms nuls. *Recherches Linguistiques de Vincennes* 12: 46–91.

Zribi-Herz, A. 1994. The syntax of nominative clitics in standard and advanced French. In *Paths towards Universal Grammar*, G. Cinque, J. Koster, J.-Y. Pollock, L. Rizzi & R. Zanuttini (eds), 453–472. Washington DC: Georgetown University Press.

Zribi-Hertz, A. 1999. Le système des possessifs en français standard moderne. *Langue Française* 122: 7–29.

Author index

Subject index

In the series *Language Acquisition and Language Disorders* the following titles have been published thus far or are scheduled for publication:

A complete list of titles in this series can be found on the publishers' website, *www.benjamins.com*

51 **PRÉVOST, Philippe:** The Acquisition of French. The development of inflectional morphology and syntax in L1 acquisition, bilingualism, and L2 acquisition. 2009. xx, 458 pp. **[Monographs on the Acquisition of Specific Languages 2]**

50 **GRINSTEAD, John (ed.):** Hispanic Child Languages. Typical and impaired development. 2009. xix, 304 pp.

49 **GARCÍA MAYO, María del Pilar and Roger HAWKINS (eds.):** Second Language Acquisition of Articles. Empirical findings and theoretical implications. 2009. ix, 272 pp.

48 **SANTOS, Ana Lúcia:** Minimal Answers. Ellipsis, syntax and discourse in the acquisition of European Portuguese. 2009. xv, 296 pp.

47 **SNAPE, Neal, Yan-kit Ingrid LEUNG and Michael SHARWOOD SMITH (eds.):** Representational Deficits in SLA. Studies in honor of Roger Hawkins. 2009. xxv, 250 pp.

46 **HAZNEDAR, Belma and Elena GAVRUSEVA (eds.):** Current Trends in Child Second Language Acquisition. A generative perspective. 2008. vi, 363 pp.

45 **GUIJARRO-FUENTES, Pedro, María Pilar LARRAÑAGA and John CLIBBENS (eds.):** First Language Acquisition of Morphology and Syntax. Perspectives across languages and learners. 2008. vi, 302 pp.

44 **SEKERINA, Irina A., Eva M. FERNÁNDEZ and Harald CLAHSEN (eds.):** Developmental Psycholinguistics. On-line methods in children's language processing. 2008. xviii, 190 pp.

43 **SAVICKIENĖ, Ineta and Wolfgang U. DRESSLER (eds.):** The Acquisition of Diminutives. A cross-linguistic perspective. 2007. vi, 352 pp.

42 **LEFEBVRE, Claire, Lydia WHITE and Christine JOURDAN (eds.):** L2 Acquisition and Creole Genesis. Dialogues. 2006. viii, 433 pp.

41 **TORRENS, Vincent and Linda ESCOBAR (eds.):** The Acquisition of Syntax in Romance Languages. 2006. viii, 422 pp.

40 **DEEN, Kamil Ud:** The Acquisition of Swahili. 2005. xiv, 241 pp.

39 **UNSWORTH, Sharon, Teresa PARODI, Antonella SORACE and Martha YOUNG-SCHOLTEN (eds.):** Paths of Development in L1 and L2 acquisition. In honor of Bonnie D. Schwartz. 2006. viii, 222 pp.

38 **FRANCESCHINA, Florencia:** Fossilized Second Language Grammars. The acquisition of grammatical gender. 2005. xxiv, 288 pp.

37 **MONTRUL, Silvina A.:** The Acquisition of Spanish. Morphosyntactic development in monolingual and bilingual L1 acquisition and adult L2 acquisition. 2004. xvi, 413 pp.

36 **BARTKE, Susanne and Julia SIEGMÜLLER (eds.):** Williams Syndrome across Languages. 2004. xvi, 385 pp.

35 **SÁNCHEZ, Liliana:** Quechua-Spanish Bilingualism. Interference and convergence in functional categories. 2003. x, 189 pp.

34 **OTA, Mitsuhiko:** The Development of Prosodic Structure in Early Words. Continuity, divergence and change. 2003. xii, 224 pp.

33 **JOSEFSSON, Gunlög, Christer PLATZACK and Gisela HÅKANSSON (eds.):** The Acquisition of Swedish Grammar. 2004. vi, 315 pp.

32 **PRÉVOST, Philippe and Johanne PARADIS (eds.):** The Acquisition of French in Different Contexts. Focus on functional categories. 2004. viii, 384 pp.

31 **MARINIS, Theodoros:** The Acquisition of the DP in Modern Greek. 2003. xiv, 261 pp.

30 **HOUT, Roeland van, Aafke HULK, Folkert KUIKEN and Richard J. TOWELL (eds.):** The Lexicon–Syntax Interface in Second Language Acquisition. 2003. viii, 234 pp.

29 **FERNÁNDEZ, Eva M.:** Bilingual Sentence Processing. Relative clause attachment in English and Spanish. 2003. xx, 294 pp.

28 **SHIMRON, Joseph (ed.):** Language Processing and Acquisition in Languages of Semitic, Root-Based, Morphology. 2003. vi, 394 pp.

27 **SALABERRY, M. Rafael and Yasuhiro SHIRAI (eds.):** The L2 Acquisition of Tense–Aspect Morphology. 2002. x, 489 pp.

26 **SLABAKOVA, Roumyana:** Telicity in the Second Language. 2001. xii, 236 pp.

25 **CARROLL, Susanne E.:** Input and Evidence. The raw material of second language acquisition. 2001. xviii, 461 pp.

24 **WEISSENBORN, Jürgen and Barbara HÖHLE (eds.):** Approaches to Bootstrapping. Phonological, lexical, syntactic and neurophysiological aspects of early language acquisition. Volume 2. 2001. viii, 337 pp.

23 **WEISSENBORN, Jürgen and Barbara HÖHLE (eds.):** Approaches to Bootstrapping. Phonological, lexical, syntactic and neurophysiological aspects of early language acquisition. Volume 1. 2001. xviii, 299 pp.

22 **SCHAEFFER, Jeannette C.:** The Acquisition of Direct Object Scrambling and Clitic Placement. Syntax and pragmatics. 2000. xii, 187 pp.

21 **HERSCHENSOHN, Julia:** The Second Time Around – Minimalism and L2 Acquisition. 2000. xiv, 287 pp.

20 **KANNO, Kazue (ed.):** The Acquisition of Japanese as a Second Language. 1999. xii, 180 pp.

19 **BECK, Maria-Luise (ed.):** Morphology and its Interfaces in Second Language Knowledge. 1998. x, 387 pp.

18 **KLEIN, Elaine C. and Gita MARTOHARDJONO (eds.):** The Development of Second Language Grammars. A generative approach. 1999. vi, 412 pp.

17 **ARCHIBALD, John:** Second Language Phonology. 1998. xii, 313 pp.

16 **HANNAHS, S.J. and Martha YOUNG-SCHOLTEN (eds.):** Focus on Phonological Acquisition. 1997. v, 289 pp.

15 **BRINKMANN, Ursula:** The Locative Alternation in German. Its structure and acquisition. 1997. x, 289 pp.

14 **CLAHSEN, Harald (ed.):** Generative Perspectives on Language Acquisition. Empirical findings, theoretical considerations and crosslinguistic comparisons. 1996. xxviii, 499 pp.

13 **ALLEN, Shanley:** Aspects of Argument Structure Acquisition in Inuktitut. 1996. xvi, 244 pp.

12 **JUFFS, Alan:** Learnability and the Lexicon. Theories and second language acquisition research. 1996. xi, 277 pp.

11 **YIP, Virginia:** Interlanguage and Learnability. From Chinese to English. 1995. xvi, 247 pp.

10 **LAKSHMANAN, Usha:** Universal Grammar in Child Second Language Acquisition. Null subjects and morphological uniformity. 1994. x, 162 pp.

9 **ADONE, Dany:** The Acquisition of Mauritian Creole. 1994. xii, 167 pp.

8 **HOEKSTRA, Teun and Bonnie D. SCHWARTZ (eds.):** Language Acquisition Studies in Generative Grammar. 1994. xii, 401 pp.

7 **MEISEL, Jürgen M. (ed.):** Bilingual First Language Acquisition. French and German grammatical development. 1994. vi, 282 pp.

6 **THOMAS, Margaret:** Knowledge of Reflexives in a Second Language. 1993. x, 234 pp.

5 **GASS, Susan M. and Larry SELINKER (eds.):** Language Transfer in Language Learning. Revised edition. 1992. x, 236 pp.

4 **ECKMAN, Fred R. (ed.):** Confluence. Linguistics, L2 acquisition and speech pathology. 1993. xvi, 260 pp.

3 **EUBANK, Lynn (ed.):** Point Counterpoint. Universal Grammar in the second language. 1991. x, 439 pp.

2 **HUEBNER, Thom and Charles A. FERGUSON (eds.):** Cross Currents in Second Language Acquisition and Linguistic Theory. 1991. viii, 435 pp.

1 **WHITE, Lydia:** Universal Grammar and Second Language Acquisition. 1989. xii, 198 pp.